Communications
in Computer and Information Science   1928

Rationale

The CCIS series is devoted to the publication of proceedings of computer science conferences. Its aim is to efficiently disseminate original research results in informatics in printed and electronic form. While the focus is on publication of peer-reviewed full papers presenting mature work, inclusion of reviewed short papers reporting on work in progress is welcome, too. Besides globally relevant meetings with internationally representative program committees guaranteeing a strict peer-reviewing and paper selection process, conferences run by societies or of high regional or national relevance are also considered for publication.

Topics

The topical scope of CCIS spans the entire spectrum of informatics ranging from foundational topics in the theory of computing to information and communications science and technology and a broad variety of interdisciplinary application fields.

Information for Volume Editors and Authors

Publication in CCIS is free of charge. No royalties are paid, however, we offer registered conference participants temporary free access to the online version of the conference proceedings on SpringerLink (http://link.springer.com) by means of an http referrer from the conference website and/or a number of complimentary printed copies, as specified in the official acceptance email of the event.

CCIS proceedings can be published in time for distribution at conferences or as post-proceedings, and delivered in the form of printed books and/or electronically as USBs and/or e-content licenses for accessing proceedings at SpringerLink. Furthermore, CCIS proceedings are included in the CCIS electronic book series hosted in the SpringerLink digital library at http://link.springer.com/bookseries/7899. Conferences publishing in CCIS are allowed to use Online Conference Service (OCS) for managing the whole proceedings lifecycle (from submission and reviewing to preparing for publication) free of charge.

Publication process

The language of publication is exclusively English. Authors publishing in CCIS have to sign the Springer CCIS copyright transfer form, however, they are free to use their material published in CCIS for substantially changed, more elaborate subsequent publications elsewhere. For the preparation of the camera-ready papers/files, authors have to strictly adhere to the Springer CCIS Authors' Instructions and are strongly encouraged to use the CCIS LaTeX style files or templates.

Abstracting/Indexing

CCIS is abstracted/indexed in DBLP, Google Scholar, EI-Compendex, Mathematical Reviews, SCImago, Scopus. CCIS volumes are also submitted for the inclusion in ISI Proceedings.

How to start

To start the evaluation of your proposal for inclusion in the CCIS series, please send an e-mail to ccis@springer.com.

Juan Carlos Figueroa-García ·
German Hernández · Jose Luis Villa Ramirez ·
Elvis Eduardo Gaona García

Editors

Applied Computer Sciences in Engineering

10th Workshop on Engineering Applications, WEA 2023
Cartagena, Colombia, November 1–3, 2023
Proceedings

Springer

Organization

General Chair

Juan Carlos Figueroa-García   Universidad Distrital Francisco José de Caldas, Colombia

Technical Chairs

Elvis Eduardo Gaona García   Universidad Distrital Francisco José de Caldas, Colombia

José Luis Villa-Ramírez   Universidad Tecnológica de Bolívar, Colombia

Program and Track Chairs

Carlos Franco   Universidad del Rosario, Colombia

Elvis Eduardo Gaona García   Universidad Distrital Francisco José de Caldas, Colombia

Germán Hernández-Pérez   Universidad Nacional de Colombia, Colombia

Publication Chair

Alvaro David Orjuela-Cañon   Universidad del Rosario, Colombia

Organizing Committee Chairs

Edwin Puertas   Universidad Tecnológica de Bolívar, Colombia

Sonia Contreras   Universidad Tecnológica de Bolívar, Colombia

Program Committee

Adil Usman   Indian Institute of Technology Mandi, India

Adolfo Jaramillo-Matta   Universidad Distrital Francisco José de Caldas, Colombia

Andres Gaona
Universidad Distrital Francisco José de Caldas, Colombia

Carlos Osorio-Ramírez
Universidad Nacional de Colombia, Colombia

De-Shuang Huang
Tongji University, China

Diana Ovalle
Universidad Distrital Francisco José de Caldas, Colombia

Diego Ismael León Nieto
Universidad Externado de Colombia, Colombia

Fabián Garay
ESINF, Colombia

Feizar Javier Rueda-Velazco
Universidad Distrital Francisco José de Caldas, Colombia

Francisco Ramis
Universidad del Bío-Bío, Chile

Guadalupe González
Universidad Tecnológica de Panamá, Panama

Gustavo Puerto-Leguizamón
Universidad Distrital Francisco José de Caldas, Colombia

Heriberto Román-Flores
Universidad de Tarapacá, Chile

I-Hsien Ting
National University of Kaohsiung, Taiwan

Jair Cervantes-Canales
Universidad Autónoma de México, Mexico

Jairo Soriano-Mendez
Universidad Distrital Francisco José de Caldas, Colombia

Javier Arturo Orjuela-Castro
Universidad Distrital Francisco José de Caldas, Colombia

Javier Sandoval
Universidad Externado de Colombia, Colombia

J. J. Merelo
Universidad de Granada, Spain

John Leonardo Vargas Mesa
Universidad del Rosario, Colombia

Jose Luís Gonzalez-Velarde
Instituto Tecnológico de Monterrey, Mexico

Lindsay Alvarez
Universidad Distrital Francisco José de Caldas, Colombia

Mabel Frías
Universidad de las Villas "Marta Abreu", Cuba

Mario Enrique Duarte-Gonzalez
Universidad Antonio Nariño, Colombia

Martha Centeno
University of Turabo, Puerto Rico

Martin Pilat
Charles University, Czech Republic

Martine Ceberio
University of Texas at El Paso, USA

Miguel Melgarejo
Universidad Distrital Francisco José de Caldas, Colombia

Nelson L. Diaz Aldana
Universidad Distrital Francisco José de Caldas, Colombia

Oscar Acevedo
Universidad Tecnológica de Bolívar, Colombia

Paulo Alonso Gaona
Universidad Distrital Francisco José de Caldas, Colombia

Rafael Bello-Pérez
Universidad de las Villas "Marta Abreu", Cuba

Rodrigo Linfati
Universidad del Bío-Bío, Chile

Roman Neruda
Charles University and Czech Academy of Sciences, Czech Republic

Sebastián Jaramillo-Isaza   Universidad Antonio Nariño, Colombia
Sergio Rojas-Galeano   Universidad Distrital Francisco José de Caldas,
                                     Colombia
Vladik Kreinovich   University of Texas at El Paso, USA
Wilson Rodríguez Calderón   ESAP, Colombia
Yesid Díaz-Gutierrez   Universidad Santo Tomás de Aquino, Colombia
Yurilev Chalco-Cano   Universidad de Tarapacá, Chile

Contents

Optimization

Artificial Intelligence

Algorithmic Trading System Using Auto-machine Learning as a Filter Rule

Edwin López[1], Germán Hernández[1], Javier Sandoval[2], and Diego León[2(✉)]

[1] Universidad Nacional de Colombia, Bogotá, Colombia
{edlopez,gjhernandezp}@unal.edu.co
[2] Universidad Externado de Colombia, Bogotá, Colombia
{javier.sandoval,diego.leon}@uexternado.edu.co

Abstract. This paper enhances the performance of an algorithmic trading system or strategy, based on technical indicators, by integrating a classification model that discriminates between potential winning and losing trades of the strategy. The features used as input for the machine learning model are generated from technical indicators at the moment a trade is opened, and are obtained through a market simulation using Open, High, Low, Close data in the Eurodollar currency.

For the search process of the appropriate classification model, two mechanisms are proposed. These are based on auto-machine learning and evolutionary algorithms, using the Tree-Based Pipeline Optimization Tool (TPOT) library, and an approach based on the Elitist Non-dominated Sorting Genetic Algorithm (NSGA-II) and TPOT. Here, the multi-objective search is guided by the accuracy metric and the System Quality Number (SQN), a metric used to evaluate trading systems.

In the conducted experiments, the classification models chosen by NSGA-II significantly enhanced the performance of the trading strategy, with 32.5% of the out-of-sample models showing positive returns and exhibiting similar in-sample and out-of-sample behavior. In contrast, with TPOT, the classifiers found tended to perform well in-sample but not consistently out-of-sample. The final strategy chosen by NSGA-II had 60–61% profitable trades both in-sample and out-of-sample, while TPOT resulted in 98% and 62%, respectively.

Keywords: Algorithmic trading · Machine Learning · Financial markets · auto-machine learning

1 Introduction

With the great technological advances in computational processing and connectivity, traders have evolved, automating many of the trading systems that were executed manually, thus giving birth to algorithmic trading (AT) in English, and this in turn opening up a range of possibilities regarding the use of methodologies based on statistics and mathematics, which are difficult to use manually in useful times to make trading decisions.

In the literature, a large number of tools have been used in AT to gain an advantage when trading, including econometric models such as ARIMA [1] and GARCH [13], through methodologies from signal processing such as Fourier transforms [10], Wavelet transforms [3], as well as, combinatorial optimization

J. C. Figueroa-García et al. (Eds.): WEA 2023, CCIS 1928, pp. 3–11, 2023.
https://doi.org/10.1007/978-3-031-46739-4_1

models such as genetic algorithms (GA) in English, reaching Machine Learning (ML) techniques showing great potential to find complex nonlinear patterns based on research from the last decade [7,9,15].

Among the variety of tools that exist to face speculation in financial markets, trading systems based on rules about technical indicators are one of those traditionally used in the industry [5], which focus on trying to exploit patterns with market logic, however, it is becoming increasingly difficult to find patterns that give advantage in the markets to operators [6,12].

Taking into account the possibilities provided by machine learning models, to find patterns, integrating machine learning with algorithmic trading systems becomes an interesting alternative, raising the question of how to integrate it and which would be the appropriate machine learning model to choose. In this sense, it is proposed to create a rule-based trading system that uses a machine learning model as part of the system.

The challenge of speculating in financial markets can be seen in the literature as reflected by [4], according to his hypothesis it is very difficult or practically impossible to obtain returns higher than the market valuation in the long term, to face this challenge speculators and researchers have used different perspectives and tools from fundamental company data in cases of stocks [14] to econometric and statistical models, as well as descriptors derived from the same prices known as technical indicators, these elements have been used both in algorithmic and discretionary speculation, where one of the approaches used are trading systems with fixed rules based on technical indicators [1,2,18], another perspective has implied the use of machine learning in various ways such as price prediction, risk management, parameter tuning and even signal detection [8].

In such a way that a favorable scenario arises to implement machine learning algorithms and especially auto-machine learning to address the problem of automatic negotiation. This document presents in the following section the two automatic trading strategies based on technical indicators and a strategy based on AUTOML as a filter rule to evaluate winning and losing trades; in the following section the experiments and results are presented and finally the conclusions and recommendations of the study are presented.

2 Proposed Trading Strategy

2.1 Base Strategy

The base strategy used is the one proposed by J. Welles Wilder Jr. in 1978, first introduced in his book "New Concepts in Technical Trading Systems" [11]. Originally designed for stocks, it can be extrapolated to other financial instruments such as currencies. To facilitate the pattern search, the strategy is refined in a single long direction. This is important as refining a strategy separately for long and short positions allows optimization of performance for each market condition [17]. Market conditions for long and short positions may differ, and therefore, strategies that perform well in some market conditions may not do so in others. By adjusting a strategy separately for long positions from short ones, one can better understand the strategy's behavior in different market conditions and make adjustments to optimize its performance. Figure 1 shows the flowchart of the base strategy, and the following steps describe it:

- A long entry signal is set when the RSI (Relative Strength Index) falls below a specified level of 30 (the default value), indicating that the asset is oversold.
- A take-profit level is established at a specific price level (e.g., 20 pips above the entry price), where the strategy will exit the long position with a profit.
- A stop-loss level is set at a specific price level (e.g., 15 pips below the entry price), where the strategy will exit the long position to limit potential loss.
- The strategy would then enter a long position when the RSI falls below 30 and exit the long position when the take-profit or stop-loss level is reached.
- After closing each trade, the strategy waits for the next RSI signal to enter another trade.

The default values proposed by the author, an RSI of 14 periods and an oversold level of 30, are used.

2.2 Trading Strategy Using Auto-machine Learning as a Filter Rule

The integration of a classification model into the foundational trading strategy is introduced as a promising enhancement to the effectiveness of investment decisions. This approach employs the inference of the classification model as an added filter, allowing for more confident initiation of a trade. Such a decision would be corroborated with market information encapsulated by the model, leading to more informed decisions and potentially reduced risk in trading operations. Moreover, the classification model can be consistently trained and optimized to accommodate market changes, thereby maintaining accuracy in its analyses.

The process of validating a potential operation through the classification performed by the machine learning model occurs if the model infers that the operation belongs to class one (1). If the classification is zero (0), the operation is disregarded. Figure 1 illustrates the flowchart of the algorithmic trading strategy, detailing the integration of the classification model.

3 Experimental Setup

For the research development, we utilized the Euro/Dollar data in OHLC (Open-High-Low-Close) format, covering the period from January 1, 2014, to March 30, 2022, as detailed in Sect. 3.1 Description of the Data Set. The following specific considerations were applied:

- The data in OHLC format was analyzed in five (5) min time windows.
- Trading was restricted to the London session hours, from 8:00 to 16:00. Any open trade at the end of the session was closed at the closing price at 16:00.
- The Metatrader 5 simulation model (MetaQuotes n.d.) was employed, based on the opening price.

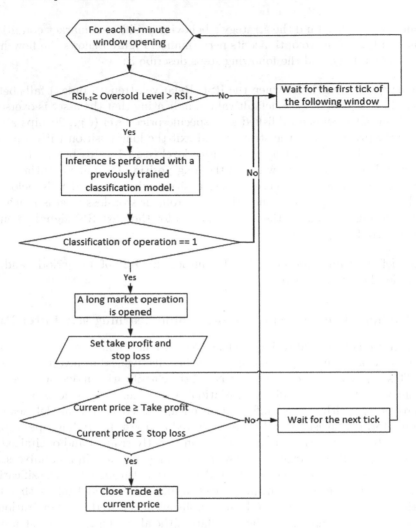

Fig. 1. Workflow of the AutoML based Strategy

The exit rules of the foundational trading strategy were determined by take profit, stop loss, and the trading day's conclusion. As there was no clear consensus on the optimal values for take profit and stop loss, the base strategy was simulated with equal values for both parameters, ranging from 2 pips to 50 pips (refer to Fig. 2). In assessing how many trades closed at the end of the day without hitting the take profit or stop loss, we aimed for a low percentage of trades deviating from the projected path. A maximum deviation of 25% was accepted, equivalent to no more than 20 pips of movement. For the experiment, a grid with take profit and stop loss values of 20 pips or less was chosen, utilizing all 2-permutations of the set $\{5, 10, 15, 20\}$, along with sets having equal values for take profit and stop loss, resulting in a total of 16 possible pairs.

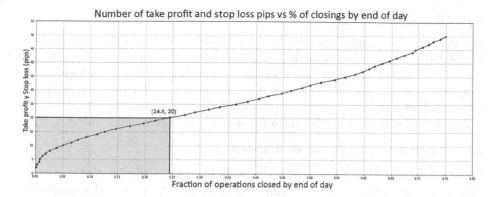

Fig. 2. Take Profit - Stop Loss Grid

3.1 Simulation Assumptions

Average prices between the bid and ask are used. Movements are measured in pips, which is a unit of measurement used to express the change in value between two currencies in a foreign exchange rate (forex). In the case of EUR/USD, it is the fourth decimal place of the currency pair. For example, moving from 1.20000 to 1.20100 would be a movement of 10 pips. The value of a pip can vary based on the currency pair and the size of the trade. A fixed spread of 1 pip is considered, which affects the profit for the trade as follows: Profit=Yes, Type of trade=Long Exit Price-Entry Price-Spread. Another case: Entry Price-Exit Price-Spread. The simulation runs each step every five minutes in the OHLC format; during the opening, technical indicators are calculated and trades are closed using the closing price as either the take profit or stop loss if any of the previous window's High, Low, or Close values exceed them, or the current window's Open value. If the price surpasses both the take profit and the stop loss in the same window, the stop loss is always considered due to the uncertainty regarding when each event occurred.

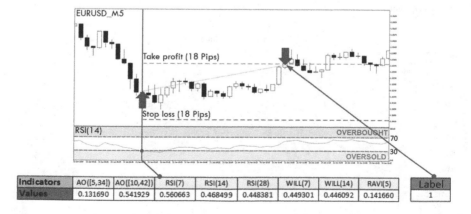

Fig. 3. Instance added as sample

3.2   Obtaining Dataset

The data set for training the classification models, tested by both the TPOT model and the proposed NSGA-II, is obtained through a simulation process with the goal of discriminating between winning and losing trades. This feature set is generated at the moment a trade is opened, and a class label is assigned once the trade is closed: one (1) if the trade was winning, and zero (0) if it ended up losing. An example of an added instance as a sample can be seen in Fig. 3.

3.3   Pipeline of the Proposed Experiment

In the experimentation process with the available data, a sequence of steps was established for each experiment, aiming to integrate the proposed algorithmic trading strategy with the classifier and its search process. Each step culminates in a trained classification model and a set of performance metrics. To enhance the accuracy of the results from the AutoML-based model, it is suggested to repeat each experiment with varying parameter values (Take profit, Stop loss) multiple times, contingent on the execution time of the classifier search algorithm. Figure 6.3 illustrates the sequence of the proposed experiment.

4   Results

In the present work, two AutoML-based approaches were employed to select a classifier to enhance the performance of a strategy, as described. The first strategy used the Python library TPOT [16] with accuracy as the metric, and the second employed NSGA-II.

Using TPOT as a mechanism to choose the classification algorithm did not yield the best results. Although training showed promising outcomes, during the out-of-sample confirmation period, only 24.3% of the final selected models displayed a positive benefit, and merely 16.6% of the models led the system to gains greater than 10 pips in the mentioned period. Additionally, an average accuracy of 95.19% in training and 60.04% in confirmation was observed, indicating overfitting in most models. Therefore, experimentation proceeded with the NSGA-II based proposal.

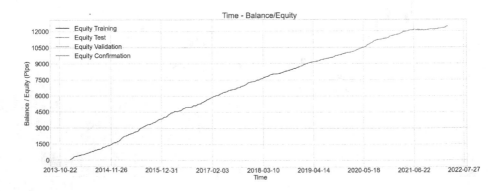

Fig. 4. TPOT trading strategy return

For the experiment with the proposed multi-objective search algorithm, each set of parameters (Take profit, Stop loss) was executed 15 times, resulting in a total of 240 runs. Out of these, 78 yielded positive profit in the confirmation period, representing 32.5% of the cases. Figure 7 shows the proportion of positive profitability per parameter set.

From all the experiments conducted using AutoML TPOT and the proposed NSGA-II, a classification model was chosen that initially exhibits uniform performance across different data partitions (see Fig. 4 and Fig. 5).

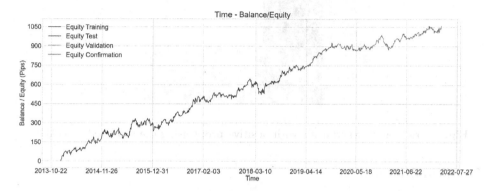

Fig. 5. NSGA II trading strategy return

In the case of the proposed NSGA-II, the base strategy without the classification model went from 2,402 operations to 1,036 (see Fig. 6), filtering out 1366 operations, of which 555 were profitable and 811 were losses. However, since 59.3% of the filtered operations were losing, the overall profit of the trading system increased, turning an algorithmic trading system that was initially losing into a potentially profitable one. For the classification model selected by TPOT, it can be seen that in the confirmation part, the model tends to reduce performance, tending to have a somewhat flat curve compared to the slope of the training part. This generates some distrust in the results for real-world application, as it may not generalize the patterns well, leading to losses in subsequent time frames.

Trading system	Measures										
	Number of operations		Profit (pips)		SQN		Max. Drawdown		% Profitable op.	
	Training Test		Training Test		Training		Training Test		Training Test	
	Validation	Confirmation	Validation	Confirmation	Test	Confirmation	Validation	Confirmation	Validation	Confirmation
Base strategy	2199 203		-2632 -78,7		-5,74	-0,57	-2724,7 -162		48,8	52,7
	2402		-2711		-5,67		-2785		49%	
Strategy with classifier chosen by NSGA-II Proposed	950 86		964,4 96		3,25	1,08	-121 -53		60%	61,62
	1036		1060.4		3,43		-121		60%	
Strategy with classifier chosen by TPOT	824 74		12141 299,7		53,73	2,15	-21 -68,5		98%	62,21
	898		12835		50.6		-105		96%	

Fig. 6. Trading strategy statistics

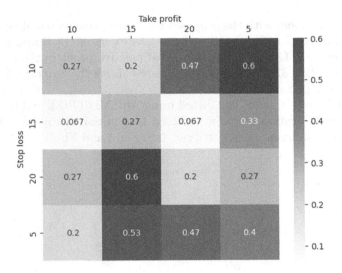

Fig. 7. Fraction of experiments with positive profit using the proposed NSGA-II

5   Conclusions

The performance of rule-based trading systems can be improved by utilizing machine learning algorithms to fulfill various functions within the system. AutoML approaches can be a significant support mechanism when facing different challenges; however, the researcher's tacit knowledge of the problem is of vital importance. This insight can contribute details that may be crucial in enhancing the performance of the final models. Attempting to find profitable patterns in a financial asset is a highly complex task due to the noise in price series. Therefore, discovering models that genuinely generalize pattern identification becomes very demanding. Consequently, it becomes an interesting alternative to guide the search by combining metrics of trading system performance and machine learning models, as the case may be. In summary, the integration of a classification model into the trading strategy improves decision-making accuracy and reduces risk in trading operations, according to the conducted experiments. It is essential to note that although the results obtained show promise in the studied foreign exchange market (euro-dollar), they cannot necessarily be extrapolated to other markets. Each market has its peculiarities and dynamics, so the validity and effectiveness of the machine learning models used in this study may vary considerably in different contexts. Further research is required to determine their applicability in other financial markets.

While the machine learning model search based on the proposed NSGA-II seems to provide good results, it can be improved by including other variables considered fixed, such as take profit and stop loss, in the solution encoding. Within the simulations, uncertainty components can be included, aiming to have models that are more resistant to the constant changes that occur in markets.

References

1. Adebiyi, A.A., Adewumi, A.O., Ayo, C.K.: Stock price prediction using the arima model. In: Proceedings - UKSim-AMSS 16th International Conference on Computer Modelling and Simulation, UKSim 2014, pp. 106–112 (2014)
2. Arce, P., Antognini, J., Kristjanpoller, W., Salinas, L.: Fast and adaptive cointegration based model for forecasting high frequency financial time series. Comput. Econ. 2017 **54**(1), 99–112 (2017). https://link.springer.com/article/10.1007/s10614-017-9691-7
3. Coggins, R., Flower, B., Dersch, D., Jabri, M., Zhang, B.L.: Multiresolution forecasting for futures trading using wavelet decompositions. IEEE Trans. Neural Netw. **12**, 765–775 (2002)
4. Fama, E.F.: Session topic: stock market price behavior session chairman: Burton G. Malkiel efficient capital markets: a review of theory and empirical work. J. Finan. **25**, 383–417 (1970)
5. Fitschen, K.: Trading system elements: entries, pp. 45–64 (2013)
6. Friedhoff, J.M., Mansouri, M.: A framework for assessing technology risks in transaction-based extended enterprises: US capital market case. IEEE Syst. J. **11**, 1505–1515 (2017)
7. Gerlein, E.A., McGinnity, M., Belatreche, A., Coleman, S.: Evaluating machine learning classification for financial trading: an empirical approach. Expert Syst. Appl. **54**, 193–207 (2016)
8. Halls-Moore, M.L.: Advanced algorithmic trading, vol. 1. QuantStar (2016)
9. Henrique, B.M., Sobreiro, V.A., Kimura, H.: Literature review: machine learning techniques applied to financial market prediction. Expert Syst. Appl. **124**, 226–251 (2019). https://doi.org/10.1016/j.eswa.2019.01.012
10. Huang, H., Zhang, W., Deng, G., Chen, J.: Predicting stock trend using Fourier transform and support vector regression. In: Proceedings - 17th IEEE International Conference on Computational Science and Engineering, CSE 2014, Jointly with 13th IEEE International Conference on Ubiquitous Computing and Communications, IUCC 2014, 13th International Symposium on Pervasive Systems, pp. 213–216 (2015)
11. Jr., J.W.W.: New concepts in technical trading systems (1978)
12. Leles, M.C.R., Mozelli, L.A., Sbruzzi, E.F., Junior, C.L.N., Guimaraes, H.N.: A multicriteria trading system based on singular spectrum analysis trading rules. IEEE Syst. J. **14**, 1468–1478 (2020)
13. Mustapa, F.H., Ismail, M.T.: Modelling and forecasting s&p 500 stock prices using hybrid Arima-Garch model, vol. 1366. Institute of Physics Publishing (2019)
14. Naseri, M.R.A., Rafiee, F.M., Moghadam, S.K.: Modeling portfolio optimization based on fundamental analysis using an expert system in the real estate industry. Int. J. Supply Oper. Manage. **7**, 39–50 (2020). https://www.ijsom.com/article_2804.html
15. Nino, J., Hernandez, G., Arévalo, A., León, D., Sandoval, J.: CNN with limit order book data for stock price prediction, vol. 1, pp. 444–457 (2019)
16. Olson, R.S., Bartley, N., Urbanowicz. R.J., Moore, J.H.: Evaluation of a Tree-based pipeline optimization tool for automating data science. (2016). http://arxiv.org/abs/1603.06212
17. Sharma, A., Bhuriya, D., Singh, U.: Survey of stock market prediction using machine learning approach. In: Proceedings of the International Conference on Electronics, Communication and Aerospace Technology, ICECA 2017 2017-January, pp. 506–509 (2017)
18. Xiong, L., Lu, Y.: Hybrid ARIMA-BPNN model for time series prediction of the Chinese stock market. In: 2017 3rd International Conference on Information Management, ICIM 2017, pp. 93–97 (2017)

An Algorithmic Trading Strategy for the Colombian US Dollar Inter-bank Bulk Market SET-FX Based on an Evolutionary TPOT AutoML Predictive Model

Andrea Cruz[1], Germán Hernández[1], Javier Sandoval[2], and Diego León[2(✉)]

[1] Universidad Nacional de Colombia, Bogotá, Colombia
{amcruzm,gjhernandezp}@unal.edu.co
[2] Universidad Externado de Colombia, Bogotá, Colombia
{javier.sandoval,diego.leon}@uexternado.edu.co

Abstract. In this paper, we introduce a competitive algorithmic trading strategy for the Colombian US dollar inter-bank bulk order-driven market, SET-FX. The strategy is underpinned by an evolutionary predictive model constructed with the Tree-based Pipeline Optimization Tool (TPOT). TPOT is a strongly-typed genetic programming-based automated machine learning tool that employs the Non-dominated Sorting Genetic Algorithm II (NSGA-II), a multi-objective evolutionary algorithm. It aims to discover machine learning models that balance maximum accuracy with minimum complexity.

Keywords: Algorithmic trading strategy · AutoML · genetic programming · TPOT

1 Introduction

Algorithmic trading strategies hinge on the capability to predict either the future price or the direction of the price of an asset. This prediction is based on the identification of patterns in market data and other complementary information. Usually, the market data consists of transaction time series, containing details such as negotiation times, prices (including open, close, high, and low), and volumes. These time series are accessible in various granularities (e.g., tick-by-tick, 1 min, 5 min, 10 min, 1 h, 1 day) depending on the access level of the entity collecting or purchasing the information.

In more sophisticated markets, agents can access not only transaction information but also limit order data. This includes information on prices and volumes at which market participants are willing to buy or sell an asset. In the Colombian US dollar inter-bank bulk market SET-FX, agents can place limit orders that convey their buying and selling intentions. Consequently, they are able to make trading decisions based not only on transaction time series but also on the current status and dynamics of limit orders.

This paper proposes the design and testing of an algorithmic trading strategy tailored for the Colombian US dollar inter-bank bulk market SET-FX. The strategy makes systematic trading decisions every second by incorporating numerous input variables extracted from the SET-FX transactions time series and limit order book (LOB) dynamics.

The remainder of this paper is organized as follows: The subsequent section provides an introduction to the Colombian US dollar inter-bank bulk market SET-FX, followed by a general description of the SET-FX LOB dynamics and information. Next, an overview of TPOT and its application in building the predictor for the proposed trading strategy is presented. Finally, we analyze the profitability of the algorithmic trading strategy proposed.

Exchange markets can be classified as dealerships, order-driven markets, or combinations of both, with some markets exhibiting a dominant characteristic.

In a dealership market, a customer's order is filled at a single price quoted by a specialist, an institutional investor tasked with providing liquidity. The quoted price for a certain quantity of the asset does not influence the price quoted for different quantities. Notable examples of dealership markets include NASDAQ and LSE.

Order-driven markets, in contrast, do not have specialized dealers. Instead, dealers are expected to quote prices by submitting limit orders and clear the market by responding to buy and sell pressure with market orders. EURONEXT is an example of such a market.

The Colombian US dollar bulk market SET-FX operates as a single asset order-driven market. In this market, institutional brokers and investment banks trade US dollars against Colombian pesos, utilizing information from the limit order and transaction books. Run by the Colombian stock market operator "Bolsa de Valores de Colombia" (BVC) in association with TP ICAP, the SET-FX market consists of 43 institutions, trading on average one and a half billion dollars per day. Market agents can submit limit orders at any price, with volumes that are multiples of 250,000 US dollars.

In this market, institutional brokers and investment banks pay a flat monthly fee of around US$2,000 per transactional client rather than per transaction. There is also a central counterparty clearinghouse where institutions deposit 10% of their total allowed long or short positions to mitigate risks such as counterparty, operational, settlement, market, legal, and default. Prior to 2019, trading was conducted by human agents interacting through a visual user interface (see Figure 1). However, in the second quarter of 2019, FIX clients were introduced to enable algorithmic trading capabilities.

The next section provides a general description of the dynamics and information within the SET-FX Limit Order Book (LOB).

2   SET-FX Limit Order Book (LOB) Dynamics and Information

The Limit Order Book (LOB) at a given moment is a register of the prices and volumes at which market participants are willing to buy and sell a financial instrument [7]. It consists of two sorted queues of orders: one containing the orders from potential buyers (known as the bid or bid side), and the other containing orders from potential sellers (referred to as the ask or sell side). Each limit order specifies the price and volume at which a participant is willing to trade.

Orders within each queue are sorted primarily by price. If multiple orders share the same price, they are further sorted by the time of arrival [21]. The bid queue is organized in descending order by price, meaning that the highest bid prices are prioritized, while the ask queue is sorted in ascending order, prioritizing the lowest selling prices. These dynamics create a structure in which market participants can gauge supply and demand at various price levels, as illustrated in Figs. 1 and 2.

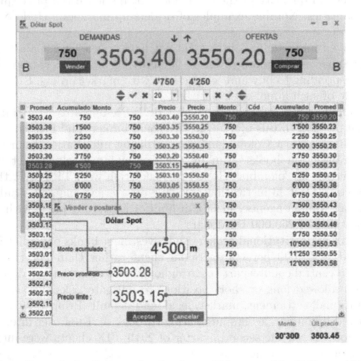

Fig. 1. Snapshot of the limit order book on February 4th 2019 at 10:20:09 A.M extracted from the SET-FX, the inter-bank exchange platform. The best fourteen prices and volumes are presented. first column shows average prices, second column shows cumulative volume, third column shows order volume and forth column shows order prices. Demandas, ofertas, monto, precio stand for bids, offers, quantity and price respectively.

Figure 1 shows a snapshot of the limit order book for the Colombian SET-FX inter-bank exchange market on February 2nd, 2011 at 10:20:09 A.M. Suppose a market agent wants to sell 750 thousand dollars at 1852.32. She has to use a limit order. The later will be placed on the sell (right) side of the limit order book right after the order to sell 250 thousand dollars at 1852.3 and before the order to sell 250 thousand dollars at 1852.33. Before the new limit order could be fulfilled, orders in from of it have to be executed or canceled.

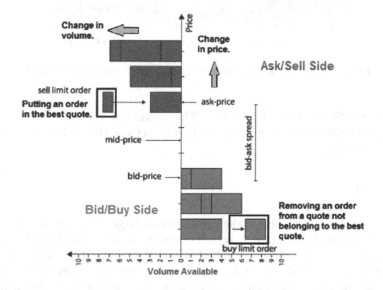

Fig. 2. LOB Events

Orders in the LOB are dynamically placed, executed, modified, and removed throughout the market negotiation period by market agents, reflecting changes in their buying and selling intentions, as shown in Fig. 2. Trading events, or transactions, also significantly influence LOB dynamics, as the orders negotiated in a transaction are removed from the LOB, further illustrated in Fig. 3. Execution of orders follows the Best Price First (BPF) mechanism, and for orders at the same price, a First In First Out (FIFO) mechanism is applied.

Various mathematical [1,4] statistical [2,15,19], and visual [8,16] representations have been employed to model, analyze, and visualize the dynamics of a limit order book (LOB) to inform trading decisions. Figure 4 illustrates a visual representation of USD/COP SET-FX LOB dynamics. The y-axis represents USD/COP exchange rates, and the x-axis represents one-minute aggregating time intervals. Red intensities depict sell volumes, and green intensities represent buy volumes. This figure also emphasizes how segments of the volume LOB dynamics can be used as predictive patterns for price movement. Figure 5 displays another heatmap visual representation of USD/COP SET-FX LOB dynamics information from March 21, 2012. Red intensities represent volume, with white spaces corresponding to zero volume and each volume unit

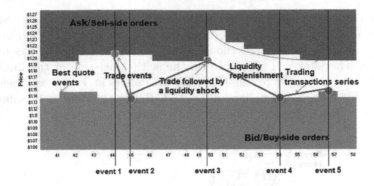

Fig. 3. LOB events that have an impact on liquidity and spread

equivalent to 250 thousand US dollars. The maximum volume, 60 on the color bar, equals 15 million US dollars. Solid black lines trace the evolution of the best buy/sell price [17].

3   TPOT

With the substantial increase in the generation of large data volumes, the use of Machine Learning (ML) models to tackle highly complex problems has gained traction across various industries, including the financial sector. This burgeoning interest has underscored the intricate challenges developers face when building effective ML models. In response, recent years have seen the development of a range of Automated Machine Learning (Auto ML) tools. These tools leverage computational power and ingenious search and optimization techniques, such as genetic algorithms, genetic programming, simulated annealing, and tabu search [20], to explore numerous alternatives. One such Auto ML tool is the Tree-based Pipeline Optimization Tool (TPOT) [12]. TPOT utilizes genetic programming to automate the construction of ML models, with a focus on incorporating inter-pretability as one of the model evaluation criteria.

The workflow to develop a machine learning model can be outlined as follows [5]:

1. Data cleaning
2. Feature engineering
   (a) Feature preprocessing
   (b) Feature selection
   (c) Feature construction
3. Model selection
4. Model training
   (a) Hyperparameter optimization
   (b) Model parameter optimization
5. Model validation

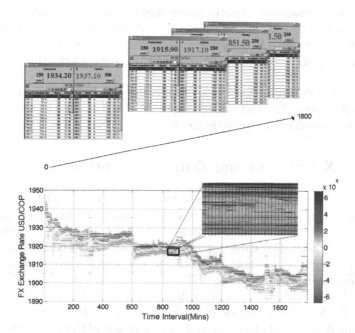

Fig. 4. A heatmap visual representation of USD/COP SET-FX LOB dynamics information, data. y-axis represents USD/COP exchange rates and x-axis captures time intervals using an aggregating one-min interval. Red intensities represented sell volumes and green intensities represents buy volumes. The zooming shows a segments of the LOB volume dynamics that can be uses as a predictive pattern for the price movement, (Color figure online)

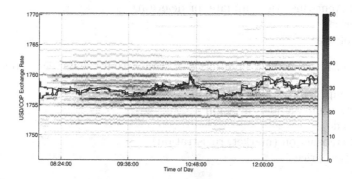

Fig. 5. A heatmap visual representation of USD/COP SET-FX LOB dynamics information from March 21, 2012. Red intensities present volume, white spaces correspond to zero volume with every volume unit equivalent to 250 thousand US dollars. Maximum volume, 60 in the color bar, is equal to 15 million US dollars. Solid black lines show best buy/sell price evolution. (Color figure online)

TPOT[1] is an open-source, genetic programming-based AutoML system that optimizes a series of feature preprocessors and machine learning models with the aim of maximizing classification or regression accuracy on a supervised task. Often, the ML models identified by TPOT outperform those developed by experts [12].

At its core, TPOT functions as a wrapper for the Python machine learning package, scikit-learn [14], and evolves using NSGA-II scikit-learn pipelines [6], which can be visualized as syntactic trees.

4   SET-FX Data Set and Data Exploration

The data set used in this study consists of six days of LOB (Limit Order Book) events, including limit order insertions, updates, deletions, and transaction events such as price, volume, and side of LOB. This information is available for replication[2]. The data was obtained from the SET-FX FIX algorithmic engine through Algocodex, a Colombian algorithmic trading company that develops trading algorithms in the SET-FX market for "Acciones y Valores," a Colombian broker that holds one of the largest positions in the SET-FX market.

The SET-FX market operates for 5 h from 8 AM to 1 PM, and each day there are approximately 14,000 LOB events, equating to one LOB event approximately every 1.29 s. Additionally, there are approximately 1,500 transactions every day, resulting in one transaction event approximately every 12 s.

The information is organized into a one-day tick-by-tick time series of LOB events, each containing:

- Time stamp
- Order unique identification
- Market side
- Type of event (insertion, update, or deletion)
- Order price
- Order volume

Combined with tick-by-tick time series of transaction events, each containing:

- Time stamp
- Transaction unique identification
- Market side
- Type of transaction (market, registration)
- Transaction price
- Volume

---

[1] http://epistasislab.github.io/tpot/.
[2] https://github.com/gjhernandezp/SetFX.

We transform this information into second-by-second granularity cumulative time series and images, using a 64-second sliding window of these time series and images to identify price trend predictive patterns as shown in Fig. 7. We also perform a multi-resolution study of the time series and images and a frequency analysis of them. Sliding 64-second windows and Haar wavelets were used to represent the time series and images. Figure 6 shows the result of applying four Haar wavelet levels, keeping only different time scale (1, 2, 4, 8, and 16 s) average coefficients of a time series.

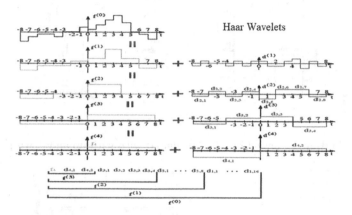

Fig. 6. Haar wavelets applied obtain different time scale (1,2,4,8 and 16 s) average coefficients of a time series

Following the approach from [18], we explore and cluster visual LOB (Limit Order Book) volume patterns that have the potential to predict price movements.

Figure 9 illustrates how LOB and transactions are associated with both upward and downward price trends.

Figure 8 presents 30 × 30 volume windows representing 30 min and 3 COP (Colombian Pesos) up and down from every mid-price. The mid-price is calculated using the lowest best buy price and the highest best sell price during the selected time window. In this representation, red signifies sell volume, and green represents buy volume.

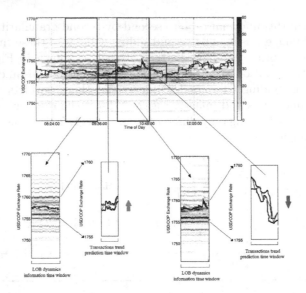

Fig. 7. How LOB and transactions are associated with with up and down price trends

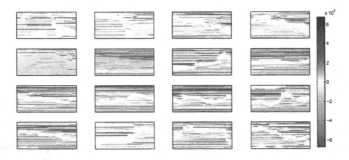

Fig. 8. 30 × 30 volume windows representing 30 min and 3 COP up and down from every mid-price calculated using lowest best buy price and highest best sell price during the selected time window. Red means sell volume and green represents buy volume.

Figure 9 displays the clustering of visual patches using K-means with 13 clusters. The bottom-most row provides a visual representation of each cluster's centroid. Clusters on the x-axis are organized according to their probability of being associated with a particular market trend. Clusters 12, 8, 7, 4, and 10 are related to upward trend movements, clusters 5, 6, 9, 3, 13, and 11 are associated with downward trend movements, and clusters 1 and 2 show a weak tendency toward downtrend regimes.

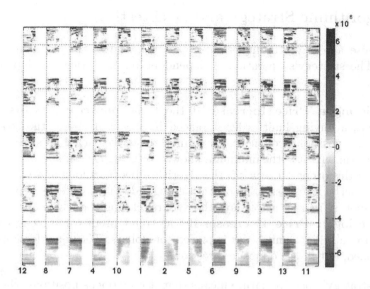

Fig. 9. Clustering of visual patches using K-means and 13 clusters. Bottom-most row presents a visual representation of every cluster's centroid. Clusters in the x-axis are organized according to their probability of being associated to a particular market trend. Clusters 12, 8, 7, 4, 10 are related to uptrend movements, clusters 5, 6, 9, 3, 13, 11 are related to downtrend movements and clusters 1, 2 showed a weak tendency to downtrend regimes.

The features considered for the analysis are categorized into LOB and transaction features. For the LOB, the features are:

- Time series of spreads (relative to the first mid-price)
- Time series of mid-prices (relative to the first mid-price)
- Time series of best buy prices (relative to the first mid-price)
- Time series of best sell prices (relative to the first mid-price)
- Time series of best buy volumes (relative to the first mid-price)
- Time series of best sell volumes (relative to the first mid-price)
- Time series of market sides (B: buy, S: sell)
- Time series of types of events (I: insertion, U: update, D: deletion)
- Time series of order prices (relative to the first mid-price)
- Time series of order volumes (relative to COP 12M)
- Time series of images representing the LOB dynamics, with a 64-second time window (64 pixels) and $10 COP granularity, quantized at $20 cents (50 pixels)

For the transaction data, the features are:

- Time series of transaction prices
- Time series of transaction volumes
- Time series of transaction market sides
- Time series of transaction types (M: market, R: registration)

5   Algorithmic Strategy and Backtesting

We propose a passive trading strategy that seeks to exploit predicted price trends. The strategy's operation is dependent on the price trend predictor's forecasts:

- **Predicting a Price Increase**: If the trend predictor forecasts a price increase, a buying limit order is placed in the book. Since the strategy is passive, a position is opened only if another market actor sells the specified amount (in our case, the minimum allowed of US$250,000) at the offered buy price. If this order is executed, the algorithm becomes long and places a new limit order at the best price on the selling side. This order is kept in place until another market actor buys the dollars, closing the whole operation.
- **Predicting a Price Decrease**: If the trend predictor forecasts a price decrease, a selling limit order is placed for dollars. The same logic as above is applied, but in the opposite direction.

The strategy's passive nature means that it only opens positions when other market actors execute the orders, rather than actively pursuing trades.

To evaluate the effectiveness of the strategy, we backtested it on both training and testing days, and also tested it on an out-of-sample day. The simulation logic used to emulate the artificial order placed by the algorithmic strategy assumes that it is executed if an order ahead in the LOB is executed. In other words, an order with a lower price must be executed on the buy side, and an order with a higher price must be executed on the sell side.

Given the promising exploration of LOB (Limit Order Book) volume visual patterns, we employed TPOT to find a competitive predictor based on the information of LOB dynamics and transactions [11]. We considered the data from the previous minute, using an up or down trend criterion based on whether the average transaction price was 20 cents higher or lower than the previous minute's closing price.

The configuration for TPOT involved 20 generations and a population size of 10, with 5-fold cross-validation. Utilizing the initial five days of the data set, TPOT found a competitive predictor with a 77% total accuracy rate, 68% accuracy for upward trends, and 69% accuracy for downward trends.

The backtesting of the algorithmic trading strategy, based on the predictive model found by TPOT, was conducted on the sixth day (2019–06–26) of the data set. The results of this backtesting are illustrated in Fig. 10.

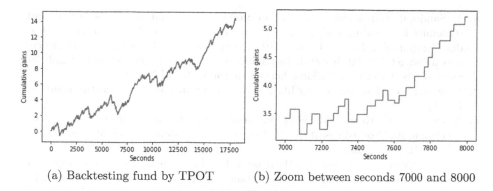

(a) Backtesting fund by TPOT   (b) Zoom between seconds 7000 and 8000

Fig. 10. Backtesting of the algorithmic trading strategy based on an predictive fund by TPOT on the 6th day (2019–06–26) of the data set.

6   Conclusion and Future Work

The algorithmic trading strategy developed for the Colombian US dollar inter-bank bulk order-driven market (SET-FX), utilizing an evolutionary predictive model constructed with TPOT, has demonstrated a high level of competitiveness. The observed gain of COP \$14 in the backtesting on the sixth day of the data set equates to approximately US\$1000 daily. Given that the positions were of US\$250,000, the result is COP \$14 × 250,000 = COP \$3.5M ≈ US\$1000.

This success suggests potential for further enhancement. Future work may explore the use of specialized time series AutoML tools, such as Auto-TS [13] or Auto_TimeSeries [9]. Additionally, the integration of reinforcement learning techniques [10] [3] could provide another avenue for improvement, possibly leading to even more robust and responsive trading algorithms.

References

1. Avellaneda, M., Stoikov, S.: High-frequency trading in a limit order book. Quant. Finan. **8**, 217–224 (2008)
2. Biais, B., Bruno, P., Hillion, S.: An empirical analysis of the order flow and order book in the Paris bourse. J. Finan. **50**(5), 1655–1689 (1995)
3. Burhani, H., Ding, G., Hernandez-Leal, P., Prince, S., Shi, D., Szeto, S.: Aiden: reinforcement learning for electronic trading (2020). https://www.borealisai.com/research-blogs/aiden-reinforcement-learning-for-order-execution
4. Cont, R., Stoikov, S., Talreja, R.: A stochastic model for order book dynamics. Oper. Res. **58**(3), 549–563 (2010)
5. Elshawi, R., Maher, M., Sakr, S.: Automated machine learning: state-of-the-art and open challenges (2019). https://arxiv.org/abs/1906.02287v2
6. Goel, A.: Are you using pipeline in scikit-learn? (2020). https://towardsdatascience.com/are-you-using-pipeline-in-scikit-learn-ac4cd85cb27f
7. Gould, M.D., Porter, M.A., Williams, S., McDonald, M., Fenn, D.J., Howison, S.D.: Limit Order Books. ArXiv e-prints (2010)

8. J. Sandoval, Hernandez, G.: Computational visual analysis of the order book dynamics for creating high-frequency foreign exchange trading strategies. Procedia Comput. Sci. **51**, 1593–1602 (2015). https://www.sciencedirect.com/science/article/pii/S1877050915010984. International Conference On Computational Science, ICCS 2015 Computational Science at the Gates of Nature

9. Lazzeri, F.: Python open source libraries for scaling time series forecasting solutions (2021)

10. Nevmyvaka, Y., Kearns, M., Feng, Y.: Reinforcement learning for optimized trade execution. In: Proceedings of the 23rd International Conference on Machine Learning, ICML2006 (2006)

11. Niño, J., Arévalo, A., Leon, D., Hernandez, G., Sandoval, J.: Price prediction with CNN and limit order book data. In: Figueroa-García, J.C., López-Santana, E.R., Rodriguez-Molano, J.I. (eds.) WEA 2018. CCIS, vol. 915, pp. 124–135. Springer, Cham (2018). https://doi.org/10.1007/978-3-030-00350-0_11

12. Olson, R.S., Bartley, N., Urbanowicz, R.J., Moore, J.H.: Evaluation of a tree-based pipeline optimization tool for automating data science. In: Proceedings of the 2016 Genetic and Evolutionary Computation Conference, GECCO 2016, pp. 485–492 (2016). https://arxiv.org/abs/1603.06212v1

13. Patil, R.: Automate time series forecasting using auto-ts (2021). https://www.analyticsvidhya.com/blog/2021/04/automate-time-series-forecasting-using-auto-ts/

14. Pedregosa, F., et al.: Scikit-learn: machine learning in python. J. Mach. Learn. Res. (2011)

15. Sandoval, J.: High frequency exchange rate prediction using dynamic Bayesian networks over the limit order book information. PhD. Thesis, Universidad Nacional de Colombia (2016)

16. Sandoval, J., Hernández, G.: Learning of natural trading strategies on foreign exchange high-frequency market data using dynamic Bayesian networks. In: Perner, P. (ed.) MLDM 2014. LNCS (LNAI), vol. 8556, pp. 408–421. Springer, Cham (2014). https://doi.org/10.1007/978-3-319-08979-9_30

17. Sandoval, J., Hernandez, G.: High-frequency trading strategies using wavelet-transformed order book information and dynamic Bayesian networks. In: Science and Information Conference (SAI), 2015, pp. 435–442 (2015)

18. Sandoval, J., Hernandez, G., Cruz, A.: Detecting informative patterns in financial market trends based on visual analysis. Procedia Comput. Sci. **80**, 752–761 (2016)

19. Slanina, F.: Mean-field approximation for a limit order driven market model. Phys. Rev. E **64**(5), 056136 (2001). https://arxiv.org/abs/cond-mat/0104547

20. Yang, X.S.: Introduction to Mathematical Optimization. Cambridge International Science Publishing (2008)

21. Yu, Y.: The limit order book information and the order submission strategy: a model explanation. In: Proceedings of the International Conference on Service Systems and Service Management, vol. 1, pp. 687–691. IEEE (2006)

Evaluating the Incidence of Different Factors on the Level of Service at Interceptions Without Traffic Lights

Mabel Frias[1]([✉])[ID], Yaima Filiberto[2][ID], Ileana Cadenas[3], Rafael Bello[4][ID], and Koen Vanhoof[5][ID]

[1] Development Department, Efimob Efficient Solutions, S.L., Vigo, Spain
m.frias@efimob.com
[2] Research and Development Department, AMV Solutions, Vigo, Spain
yaima.filiberto@amvsoluciones.com
[3] Civil Engineer Department, Universidad de Camagüey, Camaguey, Cuba
ileana.cadenas@reduc.edu.cu
[4] Computer Sciences Departament, Central University of Las Villas,
Santa Clara, Cuba
rbellop@uclv.edu.cu
[5] Business Intelligence, Faculty of Business Economics, Universiteit Hasselt,
Hasselt, Belgium
koen.vanhoof@uhasselt.be

Abstract. Considering the good performance of the Interval-valued Long-term Cognitive Networks model and the Nonsynaptic Backpropagation learning variants proposed as training learning to the method. This article is focused on the application of both proposals in the analysis of the incidence of different factors on the level of service at intersections without traffic lights.

Keywords: Interval sets · nonsynaptic learning · recurrent neural networks · Level of Service

1 Introduction

The urban explosion of cities generates traffic problems that affect the level of service and road capacity. Measuring some traffic characteristics accurately is complex, costly, and tedious. Current scientific studies focus on achieving sustainable streets that respond to increased traffic speeds and avoid street congestion. Therefore, traffic engineering is needed as a science to solve the problem in many cities where street systems have to operate beyond their capacity, resulting in accidents and congestion [6].

In Cuba, traffic has characteristics that differentiate it from other countries because different means of transport coexist, such as light vehicles (a great variety of automobiles), heavy vehicles, and animal traction vehicles. It is also characterized by high bicycle circulation. This phenomenon has been a case study for

J. C. Figueroa-García et al. (Eds.): WEA 2023, CCIS 1928, pp. 25–35, 2023.
https://doi.org/10.1007/978-3-031-46739-4_3

the Vias group of the University of Camagüey [2]. In addition, each province has specific characteristics, and Camagüey belongs to one of the first cities founded by the colonizers, with a medieval-like city and the development of many avenues. Its structure has determined that road traffic has particular characteristics [7].

The labyrinthine structure of the city is one reason that drives the research groups of Roads (Viales) and Artificial Intelligence (AIRES), both belonging to the University of Camagüey, to devote research to the improvement of Camagüey's roads. The results of these investigations provided a starting point to determine the influential parameters on the levels of service in different kinds of roads. This research proposes using a neural structure as the IVLTCN model [4] to simplify field studies. Considering the good performance of the IVLTCN model and the NSBP variants presented in the article [3], this study is aimed at the application of the IVLTCN model in the analysis of the incidence of different factors on the level of service at intersections without traffic lights.

The outline of this paper follows. Section 2 briefly describes Nonsynaptic Backpropagation Learning variants. Section 3 presents a case study where the impact of different factors on the level of service at intersections without traffic lights is evaluated through the IVLTCN model and the learning algorithm described in Sect. 2. Finally, Sect. 4 shows the general conclusions.

2   Interval-Nonsynaptic Backpropagation Learning Algorithms

Three skipped learning variants were proposed in [3] to avoid the vanishing/exploding gradient issues that might suffer the traditional propagation-based algorithms. This section briefly describes these nonsynaptic backpropagation algorithms, which are based on three variants published in [5]. These newest variants, as proposed in [5], are based on the idea that employing the same weights during the forward and backward passes is NOT essential to train a recurrent neural network.

2.1   Interval-Value Random NSBP Algorithm

The first proposal is based on the Random NSBP (R-NSBP) introduced in [5], where the weight matrix in the backward pass is replaced with a matrix comprised of normally distributed random numbers. Equation (1) and Eq. (2) show how to compute the partial derivative of the total error with respect to the neuron's activation value in the current iteration for the R-NSBP and the method described in this subsection Interval-value Random NSBP algorithm (IVR-NSBP) [3] (see Fig. 1), respectively;

$$\frac{\partial \mathcal{E}}{\partial a_i^{(t)}} = \sum_{j=1}^{M} \frac{\partial \mathcal{E}}{\partial a_j^{(t+1)}} \otimes \frac{\partial a_j^{(t+1)}}{\partial \bar{a}_i^{(t+1)}} \times \bar{w}_{ij}. \tag{1}$$

$$\frac{\partial \mathcal{E}^{\pm}}{\partial a_i^{\pm(t)}} = \sum_{j=1}^{M} \frac{\partial \mathcal{E}^{\pm}}{\partial a_j^{\pm(t+1)}} \otimes \frac{\partial a_j^{\pm(t+1)}}{\partial \bar{a}_i^{\pm(t+1)}} \otimes \bar{w}_{ij}^{\pm}. \tag{2}$$

where $\bar{w}_{ij}^{\pm}$ is the Gaussian random number generated with the following probability distribution function:

$$f(x|\mu_{ij}^{\pm}, \sigma^2) = \frac{1}{\sqrt{2\pi\sigma^2}} \otimes e^{-\frac{(x-\mu_{ij}^{\pm})^2}{2\sigma^2}} \tag{3}$$

where $\mu_{ij}^{\pm} = \bar{w}_{ij}^{\pm}$ denotes the mean and $\sigma^2 = 0.2$ represents the variance.

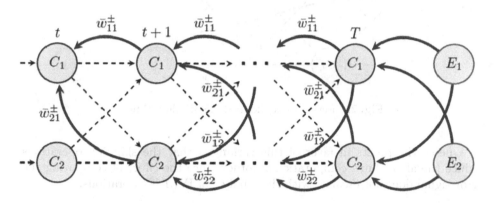

Fig. 1. Interval-value Random NSBP algorithm.

The random weights can be forced to share the same sign as the weights defined during the network construction step. On the other hand, weights in the forward pass and the nonsynaptic parameters are employed as indicated in the original NSBP learning algorithm.

2.2   Interval-Value Skipped NSBP Algorithm

The second version is a method named Interval-value Skipped NSBP algorithm (IVS-NSBP). Like its predecessor, S-NSBP [5] uses a deep learning channel to deliver the error signal directly to the current abstract hidden layer (see Fig. 2). The partial derivative of the global error concerning the neuron's output in the contemporary abstract layer can be computed by Eq. (4) in the method S-NSBP and by Eq. (5) in IVS-NSBP.

$$\frac{\partial \mathcal{E}}{\partial a_i^{(t)}} = \sum_{j=1}^{M} -(y_j(k) \ominus a_j^{(T)}) \otimes w_{ij}. \tag{4}$$

$$\frac{\partial \mathcal{E}^\pm}{\partial a_i^{\pm(t)}} = \sum_{j=1}^{M} -(y_j^\pm(k) \ominus a_j^{\pm(T)}) \otimes w_{ij}^\pm. \tag{5}$$

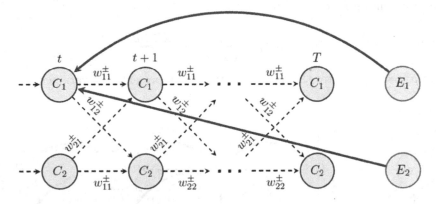

Fig. 2. Interval-value Skipped NSBP algorithm.

One of the points in favor of this variant is that the skipping operations reduce the algorithm's computational border since the effort of computing the error signal does not escalate with the number of IVLTCN iterations.

2.3 Interval-Value Random-Skipped NSBP Algorithm

The Interval-value Random-Skipped NSBP algorithm (IVRS-NSBP) [3] is a method that allows skipping operations while using random Gaussian numbers with mean $\mu_{ij}^\pm = w_{ij}^\pm$ and $\sigma^2 = 0.2$ (see Fig. 3). The IVRS-NSBP is based on the RS-NSBP [5]. A slight variance was adopted to avoid weight in the deep learning channel being too different from those used during the forward pass. This idea is formalized by the Eq. (6) in the method RS-NSBP and Eq. (7) for IVRS-NSBP.

$$\frac{\partial \mathcal{E}}{\partial a_i^{(t)}} = \sum_{j=1}^{M} -(y_j(k) \ominus a_j^{(T)}) \times \bar{w}_{ij} \tag{6}$$

$$\frac{\partial \mathcal{E}^\pm}{\partial a_i^{\pm(t)}} = \sum_{j=1}^{M} -(y_j^\pm(k) \ominus a_j^{\pm(T)}) \otimes \bar{w}_{ij}^\pm \tag{7}$$

In essence, the three variants are different from the ones proposed at [5] because now the map can handle a higher level of uncertainty due to the performance of the inference process being in a range of grey numbers and without any whitenization process. Also, just two learnable parameters associated with the generalized sigmoid transfer function are adjusted: $\lambda_i^{\pm(t)}$ and $h_i^{\pm(t)}$.

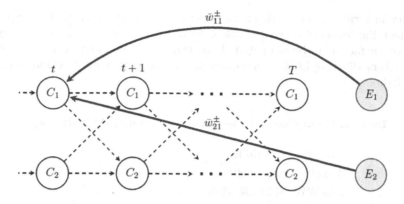

Fig. 3. Interval-value Random-Skipped NSBP algorithm.

3 Evaluating the Incidence of Different Factors on the Level of Service at Interceptions Without Traffic Lights

This section will analyze the relations among different factors affecting the level of service of intersections without traffic lights in Camagüey'. The level of service (LOS) was defined by the Highway Capacity Manual (HCM 2000) as a quality measure that describes the operational conditions within a traffic stream, generally in terms of service provided by the road to the user [1]. The factors that can affect an intersection's levels of service can be divided into two groups: Geometric characteristics such as lane widths, sidewalk widths, center divider widths, side parking, and pavement condition, and traffic characteristics such as peak hour volume, the peak intensity of the maximum demand, percentage of bicycles, percentage of animal-drawn vehicles, average stop delay, average stop delay of all vehicles and percentage of vehicles stopping.

Traffic characteristics must be studied through fieldwork to obtain the measurements, and then desk work to process the data. Although these studies do not contain complex procedures that make their calculations difficult, they are incredibly tedious. The same operations have to be repeated many times. In addition, even if you have all the time you need to make these measurements on the road, these values constantly vary because even the weather that day can affect traffic levels. Therefore, counting on a tool that allows obtaining reasonable conclusions even when the information is uncertain will speed up the work with greater reliability.

In this experiment, the IVLTCN model was used with IVS-NSBP with an uncertainty level of 0.05, and the "transitoNSI" dataset was created with 11 features and 130 instances described in Table 1. The intersections were selected in the city of Camagüey', taking ten intersections without traffic lights and diversity in terms of geometric characteristics and other essential features that can affect the levels of service. Table 2 show five scenarios that allow varying orders of the factors to be evaluated. This study aims to analyze the incidence of these factors affecting LOS from a different perspective at intersections without traffic lights.

Table 1. Description of the features of the "transitoNSI" data set

Features	Description
LaneW	Lane widths
SideWW	Sidewalk widths
CentDW	Center divider widths
PavC	Pavement Condition
MDV	Maximum demand volume (veh/h)
Intens	Maximum intensity of demand (veh/h)
PercBici	percentage of bicycles
PerVeh	percentage of vehicles
ASD	Average stop delay
ASDV	Average stop delay of all vehicles
PerVS	percentage of vehicles stopping
LOS	level of service

The first scenario shows the leading indicators analyzed by HCM 2000. In this way, how the foreign methodologies are adjusted to Cuban roads, specifically to the streets of Camagüey will be verified. In this scenario, delay parameters are evaluated together with traffic volumes.

In the second scenario, the primary geometric characteristics of the intercepted roads are collected, from lane width to pavement condition. The idea is to evaluate how these specifications affect user traffic. Scenario three summarizes the traffic characteristics of Cuban streets with a high concentration of bicycles in the vehicular flow.

Scenario four mixes geometric and traffic characteristics. In this way, the difference in the influence of the factors in the different scenarios can be observed. For the above reasons, it was decided that all the previously studied parameters would interact to analyze the problem integrated into a system of correlated actions and characteristics in scenario five. A file with the extension ".arff" is created for each scenario. That is to say, the general information is taken, multiple copies are made, and in each one, the parameters are eliminated according to the scenario to be analyzed, obtaining five ".arff" files.

Table 2. Scenarios

Scenario 1	Scenario 2	Scenario 3	Scenario 4	Scenario 5
MDV	LaneW	MDV	LaneW	LaneW
intens	SideWW	intens	SideWW	CentDW
ASD	CentDW	PerBici	CentDW	SideWW
ASDV	PavC	PerVeh	PavC	PavC
PerVS	LOS	LOS	MDV	MDV
LOS	–	–	intens	Intens
–	–	–	PerBici	PerBici
–	–	–	PerVeh	PerVeh
–	–	–	LOS	ASD
–	–	–	–	ASDV
–	–	–	–	PerVS
–	–	–	–	LOS

The following procedure will be used to carry out these experiments;

1. Build the decision system for the application domain.
2. The weight matrix is estimated according to the equation

$$w_{ji} = \frac{K \sum_k x_i(k)x_j(k) \ominus \sum_k x_i(k) \sum_k x_j(k)}{K(\sum_k x_j(k)^2) \ominus (\sum_k x_j(k))^2} \tag{8}$$

where $x_i(k)$ is the value of the i-th variable according to the k-th instance, while K is the number of cases in the data set. Afterward, these weights are transformed into interval grey numbers.

3. Configure the parameters of the IVS-NSBP learning algorithm. Recommended: learning rate $= 0.004$, momentum $= 0.8$, layer $= 3$, and the number of epochs is 200.
4. Run the IVLTCN algorithm with IVS-NSBP as the learning algorithm.
5. Calculate the $MSE^{\pm}$

$$MSE^{\pm}(X,Y) = \frac{1}{MK} \sum_{x \in X, y \in Y} \sum_{i=1}^{M} (a_i^{\pm(T)}(x) \ominus y_i^{\pm})^2 \tag{9}$$

where X is the set of corrupted patterns and Y is the set of original patterns, whereas $a_i^{\pm(T)}(x)$ is the response of the i-th neural concept in the last iteration (i.e., the abstract output layer) for the corrupted pattern $x \in X$. As a rule of thumb, the number of iterations T can equal the maximum number of variables predicted in a pattern.

The Fig. 4 shows the $MSE^{\pm}$ result for each scenario. As can be seen, the $MSE^{\pm}$ obtained by the IVLTCN+IVS-NSBP model is small.

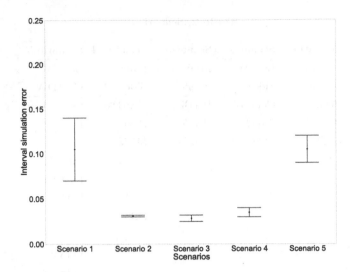

Fig. 4. Results of the $MSE^{\pm}$ for the scenarios.

Table 3 shows the activation values and the order of occurrence of the features that characterize the LOS at intersections without traffic lights. International methodologies define average delay as the leading indicator and other factors such as lane width (LaneW), maximum demand volume (MDV), and maximum intensity of demand (Intens). Corresponding to the variations made to the elements, it was determined that the percentage of bicycles (PercBici) should be taken into account in the LOS studies because it affects the circulation and incorporation of vehicles circulating on the secondary road to the main road.

In the first scenario analysis, the results correspond with those indicated by international methodologies in determining LOS, where average stop delay is the primary indicator concerning traffic volumes.

For the analysis in Scenario Two, center divider widths (CentDivW) and lane widths (LaneW) were the main factors influencing LOS. Previous research has shown that lane width is a parameter to be considered since the greater the possibility of movement, the greater the indiscipline committed by users.

The results obtained for Scenario Three clearly show that the most significant influences on LOS are the vehicle composition parameters (PercBici and PerVeh). Thus, it is demonstrated that the high concentration of bicycles on Cuba's streets, specifically in Camagüey, plays a crucial role in the LOS experienced by road users.

In scenario four, the geometric and traffic characteristics are mixed; the analysis must be different because they are now correlated, getting a little closer to the reality of what happens at intersections. From the parameters studied, it is clear that although the parameters describing the vehicle composition continue to predominate, it is important to consider the geometric characteristics CentDivW and LaneW. This shows that studies should analyze geometric and traffic characteristics to obtain adequate levels of service at intersections.

Table 3. Incidence of studied features.

Scenarios	Features	Activation values	Order of incidence
Scenario 1	MDV	[0.052 0.065]	5
	intens	[0.139 0.153]	4
	ASD	[0.9842 0.995]	1
	ASDV	[0.188 0.192]	3
	PerVS	[0.403 0.407]	2
Scenario 2	LaneW	[0.275 0.290]	2
	PavC	[0.150 0.180]	4
	CentDW	[0.298 0.301]	1
	SideWW	[0.274 0.275]	3
Scenario 3	MDV	[0.059 0.065]	4
	intens	[0.081 0.131]	3
	PerBici	[0.497 0.499]	1
	PerVeh	[0.440 0.458]	2
Scenario 4	LaneW	[0.270 0.297]	4
	SideWW	[0.274 0.275]	5
	CentDW	[0.298 0.301]	3
	PavC	[0.136 0.186]	6
	MDV	[0.053 0.063]	8
	intens	[0.050 0.136]	7
	PerBici	[0.497 0.498]	1
	PerVeh	[0.456 0.459]	2
Scenario 5	LaneW	[0.263 0.306]	7
	CentDW	[0.295 0.302]	5
	SideWW	[0.274 0.273]	6
	PavC	[0.124 0.199]	9
	MDV	[0.044 0.060]	11
	Intens	[0.144 0.151]	10
	PerBici	[0.490 0.499]	2
	PerVeh	[0.454 0.459]	3
	ASD	[0.978 0.995]	1
	ASDV	[0.170 0.192]	8
	PerVS	[0.402 0.408]	4

Scenario five is closer to reality at intersections, as it includes a broader set of measurable parameters and their interaction. More importantly, they cannot be considered isolated but are integrated into an urban structure. This experimental scenario again corroborates that the delay indicator is one of the essential aspects followed by the vehicle composition parameters (*PercBici* and *PerVeh*). Figure 5 and Table 4 show the resulting map and the weight matrix, respectively, for scenario 3.

It should be noted that these results are closely related to the data set constructed and the characteristics evaluated. It is recommended to increase the data and scenarios with new intersections or the same ones with other results in delay indicators ($ASDV$ and ASD) and MDV since traffic studies may be different each time they are performed.

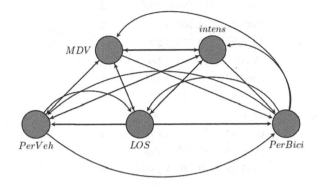

Fig. 5. Map obtained for the scenario 3.

Table 4. Weight matrix obtained for Scenario 3

	MDV	intens	PerBici	PerVeh	LOS
MDV	0	[1.206 1.306]	[−2.961 −2.861]	[2.161 2.261]	[2.057 2.157]
intens	[0.307 0.407]	0	[−1.635 −1.535]	[0.472 0.572]	[0.685 0.785]
PerBici	[−0.19 −0.09]	[−0.318 −0.218]	0	[−0.592 −0.492]	[−0.495 −0.395]
PerVeh	[−0.026 0.074]	[−0.03 0.07]	[−0.17 −0.07]	0	[−0.145 −0.045]
LOS	[−0.015 0.085]	[−0.007 0.093]	[−0.203 −0.103]	[−0.197 −0.097]	0

A correct prediction of the Level of Service at any road site allows engineers to analyze actions to promote a proper traffic organization in these areas to allow an adequate and stable flow of the different means of transport. These actions will impact the quality of the operational level experienced by drivers and pedestrians.

4   Conclusions

The model IVLTCN combined with the learning algorithm IVNSBP was applied in a real case referring to the analysis of the incidence of features that determine the level of service at significant intersections without traffic lights in Camagüey City. The vehicular flow and the geometric design of the roadway are essential elements to consider to determine the level of service at intersections. The incidence analysis in the different factors scenarios showed that delay features are the most significant element in all cases considered.

The use of a neuronal structure such as IVLTCN simplifies field studies. It makes it possible to express the variables with intervals of grey numbers, shortening the long hours of measurements on the roads that are usually necessary to obtain precise values of the variables involved in these studies.

The study developed in this article, with Artificial Intelligence techniques to analyze different scenarios, showed that the features related to delays are the most notable elements present in all scenarios where they were considered. In addition, the roadway's vehicular flow and geometric characteristics are also essential factors to consider in determining service levels at intersections without traffic lights.

References

1. Transportation Research Board, National Academies of Sciences, Engineering, and Medicine: Highway Capacity Manual 7th Edition: A Guide for Multimodal Mobility Analysis. The National Academies Press, Washington, DC (2022). https://doi.org/10.17226/26432, www.nap.nationalacademies.org/catalog/26432/highway-capacity-manual-7th-edition-a-guide-for-multimodal-mobility
2. Céspedes, L.R., Cadenas, I.F.: Incidence of vehicle composition on the level of service at non-signalized intersections in camaguey. In: Simposio Internacional de Construcciones. Convención 2021 (2021)
3. Frias, M., Nápoles, G., Filiberto, Y., Bello, R., Vanhoof, K.: Skipped nonsynaptic backpropagation for interval-valued long-term cognitive networks. In: Pichardo Lagunas, O., Martínez-Miranda, J., Martínez Seis, B. (eds.) MICAI 2022. LNCS, vol. 13612, pp. 3–14. Springer, Cham (2022). https://doi.org/10.1007/978-3-031-19493-1_1
4. Frias, M., Nápoles, G., Vanhoof, K., Filiberto, Y., Bello, R.: Nonsynaptic backpropagation learning of interval-valued long-term cognitive networks. In: 2021 International Joint Conference on Neural Networks (IJCNN), pp. 1–9 (2021). https://doi.org/10.1109/IJCNN52387.2021.9533586
5. Nápoles, G., Grau, I., Concepción, L., Salgueiro, Y.: On the performance of the nonsynaptic backpropagation for training long-term cognitive networks. In: 11th International Conference of Pattern Recognition Systems (ICPRS 2021), vol. 2021, pp. 25–30 (2021). https://doi.org/10.1049/icp.2021.1434
6. Radelat, G.: Principios de Ingeniería de Tránsito. Institute of Transportation Engineers, Washington D.C. (2003)
7. Rey, L.: Evaluación de la incidencia del reordenamiento vial en el tránsito en el centro histórico de la ciudad de camagüey (2013). Unpublished Master thesis

Physically Informed Neural Networks Applied to Financial Derivatives Valuation in Markets with Liquidity Risk

John Freddy Moreno Trujillo[✉] iD

Universidad Externado de Colombia, Bogotá, Colombia
jhon.moreno@uexternado.edu.co

Abstract. A market model with liquidity risk associated with agent trading is considered. The dynamics of prices for risky assets are described in this context, and the corresponding nonlinear partial differential equation for derivatives pricing is derived. The use of physically informed neural networks is proposed for the resolution of this equation.

Keywords: Liquidity risk · pricing derivatives · physically informed neural networks

1 Introduction

Although the pioneering derivative valuation model developed by Fisher Black and Myron Scholes in 1973 [3] is still widely used in financial practice, there are multiple criticisms that deem it unsuitable for describing the functioning of real markets due to the set of assumptions on which it is built. One typical example is the assumption of perfect liquidity of the underlying asset, which establishes that agents can trade this asset in any quantity immediately and without affecting its price. The criticism arises because it is widely recognized that not all markets are perfectly liquid, even when the underlying asset is traded in a well-established financial market. In fact, every price is subject to the so-called liquidity risk, and this source of uncertainty is considered one of the most critical risks in the current financial industry.

While there is no consensus on how to define liquidity, a considerable amount of research has focused on studying the effects of liquidity risk on asset prices (see, for example [1] or [8]). However, the development of a comprehensive model that adequately captures the impact of liquidity risk on the determination of derivative prices is still to be proposed. Consequently, an important challenge is to understand how liquidity risk influences price dynamics and derivative valuation. The purpose of this work is to present some new advances in this direction, developing the deduction of the corresponding pricing nonlinear partial differential valuation equation and proposing the use of physically informed neural networks for its resolution.

This document has 4 sections, with this introduction being the first. The second section presents the proposal for the market model with liquidity risk and carries out

J. C. Figueroa-García et al. (Eds.): WEA 2023, CCIS 1928, pp. 36–46, 2023.
https://doi.org/10.1007/978-3-031-46739-4_4

the deduction of the pricing equation. In the third section, the solution to the pricing equation using PINN (Physically Informed Neural Networks) is presented, and in the fourth section, some conclusions are provided.

2 Market Model and Pricing Equation

We consider a filtered probability space $\left(\Omega, F, P, (F_t)_{t \in [0,T]}\right)$ that model's uncertainty in the economy, where P is an empirical or market probability measure, and T is a finite time horizon. It is assumed that all stochastic processes involved are adapted to the filtration $(F_t)_{t \in [0,T]}$. The market is composed of:

- A risk-free asset with value at time t denoted by $B(t)$, associated with a constant and known interest rate $r > 0$. This asset represents the value of money in the market, and the dynamics of its price are described by the ordinary differential equation:

$$dB(t) = rB(t)dt; \quad t \in [0,T] \tag{1}$$

- A risky asset with value at time t denoted by $S(t)$, whose dynamics are characterized by the stochastic differential equation:

$$dS(t) = \alpha S(t)dt + \sigma S(t)dW(t) + \lambda(t, S(t))S(t)dN(t) \tag{2}$$

where: α is a constant representing the instantaneous expected rate of return of this asset, $\sigma > 0$ is a constant representing its instantaneous volatility, $W(t)$ is a standard Brownian motion defined on the considered probability space, $\lambda(t, S(t)) > 0$ is the term representing market illiquidity at time t, and $N(t)$ is the process describing the number of units an agent holds at time t of this asset.

If $\lambda = 0$, meaning the market is perfectly liquid, Eq. (2) reduces to the stochastic differential expression of a geometric Brownian motion, as in the classical Black-Scholes model. The term $\lambda(t, S(t))S(t)dN(t)$ in (2) describes the impact of the agent's trading strategy and the illiquidity factor on price dynamics. If $dN(t) > 0$, that is, if the agnt acquires the asset, it pushes the price upwards by an amount weighted by the market's illiquidity factor. Conversely, if $dN(t) < 0$, i.e., if the agent sells the asset, it pushes the price downwards by an amount weighted by the illiquidity factor.

- A financial derivative contracted on the risky asset, with value at time t denoted by $h(t, S(t))$, and its value at time T is $h(T, S(T)) = \Phi(S(T))$, where $\Phi(\cdot)$ is the function that describes the possible payoffs of the derivative at maturity.

In addition to these assets, the dynamics of the agent's trading strategy and their wealth process are considered.

- The agent's trading strategy is described by the number of units they hold of the risky asset at time t, denoted by $N(t)$. In the classic Black-Scholes model, it is assumed that once the agent establishes the initial quantity of units in which they take a position, they continue trading the asset according to an Itô process. In this case, we will assume that the process $N(t)$ satisfies the stochastic differential equation:

$$dN(t) = \eta(\theta - N(t))dt + \gamma dW(t) \tag{3}$$

In other words, the agent's trading strategy follows a mean-reversion process, where η is a constant representing the speed of mean reversion, θ is a constant representing the long-term number of units of the asset that the agent holds, $\gamma > 0$ is a constant representing the instantaneous volatility associated with changes in the number of units, and $W(t)$ is the same standard Brownian motion (source of randomness) associated with the asset price.

The selection of a mean-reversion process to describe the agents' trading strategy is novel in the literature and allows the incorporation of elements that are considered separately in other works, such as the permanent impact of the agent's trading speed on price dynamics. In this proposal, the trading speed is described by the constant parameter η in Eq. (3).

- The agent's wealth at time t is denoted by $Y(t)$ and is given by:

$$Y(t) = \varphi(t)B(t) + N(t)S(t) \tag{4}$$

where $\varphi(t)$ represents the amount invested or borrowed at the risk-free rate, and $N(t)$ is the number of units of the risky asset held by the agent. It is considered that the agent's trading strategy is self-financed, i.e.:

$$dY(t) = \varphi(t)dB(t) + N(t)dS(t) \tag{5}$$

This ensures the absence of arbitrage opportunities in the market (see [4]).

2.1 Dynamics of Variables in Illiquid Markets

Considering the elements of the market model, the relationship between the illiquidity factor, the agent's trading strategy, and the dynamics of asset prices is described below.

- The dynamics of the price of this asset satisfy:

$$dS(t) = S(t)[\alpha + \lambda\eta(\theta - N(t))]dt + S(t)(\sigma + \lambda\gamma)dW(t) \tag{6}$$

The trend coefficient in Eq. (6) shows the permanent effect of the agent's trading strategy on prices, as well as the effect of their trading speed, weighted by the market's illiquidity factor. In the diffusion coefficient, the effect of the volatility of the trading strategy is also captured, weighted by the illiquidity factor.

- The dynamics of the agent's wealth satisfy:

$$dY(t) = \{Y(t)r - S(t)N(t)r + N(t)S(t)[\alpha + \lambda\eta(\theta - N(t))]\}dt + N(t)S(t)(\sigma + \lambda\gamma)dW(t)$$

$$\tag{7}$$

2.2 Pricing Equation

Using subscript notation to represent the corresponding partial derivatives and applying Itô's formula, we have:

$$dh(t, S(t)) = h_t dt + h_S dS(t) + \frac{1}{2}h_{SS}(dS(t))^2$$

$$dh(t, S(t)) = \left\{ h_t + S(t)h_S[\alpha + \lambda\eta(\theta - N(t))] + \frac{1}{2}S^2(t)h_{SS}[\sigma + \lambda\gamma]^2 \right\} dt$$
$$+ S(t)h_S(\sigma + \lambda\gamma)dW(t) \tag{8}$$

The agent seeks to dynamically replicate the derivative through their trading strategy, i.e., $dY(t) = dh(t, S(t))$. By equating the diffusion coefficients in Eqs. (7) and (8), we have:

$$N(t)S(t)(\sigma + \lambda\gamma) = S(t)h_S(\sigma + \lambda\gamma)$$

From this, it follows that $N(t) = h_S$, which indicates that the agent is following a delta-hedging strategy[1]. By equating the trend coefficients in (7) and (8), considering that $Y(t) = h(t, S(t)) \equiv h$ and $N(t) = h_S$, we have

$$h_t + rS(t)h_S + \frac{1}{2}S^2(t)[\sigma + \lambda\gamma]^2 h_{SS} - rh = 0 \tag{9}$$

This is the partial differential equation that the derivative must satisfy in the framework of this market model. Note that if $\lambda = 0$, Eq. (9) reduces to the partial differential equation of the Black-Scholes model.

Considering Eq. (9), we can see that it depends on the parameter γ, associated with the dynamics of the agent's trading strategy. However, we aim to have a partial differential equation for valuation that only depends on the parameters associated with the price of the underlying asset and market illiquidity, which are the same for all agents, and not on specific characteristics of individual trading strategies. To achieve this, we start by considering that $N(t) = h_S$, which makes $N(t)$ dependent on t and $S(t)$. Applying Itô's formula to $N(t)$, we have:

$$dN(t) = \left\{ h_{St} + S(t)h_{SS}[\alpha + \lambda\eta(\theta - h_S)] + \frac{1}{2}S^2(t)h_{SSS}[\sigma + \lambda\gamma]^2 \right\} dt +$$
$$S(t)h_{SS}[\sigma + \lambda\gamma]dW(t) \tag{10}$$

by equating the diffusion coefficients of Eqs. (10) and (3), it follows that:

$$\gamma = \frac{S(t)\sigma h_{SS}}{1 - S(t)\lambda h_{SS}} \tag{11}$$

if $1 - S(t)\lambda h_{SS} \neq 0$, according to Eq. (11), the term $(\sigma + \lambda\gamma)$ is equal to:

$$\sigma + \lambda\gamma = \frac{\sigma}{1 - S(t)\lambda h_{SS}} \equiv \hat{\sigma} \tag{12}$$

and the valuation equation is:

$$h_t + rS(t)h_S + \frac{1}{2}S^2(t)\left(\frac{\sigma}{1 - S(t)\lambda h_{SS}}\right)^2 h_{SS} - rh = 0 \tag{13}$$

---

[1] In a delta-hedging strategy, the number of units of the underlying asset in which the agent takes a position to hedge their exposure is given by the partial derivative of the derivative's value with respect to the price of the underlying asset.

It is a second-order nonlinear partial differential equation that generalizes the Black-Scholes pricing equation.

Additionally, if we equate the trend coefficients in expressions (10) and (3), we have:

$$\eta(\theta - h_S) = \frac{h_{St} + \alpha S(t)h_{SS} + \frac{1}{2}S^2(t)h_{SSS}\hat{\sigma}}{1 - S(t)\lambda h_{SS}} \tag{14}$$

According to (14), we have:

$$\alpha + \lambda\eta(\theta - h_S) = \frac{\alpha + \lambda h_{St}}{1 - S(t)\lambda h_{SS}} + \frac{\lambda S^2(t)\sigma^2 h_{SSS}}{2(1 - S(t)\lambda h_{SS})^3} = \hat{\alpha} \tag{15}$$

From the previous expressions, it follows that the dynamics of the risky asset price are given by $dS(t) = \hat{\alpha}S(t)dt + \sigma\hat{S}(t)dW(t)$.

2.3 Market Illiquidity Factor

Following the works [2, 6] and [11], we consider that the market illiquidity factor takes the form:

$$\lambda(t, S(t)) = \frac{\xi}{S(t)}\left[1 - e^{-\beta(T-t)}\right] \tag{16}$$

where $\xi > 0$ is a constant coefficient that measures the impact on the asset price per unit traded. This functional form assumes that when the agent buys, the asset price goes up, and when they sell, the price goes down, with the magnitude of the impact being proportional to the number of units traded. Linearity is required to ensure the absence of arbitrage, as shown by Huberman and Stanzl in 2004 [5]. Additionally, this form implies that as time passes, private information about the asset value is revealed, so the price impact gradually decreases until it reaches zero at T, avoiding any manipulation of the price at maturity.

Starting from this functional form of the market illiquidity factor, we have that:

$$1 - S(t)\lambda h_{SS} = 1 - h_{SS}\xi\left(1 - e^{-\beta(T-t)}\right)$$

then,

$$\hat{\sigma} = \frac{\sigma}{1 - h_{SS}\xi\left(1 - e^{-\beta(T-t)}\right)}$$

which implies that $\hat{\sigma} \to \sigma$ as $t \to T$.

$$\hat{\alpha} = \frac{\alpha + \left(\frac{\xi}{S(t)}[1 - e^{-\beta(T-t)}]\right)h_{St}}{1 - h_{SS}\left(1 - e^{-\beta(T-t)}\right)} + \frac{\xi[1 - e^{-\beta(T-t)}]S(t)\sigma^2 h_{SSS}}{2[1 - h_{SS}\xi\left(1 - e^{-\beta(T-t)}\right)]^3}$$

which implies that $\hat{\alpha} \to \alpha$ as $t \to T$. Finally, the pricing equation is:

$$h_t + rS(t)h_S + \frac{1}{2}S^2(t)\left(\frac{\sigma}{1 - h_{SS}\xi\left(1 - e^{-\beta(T-t)}\right)}\right)^2 h_{SS} - rh = 0 \tag{17}$$

with $h(T, S(T)) = \Phi(S(T))$, which transforms into the classic Black-Scholes equation as $t \to T$.

3   Solution of the Pricing Equation Using Artificial Neural Networks

The notably increasing use of neural networks for function approximation and as a method for solving differential equations provides a new and efficient tool for machine learning and numerical analysis. With the aim of implementing this methodology for solving the nonlinear partial differential pricing Eq. (17), this work proposes the use of Physics-Informed Neural Networks (PINN) as an alternative approximation approach to the solution.

3.1   Physics-Informed Neural Networks (PINN)

Physics-Informed Neural Networks (PINN) were introduced by Raissi and Karniadakis in 2018 [9], Raissi, Perdikaris, and Karniadakis in 2019 [10], and Lagaris, Likas, and Fotiadis in 1998 [7] as an alternative for finding numerical solutions of partial differential equations (PDEs). This approach exploits the neural network's capacity to approximate any function along with the continuous improvements in automatic differentiation. Specifically, physics-informed neural networks are a technique in scientific machine learning that aims to solve PDEs based on a small set of data, meaning only data related to the PDE (the physics) is available instead of many pairs of independent and dependent variable values. PINNs generate approximate solutions to the PDE by training a neural network to minimize a loss function consisting of terms representing the mismatch of the conditions considered along the boundary of the spatio-temporal domain, as well as the residual of the PDE at selected points in the interior.

To describe the PINN approach to the solution $u : [0, T] \times D \to \mathbb{R}$, we consider the following generic partial differential equation (PDE):

$$\partial_t u(t, x) + \mathcal{N}[u](t, x) = 0; \ (t, x) \in (0, T] \times D \tag{18}$$

$$u(0, x) = u_0(x); \quad x \in D \tag{19}$$

where $\mathcal{N}$ is a nonlinear differential operator acting on u, $D \subset \mathbb{R}^d$ is a bounded domain, T denotes the final time, and $u_0 : D \to \mathbb{R}$ represents the initial data. It is assumed that $u(t, x) = u_b(t, x)$ for $(t, x) \in (0, T] \times \partial D$, where ∂D denotes the boundary of the domain D, and $u_b(t, x) : (0, T] \times \partial D \to \mathbb{R}$ are the boundary data available. The method constructs a neural network $u_\theta(t, x)$ to approximate the solution $u(t, x)$ of the PDE (18), where $u_\theta(t, x) : [0, T] \times D \to \mathbb{R}$ represents the function realized by a neural network with parameters θ.

The continuous-time approximation of the solution to the PDE (18) is based on the residual of the neural network u_θ defined as:

$$r_\theta := \partial_t u_\theta(t, x) + \mathcal{N}[u_\theta](t, x) \tag{20}$$

and the type of neural network considered is a multi-layer perceptron (MLP). The training of the neural network involves determining the values of the parameters (θ) that minimize the value of a cost function using gradient-based optimization methods, which require calculating the derivatives of u_θ with respect to the parameters. By incorporating the residual of the PDE (20) into the cost function that will be minimized, the PINN technique requires additional differentiations to evaluate the differential operators $\partial_t u_\theta$ and $\mathcal{N}[u_\theta]$, which can be easily obtained through automatic differentiation using tools such as TensorFlow or PyTorch in Python.

PINN approximates the solution of the PDE (18) by minimizing the cost function:

$$\phi_\theta(X) := \phi_\theta^r(X^r) + \phi_\theta^0(X^0) + \phi_\theta^b(X^b) \tag{21}$$

where X denotes the collection of training data, and the cost function $\phi_\theta(X)$ contains the following terms:

– The mean squared residuals:

$$\phi_\theta^r(X^r) := \frac{1}{N_r} \sum_{i=1}^{N_r} |r_\theta(t^r, x_i^r)|^2 \tag{22}$$

at a set of data points $X^r := \{(t^r, x_i^r)\}_{i=1}^{N_r} \subset (0, T] \times D$.

– The mean squared mismatches with respect to the initial conditions:

$$\phi_\theta^0(X^0) := \frac{1}{N_0} \sum_{i=1}^{N_0} \left| u_\theta(t^0, x_i^0) - u_0(x_i^0) \right|^2 \tag{23}$$

at a set of data points $X^0 := \{(t^0, x_i^0)\}_{i=1}^{N_0} \subset 0 \times D$.

– The mean squared mismatches with respect to the boundary conditions:

$$\phi_\theta^b(X^b) := \frac{1}{N_b} \sum_{i=1}^{N_b} \left| u_\theta(t^b, x_i^b) - u_b(t_i^b, x_i^b) \right|^2 \tag{24}$$

at a set of data points $X^b := \{(t^b, x_i^b)\}_{i=1}^{N_b} \subset (0, T] \times \partial D$.

3.2 Solution of Pricing PDE Using PINN

We consider the valuation PDE for a market with liquidity in the specific case of European call options[2]:

$$h_t + rS(t)h_S + \frac{1}{2}S^2(t)\left(\frac{\sigma}{1 - h_{SS}\xi\left(1 - e^{-\beta(T-t)}\right)}\right)^2 h_{SS} - rh = 0 \tag{25}$$

with $h(T, S(T)) = \max\{S(T) - K; 0\} \equiv (S(T) - K)^+$. We work on a bounded domain of the time t and price $S(t)$ variables, such that $t \in [0, T]$ and $S(t) \in [0, S^{max}]$, where S^{max} is a constant value that denotes the maximum possible price the asset could take within the interval $[0, T]$. We then have the following conditions associated with the PDE:

---

[2] A European call option is a type of derivative that gives its holder the right, but not the obligation, to buy a certain quantity of the underlying asset on a specific future date T and at a predetermined price K.

- If $S(t) = 0$ at any instant t, then:

$$h(t, 0) = 0 \qquad (26)$$

If at any moment in time, the price of the underlying asset reaches zero, at that moment, the call option on this asset will have no value.

- If the price of the asset is large (S^{max}) we can guarantee that the option will be exercised by its holder, hence $h(T, S(T)) = S(T) - K$. The value of this condition at t implies discounting the exercise price K, and since the no-arbitrage price of the asset at t is simply $S(t)$, we have the boundary condition:

$$h\left(t, S^{max}\right) = S^{max} - Ke^{-r(T-t)} \qquad (27)$$

- At the time T, the value of the option is determined by the cash flow generated by the option at expiration:

$$h(T, S(T)) = \max\{S(T) - K; 0\} \qquad (28)$$

We denote by $\hat{u} \equiv \hat{u}(t, S(t); \theta)$ the prediction function of our neural network for the inputs t, $S(t)$, and the parameters θ. The residual of this neural network is:

$$r_\theta := \partial_t \hat{u} + \mathcal{N}[\hat{u}]$$

where:

$$\mathcal{N}[\hat{u}] = rS(t)\widehat{u_S} + \frac{1}{2}S^2(t)\left(\frac{\sigma}{1 - \widehat{u_{SS}}\xi\left(1 - e^{-\beta(T-t)}\right)}\right)^2 \widehat{u_{SS}} - r\hat{u} \qquad (29)$$

To construct the loss function, we use the conditions (26), (27), (28), and the residual (29), remembering that the loss will be the sum of the mean squared losses based on these conditions.

- The mean squared of the residuals:

$$\phi_\theta^r(t^r, S^r(t)) := \frac{1}{N_r} \sum_{i=1}^{N_r} \left|r_\theta\left(t_i^r, S_i^r\left(t_i^r\right)\right)\right|^2 \qquad (30)$$

at a set of randomly generated points $\{(t_i^r, S_i^r(t_i^r))\}_{i=1}^{N_r} \subset (0, T] \times [0, S^{max}]$.

- The mean squared of the mismatches with respect to the conditions when the price of the asset is zero:

$$\phi_\theta^0(t^0, 0) := \frac{1}{N_0} \sum_{i=1}^{N_0} \left|\hat{u}\left(t_i^0, 0; \theta\right)\right|^2 \qquad (31)$$

at a set of points $\{(t_i^0, 0)\}_{i=1}^{N_0} \subset [0, T] \times \{0\}$.

- The mean squared of the mismatches with respect to the conditions at the derivative's expiration date:

$$\phi_\theta^b\left(T, S^b(T)\right) := \frac{1}{N_b} \sum_{i=1}^{N_b} \left|\hat{u}\left(T, S_i^b(T); \theta\right) - \left(S_i^b(T) - K\right)^+\right|^2 \qquad (32)$$

at a set of randomly generated points $\{(T, S_i^b(T))\}_{i=1}^{N_b} \subset \{T\} \times (0, S^{max})$ representing the asset price at the expiration date.

- The mean squared of the mismatches with respect to the conditions when the price of the asset reaches the maximum value considered:

$$\phi_\theta^m(t^m, S^{max}) := \frac{1}{N_m} \sum_{i=1}^{N_m} \left| \hat{u}(t_i^m, S^{max}; \theta) - \left(S^{max} - Ke^{-r(T-t_i^m)} \right) \right|^2 \qquad (33)$$

at a set of randomly generated points $(\{(t_i^m, S^{max})\}_{i=1}^{N_m} \subset (0, T] \times \{S_{max}\})$.

The loss function is given by:

$$\phi_\theta(t, S(t)) = \phi_\theta^r(t^r, S^r(t)) + \phi_\theta^0(t^0, 0) + \phi_\theta^b(T, S^b(T)) + \phi_\theta^m(t^m, S^{max}) \qquad (34)$$

The Architecture of the Neural Network

The structure considered for the implementation of the PINN technique is depicted in Fig. 1. Initially, a fully connected perceptron $(NN(t, S(t))$ is used to construct the prediction function $\hat{u}$ for the inputs t and $S(t)$. Once we have the function $\hat{u}$, we use the information from the valuation PDE (the physics) to calculate the mean squared residuals $\phi_\theta^r(t^r, S(t)^r)$, which involves computing the derivatives $\widehat{u_t}$, $\widehat{u_S}$, and $\widehat{u_{SS}}$ of the function $\hat{u}$ using automatic differentiation. We also consider the boundary conditions and the function $\hat{u}$ to calculate the mean squared mismatches $\phi_\theta^0(t^0, 0)$, $\phi_\theta^b(T, S(T)^b)$, and $\phi_\theta^m(t^m, S^{max})$.

All the results are combined in the loss function $\phi_\theta(t, S(t))$, which is minimized using gradient descent with respect to the parameters θ until the optimal set of parameters θ^* is obtained.

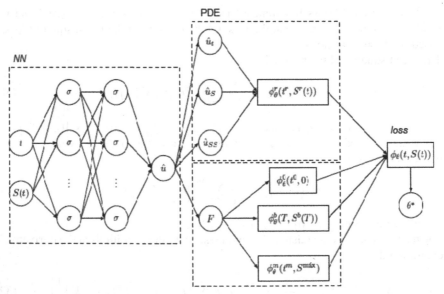

Fig. 1. Architecture considered for the implementation of the PINN technique in the process of solving the pricing PDE.

4   Generating Training Data and Solution

The next step is the creation of the training data set for the neural network, i.e., constructing the set of points at which each of the loss functions will be evaluated. We start by generating a random sample of points placed within the time-price domain. For the price, 10000 random values are generated from a uniform distribution over the interval [0, 500], and the same amount for time from the interval [0, 1]. Figure 2 shows the set of randomly generated points. We also add the set of 10,000 points generated for each of the boundary conditions of the PDE.

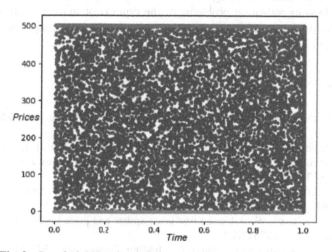

Fig. 2. Set of 10,000 points generated within the time-price domain.

Applying the proposed method for the valuation of European call options (Table 1).

Table 1. Numerical results for the calculation of the premiums for European call options using the proposed method, considering $\in [0, 500]$, $T = 1$, and a level of error associated with the cost function $\varepsilon = 10^{-8}$.

Number of iterations	Mean of $\hat{u}$ for the call option	Mean of the cost function for the call option
10	8.572	3.1437
100	4.044	3.188
200	5.6228	3.2178
300	3.7915	3.1392
400	4.3658	3.7136
1000	4.2873	1.8822
2000	4.317	3.46
5000	4.3613	1.0668

5 Conclusions

The implementation of PINN for solving the Black-Scholes PDE, it is important to highlight that while it is not an analytical procedure, its results are highly accurate when compared to the Black-Scholes formula for European options. It serves as a valuable tool when considering extensions of the valuation problem to contexts where not all assumptions are met. This is particularly relevant for cases involving semi-linear or completely nonlinear valuation PDEs, such as multiple underlying assets, illiquid markets, transaction costs, stochastic volatilities, among others.

In conclusion, machine learning techniques for solving PDEs offer a powerful alternative for addressing valuation problems in the context of market models that better mimic real-world scenarios. It is an invitation for readers to delve deeper into these tools and explore their potential applications in the financial industry.

References

1. Acharya, V., Pedersen, L.: Asset pricing with liquidity risk. J. Financ. Econ. **77**(2), 375–410 (2005)
2. Back, K.: Asymmetric information and options. Rev. Financ. Stud. **6**(3), 435–472 (1993)
3. Black, F., Scholes, M.: The pricing of options and corporate liabilities. J. Polit. Econ **81**(3), 637–654 (1973)
4. Gueant, O.: The Financial Mathematics Of market Liquidity: From Optimal Execution to Market Making. Chapman and Hall/CRC (2016)
5. Huberman, G., Stanzl, W.: Arbitrage-free price update and price-impact functions. Econometrica **72**(4), 1247–1275 (2004)
6. Kyle, A.S.: Continuous auctions and insider trading. Econometrica **53**, 1315–1335 (1985). https://doi.org/10.2307/1913210
7. Lagaris, I.E., Likas, A., Fotiadis, D.I.: Artificial neural networks for solving ordinary and partial differential equations. IEEE Trans. Neural Networks **9**(5), 987–1000 (1998)
8. Liu, W.: A liquidity-augmented capital asset pricing model. J. Financ. Econ. **82**(3), 631–671 (2006)
9. Raissi, M., Karniadakis, G.E.: Hidden physics models: machine learning of nonlinear partial differential equations. J. Comput. Phys. **357**, 125–141 (2018)
10. Raissi, M., Perdikaris, P., Karniadakis, G.E.: Physics-informed neural networks: a deep learning framework for solving forward and inverse problems involving nonlinear partial differential equations. J. Comput. Phys. **378**, 686–707 (2019)
11. Vayanos, D.: Strategic trading in a dynamic noisy market. J. Financ. **56**(1), 131–171 (2001)

Application of Hierarchical Risk Parity with Latin ADRs

Daniel Aragón Urrego[✉] [iD]

Universidad Externado de Colombia, Bogotá, Colombia
daniel.aragon@uexternado.edu.co

Abstract. This paper presents the Hierarchical Risk Parity (HRP) model and its implementation using assets of Latin American companies listed as ADRs on the NYSE. Two portfolios are optimized: HRP and Mean-Variance (MV). The in-sample results show better performance for the HRP portfolio; however, in the out-of-sample analysis, the MV portfolio outperforms with a higher Sharpe ratio and diversification ratio.

Keywords: Portfolio Optimization · Clustering Algorithms · Asset Allocation

1 Introduction

The Critical Line Algorithm (CLA) of the traditional Mean-Variance (MV) model, which allows constructing the efficient frontier of optimal investment portfolios, tends to generate concentrated and unstable solutions [9], a situation that is related to the properties that the covariance matrix must have. In particular, the MV optimization process requires the covariance matrix to be positive definite in order to obtain its inverse. However, it has been found that this matrix becomes ill-conditioned due to its high condition number. In this regard, it has been suggested that addressing these limitations could be done by incorporating additional information, as proposed in the Black-Litterman model [3]; incorporating additional constraints according to Clarke et al. [4], or by improving the numerical stability of the inverse covariance matrix following the work of Ledoit and Wolf [5]. In this sense, one possible approach is to avoid inverting the covariance matrix. Precisely, focusing on this purpose, López de Prado [7] incorporates the use of machine learning in the portfolio optimization process. This model is known as Hierarchical Risk Parity (HRP), and the objective of the following pages will be to present and implement this novel approach for constructing an optimal investment portfolio.

This document consists of five sections, with the introduction being the first one. The second section presents the problem associated with the CLA algorithm of the MV model. The third and fourth sections present the HRP approach and its implementation in the construction of a portfolio under this proposal, respectively. Finally, the conclusions are presented.

J. C. Figueroa-García et al. (Eds.): WEA 2023, CCIS 1928, pp. 47–57, 2023.
https://doi.org/10.1007/978-3-031-46739-4_5

2 Mean-Variance Model (MV): The Problem with CLA Algorithm

Markowitz [10, 11] proposed a model known as Mean-Variance (MV) for constructing optimal investment portfolios. In this model, Markowitz considers n risky assets that are characterized by the random nature of their returns: $R = (R_1, R_2, \ldots, R_n)$. From the historical series $\mathbf{R}$, the expected returns $E(R) = r = (r_1, r_2, \ldots, r_n)$ are obtained, and the variance-covariance matrix of the returns (V) is constructed. Similarly, a vector W representing the weight of each risky asset is considered: $w = (w_1, w_2, \ldots, w_n)$.

Based on this, we have the following characterization of the portfolio [6]:

$$\text{Expected portfolio return:} \quad E(\mathbf{w} \cdot \mathbf{R}) = w_1 r_1 + w_2 r_2 + \cdots + w_n r_n$$

$$\text{Portfolio risk(variance):} \quad Var(\mathbf{w} \cdot \mathbf{R}) = \sum_{i=1}^{n} w_i^2 \sigma_i^2 + \sum_{j=1, j \neq i}^{n} w_i w_j \sigma_{i,j}$$

In matrix form, the variance (σ_P^2) is equal to $\mathbf{w}^T V w$, where $\mathbf{w}$ is the $n \times 1$ vector of weights. Based on the above, two optimization problems are proposed:

- Minimize the variance (or volatility) of the portfolio subject to a given level of return:

$$min \, \mathbf{w} \Sigma \mathbf{w}^T \; s.a \; E(\mathbf{w} \cdot \mathbf{R}) \leq r_e; w_i \geq 0; \sum_{i=1}^{n} w_i = 1; \tag{1}$$

- Maximize the expected return of the portfolio given a level of risk:

$$max \, E(\mathbf{w} \cdot R) \; s.a \; \mathbf{w} \Sigma \mathbf{w}^T \leq \sigma_e \; ; w_i \geq 0; \sum_{i=1}^{n} w_i = 1 \tag{2}$$

As observed in the previous expressions, constraints are considered such as the sum of weights equal to 1 (\mathop $\sum_{i=1}^{n} w_i = 1$), as well as not allowing short sales, meaning only non-negative weights are permitted ($w_i \geq 0$).

For case (1), its solution identifies the minimum variance portfolio, which depends exclusively on the inverse of the covariance matrix, as shown in the following expression.

$$\mathbf{w} = \frac{V^{-1} 1}{1' V^{-1} 1} \tag{3}$$

It should be noted that since V is a positive definite matrix its inverse (V^{-1}) exists. In addition, it is important to consider some assumptions on which the Markowitz model is built, including:

- MV uses historical data to obtain the expected values of returns and the variance-covariance matrix, implicitly assuming that the behavior of these variables will not change, in other words, assuming a stable behavior over time.
- The need to invert the covariance matrix. In this regard, when significant changes in the asset correlations occur, large changes in the inverse matrix are observed, generating unstable estimates in expected returns and, consequently, small deviations leading to very different portfolios [12].

Research has focused on addressing this issue by proposing models that do not require inverting the covariance matrix. In particular, it is necessary for the matrix to be positive definite; however, in practice, this is not always the case since the covariance matrix is subject to large errors when it is numerically ill-conditioned, meaning it has a high condition number[1] [2]. It is important to note that a high condition number[2] makes the covariance (or correlation) matrix unstable. Additionally, the covariance matrix lacks hierarchical structure, leading to varying weights behavior [8].

In order to overcome the issue of inverting the variance-covariance matrix, the HRP approach proposed by López de Prado [7, 8] is adopted, which can be implemented through three stages: Tree clustering, Quasi-diagonalization, and Recursive bisection, which will be presented in the following section.

3   Hierarchical Risk Parity model (HRP)

The proposal presented by López de Prado [7] focuses on an asset allocation technique using graph theory and hierarchical clustering. Specifically, the author suggests that the hierarchical tree structure can be applied in portfolio composition, where the weights of assets are distributed from top to bottom and adjusted within each hierarchy. The HRP approach consists of the following three stages:

3.1   Tree Clustering

The objective of this step is to build a hierarchical tree where all assets are grouped into different levels based on their characteristics and correlations.

According to López de Prado [8], the correlation matrix is defined as:

$$\rho = \{\rho_{i,j=1,...,N}\} \tag{4}$$

With $\rho_{i,j} = \rho[X_i, X_j]$. From the correlation matrix, a new distance matrix (D), is determined, given by:

$$D(X_i, X_j) = \sqrt{0.5(1 - \rho_{\{i,j\}})} \tag{5}$$

Additionally, a matrix is established that contains the results of calculating the Euclidean distance between each pair of column vectors in the matrix D. This new matrix is known as the augmented distance matrix ($\overline{D}$):

$$\overline{D}(i, j) = \sqrt{\sum_{k=1}^{N} [D(k, i) - D(k, j)]^2} \tag{6}$$

---

[1] The condition number of a matrix is known as the "absolute value of the ratio between its maximum and minimum eigenvalues (in magnitude) [7].

[2] High correlation among asset returns will lead to a high condition number of the covariance (or correlation) matrix, causing the values of its inverse to explode. Thus, a higher condition number implies that higher relative errors in the input data result in larger relative errors in the roots of the linear system.

In (6), it is observed that $\overline{D}(i,j)$ is a function of the correlation matrix.

Based on the augmented distance matrix $\overline{D}$, a pair of assets (i^*, j^*) must be selected with the smallest distance to form the first cluster, as shown in expression (7), where U denotes the set of clusters:

$$U[1] = \arg_{\{i,j\}} \min \overline{D}(i,j) \tag{7}$$

Now, a linkage matrix is required to update the augmented distance matrix $\overline{D}$. Thus, the distance between the first cluster $U[1]$ and any other asset is determined by:

$$\overline{D}(i, U[1]) = \min\left(\overline{D}(i, i^*), \overline{D}(i, j^*)\right) \tag{8}$$

This process must be repeated for each asset in the portfolio. In this way, every time a new cluster of assets is formed, the distance matrix is updated, and this procedure is repeated until a single cluster is obtained.

3.2 Quasi-diagonalization

In the second stage, the covariance matrix is reorganized in a similar order to the arrangement of assets within the linkage matrix. Thus, starting from the formed clusters, the columns and rows of the covariance matrix are rearranged so that the largest values are located on and near the diagonal, while the smaller covariances are pushed away from the diagonal.

3.3 Recursive-Bisection

Finally, the optimal weights for each asset are determined by applying the following steps [1]:

1. The weights of the assets are denoted as:

$$w_i = 1, \forall i = 1, \ldots, N.$$

2. A top-down process is carried out, where each cluster is subdivided into 2 subclusters (V_1, V_2), starting from the final cluster $U[N]$. For each subcluster, its respective variance is obtained:

$$V_i = w^T V w, \quad i = 1, 2 \tag{9}$$

where:

$$w = \frac{diag\left(V^{-1}\right)}{trace\left(diag\left(V^{-1}\right)\right)} \tag{10}$$

When using the quasi-diagonal matrix, it makes sense to use inverse allocation weights in order to calculate the variance for the subcluster. This is because inverse variance allocation is optimal for a diagonal covariance matrix, as indicated in [1].

3. Based on the results from the previous step, a weighting factor is calculated using the new covariance matrix:

$$a_1 = 1 - \frac{V_2}{V_1 + V_2}; \quad a_2 = 1 - a_1 \tag{11}$$

4. The weighting factors mentioned in (11) are used to determine the final weights within each subcluster, so the weights of the assets in the subclusters are updated accordingly using:

$$w_1 = a_1 * w_1 \tag{12a}$$

$$w_2 = a_2 * w_2 \tag{12b}$$

5. To conclude, steps 2 to 4 are repeated for the subclusters V_1 y V_2. This ensures that each asset is assigned its respective weight within the portfolio.

As Bechis [1] points out, the weight allocation in the HRP model is top-down based on the variance within the sub-cluster, which creates competition among assets within the cluster[3] while avoiding competition with other clusters. This is the main advantage of HRP over other optimization algorithms. Furthermore, there is consistency compared to the MV model as the weights obtained through the HRP algorithm are positive ($w_1 \geq 0$), meaning there are no short sales and allowing for the complete distribution of resources ($\sum_{i=1}^{N} w_i = 1$).

4 Application and Results

4.1 Data and Results

An application of the Hierarchical Risk Parity (HRP) model will be conducted using twelve Latin American companies listed as American Depositary Receipts (ADRs) on the New York Stock Exchange (NYSE). The objective is to select actively traded stocks in the market. Specifically, assets from companies located in Chile, Colombia and Peru will be included. The data was obtained from the Yahoo Finance portal and corresponds to daily adjusted closing prices. For these assets, the in-sample analysis is conducted for the period between 01/01/2016 to 30/06/2022, and the out-of-sample analysis is conducted for the period between 01/07/2022 to 06/07/2023, resulting in 1,886 observations for each asset. It is worth noting that the price data includes the year 2020, during which the effects of the Covid-19 pandemic were experienced, as well as part of 2021, during the period of market recovery. Python will be used for implementation, following the development proposed in [7] and [14]. The portfolios will be compared based on the annualized average return, annualized volatility, annualized Sharpe ratio, and diversification ratio.

Average return corresponds to how much an investment portfolio earns or loses in a given period of time.

---

[3] Intra-cluster competition implies that the weight assigned to a cluster should be distributed among the assets within that cluster. Therefore, when considering two clusters, an asset belonging to Cluster 1 will not compete for weight allocation with assets from Cluster 2.

Volatility (or standard deviation) of returns represents the level of risk under the Modern Portfolio Theory (MPT) framework. It is a measure of the dispersion of the portfolio returns, and as such, a higher volatility implies greater risk associated with the portfolio.

Sharpe ratio corresponds to the difference between the investment return and the risk-free[4] rate (average return – risk free), divided by the standard deviation of the investment returns (Volatility). It represents the additional return that an investor receives for each additional unit of risk assumed [13].

Diversification ratio corresponds to the ratio between the weighted average of the volatilities divided by the portfolio's volatility. A higher diversification ratio indicates a more diversified portfolio, meaning that the risk is spread across different assets.

Table 1 presents information related to some key statistics of the selected assets: the selected set of assets has been subject to annualized volatilities exceeding 26%, particularly two Peruvian assets (AENZ and CPAC) which exhibit the highest figures. However, these relatively high volatilities have not been accompanied by positive average annualized returns, which is evident across all three countries and different industries.

Now, to initiate the application of the HRP model, the correlation matrix is constructed using the asset returns. From this matrix, it is notable that the lowest correlations occur between Peruvian and Chilean assets. For example, between the Peruvian asset BVN and the Chilean asset AKO-A (0.06), between AENZ from Peru and AKO-A (0.08) and ITCL (0.08) from Chile, as well as between CPAC from Peru and the Chilean assets ITCL (0.06), BSAC (0.08), and AKO-1 (0.09). It is important to note that the mentioned assets belong to different industries, including Construction & Materials, Mining, Beverages, and Banks.

Similarly, the highest correlation is observed between BSAC and BCH with a value of 0.81, which is not surprising since these two assets belong to the same country (Chile) and the same sector (banking).

Once the correlation matrix is obtained, the assets are hierarchically clustered, and using the single linkage distance, the linkage matrix is created, organizing the assets into a grouped tree structure. This is visually represented through a dendrogram. Therefore, the result of the first step of the HRP algorithm is presented in Fig. 1.

As seen in the Fig. 1, following the bottom-up process, the first two clusters formed (BCH-BSAC) and (AVAL-CIB) have in common that the assets belong to the same country and industry. Regarding the first cluster (BCH-BSAC), it can be observed that the next asset to join is CCU, reinforcing the presence of Chilean assets, albeit from a different industry. In the next level, the cluster comprises assets from three different industries with the incorporation of SQM. However, it is a Chilean cluster.

On the other hand, EC is incorporated into the AVAL-CIB cluster, resulting in a group composed of assets from Colombia, with the addition of the Oil & Gas Producers industry. The Chilean cluster (SQM-CCU-BCH-BSAC) and the Colombian cluster (EC-AVAL-CIB) will form a new subgroup with the addition of ITCL, thus concentrating 8 assets from 2 countries and 6 different industries. Finally, the last Chilean asset (AKO.A) joins the group. Furthermore, it is observed that the Peruvian assets are integrated: BVN individually and (AENZ-CPAC) as a subcluster, completing the selected asset sample.

---

[4] A risk-free interest rate of zero will be assumed.

Table 1. Selected Assets.

DR	Ticker	Country	Industry	Annualized Average Return	Annualized Volatility
Embotelladora Andina – A Shares	AKO-A	Chile	Beverages	−6.3178%	40.2016%
Banco de Chile	BCH	Chile	Banks	3.1157%	30.1799%
Banco Itau Chile	ITCL	Chile	Banks	−18.0399%	48.4017%
Banco Santander Chile	BSAC	Chile	Banks	4.1975%	32.4331%
Compania Cervecerias Unidas	CCU	Chile	Beverages	−3.4676%	26.1329%
Soc. Química y Minera de Chile – B Shares	SQM	Chile	Chemicals	27.8368%	44.1164%
Grupo Aval Acciones y Valores	AVAL	Colombia	Financial Services	−4.2698%	33.4297%
Bancolombia – Pref	CIB	Colombia	Banks	6.3044%	38.1859%
Ecopetrol	EC	Colombia	Oil & Gas Producers	13.3969%	44.7866%
Aenza S.A.A	AENZ	Peru	Construct.& Materials	−12.7384%	64.4737%
Compania de Minas Buenaventura	BVN	Peru	Mining	7.0065%	50.0751%
Cementos Pacasmayo SAA	CPAC	Peru	Construct.& Materials	−0.5786%	36.4969%

In the second part of the algorithm, it is necessary to take the correlation matrix and rearrange it according to the results of the first step, as shown in Fig. 2.

The allocation of weights is the third and final step of the HRP algorithm. This activity follows a top-down process in line with the hierarchical structure of the tree, which means that the starting point is the portfolio (represented by the top of the dendrogram). From the total assets represented by the portfolio, a bifurcation into 2 subclusters is initiated. In other words, the 100% of resources allocated to the portfolio will now be redistributed into 2 subgroups, namely: i) (AENZ-CPAC) and ii) (BVN-AKO.A-ITCL-EC-AVAL-CIB-SQM-CCU-BCH-BSAC). Next, the first subcluster is taken, and another bifurcation is performed to redistribute weight. In this case, weight is allocated to the assets AENZ and CPAC. The process is repeated, creating two new subclusters, which are: i) BVN and

ii) (AKO.A-ITCL-EC-AVAL-CIB-SQM-CCU-BCH-BSAC). This process is recursively performed until each asset is assigned its respective weight. The optimal weights obtained are presented in the Table 2.

4.2 Analysis and Comparison of Results

The results obtained after the implementation of the HRP model will be compared with the traditional mean-variance model (MV)[5]. Table 2 shows that the Chilean assets belonging to the Beverages industry account for approximately 21.95% and 46.44% in the HRP and MV models, respectively. In particular, the case of CCU stands out, as it has the lowest volatility and receives a higher weight in the MV model, highlighting the objective pursued by the Markowitz model of minimizing portfolio risk [7].

It is worth noting that both the HRP and MV models exhibit certain similarities when analyzing the results by country or industry. As an example of similarity, both portfolios assign the highest weight to Chilean assets (HRP: 60.34% and MV: 58.72%), followed by Peruvian assets (HRP: 21.55% and MV: 29.98%), and finally Colombian assets (11.29%).

On the other hand, differences can be found at the intracountry industry level. For example, assets belonging to the Chilean banking industry account for 31.46% in the HRP portfolio, while in the MV portfolio, it corresponds to 12.26%. The same occurs with the Beverages industry in the same country: 21.95% (HRP) and 46.44% (MV).

Additionally, from the optimization of the two portfolios, an in-sample exercise was carried out where the following metrics were obtained: expected annualized return, annualized volatility, annualized Sharpe ratio, and diversification coefficient (see Table 3). Given the evolution in the behavior of asset prices, particularly with periods of downturns like the one observed during the first half of 2020, it is not surprising that the results show relatively low (1.59% in HRP) and negative average annualized returns, on the order of -2.31% in the MV model.

Furthermore, this is accompanied by annualized volatilities close to 20%. However, the lower volatility is associated with the traditional model, which is consistent with its objective of minimizing portfolio risk. Given the annualized return and volatility, the annualized Sharpe ratio is higher in the HRP portfolio. However, the negative result in MV indicates that for every unit of risk, the investor loses return. On the other hand, a higher diversification coefficient is observed for the traditional Markowitz model (MV), indicating a better distribution of weights among the assets in the portfolio.

Based on the two optimized portfolios (HRP and MV), an out-of-sample exercise was conducted using daily adjusted closing prices for the period from 01/07/2022 to 06/07/2023 (Table 3 shows the results).

As observed, for both portfolios, the out-of-sample results improve compared to what was observed in the in-sample exercise: the expected annualized return increases, the annualized volatility decreases, and the annualized Sharpe ratio increases. Additionally, the diversification ratio is higher.

---

[5] The optimization of the MV portfolio will be carried out incorporating the non-negativity.restriction in the weights of the assets.

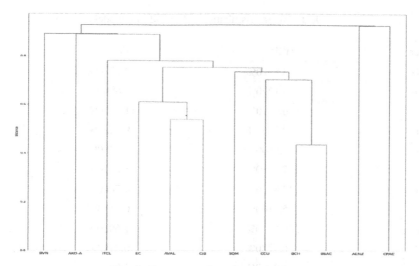

Fig. 1. Representation of grouped assets

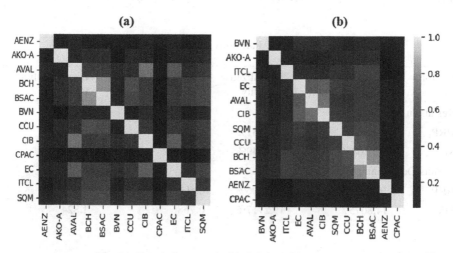

Fig. 2. Correlation matrix (**a**) Original (**b**) Reordered

When comparing the out-of-sample portfolios, MV has an advantage due to its better performance in terms of expected annualized return, which is 1.36 times the expected annualized return of HRP, and it is further accompanied by lower annualized volatility. The Sharpe ratio although positive, reflects the results of the two measures mentioned earlier, making it lower for HRP. Finally, the diversification coefficient shows that the weight distribution is better in the MV model.

Table 2. Weight distribution, HRP and MV models

Ticker	HRP	MV
AENZ	3.5120%	2.7720%
AKO-A	9.1270%	11.6800%
AVAL	6.6670%	11.1700%
BCH	9.6150%	9.3850%
BSAC	15.5500%	1.8380%
BVN	7.0780%	5.6070%
CCU	12.8200%	34.7600%
CIB	5.1100%	0.1113%
CPAC	10.9600%	21.6000%
EC	6.3280%	0.0113%
ITCL	6.2960%	1.0370%
SQM	6.9360%	0.0217%

Table 3. Portfolios performance

Portfolio	Annualized Expected Return	Annualized Volatility	Annualized Sharpe Ratio	Diversification Ratio
Results In Sample				
HRP	1.5962%	22.3831%	0.0713	1.694
MV	−2.3086%	19.8749%	−0.1162	1.709
Results Out of Sample				
HRP	10.8839%	21.4306%	0.508	1.797
MV	14.8075%	19.2717%	0.768	1.824

5   Conclusions

In this document, the HRP model has been presented as a proposal that aims to address limitations identified in the traditional Markowitz model for optimizing investment portfolios. The results show that, in the case of this set of assets, the clustering and hierarchy are characterized by being intra-industry and intra-country. Once national clusters are formed, the next observation is the creation of a binational group (Colombia-Chile), and finally, the inclusion of Peruvian assets.

The optimization of the selected assets using López de Prado's proposal in an in-sample scenario generates a portfolio that achieves improvements in terms of the expected annualized return and the Sharpe ratio compared to the results of the MV model. However, the results of the out-of-sample exercise show significant changes in the four metrics mentioned, where the traditional portfolio performs better.

References

1. Bechis, L.:. Machine learning portfolio optimization: hierarchical risk parity and modern portfolio theory. Tesis de maestría, Libera Università Internazionale degli Studi Sociali Guido Carli (2020). http://tesi.luiss.it/28022/1/709261_BECHIS_LUCA.pdf
2. Bailey, D., López de Prado, M.: The sharpe ratio efficient frontier. J. Risk **15**(2), 3–44 (2012). https://doi.org/10.21314/JOR.2012.255
3. Black, F., y Litterman, R.: Global portfolio optimization. Financ. Anal. J. **48**(5), 28–43 (1992). https://doi.org/10.2469/faj.v48.n5.28
4. Clarke, R., De Silva, H., Thorley, S.: Portfolio constraints and the fundamental law of active management. Financ. Anal. J. **58**, 48–66 (2002). https://doi.org/10.2469/faj.v58.n5.2468
5. Ledoit, O., y Wolf, M.: A well-conditioned estimator for large-dimensional covariance matrices. J. Multivar. Anal. **88**(2), 365–411 (2004). https://doi.org/10.1016/S0047-259X(03)000 96-4
6. León, D., Aragón, A., Sandoval, J., Hernández, G., Arévalo, A., Niño, J.: Clustering algorithms for risk-adjusted portfolio construction. Procedia Comput. Sci. **108**, 1334–1343 (2017). https://doi.org/10.1016/j.procs.2017.05.185
7. López de Prado, M.: Building diversified portfolios that outperform out of sample. J. Portfolio Mgmt. **42**(4), 59–69 (2016). https://doi.org/10.3905/jpm.2016.42.4.059
8. López de Prado, M.: Advances in Financial Machine Learning. John Wiley y Sons (2018)
9. López de Prado, M.: Machine Learning for Asset Managers. Cambridge University Press, UK (2020). https://doi.org/10.1017/9781108883658
10. Markowitz, H.: Portfolio selection. J. Finance **7**(1), 77–91 (1952)
11. Markowitz, H.: Portfolio Selection: Efficient Diversification of Investments. Wiley, New York (1959)
12. Michaud, R.O., Michaud, R.: Estimation error and portfolio optimization: a resampling solution. SSRN 2658657 (2007). https://doi.org/10.2139/ssrn.2658657
13. Sharpe, W.: Capital asset prices: a theory of market equilibrium under conditions of risk. J. Finance **19**(3), 425–442 (1964). https://doi.org/10.1111/j.1540-6261.1964.tb02865.x
14. Tatsat, H., Puri, S., Lookabaugh, B.: Machine Learning and Data Science Blueprints for Finance. MA, O'Reilly Medi (2020)

Experimental Analysis of a Peregrine Falcon 3D Prototype with Oscillating Feathers

Hector G. Parra[1]([⊠]) [iD], Elvis E. Gaona[1] [iD], and Hernán D. Ceron[2] [iD]

[1] Universidad Distrital Francisco José de Caldas Bogotá, Cundinamarca, Colombia
hgparrap@correo.udistrital.edu.co, egaona@udistrital.edu.co
[2] Escola de Engenharia de São Carlos, Universidade de São Paulo, São Paulo, Brasil
her-nan@sc.usp.br

Abstract. The peregrine falcon is the fastest bird in the world. Previous studies have made it possible to observe its flight conditions. One characteristic that stands out is its dorsal feathers, which allow it to generate an effect of stability in flight. The form of these feathers can contribute to the design of similar devices in wind turbines, called vortex generators. Vortex generators maintain a turbulence that modifies the zone of detachment of the boundary layer of a blade. This paper shows an experimental wind tunnel study of a falcon prototype with a hotwire sensor, 3D accelerometer and a servomechanism that allows the movement of the feathers. Measured wake wind velocity curves in transient mode showed similarities. The magnitude spectrum of the wind velocity signal measured by oscillating the feathers of the prototype showed reduction peaks in its spectral components. This indicates reduction in the vibration of the prototype at a wind velocity of 10 m/s.

Keywords: CFD transient · bio-inspired devices · rotative mesh · wind tunnel · vibration

1 Introduction

The development of wind energy systems in different parts of the world has become a wide field of research and development. Many lines of research study vibration reduction systems in wind turbines [1, 2]. Other lines study active vortex generator devices [3, 4]. Fluid dynamics simulation or CFD complements the studies and the analysis of mechanical modifications [5–7]. Current work shows the creation of mechanical improvements based on living organisms such as birds [8–10]. The special characteristics developed by some living species are applied to improve the turbulence of aerial devices [11–14]. Bioinspiration or Bio-mimetic seeks to incorporate some physiological characteristics of animal or plant species into man-made artificial systems to increase the efficiency of a system. Previous work in engineering focuses on the area of naval and aeronautical development. In the naval area, bioinspiration is being used to improve the navigation and performance of ships.

In aeronautics, the aim is to improve efficiency and reduce structural noise in aircraft and wind turbines [15]. In this paper, we will study the behavior of surface pressure by 3D

© The Author(s), under exclusive license to Springer Nature Switzerland AG 2023
J. C. Figueroa-García et al. (Eds.): WEA 2023, CCIS 1928, pp. 58–69, 2023.
https://doi.org/10.1007/978-3-031-46739-4_6

CFD simulation of a peregrine falcon, the fastest bird on the planet, and the effect of its feathers. This bird shows a flight stabilizing function with its feathers in downward flight, reaching velocities above 350 km/h (217 mph). For this reason, appreciating the feather effect and measuring it will allow the future development of devices that contribute to improve vibrations in structures such as tall buildings, flight stability of aircraft and improve the rotational noise of wind turbines.

2   Materials and Methods

The methodology consists of a numerical analysis (CFD) supported by experiments conducted to verify the numerical approach and is developed in four phases, as shown in Fig. 1. In the simulation phase, a laptop with 64GB of RAM, Core i7 processor of tenth generation and NVIDIA GFORCE GTX video card were used. In the experimental phase, a subsonic wind tunnel of the School of Engineering of Sao Carlos CAMPUS 2 with a cross-sectional area of approximately 2.5 m² was used.

Fig. 1. Methodology.

There are commercial vortex generators used on the blade surfaces of power wind turbines. The design of active vortex generators using a bio-inspired principle [16–18], can help reduce wind turbine noise and increase energy production, [19]. (Fig. 2).

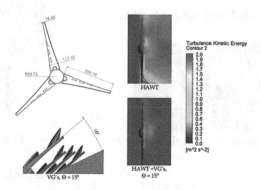

Fig. 2. Vortex Generators in Wind Turbines.

The peregrine falcon is a bird capable of reaching velocities of descent close to 350 km/h, making it the fastest aerial predator in the world [9]. These special conditions have made it an object of study for the design of aerodynamic improvements in existing aerial systems. Figure 3 shows that with the use of Scan 3D and a dissected specimen, a CAD-3D model of the bird's body and feathers is obtained. [20]. The objective is to develop a rotational mesh CFD simulation that will allow us to obtain an analysis of the dynamic behavior of wake velocity and pressure in the falcon prototype.

3   Results

With the support of the Jaime Duque Zoo in Briceño – Colombia, a 3D scan of a stuffed peregrine falcon and biological samples of its dorsal feathers were obtained.

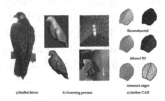

Fig. 3. 3D Scanning process.

Once the point cloud is obtained, a solid is built using MESHLAB®. The roughness of the 3D model is filtered and smoothed with MESHMIXER®, achieving a 3D solid that can be meshed to be simulated in CFD tool (see Fig. 3).

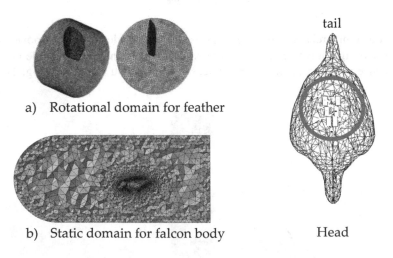

a)   Rotational domain for feather

b)   Static domain for falcon body

tail

Head

c)   Rotational domains

Fig. 4. 3D Domains with ANSYS – ICEM®.

Figure 4-a shows the meshing of the simulation domains, for the creation of the 3D finite element rotational cylindrical domains [20, 21]. These meshes allow emulating the oscillatory motion of the bird's feathers. The rotational domains are positioned in a "V" shape at the back of the 3D model of the bird (orange circle) as shown in Fig. 4c, the total number of meshes is seven, six of which are rotational, with 37867 nodes and 200114 elements, and one is a static mesh with 64.744 nodes and 355.285 elements (Fig. 4-b).

Turbulence model k-w SST
The CFD simulation of the finite volume is run through iterations of the turbulence model selected according to the nodes that are distributed by the domain or geometry of the falcon. The turbulence model selected was *kw-SST*, which allows observation of the wind behavior and its interaction with the solid surfaces of interest, as described below. The values of k and w come directly from the differential transport equations for the kinetic energy of turbulence k and angular velocity of turbulence w. The turbulence model k − w SST is shown below [22, 23, 24, 25], which includes the F1 function and the production of turbulence by the flotation effect, is shown below. P_{kb} y P_{wb} from the combined model k-w BSL. [26].

Wilcox model:

$$\frac{\partial(\rho k)}{\partial t} + \frac{\partial}{\partial x_j}(\rho U_j k) = \frac{\partial}{\partial x_j}\left(\left(\mu + \frac{\mu_t}{\sigma_{k1}}\right)\frac{\partial k}{\partial x_j}\right) + P_k - \beta' \rho k w \tag{1}$$

$$\frac{\partial(\rho w)}{\partial t} + \frac{\partial}{\partial x_j}(\rho U_j w) = \frac{\partial}{\partial x_j}\left(\left(\mu + \frac{\mu_t}{\sigma_k}\right)\frac{\partial w}{\partial x_j}\right) + \alpha_1(\frac{w}{k})P_k - \beta_1 \rho k w^2 \tag{2}$$

Transformed model k − ε:

$$\frac{\partial(\rho k)}{\partial t} + \frac{\partial}{\partial x_j}(\rho U_j k) = \frac{\partial}{\partial x_j}\left(\left(\mu + \frac{\mu_t}{\sigma_{k2}}\right)\frac{\partial k}{\partial x_j}\right) + P_k - \beta' \rho k w \tag{3}$$

$$\frac{\partial(\rho w)}{\partial t} + \frac{\partial}{\partial x_j}(\rho U_j w) = \frac{\partial}{\partial x_j}\left(\left(\mu + \frac{\mu_t}{\sigma_k}\right)\frac{\partial w}{\partial x_j}\right) + 2\rho\left(\frac{1}{\sigma_{w2}w}\right)\frac{\partial k}{\partial x_j}\frac{\partial w}{\partial x_j} + \alpha_2(\frac{w}{k})P_k - \beta_2 \rho k w^2 \tag{4}$$

BSL Model:

$$\frac{\partial(\rho k)}{\partial t} + \frac{\partial}{\partial x_j}(\rho U_j k) = \frac{\partial}{\partial x_j}\left(\left(\mu + \frac{\mu_t}{\sigma_{k3}}\right)\frac{\partial k}{\partial x_j}\right) + P_k - \beta' \rho k w + P_{kb} \tag{5}$$

$$\frac{\partial(\rho w)}{\partial t} + \frac{\partial}{\partial x_j}(\rho U_j w) = \frac{\partial}{\partial x_j}\left(\left(\mu + \frac{\mu_t}{\sigma_{w3}}\right)\frac{\partial w}{\partial x_j}\right) + (1 - F1)2\rho\left(\frac{1}{\sigma_{w2}w}\right)\frac{\partial k}{\partial x_j}\frac{\partial w}{\partial x_j} +$$
$$\alpha_3\frac{w}{k}P_k - \beta_3 \rho w^2 + P_{wb} \tag{6}$$

$$P_k = \mu_t\left(\frac{\partial U_i}{\partial x_j} + \frac{\partial U_j}{\partial x_i}\right)\frac{\partial U_i}{\partial x_j} - \frac{2}{3}\left(\frac{\partial U_k}{\partial x_k}\right)\left(3\mu_t\frac{\partial U_k}{\partial x_k} + \rho k\right) \tag{7}$$

$$P_{wb} = \frac{w}{k}((\alpha + 1)C_3 \max(0, P_{kb})\sin \Phi - P_{kb}) \tag{8}$$

where the dynamic viscosity of the fluid μ, the turbulent viscosity μt, the density of the fluid: ρ, the kinetic energy of turbulence: k, angular velocity of turbulence: w and the angle between velocity and gravity vector ϕ. [26]

F1: Function that is equal to one near the surface and decreases to a zero value outside the boundary layer.

$$\beta' = 0.09, \alpha1 = 5/9, \beta1 = 0.075, \sigma k1 = 2, \sigma w1 = 2, \sigma2 = 0.44, \beta2 = 0.085, \sigma k2 = 1,$$
$$\sigma w2 = 1/0.856.$$
(9)

With the solver CFX d ANSYS®, the values of the constants were determined from the linear combination of the three models, thus achieving the k-w BSL model. The k-w BSL model combines the advantages of Wilcox and the transformed k − ε model but cannot adequately predict the start and amount of flow separation on smooth surfaces, [26].The k − w SST model offers more accurate predictions at the onset of low-flow separation adverse pressure gradients. The SST model arises mainly because it does not consider the transport of turbulent shear stress. Appropriate behavior can be obtained by means of a limiter in the formulation of kinematic viscosity [26]. With the finite volume meshes of (Fig. 4), the static and six rotating domains (six V-shaped feathers) were configured with simulation parameters, (Table 1).

Table 1. Summary of CFD Simulation Parameter.

Simulation Parameter	Value
Simulation Type	Transient
Turbulence Model	kw-SST
Total Simulation Time	5s
Time Step	0.04 s
Loops	800
Fluid	Air at 25 °C
Wind Velocity	60 m/s
Pressure:	1 atm
Turbulence Level	5%
Velocity Subdomain Rotation	1 rev/s

Previously, a convergence analysis was conducted with 3D tetrahedral element edge sizes on feather surfaces of 10, 5, 3, 1, and 0.5 mm. Similar simulated values were observed starting from 3 mm; therefore, all meshes of the CFD simulations were configured with a maximum finite volume size of 1 mm, obtaining rotative meshes (Fig. 5).

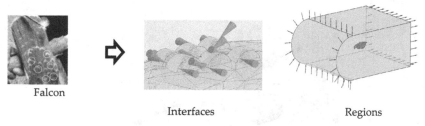

Falcon   Interfaces   Regions

Fig. 5. Static domain and rotaries subdomains.

The CFX solver is a widely used software for CFD simulation. CFX allows a quick configuration of the surfaces of a 3D domain and the selection of the turbulence model. Figure 5 shows the configuration of the fluid-to-fluid interfaces of the rotating or cylindrical domains. Six feathers can vary their angle of inclination and the air contacts the feathers. When the feathers rotate inside the bird, no variation in the behavior in the air is observed. The useful information for the analysis of the simulation is acquired when the feather is outside the bird between 0 and 90°.

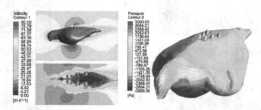

Fig. 6. Contours of velocity and pressure simulated with feather tilt angle $\Theta = 90°$.

The physical variables are post-processed using contour planes (Fig. 6). These contours show the behavior of the air velocity in the proxies to the 3D model of the falcon body, where increases in velocity (red areas) and reductions (blue areas) of the simulated wind velocity can be seen. The maximum velocity values are observed in the central part of the hawk's back and at the bottom, and the minimum values in the rear part, associated with the core of the wind wake.

The wind wake generated by the hawk has velocity values between 20–50 m/s, low velocity contours of approximately 2 m/s are observed in the rear parts of the stabilizer feathers. Figure 6 shows the simulated wind velocity contours in vertical, plane above the back of the bird (left), surface pressure contours in 3D model of the falcon (right). Figure 7 shows the surface pressure from various views and how it behaves on the bird body.

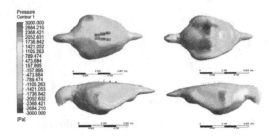

Fig. 7. Simulated surface pressure on 3D model, views: top, bottom, sides, feather tilt angle $\Theta = 90°$.

Vorticity is calculated as the curl of the velocity vector and has a value twice the rotation rate of the fluid element [26, 27]. High value contours (red) indicate areas where vorticity is higher.

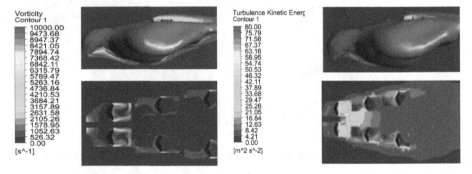

Fig. 8. Simulated vorticity and turbulence kinetic energy TKE contour planes, lateral plane, and top plane with feather tilt angle $\Theta = 90°$.

In CFD simulations [24, 25, 29], the turbulence kinetic energy or TKE can be observed by means of contour planes and indicates the amount or concentration of kinetic energy of the air in the vicinity of the solid under study [30–32]. Since the shapes of the bird's body interact with the fluid, the energy of the fluid changes as a function of the changes in the angle of inclination of the feathers. Figure 8 shows the largest kinetic energy contours observed at a 90° angle of inclination of the feathers. Near the feathers, changes in the simulated contour planes were observed as a function of the angle of inclination of the feathers. As the tilt angle increases, those of vorticity and TKE contour areas increase. Using a mathematical expression in post-processing, a curve of the simulated pressure in the transverse plane as a function of time can be constructed (Fig. 9).

$$m = \rho V A \rightarrow V = \frac{m}{\rho A} \tag{10}$$

The wake wind velocity as a function of time was obtained using a mathematical expression from the mass flow (m) (Eq. 10). The simulated velocity of the plane located at the center of the model (V) was used. The cross-sectional area of static domain (A) was divided into 3500. The density (ρ) was defined as 1.19 kg/m³ obtaining a velocity curve with values such as the velocity contours of the wind wake, as shown in Fig. 9.

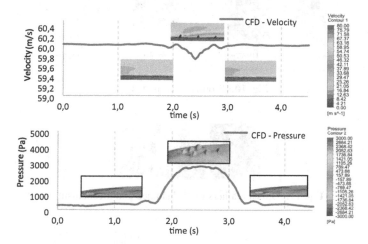

Fig. 9. Velocity and Surface Pressure.

As simulation time increases, the feather rotates, it is observed that angle changes from 0° to 90° of inclination are associated with a time range of approximately 2 s to 2.5 s (Figure 9). The expressions defined in CFD-post for the wake velocity (Eq. 11) and surface pressure (Eq. 12) curves are:

$$V_{wake} = \frac{m_{Plane1}}{\left(\frac{A_{inlet}}{3500}\right) * 1.19\left[\frac{kg}{m^3}\right]} \tag{11}$$

$$P_{falcon} = \frac{\sqrt{fx_{falcon}^2 + fy_{falcon}^2 + fz_{falcon}^2}}{A_{falcon}} + \sum_{1}^{6} \frac{\sqrt{fx_{feather\,n}^2 + fy_{feather\,n}^2 + fz_{feather\,n}^2}}{A_{feather\,n}} \tag{12}$$

After performing the CFD simulations, the experimentation phase begins with the design and construction of a prototype with the same dimensions as the simulated falcon in 3D, which is performed using a 3D printer with yellow ABS material (Fig. 10).

After the 3D printing of the falcon prototype, a servo mechanism is built to allow the vari-ation of the angular position of the dorsal feathers, so a "V" shaped arrangement is built according to those observed in the real bird (yellow circles) as shown in Fig. 11.

Figure 11 shows the construction of a servomechanism that, by means of wires, achieves the rotation of the feather support axes and thus adjusts its angle of inclination; this mechanism is connected to an embedded system with Bluetooth connectivity that allows integration to a software application developed with MATLAB. The gaps between the feathers and the bird's body were necessary to achieve movement of the feather and to achieve an inclination of 0°.

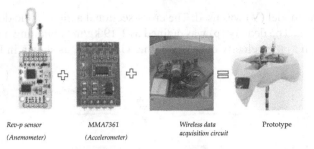

Rev-p sensor   *MMA7361*   *Wireless data*   Prototype
(Anemometer)   *(Accelerometer)*   *acquisition circuit*

Fig. 10. Prototype construction.

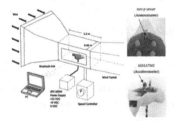

Fig. 11. Dorsal feathers in "V" shaped and mechanism.

Fig. 12. Experimental setup.

Figure 12 shows the design of the wind tunnel experiment used to validate the CFD simulations of the 3D falcon model. The Falcon prototype has a circuit and sensors that communicate wirelessly, and because of the power characteristics of the hot wire sensor or Rev-p sensor, it was necessary to use a DC ATX source with $+12V_{DC}$, $+5V_{DC}$, and $0V_{DC}$.

Fig. 13. Wind tunnel measurement protocol.

The experimental protocol is shown in the block diagram in Fig. 13. The software application developed in MATLAB communicates via Bluetooth protocol with an ESP32 or embedded system that interfaces with the hot wire sensor and 3D accelerometer, as shown in Fig. 14.

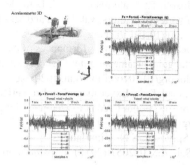

Fig. 14. MatLab App.

Figure 14 shows the wind velocity obtained with the digital anemometer sensor located in the prototype, changing the wind velocity in tunnel every 40 s by 5, 8, 10, 15, 20 m/s. The time between samples is ts = 0.005 s or sampling time. In the Figure, n is the sample number. After measuring the wake velocity, Fig. 18 is intended to show the measured acceleration experienced by the prototype falcon. The acceleration in the x-axis direction is plotted without mean value. This allows a better appreciation of the variations between each of the samples. The highest peaks in the amplitudes are associated with wind velocity of 8 m/s and 20 m/s. The color represents the angle of inclination of the feathers.

4 Conclusions

This work shows that it is possible to identify the vibration characteristics and velocities of the turbulent wake generated by a prototype using data acquisition systems and digital sensors. The 3D peregrine falcon prototype showed that the special feathers of this bird allow it to compensate or vary the vibrations it generates in high velocity descent, varying the fluctuations of its wake and changing the vibration of its structure or body. The measured mechanical vibrations of the prototype and wake wind fluctuations increase with increasing wind velocity in the tunnel. The greatest reduction in measured vibrations or accelerations is observed at a wind velocity of 10 m/s.

References

1. Deshmukh, S., Bhattacharya, S., Jain, A., Paul, A.R.: Wind turbine noise and its mitigation techniques: a review. Energy Procedia **160**(2018), 633–640 (2019). https://doi.org/10.1016/j.egypro.2019.02.215
2. Bodling, A., Sharma, A.: Numerical investigation of noise reduction mechanisms in a bioinspired airfoil. J. Sound Vib. **453**, 314–327 (2019). https://doi.org/10.1016/j.jsv.2019.02.004

3. Mystkowski, A.: Piezo-stack vortex generators for boundary layer control of a delta wing micro-aerial vehicle. Mech. Syst. Signal Process. **40**(2), 783–790 (2013). https://doi.org/10.1016/j.ymssp.2013.05.019

4. Mereu, R., Passoni, S., Inzoli, F.: Scale-resolving CFD modeling of a thick wind turbine airfoil with application of vortex generators: validation and sensitivity analyses. Energy **187**, 115969 (2019). https://doi.org/10.1016/j.energy.2019.115969

5. Lu, G., Zhou, G.: Numerical simulation on performances of plane and curved winglet – Pair vortex generators in a rectangular channel and field synergy analysis. Int. J. Therm. Sci. **109**, 323–333 (2016). https://doi.org/10.1016/j.ijthermalsci.2016.06.024

6. Zhen, T.K., Zubair, M., Ahmad, K.A.: Experimental and numerical investigation of the effects of passive vortex generators on Aludra UAV performance. Chinese J. Aeronaut. **24**(5), 577–583 (2011). https://doi.org/10.1016/S1000-9361(11)60067-8

7. Troldborg, N., Zahle, F., Sørensen, N.N.: Simulations of wind turbine rotor with vortex generators. J. Phys.: Conf. Ser. **753**, 022057 (2016). https://doi.org/10.1088/1742-6596/753/2/022057

8. Ponitz, B., Triep, M., Brücker, C.: Aerodynamics of the cupped wings during peregrine falcon's diving flight. Open J. Fluid Dyn. **04**(04), 363–372 (2014). https://doi.org/10.4236/ojfd.2014.44027

9. Ponitz, B., Schmitz, A., Fischer, D., Bleckmann, H., Brücker, C.: Diving-flight aerodynamics of a peregrine falcon (Falco peregrinus). PLoS ONE **9**(2), e86506 (2014). https://doi.org/10.1371/journal.pone.0086506

10. Gowree, E.R., Jagadeesh, C., Talboys, E., Lagemann, C., Brücker, C.: Vortices enable the complex aerobatics of peregrine falcons. Commun. Biol. **1**, 27 (2018). https://doi.org/10.1038/s42003-018-0029-3

11. Shi, S.X., Liu, Y.Z., Chen, J.M.: An experimental study of flow around a bio-inspired airfoil at Reynolds number 2.0×10^3. J. Hydrodyn. **24**(3), 410–419 (2012). https://doi.org/10.1016/S1001-6058(11)60262-X

12. Shanmukha Srinivas, K., Datta, A., Bhattacharyya, A., Kumar, S.: Free-stream characteristics of bio-inspired marine rudders with different leading-edge configurations. Ocean Engineering **170**, 148–159 (2018). https://doi.org/10.1016/j.oceaneng.2018.10.010

13. Post, M.L., Decker, R., Sapell, A.R., Hart, J.S.: Effect of bio-inspired sinusoidal leading-edges on wings. Aerosp. Sci. Technol. **81**, 128–140 (2018). https://doi.org/10.1016/j.ast.2018.07.043

14. Hassanalian, M., Throneberry, G., Abdelkefi, A.: Wing shape and dynamic twist design of bio-inspired nano air vehicles for forward flight purposes. Aerosp. Sci. Technol. **68**, 518–529 (2017). https://doi.org/10.1016/j.ast.2017.06.010

15. Drew Adam Wetzel: vortex generators for wind turbine rotor blades having noise-reducing features (2018)

16. Xia, H., Sun, Q., Liu, Y.: Energy absorption characteristics of bio-inspired honeycomb column thin-walled structure under low strain rate uniaxial compression loading. Energies **15**, 6957 (2022)

17. Vu, D.T., et al.: Solar concentrator bio-inspired by the superposition compound eye for high-concentration photovoltaic system up to thousands fold factor. Energies **15**(9), 3406 (2022). https://doi.org/10.3390/en15093406

18. Zhang, H., Sheng, W., Zha, Z., Aggidis, G.: A preliminary study on identifying biomimetic entities for generating novel wave energy converters. Energies **15**(7), 2485 (2022). https://doi.org/10.3390/en15072485

19. Dvorak, P.: Conformal vortex generator and elastomer tab let NREL test turbine produce 22% more power. https://www.windpowerengineering.com/conformal-vortex-generator-elastomer-tab-let-nrel-test-turbine-produce-22-power/ (2017). Accessed Nov. 17, 2020

20. Lattin, C.R., Emerson, M.A., Gallezot, J.D., Mulnix, T., Brown, J.E., Carson, R.E.: A 3D-printed modular device for imaging the brain of small birds. J. Neurosci. Methods **293**, 183–190 (2018). https://doi.org/10.1016/j.jneumeth.2017.10.005
21. Hongtu, Z., Ouya, Z., Botao, L., Jian, Z., Xiangyu, X., Jianping, W.: Effect of drill pipe rotation on gas-solid flow characteristics of negative pressure pneumatic conveying using CFD-DEM simulation. Powder Technol. **387**, 48–60 (2021). https://doi.org/10.1016/j.pow tec.2021.04.017
22. Heydari, M., Sadat-Hosseini, H.: Analysis of propeller wake field and vortical structures using $k-\omega$ SST Method. Ocean Eng. **204**(August 2019), 107247 (2019). https://doi.org/10.1016/j. oceaneng.2020.107247
23. van Sluis, M., Nasrollahi, S., Rao, A.G., Eitelberg, G.: Experimental and numerical analyses of a novel wing-in-ground vehicle. Energies **15**(4), 1497 (2022). https://doi.org/10.3390/en1 5041497
24. Ung, S.-K., Chong, W.-T., Mat, S., Ng, J.-H., Kok, Y.-H., Wong, K.-H.: Investigation into the aerodynamic performance of a vertical axis wind turbine with endplate design. Energies **15**(19), 6925 (2022). https://doi.org/10.3390/en15196925
25. Aziz, S., et al.: Computational fluid dynamics and experimental analysis of a wind turbine blade's frontal section with and without arrays of dimpled structures. Energies **15**(19), 7108 (2022). https://doi.org/10.3390/en15197108
26. ANSYS CFX-Solver Theory Guide, vol. 15317, no. November. (2011)
27. Whitehouse, G.R., Boschitsch, A.H.: Investigation of grid-based vorticity-velocity large eddy simulation off-body solvers for application to overset CFD. Comput. Fluids **225**, 104978 (2021). https://doi.org/10.1016/j.compfluid.2021.104978
28. Shen, Z., Yang, Z., Wang, Y.: Unsteady correlation between shear layer vorticity and acoustic refraction in low speed open-jet wind tunnel. Appl. Acoust. **182**, 108202 (2021). https://doi. org/10.1016/j.apacoust.2021.108202
29. Belamadi, R., Settar, A., Chetehouna, K., Ilinca, A.: Numerical modeling of horizontal axis wind turbine: aerodynamic performances improvement using an efficient passive flow control system. Energies **15**(13), 4872 (2022). https://doi.org/10.3390/en15134872
30. Shirzadi, M., Tominaga, Y.: CFD evaluation of mean and turbulent wind characteristics around a high-rise building affected by its surroundings. Build. Env. **225**, 109637 (2022). https://doi. org/10.1016/j.buildenv.2022.109637
31. Zeng, F., Lei, C., Liu, J., Niu, J., Gao, N.: CFD simulation of the drag effect of urban trees: Source term modification method revisited at the tree scale. Sustain. Cities Soc. **56**, 102079 (2020). https://doi.org/10.1016/j.scs.2020.102079
32. Dondapati, R.S., Rao, V.V.: Influence of mass flow rate on Turbulent Kinetic Energy (TKE) distribution in Cable-in-Conduit Conductors (CICCs) used for fusion grade magnets. Fusion Eng. Des. **88**(5), 341–349 (2013). https://doi.org/10.1016/j.fusengdes.2013.03.047

Optimal Portfolio Selection Using a Robust-Bayesian Model

Carlos Andres Zapata Quimbayo[1](✉) (iD), Diego Felipe Carmona Espejo[2] (iD), and Jhonatan Gamboa Hidalgo[3] (iD)

[1] Universidad Externado de Colombia, Bogotá, Colombia
carlosa.zapata@uexternado.edu.co
[2] Superintendencia Financiera de Colombia, Bogotá, Colombia
[3] Skandia Holding de Colombia S.A, Bogotá, Colombia

Abstract. In this paper we implement a portfolio optimization model that integrates the robust portfolio optimization approach and the Bayesian approach with the purpose of modeling the uncertainty of the estimated parameters in the expected returns and in the covariance matrix. The proposed model is implemented using the Wishart and Gamma distribution functions to model the uncertainty with ellipsoidal or quadratic type sets. To do that, we choose a portfolio made up of the shares of the USA DJI index. The results confirm the advantages of the robust approach compared to the traditional mean-variance model, both in performance evaluation and in its diversification.

Keywords: Optimal Portfolio · Robust Optimization · Bayesian Model · Uncertainty Sets

1 Introduction

The mean-variance (MV) model developed by Markowitz [1, 2] represents the most important theoretical development of the modern portfolio theory (MPT) by providing the general formulation for constructing optimal investment portfolios. However, the MV model presents important limitations [3–6], since the MV model generates low diversified portfolios and achieve low performance compared to benchmarks or compared to other more robust portfolio formulations. These limitations are due to the exclusive dependence of the MV model on historical data, which are used to obtain the parameters of expected returns and the covariance matrix, which causes a high sensitivity of the model to these parameters. These limitations have been partially overcome through the approach of robust optimization (RO) of portfolios introduced by [7, 8]. The implementation of this RO approach is based on the formulation of a maximum-minimum problem, known as the worst-case scenario. In this approach, the optimal weights of each asset are obtained when the expected returns take the worst value within the specific uncertainty set, like [9, 10] argued. Thus, by considering parameter uncertainty, RO provides a more consistent solution compared to the MV model. Furthermore, as stated by [11], the RO approach represents a significant advancement of MPT in better adapting to the dynamics of the financial market.

J. C. Figueroa-García et al. (Eds.): WEA 2023, CCIS 1928, pp. 70–79, 2023.
https://doi.org/10.1007/978-3-031-46739-4_7

Since its adoption, RO has offered an intuitive solution supported by convex optimization techniques such as quadratic programming (QP) and second-order cone programming (SOCP), considering the specification of the uncertainty sets and problem constraints [10, 11]. [8] introduced a significant number of RO formulations using convex programming. Later, [12] presented robust formulations for the MV model and portfolio Value-at-Risk (VaR) using ellipsoidal uncertainty sets, while [13] considered interval uncertainty sets for expected returns and the covariance matrix. Based on these works, there has been significant growth in RO to enhance the solutions of the MV model [14] or its extensions using risk measures such as VaR or CVaR [15, 16], as well as in performance measures [17, 18]. Thanks to advances in mathematical programming and the use of computational tools, the RO approach has been progressed, as stated by [10, 11].

On the other hand, RO can be improved from a Bayesian framework, as suggested by [19], who found that expert knowledge can be introduced into the optimization process by incorporating the investor's subjective expectations. This approach is known as Bayesian robust optimization. To do that, [19] incorporated ellipsoidal uncertainty sets from a posterior distribution function resulting from implementing a Bayesian process within the reformulation of the optimization problem to obtain the robust counterpart.

Building on these developments, this study adopts the RO and Bayesian approaches for constructing an optimal portfolio to overcome the limitations identified in the MV approach. For this purpose, the model proposed by [19] is adopted and integrated with the RO approach to achieve the construction of the robust-Bayesian portfolio (RBP). In that sense, we use the Gamma distribution function to improve the portfolio's sensitivity and diversification. The proposed model allows for achieving an RBP for a set of assets in the US market that improves the results of both the MV and RO portfolios.

2 Portfolio Theory

2.1 Mean-Variance (MV) Model

Markowitz [1, 2] developed an optimal solution for the selection of a portfolio of risky assets. The Markowitz formulation considered as inputs of the model the expected return of assets (μ_i) and covariances (σ_{ij}), under the assumption that the returns follow a normal distribution. Thus, a portfolio of n risky assets with expected return $E(R_P) = \mathbf{w}'\mu = \mu_p$ and variance $\sigma_P^2 = \mathbf{w}'\Sigma\mathbf{w}$, where $\mu \in \mathbb{R}^{n \times 1}$ is the vector of expected returns, $\Sigma \in \mathbb{R}^{n \times n}$ is the covariance matrix, and $\mathbf{w} \in \mathbb{R}^{n \times 1}$ is the vector of weights. The optimization problem is a quadratic programming (QP) problem and is solved by minimizing σ_P^2 for a given level of expected return (μ_{p0}) given by:

$$\min_{\{\mathbf{w}\}}\{\mathbf{w}'\Sigma\mathbf{w}\} \text{ s.t. } \mu'\mathbf{w} = \mu_{p0} \text{ and } \mathbf{w}'\mathbf{1} = 1 \tag{1}$$

where, $\mathbf{1} \in \mathbb{R}^{n \times 1}$ is a vector of ones. Additionally, Eq. 1 can also incorporate the restriction on negative or short weights, that is, it is solved for $\mathbf{w} \geq 0$, however, the solution is no longer analytical. Despite the developments that the MV model represents, it has important limitations. For example, using only historical data for the estimation of μ or Σ does not adequately incorporate future uncertainty, resulting in very sensitive or noisy solutions.

2.2 Portfolio Robust optimization

The RO is an optimization approach for portfolio under uncertainty introduced by [7] and [8] and represents an intuitive and efficient way to handle uncertainty for μ and Σ through uncertainty sets [10, 11]. Like the Bayesian approach, RO assumes that μ and Σ are random variables; however, RO offers an intuitive solution that can be implemented through convex programming, such as quadratic programming (QP) or second-order cone programming (SOCP). Following [20], RO involves formulating a maximum-minimum or minimum-maximum problem and solving it for the entire uncertainty set, even if μ takes its worst possible value. Since the robust counterpart requires reformulating the original optimization problem considering the uncertainty set, the most used types of uncertainty sets are interval sets and ellipsoidal or quadratic sets. The following steps are carried out to implement this: i) defining the uncertainty set for μ and Σ; ii) reformulating the original optimization problem to include the uncertainty set; and iii) solving the reformulated problem to obtain the robust optimal portfolio.

By considering the uncertainty set, RO approach provides a more robust and stable solution compared to the traditional mean-variance (MV) approach. It allows for incorporating parameter uncertainty and mitigating the adverse effects of estimation errors. Furthermore, RO can be implemented using various optimization techniques, making it versatile and practical for portfolio optimization under uncertainty. This procedure allows solving the problem that determines the worst possible realization of the parameters before solving the original portfolio selection problem. [12] developed the first comprehensive formulations of this method based on the MV model. However, as suggested [20], the formulation of the robust model depends on the objective function that describes the problem and the specified uncertainty set. For example, if we considered the quadratic utility function of the MV model and the interval-type uncertainty $\mathcal{U}_\mu$, the original optimization problem is reformulated in a max-min type as follows:

$$\max_{\{\mathbf{w}\}} \{ \min_{\{\mu \| |\mu - \hat{\mu}| \leq \delta\}} (\mathbf{w}'\mu) - \lambda \mathbf{w}'\Sigma\mathbf{w} \} \text{ s.t. } \mathbf{w}'\mathbf{1} = 1 \tag{2}$$

Therefore, the robust version of the problem is given by:

$$\max_{\{\mathbf{w}\}} \{ \mathbf{w}'\mu - \lambda \mathbf{w}'\Sigma\mathbf{w} - \delta|\mathbf{w}| \} \quad \text{s.t. } \mathbf{w}'\mathbf{1} = 1 \tag{3}$$

Now, if the ellipsoidal uncertainty set is implemented in the same objective function $\mathcal{U}_\mu = \{ \mu | (\mu - \hat{\mu})'\Sigma_\mu^{-1}(\mu - \hat{\mu}) \leq \delta^2 \}$, we obtain the following max-min problem, and the robust version of the problem are given by:

$$\max_{\{\mathbf{w}\}} \{ \min_{\{\mu | (\mu - \hat{\mu})'\Sigma_\mu^{-1}(\mu - \hat{\mu}) \leq \delta^2\}} (\mathbf{w}'\mu - \lambda \mathbf{w}'\Sigma\mathbf{w}) \} \text{s.t. } \mathbf{w}'\mathbf{1} = 1 \tag{4}$$

$$\max_{\{\mathbf{w}\}} \{ \mathbf{w}'\mu - \lambda \mathbf{w}'\Sigma\mathbf{w} - \delta\sqrt{\mathbf{w}'\Sigma_\mu\mathbf{w}} \} \text{s.a. } \mathbf{w}'\mathbf{1} = 1 \tag{5}$$

where: Σ_μ represents the diagonal matrix of the estimation errors of the covariances or uncertainty matrix. Under the assumption of a multivariate normal distribution $(\mu - \hat{\mu})'\Sigma_\mu^{-1}(\mu - \hat{\mu})$ is estimated as a χ^2 distribution with n degrees of freedom. Given the advantages of the ellipsoidal set over the interval set, as stated by [9, 12, 20, 21], this ellipsoidal set is recommended in the RO. Additionally, [9] found that robust portfolios can perform better than MV portfolios by exhibiting greater stability in their composition over time, which can significantly reduce portfolio rebalancing and thus risk losses. Transaction costs. These results highlight the advantages of the RO approach over the MV model. [11] confirmed the previous results and find that robust portfolios are superior in the design of risk management strategies. Furthermore, [20–22] also found that robust portfolios present superior results to MV portfolios in terms of performance and greater stability over time.

2.3 Bayesian Formulation of the Robust Portfolio

Meucci [19] demonstrated that the Bayesian approach can be integrated into the RO by introducing the prior probability distribution of μ and Σ, which generates an RBP. To do that, the author used ellipsoidal sets to obtain the robust counterpart by using a conjugate distribution function within the reformulation of the optimization problem. In that sense, RBP combines the investor's subjective beliefs and generates an optimal solution for the uncertainty set used. Following the same assumptions from the MV and RO models, [19] incorporates the investor's prior beliefs using a Wishart inverse-normal distribution: $\mu \sim N(v_0, \Sigma/T_0)$ and $\Sigma^{-1} \sim W\left(v_0, \Sigma_0^{-1}/v_0\right)$, where v_0 and T_0 are the hyper parameters. Furthermore, by using the ellipsoidal set of the posterior marginal distribution of μ, [19] get the estimator of the expected value of $\hat{\mu}_{ce} = \mu_1$ and the estimator of the scattering matrix $\mathbf{S}_\mu$. The uncertainty of Σ, like the previous ellipsoidal set, is also described by the estimator of the expected value of μ and the scattering matrix estimator as follows:

$$\hat{\Sigma}_{ce} = \frac{v_1}{v_1 + N + 1}\Sigma_1 \tag{6}$$

$$\mathbf{S}_\Sigma = \frac{2v_1^2}{(v_1 + N + 1)^3}\left(D_N'(\Sigma_1^{-1} \otimes \Sigma_1^{-1})D_N\right)^{-1} \tag{7}$$

where, $\otimes$ is the Kronecker product. Finally, the robust counterpart is developed. The optimal solution for the established parameters and sets of the PRB is given by:

$$\max_{\{w'\Sigma_1 w \leq \gamma_\Sigma^{(i)}\}} \left\{w'\mu_1 - \gamma_\mu\sqrt{w'\Sigma_1 w}\right\} \text{ s.t. } w'\mathbf{1} = 1 \tag{8}$$

where:

$$\gamma_\mu \equiv \sqrt{\frac{q_\mu^2}{T_1}\frac{v_1}{v_1 - 2}} \quad \text{and} \quad \gamma_\Sigma^{(i)} \equiv \frac{v^{(i)}}{\frac{v_1}{v_1+N+1} + \sqrt{\frac{2v_1^2 q_\Sigma^2}{(v_1+N+1)^3}}} \tag{9}$$

The above formulation is obtained for an inverse Wishart distribution. However, other distribution functions, such as the Gamma, can also be used. As an extension of the previous RBP, we propose a model using the Gamma distribution named as RPBg. This adjustment is made on $\mathbf{\Sigma}$, which is given by:

$$f^{\Gamma}_{\alpha,\beta,\nu,\Sigma}(\Gamma) = \frac{1}{k}|\mathbf{\Sigma}|^{-\alpha}|\mathbf{\Gamma}|^{\alpha-\frac{1}{2}(\rho+1)}\frac{1}{\beta^{\rho\alpha}}e^{\frac{-1}{\beta}tr(\mathbf{\Sigma}^{-1}\Gamma)} \tag{10}$$

where: $\mathbf{\Sigma}^{-1} \sim \mathbf{\Gamma}(\alpha, \beta, (\nu_1, \mathbf{\Sigma}_1)^{-1})$ and α and β are the shape and scale parameters, respectively. In that sense, we extended the Meucci's model by using the ellipsoidal uncertainty set. With this adjustment, we found:

$$\hat{\mathbf{\Sigma}}_{ce} = \left(\frac{\alpha}{\beta(2\alpha + \rho + 1)}\right)\Sigma_1 \tag{11}$$

$$\mathbf{S}_\Sigma = \frac{2\alpha^2}{\beta^2(2\alpha + \rho + 1)^3}(D'_N\left[\mathbf{\Sigma}_1^{-1} \otimes \mathbf{\Sigma}_1^{-1}\right]D_N)^{-1} \tag{12}$$

By incorporating these adjusted into the optimization model, the PRBg is obtained as:

$$\max_{\{\mathbf{w}'\mathbf{\Sigma}_1\mathbf{w}\leq\gamma_\Sigma^{(i)}\}}\left\{\mathbf{w}'\boldsymbol{\mu}_1 - \gamma_\mu\sqrt{\mathbf{w}'\Sigma_1\mathbf{w}}\right\} \quad \text{s.t.} \quad \mathbf{w}'\mathbf{1} = 1 \tag{13}$$

where:

$$\gamma_\mu \equiv \sqrt{\frac{\alpha q_\mu^2}{\beta T_1(2\alpha - \rho)}} \quad \text{and} \quad \gamma_\Sigma^{(i)} \equiv \frac{\nu^{(i)}}{\frac{\alpha}{\beta(2\alpha+\rho+1)} + \sqrt{\frac{2\alpha^2 q_\Sigma^2}{\beta^2(2\alpha+\rho+1)^3}}} \tag{14}$$

It should be noted that, if the RBPg model uses the parameters $\beta = 2$ and $\alpha = \nu/2$, the same results from the RBP model.

3 Numerical Implementation and Results

3.1 Data

The proposed model is implemented for the USA stock market and is taken as the Dow Jones Industrial Average (DJIA) index, which is made up of the 30 most important and representative industrial companies in the USA. In addition, the in-sample analysis period covers from January 2011 to December 2020 and the out-of-sample period covers from January 2021 to December 2022. The data sample is developed by taking the monthly adjusted closing prices of the assets and the index.

3.2 Comparison of Results

We made a comparison of the models and the proposed approach. To do that, we compared the Markowitz MV portfolio and its robust counterparts: the robust portfolio (RP), the RBP and the RBPg taking long positions ($\mathbf{w} \geq 0$) in all of cases; both in the optimal solution and in the performance evaluation in-sample and out-of-sample. Additionally, both the RBP and RBPg portfolios are implemented following the recommendations of Meucci's approach. The results obtained are presented below. Results show significant differences in portfolio composition of the traditional MV model and the robust portfolios. In addition, a notable improvement in the performance results from the RB and RBP portfolios for the out-of-sample period is identified as listed in Table 1b, as well as an improvement in all the optimal portfolios related to the benchmark (DJI), as listed in Table 1 (Fig. 1).

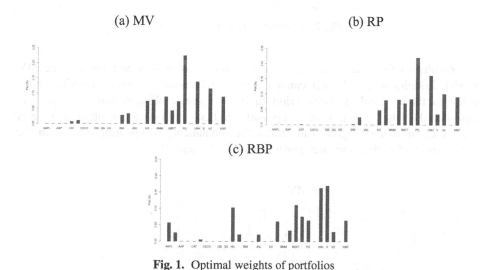

(a) MV   (b) RP

(c) RBP

Fig. 1. Optimal weights of portfolios

This performance is measured through risk-adjusted returns using the Sharpe coefficient.

Table 1. Results of the optimal portfolios

	In-sample	Out-sample						
	MV	RP	RBP	DJI	MV	RP	RBP	DJI
Return:	0.0115	0.0128	0.0169	0.0081	0.0044	0.0047	0.0051	0.0033
Risk:	0.0280	0.0281	0.0326	0.0393	0.0442	0.0452	0.0502	0.0522
Sharpe Coef.:	0.41	0.4538	0.5177	0.2058	0.0995	0.1047	0.1009	0.0636

Figure 2 shows the historical behavior of the cumulative returns for the optimal portfolios and the benchmark in the in-sample (2a) and out-of-sample (2b) periods. In both cases, a better performance of the RBPg portfolio is identified. In particular, the RBPg portfolio for the out-of-sample period is highlighted. For most of this period, this portfolio achieves a higher cumulative return and presents lower decreases than the others.

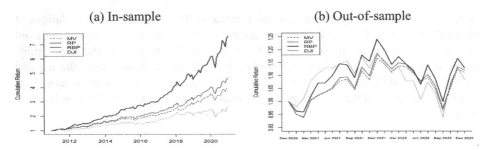

Fig. 2. Cumulative return of portfolios

Results confirm the advantages of robust portfolio models compared to the MV model. Additionally, we implemented a monthly rebalancing exercise of optimal port-folios for the in-sample analysis period. In this exercise, a rolling period of five years is considered for the calculation of the optimal weights, which gives a result of 60 updates for the entire period. Figure 3 illustrates the rebalancing or updating process in the composition of each of the three portfolios (MV, RP, and RBP).

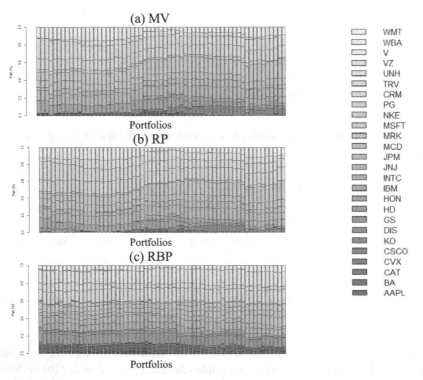

Fig. 3. Portfolio rebalancing

Figure 3a shows the frequent changes that the MV portfolio presents, which confirms the sensitivity problem that this model has compared to the estimated parameters as pointed out above. In addition, the exclusion of a large part of the assets that make up the portfolio is identified. But although the RP portfolio also has a high sensitivity, this is significantly reduced in the RBP portfolio. Figure 3c indicates a small adjustment of the weights of all the assets for the entire period. This consistency of the robust models can also be confirmed by using a concentration indicator, which is useful to identify the high deviation that portfolios can present. For this, we use the Herfindahl–Hirschman index (HHI) measured as the sum of the squares of weights of each n assets that make up the portfolio:

$$HHI = \sum_{i=1}^{n} w_i^2 \qquad (15)$$

The HHI index is calculated for all portfolios of the previous rebalancing exercise. Figure 4 shows the HHI index for the 60 portfolios. In this case, the HHI indicator is calculated for the RBP portfolio between 700 and 1050, while the indicator for the MV and RP portfolios is higher than these levels. Apart from portfolios 29–30, the RBP portfolio presents lower concentration levels or greater diversification. This is consistent with the better performance of the RBP portfolio, since, in a bearish and high-volatility period such as the one identified for the year 2022, the robust model developed from the worst-case scenario approach minimizes the potential losses that the portfolio may face. However, the variability experienced by the HHI indicator is high, which can lead to a rebalancing of portfolios, although less frequently than the RP and MV models.

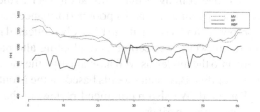

Fig. 4. HHI Index of the portfolios

On the other hand, the RBPg model is implemented following the proposed adjustment by using the gamma distribution. Figure 5 shows the results from the RBPg portfolio, and it is compared with the RBP portfolio. Figure 5a and b confirm a further diversification of the RBPg portfolio. In the first case, this is due to an increase in the assets that are part of the optimal portfolio. In the second case, a lower variability of the HHI index is observed. These results confirm the improvements of the RBP model when using gamma distribution compared to the model proposed by Meucci (2011).

(a) weights of RBP and RBPg portfolios   (b) HHI index of RBP and RBPg portfolios

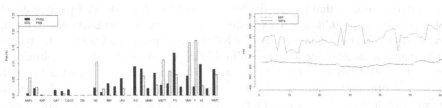

Fig. 5. RBPg portfolio results

4 Conclusions

In this work, a model integrating the RPO and Bayesian approaches was implemented for the development of an optimal portfolio to overcome the limitations of the MV model. RBP was implemented following the original proposal of Meucci (2011). However, an extension was conducted by replacing the Wishart distribution with the gamma distribution to represent the previous and subsequent distribution of the robust counterparts of the portfolio.

This new approach made it possible to build a RP for the US market based on the DJI index, whose results overcome the sensitivity and diversification problems. This means that the robust Bayesian model created a highly consistent portfolio that minimizes rebalancing over the period assessed and achieves better levels of diversification and better performance. Therefore, the proposed approach offers important advantages over Markowitz's MV model by overcoming its main limitations such as the high sensitivity of the portfolio to the estimated parameters and its poor performance outside of the sample. The advantage of the proposed model is that it can be easily replicated in different markets and asset classes. For future work, we recommend adopting alternative approaches to incorporate risk aversion into the model, as well as evaluating the model sensitivity to the distribution parameters. For this, Bayesian models based on the Monte Carlo simulation technique can be implemented. We also recommend reviewing the consistency of the model during recession and crisis periods.

References

1. Markowitz, H.: Portfolio selection. J. Fin. **7**(1), 77–91 (1952)
2. Markowitz, H.: Portfolio Selection: Efficient Diversification of Investments. Yale University Press, New Haven (1959)
3. Michaud, R.: Efficient Asset Management: A Practical Guide to Stock Portfolio Optimization and Asset Allocation. Oxford University Press (1998)
4. Chopra, V.K., Ziemba, W.T.: The effects of errors in means, variances, and covariances on optimal portfolio choice. J. Portfol. Manag. **19**(2), 6–11 (1993)
5. Best, M.J., Grauer, R.R.: Sensitivity analysis for mean-variance portfolio problems. Manag. Sci. **37**(8), 980–989 (1991)
6. Black, F., Litterman, R.: Global portfolio optimization. Financ. Anal. J. **48**(5), 28–43 (1992)
7. El Ghaoui, L., Oustry, F., Lebret, H.: Robust solutions to uncertain semidefinite programs. SIAM J. Optim. **9**(1), 33–52 (1998)

8. Ben-Tal, A.Y., Nemirovski, A.: Robust convex optimization. Math. Oper. Res. **23**(4), 769–805 (1998)
9. Fabozzi, F., Focardi, S., Kolm, P., Pachamanova, D.: Robust portfolio optimization and management. John Wiley & Sons (2007)
10. Pachamanova, D., Fabozzi, F.: Equity portfolio selection models in practice. Encycl. Financ. Models **1**(1), 61–87 (2007)
11. Kim, J.H., Kim, W.C., Kwon, D.G., Fabozzi, F.J.: Robust equity portfolio performance. Ann. Oper. Res. **266**(1–2), 293–312 (2018)
12. Goldfarb, D., Iyengar, G.: Robust portfolio selection problems. Math. Oper. Res. **28**(1), 1–38 (2003). https://doi.org/10.1287/moor.28.1.1.14260
13. Tütüncü, R.H., Koenig, M.: Robust asset allocation. Ann. Oper. Res. **132**(1–4), 157–187 (2004)
14. Garlappi, L., Uppal, R., Wang, T.: Portfolio selection with parameter and model uncertainty: a multi-prior approach. Rev. Financ. Stud. **20**(1), 41–81 (2007)
15. Zhu, S., Fukushima, M.: Worst-case conditional value-at-risk with application to robust portfolio management. Oper. Res. **57**(5), 1155–1168 (2009)
16. Zymler, S., Kuhn, D., Rustem, B.: Worst-case value at risk of nonlinear portfolios. Manag. Sci. **59**(1), 172–188 (2013)
17. Kapsos, M., Christofides, N., Rustem, B.: Worst-case robust Omega ratio. Eur. J. Oper. Res. **234**(2), 499–507 (2014)
18. Sharma, A., Utz, S., Mehra, A.: Omega-CVaR portfolio optimization and its worst-case analysis. OR Spec. **39**(2), 505–539 (2017)
19. Meucci, A.: Robust Bayesian allocation. J. Invest. Strat. **3**(2), 95–112 (2014)
20. Zapata Quimbayo, C.A.: Optimización robusta de portafolios: Conjuntos de incertidumbre y contrapartes robustas. ODEON **20**, 93–121 (2022)
21. Georgantas, A., Doumpos, M., Zopounidis, C.:Robust optimization approaches for portfolio selection: A comparative analysis. Ann. Oper. Res. 1–17 (2021). https://link.springer.com/article/10.1007/s10479-021-04177-y
22. Bertsimas, D., Brown, D.B., Caramanis, C.: Theory and applications of robust optimization. SIAM Rev. **53**(3), 464–501 (2011)

Impact of Pruning Distribution in Compressed CNN Models: A Case Study

César Pachón[1][(✉)] , César Pedraza[2] , and Dora Ballesteros[3]

[1] Doctorado en Ingeniería, Universidad Militar Nueva Granada, Bogotá, Colombia
`est.cesar.pachon@unimilitar.edu.co`
[2] Ingeniería de Sistemas, Universidad Nacional, Bogotá, Colombia
`capedrazab@unal.edu.co`
[3] Ingeniería en Telecomunicaciones, Universidad Militar Nueva Granada,
Bogotá, Colombia
`dora.ballesteros@unimilitar.edu.co`

Abstract. CNN model pruning has been one of the most widely used compression strategies in recent years to reduce model size and speed up inference time, with only a small reduction in classifier performance (e.g., accuracy, F1-score). There are numerous state-of-the-art pruning methods that focus on the selection of less important network parameters (e.g., filters, channels) to be removed from the pruned model. In the last year, some articles have focused on the automatic selection of the pruning rate (PR) per layer. However, to date, there is no experimental study that demonstrates the impact of different types of pruning rate per layer (e.g., bottom-up, top-down, uniform, bottom-up/top-down, or top-down/bottom-up) independent of the method of selecting the parameters to be pruned. Therefore, in this study, a preliminary experimental evaluation is performed for a sequential network (specifically VGG16) using random pruning, for the CIFAR10 dataset, five pruning rate per layer and ten experiments for each case. According to the results found in the fifty pruned models, it was determined that the type of PR affects the performance of the models, with bottom-up and top-down/bottom-up pruning showing poorer performance, while top-down pruning tends to have better performance. In addition, it is found that PR distributions with lower performance are associated with higher parameter reduction.

Keywords: Model compression · CNN · pruning · uniform pruning rate · adaptive pruning rate

1 Introduction

Recently, the pruning of CNN models for image classification tasks has become very important, as it allows to obtain a lighter and faster network from a trained model, with very little reduction of performance [1,2]. This allows the new pruned model to be used, for example, in an edge computing solution and/or to

J. C. Figueroa-García et al. (Eds.): WEA 2023, CCIS 1928, pp. 80–91, 2023.
https://doi.org/10.1007/978-3-031-46739-4_8

process many more images per second in applications that require it. Pruning policies include any or all of the following strategies: (1) selection of network parameters to be pruned, (2) network restructuring, (3) selection of the pruning rate (PR) per layer. Much of the state-of-the-art literature has focused on the first strategy, so the differences between pruning methods have typically centered on how the channels, filters, or neurons to be discarded in the model are selected [1]. Some work has also focused on reshaping, so that weights that are considered unrepresentative not only become zero in the pruned model, but are actually removed in the new network. For example, in terms of pruning criteria, there are methods based on the magnitude of the filters or feature maps [3–6], the gradient [7,8] or Taylor series [9], as well as the impact on the error per filter or the statistics per layer[10]. At the reshaping level, some works have proposed to restructure sequential or residual networks, allowing to significantly reduce the real parameters of the new pruned model, as well as its FLOPs [11].

Especially in the last year, there have been articles focusing on automatic calculation of the pruning rate per layer [12–15]. Each of these papers has one issue in common: they claim that uniform pruning, i.e., pruning that applies the same pruning rate to all convolutional layers in the network, is suboptimal because it degrades model accuracy to a greater extent than adaptive pruning. However, the results across papers are not consistent in terms of the type of distribution (e.g., bottom-up, top-down, uniform) that is most appropriate for a given network and dataset, or for a given filter selection method for pruning. For example, a high PR is applied to the first convolutional layer of VGG16 for CIFAR10 [12,14], as opposed to [14], which applies the lowest PR to the same convolutional layer. Or, a low PR is applied to the last convolutional layers [15], as opposed to [14], which applies the highest PR to the same convolutional layers. That is, no experiments were presented in which the filter selection criteria were fixed (e.g., random) and only the pruning rate per layer was varied for several distributions for a fixed global PR. For example, for a global PR of 50% and varying only the pruning rate per layer, it was not obvious which distribution is the best (i.e., bottom-up, top-down, uniform, bottom-up/top-down, or top-down/bottom-up), and whether there is a pattern that can be generalized across pruning methods.

In consideration of the above, the contribution of this study is as follows:

– This case study presents the impact of PR distribution using VGG16 and the CIFAR10 dataset, for a global PR of 50% and five distribution pruning rates. We show that one type of pruning distribution is not always the best for all methods of selecting the filters/neurons to be pruned. In some cases, it is very sensitive and in others, it is not.
– Our research shows that different types of pruning distributions can lead to different degrees of parameter variation, despite achieving a similar reduction in FLOPs. Furthermore, we have identified a possible correlation between accuracy loss and parameter loss in the pruned models, even when they have the same number of FLOPs.

The remainder of the study is organized as follows. Section 2 explains different types of techniques proposed for pruning in CNNs. Section 3 presents the methodology to address the case study of pruning distribution, starting from model training to pruning and retraining the pruned model. Section 4 presents the results obtained regarding the impact of the pruning distribution and method. Finally, Sect. 5 presents the conclusions of the study.

2   Pruning in CNNs

Nowadays, the compression of deep learning models has become very important due to their size (up to billions of parameters), which implies high storage costs and inference times. To accelerate these models, there are several groups of techniques that focus on network structure, network optimization, and hardware acceleration. The first group includes knowledge distillation, the second pruning and quantization, and the third memory optimization and computation reuse. At the network optimization level, pruning has proven to be effective in reducing the size (parameters) and the inference time (FLOPs) of the new model [1]. However, there are two challenges to be faced: (i) how to select the filters or neurons to prune in the network, and (ii) how to determine the pruning rate (PR) in each of the network layers [15].

Most of the state-of-the-art works have focused on the first challenge, which is to define a selection criterion for the parameters (i.e., filters/neurons, channels, layers) of the network to be pruned. Some of them have applied uniform pruning (UPR: uniform pruning rate) and others non-uniform pruning (APR: adaptive pruning rate), but without determining, first, how much impact the type of pruning rate per layer used has and, second, which distribution is better for the proposed selection criterion. However, especially in the last year, some works have evaluated the impact of pruning rate per layer within specific study sites. For instace, in [15], three networks (i.e., VGG, ResNet, y MobileNet) were evaluated on three datasets (i.e., CIFAR-10, ImageNet, y Food-101) and six pruning methods. Nevertheless, this study did not separate the impact analysis of the selection criterion from the distribution criterion because the methods used to compare each other in terms of accuracy and reduction of FLOPs disagreed in their pruning policy (i.e., in both the selection and distribution criteria). On the other hand, according to [13], when filters are pruned in the first few layers, the decrease in accuracy of the pruned model is greater. In other words, it is not advisable to have high pruning percentages in the first convolutional layers. But a limitation of this study is that it did not test different types of distributions that included pruning in all convolutional layers, as well as in the FCs of the network, with pruning values per layer that were less than 99%.

3   Methodology

The purpose of this study is to evaluate the impact of the PR distribution (i.e., bottom-up, top-down, uniform, bottom-up/top-down, or top-down/bottom-up), for the same network and dataset, while keeping the global PR fixed. The following methodology is used: (1) Selection of the network and dataset (obtain the unpruned model), (2) Theoretical calculation of FLOPs per layer (unpruned model), (3) define the Pruning Rate (PR) per layer, (4) calculate the number of FLOPs in the convolutional, pooling, and FC layers, and (5) prune and fine-tune the model and calculate its accuracy. Each step of the proposed methodology is explained below.

3.1 Selection of the Network and Dataset. Obtain the Unpruned Model

In this study, transfer learning is used to train the model on the dataset of interest and then prune it according to different pruning distributions. It is selected one of the most widely used pre-trained networks in state-of-the-art image classification methods, corresponding to VGG16, which contains an important number of parameters (more than 100 million), so that a high pruning percentage can be used to evaluate the impact of the distribution on the accuracy of the pruned model. For the dataset, CIFAR10 is selected, because it is one of the most widely used in the state-of-the-art of pruning CNNs.

The model without pruning is trained with the following hyperparameters: number of epochs equal to 40, batch size equal to 8, SGD as optimizer with learning rate of 0.001 and momentum of 0.9, and loss function of CrossEntropy-Loss. This model is used to apply the five types of pruning distributions, which are described in the last step.

3.2 Theoretical Calculation of FLOPs per Layer (Unpruned Model)

Once the network has been selected, the next step is to calculate the number of FLOPs for each of its convolutional, pooling and FC layers, according to the following equations:

$$FLOPs_{conv} = 2 \times (W_k \times H_k \times C_k) \times (W_o \times H_o \times C_o), \qquad (1)$$

where $FLOPs_{conv}$ is the number of FLOPs for a convolutional layer, W_k, H_k, and C_k correspond to the width, height and number of channels of the filter; while W_o, H_o, and C_o are the width, height, and the number of channels of the output (feature map).

For pooling layers, the number of FLOPs are obtained, according to:

$$FLOPs_{pool} = (W_o/S) \times (H_o/S) \times (C_o), \qquad (2)$$

where $FLOPs_{pool}$ is the number of FLOPs for a pooling layer, and S is the stride of the pooling operation. For both $FLOPs_{conv}$ and $FLOPs_{pool}$, the number of filters in the convolutional layer affects the number of output channels, i.e., C_o.

Finally, the number of FLOPs within FC layers are obtained, according to:

$$FLOPs_{FC^{th}} = 2 \times (neurons^{th-1} \times neurons^{th}), \qquad (3)$$

where $neurons^{th-1}$ is the number of neurons of the previous layer; and $neurons^{th}$ is the number of neurons of the current layer.

Further details of the theoretical calculation can be found in [10]. The specific values of FLOPs for VGG16 is presented in Table 2 (i.e., column entitled "original").

3.3 Define the Pruning Rate (PR) per Layer

In this study, five types of pruning distributions were evaluated, denominated PR_1 to PR_5, as follows: uniform (PR_1), bottom-up (PR_2), top-down (PR_3), bottom-up/top-down (PR_4), and top-down/bottom-up (PR_5) (See Fig. 1). Based on experimental trials, non-uniform distributions (APR: Adaptive Pruning Rate) were obtained for each of PR_2 to PR_5, ensuring that they have a comparable reduction in network FLOPs to uniform pruning (i.e. PR_1). For this study, a global PR of 50% is selected, which corresponds to a reduction of FLOPs of approximately 74.86%.

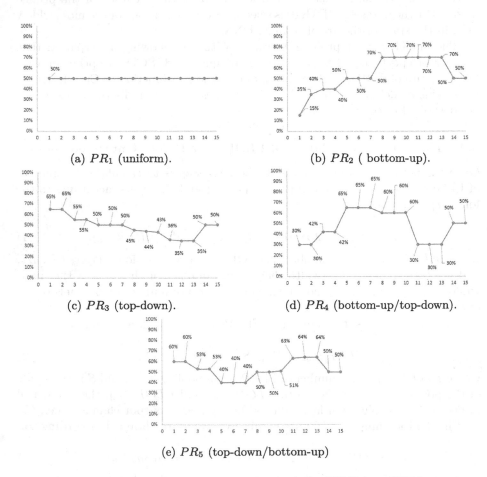

(a) PR_1 (uniform).

(b) PR_2 (bottom-up).

(c) PR_3 (top-down).

(d) PR_4 (bottom-up/top-down).

(e) PR_5 (top-down/bottom-up)

Fig. 1. Pruning distributions used in this study for VGG16 on CIFAR10.

Once the PRs per layer are defined for each of the pruning distributions, we proceed to calculate the filters and neurons that will be retained in the pruned network, as shown Table 1. Note that in all cases, the pruning rate in the last two-layers (i.e., the 14th and 15th layer) is equal to the global PR (i.e., 50%).

Table 1. Filters and neurons (retained) for the network VGG16 and the dataset CIFAR10. The values correspond to the unpruned model (i.e., "original") and five pruned models (i.e., PR_1 to PR_5). PR_1 is uniform pruning, and the others are APR-type.

Layer	original	PR_1	PR_2	PR_3	PR_4	PR_5
block1conv1	64	32	54	22	44	25
block1conv2	64	32	41	22	44	25
block2conv1	128	64	76	57	74	60
block2conv2	128	64	76	57	74	60
block3conv1	256	128	128	128	89	153
block3conv2	256	128	128	128	89	153
block3conv3	256	128	128	128	89	153
block4conv1	512	256	153	281	204	256
block4conv2	512	256	153	286	204	256
block4conv3	512	256	153	291	204	250
block5conv1	512	256	153	327	358	189
block5conv2	512	256	153	332	358	184
block5conv3	512	256	153	332	358	184
FC_1	4096	2048	2048	2048	2048	2048
FC_2	4096	2048	2048	2048	2048	2048
$FC_3(prediction)$	10	10	10	10	10	10

3.4 Calculate the Number of FLOPs in the Convolutional, Pooling, and FC Layers

From the number of filters per layer obtained in the above step, Eq. 1 and Eq. 2 are used to calculate the FLOPs of each pruned model. The values per model are shown in Table 2.

As can be seen in Table 2, these five distributions (the uniform one and the four APR types) allow us to obtain pruned models with very similar FLOPs values among them, corresponding to a reduction of about 74.8%. Therefore, the impact of pruning in terms of accuracy drop can be evaluated starting from the same original model, using the five distributions, with the random pruning method for 10 selected seeds. In this way, the results can be evaluated for each of the seeds (assuming, for example, that each seed was a pruning method), and again compacting the results by the value of the PR distribution.

Table 2. Number of FLOPs for VGG16, using the CIFAR10 dataset. The results correspond to the unpruned model and five pruned models with different pruning rate per layer. The values are in Millions.

Layer	original	PR_1	PR_2	PR_3	PR_4	PR_5
$block1conv1$	173,4	86,7	146,3	59,6	119,2	67,7
$block1conv2$	3699,4	924,8	1999,6	437,1	1748,5	564,5
$block1pool$	0,2	0,1	0,1	0,07	0,13	0,08
$block2conv1$	1849,7	462,4	703,6	283,1	735,2	338,7
$block2conv2$	3699,4	924,8	1304,2	733,6	1236,4	812,8
$block2pool$	0,1	0,05	0,06	0,04	0,058	0,047
$block3conv1$	1849,7	462,4	549,1	411,8	371,7	518,2
$block3conv2$	3699,4	924,8	924,8	924,8	447,1	1321,4
$block3conv3$	3699,4	924,8,4	924,8	924,8	447,1	1321,4
$block3pool$	0,05	0,025	0,025	0,05	0,017	0,03
$block4conv1$	1849,7	462,4	276,3	507,6	256,2	552,7
$block4conv2$	3699,4	924,8	330,3	1134,1	587,3	924,8
$block4conv3$	3699,4	924,8	330,3	1174,5	587,3	903,2
$block4pool$	0,025	0,0125	0,007	0,001	0,009	0,012
$block5conv1$	924,8	231,2	82,6	335,7	257,6	166,7
$block5conv2$	924,8	231,2	82,6	383,0	452,1	122,7
$block5conv3$	924,8	231,2	82,6	388,8	452,1	120,4
$block5pool$	0,006	0,003	0,002	0,004	0,004	0,002
FC_1	205,5	51,3	30,7	66,6	71,8	36,9
FC_2	33,5	8,4	8,4	8,4	8,4	8,4
$FC_3(prediction)$	0,08	0,04	0,04	0,04	0,04	0,04
$Total(M - FLOPs)$	30932,8	7776,67	7776,67	7774,02	7778,66	7779,8

3.5 Prune and Fine-Tune the Model. Calculate the Accuracy of the Pruned Model

In a pruning-based CNN model compression process, three main steps are performed: model training on the selected dataset, model pruning, and fine tuning of the pruned model. Section 3.1 presented the model training process, which includes the selection of the network and the dataset, as well as the definition of the training hyperparameters. Now, in this stage of the proposed methodology, model pruning and fine tuning are applied, using the same hyperparameters as in model training, except for the number of epochs, which is reduced by half.

Considering that we want to evaluate the impact of the pruning distribution on the performance of the pruned model, for the same pruning method, the inputs at this stage correspond to both the seed of the random pruning method (i.e., $seed_1$ to $seed_{10}$) and the PR value (from options PR_1 to PR_5). Below is the step-by-step pseudocode of the pruning process.

Algorithm 1: Pruning Algorithm

Input   : Original model
Output: Pruned models
PR_list ← [PR_1, PR_2, PR_3, PR_4, PR_5]
Seed_list ← [$Seed_1$, $Seed_2$, ..., $Seed_{10}$]
foreach $PR \in$ PR_list **do**
 foreach $Seed \in$ Seed_list **do**
  $model\_to\_prune \leftarrow$ original model
  $pruned\_model \leftarrow$ **prune** ($model\_to\_prune$, PR, Seed)
  $retrained\_pruned\_model \leftarrow$ **train** ($pruned\_model$, epoch = 20)
  save_model ($retrained\_pruned\_model$)

---

4   Results

This section presents the results of the fifty pruned models in terms of the type of distribution used (five options) and the seed value for random pruning (10 values). In addition, the results are evaluated considering simultaneously the seed value and the distribution method used. All pruned models were obtained from the same original model described in Sect. 3.1.

4.1   Impact by Type of Distribution

The accuracy results of the 50 pruned models are grouped by the type of distribution used, using box plots (See Fig. 2). In general, the best results are obtained when the PR_3 distribution (i.e., top-down) is applied, which means that a PR higher than the global PR is applied to the first convolutional layers (see Fig. 1c). In second place, we have the PR_4 distribution (i.e., bottom-up/top-down), in which the PR values exceeding the global PR are applied to the intermediate layers of VGG16 (see Fig. 1d). Very close, in third place, is the uniform pruning (PR_1), where the global PR is applied to all layers (see Fig. 1a). The last two positions are occupied by PR_5 (i.e., top-down/bottom-up) and $PR2$ (i.e., bottom-up). In both cases, a PR above the global PR is applied to the last convolutional layers (see Fig. 1b and Fig. 1e).

4.2   Impact by Method for Selecting Filters/Neurons to be Pruned

Similar to the analysis of the effect of type of distribution, the results of the fifty pruned models are grouped, but by the seed of the random method. This is done to determine if the method used to select the filters and neurons to be pruned also affects the model performance for the different types of pruning distributions selected in this study. The results are shown in Fig. 3.

According to the results, the highest accuracy of the pruned model obtained by each seed is very similar among them. That is, if a suitable pruning distribution is chosen for one filter selection method to be pruned, similar results can

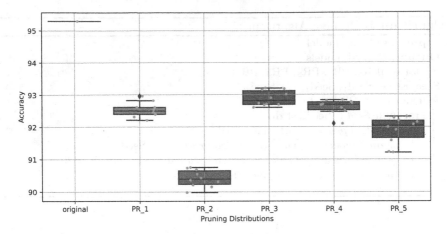

Fig. 2. Comparison between the performance of the unpruned model (i.e., original) and the models obtained by type of distribution: uniform (PR_1), bottom-up (PR_2), top-down (PR_3), bottom-up/top-down (PR_4), and top-down/bottom-up (PR_5). Each box represents the results of the ten selected seeds (i.e., pruning methods). Note that each point in the box plots corresponds to the individual performance of the seed.

be obtained for another filter selection method that has also used a distribution that is suitable for it. For example, the best result when using the 4th seed is very similar to that obtained with the 5th and 7th seeds, i.e. higher than 93%. Each seed can be viewed as a method for selecting filters and neurons to prune, so different methods can provide very close values for the accuracy of the pruned model.

But is it feasible to generalize a type of distribution that provides the best results regardless of the filter selection method to be pruned? To answer this question, it is necessary to perform a simultaneous analysis of seed vs. type of distribution, which is presented in the following subsection.

4.3   Impact by Type of Pruning Method vs Type of Distribution

For each of the seeds (i.e., filter selection methods and neurons to be pruned), the accuracy results are ordered from best to worst distribution method (see Table 3).

In seven of the ten cases, the PR_3 distribution gives the best accuracy of the pruned model, while PR_4 is better in two cases and PR_1 in one. On the other hand, the distributions with the worst performance are always the same, in penultimate place PR_5 and in last place PR_2. In other words, according to the study carried out, the accuracy of the pruned model decreases to a greater extent when the PR applied to the last convolutional layers is higher than the global PR.

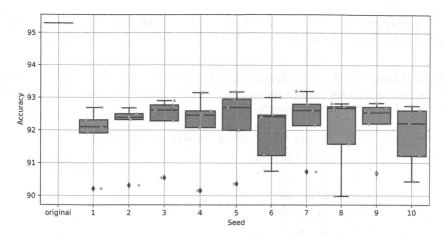

Fig. 3. Comparison between the performance of the unpruned model (i.e., original) and the models obtained by the same seed of the random pruning method: $seed_1$ to $seed_{10}$. Each box represents the results of the five selected type of distribution (i.e., PR_1 to PR_5). Note that each point in the box plots corresponds to the individual performance of the type of distribution.

Table 3. Comparison between methods for selecting filters/neurons to be pruned vs. type of distribution. For each of the columns, the best result is placed in the first row, and the worst result is placed in the last row.

$Seed_1$	$Seed_2$	$Seed_3$	$Seed_4$	$Seed_5$	$Seed_6$	$Seed_7$	$Seed_8$	$Seed_9$	$Seed_{10}$
PR_3	PR_3	PR_3	PR_3	PR_3	PR_3	PR_3	PR_1	PR_4	PR_4
PR_1	PR_4	PR_4	PR_4	PR_1	PR_4	PR_4	PR_3	PR_3	PR_3
PR_4	PR_1	PR_1	PR_1	PR_4	PR_1	PR_1	PR_4	PR_1	PR_1
PR_5	PR_5	PR_5	PR_5	PR_5	PR_5	PR_5	PR_5	PR_5	PR_5
PR_2	PR_2	PR_2	PR_2	PR_2	PR_2	PR_2	PR_2	PR_2	PR_2

4.4   Parameter Reduction vs Quality of the Pruned Model

Finally, we evaluate if there is a direct relationship between the parameter reduction and the quality of the pruned model, taking into account that each of the PRs used, although they generate the same (or very similar) reduction of FLOPs, differ in the parameter reduction. For this purpose, the amount of parameters of the pruned models is calculated for each of the distributions used, and the position occupied by the pruned model in terms of accuracy is identified. According to the results of Table 4 the models with a significant reduction of parameters, which in this case correspond to PR_2 and PR_5, will have a worse performance in terms of accuracy. Meanwhile, models with less parameter reduction, corresponding in this case to PR_3 and PR_4, perform better in terms of accuracy. However, something special happens with uniform pruning, which occupies an intermediate position in terms of parameter reduction and at the same time a position very close to PR_4 in terms of accuracy. In other words, uniform pruning is not the worst option according to the state of the art in CNNS pruning.

Table 4. Comparison between the number of parameters for each type of distribution. The ranking is a global performance through the results of the fifty pruned models. The best place is "1" and the worst place is "5".

PR	Parameters	Ranking (in terms of accuracy)
PR_1	33,589,162	3
PR_2	21,287,832	5
PR_3	42,565,743	1
PR_4	44,322,879	2
PR_5	25,803,062	4

5   Conclusions

Considering the results presented in the above section in terms of the type of distribution, two main conclusions can be drawn.

First, there is no single type of distribution that is best suited for all filter/neuron selection methods to be pruned. It was found that pruning with a high PR in the last convolutional layers of the network leads to a higher loss of accuracy in the pruned model. Moreover, contrary to what is mentioned in the state-of-the-art of pruning distribution in CNNs,it was found that uniform pruning is not the worst type of distribution. This was tested by performing a non-parametric Mann-Whitney U test comparing PR_1 with PR_2, assuming the null hypothesis that the two distributions are equal, obtaining a p-value = 0.00018, therefore the null hypothesis is rejected and it can be concluded that the difference between them is significant. In fact, for some methods, it could be the best option, taking into account both the accuracy of the pruned model and the reduction in FLOPs and parameters compared to the original (unpruned) model.

Second, when comparing the effect of the selection method of filters/neurons to be pruned with that of the type of distribution, it was found that for the same type of distribution, the results varied by up to 1% between filter/neuron selection methods. In contrast, for the same filter/neuron selection method to be pruned, the results varied by up to 3% between the distribution methods. Therefore, if the accuracy of a pruned model is to be improved, the first step is to identify which type of distribution is most appropriate for the filter/neuron selection method to be pruned, before changing the selection method.

Acknowledgements. This work has been sponsored by the Universidad Militar Nueva Granada - Vicerrectoría de investigaciones, project INV-ING-3786.

References

1. Liang, T., Glossner, J., Wang, L., Shi, S., Zhang, X.: Pruning and quantization for deep neural network acceleration: a survey. Neurocomputing **461**, 370–403 (2021)
2. Vadera, S., Ameen, S.: Methods for pruning deep neural networks. IEEE Access **10**, 63280–63300 (2022)
3. Li, H., Kadav, A., Durdanovic, I., Samet, H., Graf, H.P.: Pruning filters for efficient convnets. arXiv preprint arXiv:1608.08710 (2016)
4. Kumar, A., Shaikh, A.M., Li, Y., Bilal, H., Yin, B.P.: Pruning filters with L1-norm and capped L1-norm for CNN compression. Appl. Intell. **51**, 1152–1160 (2021)
5. He, Y., Liu, P., Wang, Z., Hu, Z., Yang, Y.: Filter pruning via geometric median for deep convolutional neural networks acceleration. In Proceedings of the IEEE/CVF Conference on Computer Vision and Pattern Recognition, pp. 4340–4349 (2019)
6. Zhang, T., Ye, S., Zhang, K., Tang, J., Wen, W., Fardad, M., Wang, Y.: A systematic DNN weight pruning framework using alternating direction method of multipliers. In: Proceedings of the European Conference on Computer Vision (ECCV), pp. 184–199 (2018)
7. Sun, X., Ren, X., Ma, S., Wang, H.: meProp: sparsified back propagation for accelerated deep learning with reduced overfitting. In: International Conference on Machine Learning, pp. 3299–3308 (2017)
8. Liu, C., Wu, H.: Channel pruning based on mean gradient for accelerating convolutional neural networks. Signal Process. **156**, 84–91 (2019)
9. Molchanov, P., Tyree, S., Karras, T., Aila, T., Kautz, J.: Pruning convolutional neural networks for resource efficient inference. In: 5th International Conference on Learning Representations (ICLR) (2017)
10. Pachón, C.G., Ballesteros, D.M., Renza, D.: SeNPIS: sequential network pruning by class-wise importance score. Appl. Soft Comput. **129**, 109558 (2022)
11. Pachón, C.G., Ballesteros, D.M., Renza, D.: An efficient deep learning model using network pruning for fake banknote recognition. Expert Syst. Appl. **233**, 120961 (2023)
12. Yang, C., Liu, H.: Channel pruning based on convolutional neural network sensitivity. Neurocomputing **507**, 97–106 (2022)
13. Liu, Y., Wu, D., Zhou, W., Fan, K., Zhou, Z.: EACP: an effective automatic channel pruning for neural networks. Neurocomputing **526**, 131–142 (2023)
14. Mondal, M., Das, B., Roy, S.D., Singh, P., Lall, B., Joshi, S.D.: Adaptive CNN filter pruning using global importance metric. Comput. Vis. Image Underst. **222**, 103511 (2022)
15. Chen, Z., Liu, C., Yang, W., Li, K., Li, K.: LAP: latency-aware automated pruning with dynamic-based filter selection. Neural Netw. **152**, 407–418 (2022)

Open-Loop Stability Analysis of Interval Dynamic Systems

Eduardo Cortés Cruz[1]([⊠]) [iD], Jorge Ivan Sofrony Esmeral[1,2] [iD],
and Jesús David Avilés Velásquez[2] [iD]

[1] Universidad Nacional de Colombia, Bogotá 11001, Colombia
{edcortescr,jsofronye}@unal.edu.co
[2] Universidad Autónoma de Baja California, 21100 Mexicali, Mexico
david.aviles@uabc.edu.mx
http://www.springer.com/gp/computer-science/lncs

Abstract. In this document, a novel approach is introduced to assess sufficient conditions for stability, contralability and observability of an LTI interval dynamic system. The suggested analysis portrays the interval dynamic system as analogous to a system containing uncertainties, where the verification of the proposed analysis is achieved by utilizing interval Gerschgorin discs for each vertex matrix originated from the interval matrix. These uncertainties are defined within well-defined bounded intervals. This work that underpins the proposed analysis is drawn from studies conducted over for more that two decades. This newly devised stability analysis technique is employed to appraise the prerequisites for open-loop stability in an interval dynamic system that characterizes the motion of fluid within a duct compromised by leakage. In line with the aforementioned exposition, this article introduces a more direct approach to evaluate the open-loop stability, controllability and observability of LTI interval systems.

Keywords: Interval dynamic systmes · stability margins · Gerschgorin discs

1 Preliminaries of Interval Arithmetic

This section presents the necessary mathematical references to understand the concept of interval analysis in relation to the concept of uncertainty, perturbations, and noise analysis.

Lemma 1 [12]. Let $x \in \mathbb{R}$ be a real (uncertain) number, represented as a bounded value in an interval of real numbers. Then, and interval number $x \in \mathbb{IR}^n$ is represented by a lower limit and an upper limit, respectively, as:

$$x^I = [\underline{x}, \overline{x}], \quad \underline{x}, \overline{x} \in \mathbb{R}^n$$

J. C. Figueroa-García et al. (Eds.): WEA 2023, CCIS 1928, pp. 92–103, 2023.
https://doi.org/10.1007/978-3-031-46739-4_9

being $\underline{x}$ and $\overline{x}$ the minimun and maximun bounded numerical values of x.

Definition 1. *Internal operations in an interval* [12]

These are the operations that can be performed on the bounded lower limit and upper limit of an interval. These operations are defined as:

- Mean value or nominal value of an interval: This designation is referred to as:

$$mid(x) = \frac{\underline{x} + \overline{x}}{2} \tag{1}$$

- width of an interval: It is defined as:

$$w = \overline{x} - \underline{x} \tag{2}$$

- Radius of an interval: The quantity that defines the tolerance of the mean value or nominal value of the interval.

$$rad(x) = \frac{\overline{x} - \underline{x}}{2} \tag{3}$$

- Absolute value: The maximum numerical absolute value within the bounds defined by the interval:

$$\max\{\underline{x}, \overline{x}\} \tag{4}$$

Lemma 2. *Interval vector*

It is an n-dimensional array of intervals, where each component forms a closed and bounded subset. It is defined as the scalar product of n intervals, which can be represented in vector form as a row vector [6,12].

$$[\mathbf{x}] = ([x_1] \times [x_2] \times ... \times [x_n])$$

Interval vectors can also be represented as:

$$[\mathbf{X}] = [\underline{\mathbf{X}}, \overline{\mathbf{X}}]$$

where: $\underline{\mathbf{X}}$ is defined as the lower limit of the vector, and $\overline{\mathbf{X}}$ is defined as the upper limit of the vector.

Lemma 3. *Interval matrix*

A matrix $\mathbf{A} = \{a_{i,j}\}$ is defined as an interval matrix if there exists a matrix $\underline{\mathbf{A}} = \{\underline{a}_{i,j}\}$ and a matrix $\overline{\mathbf{A}} = \{\overline{a}i, j\}$ such that $\underline{a}_{i,j} \leq a_{i,j} \leq \overline{a}_{i,j}$ for all $\mathbf{i}, \mathbf{j} \leq \mathbf{n}$, expressed as:

$$\mathbf{A}^{\mathbf{I}} \in [\underline{\mathbf{A}}, \overline{\mathbf{A}}]$$

1.1   Vertex Matrices

They are the finite subset of matrices contained in an interval matrix $A^I = [\underline{A}, \overline{A}]$ such that $A^I \in \mathbb{IR}^{n \times n}$, in order to determine if the interval matrix is stable or not. As mentioned, the vertices of an interval matrix form a set of matrices $\mathcal{M} \subset A^I$. The vertex matrices are obtained by taking all possible combinations of the element values from the matrices $\underline{A}$ and $\overline{A}$. Since the combinations follow a binary representation, the number of vertex matrices is 2^{n^2}, where n is the dimension of the interval matrix.

Remark 1. For more details regarding the calculation of vertex interval matrices, refer to [5]

1.2   Interval Gerschgorin Discs

Let $A^I = [\underline{A}, \overline{A}]$ be an interval matrix. The interval Gerschgorin discs are defined as the envelope of the family of circles, where each circle has its center at the corresponding component of the nominal A^I, denoted as $a_{i,i}$, and the radius is defined as follows:

$$\sum_{j \neq i} max \left(\mid \underline{a}_{i,j} \mid, \mid \overline{a}_{i,j} \mid \right)$$

Proof. The proof of this definition in [4]

2   Open Loop Stability Analysis of an Interval Dynamic System

In this section, we propose a method for evaluating the stability conditions in open loop, taking into account the mathematical properties of interval matrices studied mainly by [1, 2, 10], and the analytical study conducted by [3, 4] and [5]. Additionally, we propose the necessary and sufficient conditions for evaluating the controllability and observability conditions for the B^I and C^I interval matrices.

2.1   Open Loop Stability for the A Interval Matrix

Consider the interval dynamic system:

$$\dot{x}^I(t) = A^I x^I(t) + B^I u^I(t)$$
$$y^I(t) = C^I x^I(t)$$

(5)

where $u^I(t)$ is the bounded interval input signal with known extreme values and defined as $u^I(t) = [\underline{u}, \overline{u}]$, and the interval matrices A^I and B^I expressed as:

$$A^I = [\underline{A}, \overline{A}] = [A - \triangle A, A + \triangle A]$$

$$B^I = [\underline{B}, \overline{B}] = [B - \triangle B, B + \triangle B]$$

$$C^I = [\underline{C}, \overline{C}] = [C - \triangle C, C + \triangle C]$$

To evaluate the open-loop stability of the interval system described in Eq. (5), we will present a new analysis to obtain the necessary and sufficient conditions for the A^I interval matrix:

1. Necessary condition: The square matrix $\mathbf{A} \in \mathbb{R}^{n \times n}$ representing the parameters of the dynamic system must be full rank.
2. If the previous condition is satisfied, the next step is to verify if the uncertainty value $\triangle A$ added to the matrix A to make it an interval matrix A^I does not cause singularity. The necessary condition to verify this is through sensitivity analysis as presented by [2]:

$$\| \triangle A \| < 1/ \| A^{-1} \|$$

3. After confirming the interval mathematical analysis that establishes the complete range conditions for the interval matrices, we will proceed to analyze the stability of the dynamic system. This will be done by assessing the stability margin denoted as M, which is detailed in the method presented in [3] and outlined as follows:
Consider the matrix A^I defined as $A = A_o + \triangle A$, where A_o represents the nominal matrix and $| \delta A | \leq \triangle A$ accounts for the associated uncertainty. Utilizing the transformation matrix T, the Jordan form matrix $A_j = T^{-1} A_o T$ is obtained, with T expressed in terms of the Jordan form matrix. Drawing upon these two aforementioned concepts, a set matrix

$$F \triangleq A_j - \Lambda - | T^{-1} | \triangle A | T |= [f_{i,j}]$$

is constructed, where Λ is the eigenvalues matrix of A_o

Now we will present the following theorems that enable the analysis of the stability conditions stated for the A interval matrix.

Theorem 1. The eigenvalues of the interval matrix $A^I = [\underline{A}, \overline{A}]$ are included in the union of discs whose centers are the eigenvalues $\lambda_{i,i}$ of the matrix A_o and whose radii are given by:

$$\sum_{j=1}^{n} f_{i,j} \; \forall \; i = 1, 2, \cdots, n$$

Theorem 2. The eigenvalues of the interval matrix A^I are stable if

$$\mathbb{R}(\lambda_{i,i}) + \Sigma_{j=1}^{n} f_{i,j} < -M$$

$\forall i = 1, \cdots, n$, with M being the mentioned stability margin.

Proof. The proofs of these theorems are provided in [3]

2.2 Controlabillity Conditions

Now we will evaluate the necessary and sufficient conditions for assessing the controllability conditions of the interval system presented in (5) by evaluating the full rank conditions of the B^I interval matrix.

Necessary and sufficient conditions of the full rank:
    The condition for the rectangular matrix B, is defined from the criterion exposed by [10]

Theorem 3. Let an interval $n \times m$ matrix B be such that $n \geq m$, the mid-value matrix mid B have full rank, and

$$\rho \left[|\, (midB)^{\dagger} \,|\, (radB) \right] < 1$$

where

$$(midB)^{\dagger} = \left[(midB)^{T} \, (midB) \right]^{-1} (midB)^{T}$$

and

$$radB = \Delta B$$

where ρ denotes the spectral radius.

Proof. The proof of this theorem is defined from theorem 3 in [10]

2.3 Observability Analysis

For this analysis, it is necessary to evaluate the C^I interval matrix as follows:

Corollary 1. *Let an interval $q \times n$ matrix C be such that $q \leq n$, the midpoint matrix midC have full rank, and*

$$\rho \left(radC \,|\, mid\,(C)^{\dagger} \,| \right) < 1$$

where $\rho\,(\cdot)$ means taking of the spectral radius. Then the C interval matrix has full rank.

Proof. The proof of this collorary is defined in [10]

Conclusión

The criteria established in this section will allow us to evaluate whether a dynamic system described by Eq. (5) can be open-loop stable, based on the magnitude of the uncertainties ΔA. Furthermore, these criteria will assist in determining whether the interval system satisfies the conditions for controllability and observability, as determined by the uncertainties defined by ΔB and ΔC, respectively.

In the next section, this criterion is applied to evaluate the interval dynamic system that describes the movement of fluid in a horizontal duct in the presence of a leak.

3 Analytical Model of the Dynamic System of a Fluid Moving in a Horizontal Duct

3.1 Behavior of the Fluid in Steady-State Conditions with Varying Friction Parameter f_1.

The friction factor f_1 refers to the physical properties of the fluid within its movement along the duct, in the absence and presence of leaks. Depending on the value of the friction factor: f_1 [9,13], it will affect the behavior of the fluid's outlet flow rate: Q_{out}. The equation that defines the analytical characteristics of the friction factor f_r is:

$$f_r = \frac{1.325}{\left[ln\left(\frac{\varepsilon}{3.7D_o} - \frac{5.74}{R_e^{0.9}} \right) \right]^2} \tag{6}$$

where ε is a roughness coefficient associated with the duct's construction material, which in this case has a value of 0.046. R_e is the Reynolds number, which defines the dynamic behavior of the fluid's motion in the duct. The Reynolds number R_e is defined by physical properties of the fluid, such as fluid viscosity ν, and the diameter of the duct's cross-sectional area through which the fluid flows, D_o. The equation defining the Reynolds number is:

$$R_e = \frac{4Q}{\pi D_o \nu} \tag{7}$$

3.2 Characteristics of the Fluid in the Pipeline in the Presence of Leaks

The fluid characteristics analyzed in this study took into account the physical considerations outlined in [9], resulting in the derivation of the following equations:

$$\frac{\partial H}{\partial t} + \frac{\nu^2}{g\mathcal{A}} \frac{\partial Q}{\partial z} = 0$$

$$\frac{1}{\mathcal{A}} \frac{\partial Q}{\partial t} + g\frac{\partial H}{\partial z} + \frac{fQ|Q|}{2D_0\mathcal{A}^2} = 0 \tag{8}$$

Obtaining analytical solutions for the equation sets given in (8) is unfeasible because of the infinite dimensionality of the model. Consequently, in view of these limitations, we advocate employing the efficient Finite Difference method as a solution for (8). This method has yielded favorable results for systems of this nature, as demonstrated, for instance [9]

Based on the aforementioned considerations, we derive the following finite difference equations:

$$\dot{Q}_i = -g\mathcal{A}\frac{(H_{i+1}-H_i)}{\Delta z_i} - \mu Q_i^2$$

$$\dot{H}_{i+1} = -\frac{\nu^2}{g\mathcal{A}}\frac{(Q_{i+1}-Q_i+Q|_{H_f})}{\Delta z_i} \tag{9}$$

where $\mathcal{A}$ is the cross-sectional area of the duct, $\mu = \frac{f}{2\phi\mathcal{A}}$, where ϕ is the diameter of the duct, f is the friction factor, ν is the fluid velocity in the duct, and g is the acceleration due to gravity. The expression $Q|_{H_f}$ describes the flow rate associated with the leak pressure H_f, given by: $Q|_{H_f} = \lambda\sqrt{H_f}$.

With the finite difference model presented, the duct is divided into the smallest discrete difference, which consists of two sections. The duct with a leak is represented as shown in the following Fig. 1:

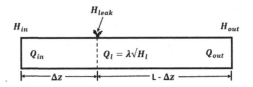

Fig. 1. Fluid moving in the duct with a leak.

3.3   State Variable Representation

The dynamic system of the fluid with a leak using finite differences is represented as:

$$\dot{Q}_1 = -g\mathcal{A}\frac{(H_{2|f}-H_1)}{\Delta z} - \mu Q_1^2$$

$$\dot{H}_{2|f} = -\frac{\nu^2}{g\mathcal{A}\Delta z}\left(Q_2 + \lambda\sqrt{H_{2|f}} - Q_1\right) \tag{10}$$

$$\dot{Q}_2 = -g\mathcal{A}\frac{(H_3-H_{2|f})}{\Delta z} - \mu Q_2^2$$

where the input vector is $u = [H_1, H_3]$ and the output vector is $y = [Q_1, Q_2]$. Therefore, the nonlinear analytical model shown in (9) is expressed as:

$$\begin{bmatrix} \dot{Q}_1 \\ \dot{H}_{2|f} \\ \dot{Q}_2 \end{bmatrix} = f_{NL}\left(Q_1, H_{2|f}, Q_1\right) + g_{NL}\left(H_1, H_3\right) \qquad (11)$$

being:

$$f_{NL}\left(Q_1, H_{2|f}, Q_2\right) = \begin{bmatrix} -\mu Q_1^2 - \frac{g\mathcal{A}H_{2|f}}{\Delta z} \\ \frac{\nu^2}{g\mathcal{A}}Q_1 - \frac{\nu^2}{g\mathcal{A}}\sqrt{H_{2|f}} - \frac{\nu^2}{g\mathcal{A}}Q_2 \\ \frac{g\mathcal{A}H_{2|f}}{L-\Delta z} - \mu Q_2^2 \end{bmatrix}$$

and

$$g_{NL}\left(H_1, H_3\right) = \begin{bmatrix} \frac{g\mathcal{A}H_1}{\Delta z} \\ 0 \\ -\frac{g\mathcal{A}H_3}{L-\Delta z} \end{bmatrix}$$

The nonlinear model presented in (10) is linearized using the equilibrium point-based linearization method [11]. Applying this approach, we derive the following state equations:

$$A = \begin{bmatrix} -2\mu Q_{1e} & -\frac{g\mathcal{A}}{\Delta z} & 0 \\ \frac{\nu^2}{g\mathcal{A}} & -\frac{\nu^2}{2g\mathcal{A}\sqrt{H_{2|fe}}} & \frac{-\nu^2}{g\mathcal{A}} \\ 0 & \frac{g}{L-\Delta z} & -2\mu Q_{2e} \end{bmatrix}$$

where Q_{1e}, $H_{2|fe}$, and Q_{2e} are the equilibrium points found when the nonlinear function $f_{NL}\left(Q_1, H_{2|f}, Q_1\right) = 0$ [11], $\mu = \frac{f_r}{2D_0\mathcal{A}}$

The matrix B is obtained by evaluating the Jacobian of the nonlinear function $g_{NL}\left(H_1, H_3\right)$.

$$B = \begin{bmatrix} \frac{g\mathcal{A}}{\Delta z} & 0 \\ 0 & 0 \\ 0 & -\frac{g\mathcal{A}}{L-\Delta z} \end{bmatrix}$$

The matrices C and D are obtained as follows:

$$C = \begin{bmatrix} 1 & 0 & 0 \\ 0 & 0 & 1 \end{bmatrix} \qquad D = \begin{bmatrix} 0 & 0 \\ 0 & 0 \end{bmatrix}$$

Based on the linearized model that has been presented, the following numerical values were used, taking reference data from [9,14], for the simulation:

Table 1. Test pipeline parameters.

Pipeline diameter ϕ.	0.25 m
Pipeline length $L = \Delta z_1$	132.56 m
Cross-sectional area of the Pipeline $\mathcal{A}$	0.0491 m^2
Fluid velocity in the pipeline ν	376 m/s
upstream pressure head: H_{in}	6.5 m
downstream pressure head: H_{out}	3.8 m
friction factor: f_r	0.0181076

3.4   Interval Linearized Dynamic System with a Leak

The matrices A and B were represented in the form of interval matrices, incorporating uncertainties linked to the physical parameters of both the fluid and the pipeline, such as the friction factor f and the cross-sectional area $\mathcal{A}$, respectively. These interval matrices are defined as follows:

$$\mathbf{A^I} = [\mathbf{A} - \mathbf{\Delta A}, \mathbf{A} + \mathbf{\Delta A}]$$

$$\mathbf{B^I} = [\mathbf{B} - \mathbf{\Delta B}, \mathbf{B} + \mathbf{\Delta B}]$$

Now we proceeded to perform the open-loop stability analysis of the interval dynamic system of the fluid moving in a horizontal duct, taking into account the numerical data obtained from Table 1. The numerical values of the matrices were as follows:

$$A^I = \begin{bmatrix} [-0.4286, -0.3877] & [-3.8566, -3.8566] & [0, 0] \\ [7.4812, 7.4812] & [-0.0025, -0.0025] & [-14.9625, -14.9625] \\ [0, 0] & [7.9401, 7.9401] & [-0.42857, -0.3877] \end{bmatrix}$$

$$B^I = \begin{bmatrix} [0.0724, 0.1207] & [0, 0] \\ [0, 0] & [0, 0] \\ [0, 0] & [-0.0880, -0.1467] \end{bmatrix}$$

$$C = \begin{bmatrix} 0.0313 & 0 & 0 \\ 0 & 0 & 0.0625 \end{bmatrix}$$

$$D = \begin{bmatrix} 0 & 0 \\ 0 & 0 \end{bmatrix}$$

3.5   Open-Loop Stability Analysis of the Interval Dynamic System

For the analytical concepts presented in Sect. 2 of this article, we developed a program in Matlab. We conducted computer simulations using this program to evaluate the open-loop stability of the interval dynamic system described in the example. The results of these simulations are shown in the following figures.

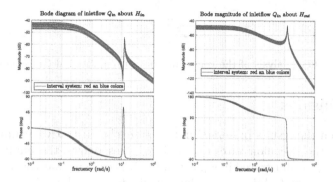

Fig. 2. Bode diagram Q_{in} about H_{in} and H_{out}

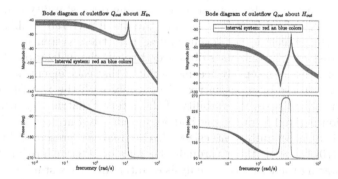

Fig. 3. Bode diagram Q_{out} about H_{in} and H_{out}

And finally, an open-loop stability analysis was performed using the Gerschgorin interval disks to evaluate the stability of the vertex matrices associated with the interval matrix A^I. The results obtained are presented in Fig. 6.

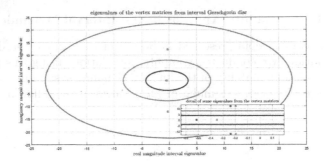

Fig. 4. Stability analysis of the vertex matrices using interval Gerschgorin discs

4   Conclusions

Drawing from the results presented in this article's illustrative example, we can observe how the inlet flow rates Q_{in} and Q_{out} respond to the input conditions $u = [H_{in}, H_{out}]$ as illustrated in Figs. 2 and 3. It is evident that the uncertainties, denoted as ΔA and ΔB, satisfy the criteria for open-loop interval stability. This indicates the system's stability even in the presence of uncertainties when operating in an open-loop configuration, as indicated by the use of the green color.

The presented simulations utilize the theoretical framework to demonstrate the expedited nature of this approach in assessing open stability conditions for complex interval dynamic systems, such as the one illustrated. Unlike the referenced works [14], which do not specifically address these systems.

Figure 4 displays the outcomes obtained through the utilization of the Interval Greschgorin discs concept. It becomes evident that each eigenvalue of the vertex matrix within the interval matrix A^I complies with the Hurwitz condition. This observation validates the stability of the interval matrix A^I, corroborating the conclusion derived from the methodology delineated in Sect. 2.

This article successfully synthesizes all the analyses presented by Rhon [1] and Shary [10], viewing them through the lens of interval arithmetic theory and incorporating the theoretical analysis of interval matrix stability using Gerschgorin discs, as introduced by Xu et al. [4], Juang et al. [3], and Wang et al. [7].

References

1. Rohn, J.: Positive definiteness and stability of interval matrices. SIAM J. Matrix Anal. Appl. **15**(1), 175–184 (1994)
2. Assem, Sensitivity analysis in linear systems, Department of Engineering Mathematics Cairo University Giza/Egypt (1986)
3. Juang, Y.-T., Shao, C.-S.: Stability analysis of dynamic interval systems. Int. J. Control **49**(4), 1401–1408 (1989)
4. Xu, S.-J., Rachid, A.: Generalized Gerschgorin disc and stability analysis of dynamic interval systems. In: UKACC International Conference on Control 1996 (Conference Publication No. 427), vol. 1, pp. 276–280 (1996)

5. Estrada, R., Antonio, J.: Análisis de estabilidad de sistemas lineales en variables de estado con incertidumbre paramétrica. Universidad Autónoma de Nuevo León (1994)
6. Tornil, S.: Detección robusta de fallos utilizando análisis intervalar. Universitat Politècnica de Catalunya (UPC) (2006)
7. Wang, K., Michel, A.N.: On sufficient conditions for the stability of interval matrices. Syst. Control Lett. **20**(5), 345–351 (1993)
8. Yedavalli, R.K.: Stability analysis of interval matrices: another sufficient condition. Int. J. Control **43**(3), 767–772 (1986)
9. Torres, L.: Location of leaks in pipelines using parameter identification tools. arXiv e-prints, arXiv-1406 (2014)
10. Shary, S.P.: On full-rank interval matrices. Numer. Anal. Appl. **7**, 241–254 (2014)
11. Khalil, H.K.: Nonlinear Systems, 3rd edn. Prentice Hall (2002)
12. Moore, R.E., Kearfott, R.B., Cloud, M.J.: Introduction to Interval Analysis. SIAM (2009)
13. Bermúdez, J.-R., López-Estrada, F.-R., Besançon, G., Valencia-Palomo, G., Torres, L., Hernández, H.-R.: Modeling and simulation of a hydraulic network for leak diagnosis. Math. Computat. Appl. **23**(4), 70 (2018)
14. Visairo, N., Verde, C., Gentil, S.: Localización de múltiples fugas en ductos considerando restricciones físicas. In: Memorias del Congreso Nacional de Control Automático (2003)

Acquisition of Motor Images of the Left and Right Hand by Means of the Emotiv EPOC+ Headset for Their Classification Using the EEGNet Neural Network

Johan Sebastián Castellanos-Delgado, Luisa Gallo-Sánchez[✉], and David Gonzalez-Morales

Facultad de Ingeniería, Universidad de Ibagué, Carrera 22 Calle 67, 730002 Ibagué, Colombia
luisa.gallo@unibague.edu.co

Abstract. The Brain-Computer Interface (BCI) system provides a channel between the brain and an electronic device. One problem with such devices is the desynchronization between the signal obtained and the actions of neuroprostheses. The main objective of this research is to control a subject-dependent prosthetic simulation using signals from motor imagery (MI) obtained from two completely healthy individuals through the EMOTIV EPOC+ headset. For signal processing, a preprocessing and a classifier with a convolutional neural network (CNN) are applied. Using the EEGNet architecture, a classifier of up to 77.9% was obtained. In this work, a subject selection methodology has been developed in order to save time in data acquisition and improve data quality.

Keywords: Deep learning · Motor imagery · Electroencephalogram · Motor imagery classification · Brain-Computer Interface

1 Introduction

Humans are greatly affected by the amputation of any limb. For example, the hand physically performs precise, heavy, and fast operations, using 27 degrees of freedom for all its movements [1] affecting a very important limb for the humans. Psychologically and neurologically, people also have complications after the amputation of any limb. For example, phantom limb pain affects between 50% and 80% of the amputated population. It is considered a psychological pain due to a memory of pain that involves sensory and affective components [2], and neurological due to reorganization in the primary somatosensory cortex (S1) [3].

The human hand is controlled by neural evoked potentials that stimulate the central nervous system, sending stimuli from the brain to the spinal cord. Thanks to Brodmann's research, which refers to the areas of the cerebral cortex [4] the affected area of the brain can be identified by an external stimulus. For example, the motor movement of the body mainly affects the primary motor cortex, finding stimuli in the contralateral area of the movement of a limb. This means that the central nervous system is asymmetrical in

© The Author(s), under exclusive license to Springer Nature Switzerland AG 2023
J. C. Figueroa-García et al. (Eds.): WEA 2023, CCIS 1928, pp. 104–114, 2023.
https://doi.org/10.1007/978-3-031-46739-4_10

humans and most animals [5]. The motor area of the brain is activated with both the performed and imagined movement. This means that it is not necessary to make the movement of any limb for the motor area of the brain to be activated. The intention to perform an action is known as motor imagery signals. Thanks to this advancement, neuroprosthetics can be implemented in people with amputations.

Motor imagery, like real movements, has a high degree of similarity [6], This is why researchers have paid so much attention to this type of signal. There are two types of imagery [7]. The first is visual imagery (VI), which involves a visual representation of a limb with a clear and vivid image. The second is the kinesthetic imagery (KI), which involves feeling the movement without the need to visualize it [8]. A notable characteristic between these two types of imagery is Fitts' law [9]. KI follows Fitts' law, which states that the associated movements show the same limitations as the movements during execution. On the contrary, in VI, people can imagine movements that exceed the physiological limitations of humans. Studies have shown that several areas of the cortex are activated during the motor imagery task [10–12]. These regions include the following: supplementary motor area, superior and inferior parietal lobe, dorsal and ventral lateral premotor cortex, prefrontal areas, primary motor cortex (M1), primary sensory cortex, secondary sensory area, insular cortex, anterior cingulate cortex, superior temporal gyrus, basal ganglia, and cerebellum. It should be noted that this conclusion was reached thanks to functional magnetic resonance imaging (fMRI) data [6].

Imagined movements generate sensory stimuli that can changes in neuronal activity over time, these are called event-related potentials (ERPs). These event-related phenomena represent specific frequency changes of ongoing EEG activity and consist of the decrease or increase of potentials in frequency bands of the sensorimotor rhythms, that is, mu (μ) and beta (β) [13]. These relationships are called event-related desynchronization (ERD), which describes the attenuation or blocking of short-duration (phasic) and regionally localized amplitude of the oscillations in the alpha and beta bands that occurs in direct relation to an event [14], and event-related synchronization (ERS), which describes the phasic and regionally localized increase in the activity of the alpha and beta bands in the form of bursts. It is usually seen more clearly in the beta band and it is posterior to the event.

Brain-computer interfaces (BCIs) provide an alternative mode of communication between the human brain and external devices that provide the user with control and communication [15]; BCIs are able to interpret electroencephalographic signals for subsequent control of a device. Several neuronal capture techniques can be used, among the easiest and most economical is electroencephalography, it is popularly used by scientists due to its non-invasive nature and high temporal resolution [16]. One of the most affordable headsets to the public is the EMOTIV EPOC+ [17].

The main interest of this research is to implement the bases for a field that is little known in our country and region, in order to be able to motivate and support future research in the process of acquisition, preprocessing and classification of IM, ultimately benefitting a large population of people who need neuroprosthetics to improve their quality of life. Specifically, it is intended through the acquisition of EEG, to determine the intention of movement and discriminate between the right and left hand.

2 Methodology

2.1 Data Acquisition

The Emotiv EPOC+ headset is a wireless EEG that includes 14 sensors located at positions AF3, F7, F3, FC5, T7, P7, O1, O2, P8, T8, FC6, F4, F8, AF4 positions of the standard 10–20 EEG positioning system [18]. The headset communicates with a computer via Bluetooth in the 2.4 GHz band using a supplied proprietary USB dongle. The internal sampling rate is 2048 Hz, which is downsampled to 128 Hz, which is the frequency provided to any external application.

A Python 3 server called CyKit was implemented to deliver raw and real-time data from the headset. The data is transmitted and captured by this server, which hosts and transmits it through the local server. The data reception algorithm was made by Warren and is published on GitHub [19]. Additionally, the OpenVibe software will be used as the main software for the visualization and recording of EEG signals in this research.

2.2 Subject Selection

The ability to imagine movements can be assessed using special questionnaire scales. The Motion Imagery Questionnaire (MIQ) and Vividness of Motor Imagery Questionnaire (VMIQ) scales are based on questions that address the ease with which certain movements of the upper and lower extremities can be imagined on 7- and 5-point scales, respectively. Scores on these tests support a direct relationship with motor ability[20].

The evaluation questionnaire [21] was used to assess 5 volunteers, 3 men and 2 women, of whom one from each gender with the highest score was chosen. This was done in order to save time in data acquisition and to be able to obtain good-quality data. This is possible since the focus of this research is subject-dependent.

To further improve the quality of the data, the 2 subjects underwent motor training based on motor imagery. Previous studies have shown the possibility of learning motor skills and also of neuronal reorganization of cortical structures, i.e., use-dependent plasticity, as shown in [22].

The motor training regimen involved 40 imaginations per session, consisting of 20 imaginations for the right hand and 20 for the left hand. The imaginations must be kinesthetic and visual. Two sessions are performed per day; the first after the person wakes up, and the other before going to sleep, for a week. These times were chosen because the brain is in a deep learning state.

2.3 Experiment Format

The two volunteers underwent 17 sessions, each of which consisted of two different test formats, one for the right hand and one for the left hand. Each volunteer performed 20 trials in each format. During motor imagery, the person was instructed not to blink, swallow, move their tongue, or make facial gestures (move their lips, move their nose, frown, etc.).

OpenVibe provides a graphical interface that performs the entire experiment visualization procedure. Once data recording begins, a black window with a green cross in the center appears, at which time the person should prepare for the imagery. Then a red arrow will appear, indicating motor imagery. If the arrow is pointing to the right, the right hand should be imagined, and to the left for the left hand. Once motor imagery has finished, the green cross will appear again, but this time it indicates the end of the session, followed by a 2-s break. This scheme is shown in Fig. 1.

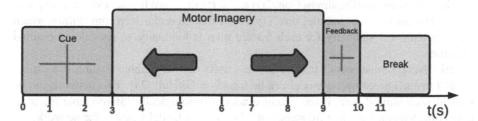

Fig. 1. Experimental diagram.

2.4 Data Preprocessing

EEG signals have a low signal-to-noise ratio (SNR) and contain several frequency components irrelevant to MI, so frequency filtering was performed from 8 to 30 Hz to obtain the alpha and beta bands, as these bands contain features relevant to MI. In addition, common average referencing (CAR) was performed for each electrode to eliminate information coming from other parts of the brain, different from the area where the electrode is located.

2.5 Classification

A CNN was implemented with the EEGNet architecture [23], which is a compact neural network for EEG-based BCI. It works with known feature extraction concepts for BCI such as the common spatial filter, and the construction of filter banks. EEGNet is capable of classifying sensorimotor rhythms (SMR) (Fig. 2).

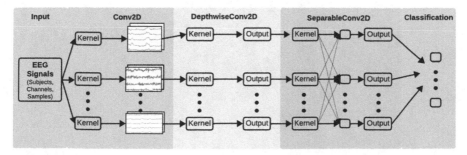

Fig. 2. EEGNet architecture.

The data matrix was expanded to four dimensions, meeting the dimension of the input matrix. This matrix must have the shape (a, b, c, d), where (a) and (b) give the shape of the matrix of all the data to be trained, (c) and (d) give the shape of the individual signal contained in the matrix.

The Conv2D layer is a temporal convolution that is dedicated to learning frequency filters. The feature maps obtained in this stage serve as input for the other layer, which is a deep convolution (DepthwiseConv2D) and serves to learn frequency-specific spatial filters. The last layer (SeparableConv2D) is a combination of a deep convolution, which learns a temporal summary for each feature map individually, to provide an optimal classifier.

EEGNet is robust enough to learn a wide variety of interpretable features in a variety of BCI tasks. The complete model can be found on GitHub [24]. This network can be trained with limited data, it can produce neurophysiologically interpretable features, data collected at a sampling frequency of 128 Hz must be delivered to the network.

2.6 Control of the Prosthetic Simulation

The hand used is controlled by an Arduino Uno. A serial communication protocol was implemented using the Python Pyserial library, for communication between the Arduino and the neural network programmed in Python. The purpose is to enable the hand to move if the neural network recognizes input from motor imagery.

3 Test and Results

3.1 Data Acquisition

The recording tests were performed in a home room, making sure that it was in the morning to avoid noise, distractions, and brain fatigue. The data collection was mainly done by respecting the electrode positioning proposed by the Emotiv Company, this positioning is not favorable because there are no electrodes that cover the main motor areas for motor imagery, the solution was to modify the normal positioning, and take the electrodes that are most involved in the motor areas of the brain, the result is shown in Table 1.

Table 1. Electrode positioning

Emotiv Positioning	Modified Positioning
AF3	F1
F7	FC5
F3	FC1
FC5	C3
T7	CP5
T8	CP6
FC6	C4
F4	FC2
F8	FC6
AF4	F2

3.2 Feature Extraction

In Fig. 3, parts of the signal that at first glance are considered MI features are highlighted with in a box, ERD and ERS are seen in the epochs, as demonstrated in [14]. In addition, it is very important to know that ERD and ERS are variable between subject, session, and epoch. This means that the ERD or ERS recorded in epoch 10 will not be the same as the ERD or ERS recorded in epoch 11 [14]. This is largely due to the plasticity of the brain.

In order to visualize ERD and ERS in [14], it is suggested that it is best to take multiple data and average them. To demonstrate, some sessions were averaged. ERD and ERS can be visualized in a scaleogram using the wavelet transform, as shown below, Fig. 4a shows an average of session 15 of subject 1, imagining the right hand. Figure 4b shows an average of the same session, but imagining the left hand.

When a movement is imagined, the brain areas that are activated are contralateral to the movement, Therefore, in Fig. 4a, the right hand was imagined, which means that the C3 electrode is the one with the most information about this imagination. As can be seen, the decrease in power between the 2.5 and 5 s of the C3 electrode refers to an ERD, which is not observed in the C4 electrode since there is an increase in potential that remains. From the 5th to the 6th second of the C3 electrode, the increase in potential can be seen, which is equivalent to an ERS, and in the C4 electrode it is not seen with great magnitude.

In In Fig. 4b, the left hand was imagined, which means that the C4 electrode records the ERD and ERS. For the C4 electrode, an ERD is evident from 1.5 to 3.5 s, and an ERS is seen from 5 to 6 s. The opposite is evident in the C3 electrode.

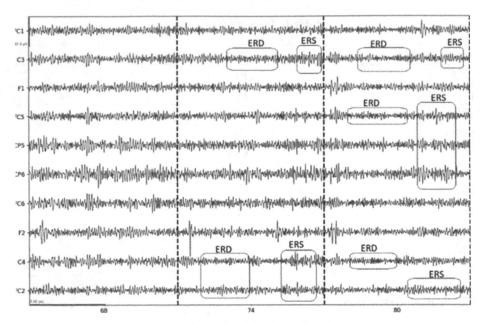

Fig. 3. ERD and ERS over time.

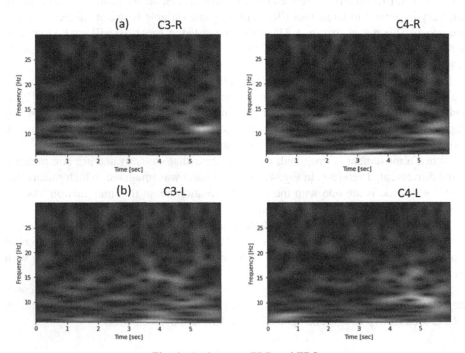

Fig. 4. Scaleogram ERD and ERS

3.3 Classification

The behavior of the neural network training and testing can be seen in Fig. 5. On the right side are the training data and on the left side are the test data. The figure shows a training of 2000 epochs, which was chosen because the training and testing generate a lot of noise. To save the model, a callback was used. The criterion used was the test accuracy, and the best weight that the network could learn in the entire period of epochs was saved. The training and testing data were divided into 70–30.

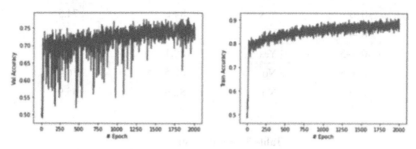

Fig. 5. Training and testing behavior.

Table 2 shows the results of several proposed trainings for the data of subject 1, varying some criteria to see the behavior of the network and thus obtain the best possible trained network. The criteria used were the following: number of electrodes, epoch time, and data preprocessing with bandpass filter and CAR. The electrodes varied between 10 or 2, the first takes all the electrodes that were recorded in the experiment and the second only collects the C3 and C4 electrodes, since topographically they are the ones that capture the most hand signals in the motor area. For the second criterion, several epochs were taken, taking into account that the ERD and ERS are not the same in each experiment, as shown above. The table shows the percentages obtained by each training and test.

The same procedure mentioned above was performed for subject number 2, the results are shown in Table 3.

To test the network with data it has never seen before and conclude that the network can indeed classify EEG IM signals, it was decided to retrain a network with the most outstanding criteria for each subject. This time, the data will be divided into 3 parts: training data, test data, and validation data, in the following order 70–20-10. The results are shown in Table 4. The best classification on data the network has never seen before was obtained by subject 2 with a result of 77.9%.

Table 2. Result of subject 1.

Number of electrodes	Epoch time (s)	With bandpass filter and CAR	Training accuracy (%)	Testing accuracy (%)
10	0.5–5	Yes	85.9	76.5
10	1–5	Yes	83	67.6
10	0–6	Yes	91.8	77
10	0–4	Yes	83.2	76.5
2	0–6	Yes	84.2	74.5
2	0–4	Yes	81.3	66.7
2	0.5–5	Yes	82.1	70.6
10	0.5–5	No	68.5	56.4
10	0–6	No	82.6	55.9

Table 3. Result of subject 2.

Number of electrodes	Epoch time (s)	With bandpass filter and CAR	Training accuracy (%)	Testing accuracy (%)
10	0.5–5	Yes	69.5	57.8
10	1–5	Yes	77.7	59.9
10	0–6	Yes	65.8	60.3
10	0–4	Yes	84.9	57.8
2	0–6	Yes	78.8	62.3
2	0–4	Yes	59.7	58.8
2	0.5–5	Yes	67.6	60.2
10	0.5–5	No	80	74.5
10	0–6	No	86.6	77.9

Table 4. Best networks depending on each subject.

Number of electrodes	Epoch time (s)	With bandpass filter and CAR	Training accuracy (%)	Testing accuracy (%)	Validation accuracy (%)
10	0–6	Yes	95	80.9	70.58
10	0–6	No	84.2	80.1	77.9

4 Conclusions

This research implemented a low-cost EEG headband for a motor imagery classification problem. The results of this study suggest that the Emotiv EPOC+ headband may be of interest for the development of motor imagery BCI applications, as these low-cost devices show comparable results in BCI applications.

All people are different, both anatomically and psychologically. In motor imagery signals, psychology has a significant impact on mood. Despair and stress can lead to these signals being misinterpreted. Anatomically, the brain is considered to be another fingerprint, and this is closely linked to neuroplasticity. As a result, the results showed that the data from each person differs in classification. Even using the same preprocessing and data classification for each subject, the results were different.

Due to the subject's dependency, in this study the EEG data preprocessing was necessary for subject number one. This may be related to noise captured from the outside, by their anatomy, or caused by the subject during motor imagery. For this reason, the neural network was unable to interpret a pattern in the signals. It was decided to perform data preprocessing before entering the network. This improved the classification, making the network interpret a differential pattern between each imagination for subject one.

The purpose of this research work was to control a subject-dependent prosthetic simulation using the commercial EMOTIV EPOC+ headband through IM signals. Therefore, it was not necessary to create a database with several people, since the ability of the network to classify data with independence from the subject was not being evaluated. Likewise, the people with the best imagination capabilities were chosen and trained to obtain good quality signals and optimize research efficiency.

References

1. Constantine, A., Asanza, V., Loayza, F.R., Peláez, E., Peluffo-Ordóñez, D.: BCI system using a novel processing technique based on electrodes selection for hand prosthesis control. IFAC-PapersOnLine **54**(15), 364–369 (2021). https://doi.org/10.1016/j.ifacol.2021.10.283
2. Herta, F., Lone, N., Troels Staehelin, J.: Phantom limb pain: a case of maladaptive CNS plasticity? Nat. Rev. Neurosci. **7**, 873–881 (2006). https://doi.org/10.1038/nrn1991
3. Andoh, J., et al.: Assessment of cortical reorganization and preserved function in phantom limb pain: a methodological perspective. Sci. Rep. **10**, 11504 (2020). https://doi.org/10.1038/s41598-020-68206-9
4. Zilles, K.: Brodmann: a pioneer of human brain mapping—his impact on concepts of cortical organization. Brain **141**(11), 3262–3278 (2018). https://doi.org/10.1093/brain/awy273
5. Lapraz, F., et al.: Asymmetric activity of NetrinB controls laterality of the Drosophila brain. Nat. Commun. **14**, 1052 (2023). https://doi.org/10.1038/s41467-023-36644-4
6. Solodkin, A., Hlustik, P., Chen, E., Small, S.: Fine modulation in network activation during motor execution and motor imagery. Cereb. Cortex **14**(11), 1246–1255 (2004). https://doi.org/10.1093/cercor/bhh086
7. Jin Yang, Y., Jeong Jeon, E., Sic Kim, J., Kee Chung, C.: Characterization of kinesthetic motor imagery compared with visual motor imageries. Sci. Rep **11**, 3751 (2021). https://doi.org/10.1038/s41598-021-82241-0
8. Zapała, D., Iwanowicz, P., Francuz, P., Augustynowicz, P.: Handedness effects on motor imagery during kinesthetic and visual-motor conditions. Sci. Rep. **11**, 13112 (2021). https://doi.org/10.1038/s41598-021-92467-7

9. Fitts, P.M.: The information capacity of the human motor system in controlling the amplitude of movement. J. Exp. Psychol.: Gen. **121**(3), 262–269 (1992). https://doi.org/10.1037//0096-3445.121.3.262
10. Henrik Ehrsson, H., Geyer, S., Naito, E.: Imagery of voluntary movement of fingers, toes, and tongue activates corresponding body-part-specific motor representations. J. Neurophysiol. **90**(5), 3304–3316 (2003). https://doi.org/10.1152/jn.01113.2002
11. Mokienko, O., Chervyakov, A., Kulikova, S., Bobrov, P.: Increased motor cortex excitability during motor imagery in brain-computer interface trained subjects. Front. Comput. Neurosci. **7**(168), 1–7 (2013). https://doi.org/10.3389/fncom.2013.00168
12. Hanakawa, T., Parikh, S., Bruno, M., Hallett, M.: Finger and face representations in the ipsilateral precentral motor areas in humans. J. Neurophysiol. **93**(5), 2950–2958 (2005). https://doi.org/10.1152/jn.00784.2004
13. Pfurtscheller, G., Lopes da Silva, F.: Event-related EEG/MEG synchronization and desynchronization: basic principles. Clin. Neurophysiol. **110**(11), 1842–1857 (1999). https://doi.org/10.1016/S1388-2457(99)00141-8
14. Pfurtscheller, G.: Event-related synchronization (ERS): an electrophysiological correlate of cortical areas at rest. Electroencephalogr. Clin. Neurophysiol. **83**(1), 62–69 (1992). https://doi.org/10.1016/0013-4694(92)90133-3
15. Wolpaw, J.R., et al.: Brain-computer interface technology: a review of the first international meeting. IEEE Trans. Rehab. Eng. **8**(2), 164–173 (2000). https://doi.org/10.1109/TRE.2000.847807
16. Phadikar, S., Sinha, N., Ghosh, R.: Unsupervised feature extraction with autoencoders for EEG based multiclass motor imagery BCI. Expert Syst. Appl. **213**, 118901 (2023). https://doi.org/10.1016/j.eswa.2022.118901
17. T. l. d. reservados, «Emotiv,» Emotiv. https://www.emotiv.com/epoc/ (2011). Último acceso: 10 Enero 2023
18. Benitez, S.D., Toscano, S., Silva, A.: On the use of the Emotiv EPOC neuroheadset as a low-cost alternative for EEG signal acquisition. In: IEEE Colombian Conference on Communications and Computing, pp. 1–6 (2016). https://doi.org/10.1109/ColComCon.2016.7516380
19. Warren: GitHub. https://github.com/CymatiCorp/CyKit 27 Diciembre 2018. Último acceso: 14 Octubre 2022
20. Chernikova, L.A., Mokienko, O.A., Frolov, A.A., Bobrov, P.D.: Motor imagery and its practical application. Neurosci. Behav. Physiol. **44**(5), 483–489 (2014). https://doi.org/10.7868/s0044467713020056
21. Gregg, M., Hall, C., Butler, A.: The MIQ-RS: a suitable option for examining movement imagery ability. Evi.-Based Complement. Altern. Med. **7**(2), 249–257 (2010). https://doi.org/10.1093/ecam/nem170
22. Lebon, F., Papaxanthis, C., Gaveau, J., Ruffino, C.: An acute session of motor imagery training indices use-dependent plasticity. Sci. Rep. **9**, 20002 (2019). https://doi.org/10.1038/s41598-019-56628-z
23. Lawhern, V., Solon, A., Waytowich, N., Gordon, S., Hung, C., Lance, B.: EEGNet: a compact convolutional neural network for EEG-based brain-computer interfaces. Neural Eng. **15**, 056013 (2018). https://doi.org/10.1088/1741-2552/aace8c
24. Lawhern, V., Solon, A., Waytowich, N., Gordon, S., Hung, C., Lance, B.: GitHub. https://github.com/vlawhern/arl-eegmodels (2018). Último acceso: 15 Febrero 2023

Natural Language Contents Evaluation System for Multi-class News Categorization Using Machine Learning and Transformers

Duván A. Marrugo, Juan Carlos Martinez-Santos, and Edwin Puertas(✉)

Universidad Tecnológica de Bolívar, Cartagena de Indias, Colombia
{marrugod,jcmartinezs,epuerta}@utb.edu.co

Abstract. The exponential growth of digital documents has come with rapid progress in text classification techniques in recent years. This paper provides text classification models, which analyze various steps of news classification, where some algorithmic approaches for machine learning, such as Logistic Regression, Support Vector Machine, and Random Forest, are implemented. In turn, the uses of Transformers as classification models for the solution of the same problem, proposing BERT and DistilBERT as possible solutions to compare for the automatic classification of news containing articles belonging to four categories (World, Sports, Business, and Science/Technology). We obtained the highest accuracy on the machine learning side, with 88% using Support Vector Machine with Word2Vec. However, using Transformer DistilBERT, we got an efficient model in terms of performance and 91.7% accuracy for classifying news.

Keywords: Text Classification · Automatic Classification · News Classification · Transformer · Machine Learning · Deep Learning

1 Introduction

There is a large amount of data stored in electronic format. With this data, the need has arisen for similar means that can interpret and parse similar data and extract valuable data, which we can use to assist decision-making [2]. Furthermore, we use information digging to remove concealed data from big data sets, an exceptionally integral asset utilized for this reason. According to a report by the consulting firm IDC, in 2025, the volume of data will reach 175 zettabytes, which means the equivalent of 175 times the information generated in 2011 [24].

News information was readily and rapidly available in the last decade. As a result, news is now easily affordable through content providers such as online news services. As mentioned in Ofcom's report on news consumption in 2020 [6], 65% of adults use the Internet as a news platform, compared to 41% in 2016, indicating a significant increase in the availability and growing popularity of online news [5].

J. C. Figueroa-García et al. (Eds.): WEA 2023, CCIS 1928, pp. 115–126, 2023.
https://doi.org/10.1007/978-3-031-46739-4_11

Classifying news text automatically assigns a text news document to a defined class of news items from predefined categories. Different approaches to machine learning, such as artificial neural networks, support vector machines, and decision techniques, can be used to solve the text classification problem [25]. Researchers have approached text classification using various clustering methods, Naive Bayes classifier [3], support vector machines with word2vec, and TF-IDT approaches [15]. There have also been several novel approaches to artificial neural networks. As seen in [14,20,21], neural has fruitfully carried out sentiment analysis.

Approaches are using Recurrent Neural Networks (RNN) to solve NLP problems. The success of RNNs is due to the Long Short Term Memory (LSTM) [7]. Moreover, the incredible versatility of these networks makes it possible to resolve a diversity of problems [13]. Authors in [23] introduce a novel model architecture, Transformer, to counter these two limitations. Furthermore, their proposed technique discards the recurrent architecture to depend solely on the attentional mechanism [12].

This paper presents the solution of new classifiers from a Machine Learning perspective, implementing after preprocessing, feature extraction, and three supervised classification methods for developing news classification models. Furthermore, Transformer models Bert and DistilBert will use the pre-trained language representation. Training data will be used for both, choosing the one with the best performance in terms of accuracy. This work is as follows: First, it overviews the related work on text categorization. Next, it describes the methodology implemented for classification models. Then, it presents experimental validation. Finally, it summarizes conclusions and future work.

2   Related Work

Nowadays, several studies focus on solving the categorization problem of news articles in different languages using machine learning methods. For example, in [4], in real-time, the authors evaluated the performance of machine learning-based methods for English news from the BBC website to classify them into five topics: business, entertainment, politics, sports, and technology. The classifiers selected for the analysis were Naïve Bayes (NB), Logistic Regression (LR), Support Vector Machine (SVM), Decision Tree (DT), and Random Forest (RF). In addition, they used TF-IDF for feature extraction, with the LR method obtaining the highest accuracy of 95.5%.

As before, in [8], the authors evaluated the performance of the BBC corpus news. They used NB, Multilayer Perceptron Neural Network, DT, and RF classifiers. The same feature extraction method, TF-IDF, was implemented. The best-performing way was NB, with 96.8% accuracy. Next, four machine learning methods, SVM, NB, k-Nearest Neighbors (kNN), and Convolutional Neural Network in [9], were applied to analyze text representation models using feature extraction, bag-of-words, and n-gram methods. Using the SVM model with bag-of-words for the 20 Newsgroups and AG's News corpora, an accuracy of 90.8% and 85.14%, respectively, was obtained.

In [16], authors used three text corpora. The first one includes Women, litera-ture, sports, and campus news. The second corpus includes sports, constellation, games, and entertainment news. They obtained as F1 results for corpus 1 and 2 the best results through SVM: 0.86 and 0.71, respectively. For the last corpus, the best estimation was through LR, with an F1 of 0.63.

In [19], authors developed models using ten machine learning methods and pondered the text employing TF-IDF to classify news articles with the Middle East, technology, sports, and business topics. First, they obtained SVM as the best-performing method, with F1 = 97.9. Then, based on the corpora AR-5, KH-7, AB-7, and RT-40, whose names correspond to the number of topics, nine neural network models were implemented [11].

Nowadays, the use of pre-entrant linguistic models is growing, as is the par-ticular case of BERT (Bidirectional Encoder Representations from Transform-ers) [10], which is like DistriBERT [22]. These contextual representation models, useful for text classification tasks, provide a contextual representation of words different from word-based embedding models, such as word2vec [17] and GloVe [18], where a unique word embedding is produced for each word, regardless of the context.

3   Methodology

3.1   Dataset Description

To solve the multiclass text classification problem, a text corpus from a com-petition proposed by the National Yang-Ming Chiao Tung University (NYCU) of Kaggle [1], which linked 58 participants, was used. Given the title and con-tent of the news item, we train a model using Transformers to correctly classify the news item into four different categories: World, Sports, Business, and Sci-ence/Technology, which records information on 2000 training samples and 400 test samples. The baseline required for the use of a Transformer was 15%. In turn, the dataset provides four columns of information: ID, Category, Title, and Description. Therefore, the data could be more balanced. For example, sports and world news represent 27% of the dataset, while business represents 25% and sci-tech news 21%.

3.2   Classification Process

Figure 1 visually represents the classification process. It begins with reading the dataset stored in CSV files and organizing it into a data frame with four corresponding columns, as explained in Subsect. 3.1. Subsequently, data prepro-cessing takes place. We conducted an exploratory analysis to identify keywords, acronyms, and abbreviations facilitated by n-gram analysis for feature selection. We analyzed this using Bag of Words (BoW), Term Frequency-Inverse Doc-ument Frequency (TF-IDF), and Word2Vec methods. These approaches offer advantages such as resource and time efficiency and enhanced prediction accu-racy for the model.

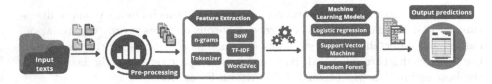

Fig. 1. News classification Machine Learning framework.

3.3 Pre-processing

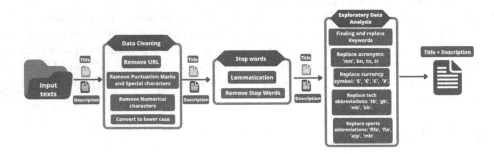

Fig. 2. Data cleaning pipeline.

Data Cleaning. Preprocessing operations consist of cleaning and normalizing the input data to improve the results of the feature extraction stage, i.e., regardless of whether they are manually constructed or automatically learned (in deep learning methods). As shown in the Data Cleaning section in Fig. 2, we focus on eliminating four essential issues: URLs, numeric characters, lowercase conversion, and punctuation marks.

Exploratory Data Analysis. To further normalize the data and reduce the feature space, we implemented additional procedures such as converting all text to lowercase and normalizing slang words and abbreviations. To assess the relationships between words within each news item, we conducted two types of analyses:

- In the Univariate Analysis, we identified words like 'bn' (converted to 'billion'), 'snday' (normalized to 'sunday'), 'qot', and 'bsness' (expanded to 'business'). These words were either replaced with their expanded meanings or removed as necessary. Interestingly, this step led to a slight increase in model accuracy, approximately 0.01%, compared to not performing it.

– In the Bivariate Analysis, we employed bigram and trigram analysis to examine word relationships. This analysis unveiled modifications in certain words, such as currency symbols (e.g., "$" to 'dollar', '€' to 'euro') and abbreviations (e.g., 'tb' to 'terabyte', 'gb' to 'gigabyte'). We also observed transformations like 'mn' to 'million', 'bn' to 'billion', and 'tn' to 'trillion'. These normalization techniques contributed to refining the data and enhancing its accuracy.

3.4 Feature Extraction

Our feature extraction approach employed three distinct methods: Bag-of-Words (BoW), TF-IDF (Term Frequency-Inverse Document Frequency), and Word2Vec. For Bag-of-n-grams and TF-IDF, we focused on capturing consecutive word sequences of length "n", denoting 2 and 3 as bigrams and trigrams, respectively. The parameter settings encompassed a frequency range from 1 to 500, an n-gram range spanning (1, 3), and the 'word' analyzer. In the case of Word2Vec, we opted for the Skip-gram model. We conducted meticulous parameter tuning, encompassing factors like the number of features, context window size, and negative sampling, among others, to ensure optimal performance in alignment with prior research findings.

3.5 Classification Using Supervised Algorithms

Initially, we conducted random oversampling with careful control over randomness, setting a specific random state (Random State) to 42. Following this, we implemented cross-validation through random permutation (Shuffle Split) to create a training dataset, accounting for 80% of the total data, and a test dataset, representing the remaining 20%.

We chose three classifiers for our news classification task: Logistic Regression (LR), Random Forest, and Support Vector Machine (SVM) with an RBF kernel, based on their demonstrated effectiveness in previous research. We fine-tuned LR using the 'lbfgs' optimizer with an inverse regularization strength of 1.0, allowing a maximum of 600 iterations for convergence. Random Forest, an ensemble method, incorporated 200 decision tree classifiers, each with a maximum depth of 200, to improve prediction accuracy and prevent overfitting. In the case of SVM, we utilized the 'rbf' kernel for multi-dimensional operations, applied an 'l2' penalty to avoid sparse coefficient vectors, and set the random state to 0 for consistency. These classifiers, each with its specific configuration, were applied to address our news classification task effectively.

3.6 Transformers

Architecture: The critical component of this architecture is the self-attention layer (A), which intuitively allows the encoder to look at other words in the input sentence whenever processing one of its words. Stacking multiple layers of this type creates a multi-head attention (MHA) layer, as shown in Fig. 3. Then, we condensed the individual outputs into a single matrix by concatenating the head outputs and passing the result through a linear layer.

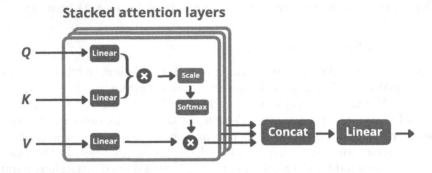

Fig. 3. The multi-head attention layer used in the Transformer architecture.

– **Encoder:** In the encoding part, the input embeddings are multiplied by three separate weight matrices, as indicated in Eq. 1, Q (queries), K (keys), and V (values), to generate different word representations.

$$Q = X \cdot W_Q$$
$$K = X \cdot W_K \tag{1}$$
$$V = X \cdot W_V$$

W_Q, W_K, $W_V \in \Re^{dim \times d_k}$ are the learned weight matrices. Eventually, we obtain the representation of each word by multiplying the scaled term with the V matrix containing the input representation. We define this operation in Eq. 2.

$$Z = A(Q, K, V) = S\left(\frac{Q \cdot K^T}{\sqrt{d_k}}\right) \cdot V \tag{2}$$

Here, S represents the softmax function.

– **Decoder:** During the decoding phase, every decoder layer receives the output of the encoder (the K and V matrices) and the output of the previous decoder layer. Additionally, we modified the self-attention layers into what we defined as "Masked" self-attention layers. The masked MH self-attention layer ensures the use of only the self-attention scores. We do it by adding a factor M to the word embeddings in Eq. 3. We set M to -inf for masked positions and 0 otherwise.

$$Z = S\left(\frac{Q \cdot K^T + M}{\sqrt{d_k}}\right) \cdot V \tag{3}$$

– **Preprocessing:** For performing the preprocessing, we should note that the two proposed models, BERT and DistilBert, based on deep neural network architectures, include similar steps for removing special characters, lemmatization, and stop word removal. In addition, tokenized documents are truncated or padded with a given number of tokens to ensure that the model receives uniformly sized input samples (i.e., with the same number of tokens).

As mentioned above, we will develop the problem using pre-trained BERT and DistilBERT for automatic news categorization and test different optimizer methods. Table 1 shows the parameters used for each architecture.

Table 1. Hyperparameters used in both models

BERT		DistilBert	
vocab size	128000	vocab size	128000
hidden size	768	hidden size	768
num hidden layers	12	num hidden layers	6
num attention heads	12	num attention heads	12
intermediate size	3072	intermediate size	3072
hidden dropout prob	0.1	hidden dropout prob	0.1
attention probs	0.1	attention probs	0.1
dropout prob	0.1	dropout prob	0.1
max position embeddings	512	Seq classif dropout	0.2
type vocab size	2	type vocab size	2
initializer range	0.02	initializer range	0.02
interaction	32	interaction	20
Optimizer	Adam Optimizer	Optimizer	Adamax Optimizer

4   Experimental Results

We performed testing on 55% of the test data as suggested by the competition parameters set by National Yang Ming Chiao Tung University (NYCU).

4.1   Machine Learning Results

Following the feature extraction process outlined in the preceding section, we evaluated each classifier with various feature extraction methods, and the results are in Table 2. As anticipated, Word2Vec emerged as one of the feature extraction models contributing significantly to the model's overall performance. The best results among the three proposed machine learning models, according to the predefined metrics, were achieved using Word2Vec.

The top-performing machine learning model was the Support Vector Machine (SVM), employed based on the premise that it worked well with Word2Vec. During development, we tested three kernel types: 'linear,' 'poly,' and 'rbf,' to find the best approximation to align with the probability estimates derived from Word2Vec. The Radial Basis Function (RBF) Kernel was the most suitable task. Nevertheless, it is noteworthy to mention that prior expectations suggested that the linear Kernel would yield superior classifier performance.

Table 2. Performance of the Classifiers

Algorithm	Feature Extraction	Accuracy	Precision	Recall	F1
Support Vector Machine	Word2Vect	0,88	0,88	0,88	0,88
LogisticRegression	Word2Vect	0,86	0,86	0,86	0,86
RandomForest	Word2Vect	0,86	0,86	0,87	0,86
Support Vector Machine	TF-IDF	0,83	0,83	0,83	0,82
LogisticRegression	TF-IDF	0,82	0,82	0,82	0,82
LogisticRegression	Bag-of-Words	0,81	0,81	0,81	0,81
Support Vector Machine	Bag-of-Words	0,8	0,8	0,81	0,8
RandomForest	TF-IDF	0,75	0,76	0,75	0,75
RandomForest	Bag-of-Words	0,74	0,76	0,74	0,74

4.2 Transformers Results

The previously described construction of the BERT and DistilBERT models resulted in two models with accuracies of 0.92 and 0.917, respectively. Since we conducted both the analysis and training, accuracy and loss are the primary metrics in Figs. 4 and 5. The accuracy trends during training for each iteration are observable, with each model utilizing a different number of iterations. Specifically, the BERT model employed 32 iterations, while DistilBERT used 20. To assess the efficiency of each model in achieving their maximum accuracy levels, we implemented EarlyStopping with a patience of 5 and obtained this information, as presented in Table 3. It is worth noting that while the BERT model achieves higher accuracy than DistilBERT, considering the number of iterations it takes to reach maximum accuracy is crucial. Based on the duty cycle percentage required to attain its maximum accuracy, DistilBERT emerges as the more efficient model, achieving similar accuracy to BERT in a shorter duty cycle. However, it is noteworthy to comment on the significance of this observation despite the highest accuracy.

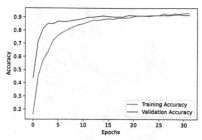

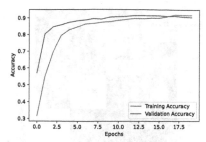

(a) Accuracy BERT model with 32 spochs.

(b) Accuracy DistilBERT model with 20 spochs.

Fig. 4. Training and validation accuracy.

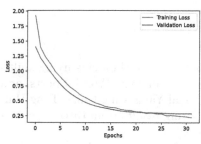

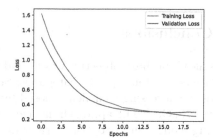

(a) Loss BERT model with 32 spochs.

(b) Loss DistilBERT model with 20 spochs.

Fig. 5. Training and validation loss.

In Fig. 6a, it is evident that DistilBERT does not achieve equal or higher precision than BERT. However, it excels in predicting the science/technology and business categories with a minimum percentage error of 2.25% when considering the dataset. Furthermore, DistilBERT is highly effective in predicting the sports category, which comprises a significantly larger volume of data than the other classes, namely science/technology and business.

Table 3. Efficiency comparison measured over the duty cycle.

Model	interactions	Loss	Accuracy	Duty cycle
BERT	30/32	0.2889	0.92	93.17 %
DistilBERT	15/20	0.3045	0.917	75 %

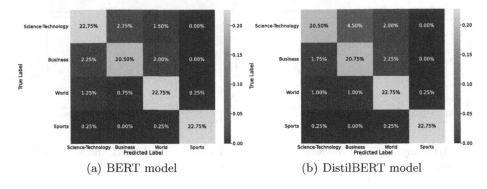

(a) BERT model   (b) DistilBERT model

Fig. 6. Transformer model confusion matrices for news classification.

5   Conclusions

The study's primary objective was to find an optimal model for classifying multi-class texts into four specific categories: Science/Technology, World, Sports, and Business, addressing a challenge posed by National Yang Ming Chiao Tung University (NYCU). The approach involved comparing results from three machine-learning models and two Transformer models.

Machine Learning models explored various feature extraction methods to enhance news classification accuracy. The top-performing model was Support Vector Machine in conjunction with Word2Vec, achieving an accuracy of 88%, surpassing other models. Word2Vec consistently proved to be the best feature extractor, enhancing accuracy by 1% to 2% across models, with sports news classification showing the highest precision and AUC.

Two Transformer models, BERT and DistilBERT, were also evaluated. DistilBERT emerged as the more efficient model, offering faster and more accurate news classification despite having slightly lower accuracy than BERT. Ultimately, DistilBERT was the preferred classifier with an accuracy of 91.7%, outperforming other models.

Comparing the results with 58 other participants, the Machine Learning model ranked seventh, while the Transformer model claimed the top position with a marginal accuracy difference of 0.01%.

For future work, there are plans to optimize the model further. Additionally, a multilingual model capable of classifying news in English, Mandarin, Spanish, and Hindi, the world's most spoken languages according to the BBC, will be developed.

References

1. lab 912, M.: Deeplearning hw2 transformer (2022). https://kaggle.com/competitions/deeplearning-hw2-transformer

2. Ahmed, J., Ahmed, M.: Online news classification using machine learning techniques. IIUM Eng. J. **22**, 210–225 (2021). https://doi.org/10.31436/iiumej.v22i2. 1662, https://journals.iium.edu.my/ejournal/index.php/iiumej/article/view/1662

3. Ahmed, J., Ahmed, M.: Online news classification using machine learning techniques. IIUM Eng. J. **22**, 210–225 (2021). https://doi.org/10.31436/iiumej.v22i2. 1662, https://journals.iium.edu.my/ejournal/index.php/iiumej/article/view/1662

4. Patro, A., Mahima Patel, R.S., Save, D.J.: Real time news classification using machine learning. Int. J. Adv. Sci. Technol. **29**(9s), 620–630 (2020)

5. Barua, A., Sharif, O., Hoque, M.M.: Multi-class sports news categorization using machine learning techniques: resource creation and evaluation. Procedia Compute. Sci. **193**, 112–121 (2021). https://doi.org/10.1016/j.procs.2021.11. 002, https://www.sciencedirect.com/science/article/pii/S1877050921021268. 10th International Young Scientists Conference in Computational Science, YSC2021, 28 June–2 July 2021

6. Blackledge, C., Atapour-Abarghouei, A.: Transforming fake news: robust generalisable news classification using transformers (2021). https://doi.org/10.48550/ ARXIV.2109.09796, http://arxiv.org/2109.09796

7. Cho, K., et al.: Learning phrase representations using RNN encoder-decoder for statistical machine translation (2014). https://doi.org/10.48550/ARXIV.1406.1078, http://arxiv.org/1406.1078

8. Deb, N., Jha, V., Panjiyar, A., Gupta, R.: A comparative analysis of news categorization using machine learning approaches. Int. J. Sci. Technol. Res. **9**, 2469–2472 (2020)

9. Devi, J.S., Bai, D.M.R., Reddy, C.: Newspaper article classification using machine learning techniques. Int. J. Innov. Technol. Explor. Eng. **9**(5), 872–877 (2020). https://doi.org/10.35940/ijitee.e2753.039520, https://dx.doi.org/10.35940/ijitee.E2753.039520

10. Devlin, J., Chang, M.W., Lee, K., Toutanova, K.: BERT: pre-training of deep bidirectional transformers for language understanding (2018). https://doi.org/10. 48550/ARXIV.1810.04805, http://arxiv.org/1810.04805

11. Elnagar, A., Al-Debsi, R., Einea, O.: Arabic text classification using deep learning models. Inf. Process. Manag. **57**(1), 102121 (2020). https://doi.org/ 10.1016/j.ipm.2019.102121, https://www.sciencedirect.com/science/article/pii/ S0306457319303413

12. Gillioz, A., Casas, J., Mugellini, E., Khaled, O.A.: Overview of the transformer-based models for NLP tasks. In: 2020 15th Conference on Computer Science and Information Systems (FedCSIS), pp. 179–183 (2020). https://doi.org/10.15439/ 2020F20

13. Greff, K., Srivastava, R.K., Koutnik, J., Steunebrink, B.R., Schmidhuber, J.: LSTM: a search space odyssey. IEEE Trans. Neural Netw. Learn. Syst. **28**(10), 2222–2232 (2017). https://doi.org/10.1109/tnnls.2016.2582924

14. Kosheleva, O., Kreinovich, V., Shahbazova, S.: Type-2 fuzzy analysis explains ubiquity of triangular and trapezoid membership functions. In: Shahbazova, S.N., Kacprzyk, J., Balas, V.E., Kreinovich, V. (eds.) Recent Developments and the New Direction in Soft-Computing Foundations and Applications. SFSC, vol. 393, pp. 63–75. Springer, Cham (2021). https://doi.org/10.1007/978-3-030-47124-8_6

15. Lilleberg, J., Zhu, Y., Zhang, Y.: Support vector machines and word2vec for text classification with semantic features. In: 2015 IEEE 14th International Conference on Cognitive Informatics & Cognitive Computing (ICCI*CC), pp. 136–140 (2015). https://doi.org/10.1109/ICCI-CC.2015.7259377

16. Luo, X.: Efficient English text classification using selected machine learning techniques. Alex. Eng. J. **60**(3), 3401–3409 (2021). https://doi.org/10.1016/j.aej.2021. 02.009, https://www.sciencedirect.com/science/article/pii/S1110016821000806

17. Munikar, M., Shakya, S., Shrestha, A.: Fine-grained sentiment classification using BERT. In: 2019 Artificial Intelligence for Transforming Business and Society (AITB), vol. 1, pp. 1–5 (2019). https://doi.org/10.1109/AITB48515.2019.8947435

18. Pennington, J., Socher, R., Manning, C.: GloVe: global vectors for word representation. In: Proceedings of the 2014 Conference on Empirical Methods in Natural Language Processing (EMNLP), pp. 1532–1543. Association for Computational Linguistics, Doha (2014). https://doi.org/10.3115/v1/D14-1162, https://www.aclanthology.org/D14-1162

19. Qadi, L.A., Rifai, H.E., Obaid, S., Elnagar, A.: Arabic text classification of news articles using classical supervised classifiers. In: 2019 2nd International Conference on new Trends in Computing Sciences (ICTCS), pp. 1–6 (2019). https://doi.org/ 10.1109/ICTCS.2019.8923073

20. Rustamov, S.: A hybrid system for subjectivity analysis. Adv. Fuzzy Syst. **2018**, 1–9 (2018). https://doi.org/10.1155/2018/2371621

21. Rustamov, S., Mustafayev, E., Clements, M.: Context analysis of customer requests using a hybrid adaptive neuro fuzzy inference system and hidden Markov models in the natural language call routing problem. Open Eng. **8**, 61–68 (2018). https:// doi.org/10.1515/eng-2018-0008

22. Sanh, V., Debut, L., Chaumond, J., Wolf, T.: DistilBERT, a distilled version of BERT: smaller, faster, cheaper and lighter (2019). https://doi.org/10.48550/ ARXIV.1910.01108, http://arxiv.org/1910.01108

23. Vaswani, A., et al.: Attention is all you need (2017). https://doi.org/10.48550/ ARXIV.1706.03762, http://arxiv.org/1706.03762

24. Yang, Y., Chen, X., Tan, R., Xiao, Y.: IoT Technologies and Applications, pp. 1–60. Wiley (2021). https://doi.org/10.1002/9781119593584.ch1

25. Yıldırım, S., Jothimani, D., Kavaklıoğlu, C., Başar, A.: Classification of "hot news" for financial forecast using NLP techniques. In: 2018 IEEE International Conference on Big Data (Big Data), pp. 4719–4722 (2018). https://doi.org/10.1109/BigData. 2018.8621903

Automatic Assessment of Voice Disorders Using Phase Plots

N. R. Calvo-Ariza[1]([⊠]) [iD], T. Arias-Vergara[1,2] [iD], and J. R. Orozco-Arroyave[1,2] [iD]

[1] GITA Lab. Faculty of Engineering, University of Antioquia UdeA,
Medellín, Colombia
`nestor.calvo@udea.edu.co`
[2] Pattern Recognition Lab, Friedrich-Alexander-Universität Erlangen-Nürnberg,
Erlangen, Germany

Abstract. The early detection of pathologies is a significant challenge in the healthcare sector and often requires the involvement of multiple specialists in different areas. The analysis of bio-signals, such as speech, gait, and video, has shown promising results in detecting pathologies. In this study, we propose using phase plots extracted from electroglottographs (EGG) and acoustic signals to detect voice disorders automatically. The method consists in using the visual information provided by the plots and processing the information with convolutional neural networks for quantitative analysis of voice quality. We test our approach with EGG and acoustic signals from the Saarbruecken Voice Database (SVD), which contains recordings of 687 controls and 1186 patients diagnosed with 71 different voice pathologies. In addition to the phase plots, state-of-the-art features were computed for quantitative assessment. An 85 % accuracy was obtained when we combined the proposed phase plots with filter-bank features.

Keywords: Voice disorders · EGG signals · Acoustic signals · Phase plots · Machine learning · Deep learning

1 Introduction

Voice disorders occur when the quality, pitch, and other aspects differ according to different factors [3]. Detecting these pathologies can be challenging due to various causes that can originate the pathology and different disorders that share effects on the body [16]. The detection, diagnosis, and treatment of voice pathologies have improved over time, thanks to the involvement of multiple disciplines such as neurology, psychiatry, laryngology, and others [4].

Over the last few years, automatic tools have been used to help physicians in the diagnosis, thanks to automatic analysis of different signals such as voice, writing, and video [17] obtained from the patient in combination with machine learning and deep learning techniques. More specifically, in the field of automatic speech analysis, numerous studies have been dedicated to detecting voice

J. C. Figueroa-García et al. (Eds.): WEA 2023, CCIS 1928, pp. 127–138, 2023.
https://doi.org/10.1007/978-3-031-46739-4_12

disorders. These works often involve comparing different features and classification algorithms to identify the most suitable ones for the task. For instance, in [10] the authors utilized mel-frequency cepstral coefficients (MFCC) as well as noise-related features to represent the speech signal, this representation is then used to create a Gaussian mixture model (GMM) to classify between two classes, healthy vs. voice disorder; the work uses different vowels as well as the fusion of them, but the work only considered the speech recordings of the SVD, but did not consider the information of the EGG signals that are provided in the same corpus. In [15], authors compared the performance of different machine learning models such as Random Forest (RF), Support Vector Machine (SVM), Gradient Boost (GB), and K-Nearest Neighbors (KNN) for the classification between healthy and 3 different voice pathologies. Other measures are also used in different studies like jitter, shimmer, noise-related features, among others [5]. The classification process has also evolved recently, there are works that use deep learning approaches, where the audio signal is commonly transformed into a spectrogram that is automatically processed by convolutional neural networks (CNN) [11] in combination with classical models such as SVM [1]. Deep learning models have also been used [23, 25].

Another signal that is useful for evaluating and detecting voice disorders is the EGG, also known as the glottal signal. This signal captures the opening and closing movements of the glottis during speech production. Works that use the EGG signal vary depending on the method to obtain or capture the signal. In [6], the EGG signal was captured by electrodes placed on the neck. However, sometimes this is not possible, so techniques to recreate the glottal signal from the speech signal are also used [8,9,13]. Once the glottal signal is extracted, some authors measure quotients originally designed for speech, like jitter and shimmer. Other works apply typical speech features like MFCCs [8,13].

Regarding the access to data to create and evaluate models. Multiple works use private databases [5,8,15], but others (actually the majority) use public databases like the SVD [1,10,23,25]. This corpus has a high amount of subjects suffering from different pathologies, as well as different tasks. Besides, the corpus includes both EGG and speech signals. The main drawback of this database is its unbalance in age and gender between pathological and healthy participants. According to our literature research, none of the studies specifically focused on ensuring a balanced distribution of age and gender. As a result, the potential influence of these variables on the models' performance is not explicitly addressed. Further considerations regarding dataset balance in terms of age and gender may be valuable to mitigate any biases or confounding factors that these variables might introduce.

In this work, we propose a method for the automatic analysis of voice disorders using phase plots. These plots were first proposed in [24] as a visualization method to analyze abnormal vibrations of the vocal folds from glottal area waveforms obtained with high-speed video endoscopy (HSV) data. However, the plots were not used for objective analysis of voice disorders. Then in [2], it was proposed to use shape-based parameters (e.g., size of the glottal cycles, inter-cycle variability, and intra-cycle consistency) for quantitative analysis using the phase plots. These voice parameters proved suitable for analyzing vocal folds vibration; however, the main limitation is that HSV data of the vocal folds are required for analysis. We propose to extract the phase plots from the acoustic and EGG signals and use CNN to analyze voice disorders quantitatively. Additionally, we compute phonation, articulation, non-linear dynamics, and filterbank features as the baseline for comparison with our proposed approach. Automatic analysis is performed on signals from the sustained phonation of vowels from the corpus SVD. A subset of the corpus was taken to guarantee age and gender balance.

2   Data

The SVD is a German database that contains acoustic and EGG recordings of different voice pathologies and healthy subjects [21]. The database contains more than 2000 recordings sessions; each session contains the sustained vowels /a/, /i/, and /u/, as well as the short phrase "Guten Morgen, wie geht es Ihnen?". In this study, we used a subset of the SVD to balance the dataset according to age and sex. Furthermore, we only considered acoustic and EGG recordings of the sustained phonation of the vowel /a/. Table 1 shows the demographic information of the data used in this study. The recordings are sampled at 50 kHz with a 16-bit resolution.

Table 1. Demographic information of subjects in SVD database after balance in age and gender.

	Subjects with a pathology		Healthy subjects	
	Male	Female	Male	Female
# of participants	159	115	165	115
Age [years]	39.61 ± 11.10	39.38 ± 14.42	37.05 ± 11.13	38.34 ± 14.47
Age range [years]	24–69	24–84	19–70	19–82

3   Methods

As described in the introduction, most of the work in the literature has considered spectral analysis, non-linear dynamics, perturbation, noise, energy, and pitch-based features to characterize voice problems. Thus, we compare our approach with state-of-the-art features (baseline) to show its suitability for objectively analyzing voice disorders. We begin this section by describing the proposed phase plot analysis and then the baseline features used for the objective analysis of voice signals.

3.1   Phase Plot Analysis

In general, phase plots can be obtained by plotting the real and imaginary parts of an analytic signal of the form

$$z(t) = x(t) + jy(t) \tag{1}$$

where $x(t)$ is the acoustic/EGG signal and $y(t)$ is the imaginary part obtained with the Hilbert transform. As shown in [2], when the phase plots are extracted from glottal signals, and glottal cycles are represented as elliptical trajectories superimposed in a 2D plane. In the case of acoustic signals, the phase plots result in more complicated shapes due to the non-linearities present in the signal.

Middle part of Fig. 1 shows an example of the phase plot extracted from a segment of a sustained phonation.

From the Figure, it can be observed that analyzing abnormal vibration in the signal can be difficult due to the complexity of the plot, which is the result of the components (e.g., harmonics) that compose the acoustic signal. Thus, we propose the following procedure to perform analysis with phase plots:

1. Extract the temporal fine structure (TFS) [12] of the acoustic/EGG signal to reduce the complexity of the phase plot. The TFS is obtained by dividing the acoustic/EGG signal by the amplitude envelope of the signal, i.e., the magnitude of the analytic signal. Top part of Fig. 1 shows an example.
2. Compute the Hilbert transform of the resulting TFS to obtain $z'(t) = x'(t) + jy'(t)$ and plot the real and imaginary parts to get the phase plot, i.e., $x'(t)$ vs. $y'(t)$.Middle part of Fig. 1 shows an example.
3. Transform the resulting phase plot into an image with dimensions 256×256. For this, the phase plot is converted into a heatmap by computing a bidimensional histogram of the phase plot with 248 bins and applying a 2D Gaussian filter with a standard deviation of 12 to smooth the data points. Bottom part of Fig. 1 shows an example.

An example of the phase plots (as heatmaps) obtained from the recordings of a healthy control and a patient can be observed in Fig. 2. It can be observed that the phase plot of the patient is more "noisy" than the one of the healthy subjects.

The quantitative analysis of the proposed phase plots is performed by training a CNN and then using embeddings of the last layers as a feature vector. The details of the architecture used in this study are given in Sect. 3.3.

3.2   Baseline Features

Filterbank Analysis: With this set of features, we aim to provide a time-frequency representation of voice signals that encodes the frequency components similarly to the basilar membrane in the human ear, i.e., encode the spectral information of the sounds in different non-linearly spaced frequency bands. For this, we considered three different filterbank-based features: Mel Frequency Cepstral Coefficients, Bark Frequency Cepstrum Coefficients (BFCC), and Gamma-tone Frequency Cepstrum Coefficients (GFCC).

MFCCs: Mel is a perceptual scale proposed by [20] to measure how different tones are perceived by the human ear. Triangular filters are applied to the log-power spectrum in the Mel-scale to obtain the Mel-spectrum, a "compressed" and nonlinear representation of the Short-Time Fourier Transform (STFT).

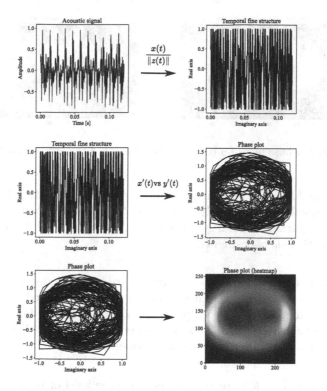

Fig. 1. Steps to obtain phase plots

To obtain the MFCCs, the filter bank is applied to the STFT. Then, the logarithm of the sum of the energy in each frequency band is calculated. Then, the discrete cosine transform (DCT) is applied, generating N number of cepstral coefficients for each window, N is the number of filters selected from the filter bank. We considered 20 coefficients.

BFCCs: BFCCs follow a similar process as MFCCs, with the main difference being the scale used and the set of filters. This new scale can be seen in Eq. 2, where f is the frequency value in Hertz. These coefficients seek to mimic the human ears' frequency response, and this set of coefficients has shown to be helpful and sometimes better than MFCCs.

$$\text{BARK}(f) = 13 \cdot \arctan(0.00076 \cdot f) + 3.5 \cdot \arctan\left(\left(\frac{f}{7500}\right)^2\right) \quad (2)$$

GFCCs: The frequency scale of the Gammatone filterbank is based on the Equivalent Rectangular Bandwidth (ERB) and the shape of the filterbank is obtained as the multiplication of sine and gamma functions. The center frequencies can be calculated as:

$$f_c = -\alpha + (f_H + \alpha)e^{m\frac{(-\log(f_H+\alpha)+\log(f_L+\alpha))}{M}}, \text{ with } \alpha = \text{EarQ*minBW} \quad (3)$$

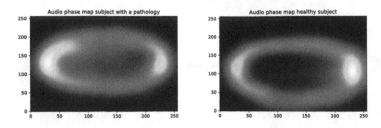

Fig. 2. Phase plot of a patient (left) and a healthy subject (right)

where m is an M-dimensional array of integer values $m = \{1, 2, 3 \ldots M\}$, f_L is the lower frequency (e.g. $f_L = 50$ Hz), f_H is the upper frequency (e.g. $f_H = 8$ kHz), and the parameters EarQ $= 9.26449$ and minBW $= 24.7$ can be changed if another ERB scale is desired [7].

Non-linear Features: Non-linear features are used to measure how chaotic or unpredictable the signal is. These features are mainly used because studies have shown nonlinearity in speech production, e.g., pressure flow at the glottis, vocal fold collisions, etc. In this work, we computed Sample Entropy, Largest Lyapunov Exponent (LLE), and Hurst Exponent (HE).

Sample Entropy: This feature aims to measure the level of regularity or unpredictability in a time series data. It is used to quantify a signals' complexity by calculating the likelihood that similar patterns will repeat themselves inside the signal. To calculate sample entropy, the signal is delayed by a value of m; this new vector is then compared with the original one using the absolute distance between scalars. Those scalars where the absolute distance between them is lower than a tolerance r are considered similar. The tolerance was set to $0.2 * std(segment)$ with std being the standard deviation.

LLE: This feature quantifies the predictability or stability of a system in the presence of changes [22]. It is computed based on the concept of attractors, with the exponents defined as the average differences between neighboring points in the attractor. Distances below a predefined threshold ϵ are stored, and the highest of these exponents is selected as the feature. The exponent provides a quantitative measure of the level of chaos or irregularity present in the signal. It has the potential to differentiate between standard speech and speech affected by a disorder.

HE: This feature quantifies the "long-term memory" or the presence of long statistical dependencies in a time series that are not attributed to cycles. By computing this exponent, we can assess self-similarities and determine the resemblance of a sustained vowel signal to its initial portion. The range of values for this exponent typically spans from 0 to 1. A value of 0.5 corresponds to a random process, while values greater than 0.5 indicate the presence of positive autocorrelation, and values less than 0.5 suggest negative autocorrelation.

Articulation Features. Articulation features are designed to model how humans use speech organs (such as lips, tongue, and jaw) to produce speech sounds. In this study, we utilized the DisVoice toolkit for extracting these features [14,19]. The DisVoice toolkit offers the capability to extract 122 descriptors; however, we focused on the first and second formant frequencies and their respective derivatives. To ensure consistent feature vector lengths, statistical functionals, including mean, standard deviation, skewness, and kurtosis, were computed for each feature using a predefined window size. Consequently, a total of 28 articulation features were obtained.

Phonation Features. Phonation features are used to find or model abnormal patterns in the vocal fold vibration [19]; some of these features are the fundamental frequency, jitter, shimmer, amplitude perturbation quotient (APQ), and pitch perturbation quotient (PPQ), among others. Similarly to the articulation features, four statistical functionals were calculated per feature.

Fundamental Frequency (F0): The fundamental frequency of a periodic signal is the inverse of the period; in the case of speech signals (non-periodic signals), it is defined as the rate of the vibration of the vocal folds.

Temporal and Amplitude Perturbations: Jitter refers to the temporal perturbation or variation in the fundamental frequency between periods, while shimmer quantifies the variation in the amplitude of the speech signal or the maximum peak. Jitter is computed as the average difference between two consecutive periods divided by the average period length. On the other hand, shimmer is calculated as the average difference between the amplitudes of consecutive speech cycles divided by the average amplitude value.

Pitch and Amplitude Perturbation Quotient: Both are usually refered as PPQ or APQ and a number, e.g., PPQ5. PPQ it's defined as the ratio of disturbance within the number of periods divided by the average period, e.g. PPQ5 represents the ratio within five (5) periods. On the other hand, APQ represents the amplitude disturbance within periods.

3.3   Classifiers

We considered two classifiers to automatically detect voice problems from the acoustic/EGG signals: a CNN and a Support Vector Machine. The CNN was used to obtain the feature vectors (embeddings) from the phase plots, and the SVM was used to classify patients vs. healthy controls.

Convolutional Neural Networks (CNNs) are widely employed in computer vision and video recognition tasks due to their ability to automatically extract hierarchical patterns from raw pixel data. In this research, a CNN architecture consisting of three convolutional layers is utilized to extract patterns from phase plot heat maps. Each layer contains a set of filters that convolve over the input image, highlighting local information. The convolutional layers have 64, 32, and 16 kernels respectively, with a kernel size of 3×3 except for the second layer, as shown in Fig. 3. Rectified Linear Unit (ReLU) activation functions are employed in all layers. Max pooling with a pool size of 2×2 is applied after each convolution. The last layer before the fully connected layer is flattened, and different sizes (128, 256, and 512) are tested for the first fully connected layer, which will serve as embeddings for the phase diagrams. The network is trained using an ADAM optimizer with a batch size of 4 and 100 epochs. To prevent overfitting, an early stopping algorithm with a patience of 5 is implemented.

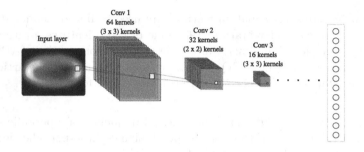

Fig. 3. CNN architecture

Support Vector Machines, a popular supervised learning method, are chosen as the classifier in this research. SVMs excel at creating hyperplanes to separate data points. Two key parameters, namely C and γ, are used to construct these hyperplanes. The regularization parameter C balances between accuracy and overfitting, with higher values indicating a more tailored model that might overfit. On the other hand, γ determines the proximity of the decision boundary to the data, with lower values resulting in a softer decision boundary but reduced accuracy.

SVMs operate by transforming data into a high-dimensional feature space for effective separation [18]. While this transformation can be computationally expensive, SVMs employ kernels that enable efficient feature evaluation. The research evaluates two kernel options: linear and radial basis function (RBF) kernels, which are commonly used in SVM applications.

4   Experiments and Results

The primary objective of this study is to demonstrate the effectiveness of phase plots as features for voice pathology classification. To establish a baseline for comparison with state-of-the-art features, multiple experiments were conducted using only the vowel /a/. The classifier of choice is Support Vector Machine (SVM), requiring hyperparameter optimization. Ten-fold cross-validation was employed, with 80% of the 554 samples allocated to the training set and the remaining 20% to the test set.

The experimental process involved training the model on the training set to identify the best parameters specific to that set of features. Subsequently, the model was tested on the remaining subjects within the fold. Importantly, the ten-fold cross-validation was subject-independent, ensuring that no data from the same subject appeared in both the training and test sets of the same fold. The ten folds were created once and remained consistent across different experiments. A grid search algorithm was employed to determine the optimal values for the hyperparameters: C, γ, and the choice of kernel. The experiments involved evaluating the following parameter values: $\gamma = 0.0001, 0.001, 0.01, 0.1, 1, 10$ and $C = 0.01, 0.1, 1, 10, 100, 1000$. Two types of kernels, linear and radial basis function, were considered. This process was repeated for each fold, resulting in ten sets of parameters. To obtain a single model, the mode (most frequently occurring value) of these ten parameter sets was determined, and it became the final set of parameters for the model.

Using the fixed set of parameters, the new model was trained and tested on each fold. Accuracy, sensitivity (recall), and specificity metrics were calculated for each iteration. Accuracy reflects the model's overall predictive performance for both positive and negative instances, accounting for the class imbalance. Sensitivity measures the model's ability to correctly identify positive cases, while specificity quantifies the correct identification of negative instances. After the ten-fold iteration, the mean and standard deviation of these metrics were calculated to obtain the final results for the specific feature set.

4.1 Results

Experiments were performed using EGG and speech individually, all the features were extracted for both signals, and an SVM was trained for each combination. Table 2 shows the best parameters found and the models' accuracy, sensitivity, and specificity with those parameters.

We can notice that we obtained models with good accuracy but low sensitivity; this means that the models are unable to classify a person as a healthy subject using only one set of features.

Early Fusion with Embeddings of Phase Plots. To improve the previous results, an early fusion approach was used; this fusion will allow us to introduce more information about the subject by concatenating different feature sets. All the classical features are fused, but the main idea is to fuse the information from the phase plots. We need to extract the information that the CNN returns after the convolutional process. Similarly to the last experiment, accuracy, sensitivity, and specificity are reported to obtain the best model; the models with the best results can be seen in Table 3.

Table 2. Results and best parameters for each feature in each modality

Modality	Feature	C	γ	Kernel	Accuracy	Sensitivity	Specificity
EGG	Non-linear	1	0.01	rbf	0.59 ± 0.02	0.25	0.96
	MFCC	0.01	0.001	linear	0.66 ± 0.09	0.45	0.84
	BFCC	**0.01**	**0.001**	**linear**	**0.68 ± 0.07**	**0.43**	**0.83**
	GFCC	1	0.001	rbf	0.64 ± 0.08	0.24	0.87
	Phonation	100	1	rbf	0.63 ± 0.08	0.44	0.75
	Articulation	0.01	0.001	rbf	0.54 ± 0.14	0.21	0.77
Audio	Non-linear	10	0.1	rbf	0.61 ± 0.05	0.18	0.87
	MFCC	0.01	0.001	rbf	0.62 ± 0.07	0.24	0.95
	BFCC	**0.1**	**0.001**	**linear**	**0.74 ± 0.08**	**0.74**	**0.74**
	GFCC	10	0.001	rbf	0.64 ± 0.09	0.13	0.95
	Phonation	0.01	0.1	rbf	0.62 ± 0.07	0.5	0.77
	Articulation	0.1	0.001	rbf	0.62 ± 0.09	0.12	0.96

Table 3. Best results obtained with early fusion

Feature 1	Feature 2	Accuracy	Sensitivity	Specificity
GFCC Audio	MFCC Audio	0.85	0.64	0.91
GFCC Audio	BFCC EGG	0.85	0.66	0.93
Embeddings with EGG and layer size 512	BFCC EGG	**0.85**	**0.84**	**0.85**
Embeddings with Audio and layer size 128	GFCC EGG	0.85	0.79	0.84

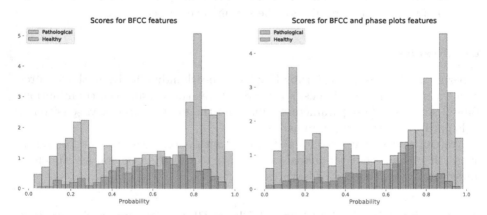

Fig. 4. Score distribution with BFCC features (left) and the fusion with phase plot (right)

The results presented in Table 3 demonstrate the effectiveness of the fusion strategy in enhancing the accuracy of our models. A comparison between the fused features and the more classical ones reveals a notable improvement in accuracy, sensitivity, and specificity, resulting in a more robust and comprehensive model. Furthermore, the benefits brought by the phase plots are visually evident in Fig. 4. This illustration depicts a histogram score distribution, representing the probability distribution of the Support Vector Machine (SVM). In the classification process, each sample is assigned a probability of belonging to the positive class (pathological), resulting in the emergence of two Gaussian distributions (one for each class). The closer the mean of each gaussian distribution is to zero and one the better our model is. This allows us to say that the fused features exhibit a significantly improved distribution, particularly among the healthy subjects, in contrast to the distribution observed when using a model trained solely on BFCC features.

5   Conclusion

This paper proposes a new methodology for automatically evaluate voice disorders using phase plots extracted from voice and EGG signals. We estimated the TFS using the Hilbert transform and then obtained the phase plot from the analytic signal. To analyze the bi-dimensional data, we transformed the resulting plot into an image (heatmap) using a 2D histogram and a Gaussian filter. Additionally, we used state-of-the-art features commonly used for quantitative analysis of voice disorders as a baseline. According to the results, using the phase plots combined with filter bank features (Bark scale) yielded the highest performance, which shows the suitability of the proposed approach to capture abnormal oscillations in the acoustic and EGG signals.

One of the limitations of this study is that the phase plots were computed from the complete signal; thus, it is not possible to capture dynamic information that might be important to assess voice quality, e.g., the onset of phonation. However, this approach allows analyzing abnormal vibrations in the whole signal. Thus, in future work, we will consider frame-wise analysis to extract the phase plots and capture within signal variability.

Acknowledgement. This work was funded by CODI at UdeA grant #PI2023-58010.

References

1. Alhussein, M., Muhammad, G.: Voice pathology detection using deep learning on mobile healthcare framework. IEEE Access **6**, 41034–41041 (2018)
2. Arias-Vergara, T., Döllinger, M., Schraut, T., Khairuddin, K.A.M., Schützenberger, A.: Nyquist plot parametrization for quantitative analysis of vibration of the vocal folds. J. Voice (2023)
3. Boone, D.R., McFarlane, S.C., Von Berg, S.L., Zraick, R.I.: The voice and voice therapy (2005)
4. Carding, P.: Voice pathology in the United kingdom. BMJ **327**(7414), 514–515 (2003)
5. El Emary, I., Fezari, M., Amara, F.: Towards developing a voice pathologies detection system. J. Commun. Technol. Electron. **59**, 1280–1288 (2014)

6. Fabris, C., De Colle, W., Sparacino, G.: Voice disorders assessed by (cross-) sample entropy of electroglottogram and microphone signals. Biomed. Signal Process. Control **8**(6), 920–926 (2013)

7. Glasberg, B.R., Moore, B.C.: Derivation of auditory filter shapes from notched-noise data. Hear. Res. **47**(1–2), 103–138 (1990)

8. Kadiri, S.R., Alku, P.: Analysis and detection of pathological voice using glottal source features. IEEE J. Select. Top. Signal Process. **14**(2), 367–379 (2019)

9. Kohler, M., Vellasco, M.M., Cataldo, E., et al.: Analysis and classification of voice pathologies using glottal signal parameters. J. Voice **30**(5), 549–556 (2016)

10. Martínez, D., Lleida, E., Ortega, A., Miguel, A., Villalba, J.: Voice pathology detection on the saarbrücken voice database with calibration and fusion of scores using MultiFocal toolkit. In: Torre Toledano, D., et al. (eds.) IberSPEECH 2012. CCIS, vol. 328, pp. 99–109. Springer, Heidelberg (2012). https://doi.org/10.1007/978-3-642-35292-8_11

11. Mohammed, M.A., et al.: Voice pathology detection and classification using convolutional neural network model. Appl. Sci. **10**(11), 3723 (2020)

12. Moon, I.J., Hong, S.H.: What is temporal fine structure and why is it important? Korean J. Audiol. **18**(1), 1 (2014)

13. Muhammad, G., et al.: Voice pathology detection using interlaced derivative pattern on glottal source excitation. Biomed. Signal Process. Control **31**, 156–164 (2017)

14. Orozco-Arroyave, J.R., et al.: Neurospeech: an open-source software for Parkinson's speech analysis. Digit. Signal Process. **77**, 207–221 (2018)

15. Pham, M., Lin, J., Zhang, Y.: Diagnosing voice disorder with machine learning. In: 2018 IEEE International Conference on Big Data (Big Data), pp. 5263–5266. IEEE (2018)

16. Sataloff, R.T.: Professional voice. The science and art of clinical care, pp. 179–183 (1991)

17. Savitt, J.M., Dawson, V.L., Dawson, T.M., et al.: Diagnosis and treatment of Parkinson disease: molecules to medicine. J. Clin. Invest. **116**(7), 1744–1754 (2006)

18. Schölkopf, B., Smola, A.J., Bach, F., et al.: Learning with Kernels: Support Vector Machines, Regularization, Optimization, and Beyond. MIT press, Cambridge (2002)

19. Vásquez-Correa, J.C., Orozco-Arroyave, J., Bocklet, T., Nöth, E.: Towards an automatic evaluation of the dysarthria level of patients with Parkinson's disease. J. Commun. Disord. **76**, 21–36 (2018)

20. Volkmann, J., Stevens, S., Newman, E.: A scale for the measurement of the psychological magnitude pitch. J. Acoust. Soc. Am. **8**(3), 208–208 (1937)

21. Woldert-Jokisz, B.: Saarbruecken voice database (2007)

22. Wolf, A., Swift, J.B., Swinney, H.L., Vastano, J.A.: Determining lyapunov exponents from a time series. Phys. D **16**(3), 285–317 (1985)

23. Xie, X., Cai, H., Li, C., Ding, F.: A voice disease detection method based on MFCCs and shallow CNN. arXiv preprint arXiv:2304.08708 (2023)

24. Yan, Y., Ahmad, K., Kunduk, M., Bless, D.: Analysis of vocal-fold vibrations from high-speed laryngeal images using a Hilbert transform-based methodology. J. Voice **19**(2), 161–175 (2005)

25. Zakariah, M., Ajmi Alotaibi, Y., Guo, Y., Tran-Trung, K., Elahi, M.M., et al.: An analytical study of speech pathology detection based on MFCC and deep neural networks. Computat. Math. Methods Med. 2022 (2022)

Medical Image Compression Techniques Comparison Using Open-Source Libraries

Juan P. D'Amato[1,2]([✉]) [iD] and Mauricio Oliveto[1]

[1] Pladema Institute, Campus Universitario, UNICEN, Tandil, Argentina
juan.damato@gmail.com
[2] National Scientific and Technical Research Council, CONICET,
Buenos Aires, Argentina
http://www.pladema.net

Abstract. Digital Imaging and Communications in Medicine (DICOM) has become the de facto standard for the exchange and storage of medical images. With the increasing use of imaging modalities and the growing size of image datasets, efficient compression techniques have become essential to address storage, transmission, and processing requirements. This paper provides an overview of DICOM image compression, particularly based on MRI cases, discussing the various techniques and challenges associated with it. It explores both lossless and lossy compression methods (like FIT, that was developed by this group), their impact on image quality, and the trade-offs between compression ratio and performance. Furthermore, it highlights the importance of considering regulatory requirements, interoperability, and the potential impact on clinical workflows when implementing DICOM image compression solutions .

Keywords: Medical image · fast compression · parallel implementation

1 Introduction

Nowadays, more data is captured for every person at any moment. In particular in health, large images of hundreds of megabytes, like Magnetic resonance imaging (MRI) or Computed topographies (CT) are generally used for different clinical studies through different stages. For handling such images from thousands of patients, distributed systems are necessary. Several challenges arise due to the increasing volume and complexity of medical imaging data. Firstly, storage capacity becomes a significant concern as the size of image databases grows exponentially. Scalable and cost-effective storage solutions are needed to accommodate the ever-expanding collection of images. Secondly, efficient indexing and retrieval mechanisms are required to enable quick and accurate access to specific images or patient studies within the database. The challenge lies in developing robust metadata management systems that can handle large-scale indexing and search operations effectively. Thirdly, data integrity and security are critical considerations. Protecting sensitive patient information and ensuring data

J. C. Figueroa-García et al. (Eds.): WEA 2023, CCIS 1928, pp. 139–150, 2023.
https://doi.org/10.1007/978-3-031-46739-4_13

integrity in a large image database require implementing robust access controls, encryption techniques, and mainly backup strategies.

Additionally, image data standardization and interoperability are necessary when integrating images from various imaging modalities, equipment vendors, and healthcare institutions. Harmonizing data formats, ensuring compliance with industry standards such as DICOM, and resolving data inconsistencies become crucial tasks.

Lastly, the computational demands for processing and analyzing large image databases are significant. Efficient computational infrastructure and powerful algorithms are needed for tasks such as image analysis, pattern recognition, and machine learning-based applications. This gains particular interest, when this data is used as input to intelligent processing based on last complex Convolutional models [1].

Overcoming these challenges requires a combination of advanced storage solutions , robust metadata management systems, stringent security measures, data standardization efforts, and powerful computing resources to enable efficient management and utilization of large image databases in the medical domain

1.1   The Role of Data Compression in PACS

Image compression techniques play a vital role in addressing such challenges and they are essential in the medical domain. Picture Archiving and Communication Systems (PACS) and Electronic Health Record (EHR) systems are used in modern healthcare infrastructure. These systems handle large volumes of medical image data and require efficient storage and retrieval mechanisms. In such systems, image compression enables seamless integration of medical images within these systems, ensuring faster access to patient data, improved system performance, and enhanced overall workflow efficiency, even when the systems are deployed in a cloud. Such systems was first presented in [10]. Also, image compression techniques reduce the file sizes, enabling more efficient utilization of storage resources. This is particularly important for long-term archiving, where large volumes of images need to be stored for extended periods [9].

By reducing storage requirements and transmission bandwidth, image compression can lead to cost savings in terms of infrastructure, hardware, and network resources. Efficient utilization of storage capacity and optimized network utilization can result in reduced hardware and maintenance costs, enabling healthcare organizations to allocate resources more effectively.

The HIPAA (Health Insurance Portability and Accountability Act) in the United States, have stringent guidelines regarding the storage, transmission, and protection of patient data, including medical images. Compression techniques can help in ensuring compliance with regulatory requirements by providing secure and efficient methods of handling sensitive patient information.

In summary, image compression is a crucial requirement in the medical domain due to the need for efficient storage, faster transmission, seamless integration with healthcare systems, preservation of diagnostic quality, and enhanced collaboration. Image compression techniques contribute to cost-effective health-care delivery, at the same time it can optimize back-up processes, necessary for keeping data through different years.

For these reasons, an evaluation of different existing algorithms is carried out. Here, we describe different known algorithms and the FIT algorithm that we have developed in different image cases. This document is structured in four sections, as follows: Section 2 summarizes some of the existing works and proposals in the area; Sect. 3 gives a description of the proposed algorithm and its variants; Sect. 4 displays some proofs and examples, and Sect. 5 presents the final conclusion.

2 Background

Digital Imaging and Communications in Medicine (DICOM) is a widely adopted standard for the management, exchange, and storage of medical images and related information, as explained in [11]. It was developed by the American College of Radiology (ACR) and the National Electrical Manufacturers Association (NEMA) to ensure interoperability and facilitate seamless communication between various medical imaging devices and systems. DICOM encompasses a comprehensive set of rules, data structures, and protocols that define how medical images and associated data should be acquired, stored, transmitted, displayed, and archived. It provides a standardized framework for image acquisition, storage, retrieval, and sharing across different healthcare settings and technologies, including radiology, cardiology, pathology, and more.

The key components of DICOM include:

1. Image Data: DICOM defines a standardized format for encoding medical images, allowing for consistent representation across different imaging modalities such as X-ray, computed tomography (CT), magnetic resonance imaging (MRI), ultrasound, and nuclear medicine. It ensures that images contain all metadata, including patient information, acquisition parameters, and clinical annotations.
2. Communication Protocols: DICOM specifies a set of network protocols and services that enable the exchange of medical images and associated information between different compliant devices. These protocols ensure reliable transmission, various data transfer modes (e.g., store, query, retrieve), and mechanisms for network security and authentication.
3. Data Elements and Structured Reporting: DICOM defines a comprehensive data dictionary that includes a standardized set of attributes and elements used to describe medical images, and metadata. This structured approach allows for consistent and meaningful reporting of findings, enabling effective communication among healthcare professionals.
4. Workflow Integration: DICOM facilitates the integration of medical imaging devices and systems with other healthcare ones, such as picture archiving and communication systems (PACS) and electronic health record (EHR) systems. This integration enables seamless access to images and associated data.

https://es.overleaf.com/project/64e89d571c20533b5e2c3a00

As new users demands more accessibility to their own data, systems trends to move to cloud platforms [4,12], where they have to interoperate with other existing devices, users and systems. A typical PACs server architecture is present in Fig. 1

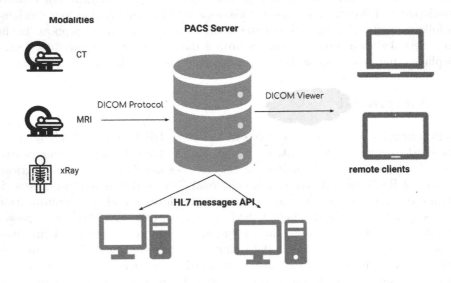

Fig. 1. An architecture of a PACs server

It is important for healthcare professionals, researchers, and technology vendors to understand the principles and capabilities of DICOM to ensure effective utilization of medical imaging data, promote interoperability, and enhance patient care across the healthcare ecosystem. Integrate new algorithms into existing systems, demands to change the data flow and to evaluate the implementation impact. Particularly, the systems should consider:

1. Balancing compression CPU effort and obtained size
2. Performance evaluation and benchmarking
3. Balancing compression ratio and diagnostic accuracy
4. Validation and compliance testing
5. Choosing appropriate compression parameters
6. Understanding the effect of compression on clinical interpretation

2.1 MRI and CT Representation

The largest DICOMs files are those which contains CTs or MRI information. MRI images and CTs are composed of a three-dimensional grid of picture elements, known as voxels. Each voxel represents a specific location within the imaged volume and contains information about the signal intensity at that location. The voxels are arranged in a regular grid pattern along the x, y, and z axes.

The three-dimensional volume of an MRI scan is typically divided into a series of thin two-dimensional slices. These slices represent cross-sectional views of the imaged anatomy. Each slice contains a matrix of voxels, forming a two-dimensional grid. Scanners can acquire images with varying spatial resolutions, depending on factors such as voxel size and field of view (FOV). Higher resolution images contain smaller voxels, resulting in finer anatomical details but potentially requiring more storage space.

The primary information stored in each voxel is the signal intensity, which corresponds to the strength of the signal received at that point in a normalized space. Different tissues exhibit varying signal intensities, forming the basis for tissue contrast in MRI images. Intensity is generally represented as a 16-bit signed value. Generally, common image compressors that do not support that format, so different transformations should be applied.

3   Proposal

Lossless and lossy compression algorithms are two approaches used to reduce the file size of digital data, including images, while aiming to preserve the integrity of the original information. Lossless compression algorithms aim to achieve maximum data reduction without any loss of information. They utilize encoding techniques that allow for perfect reconstruction of the original data. These algorithms identify redundancies and patterns within the data and represent them using more efficient coding schemes. Most known algorithms for images are ZIP or PNG. We also consider ZSTD [3]. Zstandard or ZSTD is a fast lossless compression algorithm developed by Meta, providing high compression ratios using dictionaries. The reference library offers a very wide range of speed/compression trade-off, and is backed by an extremely fast decoder . Dictionaries could be dynamically calculated or pre-computed (specially useful when the data is of the same kind).

On the other hand, lossy compression algorithms prioritize achieving higher compression ratios by selectively discarding or approximating data that is deemed less perceptually significant. These algorithms exploit the limitations of human perception to eliminate or reduce redundant or irrelevant information. Some of the most known lossy algorithms are JPG for images or H264 for video as mentioned in [5].

Additionally, we have developed a lossy algorithm called FITDepth, or FIT, previously presented in [2]. This proposal was initially designed for depth infrared images (like the ones obtained by LIDAR cameras) focused on speed, but also on keeping reasonably good quality reconstructions after encoding. As captured images with these cameras represent a 3D scene, each row of such image is part of an object's surface, like an iso-surface. Our idea is to treat each depth image row separately and to describe it as a set of polynomial functions. The proposed algorithm evaluates each pixel in a sequential way, from left to right, and represented as splines. Each separated spline is evaluated to find the parameters of the function that best fits the pixels.

The difference between the original image, and the one obtained after decompression using a lossy method is called "residual". This residual is a matrix of the same size as the original image, with negative and positive values. For increasing the quality of the reconstruction, the residual could be preserved in a secondary file, either in its original precision or reduced by a quantization factor.

Independently of the algorithm used, the PACs server should include both operations: encryption and decryption, either when reading a file or when storing. Such scheme is presented in Fig. 2

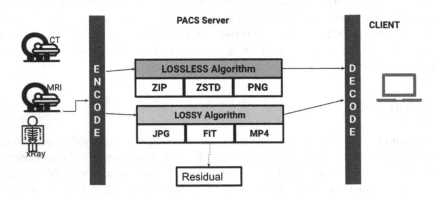

Fig. 2. Different algorithms available for compression

3.1   Image Compression Techniques Applied to MRI and CT Using FIT

For image compression, there are plenty of solutions and algorithms that can be used every day. These algorithms can be characterized in "Lossless" or "lossy" compression. The most common lossless Compression are based on one of this lists: Run-length encoding (RLE), Huffman coding or Predictive encoding techniques. On the other hand, lossy compression is based on transform-based methods (e.g., Discrete Cosine Transform), Wavelet-based methods, Fractal-based methods among others.

Our algorithm, FIT, is supposed to be implemented using parallel technology. For this purpose, we have an own scheme that handles the process memory, as it is explained our work. For each spline, a polynomial regression model in a general form is used as a fitting function. The vector of estimated polynomial regression coefficients is obtained using the "ordinary least squares estimation". The difference between estimation and real image is stored in a separated structure.

3.2   Lossless Compression Basis

To get the best compression rate and performance, we propose to apply a dictionary-based compression algorithm (This step could also be applied in lossy compression). In our implementation, the open-source library of [3] is used.

For keeping a high framerate, our proposal is to pre-train this algorithm with several compressed images using our algorithm to generate a default dictionary file with existing library tools. Later, during encoding—in case this step is enabled—,this computed dictionary is used. Using this pre-trained dictionary really improves the speed (it is faster) and the compression size (output is smaller) in both cases.

3.3   Lossy Image Compression Basis and Residual

JPEG and JPEG2000 are the most known image compression standards that employ different compression techniques to reduce the file size of digital images while balancing image quality [6]. In the case of JPEG, it utilizes a lossy compression algorithm based on the Discrete Cosine Transform (DCT). The image is divided into blocks, and the DCT is applied to each block to transform it into frequency coefficients. Quantization is then performed, which discards some of the less visually significant coefficients based on a specified quantization table. By selectively discarding coefficients, JPEG achieves higher compression ratios but introduces some loss of image quality. JPEG offers high compression ratios at the cost of some loss in image quality. Our algorithm FIT, also is considered as a "lossy image compressor".

For image sequences, a H264 video encoder based could also be useful. Such method, based on temporal block encoding, could not only compress a frame (intra frame) but also consecutive frames (inter frames). In all the cases, for preserving the most data possible, the difference between the original image and the compressed one, is also stored, called as "residual". This residual is stored using a linear fixed quantization (dividing each element by a constant) and also compressed using the ZSTD algorithm.

4   Results and Discussion

In order to compare the proposed methods of compression, ten (10) different MRI cases, were used based on the [8] database. Each sequence is composed of more than 150 frames of 512×512 resolution. All of them were up body regions, used for coVid influence detection. For measuring the quality of the encoding/decoding method, the peak signal-to-noise ratio (PSNR) was used. The PSNR, that has also been proposed in most of other related works, is defined as Eq. 1

$$\text{PSNR} = 10 \log_{10} \frac{(2^d - 1)^2 WH}{\sum_{i=1}^{W} \sum_{j=1}^{H} (p[i,j] - p'[i,j])^2} \qquad (1)$$

where d is the bit depth of pixel, W is the image width, H is the image height, and $p[i,j]$, $p'[i,j]$ is the ith-row jth-column pixel in the original and compressed image, respectively.

Moreover, the compression rate - as the comparison between the original size and the one resulting after applying the method - was also used. The third metric used was the Frames-per-second that can be reached while encoding. In addition to our implementation, the same sequences were compressed using an intra-coded mode of JPEG2000 coding standards, both in lossless and lossy modes. The PNG format, which is one of the fastest formats, was used. Finally, Jasper libraries were used for JPEG2000 [7]. All tests were run strictly on parallel CPU.

4.1 Lossless Compression Comparison

With regards to performance, the benchmark was run on a Intel i7 12650 with 32 GB RAM laptop. Such device was tested with 100 frames, and the average times were obtained. The lossless algorithms tested in this case were PNG, a typical ZIP and the ZSTD, like shown in Fig. 3.

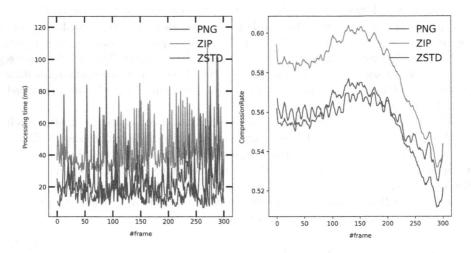

Fig. 3. (Left) Processing time per frame (right) Compression rate

Here, we can observe that ZSTD seems to be faster than the other methods.

4.2 Lossy Compression Comparison

Then, lossy compression algorithms, like FIT, JPG and MP4 were evaluated and presented in Fig. 4 using the same data.

In this case, it was observed that compression rate of FIT algorithm slighty change in the middle planes of the volumetric image. Observing in detail some sample planes (0, 150 and 290), rendered in Fig. 5, we can observe that the image corresponding to plane 150 has much more information than the other 2. So, it can be resumed that this algorithms depends on the amount of surfaces (it was also discussed in the original paper)

On the other hand, MP4 and JPG works relatively stable, as it always encode the image in the same format. There observed some peaks that are related to

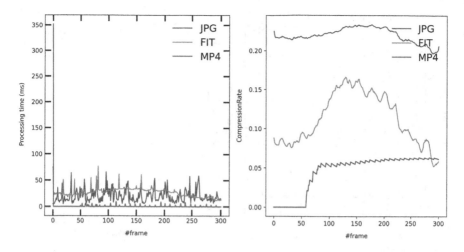

Fig. 4. (Left) Processing time per frame (right) Compression rate

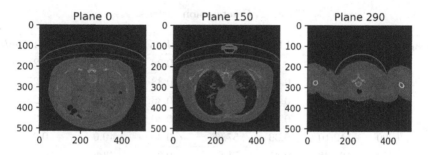

Fig. 5. Different planes

the time the files are written to the hard disk. This could be improved in the future using non-blocking writing.

Finally, we evaluate decompression time using Residual component and quality metric based on PSNR. As it can be observed in Fig. 6 , FIT and MP4 are very fast for decoding, but they have lower quality (a good expected quality in such images should be above 40).

4.3   Evaluation of Multiple Images

At a later stage, several images were processed using the lossy approach with several configurations. Residual was quantized using a 128 factor. All of these results are presented in Table 1.

For comparing the lossy version, the linear combination of SPEED, compression RATE and PSNR was used, keeping the lower values at their best. It was observed that, in homogeneous scenes (like 1, 2, 3 and 8), the JPEG2000 format tends to work better than our algorithm. In all other cases (scenes 0, 4, 5, 6 and 7), our algorithm worked better in producing a better reconstruction quality (PSNR) and a minimal compression rate.

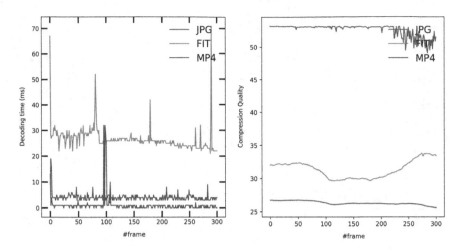

Fig. 6. (Left) Decompression time per frame (right) Image quality

Table 1. Compression metrics.

Image	Planes	FIT_{CTime}	FIT_{Rate}	JPG_{CTime}	JPG_{Rate}	$MP4_{CTime}$	$MP4_{Rate}$
1	301	91.601	0.32	53.92	0.28	20.8	0.21
2	200	140.05	0.48	52.88	0.38	31.3	0.27
3	200	129.26	0.43	70.68	0.36	36.3	0.25
4	270	112.85	0.35	61.65	0.30	35.0	0.22
5	290	112.10	0.36	57.66	0.30	40.0	0.22
6	213	123.38	0.41	71.65	0.35	43.5	0.25
7	249	136.69	0.47	57.77	0.38	48.3	0.27
8	301	100.98	0.33	40.99	0.29	39.2	0.22
9	256	104.00	0.36	39.31	0.29	32.9	0.21

As it can be observed, the performance of the depth coding algorithm showed better outcomes than the other methods. The key is to choose a good compression library. No deeper analysis was carried out.

In all cases, the linear fit reached top-frame rate. When residual was added, the performance fell dramatically. This happened because ZSTD has a one-thread implementation. When a higher polynomial function was evaluated, the gain in quality was not that notable with respect to the loss of speed. Our algorithm works in an asymmetrical way (since decoding is about 10 times faster than encoding). This is a good feature in algorithms of said kind, especially when decoding occurs in a low-profile hardware or when it is necessary to handle many cameras.

4.4   Decompression Time

One key factor in PACs systems is lattency, what it means, the time measure between the moment an image is requested unitl the time it is given to the final user. For such reason, decompression and output format are fundamental. That is why we also evaluate the decompression step, as it is presented in Table 2.

Table 2. Decompression metrics.

Image	Planes	FIT_{DTime}	FIT_{PSNR}	JPG_{DTime}	JPG_{PSNR}	$MP4_{DTime}$	$MP4_{PSNR}$
1	301	26.57	54.53	4.11	56.61	2.03	54.65
2	200	29.82	55.27	4.91	56.56	1.07	54.39
3	200	29.75	55.19	5.68	55.33	1.35	53.28
4	270	29.94	54.76	4.78	56.75	0.74	54.64
5	290	28.08	54.69	5.34	56.66	1.01	54.57
6	213	27.51	54.99	5.54	56.89	1.79	54.72
7	249	29.86	55.42	4.47	56.99	1.00	54.70
8	301	27.28	54.72	4.18	55.25	0.86	53.30
9	256	28.25	54.76	4.01	56.75	0.99	54.64

It was observed that MP4 keeps a good balance between quality and performance.

5   Conclusions

In this work, the evaluation of different compression algorithms was presented. The main idea was to evaluate different metrics, such as processing time, quality and compression rate for taking into account in PACs. Since DICOM images have critical information, it was very important to preserve as much features as possible. Also, an own proposed lossy compression method was tested. The method was then compared to JPEG and MP4 formats.

It was found that a lossy compression algorithm could be used with residual storing, having a perfect balance between speed and compression rate. Despite our best efforts—and contrary to earlier results—,there is still more work to do in the evaluation of different configurations and in many different situations. Our next work will explore the implementation of such methods in GPU to get a better speed-up and defining a unique descriptor for automatically parametrizing the algorithms, balancing between quality and speed. Also, it would be interesting to use generative machine-learning models (GANs) to complement the compression strategies.

References

1. Hostin, M., Ogier, A., Nicolas, P., Bellemare, M.: Combining loss functions for deep learning bladder segmentation on dynamic MRI, pp. 1–4 (2021). https://doi.org/10.1109/BHI50953.2021.9508559
2. D'Amato, J.P.: FitDepth: fast and lite 16-bit depth image compression algorithm. J Image Video Proc. **2023**, 5 (2023). https://doi.org/10.1186/s13640-023-00606-z
3. Kucherawy, M.: (Facebook), Zstandard Compression and the 'application/zstd' Media Type. https://datatracker.ietf.org/doc/html/rfc8878
4. Yan, C., Gong, B., Wei, Y., Gao, Y.: Deep multi-view enhancement hashing for image retrieval. IEEE Trans. Pattern Anal. Mach. Intell. **43**(4), 1445–1451 (2020)
5. Wang, B., et al.: Highly parallel HEVC decoding for heterogeneous systems with CPU and GPU. Sign. Process. Image Commun. **62**, 93–105 (2017). https://doi.org/10.1016/j.image.2017.12.009
6. Yan, C., et al.: A highly parallel framework for HEVC coding unit partitioning tree decision on many-core processors. IEEE Signal Proc. Letters **21–5**, 573–576 (2014). https://doi.org/10.1109/LSP.2014.2310494
7. Skodras, A., Christopoulos, C., Ebrahimi, T., The, J.P.E.G.: still image compression standard. IEEE Signal Process. Mag. **18**(5), 36–58 (2000). https://doi.org/10.1109/79.952804
8. Paiva, O.: 2020. CORONACASES.ORG - Helping Radiologists To Help People In More Than 100 Countries! — Coronavirus Cases. [online] Coronacases.org
9. França, R.P., Monteiro, A.C.B., Arthur, R., Iano, Y.: An overview of the impact of PACS as health informatics and technology e-health in healthcare management. Cogn. Syst. Signal Process. **2022**, 101–128 (2021). https://doi.org/10.1016/B978-0-12-824410-4.00007-6
10. Kimura, M.: PACS and patient data management systems. Comput. Methods Programs Biomed. **36**(2–3), 107–112 (1991). https://doi.org/10.1016/0169-2607(91)90056-y
11. López, D., Barreras, L., Orozco, A.: Implementación de estándares DICOM SR y HL7 CDA para la creación y edición de informes de estudios imagenológicos. Revista Cubana de Informática Médica. **6**, 71–86 (2014)
12. Kawa, J., et al.: Design and Implementation of a cloud PACS architecture. Sensors. **22**, 8569 (2022). https://doi.org/10.3390/s22218569

Implementation of a Reinforced Learning Algorithm in a Simulation Environment for Path Planning of a Robot Manipulator with 3 Degrees of Freedom

W. Fernando Latorre[1]($\boxtimes$), F. Camilo Castro[2], Y. Patricia Caviativa[1,2],
J. Carlos Amaya[1,2], and F. Alberto Sanz[1,2]

[1] Universidad Manuela Beltrán, Bogotá, Colombia
`fernado.latorre@academia.umb.edu.co`
[2] vicerrectoría de investigación, San Pedro, Costa Rica
`{Fabian,Castro}@docentes.umb.edu.co`

Abstract. Nowadays, robots are trying to become more and more intelligent by using more modern algorithms than those previously used based on traditional mathematics. Therefore, a robotic manipulator can learn from the experience it gains from the environment. Reinforcement learning will allow a robotic device to learn based on its experience, every time it performs a movement it will keep a record which it will compare in a future action to determine if it is a correct way to reach the target or if it finds a better way to do it. This will make the robot more efficient as it will search for an optimal way to perform its trajectory. To implement this reinforced learning, trajectory planning will be used to monitor the different movements of a three-degree-of-freedom manipulator robot in a workspace. These trajectories will be generated according to the actions performed by the robot, taking into account its workspace, the dimensions of the robotic manipulator and its maximum range of motion in a predetermined area. The trajectories obtained will be saved and will support learning to move, i.e., the robot will have the ability to analyze and compare each trajectory, determining which is the most optimal to perform its programmed task and then execute it.

Keywords: Artificial intelligence · path planning · reinforcement learning · robot manipulator

1 Introduction

In recent years the use of robotic devices has increased in different areas, some of these are industrial automation and medicine, this in order to reduce errors in jobs that require high precision and have a greater capacity for performance and increasing complexity in their tasks having to increase the level of computational intelligence to these systems for decision making and responses to the functions

vicerrectoría de investigación UMB.

J. C. Figueroa-García et al. (Eds.): WEA 2023, CCIS 1928, pp. 151–162, 2023.
https://doi.org/10.1007/978-3-031-46739-4_14

to be performed. Robot manipulators have provided a great help in different types of jobs that depend on trajectory planning of the robotic manipulator and its configuration of algorithms based on traditional mathematical models of direct and inverse kinematics and constantly require human supervision. Model-free algorithms as reinforced learning avoid the need to model the environment or dynamics by learning a direct policy mapping between states and actions [1]. Policy is learned through experience, so we consider model-free methods to be "experience-based". Model-based methods typically learn a dynamic model and reward function to predict the next state and next reward given the current state and a potential next action. These results can be used sequentially to predict future expected rewards for a set of actions [3].

This research is integrated into a macro project of the Universidad Manuela Beltrán UMB, which focuses on a surgical robot in assisting mastoidectomy for trajectory planning in the drilling process in the first phase of the surgical process. This project is limited to the simulation of a robotic manipulator using reinforced learning algorithms in order to learn movements that generate trajectories through experience gained from the environment and free from traditional models such as direct and inverse kinematics. To select the reinforced learning algorithm in the robotic simulation environment, the behaviour of three algorithms DQN, A2C, PPO implemented in the open AI gymnasium library on the Lunar platform is studied and once the algorithm to be used is selected, it is evaluated in the robotic manipulator simulator in a virtual environment comparing its performance with the data obtained to achieve the desired movements and configurations.

2   Background

2.1   Preliminaries

We study reinforced learning applied to path planning in three degrees of freedom manipulator robot, where the problem has a closed solution trying to give a solution with deterministic policy gradient algorithms, we selected three algorithms of this family for its simplicity and easy programming to interact with a robotics simulator (GAZEBO).

Deep Deterministic Policy Gradient (DDPG). Is an algorithm that simultaneously learns a Q-function and a policy. It uses data outside the policy and the Bellman equation to learn the Q-function and uses the Q-function to learn the policy [5]. This approach is closely related to Q-learning and is motivated in the same way: if you know the optimal action-value $Q^*(s, a)$ function then in any given state $a^*(S)$, the optimal action can be found by solving:

$$L(\theta, D) = E_{(s,a,s',d)} = \left[(Q_\theta(s,a)) - (r + \gamma(1-d))max_{a'}Q_\theta(s', a')^2\right] \quad (1)$$

DDPG interleaves the learning of an approximator of $Q^*(s, a)$ with the learning of an approximator of $a^*(s)$, and does so in a way that is specifically tailored for continuous action space environments. Starting point for learning an approximator of $Q^*(s,a)$ Suppose the approximator is a neural network $Q_\theta(s,a)$, with theta- parameters, and we have collected a set D of (s',r',a',d') transitions (where d indicates whether the state s' is terminal). We can set up a mean squared Bellman error function (MSBE)Q_θ, which tells us approximately how close it is to satisfying the Bellman equation:

$$a^* = arg\max_a Q^*(s,a) \tag{2}$$

Pseudocode

Algorithm 1. Deep Deterministic Policy Gradient.

1: Input: initial policy parameters θ, Q-function parameters ϕ, empty replay buffer D

2: Set target parameters equal to main parameters
$\theta_{\mathbf{targ}} \leftarrow \theta$, $\phi_{\mathbf{targ}} \leftarrow \phi$
3: **repeat**
4:    Observe state s and select action
$a = clip(\mu_\theta(s) + \epsilon, a_{Low}, a_{High})$ where $\epsilon \sim \mathbf{N}$
5:    Execute a in the environment
6:    Observe next state s', reward, r, and done signal d to indicate whether s' is terminal
7:    IF s' is terminal, reset environment state.
8:    **if** it's time to update **then**
9:       **for** however many updates **do**
10:          Randomly sample a batch of transitions
$B = (s,a,r,s',d)$ from D
11:          Compute targets

$$y(r,s',d) = r + \gamma(1-d)Q_{\phi targ}(s', \mu_{\theta targ}(s'))$$

12:          Update Q-function by one step of gradient descent using

$$\nabla_\phi \frac{1}{|B|} \sum_{(s,a,r,s',d)} (Q_\phi(s,a) - y(r,s',d))^2$$

13:          Update policy by one step of gradient ascent using

$$\nabla_\phi \frac{1}{|B|} \sum_{(s \in B)} Q_\phi(s, \mu_\theta(s))$$

14:          Update target networks with

$$\phi_{targ} \leftarrow \rho\phi_{targ} + (1-\rho)\phi$$
$$\theta_{targ} \leftarrow \rho\theta_{targ} + (1-\rho)\theta$$

15:       **end for**
16:    **end if**
17: **until** convergence

Asynchronous Methods for Deep Reinforcement Learning (A2C).
The general architecture of critical actor reinforcement learning performs asynchronous training of learning agents in a distributed environment, in each process contains an actor acting from its own environment, an independent replay memory and a learner that samples data from the independent replay memory and a learner that samples data from the replay memory and calculates gradient loss with respect to the policy parameters, the gradients are sent asynchronously to a central parameter server to update a central copy of the model [2].

Pseudocode

Algorithm 2 Asynchronous advantage actor-criti for each actor-learner thread

---

1: //Assume global shared θ, θ^-, and counter $T = 0$.
2: Initialize thread step counter $t \leftarrow 0$
3: Initialize network wweights $\theta^- \leftarrow \theta$
4: Initialize network gradients $d\theta \leftarrow 0$
5: Get initial state s
6: **repeat**
7:     Take action a with $\epsilon - greedy$ policy based on $Q(s, a; \theta)$
8:     Receive new state s' and reward r

$$y = \begin{cases} r & for\ terminal\ s' \\ r + \gamma max_{a'} Q(s', a'; \theta^-) & for\ non\ terminal\ s' \end{cases}$$

   Accumulate gradients wrt $\theta : d\theta \leftarrow d\theta + \frac{\partial(y - q(s,a;\theta))^2}{\partial\theta}$
9:     $s = s'$
10:    $T \leftarrow T + 1\ and\ t \leftarrow t + 1$
11:    **if** T mod $I_{targ} == 0$ **then**
12:        Update the target network $\theta^- \leftarrow \theta$
13:    **end if**
14:    **if** t mod $I_{AsyncUpdate} == 0$ or s is terminal **then**
15:        Perform asynchronous update of θ using $d\theta$
16:        Clear gradients $d\theta \leftarrow 0$.
17:    **end if**
18: **until** $T > T_{max}$

Proximal Policy Optimization Algorithms (PPO). This algorithm combines ideas of A2C (having multiple actors) and TRPO (this one uses a region of truth to improve the actor). The main idea is that after an update, the new policy should not be too far from the old policy. For that, PPO uses clipping to avoid too big an update. For the implementation of the PPO, an automatic differentiation is used where the loss and multiple steps of ascent of stochastic gradients are built for each objective. Most techniques for calculating variance advantage function estimators reduce the learned state value function $V(s)$; e.g., generalized advantage estimation or finite element estimators. When using a neural network architecture that shares parameters between a policy and a function value we must use a loss function that combines the policy value and the function value and the entropy bonus can be increased to ensure sufficient exploration. The following mathematical model combines the loss and the value function that is maximized at each iteration [4].

$$L_t^{CLIP+VF+S}(\theta) =$$
$$\hat{E}_t \left[L_t^{CLIP+VF+S}(\theta)_{C1} L_t^{VF}(\theta) +_{C2} S \left[\Pi_\theta \right] (s_t) \right] \tag{3}$$

where L^{CLIP} is the loss, C_1, C_2 are coefficients, and S denotes an entropy bonus, and L_t^{VF} is a squared-error loss $(V_\theta(s_t - V_t^{targ})^2$

Algorithm 3 PPO, Actor-Critic Style

1: **for** iteration=1,2,.... **do**
2:      **for** actor=1,2,....,N **do**
3:          Run policy $\pi_{\theta_{old}}$ environment for T timesteps
4:          Compute advantage estimates $\hat{A}_1, ..., \hat{A}_t$
5:      **end for**
6:      Optimize surrogate L wrt θ,with K epochs and minibatch size $M \leq NT$
7:      $\theta_{old} \leftarrow \theta$
8: **end for**

---

3   Implementation Algorithms

For the development of the research, different reinforcement learning algorithms are tested by performing simulations with the lunar Lander environment to determine their operation, iterations and rewards generated in each one of them. The DQN, A2C and PPO algorithms are used; which are implemented in the selected environment where 3000 iterations are generated, generating a reward for each one and thus determine its operation and effectiveness.

3.1   DQN Algorithm in Lunar Lander Environment

The DQN algorithm is used in the lunar Lander environment, generating 3000 iterations hoping to obtain the highest possible reward, a process that lasted 40 min for training. This algorithm will make several simulations where the ship will have to land in the correct area, if it does, it will have a positive reward, otherwise a negative reward. This algorithm will learn from the simulations carried out previously to increase its positive reward until it achieves its objective, learning to land in the selected area (Fig. 1)

At the end of the training of this algorithm, the learning is obtained in the 3000 iterations carried out.

The training the algorithm obtains negative rewards in the range of 500 to 800 where it has not learned to land in the middle of the two flags.

Fig. 1. (a) Release cost (b) WIP-holding cost

3.2   A2C Algorithm in Lunar Lander Environment

The A2C algorithm uses actor-critical algorithms for its simulations, in this case the luna Lander environment will be used to carry out the simulation with 3000 iterations where the ship must land in the assigned area modifying the network through the results obtained in its past iterations. This training process took approximately 30 min to be able to perform 4 simulations at the same time, obtaining 4 different rewards.

This algorithm provides us with a better training speed, but it is observed that the rewards that are generated do not reach their maximum value and it does not achieve its main objective of obtaining and maintaining the highest possible reward. Hence the name Actor-Critic where Policy Network will act as the main hero and the State-Value Network as the critic. If you have read about GANs, this concept may sound a bit familiar where we have a generator and discriminator involved in an adversarial system.

3.3   PPO Algorithm in Lunar Lander Environment

The PPO algorithm is used in the lunar Lander environment, generating 3000 iterations hoping to obtain the highest possible reward. This training is achieved in a time of 30 min by being able to perform 4 simulations at the same time. This algorithm will do several simulations with not so big updates where the ship will have to land in the correct zone, if it does it will have a positive reward, otherwise a negative reward. This algorithm through each update will change its policy until it achieves its objective.

He rewards generated by the PPO algorithm in some iterations reach their maximum value, but do not maintain it, causing their next iteration to get a different and lower reward. At the end of the training he does not obtain or keep the highest possible reward

4   Choice of Algorithm to Implement

When carrying out the simulations with these three algorithms, the DQN algorithm is selected, which with the same number of iterations carried out in comparison with the A2C and PPO algorithms achieves the highest reward in a smaller number of attempts, thus demonstrating that this algorithm provides us with a greater effectiveness, learning from its previous iterations and using this information to maintain optimal performance. The DQN algorithm offers us fast and reliable learning since approximately from iteration 800 it achieves its maximum reward and maintains it until the end of the training, achieving the final objective, which in the Lunar Lander environment is to make the spacecraft land in the designated area (Fig. 2).

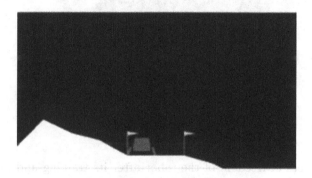

Fig. 2. reward 4 PPO algorithm.

5   Implementation of the Selected Algorithm

For the implementation of the DQN algorithm, a robotic model provided by the gazebo software is used, which allows it to be programmed and configured as needed. This robotic prototype has 6 degrees of freedom, but for the implementation of the DQN algorithm only 3 degrees of freedom will be used, which will be the rotation of the base, joint 1 of the robot and joint 2 of the robot. This the robot comes configured in an initial vertical position and is located on a table simulating a real work environment (Fig. 3).

For the programming of the DQN algorithm, the OpenAI Python libraries are used, which allow the stabilization and configuration of robotic models by reducing errors or noisy performance generally produced in any simulation. The Pytorch learning library is also used, which is used in robotics applications for device configuration and implementation of reinforcement learning algorithms thanks to its possibility of creating data layers and architectures through the Python programming language.

This programming allows the robotic manipulator to learn through his experience using the DQN reinforcement learning algorithm (see annex E) reaching the desired point thanks to his training through rewards; getting your greatest value to achieve your goal.In the following image you can see the position of the

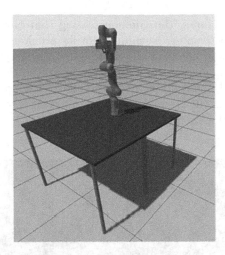

Fig. 3. Gazebo robotic prototype.

3 selected degrees of freedom of the robot after its training and location selection, which is achieved using the DQN algorithm that generates the different trajectories necessary for the robot to go to the position assigned (Table 1).

Table 1. Degree of freedom configuration.

Position	Base Joint	Joint 1	Joint 2
Figure 15	0°	90°	0°
Figure 16	90°	90°	0°
Figure 17	−90°	90°	0°
Figure 18	−160°	90°	0°
Figure 19	0°	0°	−90°
Figure 20	0°	−90°	−90°
Figure 21	−90°	−90°	−90°
Figure 22	−45°	−45°	−45°
Figure 23	90°	−45°	90°
Figure 24	−30°	30°	−30°

When carrying out the trajectory planning with the DQN algorithm and after its training, it gives us the following relationship of reward, loss, average Q and epsilon corresponding to the movement generated by the robot (Figs. 4, 5, 6).

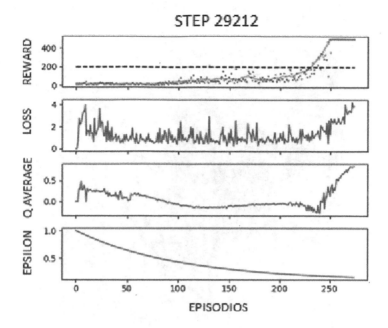

Fig. 4. Training rewards.

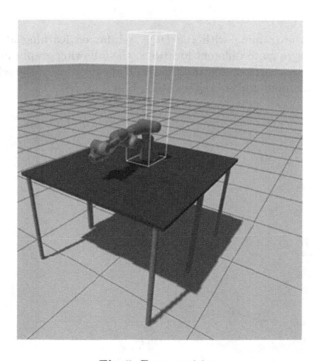

Fig. 5. Front position.

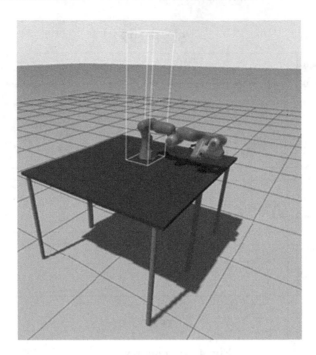

Fig. 6. Position to the right.

At the end of the training with the DQN reinforced learning algorithm and getting the robot to go to different locations, the following graphs are generated where the trajectory curve made and the speed of execution of the selected joints of the robotic manipulator are represented (Figs. 7, 8, 9)).

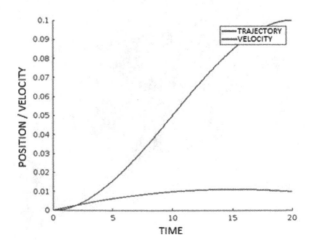

Fig. 7. Base joint.

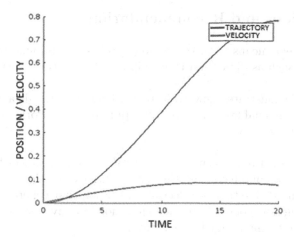

Fig. 8. Joint 1.

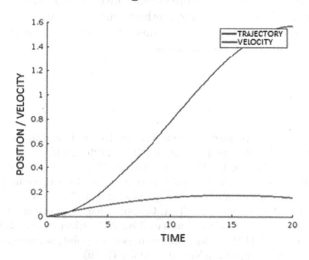

Fig. 9. Joint 2.

6   Analysis and Interpretation of the Results

By using the DQN reinforcement learning algorithm, it is evident that it is possible for a robotic manipulator through trajectory planning training to be able to perform movements through his experience with previous movements, and learn from his mistakes; this is reflected in the reward obtained by the robotic manipulator in fig. 39. The data obtained in the robot simulation reflects the information obtained when the DQN algorithm was simulated in a Lunar Lander virtual environment where it also obtained a positive reward and learned to get to the right place. The ability of the robotic manipulator to reach the desired position in a short time with a stable speed is also evidenced, as seen in Figs. 29, 30 and 31 .

7   Conclusions and Recommendations

There are different means of programming a robotic manipulator, be it traditional methods such as direct and inverse kinematics or trajectory planning.

This work demonstrates how trajectory planning through a reinforcement learning algorithm enables a robotic manipulator to perform a certain task through its learning.

There are different reinforcement learning algorithms with which training can be carried out to accomplish a certain task. You have to select the appropriate one for what is needed, either by selecting the action that generates the greatest value, calculating how good it is to take an action in a given state or by limiting the change made to the policy in each state.

Just as there are methods of direct and inverse kinematics or trajectory planning, greater advances and new methods for the configuration of robotic manipulators will emerge every day, we must be aware of these advances to use the most effective according to our needs.

References

1. Engstrom, L., et al.: Implementation matters in deep policy gradients: a case study on PPO and TRPO. arXiv preprint arXiv:2005.12729 (2020)
2. Kwon, Y., Saltaformaggio, B., Kim, I.L., Lee, K.H., Zhang, X., Xu, D.: A2c: self destructing exploit executions via input perturbation. In: Proceedings of The Network and Distributed System Security Symposium (2017)
3. Li, X., Chen, G., Wu, G., Sun, Z., Chen, G.: Research on multi-agent D2D communication resource allocation algorithm based on A2C. Electronics **12**(2), 360 (2023)
4. Wijmans, E., et al.: DD-PPO: learning near-perfect pointgoal navigators from 2.5 billion frames. arXiv preprint arXiv:1911.00357 (2019)
5. Zhang, R., Xiong, K., Lu, Y., Gao, B., Fan, P., Letaief, K.B.: Joint coordinated beamforming and power splitting ratio optimization in mu-miso SWIPT-enabled HetNets: a multi-agent DDQN-based approach. IEEE J. Sel. Areas Commun. **40**(2), 677–693 (2021)

Machine Learning for Rice (*Oryza sativa* L.) Phenological Identification

Martha P. Valbuena-Gaona[1]([⊠]) and Laura A. Valbuena-Gaona[2]

[1] Department of Research and Development, Procalculo, Bogota, Colombia
mvalbuena@procalculo.com
[2] Department of Agronomy, National University of Colombia, Bogota, Colombia

Abstract. Rice is one of the most important crops worldwide because of its nutritional value. Panama is one of the highest rice consumers in the world and the second-largest producer in Central America. Crop phenology is correlated with yield, so it is important to monitor it in a decision-making system. For that, machine learning has shown good results in monitoring crops, so this work aims to identify the phenological state of rice crops using machine learning.

The project was developed in Alanje, Panama, where local farmers collected phenological data for five months. The satellite data was obtained from Planet Scope, and images contained 8 bands and 3 m resolution. In addition, using the bands, spectral indexes were calculated. All data was processed using the Pycaret library in Python. The spectral indexes were eliminated from the final model because of their large correlation with bands. After running the automation function in Pycaret, Linear Discriminant Analysis was obtained as the best model for our data with 96.11% accuracy. Planet Scope images are optimal for monitoring phenology in rice crops due to their high resolution and the homogeneity of rice crops.

Keywords: Artificial intelligence · neural network · Panama · Planet Scope · spectral imagery · spectral signature

1 Introduction

Rice (Oryza sativa L.) is an Asian semi-aquatic grass and one of the most important crops worldwide because of its nutritional value, supplying more than 20% of the calories consumed by the population [1, 2]. Panama has one of the highest rice consumption in the world with 74 kg/year per capita; so it is not surprising that it is the second-largest producer in Central America, after Costa Rica, responsible for 22% of the region's rice production [3]. One of the most critical limitations in crop production, including rice, is the lack of decision-making, depending on changing external conditions like climate, soils, fertilizers availability, and others [4]; phenological phases in rice define yield because of the correlation between growth and development and respiration and photosynthesis taxes, that leads to dry matter accumulation [5]. Phenology causes changes in the plant, and as it changes, so do its requirements, so it would be essential in a

© The Author(s), under exclusive license to Springer Nature Switzerland AG 2023
J. C. Figueroa-García et al. (Eds.): WEA 2023, CCIS 1928, pp. 163–172, 2023.
https://doi.org/10.1007/978-3-031-46739-4_15

decision-making process for scheduling applications, processes, and activities related to the crop [4]. Climate pressure in crop growing has been studied for several years, being able to advance or delay harvests depending on factors like temperature, precipitation, photoperiod, and CO_2 concentration [6].

Taking into account the climate change conditions, it is necessary to establish a monitoring system, to identify the crop's phenological state and be able to define proper management.

Machine learning, as its name implies, is a science field from artificial intelligence that gives machines the ability to learn from data and improve over time without being strictly programmed [7]; this has allowed machine learning to be used in many fields such as agriculture, due to its versatility, ease of use and accuracy. For example, Suchithra and Pai (2020) designed a classification model, with an accuracy of approximately 90%, to predict soil parameters to reduce fertilization inputs [8]. Alagumariappan, et al. (2020) created a real-time decision-support system based on a camera sensor to detect plant disease in the field, with a sensibility of 95% with an extreme learning machine classifier [9]. Badage (2018) generated a monitoring system for early disease detection using remote sensing images and machine learning [10]. In addition, several works linked machine-learning processes to the phenological state in crops like Guo, et al. (2021) which designed a model to predict yield based on climatic, geographic, and phenology variables in rice crops, including sowing, emergence, three leaves, transplanting, turning green, tiller, booting, heading, flowering, milky and mature; lighting the importance of phenology in crop production [5]. Dai, et al. (2019) created a model for leaf unfolding date prediction under global warming conditions [11]. Czernecki, et al., (2018) created a phenological phases monitoring model using satellite (Spectroradiometer-derived products) and meteorological datasets, the phenological phases were related to the BBCH scale [12]. These works also show the usefulness of machine learning in monitoring phenology and create the necessity of improving models to detect changes in phenology for decision-making.

Taking into account the above, this paper seeks to highlight the role of machine learning techniques on the study of plant growth and development, creating a model to identify the phenological state of rice crops. In addition, the results of the model are presented in a georeferenced visualization in order to optimize area-based decision-making.

2   Methods

Farmers in the Alanje region of Panama collected data on crop yields over five months. Each crop had different phenology due to varying sowing dates. Table 1 displays the number of samples taken in the field per phenological state.

PlanetScope is a satellite constellation that captures everyday imagery of each point in the world. The third generation of PlanetScope sensors, known as SuperDove or PSB.SD, is currently in orbit and is producing daily imagery with 8 spectral bands (coastal blue, blue, green 1, green 2, red, yellow, red edge, and near-infrared) with a spatial resolution of three meters. These satellites were launched in early 2020 and started producing imagery in mid-March 2020 [13].

Table. 1. Number of samples taken per phenological state.

CLASS	SAMPLES NUMBER
3 weeks	31
8 weeks	23
10 weeks	31
12 weeks	30
15 weeks	31
17 weeks	15
Water	30
Buildings	32
Clouds	31

For this investigation, one Planet imagery per phenological state was downloaded. These images were powered by Planet and distributed by Procalculo. Figure 1 shows the spectral resolution of Planet Imagery taken by the satellite Super Dove.

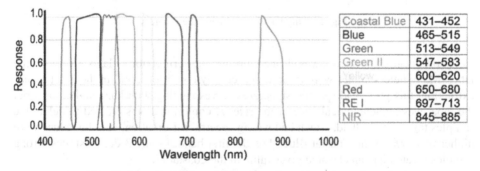

Fig. 1. Spectral signature of rice crop from PlanetScope image.

The points taken on the field match with a pixel of the Planet Imagery. In the software ArcGIS Pro, with the tool known as "Multi Values to Point" which extracts the value of each pixel in the eight bands, the graphic generated is called Spectral Signature. The electromagnetic spectrum interacts with matter in a balanced relationship that indicates that the light reaching a body will be proportional to the light that is transmitted, absorbed, and reflected in the body per unit of time [14]. The Spectral Signature comes from the measurements of the relationship between the incident and reflected radiation flux and the electromagnetic spectrum longitude. Each material or land cover has a specific spectral signature. For this reason, the use of spectroscopy is helpful in areas like agriculture, geology, and environmental studies.

The first step consisted of the generation of training data. The data acquired on the field corresponds to the phenological states of the rice. In addition, other land covers like forests, clouds, water bodies, and buildings were detected in the area of interest. To improve the results of the classification, many samples of each land cover were extracted and incorporated into the samples for the training and testing model. Figure 2 displays the samples located in the images.

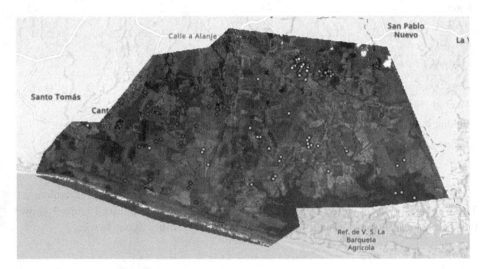

Fig. 2. Samples located inside the imagery

Subsequently, the dataset was cleaned through the verification of land cover with the label. Many field samples were taken under cloudy conditions, and in the pixel values extraction, this point had spectral signatures corresponding with haze and clouds, but the label was a phenological state of the rice. A conditional was created to delete the samples taken on the field, which had wrong spectral information, and the values were higher than 600 in the Coastal Blue, thus the first band. Figure 3 demonstrates wrong samples located had an elevated pixel value in the coastal blue.

The spectral indexes are mathematical formulas of spectral bands that extract information about the land cover features. In agriculture, the indexes indicate the health, water composition, age, and other characteristics of the vegetation [15]. The indexes calculated for the incorporation in the model were: Normalized Differential Vegetation Index (NDVI), Soil Adjusted Vegetation Index (SAVI), Green Normalized Differential Vegetation Index (GNDVI), Modified Soil Adjusted Vegetation Index (MSAVI), Green-Red Vegetation Index (GRVI), Modified Green-Red Vegetation Index (MGRVI), Red edge for chlorophyll (ReCl), Optimized Soil Adjusted Vegetation Index (OSAVI), Enhanced vegetation index (EVI), Structure Insensitive Pigment Index (SIPI), Green Chlorophyll Index (GCI).

Pycaret is a basic and easy-to-use open-source machine-learning framework developed in Python. It assists users from the beginning of data preparation to the finish of model analysis and implementation [16]. This library was used in this study for the training, testing, and classification of the rice phenology with spectral data obtained from

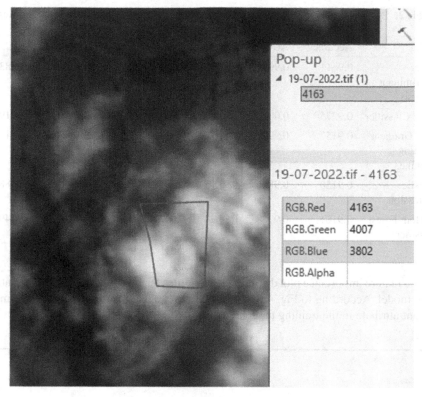

Fig. 3. Spectral values taken in a cloud

Planet Imagery. Pycaret compares different Machine Learning algorithms for classification through the testing date, using 30% of the samples. The 70% remaining was used for the training model.

With the best model selected, it is necessary to validate with a confusion matrix, which is a graphic that shows on Axis X the truth label samples, and on Axis Y are located the predicted labels. The main diagonal indicates the number of correct classifications, while the number of elements located outside the main diagonal is erroneously labeled. Pycaret allows the identification of the most important features used in the classification model to avoid correlation between attributes.

Finally, the trained and tested model could classify Planet Imagery located in rice-producing areas, differentiating between other coverages such as forest, water, buildings, and clouds.

3   Results

The first model includes the eight bands from the imagery and the spectral indexes presented in Table 1. Using the Python library known as PyCaret, fifteen models were compared, and the Linear Discriminant Analysis achieved the best precision. Table 2 displays the accuracy and other precision indicators.

Table 2. Pycarets automatically function for choosing the best model with spectral indexes.

Model	Accuracy	AUC	Recall	Prec	F1	Kappa	MCC
Linear Discriminant Analysis	0.9611	0.9933	0.9611	0.9620	0.9549	0.9558	0.9583
Ridge Classifier	0.9275	0.0000	0.9275	0.9337	0.9174	0.9177	0.9219
Light Gradient Boosting Machine	0.9157	0.9921	0.9157	0.9282	0.9039	0.9043	0.9115
Logistic Regression	0.9150	0.9866	0.9150	0.9277	0.9072	0.9035	0.9088
Random Forest Classifier	0.9101	0.9768	0.9101	0.9222	0.9006	0.8979	0.9049

The feature importance plot displays the attributes that provide the most information to the model. According to Fig. 4, the information extracted from the band is the most relevant attribute in the training model.

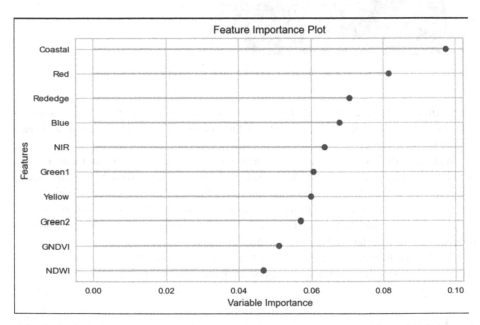

Fig. 4. Variable importance from Linear Discriminant Analysis model with spectral indexes.

Due to the low information provided by the features that correspond to spectral indexes, a second model was run. The results of the precision are displayed in Table 3, and the model with better accuracy is one more time, the Linear Discriminant Analysis.

Table 3. Pycarets automatically function for choosing the best model without spectral indexes.

Model	Accuracy	AUC	Recall	Prec	F1	Kappa	MCC
Linear Discriminant Analysis	0.9611	0.9965	0.9611	0.9713	0.9589	0.9559	0.9578
Extra Trees Classifier	0.9324	0.9773	0.9324	0.9347	0.9194	0.9233	0.9284
Random Forest Classifier	0.9209	0.9731	0.9209	0.9265	0.9086	0.9103	0.9159
Logistic Regression	0.9092	0.9862	0.9092	0.9116	0.8969	0.8967	0.9027
Quadratic Discriminant Analysis	0.9046	0.9901	0.9046	0.8955	0.8845	0.8913	0.8994

The feature importance plot corresponds to Fig. 5. In this case, the most important features were both green and yellow.

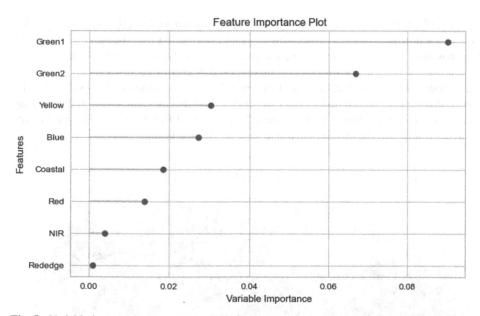

Fig. 5. Variable importance from Linear Discriminant Analysis model without spectral indexes.

The confusion matrix is a tool used to evaluate the accuracy of a classification model. The main diagonal of the matrix shows the number of samples that were classified correctly, while the elements outside the main diagonal represent the samples that were labeled incorrectly. In other words, the confusion matrix provides a summary of the model's performance by showing how many positive and negative events were predicted correctly or incorrectly. In this case, only two samples were labeled incorrectly, while 75 samples were classified correctly. Figure 6 displays the confusion matrix for the Linear Discriminant Analysis model without indexes.

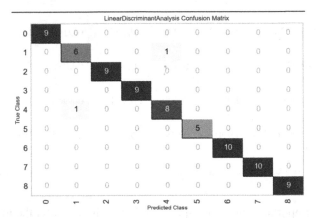

Fig. 6. Confusion matrix for Linear Discriminant Analysis model without spectral indexes.

Finally, the script includes the Python library known as Rasterio, which allows for the extraction, analysis, and processing of pixel information from imagery. Numpy and Pandas are Python tools that enable the processing, analysis, and organization of data for statistical analysis. In this case, the image could be converted into a data frame where each row represents a pixel, and the different columns correspond to the spectral bands. With this format, the trained model can predict the labels for each row, generating an image with a unique band that represents the labels in different colors. The land cover classifications and the phenological rice state are shown in Fig. 7.

Fig. 7. Classification obtained from Linear Discriminant Analysis model.

4   Discussion

The use of PyCaret, a Python library, allows for the comparison and selection of the best machine learning model using many metrics. The model that achieved the best precision in all the metrics was the Linear Discriminant Analysis Model, which contained only the spectral information extracted from the bands, without spectral indexes. In accuracy, models with and without spectral indexes achieved a 96.11% precision, but in metrics such as AUC, Kappa, Recall, F1, and MCC, the best results were obtained by the model without indexes.

Autocorrelation is generated when two attributes explain the same thing, thus a feature is not providing information to the model. Autocorrelation could generate noise and lower the model's precision. Spectral indexes are calculated with the spectral information of the bands. For this reason, the model trained with indexes and pixel values is less precise due to the autocorrelation caused by the analysis including spectral indexes.

Linear Discriminant Analysis is a popular and simple classification tool that often outperforms more sophisticated modern machine learning techniques in remote sensing [17]. The critical principle of this algorithm is to optimize the separability between the two classes to identify them in the best way possible, constructing a new linear axis and projecting the data points on that axis [18].

The spectral signature generated from the pixel value of the Planet Imagery turns out to be detailed and accurate. Crop's reflectance in the visual spectrum and the red edge and near-infrared provide information about the health, humidity, phenology, and chemical requirements such as fertilizer. Each phenological state of the crops has a different spectral signature, and for this reason, it is very important to include the age in the crop identification.

The machine learning model tries to find a general behavior of each class, and if the analyst includes samples without spectral coincidence, the model is going to fail. With the machine learning model classifier, the model achieved 96.11% precision for identifying land covers like clouds, forests, water, and the phenological states of the rice crop. With other field samples, the creation of a spectral library would be a reality. The model can incorporate more information about other crops, and subsequently, a Planet Imagery with any crop would be classified.

An important factor that allowed the high precision reached was the homogeneity of the crops and the other land covers. The crops used to be sown in large parcels, generating that satellite imagery with a medium resolution like Landsat or Sentinel could analyze crops.

The use of 3-m Planet Imagery with 8 bands is effective in identifying the phenological state of rice crops due to their large homogeneity. This allows for high accuracy in the model due to the details in the spectral signature. However, working with spectral indexes is not significant because of the high correlation with the image bands, leading to noise in the final model and less precision due to redundant variables. The Pycaret library is helpful in improving accuracy by selecting the best models based on metrics like accuracy, AUC, Recall, F1, Kappa, and MCC. Despite having a high accuracy rate of 96.11%, the model struggles with identifying clouds and buildings due to their spectral signature. Therefore, it is important to continue training the model to improve accuracy.

References

1. Muthayya, S., Sugimoto, J.D., Montgomery, S., Maberly, G.F.: An overview of global rice production, supply, trade, and consumption. N. Y. Acad. Sci. **1324**, 7–14 (2014)
2. Fukagawa, N., Ziska, L.: Rice: importance for global nutrition. J. Nutr. Sci. Vitaminol. **65**, S2–S3 (2019)
3. USDA. Panama, Costa Rica, and Nicaragua Rice Production (2017)
4. Adeluyi, O., Harris, A., Verrelst, J., Foster, T., Clay, G.D.: Estimating the phenological dynamics of irrigated rice leaf area index using the combination of PROSAIL and Gaussian process regression. Int. J. Appl. Earth Obs. Geoinformation **102** (2021)
5. Guo, Y., et al.: Integrated phenology and climate in rice yields prediction using machine learning methods. Ecol. Indic. **120**, 106935 (2021)
6. Alvarado, M.A., Foroughbakhch, R., Jurado, E., Rocha, A.E.: Cambio climático y la fenología de las plantas. Ciencia UANL **5**, 493–500 (2002)
7. Liakos, K., Busato, P., Moshou, D., Pearson, S., Bochtis, D.: Machine learning in agriculture: a review. Sensors **18**(8), 2674 (2018)
8. Suchithra, M.S., Pai, M.L.: Improving the prediction accuracy of soil nutrient classification by optimizing extreme learning machine parameters. Inf. Process. Agric. **7**, 72–82 (2020)
9. Alagumariappan, P., Dewan, N.J., Muthukrishnan, G.N., Raju, B.K., Bilal, R.A., Sankaran, V.: Intelligent plant disease identification system using machine learning. Eng. Proc. **2**(1), 49 (2020)
10. Badage, A.: Crop disease detection using machine learning: Indian agriculture. Int. Res. J. Eng. Tech. (IRJET) **5**, 866–869 (2018)
11. Dai, W., Jin, H., Zhang, Y., Liu, T., Zhou, Z.: Detecting temporal changes in the temperature sensitivity of spring phenology with global warming: application of machine learning in phenological model. Agr. For. Meteorol. **279**, 107702 (2019)
12. Czernecki, B., Nowosad, J., Jablonska, K.: Machine learning modeling of plant phenology based on coupling satellite and gridded meteorological dataset. Int. J. Biometeorol. **62**, 1297–1309 (2018)
13. Planet. Planet imagery product specifications (2022)
14. Sánchez-Galán, J.E., Barranco, F.R., Reyes, J.S., Quirós-McIntire, E.I., Jiménez, J.U., Fábrega, J.R.: Using supervised classification methods for the analysis of multi-spectral signatures of rice varieties in panama. Adv. Sci., Technol. Eng. Syst. J. **6**(2), 552–558 (2021). https://doi.org/10.25046/aj060262
15. Li, J., Pei, Y., Zhao, S., Xiao, R., Sang, X., Zhang, C.: A review of remote sensing for environmental monitoring in China. Remote Sens. **12**(7), 1130 (2020). https://doi.org/10.3390/rs12071130
16. Whig, P., Gupta, K., Jiwani, N., Jupalle, H., Kouser, S., Alam, N.: A novel method for diabetes classification and prediction with Pycaret. Microsyst. Technol. (jun) (2023). https://doi.org/10.1007/s00542-023-05473-2
17. Suesse, T., Brenning, A., Grupp, V.: Spatial linear discriminant analysis approaches for remote-sensing classification. Spat. Stat. **57**, 100775 (2023). https://doi.org/10.1016/j.spasta.2023.100775
18. Deepika, C., Gnanamalar, R.P., Thangaraj, K., Revathy, N., Karthikeyan, A.: Linear discriminant analysis of grain quality traits in rice (Oryza sativa L.) using the digital imaging technique. J. Cereal Sci. **109**, 103609 (2023). https://doi.org/10.1016/j.jcs.2022.103609

wGMU: A Novel Fusion Strategy to Identify the Important Parts of Sentence for Relation Classification

D. Escobar-Grisales(✉)📶, S. A. Moreno-Acevedo📶, C. D. Rios-Urrego📶,
and J. R. Orozco-Arroyave📶

GITA Lab. School of Engineering, University of Antioquia UdeA, Medellín, Colombia
daniel.esobar@udea.edu.co

Abstract. The progress in Natural Language Processing (NLP) has
increased the research community's interest in addressing different
aspects of Information Extraction (IE). Relation Classification (RC) is
one of the topics within IE that involves the identification and classification of semantic relationships present between two entities mentioned
in a given text. Typical approaches require the use of complex deeplearning multi-task architectures. With the aim of addressing the same
problem but without requiring huge amounts of data and sophisticated
deep models, this work explores the possibility of splitting sentences by
dividing them into five tokens: three context tokens (initial, intermediate, and final) and two entity tokens (head and tail). Additionally,
this paper introduces a new information fusion strategy called weighted
Gated Multimodal Unit (wGMU), which combines the token representations to obtain a sentence representation. This approach enables the
analysis of the im- importance of each token that composes the sentence
in the RC. According to F1-score, the wGMU strategy outperforms the
early fusion strategy by up to 6% and the approach based on the original
GMU by up to 14%. Moreover, the contribution analysis indicates that
the final context token is not crucial in the RC task. Hence, excluding
this representation, the model complexity can be reduced.

Keywords: Natural Language Processing · Relation Classification ·
Deep Learning · Fusion Strategy

1 Introduction

NLP has benefited from great advances in Artificial Intelligence and Pattern
Recognition, enabling the automatic recognition of Named Entities, i.e., Named
Entity Recognition (NER). However, apart from the interest in recognizing entities within a text, it is also necessary to develop methods to automatically identify and classify semantic relationships present between entities mentioned in a

---

D. Escobar-Grisales, S. A. Moreno-Acevedo—These authors contributed equally to this
work.

J. C. Figueroa-García et al. (Eds.): WEA 2023, CCIS 1928, pp. 173–184, 2023.
https://doi.org/10.1007/978-3-031-46739-4_16

given text, i.e., Relation Classification (RC). RC methods focus on identifying semantic relations that exist between two or more entities in a sentence, enabling a broad range of applications including support in clinical decision making [1], drug discovery [21], economic management [7], and others. RC is also considered a fundamental topic to support other areas like knowledge graphs, natural dialogue systems, and natural language understanding.

Several architectures have been proposed in the literature to create RC models. Typically, the models follow a multi-task approach, where only one model is trained before its fine-tuning to make it suitable for several tasks. Well-known applications include Named Entity Recognition (NER), question answering, RC, and others. It is also known that multi-task improves the generalization capability of the models [13]. For instance, DeepStruct was introduced in [14], where different NLP tasks related to document analysis were tested, including classifying and extracting relationships between entities. Following a multi-task approach to perform the classification of relationships within texts, i.e., RC, the authors achieved F1-scores of up to 76.8% working with documents of the TACRED dataset. In [16], the authors introduced the K-Adapter framework, which uses an adapter to inject multiple kinds of knowledge into a pre-trained model. This approach takes advantage of all available information, for instance: linguistic knowledge obtained via dependency parsing. In this paper, the authors also used the multi-task approach, and different NLP tasks were evaluated. Results showed an F1-score of up to 72.4% for RC also in texts of the TACRED dataset.

Other approaches combined Recurrent Neural Networks (RNNs) and Convolutional Neural Networks (CNNs) to model temporal and spatial information [18]. In [19], the authors used Word2Vec model to obtain a numerical representation of the words in the text. These representations feed a Bi-directional Long-short Term Memory (Bi-LSTM) followed by a Convolutional Neural Network (CNN). F1-scores of up to 60% were achieved in the KBP37 database. The authors improved this architecture in [20] by incorporating a fusion strategy based on attention mechanisms.

The above-mentioned works rely on accessing big amounts of data and are based on complex deep models. In contrast, a simpler architecture was proposed in [11]. The authors addressed both challenges at the same time by working with limited data and implementing a simple architecture with an early-fusion strategy. The approach divides a sentence into three contexts: initial, intermediate, and final, and also into two entities: head and tail. The authors implement a one-dimensional CNN, which was fed by embeddings computed based on Bidirectional Encoder Representations from Transformers (BERT) [3] to obtain a sentence-wise representation. The classification was done by a fully connected layer, where the concatenation of all sentence parts (i.e., early fusion) was used as input.

According to our literature review, other fusion strategies have not been explored in the context of RC. The majority of highly accurate models require large amounts of data to be trained in a multi-task setting. However, in real-world applications, there is often insufficient data. Therefore, methodologies like those based on various sentence partitions have been proposed to work with limited data. Nevertheless, these strategies do not consider the fact that each part of the sentence may be contributing differently to the final model. Conversely, existing methods assign equal importance to each part of the sentence.

Our research explores the sentence representation proposed in [11] and introduces a novel fusion strategy, namely wGMU. This approach enables the analysis of the significance of each part of the sentence (token) in a given text. The proposed method is evaluated in the SemEval 2010 task 8 dataset [6]. Results indicate that dividing the sentence into tokens enhances the model's comprehension when dealing with limited data.

The rest of the paper is as follows: Sect. 2 describes the corpora considered for this study. Section 3, presents the methods used in the study. Section 4 shows the results and analysis of the study, and finally, Sect. 5 contains the conclusions and future work.

2   Data

2.1   SemEval 2010 Task 8

The SemEval 2010 Task 8 dataset is a benchmark dataset used for evaluating relation extraction methods. The dataset consists of a collection of sentences taken from news articles grouped into 2 files, one for training with 8000 sentences and the other one for testing with 2717 sentences. Its aim is to determine the semantic relationship between pairs of elements in a given sentence. Table 1 summarizes the relationships present in the dataset and provides some examples where the entities of interest are underlined.

3   Methods

Figure 1 summarizes the general methodology proposed in this work. First, the sentence is split into five tokens, including three context tokens (initial, intermediate, and final) and two entity tokens (head and tail). The RoBERTa pretrained model is used to obtain a numerical representation for each word in the sentence, resulting in a dynamic representation $M \in \mathbb{R}^{n \times d}$ for each token, where n is the number of the words that composed each token and d is the word-embedding dimension. Based on the methodology proposed in [11], we obtained a static representation for context tokens using a CNN-based approach. For entity tokens, we computed the average embedding of the dynamic representation. A *tanh* is afterward applied to create a soft representation of the averaged embeddings. To combine the information from the five tokens, we used three different approaches: (i) the baseline is created by concatenating the token's representations, (ii) standard GMU's are created, and (iii) the weighted version of the GMU's are introduced, namely wGMU. A fully connected layer is utilized to classify the relationship between the two entities in the sentence.

Table 1. Relations of the SemEval 2010 task 8 dataset

Relation	Definition	Example
Product-Producer	A producer causes a product to exist.	The *sugar factory* in Ipswich was built in 1925.
Cause-Effect	An event or object leads to an effect.	The *burst* has been caused by water hammer *pressure*.
Content-Container	An object is physically stored in a delineated area of space.	The *key* was in a *chest*.
Component-Whole	An object is a component of a larger whole.	The *introduction* in the *book* is a summary of what is in the text.
Entity-Destination	An entity is moving towards a destination.	*People* have been moving back into *downtown*.
Instrument-Agency	An agent uses an instrument.	A *telescope* assists the *eye* chiefly in two ways.
Entity-Origin	An entity is coming or is derived from an origin.	The *staff* was removed from his *position*.
Message-Topic	A message, written or spoken, is about a topic.	The *chapters* in this book investigate *issues* and communities.
Member-Collection	A member forms a nonfunctional part of a collection.	*Fish* swim in a *shoal*, but they fall one by one.

3.1 Generation of Tokens

Sentences were divided into five tokens, where a token is a set of words. The words that precede the first entity form the initial context token, the words between the entities of a sentence form the intermediate context token, and the words following the last entity form the final context token. The first entity in the sentence is the head entity token, and the second one is the tail entity token. Initial, intermediate, and final context tokens have 5, 4, and 7 words on average, respectively. We compute the third quartile of the distribution of words in each context token because these values allow us to set the dimension of the embedding matrix that will be used as input to the CNN. This approach has been used in other methodologies that addressed NLP problems based on a CNN [5]. The number of words in the third quartile is 7, 5, and 11, for the initial, intermediate, and final tokens, respectively. Entities in the sentences of the corpus usually have one, two, or three words; for this reason entities are not analyzed by a CNN.

3.2 RoBERTa

RoBERTa [12] is a pre-trained NLP model that was developed as an improvement to the BERT model. This model includes modifications in its masking and optimization mechanisms, which have led to significant improvements in

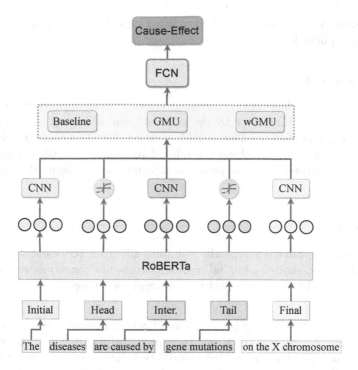

Fig. 1. General methodology

its performance. RoBERTa is composed of 24 Transformer blocks, which are made up of 16 self-attention heads and a fully connected layer containing 1024 units. The key advantage of RoBERTa is its ability to work with multiple languages. This model was pre-trained with 2.5 TB of text data from the Common Crawl corpus [17], which includes text in 100 different languages. This extensive pre-training has allowed RoBERTa to compute text representations in multiple languages, making it a valuable tool for multilingual NLP tasks.

3.3 CNN

CNNs have been widely used in different image processing task [9], however recently has been used to address different NLP task, including sentence/document classification [15], sentiment analysis [8], market segmentation [4], and others. A static representation for a document (sentence, paragraph, and other) based on word representations that form the embedding matrix M can be obtained using a CNN. The convolution is developed along the sequence of words in one dimension (i.e., vertically), and the filter's size in the convolution defines the semantic relationships analyzed among the words. In this work, based on the third quartile of words in the context tokens, we defined the kernel size to map *tri*-gram semantic relationships. CNN is only applied in context tokens because these tokens are composed of several words, while entity tokens are composed of one or three words. When entity tokens are composed of more than one word, we computed the average word embedding and a *tanh* activation function is applied; following the methodology proposed [11]

3.4 Fusion Strategies

In the relationship classification between entities, it is important to consider not only the words that refer to the entities themselves but also other non-entity words in the sentence that provide context [10]. The context tokens help in determining how entity tokens are related to each other. We consider three different fusion strategies to combine the information of tokens that composed the sentence.

3.5 Baseline

State-of-the-art approaches typically combine all token representations following an early-fusion strategy, i.e., all representations are concatenated before the classification. In this work, we used this strategy as a baseline.

GMU: This architecture was proposed in [2], where the main idea is to combine the advantages of early and late fusion by using multiplicative gates to selectively integrate information from multiple modalities. These gates allow the model to dynamically adjust the contribution of each modality to the final output according to the relevance and complementary information provided by each modality. First, the representation of each modality feeds a fully-connected layer with an activation function tanh. Then, for each modality, a gate layer with σ activation function controls the contribution of each modality. Figure 2 shows the original GMU architecture for k modalities. Notice that each modality has a weight vector $\mathbf{z}_k$, which controls the contribution of the modality k. However, the $\mathbf{z_k}$ vector is not normalized with respect to the other $\mathbf{z}$ vectors from the other modalities; thus, the contribution from each modality is not comparable, i.e., it is not possible to intelligently select the amount of relevant information per modality. In this study, each token is considered a modality. We aim to find an intermediate representation that appropriately combines the information from context tokens (initial, intermediate, and final) and entity tokens (head and tail).

wGMU: We proposed a modification of the original GMU to ensure that the sum of the weights vector $\mathbf{z}$ in the fusion will be equal to the unit vector. Therefore, we defined a modification to the Softmax function.

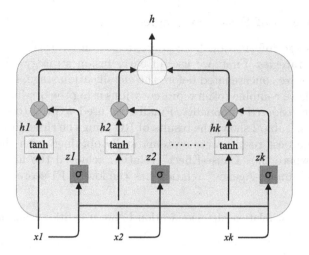

Fig. 2. Original GMU. Figure adapted from [2]

The standard Softmax activation function is defined as:

$$S(\mathbf{x})_i = \frac{e^{x_i}}{\sum_{j=1}^{k} e^{x_j}},\tag{1}$$

where $i = 1, 2, ..., k$ and $\mathbf{x} = (x_1, x_2, ..., x_k)$. This definition is useful when $\mathbf{x}$ is a vector. However, when $\mathbf{x}$ is a matrix $\mathbf{X} \in \mathbb{R}^{n \times m}$ the Softmax function definition can be rewritten as

$$S(\mathbf{X})_{ij} = \frac{e^{x_{ij}}}{\sum_{k=1}^{n} e^{x_{kj}}},\tag{2}$$

where $i = 1, 2, ..., n$ and $j = 1, 2, ..., m$. In this study, we form a weight matrix $\mathbf{Z} \in \mathbb{R}^{n \times m}$, where n is the number of modalities and m is the dimension of each weights vector $\mathbf{z}$. We replace the σ activation function with the Softmax activation function adapted to matrices in the original GMU. This variation allows us to train each vector of weights $\mathbf{z}$ considering the simultaneous contribution of the other modalities in the combination. In addition, it also allows greater interpretability in order to define which modality/token contributes the most to the combination.

4   Experiments and Results

We defined two main experiments for RC. Initially, we compare three fusion strategies to combine the information from context and entity tokens. Next, we analyzed the contribution of each token using the weights vectors calculated with the wGMU.

4.1 Comparison of Fusion Strategies

In order to merge information from context and entity tokens, we considered three fusion strategies. First, we use an early fusion strategy where all token representations are concatenated before the classification stage, i.e., the baseline model. Second, we combine token representations using the original GMU, where each token is considered a modality. Finally, we used wGMU to combine token representations. Table 2 shows the results of RC using the three fusion strategies. Notice that the best results were systematically obtained with the wGMU for all relations, where the "Cause-Effect" relation achieved the highest F1-score, while the "Instrument-Agency" relation has the lowest F1-score.

Table 2. Results in relationship classification between entities using different fusion strategies.

	Baseline			Original GMU			wGMU		
	Precision	Recall	F1-score	Precision	Recall	F1-score	Precision	Recall	F1-score
Product-Producer	56.1	68.0	61.4	47.9	65.4	55.3	71.4	73.6	**72.5**
Cause-Effect	84.5	85.1	84.8	77.2	86.6	81.6	86.7	83.5	**85.1**
Content-Container	70.7	72.9	71.8	67.6	78.1	72.5	72.4	85.9	**78.6**
Component-Whole	65.8	78.8	71.7	70.6	68.6	70.0	77.1	73.4	**75.2**
Entity-Destination	74.4	68.8	71.5	68.2	50.7	58.2	81.3	84.6	**82.9**
Instrument-Agency	62.9	53.2	57.6	57.4	44.9	50.4	76.3	55.8	**64.4**
Entity-Origin	67.5	59.7	63.4	77.6	22.9	35.3	78.7	68.6	**73.3**
Message-Topic	73.3	74.7	74.0	64.9	61.7	63.3	77.3	84.7	**80.8**
Member-Collection	81.0	76.8	78.9	76.9	75.5	76.2	77.0	84.5	**80.6**
Average	70.7	70.9	70.6	67.6	61.6	62.5	77.6	77.2	**77.0**

The F1-score comparison between different fusion strategies is presented in Fig. 3. According to the F1-scores, the best results for each relation were obtained using the wGMU. This approach outperformed the GMU by up to 38%, 24%, 17% for the relations "Entity-Origin", "Entity-destination", and "Product-Producer", respectively.

4.2 Token Contribution Analysis

The wGMU allows analyzing the contribution of the modality/token k based on the weights vector z_k. The normalization of the weight vector k with respect to the weight vectors of other modalities enables values in z_k to be close to 1, indicating a high contribution from modality/token k in the combination. We computed the average of each z vector for each token and for all samples in the test set. Figure 4.A shows the boxplot for the weights from each token in

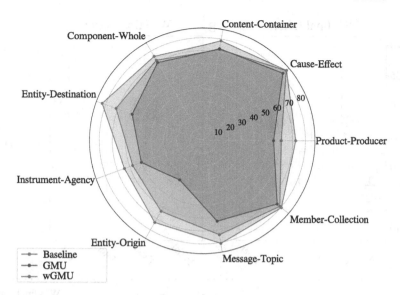

Fig. 3. F1-score (%) of RC between two entities for different fusion strategies: Baseline, GMU, wGMU

the sentence. Notice that the initial context token and final context token have, on average, a lower contribution compared to the average contribution of other tokens. To validate the importance of the different tokens, we conducted an experiment with the wGMU model using only the intermediate token context and two entity tokens (head and tail). However, the results were worse than the ones in the baseline. Therefore, we conducted another experiment with the same wGMU model, but without considering the final context token. Figure 4.B shows the boxplot for the experiment with four tokens, where all tokens tend to increase their contribution to the fusion. Notice that the initial context token has the largest increase. Figure 4.C shows a comparison of the model with the final context token and the model without this context token. Both models yield a similar F1-score for all classes, demonstrating that the final context token is not crucial for classifying relationships discussed in this paper. Notice that the final token is larger than the rest of the tokens; therefore, the model complexity can be reduced when this representation is not considered.

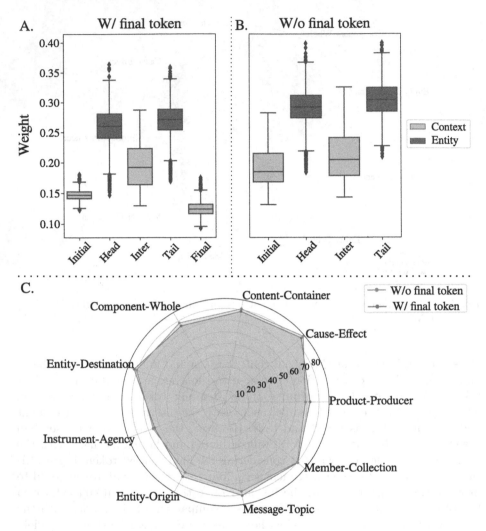

Fig. 4. Analysis of the average contribution of the tokens in the sentences of test set. **A** Boxplot of the token weights in the adapted GMU considering all tokens in the sentence. **B** Boxplot of the token weights in the adapted GMU without considering the context token "final". **C** F1 score (%) comparison between the adapted GMU with all tokens and without context token "final".

5   Conclusions

In this study, we addressed the RC between entities by dividing a sentence into five tokens, including three context tokens (initial, intermediate, and final) and two entity tokens (head and tail). First, we employed the method proposed in [11] to obtain numerical representations of each token. Then, representations from tokens that composed the sentence were combined using three different fusion strategies: early fusion (baseline), an approach based on GMUs, and our proposed approach called wGMU. Finally, the resulting sentence representation feeds a fully-connected layer for RC. We tested our approach in The SemEval 2010 Task 8 dataset.

The wGMU approach achieves an average F1-score of 77% in the classification of 9 relations. This result outperforms the baseline strategy by up to 7% and the GMU approach by up to 15%. The wGMU strategy obtained better results than the baseline, and GMU approaches for all relations, particularly in the "Product-Producer," "Entity-Destination," and "Entity-Origin" relationships. Furthermore, we conducted an analysis to assess the contribution of tokens to the RC task, which was based on the weight vectors computed by the wGMU. Results indicate that the context token "final" had a lower contribution to the combination of all token representations. Interestingly, the F1-score remained similar when the context token "final" was not considered in the wGMU model. This result showed that wGMU was able to identify a specific part of the sentence which does not provide significant information in the RC.

Results show that wGMU is suitable for adequately weighting the tokens composing a sentence, enhancing the model's performance for RC. Furthermore, this approach allows to identify parts of the sentence that are not relevant to the classification task. Therefore, this information could be excluded to reduce model complexity. Future experiments will include other datasets that exhibit issues such as class imbalance or a smaller amount of data. Moreover, we will test the wGMU in other problems, especially those that involve analyzing multiple sources of information.

Acknowledgements. This work was funded by UdeA grant # PI2023-58010.

References

1. Agosti, M., et al.: A relation extraction approach for clinical decision support. arXiv preprint arXiv:1905.01257 (2019)
2. Arevalo, J., et al.: Gated multimodal units for information fusion. arXiv preprint arXiv:1702.01992 (2017)
3. Devlin, J., et al.: Bert: pre-training of deep bidirectional transformers for language understanding. arXiv preprint arXiv:1810.04805 (2018)
4. Escobar-Grisales, D., et al.: Author profiling in informal and formal language scenarios via transfer learning. TecnoLógicas **52**, 212–225 (2021)
5. Escobar-Grisales, D., et al.: Colombian dialect recognition based on information extracted from speech and text signals. In: Proceedings of ASRU, pp. 556–563. IEEE (2021)
6. Hendrickx, I., et al.: Semeval-2010 task 8: multi-way classification of semantic relations between pairs of nominals. arXiv preprint arXiv:1911.10422 (2010)
7. Jabbari, A., et al.: A French corpus and annotation schema for named entity recognition and relation extraction of financial news. In: Proceedings of LREC, pp. 2293–2299 (2020)
8. Kim, H., Jeong, Y.S.: Sentiment classification using convolutional neural networks. Appl. Sci. **9**(11), 2347 (2019)

9. Krizhevsky, A., et al.: Imagenet classification with deep convolutional neural networks. Commun. ACM **60**(6), 84–90 (2017)
10. Li, X., et al.: Eine: relation classification by enhancing the impact of non-entity words. In: Proceedings of MLNLP, pp. 68–73 (2022)
11. Liu, J., et al.: Relation classification via BERT with piecewise convolution and focal loss. Plos one (9), e0257092 (2021)
12. Liu, Y., et al.: Roberta: a robustly optimized BERT pretraining approach. arXiv preprint arXiv:1907.11692 (2019)
13. Ruder, S.: An overview of multi-task learning in deep neural networks. arXiv preprint arXiv:1706.05098 (2017)
14. Wang, C., et al.: Deepstruct: pretraining of language models for structure prediction. arXiv preprint arXiv:2205.10475 (2022)
15. Wang, G., et al.: Joint embedding of words and labels for text classification. arXiv:1805.04174 (2018)
16. Wang, R., et al.: K-adapter: Infusing knowledge into pre-trained models with adapters. arXiv preprint arXiv:2002.01808 (2020)
17. Wenzek, G., et al.: CCNet: extracting high quality monolingual datasets from web crawl data. In: Proceedings of LREC, pp. 4003–4012. European Language Resources Association, Marseille, France (2020)
18. Wiest, L.: Recurrent neural networks-combination of RNN and CNN. Published on 7 (2017)
19. Zhang, L., Xiang, F.: Relation classification via BILSTM-CNN. In: Tan, Y., Shi, Y., Tang, Q. (eds.) DMBD. LNCS, vol. 10943, pp. 373–382. Springer, Cham (2018). https://doi.org/10.1007/978-3-319-93803-5_35
20. Zhang, X., et al.: A combination of RNN and CNN for attention-based relation classification. Procedia Comput. Sci. **131**, 911–917 (2018)
21. Zheng, S., et al.: Text mining for drug discovery. Bioinf. Drug Disc., 231–252 (2019)

Effect of Preprocessing in Deep Learning Systems to Aid the Diagnosis Using X-Ray Pulmonary Images

Luis-Ramón Barrios-Roqueme[ID], Hernando Altamar-Mercado[ID], and Alberto Patiño-Vanegas[✉][ID]

Facultad de Ciencias Básicas, Universidad Tecnológica de Bolivar, Cartagena, Colombia
{lroqueme,haltamar,apatino}@utb.edu.co

Abstract. The main objective of this research is to analyze the effect of applying some image preprocessing techniques on the performance of convolutional neural networks for the classification of COVID19, Pneumonia, and Normal patients from chest X-ray images. The normal category corresponds to patients without COVID-19 and/or without pneumonia. The preprocessing applied to the images are Global Histogram Equalization, Contrast-Limited Adaptive Histogram Equalization, pseudo colorization HSV, and pseudo colorization JET. The trained architectures were VGG16, ResNet50, MobileNet, and Xception. According to the metrics, it was observed that all the trained models improved their performance in classification when one of the image preprocessing techniques was used before being evaluated. The combination (model and preprocessing) with the best performance for each category was also determined. Finally, with this combination, a probability threshold was proposed to classify a given image.

Keywords: X-Ray · COVID-19 · Histogram equalization · HSV · JET

1 Introduction

Chest radiographs or X-rays (Rx) and computed tomography are alternative, rapid, and sensitive methods of detection of pulmonary viral infection diseases, which can show visual indicators related to viral infection [11]. Chest images with Rx acquire great value in the diagnosis and prognosis of patients with suspected pneumonia or COVID-19, but often the physical signs in the chest examination are minimal and the X-ray can be normal in the early stages of the disease, making it difficult to differentiate from other pulmonary viral infections such as pneumonia, which can lead to delays in diagnosis and increased chance of disease spread [18]. On the other hand, when the patient has respiratory complications, the diagnosis is difficult when the Rx image of the lungs is not of good quality. The quality of the image can be related to the lack of inspiration, the breast prominence, and the bad positioning of the patient that can cause the scapulae

© The Author(s), under exclusive license to Springer Nature Switzerland AG 2023
J. C. Figueroa-García et al. (Eds.): WEA 2023, CCIS 1928, pp. 185–194, 2023.
https://doi.org/10.1007/978-3-031-46739-4_17

and the soft tissues to be projected on the pulmonary region, increasing the density of the periphery of the lung and simulating Ground-Glass Opacity (GGO); which is a characteristic of Rx images of patients with pneumonia. Thus, the detection of viral infection in a chest image is not a visually easy task for health specialists. Fortunately, Deep Learning (DL) techniques as a computational tool have been used in many Rx image segmentation and data classification applications for the detection and diagnosis of respiratory syndromes with promising results. Some previously trained artificial neural network models have been used together with automatic segmentation, image feature extraction methods, and classifiers based on machine learning such as the K nearest neighbors (KNN), support vector machines (SVM), and the classifier based on Bayes' theorem, among others [6,15]. In other work, the performance of Convolutional Neural Network (CNN) has been studied using Global Histogram Equalization (HE) and pseudo-coloring (or false color) improving the performance of the models [12,13].

We propose the use of CNN to identify Pneumonia and COVID19 diseases from chest X-rays. Thus, we avoid first extracting the characteristics of each disease, since in these networks the extraction of the characteristics is carried out automatically in the training stage. In addition, keeping in mind that the region of interest is focused on the lungs, we have used the Contrast Limited Adaptive Histogram Equalization (CLAHE) technique. The parameters are adapted to the characteristics of each region, to highlight the specific details of each disease in the lung area. In this way, we avoid carrying out a previous segmentation. To carry out the research we have chosen four pre-trained convolutional neural networks because they can be adjusted more easily and quickly than training them from scratch. The VGG16, ResNet50, MobileNet and Xception convolutional neural network architectures were chosen, which presented good performance in similar problems [6,7,12]. Thus, our research focused on verifying if the four CNN architectures improve their performance using CLAHE, compared to the other processing reported with the best performance (HE, HSV Colormap, and JET Colormap).

2 Method

The main objective of this research is to analyze the effect of applying image pre-processing with HE, CLAHE, HSV colormap and JET on the performance of VGG16, ResNet50, MobileNet, and Xception convolutional neural networks for the classification of COVID19, Pneumonia and Normal patients from chest x-ray images. The normal category corresponds to patients without COVID-19 and/or without Pneumonia.

First, it is necessary to determine which CNN architecture presents the best performance without performing any type of preprocessing. For this, it is analyzed if there is a significant difference between the architectures that present similar performance through an analysis of the ROC curve. Then, it is determined which is the CNN architecture that presents the best performance when preprocessing is performed with the CLAHE technique. It is then determined which CNN architecture and which preprocessing techniques give the best performance. Finally, the performance of the two best models obtained when using and when not using preprocessing is compared through an analysis of the ROC curve. This method is illustrated in Fig. 1.

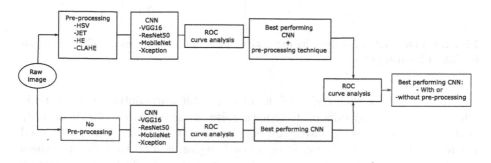

Fig. 1. Flowchart: Illustration of the method.

2.1   Image Preprocessing

The importance of image preprocessing systems lies in the reduction of costs and the time required to reach a viable implementation of the classification systems [8]. Below is a brief description of the image preprocessing techniques used in this work to apply to chest X-ray images before being used in training:

Histogram Equalization (HE): A technique of adjusting the grayscale of an image so that the histogram of the input image is mapped to a smooth grayscale histogram [5]. The Fig. 2 shows an original chest X-ray image with its respective histogram and the image when histogram equalization is applied. It is observed that histogram equalization results in an increase in the dynamic range of gray values producing better contrast. The histogram equalization of an image is a global procedure, that is, the transformation is calculated using the histogram of the complete image, which can generate regions with low contrast because localized information of the image is not considered [17].

Contrast Limited Adaptive Histogram Equalization (CLAHE): Adaptive histogram equalization is a technique that differs from ordinary histogram equalization in that it calculates several histograms, each corresponding to a different section of the image, and uses them to redistribute the luminance values in each region. Therefore, it is suitable for improving local contrast. In order to eliminate the noise in the borders between the image regions, bilinear interpolation is applied [14]. The problem with using the adaptive histogram equalization

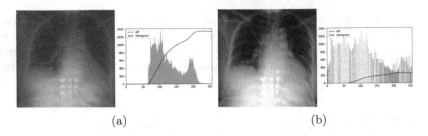

(a)   (b)

Fig. 2. (a) Original image with its respective histogram and (b) image after the equalization of its histogram

technique is that in each region of the image, a different contrast value is redistributed and it is very difficult to remove noise at the edges. For this reason, the contrast-limited adaptive histogram equalization (CLAHE) technique is used, where the distribution of gray levels in each region is used to define the shape of the histogram that produces the best quality result by effectively suppressing amplification of noise and accelerating the operation of the bilinear interpolation algorithm for the elimination of noise at the edges of each region. Figure 3a illustrates an original chest X-ray image and Fig. 3b the image when CLAHE is applied. Unlike the result obtained with the global histogram equalization technique (see Fig. 2b), a better contrast is observed throughout the image.

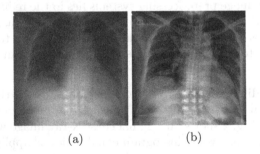

(a)   (b)

Fig. 3. (a) Original chest radiograph image and (b) after applying the Contrast Limited Adaptive Histogram Equalization (CLAHE) technique.

Color-Map: This is a simple way to pseudo-color/false-color a grayscale image using the color scales. This is necessary because human perception is not designed to observe small changes in grayscale images. Human eyes are more sensitive to observing changes between colors, so it is often necessary to recolor grayscale images to see more detail [4]. The procedure is also ideal for highlighting features before training.

In this investigation, two color models HSV and JET are applied. The HSV (Hue, Saturation, Value) model, is a non-linear transformation of the RGB color space and the JET model is a type of gray color [2]. The Fig. 4 shows an original chest X-ray image and when HSV and JET color maps are applied to it, respectively. It is observed that in each pseudocolor details are highlighted that are not observed in the other, but the JET color-map allows to better highlight the details in the lungs.

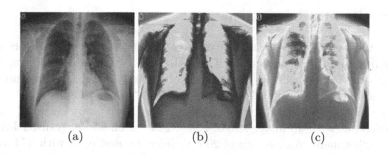

(a)   (b)   (c)

Fig. 4. (a) Grayscale image, (b) Color-map HSV and (c) Color-map JET.

2.2   Database

The data is taken from two free databases published on the kaggle.com website called "Chest X-Ray Images (Pneumonia)" and "COVID-19 Radiography Dataset". The "Chest X-Ray Images (Pneumonia)" data set consists of 5216 X-ray images labeled into two categories (Pneumonia and Normal) corresponding to pediatric patients of boys and girls from Guangzhou (China) [1,10]. The "COVID-19 Radiography Dataset" consists of 21164 X-ray images labeled into four categories (COVID-19, Lung Opacity, Normal, and Viral Pneumonia) and was created by a team of researchers from Qatar University, Doha, Qatar, and the University of Dhaka, Bangladesh, along with their collaborators from Pakistan and Malaysia [3]. In both databases, the data sets present a marked unbalance between the categories, which could bias the prediction results towards the category with the largest number of images. To balance the database in such a way that all categories will have the same number of images, images classified into the COVID-19, pneumonia, and normal categories were selected from the different databases. After being unified, refined, and balanced, the database was made up of 2400 × 2400 images for each category for a total of 7200, distributed like this: Training (70%), Validation (20%) y Test (10%).

2.3   Statistical Analysis of the ROC Curve

To rigorously determine if there was a significant difference between the CNN architectures that presented similar performance, an analysis of the ROC curve was performed. The area under the ROC curve (AUC), estimates the ability to distinguish or "discriminate" between cases and non-cases in a test. The Youden statistic is used to determine the optimal cut-off point of the ROC curve that maximizes the rate of true positives with respect to the rate of false positives ($Youden = Sensitivity + Specificity - 1$) [16]. In this work, we have followed the method of comparing the area under the ROC curve as a statistical test proposed by Hanley [9].

3   Results and Discussion

Initially, the performance results of each of the chosen models are presented, without using image preprocessing. Then, the results are presented using image preprocessing. Finally, the performance results of the models are presented taking into account the optimal threshold established in the ROC curve.

In the first stage (with the original images without preprocessing), training was carried out with an image size of 224×224, batch size 8, transfer learning, and fine adjustment. An average of 20 epochs were used each with 374 average iterations. The initial learning rate was 1×10^{-2}, it was set to decrease during training when the validation loss stopped improving every 5 steps. In the second stage, the models are trained again with the configurations established in the previous stage, but this time pre-processing is applied to the images.

3.1   Evaluation of the Models Without Using Image Preprocessing

Table 1 shows the performance metrics of each trained model when evaluated with the test set. The model with the best performance when the images have not been processed is MobileNet with an Accuracy of 90.52% and AUC of 0.907.

Table 1. Results of the evaluation of each model using images without preprocessing.

Model	Accuracy (%)	Loss	Presición	Recall	AUC
MobileNet	90.52	0.6042	0.79	0.76	0.907
ResNet50	78.04	1.0535	0.66	0.55	0.774
VGG16	69.41	1.3142	0.51	0.54	0.695
Xception	60.94	1.1051	0.41	0.41	0.651

3.2   Evaluation of Models with Image Preprocessing Techniques

According to the results observed in Table 2, all the implemented models improved performance in the classification of patients with the application of chest image preprocessing techniques. Specifically, it was found that the ResNet50 model with the CLAHE and color map JET preprocessing techniques are the ones with the best performance for the correct classification of the images in the different categories.

Table 2. Evaluation of models with image pre-processing techniques

Model	Technique	ACC	Loss	Precision	Recall	AUC
ResNet50	CLAHE	99.96	0.0369	0.99	0.99	1.000
	JET Colormap	98.87	0.2011	0.93	0.92	0.995
	HSV Colormap	95.56	0.4557	0.89	0.86	0.984
	HE	96.33	0.3796	0.87	0.86	0.965
MobileNet	CLAHE	99.79	0.0475	0.99	0.99	0.999
	JET Colormap	96.82	0.3449	0.90	0.89	0.985
	HSV Colormap	95.92	0.4181	0.86	0.84	0.975
	HE	92.53	0.5653	0.76	0.76	0.921
VGG16	CLAHE	95.79	0.4280	0.86	0.85	0.961
	HSV Colormap	93.26	0.5102	0.83	0.80	0.949
	JET Colormap	84.30	0.7781	0.77	0.71	0.903
	HE	78.80	0.8702	0.62	0.62	0.785
Xception	CLAHE	88.31	0.6964	0.72	0.73	0.698
	JET Colormap	78.87	0.8396	0.45	0.53	0.667
	HE	67.62	1.0604	0.31	0.47	0.640
	HSV Colormap	76.34	0.8830	0.47	0.52	0.557

In this sense, it is interesting to prove that the CLAHE image processing technique presents better performance in all categories than the JET color map technique using ResNet50.

Analysis of the Effect of Preprocessing for Each Category. For this, the classification probability given by the model for each category was used. The AUC analysis was carried out as a bivariate model, where the category of interest takes a value of 1 and the rest of the categories a value of 0. For example, if the effect of preprocessing with CLAHE on images with COVID-19 is going to be studied, the label for COVID-19 is 1 and the rest of the images (Pneumonia and Normal) are labeled as 0. With 95% confidence, the performance of each category was compared according to the preprocessing technique.

The graphs of the comparison of the ROC curves and the AUC of the models implemented with ResNet50 and the CLAHE image preprocessing techniques (colored in pink) and the color map (colored in turquoise) can be seen in Fig. 5. Based on the $p-values$ and with 95% confidence, the AUC of the model implemented with ResNet50 and the CLAHE technique differs significantly from the AUC of the model implemented with ResNet50 and the JET color map technique. Therefore, the model implemented with ResNet50 and the CLAHE technique has a better ability to correctly classify images into the categories COVID-19, Pneumonia, and Normal.

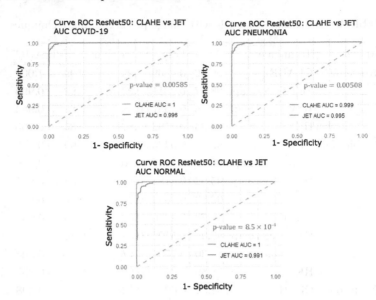

Fig. 5. ROC curves comparison: ResNet50 + CLAHE Vs. ResNet50 + JET color map.

The Optimal Cut-Off Points with ResNet50 and Color Map JET. Based on the area under the ROC curve for each of the categories and the estimated calculation of the Youden statistic (see Fig. 6), the following classification thresholds are suggested for images preprocessed with CLAHE and the ResNet50 architecture (see Table 3):

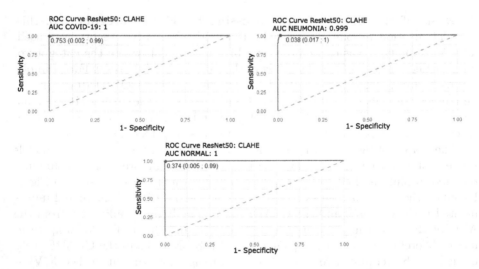

Fig. 6. ROC curve and optimal cut-off point in each category for ResNet50 + CLAHE.

From the results, the following can be deduced: (i) The threshold of 0.753 in the COVID-19 category suggests that if the system classifies an image with a probability greater than or equal to 75.3% in this category, it can be inferred with 95% confidence that the image is correctly classified in the COVID-19 category, (ii) The threshold of 0.038 in the Pneumonia category suggests that if the system classifies an image with a probability greater than or equal to 3.8% in this category, it can be inferred with 95% confidence that the image is correctly classified in the Pneumonia category; and (iii) The threshold of 0.374 in the Normal category suggests that if the system classifies an image with a probability greater than or equal to 37.4% in this category, it can be inferred with 95% confidence that the image is correctly classified in the Normal category.

Table 3. The optimal cut-off points with ResNet50 and color map JET.

Category	Youden
COVID-19	0.753
Pneumonia	0.038
Normal	0.374

4   Conclusions

In this work, a study was carried out on the preprocessing of chest X-ray images in the performance of convolutional neural networks, to classify patients in the COVID-19, Pneumonia, and Normal categories. The image preprocessing approaches that were chosen are global histogram equalization (HE), contrast-limited adaptive histogram equalization (CLAHE), pseudocoloring with a HSV map, and pseudo colorization with a JET map. The chosen neural network architectures are VGG16, ResNet50, MobileNet, and Xception. For the training, a balanced and manually refined database was used. For the analysis of the performance of the CNNs with and without image preprocessing, the statistical analysis of the AUC in the different categories was used. The model implemented with the MobileNet architecture without preprocessing of chest X-rays has a better ability to correctly classify patients into the COVID-19, Pneumonia, and Normal categories. All the implemented models significantly improved the performance in the classification of patients with the application of chest image preprocessing techniques. The model with the ResNet50-type architecture when using the CLAHE preprocessing technique is the best performing for the classification of patients into the COVID-19, Pneumonia, and Normal categories. However, ResNet50 with Colormap JET also presents a similar performance.

References

1. Chest X-Ray Images (Pneumonia)—Kaggle. https://www.kaggle.com/datasets/
2. Color Jet. http://www.colores.org.es/jet.php
3. COVID-19 Radiography Dataset—Kaggle. https://www.kaggle.com/datasets
4. OpenCV: ColorMaps in OpenCV. https://docs.opencv.org/
5. Acharya, T., Ray, A.K.: Image Processing Principles and Applications. IEEE (2015). http://www.wiley.com/go/permissi
6. Civit-Masot, J., Luna-Perejón, F., Morales, M.D., Civit, A.: Deep learning system for COVID-19 diagnosis aid using X-ray pulmonary images. Appl. Sci. **10**(13) (2020). https://doi.org/10.3390/app10134640
7. Farag, H.H., Said, L.A., Rizk, M.R., Ahmed, M.A.E.: Hyperparameters optimization for ResNet and Xception in the purpose of diagnosing COVID-19. J. Intell. Fuzzy Syst. **41**(2), 3555–3571 (2021). https://doi.org/10.3233/JIFS-210925
8. Gonzalez, R.C., Woods, R.E.: Digital Imagen Processing Using MATLAB (2009). http://www.gatesmark.com/
9. Hanley, J.A., McNeil, B.J.: A method of comparing the areas under receiver operating characteristic curves derived from the same cases. Radiology **148**(3), 839–843 (1983). https://doi.org/10.1148/radiology.148.3.6878708
10. Kermany, D.S., et al.: Identifying medical diagnoses and treatable diseases by image-based deep learning. Cell **172**(5), 1122–1131 (2018). https://doi.org/10.1016/j.cell.2018.02.010
11. Li, Y., Xia, L.: Coronavirus disease 2019 (COVID-19): role of chest CT in diagnosis and management. Am. J. Roentgenol. **214**(6), 1280–1286 (2020). https://doi.org/10.2214/AJR.20.22954
12. Rahaman, M.M., et al.: Identification of COVID-19 samples from chest X-Ray images using deep learning: a comparison of transfer learning approaches. J. X-Ray Sci. Technol. **28**(5), 821–839 (2020). https://doi.org/10.3233/XST-200715
13. Sethy, P.K., Behera, S.K., Anitha, K., Pandey, C., Khan, M.R.: Computer aid screening of COVID-19 using X-ray and CT scan images: an inner comparison. J. X-Ray Sci. Technol. **29**(2), 197–210 (2021). https://doi.org/10.3233/XST-200784
14. Smith, P.: Bilinear interpolation of digital images. Ultramicroscopy **6**(2), 201–204 (1981). https://doi.org/10.1016/0304-3991(81)90061-9
15. Tsiknakis, N., et al.: Interpretable artificial intelligence framework for COVID-19 screening on chest X-rays. Exp. Ther. Med. **20**(2), 727–735 (2020). https://doi.org/10.3892/etm.2020.8797
16. Youden, W.J.: Index for rating diagnostic tests. Cancer **3**(1), 32–5 (1950). https://doi.org/10.1002/1097-0142(1950)3:1⟨32::aid-cncr2820030106⟩3.0.co;2-3
17. Yu, Z., Bajaj, C.: A fast and adaptative method for image contrast enhancement. Department of Computer Sciences, University of Texas at Austin, pp. 1001–1004 (2004)
18. Zhu, N., et al.: A novel coronavirus from patients with Pneumonia in China, 2019. N. Engl. J. Med. **382**(8), 727–733 (2020). https://doi.org/10.1056/nejmoa2001017

Topological Data Analysis to Characterize Fluctuations in the Latin American Integrated Market

Andy Domínguez Monterroza[1]($\boxtimes$)(iD), Alfonso Mateos Caballero[2](iD),
and Antonio Jiménez-Martín[2](iD)

[1] Programa de Ciencia de Datos, Facultad de Ciencias Básicas, Universidad
Tecnológica de Bolívar, Cartagena de Indias, Colombia
adominguez@utb.edu.co
[2] Decision Analysis and Statistic Group, Departamento de Inteligencia Artificial,
Universidad Politécnica de Madrid, Madrid, Spain
{alfonso.mateos,antonio.jimenez}@upm.es

Abstract. Topological data analysis (TDA) is a recent data science technique that provides tools to describe the shape of complex multivariate data based on well-established notions in the field of algebraic topology. In this study, we apply TDA to analyze the stability and changes in the topological structure of the Integrated Latin American Market (MILA), being the analysis of extreme events among the most relevant features of study in financial markets. Our findings reveal that the topological descriptor of the persistent homology norm of dimension 1, computed from the set of multivariate financial time series of MILA's major indices, effectively characterizes fluctuations and captures events of interest (e.g., crises like COVID-19) in the market dynamics. This research demonstrates the capability of TDA in analyzing and understanding the market structure, contributing valuable insights for risk assessment and decision-making processes in financial markets.

Keywords: Topological data analysis · Market dynamics · Integrated Latin American market

1 Introduction

Financial crises impact many aspects of the social and economic life of nations. One interest that has gained much attention from academics and researchers is to study market behavior under financial crises and to propose tools to detect early warning signals. One aspect of great interest is the study of extreme events

This work was supported by the Spanish Ministry of Science and Innovation projects PID2021-122209OB-C31 and RED2022-134540-T.

since often trigger impacts in financial and social terms. For instance, the Covid-19 pandemic has had repercussions in many aspects of our daily lives, having significant implications in the global financial sphere. Financial crises frequently affect the dynamics of the series of asset prices in the financial markets.

In this paper we focus on the Integrated Latin American Market (MILA). MILA is the result of the integration of the Stock Exchanges of Colombia, Lima, Mexico, and Santiago de Chile. It represents a facet of the trade and economic collaboration among the member nations of the Pacific Alliance, which includes Chile, Colombia, Peru, and Mexico. Few studies have investigated the MILA market dynamics during the recent crisis caused by Covid-19.

We propose that the topological information contained in multidimensional space constituted by the primary indices of the MILA market could be valuable for quantifying changes in market dynamics. We hypothesize that distinct topological features emerge during varying market states. We contend that topological data analysis (TDA) holds the potential to effectively elucidate these changes.

TDA is a recent technique in data science that allows studying the shape of a high-dimensional dataset through the lens of algebraic topology. The idea behind topological data analysis is to construct a point cloud and from it by a filtering process build simplicial complexes and compute the persistent homology on them. The persistent homology captures the topological features describing the point cloud as the filtering parameter increases leading to the formation of the simplicial complexes.

One way to monitor the persistence of topological features is the persistence diagram, which shows the coordinates of the topological features of the different homology classes that are calculated on the simplicial complexes. These reflect the life-time of the features.

Peter Bubenik [1] introduced a topological descriptor called *persistence landscapes*, which are sequences of piecewise-linear functions defined on the persistence diagrams, offering advantages for ease of computation and can provide insights for statistical analysis and machine learning.

An approach to examine the topological evolution of point cloud homology is to compute the first and second-order norms of the persistence landscape function. The first-order norm entails adding the absolute values of the elements within the landscape persistence function, while the second-order norm involves calculating the square root of the sum of the squared values of the elements of the landscape persistence function.

We apply TDA on the MILA market. Specifically, we compute the norms of the topological descriptor and the persistence landscape on the multivariate point cloud of the main financial indices of the MILA market. The results derived reveal the dynamic changes in the market's topological structure during the analyzed time period and demonstrate that the persistence landscape norms successfully characterizes the fluctuations due to the extreme event influenced by the Covid-19 pandemic.

This work is structured as follows. In Sect. 2 we make a review of the use of TDA in financial markets. In Sect. 3 the methods and data used for the analysis of the MILA market are described, including the construction of the point cloud from the main index series that compose the MILA market and the subsequent filtering process to obtain the simplicial complexes and the subsequent computation of the persistence landscape and its norms. Finally, some conclusions are provided in Sect. 3.

2   TDA in Financial Markets

In recent years, TDA has been applied to study various contexts in financial markets. Gidea and Katz [2] characterized the financial crises of the Dotcom crash and Lehman Brothers bankruptcy through the lens of TDA, finding that persistent homology can characterize abrupt transitions such as those that occur in financial markets during analyzed financial crises. Additionally, Gidea *et al.* [3] employed a similar methodology to characterize critical transitions in the cryptocurrency market using persistent homology.

Other recent studies have shown that TDA plausibly captures the slow response to price through topological changes in the time series. In [4], persistent homology is used to detect early warning signals of financial crises in the Singapore, Malaysia, and US markets. The results compare the L^1 norms of the persistence landscape with the residuals of the analyzed time series, demonstrating that the L^1 norms of the persistence landscape obtained from the calculation of persistent homology are indicators that can provide early warning signals. Likewise, early warning signals using persistent homology and critical slowing down in US financial crises is studied in [5], and the results show that the L^p-norm time series are more likely to increase before financial crises.

In [6] also shows changes in persistent homology over multivariate distributions, evaluating the effects between the covariance of time series and the average value of the L^p-norm of persistence landscapes. On the other hand, the analysis of complex networks based on correlation using persistent homology was performed in [7] to detect early signals of critical transitions in financial markets. The conclusion is that persistent homology is a powerful tool for studying the topological changes in the correlation network of stocks and shows the presence of early warning signals of critical transitions.

Persistent homology has also been applied in the development of improved portfolio investment strategies. In [8], a new strategy based on the L^1 norms of persistence landscape to filter assets is developed, leading to more optimal and robust portfolios.

3   Analysis of the MILA Market on the Basis of TDA

In this section, we describe the methodology we have used for the analysis of the MILA market on the basis of TDA techniques, which is shown Fig. 1. It consists of four steps, described in the following subsections, including the MILA data adquisition and pre-processing (Sect. 3.1), the construction of the point cloud to extract the topological information associated with multidimensional time series (Sect. 3.2), the application of persistent homology, which provides relevant information about the changes in the topological structure of a space over a filtration process (Sect. 3.3), and finally the computation of persistence landscapes on the basis of L^p norms (Sect. 3.4).

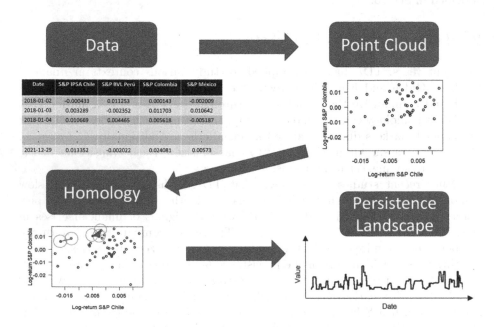

Fig. 1. Research framework

3.1   Data Adquistion and Pre-processing

The Integrated Latin American Market (MILA) emerges from the integration of the stock exchanges of Colombia, Lima, Mexico, and Santiago de Chile. It constitutes a part of the trade and economic participation endeavors among the member countries of the Pacific Alliance, composed of Chile, Colombia, Peru, and Mexico.

The daily time series of the four main indexes of the MILA market, S&P IPSA Chile, S&P BVL Perú, S&P Select Colombia, and S&P BMV Total México from January 1, 2018 to December 30, 2020 were obtained from www.spglobal.com. The time period was chosen around the Covid-19 pandemic to assess whether the topological approach enables capturing changes in the dynamics of the MILA market due to the pandemic's impact.

The S&P IPSA Chile index seeks to measure the performance of the largest and most liquid stocks listed on the Santiago Exchange. The S&P BMV Total

México Index is designed to serve as a broad benchmark for the Mexican equities market. The index is designed to measure the performance of Mexico-domiciled stocks, including real estate investment trusts and mortgage trusts, that are listed on the Mexican Stock Exchange. The S&P Select Colombia index is designed to provide exposure to the largest and most liquid stocks domiciled in Colombia. Finally, the S&P BVL Perú General index is a modified market cap-weighted index that is designed to serve as the broad benchmark for the Perú stock market.

For each index, logarithmic returns were computed as $r_{ij} = ln(P_{ij}/P_{ij-1})$, where P_{ij} represents the closing values of index i on day j (see Fig. 2).

Table 1 provides some statistics of the log-return of the four indices under consideration.

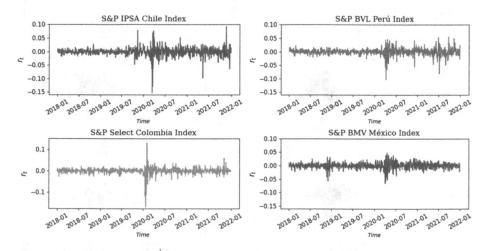

Fig. 2. Log-return of MILA indices.

3.2   Point Cloud

Point clouds are constructed to extract the topological information associated with multidimensional time series (see Fig. 3). A detailed description of the procedure used in this work on how persistent homology of multivariate series is computed is available at [2].

First, a time series X, with d values for each unit of time, is considered, and a sliding window of size w is fixed. Each window forms a point cloud of size w, and a point in the point cloud is given by $(x_1, x_2, ..., x_d)$ in $\mathbb{R}^d$ (see Fig. 1). Then, for each window w, TDA is applied, and the persistent homology of class 1 is calculated, which provides information about the topological structure of the loops in the simplicial complexes that form as the filtration parameter (radius of the disk at each point in the point cloud) varies.

Table 1. Statistics summary of log-return indices.

	S&P Chile	S&P Colombia	S&P Perú	S&P México
mean	0.000418	0.000069	−0.000017	0.000038
std	0.015197	0.014575	0.012287	0.010943
kurtosis	20.229734	37.728770	11.141234	4.554630
min	−0.152622	−0.167413	−0.103319	−0.065554
max	0.092506	0.129198	0.055775	0.047581

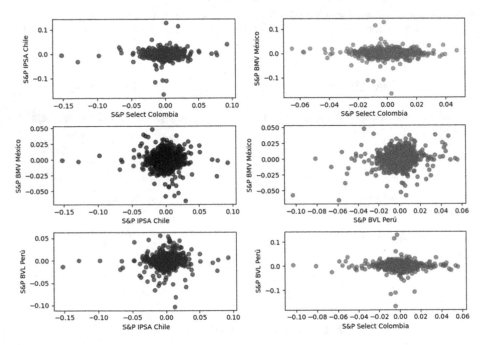

Fig. 3. Point cloud on R^2

Subsequently, the corresponding persistent landscape and its L^p norms (L^1 and L^2) are calculated to study the changes in the topological structure over time in the multidimensional time series. Here, d is equal to 4 and corresponds to the log-returns series of the indices of the countries that compose MILA market: S&P IPSA Chile, S&P BVL Perú, S&P Select Colombia, and S&P BMV Total México indices.

The sliding window in this study has a size of $w = 25$ trading days and $w = 50$, $w = 100$ and $w = 150$ trading days to study monthly, bi-monthly, quarterly and semi-annually changes in the topological structure of the market, respectively.

3.3   Persistent Homology

One of the main tools in algebraic topology is *homology*, which has played a crucial role in the development of TDA and computational topology applications. Homology provides information about a topological space that is invariant under continuous deformations, supplying relevant information about the topological structure of a space.

Persistent homology provides relevant information about the changes in the topological structure of a space over a filtration process, allowing to capture the topological features of complex data in low dimensions. Homological dimension 0 represents connected components, dimension 1 represents holes, dimension 2 represents voids, and so on. In this work, the 1-dimension homology H_1 is computed.

3.4   Persistence Landscapes

The L^p norms (L^1 and L^2) of the persistence landscapes were computed on simplicial complexes with varying window size re-construed from cloud points are depicted (see Figs. 3 and 4).

The L^1 and L^2 norms of the persistence diagram (see Figs. 4 and 5) depict the evolution of the topological structure of the abstract space constructed from the four market indices of MILA. For the fixed parameters of a window size of $w = 25$ trading days and $w = 50$, $w = 100$, $w = 150$ trading days, an atypical variation in the topological information of the market associated with the global Covid-19 pandemic is observed.

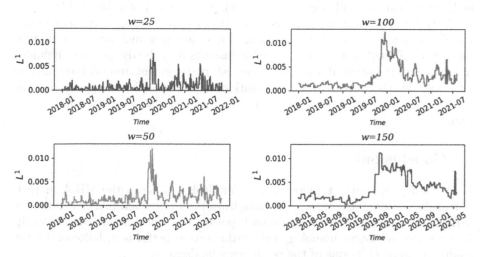

Fig. 4. Persistence landscape L^1 for various sliding windows w

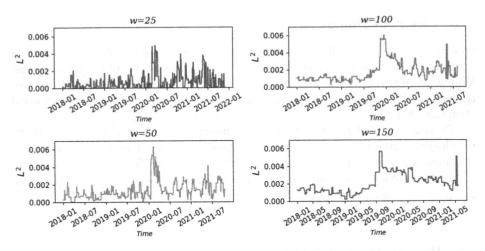

Fig. 5. Persistence landscape L^2 norm for various sliding windows w

This suggests that the L^1 and L^2 norms provide valuable insights into the dynamic changes in the market's topological structure during the analyzed period, highlighting the impact of the Covid-19 pandemic on the market's topological features. These results highlight the usefulness of topological data analysis techniques for understanding and characterizing the behavior of markets in the face of extreme events.

These results are consistent with findings from related studies [2, 10] that demonstrate how persistent homology effectively characterizes abrupt transitions in financial markets. This characteristic highlights the potential of TDA, particularly of persistent homology, as a tool that can potentially serve as an early warning indicator for abrupt transitions. These findings underscore the promising nature of TDA in providing valuable insights into the dynamics of financial markets and its potential applications in risk management and decision-making processes. Further research and exploration of persistent homology in financial contexts are warranted to fully exploit its capabilities as an early warning systems.

4   Conclusions

In this study, we apply topological data analysis (TDA) in the MILA market. A transformation of the time series data from the three main markets indices of MILA into an abstract space based on topology was constructed. Subsequently, 1-dimension persistent homology calculations were performed, followed by the computation of L^p norms of the persistence landscapes.

The results derived point out that topological descriptors such as the norm of persistent homology of the topological space derived from the set of multivariate financial time series of assets can effectively characterize fluctuations and capture significant events (such as the COVID-19 crisis) in the market dynamics. These findings demonstrate the potential of utilizing topological features to understand and analyze complex market behavior, particularly during periods of volatility or crisis. Incorporating topological descriptors into financial analysis can enhance our ability to detect and interpret relevant market events, leading to improved risk management and decision-making processes.

The L^p norms of the persistence landscapes are topological features that can be incorporated into a machine learning framework to develop forecasting models for financial time series. We propose as future research work the exploration of the potential of combining TDA with machine learning techniques to leverage these features for improved prediction accuracy in financial forecasting tasks.

References

1. Bubenik, P.: Statistical topological data analysis using persistence landscapes. J. Mach. Learn. Res. **16**, 77–102 (2015)
2. Gideam, M., Katz, Y.: Topological data analysis of financial time series: landscapes of crashes. Phys. A **491**, 820–834 (2018)
3. Gidea, M., Goldsmith, D., Katz, Y., Roldan, P., Shmalo, Y.: Topological recognition of critical transitions in time series of cryptocurrencies. Phys. A **548**, 123843 (2020)
4. Ismail, M.S., Md Noorani, M.S., Ismail, M., Abdul Razak, F., Alias, M.A.: Early warning signals of financial crises using persistent homology. Phys. A **586**, 126459 (2022)
5. Ismail, M.S., Md Noorani, M.S., Ismail, M., Abdul Razak, F.: Early warning signals of financial crises using persistent homology and critical slowing down: evidence from different correlation tests. Front. Appl. Math. Stat. **8**, 126459 (2022)
6. Aromi, L.L., Katz, Y.A., Vives, J.: Topological features of multivariate distributions: dependency on the covariance matrix. Commun. Nonlinear Sci. Numer. Simul. **103**, 105996 (2021)
7. Gidea, M.: Topological data analysis of critical transitions in financial networks. In: Shmueli, E., Barzel, B., Puzis, R. (eds.) NetSci-X 2017. SPC, pp. 47–59. Springer, Cham (2017). https://doi.org/10.1007/978-3-319-55471-6_5
8. Goel, A., Pasricha, P., Mehra, A.: Topological data analysis in investment decisions. Expert Syst. Appl. **147**, 113222 (2020)
9. Ismail, M.S., Hussain, S.I., Noorani, M.S.M.: Detecting early warning signals of major financial crashes in bitcoin using persistent homology. IEEE Access **8**, 202042–57 (2020)
10. Baitinger, E., Flegel, S.: The better turbulence index? Forecasting adverse financial markets regimes with persistent homology. Fin. Markets. Portfolio Mgmt. **35**, 277–308 (2021)
11. Majumdar, S., Laha, A.K.: Clustering and classification of time series using topological data analysis with applications to finance. Expert Syst. Appl. **162**, 113868 (2020)

Implementation of the Chaotic Systems Lorenz, Rössler, and Chen on an 8 Bit Microcontroller

Eberto Benjumea[1]([✉]) [ID], Fabio Vega[1,2] [ID], Erik Barrios[1,3] [ID], Angie Vitola[1] [ID],
and J. L. Villa[1] [ID]

[1] Universidad Tecnológica de Bolívar, Km 1 Via Turbaco, Cartagena, Colombia
{ebenjumea,fvega,erbarrios,vitolaa,jvilla}@utb.edu.co
[2] Grupo de Óptica e Informática, Universidad Popular del Cesar,
Valledupar, Colombia
[3] Esc. de Ciencias Básicas, Tecnología e Ingeniería, Universidad Nacional Abierta
y a Distancia, Corozal, Colombia
http://www.utb.edu.co

Abstract. In the present work, dynamic systems of a chaotic nature are addressed, specifically an lysis and implementation of the Lorenz chaotic system is carried out. In the first instance, the behavior of the system in continuous time and its discretization are exhibited. Subsequently, the simulations of the chaotic system using the Matlab tool are presented. For the implementation, an Arduino Mega 2560 was used, where the digital ports were coupled to an array of resistors $R - 2R$, which serves as a DAC (Digital to log Converter). The Rössler and Chen chaotic systems were also implemented with this hardware. The behavior of the signals was verified through an oscilloscope and contrasted with the simulations carried out, obtaining highly satisfactory results.

Keywords: Chaotic systems · Embedded systems · Lorenz attractor · Rössler attractor · Chen attractor

1 Introduction

Chaotic systems have found application in different fields of science, beyond physics and mathematics; biology, chemistry, engineering, and even economics have found tools to study their own systems [1]. The dynamic behavior of a deterministic chaotic system has different characteristics from those of a purely random system, and throughout the second half of the 20th century, scientists were finding and defining these characteristics. The most important of these is sensitivity to initial conditions: two initially very close states eventually gave rise to entirely separate future states. Although the sensitivity to the initial needs was foreseen by Poncairé, Edward Lorenz was the first to develop a deterministic chaotic system that possessed this property, starting from a series of differential equations, which simulated a kind of "toy atmosphere". The latter was the one who coined the expression "Butterfly Effect". In addition to sensitivity to initial

© The Author(s), under exclusive license to Springer Nature Switzerland AG 2023
J. C. Figueroa-García et al. (Eds.): WEA 2023, CCIS 1928, pp. 204–215, 2023.
https://doi.org/10.1007/978-3-031-46739-4_19

conditions, deterministic chaotic systems exhibit other characteristic properties such as recurrence, self-similarity, and fractality [2]. There are multiple applications for chaotic systems, where it is possible to highlight signal processing and information security [3], highlighting works that have been developed under this proposal to encrypt audio signals, and digital signals, including images, among others [4].

The objective of this work is to apply dynamic systems of a chaotic nature to a particular physical system, emphasizing the use of lysis tools and the correspondence between the behavior exhibited by the physical system and the lysis of the system's mathematical model. Therefore, the development and implementation of a low-cost chaotic system based on the Lorenz differential equations system discretized in a simple microcontroller is addressed. Due to the above, it may be advantageous to have a chaotic system or several of them, embedded in a small component from which the states of these systems can be available for synchronization or control purposes in a secure wireless communications system, or electronic security systems: such as electric door controls, or secure car or home alarms. Understanding that the advantage of having one or more systems embedded in a single microcontroller is mainly their size or portability.

The system consists of a low-cost microcontroller and a resistive array as DACs. Since the microcontroller can be programmed in C language, the program can be easily reconfigurable, and adapted to different chaotic systems, for example, Rossler and Chen as we will show.

The document is organized as follows. Section 2 presents the mathematical model used, carrying out an lysis in Matlab of the behavior of the system in continuous time. Also, it includes the lysis of equilibrium points, eigenvalues estimation, and bifurcation diagram. In Sect. 3 we present the hardware implementation, including the systems discretization, the algorithm, and the implementation in an Arduino Mega 2560. Then, the results are shown in Sect. 4, and we compare the results of the simulation and implementation. Finally, the relevant conclusions of the work are presented.

2 Mathematical Model

The Lorenz system is presented below, which consists of three first-order nonlinear ordinary differential equations.

$$x'(t) = -\sigma x(t) + \sigma y(t) \tag{1}$$
$$y'(t) = \rho x(t) - y(t) - x(t)z(t) \tag{2}$$
$$z'(t) = x(t)y(t) - bz(t), \tag{3}$$

where, σ is the Prandtl number, ρ is the Rayleigh number, and b is another parameter that is related to the physical size of the system. In this system, it is assumed that the three parameters are positive, in addition, $\sigma > b + 1$.

2.1   System Behavior Lysis

Starting from the Lorenz equations, it is necessary to understand system behavior by lyzing the equilibrium points, bifurcations, and response characterization.

Fixed Points. The fixed points are determined when $f'(t) = 0$, for our lysis, we must find the solution of the following system of equations:

$$-\sigma x + \sigma y = 0 \tag{4}$$

$$\rho x - y - xz = 0 \tag{5}$$

$$xy - bz = 0 \tag{6}$$

It is easy to verify that the point $[0, 0, 0]$ is an equilibrium point of the system. From Eq. (4) we have that $x = y$, and replacing in Eq. (5) and factoring, we obtain Eq. (7).

$$x(\rho - 1 - z) = 0 \tag{7}$$

Now, having $z = \rho - 1$, $y = x$ and replacing both in Eq. (6) results in Eq. (8).

$$x^2 - b(\rho - 1) = 0 \tag{8}$$

$$x_{12} = \pm\sqrt{b(\rho - 1)} \tag{9}$$

Given the above, we have the three equilibrium points in Eq. (10), where it can be evidenced that there is a bifurcation in $\rho = 1$.

$$p_1 = \begin{bmatrix} 0 \\ 0 \\ 0 \end{bmatrix} ; p_2 = \begin{bmatrix} \sqrt{b(\rho - 1)} \\ \sqrt{b(\rho - 1)} \\ \rho - 1 \end{bmatrix} ; p_3 = \begin{bmatrix} -\sqrt{b(\rho - 1)} \\ -\sqrt{b(\rho - 1)} \\ \rho - 1 \end{bmatrix} \tag{10}$$

Characterization of Fixed Points. Fixed points can be characterized using the Jacobian of the nonlinear system and exploring their eigenvalues. Equation (11) is the Jacobian of the nonlinear system in Eq. (4, 5, 6).

$$A = \begin{bmatrix} -\sigma & \sigma & 0 \\ \rho - z & -1 & -x \\ y & x & -b \end{bmatrix} \tag{11}$$

From Eq. (11) the calculation of the eigenvalues for $p_1 = [0, 0, 0]$.

$$A_{p_1} = \begin{bmatrix} -\sigma & \sigma & 0 \\ \rho & -1 & 0 \\ 0 & 0 & -b \end{bmatrix} \qquad (12)$$

$$\lambda I - A = \begin{bmatrix} (\lambda + \sigma) & -\sigma & 0 \\ -\rho & (\lambda + 1) & 0 \\ 0 & 0 & (\lambda + b) \end{bmatrix} \qquad (13)$$

The characteristic polynomial is given by Eq. (13).

$$p(\lambda) = (\lambda + \sigma)(\lambda + 1)(\lambda + b) - \rho\sigma(\lambda + b) = 0 \qquad (14)$$

$$(\lambda + b) = 0; (\lambda + \sigma)(\lambda + 1) - \rho\sigma = 0$$

$$\lambda_1 = -b; \lambda^2 + \lambda(1 + \sigma) + \sigma(1 - \rho) = 0$$

Applying the general equation for solving quadratic equations we obtain Eq. (14).

$$\lambda_{2,3} = \frac{-(1 + \sigma) \pm \sqrt{(1 + \sigma)^2 - 4\sigma(1 - \rho)}}{2} \qquad (15)$$

Note that when $\rho = 1$ Eq. (15) is:

$$\lambda_1 = -b \; ; \; \lambda_2 = -(1 + \sigma) \; ; \; \lambda_3 = 0 \qquad (16)$$

Thus, it is possible to infer that for $0 \leq \rho < 1$ the eigenvalues are real less than zero, which makes the system attract or sink at the point $p_1 = [0, 0, 0]$.

Next, we will restrict the study to the special case of the Lorenz system where the parameters are given by $\sigma = 10$, $b = 8/3$ and $\rho = 28$. Historically, these are the values that Lorenz used when he first found phenomena in this system [5]. Therefore, the points found before would be given by Eq. (16).

$$p_1 = \begin{bmatrix} 0 \\ 0 \\ 0 \end{bmatrix} ; p_2 = \begin{bmatrix} \sqrt{(8/3)(27)} \\ \sqrt{(8/3)(27)} \\ 27 \end{bmatrix} ; p_3 = \begin{bmatrix} -\sqrt{(8/3)(27)} \\ -\sqrt{(8/3)(27)} \\ 27 \end{bmatrix} \qquad (17)$$

Simplifying Eq. (16) we obtain Eq. (17).

$$p_1 = \begin{bmatrix} 0 \\ 0 \\ 0 \end{bmatrix} ; p_2 = \begin{bmatrix} 6\sqrt{2} \\ 6\sqrt{2} \\ 27 \end{bmatrix} ; p_3 = \begin{bmatrix} -6\sqrt{2} \\ -6\sqrt{2} \\ 27 \end{bmatrix} \qquad (18)$$

Taking into account that $6\sqrt{2} \approx 8.48528$, in Fig. 1a it is possible to show the detection of equilibrium points on the Lorenz attractor. Likewise, Fig. 1a presents the vector field of the system with its respective solutions.

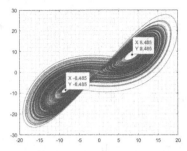

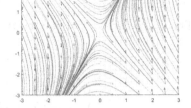

(a) Detection of equilibrium points for $p_1 = (0,0,0)$, $p_{2,3} = (\pm6\sqrt{2},\pm6\sqrt{2},27)$

(b) Solutions of the Lorenz system over its vector field

Fig. 1. Detection of equilibrium points and Solutions of the Lorenz

2.2 Simulation in Matlab

For the design and simulation of the Lorenz chaotic system, the Simulink application of the Matlab tool was used under version R2019b.

In Fig. 2 two identical subsystems of Lorenz differential equations and their internal design are presented. The objective is to simulate two systems with relatively close initial conditions to observe their response over time. Figure 3 uses a starting point of $p_1 = [0,2,0]$ for subsystem 1, and $p_2 = [0,2.01,0]$ for subsystem 2.

It is possible to confirm the paradigm of chaotic systems, where the susceptibility of the systems to their initial conditions is evident. Additionally, Fig. 4 is presented; note that although both solutions have very different initial conditions, that is, $p_1 = [0,2,0]$ and $p_2 = [0,-2,0]$, the solutions eventually tend to revolve around the same two points, hence the name Lorenz attractor. Finally, Fig. 5 shows the graph of bifurcations made in Matlab.

3 Hardware Implementation

In this section we introduced de discretized system, then we describe the implementation in a microcontroller.

3.1 System Discretization

To implement the algorithm in an embedded system, we use the Gauss derivative approximation for discrete systems:

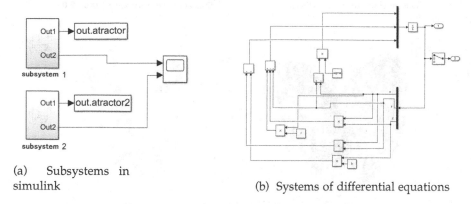

(a)   Subsystems   in
simulink

(b) Systems of differential equations

Fig. 2. Design of the Lorenz equation system in Simulink.

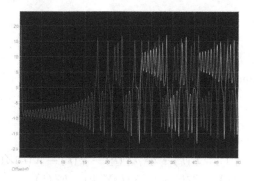

Fig. 3. x-signal for nearby initial conditions.

$$\frac{df(x, y, z)}{dt} \approx \frac{f(k) - f(k - 1)}{t_s} \tag{19}$$

where t_s must be related to the time between samples. From here we can define
the discrete function as:

$$f(k) = f(k - 1) + t_s * \frac{df(x, y, z)}{dt} \tag{20}$$

where $f(k - 1)$, Implies an initial value for the initial of the iterations, in the
numerical approximation to start the computation. The sampling period t_s must
be such that it satisfies the Nyquist theorem for signal reconstruction and such
that $t_s = 0.1/|\lambda| \, max$. [6] Computing the expression for the eigenvalues given
by [7], the value $|\lambda| \, max = 22.8277$ is obtained. and choosing a sample for 10
times the maximum frequency, the sampling period complies with $t_s = 0.00438$
[8,9]. The sampling period affects the stability and dynamics in the discretization
process as can be seen in the work [8].

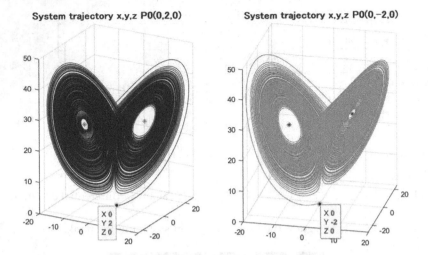

Fig. 4. Simulink.

The discrete-time differential equation for the third-order chaotic Lorenz system becomes:

$$X(k+1) = X(k) + t_s(-\sigma X(k) + \sigma Y(k)) \tag{21}$$
$$Y(k+1) = Y(k) + t_s(\rho X(k) - Y(k) - X(k)Z(k)) \tag{22}$$
$$Z(k) = Z(k) + t_s(X(k)Y(k) - bZ(k)) \tag{23}$$

where $X(k)$, $Y(k)$ y $Z(k)$ they form the current state of the system, and t_s is the sampling time.

For the chaotic Rössler system it remains:

$$X(k+1) = X(k) + t_s(Y(k) + Z(k)) \tag{24}$$
$$Y(k+1) = Y(k) + t_s(X(k) - aY(k)) \tag{25}$$
$$Z(k+1) = Z(k) + t_s(b + Z(k)(X(k) - c)) \tag{26}$$

For Chen's chaotic system it would be:

$$X(k+1) = X(k) + at_s(Y(k) - X(k)) \tag{27}$$
$$Y(k+1) = Y(k) + t_s((c-a)X(k) - X(k)Z(k) + cY(k)) \tag{28}$$
$$Z(k+1) = Z(k) + t_s(X(k)Y(k) - bZ(k)) \tag{29}$$

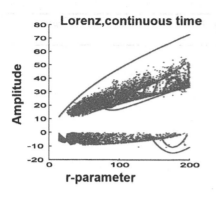
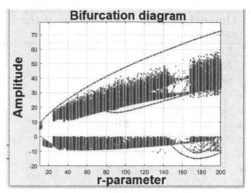

Fig. 5. bifurcation comparison

3.2 Microcontroller Implementation

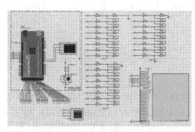

(a) Schematic of the oscillators in Proteus.

(b) Lorenz oscillator electronic circuit with Arduino

Fig. 6. Lorenz oscillator implementation on arduino Mega 2560

Figure 6a shows the electronic circuit used to implement the chaotic Lorenz oscillator. An Arduino Mega 2560 was used, where the digital ports A, C, and L were coupled to an array of resistors $R - 2R$, which acted as a digital-to-log converter (DAC). This arrangement was selected because it is simple to configure and inexpensive. The calculated values of variables $x(t)$, $y(t)$, and $z(t)$ are written to the named ports every 4.38 ms. Thus, the DAC outputs were obtained from resistors labeled $R48$, $R20$, and $R50$. Because the system outputs are log, it is possible to obtain the output in the discrete mode. Once the digital ports are written, the three variables are sent via a serial port under a simple position control. Additionally, a TFT LCD screen shown in Fig. 6a was used only for the status display. Finally, Fig. 6b shows the physical implementation of the electronic circuit of the oscillator.

On the other hand, Algorithm 1 was adopted to test the arrangement in the Arduino environment, where the initial conditions of the oscillator $[x1, y1, z1]$, were chosen arbitrarily, taking care that they are different from zero.

Algorithm 1: Implementation of the Lorenz system in arduino Mega 2560.

Data: σ, b, r, t_s, x_1, y_1, z_1
Result: x, y, z

1 **while** *1* **do**
2   Solve $x \leftarrow Eq.(18)$;
3   Solve $y \leftarrow Eq.(19)$;
4   Solve $z \leftarrow Eq.(20)$;
5      $cx = 5(x + 20)$;
6      $cz = 2((z + 30))$;
7      $cy = 5(y + 20)$;
8      $PORTA = cx$;
9      $PORTC = cy$;
10      $PORTL = cz$;

11 **return** x, y, z

The Arduino code for Lorenz, Rössler, and Chen chaotic oscillators implementation can be downloaded from: https://github.com/vegaapp/MCUcaoticsystem.

4   Results and Discussion

The data used were generated using the Matlab environment and stored in a mat file for future manipulation. Likewise, the behavior of the signals was verified through an oscilloscope, and the results are shown in Fig. 7; where Fig. 7a illustrates the oscilloscope reading of the x (yellow) and y (blue) signals; Fig. 7b shows the oscilloscope reading of the x (yellow) and z (blue) signals, and Fig. 7c shows the reading of the oscilloscope of the y (yellow) and z (blue) signals. In Fig. 10, you can see the data acquired in real-time for each of the signals x, y, and z and their combinations xy, xz and yz of the three chaotic systems implemented.

Additionally, it was possible to evaluate the operation of the electronic circuit by comparing the implementation data with those obtained in the simulation. In Fig. 8 you can see the signals x, y generated both by the implementation and in the simulation: It is noteworthy that the initial conditions were different, and their results are consistent with the theoretical lyses set out in previous sections according to the shape of the expected signal. Therefore, Fig. 9 shows the representations in three dimensions ($3D$) of the signals x, y, z. Initially, they are shown separately; then, we overlap the variables to confirm the existence of points on which, regardless of the initial conditions, the solutions tend to rotate around them, which corresponds to the Lorenz attractor.

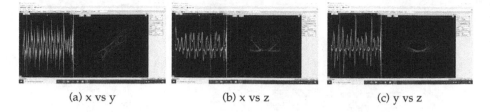

(a) x vs y   (b) x vs z   (c) y vs z

Fig. 7. Display on the oscilloscope Lorenz chaotic oscillator (Color figure online)

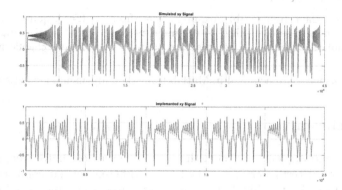

Fig. 8. Comparison between the implementation and the simulation of the signals x and y

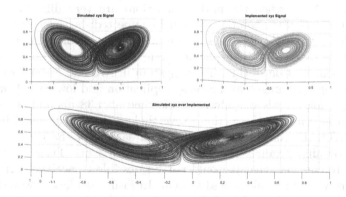

Fig. 9. Comparison of the xyz signal implemented over simulated.

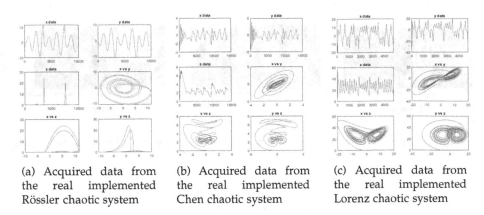

(a) Acquired data from the real implemented Rössler chaotic system

(b) Acquired data from the real implemented Chen chaotic system

(c) Acquired data from the real implemented Lorenz chaotic system

Fig. 10. Display data acquired in Matlab from the implemented chaotic systems

5   Conclusions

Simulations and implementation of the chaotic Lorenz oscillator were presented, in which several tests were performed using different initial conditions, which allowed us to verify two highly relevant facts. First, when the initial conditions are very close to each other, the responses of the systems are identical only for a determined time, since later, the solutions are quite far apart from each other (Note Fig. 3). Now, when the initial conditions are very different, very little relationship between the solutions would be expected; however, it was possible to show that eventually, all the solutions tended to revolve around the same pairs of points (See Fig. 4); this phenomenon is known as the Lorenz attractor.

The implementation of this chaotic system in Arduino Mega 2560 was successful, offering advantages such as easy replication and low cost. However, the generation of log signals was always performed at 4.38 ms and there were no decreases or increases in this period. Nevertheless, during the acquisition of the data in MATLAB, the acquisition time of a sample of the three signals was measured, obtaining values between 1.3 ms and 3.3 ms. These measurements allowed us to conclude that it would not be possible to achieve periods of less than 3.3 ms with the implemented system. In future studies, it would be interesting to explore the behavior of the signals and the limiting conditions of the implemented system before different generation periods. In addition, because the acquired data were obtained directly from the microcontroller via a serial port, it would be beneficial to physically acquire the data at the output of the converter to establish its impact on the signals.

A link to the video of the results is http://www.youtube.com/watch?v=CH_Q9EZ3tKY&feature=youtu.be.

Acknowledgments. The authors gratefully acknowledge the financial support received from Universidad Tecnológica de Bolívar. Additionally, E. Benjumea, F. Vega, and E. Barrios express their sincere gratitude to the Ministerio de Ciencia y Tecnología

Minciencias and Sistema General de Regalías (Programa de Becas de Excelencia) for granting them a PhD scholarship.

References

1. Escot Mangas, L.: Dinámica económica caótica: una aplicación al estudio del ciclo y el crecimiento económico. Universidad Complutense de Madrid, Servicio de Publicaciones (2003)
2. Izquierdo, A.P.: La teoría del caos: Las leyes de lo impredecible. RBA Libros (2019)
3. Kocarev, L.J., Halle, K.S., Eckert, K., Chua, L.O., Parlitz, U.: Experimental demonstration of secure communications via chaotic synchronization. Int. J. Bifurcat. Chaos 2(03), 709–713 (1992)
4. Bustos, A.Y.A.: Synchronization of discrete-time chaotic oscillators. Ph.D. thesis, Centro de Investigación Científica y de Educación Superior de Ensenada (2005)
5. Hirsch, M.W., Smale, S., Devaney, R.L.: Differential Equations, Dynamical Systems, and an Introduction to Chaos. Academic Press (2012)
6. Haugen, F.: Model forms and time-response calculations. In: Dynamic Systems: Modeling, Analysis and Simulation, pp. 50–73 (2004)
7. Lorenz, E.N.: Deterministic nonperiodic flow. J. Atmos. Sci. 20, 130–141 (1963)
8. Chiu, R., Mora-González, M., López-Mancilla, D.: Chaotic oscillators implemented into a PIC18F microcontroller. Nova Scientia 6(12), 60–77 (2014)
9. Chiu, R., Mora-Gonzalez, M., Lopez-Mancilla, D.: Implementation of a chaotic oscillator into a simple microcontroller. IERI Procedia 4, 247–252 (2013)

Enhancing Impaired Waist-to-Height Ratio Classification Using Neural Networks

Erika Severeyn[1]([✉])[iD], Alexandra La Cruz[2][iD], and Mónica Huerta[3][iD]

[1] Universidad Simón Bolívar, Caracas, Venezuela
severeynerika@usb.ve
[2] Universidad de Ibagué, Ibagué, Colombia
alexandra.lacruz@unibague.edu.co
[3] Universidad Politécnica Salesiana, Cuenca, Ecuador
mhuerta@ups.edu.ec

Abstract. Obesity is a condition characterized by the excessive accumulation of adipose tissue. However, directly measuring adiposity can be challenging, especially in epidemiological and clinical settings. Therefore, simple anthropometric measurements are commonly used to assess fat quantity and distribution. The Body Mass Index (BMI) is a widely used measure for estimating total fat quantity. Additionally, indicators such as waist circumference and waist-to-height ratio (WHtR) provide valuable insights into the distribution of visceral, central, or abdominal fat. These measurements play a crucial role in understanding and evaluating health risks associated with obesity. This study utilized a dataset consisting of 1978 participants, anthropometric measurements, including height, weight, body circumferences, and body folds, were collected from each participant. The research aimed to classify individuals with impaired WHtR using artificial neural networks (ANNs) based on anthropometric parameters. Multiple tests were conducted using Monte Carlo cross-validation with different training and testing ratios. The architecture of the ANN was modified by varying the number of hidden layers. The results showed an accuracy exceeding 82.4%. The sensitivity values consistently surpassed 79.9%, indicating the model's effective detection of positive cases. The model also demonstrated excellent specificity, with a score exceeding 85%. Positive and negative predictive values showed slight improvements as the training data expanded. The F1 score, which considers both precision and sensitivity, was above 0.794, indicating a favorable balance in classifying individuals with impaired WHtR. The model's performance remained consistent across different training-test splits, suggesting stability and reliability in its predictions.

Keywords: Monte Carlo Cross Validation · Artificial Neural Networks · Waist to Height Ratio

Supported by Universidad de Ibagué, Universidad Politécnica Salesiana, and Universidad Simón Bolívar.

J. C. Figueroa-García et al. (Eds.): WEA 2023, CCIS 1928, pp. 216–227, 2023.
https://doi.org/10.1007/978-3-031-46739-4_20

1   Introduction

Obesity has reached alarming levels among adults, adolescents, and children. Excess weight and obesity, along with a sedentary lifestyle and a family history of cardiovascular disease [6], contribute to a significant prevalence of metabolic disorders such as Metabolic Syndrome (MS) [23,25], Insulin Resistance (IR) [33, 34], atherosclerosis [41], and impaired glucose tolerance [14,32]. These conditions significantly increase the risk of developing type 2 diabetes and cardiovascular disease [24]. The high prevalence of cardiovascular diseases (CVD) and diabetes poses a significant public health concern, as they are the primary causes of disability and mortality in many countries worldwide.

The excessive accumulation of adipose tissue characterizes obesity [21]. However, in epidemiological and clinical contexts, assessing fat quantity and distribution relies on simple anthropometric measurements due to the challenges posed by direct adiposity measurement [20]. The Body Mass Index (BMI) [3] is a prevalent measure for estimating total fat quantity. Moreover, indicators such as Waist Circumference (WC), Waist-to-Hip Ratio (WHR), and the more recently introduced Waist-to-Height Ratio (WHtR) offer valuable insights into the distribution of visceral, central, or abdominal fat [10]. These measurements play a crucial role in understanding and assessing obesity-related health risks.

While WC is considered a valuable indicator for CVD, IR, and MS, its usefulness is limited due to variations in diagnostic cut-off points based on ethnic and racial backgrounds [22]. The literature suggests that a better predictor in this regard is the WHtR, which is a universal index with gender-specific variations. A WHtR value of 0.50 or higher is associated with cardiometabolic risk in individuals aged 18 and above [8]. Young adults with a normal BMI and a WHtR above 0.50 exhibit elevated IR, insulin plasma concentration, triglyceride levels, and lower HDL cholesterol levels compared to those with a WHtR below 0.50 [17]. Furthermore, research evaluating the predictive value of WHtR as a predictor of coronary heart disease has shown a higher prevalence of this disease among individuals with a WHtR of 0.50 or higher (indicating abdominal obesity) [4].

Various research studies demonstrate the potential of integrating machine learning into medical tasks, including disease diagnostics and personalized treatment provision. Incorporating machine learning techniques into clinical information processing offers several advantages. Firstly, it enables the analysis of datasets with high dimensionality. Additionally, it allows for analyzing information in diverse formats, such as images [9,15] and electrical data [19]. Moreover, machine learning algorithms can identify intricate patterns and relationships within the data [26].

The application of artificial neural networks (ANN) in the diagnosis of obesity [30], MS [37], and metabolic diseases have shown promising results in the field of medical research. ANNs, known for their capacity to learn and recognize complex patterns, have been used to analyze large datasets of various metabolic parameters, including BMI [28], WC [38], blood glucose levels [27] and lipid profiles [11]. By training these networks with relevant data, they can effectively identify patterns and relationships that contribute to diagnosing obesity, MS, and related metabolic disorders. The integration of neural networks in this diagnostic process has the potential to enhance accuracy and efficiency, ultimately leading to improved patient outcomes and personalized treatment strategies.

Hence, the primary objective of this research is to utilize anthropometric parameters and the ANN technique as a classifier to categorize individuals with impaired WHtR. A comprehensive database comprising 1978 subjects was employed, encompassing 26 different anthropometric variables for achieving this goal. The subsequent section of this study provides a detailed account of the methodology used. Section 3 elaborates on the main findings obtained from the analysis. Furthermore, Sects. 4 and 5 delve into the discussion of these findings and present the concluding remarks, respectively. By employing the ANN technique and leveraging the extensive dataset, this study aims to contribute to the understanding and identifying individuals with impaired WHtR, thereby aiding in the diagnosis and management of related health conditions.

2   Methodology

2.1   Database

The dataset used in this study comprises a total of 1978 individuals, with 678 being male and the remaining participants being female. The Nutritional Evaluation Laboratory of Simón Bolívar University collected this dataset between 2004 and 2012 [12]. The data collection protocol included 28 anthropometric measurements, covering parameters such as height, weight, body circumferences, and body folds. Carefully recorded, these measurements were part of the comprehensive assessment during the data collection period. Together with a wide range of anthropometric variables, this dataset provides a robust foundation for analyzing and investigating various aspects of body composition and nutritional evaluation. Additionally, Eq. (1) calculated the WHtR.

$$WHtR = \frac{Waist}{Height} \tag{1}$$

where *Waist* is the circumferential perimeter of the waist (measured in centimeters) and the *Height* is the tall (measured in centimeters) [5,7]. In this research, the inclusion criteria for impaired WHtR were based on [4,16], where a WHtR above 0.5 is considered indicative of an increased risk of health issues like obesity, cardiovascular diseases, and metabolic disorders.

All methodologies employed in this research adhered to the ethical guidelines set forth by the Bioethical Committee of Simon Bolívar University, following the principles outlined in the 1964 Helsinki Declaration and its subsequent revisions or any equivalent ethical standards. Before they participated in the study, all subjects provided their informed consent by signing the necessary documentation. This ensured that the participants were fully aware of the nature of the study, its objectives, and any potential risks or benefits associated with their involvement. By upholding these ethical standards and obtaining informed consent, the study aimed to protect the rights, privacy, and well-being of the individuals involved.

2.2 Classifier Assessment Metrics

In order to evaluate the ANNs classifiers, the true positives (TP), false positives (FP), true negatives (TN), and false negatives (FN) were measured [35]. The accuracy (ACC), specificity (SPE), sensitivity (SEN), positive predictive value (PPV), negative predictive value (NPV), and F1 score (F1) were calculated using the Eqs. (2), (3), (4), (5), (6), and (7) respectively.

$$ACC = \frac{(TP+TN)}{(TP+FP+TN+FN)} \tag{2}$$

$$SEN = \frac{TP}{(TP+FN)} \tag{3}$$

$$SPE = \frac{TN}{(TN+FP)} \tag{4}$$

$$PPV = \frac{TP}{(FP+TP)} \tag{5}$$

$$NPV = \frac{TN}{(FN+TN)} \tag{6}$$

$$F1 = 2\,\frac{(PPV)\,(SEN)}{(PPV+SEN)} \tag{7}$$

2.3 ANN Implemented

Artificial neural networks (ANNs) are computational frameworks that draw inspiration from the intricate structure and functional mechanisms of the human brain. Comprising interconnected nodes, often referred to as "neurons", these networks possess the ability to process and transmit information. Engineers specifically design ANNs to acquire knowledge and generate predictions by discerning intricate patterns within complex datasets. This learning process, commonly known as training, enables ANNs to uncover underlying relationships and make accurate predictions based on the acquired knowledge [39].

ANNs can detect and categorize patterns present in data by training to identify and classify input patterns by analyzing their inherent features and attributes [2]. ANNs find utility in various applications, including image recognition, speech recognition, and data analysis. They consist of multiple interconnected layers of nodes, or neurons, which process and evaluate the input data [2]. During the training phase, the network adjusts the weights and biases of its connections to optimize its capability for pattern recognition and classification. Once trained, the network can effectively classify new and unseen patterns based on the knowledge it acquired during training [42].

ANNs have emerged as highly effective instruments in diverse domains, encompassing computer vision, natural language processing, and bioinformatics. They facilitate automated and efficient examination of intricate data, enabling tasks like object recognition, handwriting recognition, and disease diagnosis [13].

Monte Carlo Cross Validation (MCCV). The MCCV, widely employed in machine learning, evaluates model performance. It entails conducting the cross-validation process multiple times using distinct data splits. This methodology effectively reduces performance estimate fluctuations and offers a more dependable evaluation of the model's generalization. By averaging the outcomes across numerous iterations, MCCV provides a reliable measure of the model's anticipated performance on unseen data [1]. This method is notably effective when dealing with limited data or in cases of significant variability in performance estimates.

Characteristics of ANN Implemented. In this study, a feedforward neural network was employed in conjunction with a training function that effectively updates weight and bias values using the scaled conjugate gradient technique to classify individuals with impaired WHtR. This approach allows the network to iteratively adjust its weights and biases, facilitating effective navigation through complex and multidimensional input spaces. This adaptive capability enhances the network's flexibility and promotes robust learning from the available data. To further improve classification accuracy, a Monte Carlo cross-validation (MCCV) technique was implemented [36]. Figure 1 depicted the methodology research followed in this study.

The feedforward neural network classifier was trained and tested, first, randomly dividing the dataset into two groups: one for training and the other for testing. This random partitioning was repeated 100 times to ensure the reliability and robustness of the results. In each iteration, the different performance metrics were calculated. The partitions processed were for 90% training and 10% testing, 80% training and 20% testing, 70% training and 30% testing, 60% training and 40% testing, and 50% training and 50% testing. The random partitioning allows a comprehensive evaluation of the ANN's performance under various training and testing scenarios.

Furthermore, the procedure was repeated for the feedforward neural networks with different numbers of hidden layers, ranging from 10 to 100 layers. This extensive analysis enabled a thorough examination of the ANN's performance across different configurations.

2.4   Statistical Tests

In order to make a statistical comparison of the metrics from each experiment, the researchers utilized the Mann-Whitney U test. This particular test was selected because it assumes that the samples being compared are not paired and have distributions that deviate from the normal distribution. The statistical significance was given considering a p-value lower than 5%, as stated by [18]. Tables 1, 2, 3, 4, and 5 are presented as mean and standard deviation values (mean $\pm$ STD).

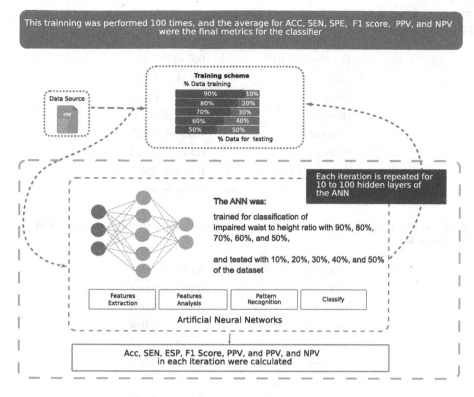

Fig. 1. General methodology schematics for the ANN classification.

3   Results

Tables 1, 2, 3, 4, and 5 present the area under the ROC curve of ANNs classification, accuracy, sensitivity, specificity, positive predictive value, negative predictive value, and F1 score obtained from applying ANNs to classify subjects with impaired WHtR. These results correspond to different training and testing percentage values used in the experiments and the best amount of hidden layer in ANN.

4   Discussion

This research used ANNs to classify impaired WHtR based on anthropometric parameters. In order to achieve this classification, several testing was conducted using MCCV (Monte Carlo cross-validation) with different ratios for training and testing. Furthermore, the ANN architecture was modified by varying the number of hidden layers. The performance of the model was evaluated using various metrics, including accuracy, sensitivity, specificity, positive predictive value, negative predictive value, and F1 score.

Table 1. Monte Carlo cross-validation test results for 90% training and 10% test and 70 hidden layers.

Training%-Test%	90%-10%
AUC	0.903 ± 0.023
Sensitivity	0.799 ± 0.065
Specificity	0.875 ± 0.050
Accuracy	0.843 ± 0.025
F1 Score	0.815 ± 0.033
Negative Predictive Value	0.850 ± 0.037
Positive Predictive Value	0.839 ± 0.048

Table 2. Monte Carlo cross-validation test results for 80% training and 20% test and 70 hidden layers.

Training%-Test%	80%-20%
AUC	0.900 ± 0.014
Sensitivity	0.797 ± 0.059
Specificity	0.860 ± 0.048
Accuracy	0.833 ± 0.017
F1 Score	0.806 ± 0.023
Negative Predictive Value	0.848 ± 0.033
Positive Predictive Value	0.821 ± 0.044

Table 3. Monte Carlo cross-validation test results for 70% training and 30% test and 70 hidden layers.

Training%-Test%	70%-30%
AUC	0.899 ± 0.014
Sensitivity	0.798 ± 0.047
Specificity	0.852 ± 0.044
Accuracy	0.829 ± 0.016
F1 Score	0.804 ± 0.020
Negative Predictive Value	0.846 ± 0.026
Positive Predictive Value	0.813 ± 0.037

The analysis of accuracy revealed that the model's predictive performance exhibited a marginal enhancement with an increase in the percentage of training data. Nevertheless, no statistically significant differences were observed between each experiment. This implies that the model's performance remained stable across various training ratios. Generally, the accuracy metric is an evaluator for a classification model's ability to predict the class labels of the data. In this

Table 4. Monte Carlo cross-validation test results for 60% training and 40% test and 50 hidden layers.

Training%-Test%	60%-40%
AUC	0.898 ± 0.013
Sensitivity	0.787 ± 0.040
Specificity	0.860 ± 0.035
Accuracy	0.828± 0.015
F1 Score	0.799 ± 0.018
Negative Predictive Value	0.840 ± 0.023
Positive Predictive Value	0.814 ± 0.034

!t

Table 5. Monte Carlo cross-validation test results for 50% training and 50% test and 30 hidden layers.

Training%-Test%	50%-50%
AUC	0.895 ± 0.012
Sensitivity	0.784 ± 0.039
Specificity	0.855 ± 0.035
Accuracy	0.824 ± 0.013
F1 Score	0.794 ± 0.017
Negative Predictive Value	0.838 ± 0.021
Positive Predictive Value	0.808 ± 0.034

specific study, the model achieved an impressive level of classification accuracy, surpassing 82.4% [29].

Concerning the sensitivity, our experiments consistently showed that using a 90% for training and 10% for testing split resulted in values exceeding 79.9%, indicating the model's effective and accurate detection of positive cases. The consistent sensitivity observed across all experiments suggests that our model is a good classifier identifying individuals with impairments [29].

The measure of specificity refers to the accurate identification of the true negative cases by the model [29]. Our research findings demonstrate a slight enhancement in specificity as the training dataset expands. The model showcases excellent performance in correctly categorizing negative cases, as evidenced by its impressive score exceeding 85%.

As the amount of training data increases, the PPV, also known as precision, exhibits a slight improvement. PPV reflects the proportion of predicted positive instances that are truly positive. A high PPV value exceeding 80.8% indicates that the likelihood of false positives in the model's predictions is only 19.2% citeumberger2017understanding. False positives may lead to unnecessary medical treatments for subjects with normal WHtR.

Similarly, NPV represents the proportion of predicted negative instances that are truly negative. The results indicate a slight increase in NPV as the training data expands. With an NPV exceeding 83.8%, the model effectively identifies negative instances, with only a 16% probability of false negatives in its predictions [31]. False negatives can result in delayed or missed diagnoses, preventing patients from receiving timely treatment and care. This can lead to developing obesity, and MS among others.

The F1 score is a metric that assesses a classification model's performance by considering both precision and sensitivity. It provides an overall evaluation of how well the model achieves a balance between accurately identifying positive instances (precision) and capturing all relevant positive instances (sensitivity) [40]. In this particular study, obtaining an F1 score above 0.794 suggests that the model exhibits a favorable balance between precision and sensitivity when classifying impaired WHtR subjects. This indicates that the model can accurately identify positive instances while also capturing a significant proportion of the actual positive instances.

It is important to highlight that the standard deviations associated with accuracy, specificity, positive predictive values, and F1 score values are relatively low. This indicates that the model's performance remains consistent across multiple runs, regardless of different training-test splits of the database. The low standard deviations suggest that the results are reliable and not significantly affected by random variations. In other words, the model's performance can be considered stable and not heavily influenced by chance fluctuations in the data.

5   Conclusions

In conclusion, this research utilized ANNs to classify impaired WHtR based on anthropometric parameters. Multiple tests were conducted using MCCV with different training and testing ratios, and the ANN architecture was modified by varying the number of hidden layers. The model exhibited an impressive level of classification accuracy, surpassing 82.4%. Sensitivity values consistently exceeded 79.9%, indicating the model's effective detection of positive cases. The model also demonstrated excellent specificity, with a score exceeding 85%. Positive and negative predictive values showed slight improvements as the training data expanded. The F1 score, which considers both precision and sensitivity, was above 0.794, indicating a favorable balance in classifying impaired WHtR subjects. The model's performance remained consistent across different training-test splits, suggesting stability and reliability.

In future work, we will apply this methodology to different demographic groups, cultural contexts, or environmental conditions. By doing so, we can gain a deeper understanding of the model's generalizability and identify any potential biases or limitations that may arise in specific contexts.

Acknowledgment. The Research Direction of Universidad de Ibagué from Ibagué Colombia, the Vice-rectorate of Research of Universidad Politécnica Salesiana from Cuenca, Ecuador, and the Research and Development Deanery of the Universidad Simón Bolívar (DID) from Caracas, Venezuela are the main founded of this project.

References

1. A. Ramezan, C., A. Warner, T., E. Maxwell, A.: Evaluation of sampling and cross-validation tuning strategies for regional-scale machine learning classification. Remote Sens. **11**(2), 185 (2019)
2. Abiodun, O.I., et al.: Comprehensive review of artificial neural network applications to pattern recognition. IEEE Access **7**, 158820–158846 (2019)
3. Al-Ghamdi, S., et al.: Prevalence of overweight and obesity based on the body mass index; a cross-sectional study in Alkharj, Saudi Arabia. Lipids Health Dis. **17**(1), 1–8 (2018)
4. Alshamiri, M.Q., Habbab, M.A., Al-Qahtani, S.S., Alghalayini, K.A., Al-Qattan, O.M., El-Shaer, F., et al.: Waist-to-height ratio (WHTR) in predicting coronary artery disease compared to body mass index and waist circumference in a single center from Saudi Arabia. Cardiol. Res. Pract. **2020** (2020)
5. Ashwell, M., Gunn, P., Gibson, S.: Waist-to-height ratio is a better screening tool than waist circumference and BMI for adult cardiometabolic risk factors: systematic review and meta-analysis. Obes. Rev. **13**(3), 275–286 (2012)
6. Berthoud, H.R., Morrison, C.D., Münzberg, H.: The obesity epidemic in the face of homeostatic body weight regulation: what went wrong and how can it be fixed? Physiol. Behav. **222**, 112959 (2020)
7. De Koning, L., Merchant, A.T., Pogue, J., Anand, S.S.: Waist circumference and waist-to-hip ratio as predictors of cardiovascular events: meta-regression analysis of prospective studies. Eur. Heart J. **28**(7), 850–856 (2007)
8. Gibson, S., Ashwell, M.: A simple cut-off for waist-to-height ratio (0·5) can act as an indicator for cardiometabolic risk: recent data from adults in the health survey for England. Br. J. Nutr. **123**(6), 681–690 (2020)
9. Giger, M.L.: Machine learning in medical imaging. J. Am. Coll. Radiol. **15**(3), 512–520 (2018)
10. Gu, Z., et al.: Body mass index, waist circumference, and waist-to-height ratio for prediction of multiple metabolic risk factors in Chinese elderly population. Sci. Rep. **8**(1), 1–6 (2018)
11. Hatmal, M.M., et al.: Artificial neural networks model for predicting type 2 diabetes mellitus based on VDR gene Foki polymorphism, lipid profile and demographic data. Biology **9**(8), 222 (2020)
12. Herrera, H., Rebato, E., Arechabaleta, G., Lagrange, H., Salces, I., Susanne, C.: Body mass index and energy intake in venezuelan university students. Nutr. Res. **23**(3), 389–400 (2003)
13. Iqbal, N., Kumar, P.: From data science to bioscience: emerging era of bioinformatics applications, tools and challenges. Procedia Comput. Sci. **218**, 1516–1528 (2023)
14. Kawasaki, M., et al.: Obesity and abnormal glucose tolerance in offspring of diabetic mothers: a systematic review and meta-analysis. PLoS ONE **13**(1), e0190676 (2018)
15. Ker, J., Bai, Y., Lee, H.Y., Rao, J., Wang, L.: Automated brain histology classification using machine learning. J. Clin. Neurosci. **66**, 239–245 (2019)

16. Li, Z., Liu, F., Yang, W., Peng, S., Zhou, J.: A survey of convolutional neural networks: analysis, applications, and prospects. IEEE Trans. Neural Netw. Learn. Syst. (2021)
17. Liu, P.J., Ma, F., Lou, H.P., Zhu, Y.N.: Comparison of the ability to identify cardiometabolic risk factors between two new body indices and waist-to-height ratio among Chinese adults with normal BMI and waist circumference. Public Health Nutr. **20**(6), 984–991 (2017)
18. Marusteri, M., Bacarea, V.: Comparing groups for statistical differences: how to choose the right statistical test? Biochemia Medica **20**(1), 15–32 (2010)
19. Minchole, A., Camps, J., Lyon, A., Rodríguez, B.: Machine learning in the electrocardiogram. J. Electrocardiol. **57**, S61–S64 (2019)
20. Nimptsch, K., Konigorski, S., Pischon, T.: Diagnosis of obesity and use of obesity biomarkers in science and clinical medicine. Metabolism **92**, 61–70 (2019)
21. World Health Organization: Overweight and obesity (2020)
22. Owolabi, E.O., Ter Goon, D., Adeniyi, O.V., Ajayi, A.I.: Optimal waist circumference cut-off points for predicting metabolic syndrome among low-income black South African adults. BMC. Res. Notes **11**(1), 1–5 (2018)
23. Perpinan, G., Severeyn, E., Wong, S., Altuve, M.: Cardiac autonomic modulation in response to a glucose stimulus. Med. Biol. Eng. Comput. **57**, 667–676 (2019)
24. Piché, M.E., Tchernof, A., Després, J.P.: Obesity phenotypes, diabetes, and cardiovascular diseases. Circ. Res. **126**(11), 1477–1500 (2020)
25. Piuri, G., et al.: Magnesium in obesity, metabolic syndrome, and type 2 diabetes. Nutrients **13**(2), 320 (2021)
26. Polignano, M., Suriano, V., Lops, P., de Gemmis, M., Semeraro, G.: A study of machine learning models for clinical coding of medical reports at CodiEsp 2020. In: CLEF (Working Notes) (2020)
27. Pradhan, N., Rani, G., Dhaka, V.S., Poonia, R.C.: Diabetes prediction using artificial neural network. In: Deep Learning Techniques for Biomedical and Health Informatics, pp. 327–339. Elsevier (2020)
28. Shahid, N., Rappon, T., Berta, W.: Applications of artificial neural networks in health care organizational decision-making: a scoping review. PLoS ONE **14**(2), e0212356 (2019)
29. Shreffler, J., Huecker, M.R.: Diagnostic testing accuracy: sensitivity, specificity, predictive values and likelihood ratios (2020)
30. Snekhalatha, U., Sangamithirai, K., et al.: Computer aided diagnosis of obesity based on thermal imaging using various convolutional neural networks. Biomed. Signal Process. Control **63**, 102233 (2021)
31. Umberger, R.A., Hatfield, L.A., Speck, P.M.: Understanding negative predictive value of diagnostic tests used in clinical practice. Dimens. Crit. Care Nurs. **36**(1), 22–29 (2017)
32. Velásquez, J., Severeyn, E., Herrera, H., Encalada, L., Wong, S.: Anthropometric index for insulin sensitivity assessment in older adults from ecuadorian highlands. In: 12th International Symposium on Medical Information Processing and Analysis, vol. 10160, pp. 225–234. SPIE (2017)
33. Vintimilla, C., Wong, S., Astudillo-Salinas, F., Encalada, L., Severeyn, E.: An aide diagnosis system based on k-means for insulin resistance assessment in eldery people from the ecuadorian highlands. In: 2017 IEEE Second Ecuador Technical Chapters Meeting (ETCM), pp. 1–6. IEEE (2017)
34. Wondmkun, Y.T.: Obesity, insulin resistance, and type 2 diabetes: associations and therapeutic implications. Diabetes Metab. Syndr. Obes. Targets Ther. **13**, 3611 (2020)

35. Xu, J., Zhang, Y., Miao, D.: Three-way confusion matrix for classification: a measure driven view. Inf. Sci. **507**, 772–794 (2020)
36. Xu, Q.S., Liang, Y.Z.: Monte Carlo cross validation. Chemom. Intell. Lab. Syst. **56**(1), 1–11 (2001)
37. Xu, W., et al.: Identifying metabolic syndrome easily and cost effectively using non-invasive methods with machine learning models. Diabetes Metab. Syndr. Obes. 2141–2151 (2023)
38. Yu, J., Xie, X., Zhang, Y., Jiang, F., Wu, C.: Construction and analysis of a joint diagnosis model of random forest and artificial neural network for obesity. Front. Med. **9**, 906001 (2022)
39. Yu, Y., Si, X., Hu, C., Zhang, J.: A review of recurrent neural networks: LSTM cells and network architectures. Neural Comput. **31**(7), 1235–1270 (2019)
40. Zhang, D., Wang, J., Zhao, X.: Estimating the uncertainty of average F1 scores. In: Proceedings of the 2015 International Conference on the Theory of Information Retrieval, pp. 317–320 (2015)
41. Zhang, X., et al.: IGE contributes to atherosclerosis and obesity by affecting macrophage polarization, macrophage protein network, and foam cell formation. Arterioscler. Thromb. Vasc. Biol. **40**(3), 597–610 (2020)
42. Zhang, Z., Yang, K., Qian, J., Zhang, L.: Real-time surface EMG pattern recognition for hand gestures based on an artificial neural network. Sensors **19**(14), 3170 (2019)

Application of Artificial Intelligence Tools, Data Processing, and Analysis in the Forecasting of Level and Flow Variables in Wells with Little Data from the Morroa Aquifer

Carlos Cohen Manrique[1]($\boxtimes$) (iD), J. L. Villa[2] (iD), A. A. Month[3] (iD),
and G. Perez Velilla[3] (iD)

[1] Universidad Tecnologica de Bolivar, COL (DocTC-CECAR/Sjo), Cartagena, Colombia
`carlos.cohen@cecar.edu.co`
[2] Universidad Tecnologica de Bolivar, COL, Cartagena, Colombia
`jvilla@utb.edu.co`
[3] CARSUCRE, Sincelejo, Colombia

Abstract. Aquifers are one of the main source of plain water in many places in the world and its monitoring and control are crucial for their sustainability. This article presents the application of data science and artificial intelligence tools to predict variables related to water levels and flow rates in confined aquifers, dealing with scarce, noisy, and outlier- prone data. The case study focuse on some measurement wells within the Morroa aquifer, main source of plain water in the Sucre Department in Colombia. In this research, several tools were employed to address missing data (Multiple Imputation), data smoothing (Whittaker Smoother), and predictive analysis using Neural Networks (LSTM) to establish the behavior of water level and flow variables. The obtained results suggest the feasibility of using these tools for larger data samples across the piezometer network of the mentioned aquifer.

Keywords: Groundwater level · noisy data · data imputation · data smoothing

1 Introduction

In recent years, the importance of groundwater reservoirs, known as aquifers, for the sustainability of life throughout the world has been increasing. Many places in the world depend on them as the sole and exclusive source of drinking water for their inhabitants and for the agricultural and business sectors.

Colombia, despite being one of the richest countries in the world in terms of water, has many extremely dry places within its geography with very few possibilities of having the availability of the precious liquid in an easy and abundant way. For this reason, the conservation of the country's diverse water sources, both surface and underground, has become an important national policy, strengthening the conservation and preservation

J. C. Figueroa-García et al. (Eds.): WEA 2023, CCIS 1928, pp. 228–239, 2023.
https://doi.org/10.1007/978-3-031-46739-4_21

of the flora and fauna established in all regions. In this same sense, constitutionally the right to access drinking water in the country is fundamental [1].

The department of Sucre is located in the northern part of Colombia and historically, in spite of having geography suitable for settlements: surrounded by savannas, hills, hilly landscapes, and semi-forested regions, favorable for the existence of long-lasting water reservoirs, it has been a region hit by the scarcity of drinking water for its almost one million inhabitants, despite the fact that it has a very important groundwater system, composed of the aquifers of Betulia, El Roble, Morroa, Morrosquillo, San Cayetano and Toluviejo, which cover almost the entirety of its geography [2]. The most important of them all due to its extension, water quality, and the large populations that have historically depended almost exclusively on its resources (including the capital city, Sincelejo), is the Morroa aquifer; which has more than 1120 km^2 is undoubtedly the most important source of drinking water for the inhabitants of the Sucre savannas, and is located between the departments of C'ordoba, Bol'ivar and the department of Sucre, as can be seen in Fig. 1.

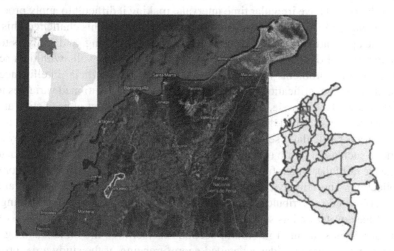

Fig. 1. Area of the Morroa aquifer on the Colombian Caribbean Coast.

Despite all of the above and despite being a true vital treasure for hundreds of thousands of people settled along the aquifer zone, it is currently the second most over-exploited confined aquifer in the world and has also been exposed to high pollution loads due to anthropogenic activities, dumping and poor social practices in waste management. For all these reasons, it is urgent to follow strategies and technological, social and economic activities aimed at improving the management of the aquifer in order to help reduce the impact that year after year undermines the sustainability of this important water pantry.

The entity in charge of managing the aforementioned aquifers in the department of Sucre is CARSUCRE, a governmental agency that has undertaken numerous efforts to address this challenge [3–5]. In fact, in line with the above, CARSUCRE has identified that the Morroa aquifer faces two main problems that threaten its current state: overexploitation and the risk of contamination due to human activities. Overexploitation has been evidenced by the concentration of wells in a specific area (legal and illegal), the constant extraction of water from these wells, and the continuous decrease of the water level in them. These factors combined represent a serious threat to the sustainability of this valuable water resource.

To ensure sustainable groundwater management, it is essential to accurately identify variations in aquifer storage over time. This process begins by analyzing historical water level records in monitoring wells. However, it is common to face a shortage of water level data, especially in developing regions or regions with limited access to technology [6]. Due to these circumstances, for about two decades, extensive monitoring has been carried out in certain extraction wells located in CARSUCRE's jurisdiction. In order to measure and determine flow-related variables, the volume of water extracted in these wells, and the static and dynamic levels of the aquifer's water layers, a network of carefully arranged piezometers was implemented. However, due to the manual nature of the sensing processes and the extensive distances involved, the data collected to date lack periodicity and have irregular time intervals, making it difficult to apply processing and forecasting tools for decision-making. In order to address this challenge, this paper explores the application of artificial intelligence, data processing, and analysis tools in the management of dynamic level and flow variables in some wells with data scarcity and inherent noise problems in the Morroa Aquifer. These artificial intelligence tools could facilitate the identification of correlations between the mentioned variables in each of the studied wells. Likewise, they would allow the carrying out of predictive analyses under possible scenarios that the region could face. It is relevant to mention that this area of the country is particularly sensitive to being affected with certain frequency by natural phenomena such as El Nin~o (characterized by low rainfall) or La Nin~a (characterized by excessive rainfall), which further aggravates the need for a systematic and consistent data collection. The effective implementation of these artificial intelligence and data analysis tools would contribute significantly to management and decision-making in the context of the aquifer and its sustainable use in the region.

This article is structured in several sections to facilitate the understanding of the study. The first section provides a detailed georeferencing of the study area, providing a key geographical perspective to contextualize the results. This is followed by a brief but comprehensive literature review, examining techniques previously applied in scenarios similar to the one presented in this paper, thus allowing a better understanding of the current proposals. The second section focuses on the description of the variables and data used in the research. The characteristics of the data are detailed, addressing aspects such as sparsity, noise, and the presence of outliers, which provides a fundamental frame of reference to understand the complexity of the analysis. Subsequently, in the third section, the results obtained through the implementation of data science and artificial intelligence tools are systematically presented. These results are accompanied by fundamental discussions, in which the findings are examined in depth, highlighting their relevance in the context of the hydrological problem addressed.

1.1 Literature Review

Many authors have been proposing a variety of tools to model, analyze and predict variables related to dynamic and static levels, volumes, and flows in groundwater bodies. The main objective is to understand and estimate their capacity, as well as the water balance between recharge and abstraction due to consumption. For example, authors such as [7] developed a cost function for robust training of recurrent neural network models using groundwater-level data affected by outliers and noise. In this study, the optimal cost function is based on the trimmed least squares (LTS) method with asymmetric weighting (AW) and the Whittaker smoother (WS), which present different mechanisms for the detection and rejection of noise or outliers. These authors achieved that their developed cost function can potentially be employed in many hydrogeological applications, such as monitoring groundwater resources, predicting and analyzing water tables, and identifying changes in aquifer processes. All of these field applications where the data are susceptible to external influences or exhibit measurement problems. In [6] the authors developed an imputation method to approximate missing observations of monthly average water table levels in individual wells since 1948. To impute missing water table levels in individual wells, two global data sources: the Palmer Drought Severity Index (PDSI) and the Global Land Data Assimilation System (GLDAS) were used to perform regressions. In addition to the meteorological datasets, four additional features were generated, and temporal data were coded into 13 parameters representing the month and year of observation. This extension of previous work used inductive bias to inform models about water table trends and structures from existing observations using prior estimates of water table behavior. The method was demonstrated in the Beryl-Enterprise aquifer in Utah (USA) and the imputed results followed trends in observed data and hydrogeologic principles, even over long periods without observed data. On the other hand, [8]. In this study, the LightGBM model was applied to make predictions of water levels along the lower Columbia River. The model inputs consisted of the flows of two upstream rivers (Columbia and Willamette rivers) and tidal characteristics, including the tidal range at the estuary mouth (Astoria) and tidal components. The model was optimized by selecting appropriate parameters. The results obtained showed that the LightGBM model was able to achieve high accuracy in its predictions, demonstrating very good mean square error values. Furthermore, it was observed that these predictions were statistically superior to those obtained by physics-based models, such as the non stationary tidal harmonic analysis model. [9] employs a graph neural network (GNN) in order to forecast groundwater dynamics, representing each well as a node within the graph in the southwestern area of British Columbia in Canada. Spatial information is extracted from an interconnected network through the use of graph convolution layers, incorporating a self-adaptive adjacency matrix. [10] combined neural networks, digital elevation models, and fitted reflectance product' (MOD43B4) using the CMRSET algorithm to study large-scale spatiotemporal trends. The distinctive aspect proposed in this article compared to the mentioned studies lies in the quality of the obtained data. As the data is not acquired at regular time intervals and is highly susceptible to noise due to the lack of well monitoring through sensors, but rather through manual means. The nature of manually acquiring the data introduces uncertainty and additional challenges in the analysis and processing, thus prompting the need to address the problem with data science and artificial intelligence approaches capable of dealing with these specific characteristics of the dataset.

2   Materials and Methods

Figure 2 shows the key stages of the investigation. Data collection was carried out directly by the competent entities in the wells listed in Table 1, using piezometers to determine aquifer levels and macro meters to obtain information on the extraction flow rate. After the information capture phase, validations were carried out with experts to ensure the quality of the data, filtering out any atypical data or data with excessive noise levels due to errors in measurement or systematization. Next, the data from each well was processed and analyzed individually, obtaining information on the three variables mentioned for the years 2020, 2021, and 2022.

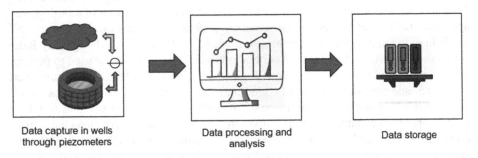

Data capture in wells through piezometers   Data processing and analysis   Data storage

Fig. 2. Stages of data processing for each well.

The information obtained from the wells presented significant challenges due to the lack of data in the collected samples. The measurement frequency in the wells was approximately 45 days, resulting in several missing data points in the samples, complicating the reliable assessment of the variables. To address this issue of missing data in the research, the multiple imputation method using neural networks [14] was employed, which provides various mechanisms for detecting and handling noise or outliers. A Multilayer Perceptron Artificial Neural Network model was used, consisting of two fully connected neuron layers (Dense) with ReLU activation in the first layer (64 neurons), a hidden layer (10 neurons), and a linear output layer (Dense(1)). The model is trained using Mean Squared Error (MSE) as the loss function and the Adam optimizer. This methodology was chosen because artificial neural networks have demonstrated greater efficiency in reducing imputation error compared to other widely used analysis techniques, especially when there is significant correlation with other recorded variables [15].

Furthermore, to deal with noisy data, the Whittaker Smoother (WS) was applied due to its mechanism for detecting and rejecting noise or outliers [7]. WS, as a special application of the B-spline technique, is described in the literature as a method that smoothly fits observed data by minimizing discrepancies between observed and smoothed values [16]. Due to the nature of the data, a WS with lambda = 0.2 (smoothing level control parameter), defined through trial and error, was used, based on observations of how well it tracked the original data.

The objective of this WS is to find the smoothed values that minimize the sum of squares function, and it facilitates the analysis of the data and the detection of underlying patterns or trends (see Fig. 3).

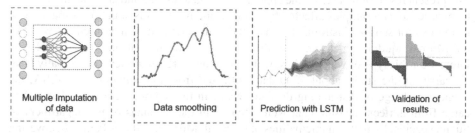

Fig. 3. Tools used in the study.

The prediction stage was carried out using a Long Short-Term Memory (LSTM) neural network with the aim of addressing the challenge of estimating future values of variables of interest included in the research [17] and [18]. Specifically, the focus was on achieving an accurate estimation of dynamic water level (expressed in meters), discharge rate (measured in liters per second), and delivered volume (quantified in cubic meters per second) for the wells in Table 1. These neural network-based techniques, backed by their inherent ability to capture sequential patterns and temporal dependencies, proved to be effective tools in predicting the mentioned variables, thus providing a more comprehensive and accurate understanding of the underlying hydrological behavior in the study.

The neural network model consisted of two hidden layers, each containing 10 neurons, and to facilitate the training process, the discharge rate and dynamic water level data were normalized. Subsequently, the model was compiled using the "Adam" optimizer and the "MSE" (Mean Squared Error) loss function [19]. After completing the training, utilizing 65% of the data, the model was used to make predictions of the dynamic water level based on new discharge rate values. An analysis was conducted to verify if these levels, in both extreme and conventional situations, exceeded the maximum specified values listed in Table 1. This evaluation allowed the identification of potential scenarios in which the dynamic water level could surpass the established limits, providing valuable information for decision-making and efficient water resource management.

Lastly, an exhaustive analysis was performed on the data provided by the predictors, which were validated by experts in the field. Additionally, the cleansed data corresponding to each well was carefully cross-referenced and integrated to obtain the necessary information related to the variables considered in the study. This procedure provided a comprehensive and detailed insight into the patterns and relationships present in the data, revealing crucial information for understanding the dynamics of the analyzed variables. Through the use of specialized techniques and algorithms, significant and relevant insights were extracted, forming a solid foundation for decision-making and effectively managing critical situations or adverse scenarios that may arise in the supply of potable water.

3 Data Description

The present research focuses on the application of data science and artificial intelligence techniques to data samples affected by scarcity and noise. This situation is mainly due to the lack of sensory instrumentation in the extraction and/or measurement wells of the Morroa aquifer, which makes it difficult to capture in real-time the variables of interest for this type of water bodies, which have an increasing relevance globally [11]. To carry out the study, about 1200 data collected from the network of ADESA, the agency in charge of distributing drinking water in the region, were used. These data came from thirteen measurement wells located in the savannas of the department of Sucre, specifically in the municipalities of Corozal, Morroa, and Los Palmitos, covering an area of approximately 42 km². The variables selected to apply these techniques are the static level and dynamic level in the aquifer recharge zones, as well as the volume of extraction and the flow supplied to the companies in charge of water distribution. The objective is to establish, based on the data obtained, correlations between these variables, and, in this way, to be able to predict their behavior in various possible scenarios.

This information is crucial to anticipate aquifer levels, being the piezometric level the most important variable to be controlled by regulatory agencies. The study of dynamic level, static level, and flow rates in groundwater aquifers is of vital importance in the field of hydrology and water resources monitoring. These parameters provide key information on the health and availability of water in an aquifer, allowing effective and sustainable management of this vital resource. By way of clarification, in aquifers, static level refers to the natural state of the groundwater position [12], without abstraction. On the other hand, the dynamic level refers to the level reached by the water inside the well under pumping conditions [13]. In addition, the flow rate represents the amount of liters per second that are pumped or extracted from each of the wells connected to the aquifer, for subsequent distribution or use in agricultural or industrial activities.

Table 1 shows the list of wells selected for this study, which have data on dynamic level, static level, flow rates delivered to the water distribution company, and volume delivered. These data were subjected to an exhaustive analysis of statistical behavior and validation to ensure their reliability and accuracy. For this purpose, the Regressor package of the R-Studio® software, a tool specialized in the construction and evaluation of regression models, was used. Using this methodology, the relationships between the predictor variables and the response variable were explored, thus making it possible to generate accurate forecasts and estimates. The regression approach used is based on the model's ability to capture patterns and trends in the data, and then apply it to make reliable predictions.

Table 1. Wells monitored for the present study.

Identification	Number Well	Location	Flow Rate Delivered (lt/s)
44-IV-D-PP-31	32	Corozal	20
44-IV-D-PP-35	36	Corozal	25
44-IV-D-PP-38	02	Corozal	45
44-IV-D-PP-37	01	Corozal	45
44-IV-D-PP-42	03	Corozal	35
44-IV-D-PP-43	43B	Corozal	18
44-IV-D-PP-44	45	Corozal	20
44-IV-D-PP-46	46	Corozal	120
44-IV-D-PP-47	47	Betulia	100
44-IV-D-PP-48	48B	Los Palmitos	80
44-IV-D-PP-51	51	Los Palmitos	60
44-IV-D-PP-16	40	Corozal	14
44-IV-D-PP-01	35	Corozal	35

4 Results and Discussion

The application of multiple imputation and the WS smoother gave very good results, and contributed to mitigating the sudden changes detected, which allowed obtaining a clearer and more stable trend in the observations, thus improving the response of the system and preparing it for the next stage of training and prediction of the dynamic level and flow variables in the wells studied.

Figure 4 shows the results of the applied techniques: multiple imputation (blue), the smoother, and the neural predictor (red). It can be seen that the trend of the dynamic level in well 32 is decreasing with time. Considering that in 2021 and the initial part of 2022 the region experienced the occurrence of the La Nin˜a phenomenon, it can be inferred that this particular well was affected, as evidenced by the marked change that occurred in 2021.

In the same vein, it can be observed in Table 2 that the WS reasonably "follows" the behavior of the measured data, even when they do not adhere to a predictable or marked pattern, as seen in wells 32 and 45B, where the dynamic level oscillates. Meanwhile, in wells 35 and 51, a clear upward trend in the dynamic level is evident. As for the prediction, it is clear that only well 32 shows a tendency for a decrease in the dynamic level, while wells 48B and 51 exhibit an increasing trend. Well, 35 displays a more stable future behavior with values very close to those recorded in the last year, despite coming from a pronounced increasing trend. Regarding the results of the statistical analysis, several metrics were evaluated, including the coefficient of determination R^2. It is evident that most of the R^2 values are that are less than 1, which indicates that the model significantly explains the proportion of variability present in the analyzed data, demonstrating a close and accurate fit of the WS model to the observed real values. Thus, the trend of the

WS smoother follows that of the predictor in defining future values for the evaluated variables. Results comparable to those obtained in [9, 18] and [19].

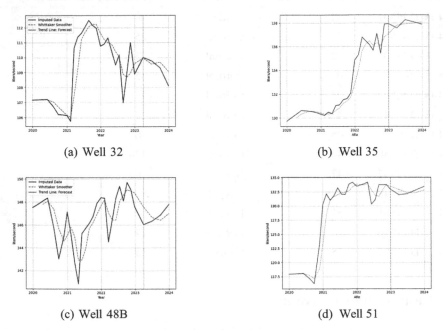

(a) Well 32   (b) Well 35

(c) Well 48B   (d) Well 51

Fig. 4. Imputed, smoothed and predicted dynamic level data for the evaluated wells.

Regarding the flow rate, it is also noteworthy how the Whittaker smoother establishes the trend of the original data, even in the presence of noisy signals indicating significant and abrupt changes. Moreover, thanks to the effective performance of the WS, the predictor (red line) consistently exhibits a clear downward trend in the majority of cases, based on the well data, indicating a reduction in the flow rate delivered by the evaluated wells. This reduction can be largely attributed to extraction challenges and the current water stress experienced by nearly all locations within the Morroa aquifer (see Fig. 5).

In Table 3, we present the results obtained from evaluating the data using R-Studio's Regressor software, employing various data analysis tools such as RF, CART, GPR, SVR, and LASSO. The selection of wells was based on two fundamental reasons. Firstly, we considered their geographical location in the central area of the aquifer, which is known to be heavily exploited and faces significant challenges related to overexploitation and contamination. Secondly, we prioritized wells with fewer missing data points in their measurements. When MSE is Mean Squared Error and ER is Relative Error.

The original data sample exhibits a strong correlation between the variables under evaluation, namely the dynamic water level and the flow rate. However, despite the favorable correlations found in most of the techniques assessed, the mean squared errors, mean absolute errors and relative errors show unsatisfactory behaviors with considerably elevated values. This indicates a substantial disparity, insufficient or noisy data, or even

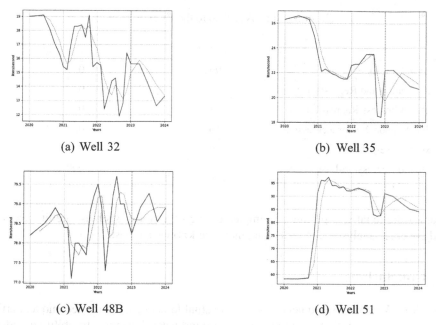

(a) Well 32   (b) Well 35

(c) Well 48B   (d) Well 51

Fig. 5. Imputed, smoothed and predicted flow data for evaluated wells.

Table 2. Errors obtained by the data samples.

Well	Dynamic Level	Flow rate
32	0.78	0.75
35	0.96	0.75
43B	0.56	0.63
51	0.89	0.86

the presence of outliers in the data. Therefore, the smoother proved to be a fundamental tool in our investigation.

As a form of discussion, this research proposes the utilization of data science and artificial intelligence tools in hydrological applications such as groundwater aquifers. In these contexts, data scarcity and technological difficulties due to the lack of permanent monitoring in wells pose significant challenges, leading to possible errors in field data collection and systematization. In this regard, the utility of data-driven models for large-scale groundwater dynamics has been demonstrated. The developed methods are computationally efficient and provide a means for conducting simple and interpretable assessments of water resources.

It is worth mentioning that, for such applications, reliability can be improved with a more robust and high-quality database. One approach to achieve this is by expanding the time window applied to the variables of interest, encompassing a larger number of

Table 3. AI tools applied to the data obtained.

ID	MSE	ER	Correlation
Random Forests	2.96	6.65	0.98
Classification and Regression Trees	4.79	10.77	0.97
Gaussian Process Regression	7.74	17.38	0.96
Radial-Support Vector Regression	6.16	13.84	0.95
K Nearest Neighbors	5.36	12.05	0.91
Penalized Regression-Lasso	9.96	22.37	0.88

years. Additionally, exploring and implementing other tools, such as satellite imagery and coverage analyses, can further augment the knowledge base.

5 Conclusions

The WS (Whittaker Smoother) serves as a valuable data smoothing technique, particularly in hydrological applications such as groundwater dynamics. Its ability to reduce noise and fluctuations in time series and other data with undesired variations provides a clearer and more precise view of the behavior of the variables of interest. Given the nature of hydrological applications, where data quality can be compromised by various factors, the WS becomes an effective solution to mitigate the effects of data scarcity, measurement errors, or the lack of continuous monitoring at specific points of interest. By applying the WS, researchers and professionals can enhance data quality and reliability, leading to a better understanding and forecasting of hydrological phenomena and, ultimately, more efficient and sustainable water resource management.

In this research, several tools were employed to address missing data (Multiple Imputation), data smoothing (Whittaker Smoother), and predictive analysis using Neural Networks (LSTM) to establish the behavior of water level and flow variables in some wells within the Morroa aquifer. The obtained results align with the challenges of overexploitation that this crucial water resource in the Sucre region has been facing.

Acknowledgments. The authors would like to extend their sincerest gratitude to the Corporaci´on Aut´onoma Regional de Sucre for their invaluable collaboration in the development of this document. The generous provision of essential information and the valuable technical guidance provided have been of vital significance for the accomplishment and enrichment of this manuscript.

References

1. Pérez, A.J., et al.: Assessing sub-regional water scarcity using the groundwater footprint. Ecological Indicators **2**(5), 32–39 (2019)
2. Navarro Mercado, J.L.: Monitoreo de las obras piloto de recarga artificial en el acuífero Morroa, departamento de Sucre, Colombia (Bachelor's thesis, Universidad Eafit) (2020)

3. Lopez Ramırez, S.E.: Actualizacion del modelo numerico del acuıfero Morroa utilizando Visual Modflow Flex (2015)
4. Month, A.E.Á., Velilla, G.A.P., Month, J.A.Á.: Statistical analysis of water resource management in the morroa aquifer in the department of sucre. J. Pharm. Negative Results 5268–5277 (2022)
5. De Aguas, Grupo Ppias. Estudio tecnico del Acuifero Morroa. Carsucre (2023)
6. Ramirez, S.G., Williams, G.P., Jones, N.L.: Groundwater level data imputation using machine learning and remote earth observations using inductive bias. Remote Sens. **14**(21), 5509 (2022)
7. Jeong, J., Park, E., Chen, H., Kim, K.-Y., Han, W.S., Suk, H.: Estimation of groundwater level based on the robust training of recurrent neural networks using corrupted data. J. Hydrol. **582**, 124512 (2020)
8. Gan, M., Pan, S., Chen, Y., Cheng, C., Pan, H., Zhu, X.: Application of the machine learning lightgbm model to the prediction of the water levels of the lower columbia river. J. Mar. Sci. Eng. **9**(5), 496 (2021)
9. Bai, T., Tahmasebi, P.: Graph neural network for groundwater level forecasting. J. Hydrol. **616**, 128792 (2023)
10. Pagendam, D., Janardhanan, S., Dabrowski, J., MacKinlay, D.: A log-additive neural model for spatio-temporal prediction of groundwater levels. Spat. Stat. **55**, 100740 (2023)
11. Scanlon, B.R., et al.: Global water resources and the role of groundwater in a resilient water future. Nat. Rev. Earth Environ. **4**(2), 87–101 (2023)
12. Orellana, F., Rivera, D., Montalva, G., Arumi, J.L.: InSAR-based early warning monitoring framework to assess aquifer deterioration. Remote Sens. **15**(7), 1786 (2023)
13. Behera, A.K., Pradhan, R.M., Kumar, S., Chakrapani, G.J., Kumar, P.: Assessment of groundwater flow dynamics using MODFLOW in shallow aquifer system of Mahanadi delta (east coast) India. Water **14**(4), 611 (2022)
14. Choi, J., Dekkers, O.M., le Cessie, S.: A comparison of different methods to handle missing data in the context of propensity score analysis. Eur. J. Epidemiol. **34**, 23–36 (2019)
15. Han, J., Kang, S.: Dynamic imputation for improved training of neural network with missing values. Expert Syst. Appl. **194**, 116508 (2022)
16. Liang, Jieyu, et al.: Using enhanced gap-filling and whittaker smoothing to reconstruct high spatiotemporal resolution NDVI time series based on Landsat 8, Sentinel-2, and MODIS imagery. ISPRS Int. J. Geo-Information **12**(6), 214 (2023)
17. Yang, X., Zhang, Z.: A CNN-LSTM Model based on a meta-learning algorithm to predict groundwater level in the middle and lower reaches of the heihe river, China. Water **14**(15), 2377. (2022). Lin, H., Gharehbaghi, A., Zhang, Q., Band, S.S., Pai, H.T., Chau, K.W., Mosavi, A.: Time series-based groundwater level forecasting using gated recurrent unit deep neural networks. Engineering Applications of Computational Fluid Mechanics **16**(1), 1655–1672 (2022)
18. Sreekanth, P.D., Geethanjali, N., Sreedevi, P.D., Ahmed, S., Kumar, N.R., Jayanthi, P.K.: Forecasting groundwater level using artificial neural networks. Curr. Sci. **96**(933), 939 (2009)
19. Kaya, Y.Z., Ünes, F., Demirci, M., Ta¸sar, B., Var¸cin, H.: Groundwater level prediction using artificial neural network and M5 tree models. Aerul si Apa Componente ale Mediului 2018, 195–201 (2018)

Voltage Regulation for Microgrids Based on a Data-Driven Predictor

Vladimir Toro$^{(\boxtimes)}$ ⓘ, J. A. Rodriguez-Gil ⓘ, and E. Mojica-Nava ⓘ

Departamento de Ingeniería Eléctrica y Electrónica, Universidad Nacional de
Colombia, Bogotá, Colombia
{bwtorot,jharodriguezgi,eamojican}@unal.edu.co

Abstract. This paper presents a data-driven control algorithm for voltage regulation in an MG. Using the V-Q decoupling model for microgrids, the voltage at each inverter is represented by a nonlinear equation, which depends on the inverter's impedance and reactive power. The nonlinear model is represented as a linear one in the Koopman space or lifted space using the EDMD algorithm and data collected from simulation experiments. To control the voltage at each inverter is proposed a MPC design that uses the Koopman linear representation of the problem. The algorithm is solved by using ADMM in a distributed form following a tracking scheme. This design allows minimizing the computation time and the control effort while tracks the voltage reference value. The algorithm is proved to load changes.

Keywords: Koopman · ADMM · distributed · Microgrid · MPC

1 Introduction

The widespread growth of energy resources (DERs), especially renewable ones, has increased the worries about their effect on the quality and stability of the utility network. Most of the DERs work interfaced with power converters. In alternating current (AC) systems, the inverter should define the amplitude and frequency of the generated signal while keeping the power supply [3]. The microgrid (MG) is the answer for the proper connection and integration of several DERs. It can work with the utility network as a controllable power source that follows the frequency and voltage magnitude imposed for the utility, known as the grid-following form. Also, the MG can work as an isolated unit where the reference values for frequency and voltage magnitude are set by the MG itself, known as the grid-former form [7]. For an AC MG, voltage regulation should be

Vladimir Toro is supported by Colciencias 754-2016.
J. A. Rodriguez-Gil is supported by Universidad Nacional de Colombia and Minciencias, with project "Programa de Investigación en Tecnologías Emergentes para Microredes Eléctricas Inteligentes con Alta Penetracion de Energías Renovables" Contract 80740-542-2020.

J. C. Figueroa-García et al. (Eds.): WEA 2023, CCIS 1928, pp. 240–250, 2023.
https://doi.org/10.1007/978-3-031-46739-4_22

done by tracking a reference value for the magnitude and regulating the reactive power.

A MG consists of several DERs working in parallel where the inverters should establish the reference values while keeping the power requirements when working in islanded mode. A hierarchical control is used to control the MGs devices from the electronic devices at each inverter until global parameters to achieve collective behaviors [6]. Following the hierarchical frame, the primary level usually involves the current and voltage controllers, the protections, and the proportional control strategy for the inverter's connection in parallel, known as droop-control. The secondary control level fulfills global objectives, such as voltage and frequency regulation for the set of inverters, and might include optimization strategies. The secondary control action can be either centralized or distributed. The last strategy is preferred in scenarios where communication among inverters is unavailable, or where distances made communications expensive and inclined to failures [9].

Several distributed strategies have been proposed for voltage regulation, most of them relying on using integrators with a consensus strategy. For voltage regulation, voltage and reactive power measurements from each inverter's neighbors set are gathered and compared to generate the control signal. However, in many cases, the controller can not regulate the voltage property when there are fluctuations in the reactive power [1]. One alternative is the design of Model Predictive Control (MPC), it uses a model that gathers information about voltage and reactive power for voltage regulation and optimization, such as minimization of the control cost and the difference between the voltage and its reference value.

The voltage at each inverter is modeled by a nonlinear differential equation, that can be problematic to solve at each iteration in an MPC design. One alternative is linearizing the nonlinear equation at one operation point. However, this can limit the performance of the controller. On the other hand, a nonlinear system can be represented as a linear one in the observables's space by using the composition operator, better known as the Koopman operator. This operator uses measurements from the system known as observables to represent the system in a lifted space using a set of generally non-linear basis functions. The Koopman operator can be approximated by using data-driven algorithms. In this case, the approximation is good enough for a time window suitable for MPC design [10].

The distributed nature of the power system requires that control algorithms can be adjusted when inverters are connected or disconnected from the MG. That plug-and-play capacity is given by the distributed control algorithm. Also, it is necessary to solve an optimization problem at each sample time. Some algorithms perform better to solve optimization problems faster and with limited resources. The Alternating Direction Multipliers Method (ADMM) is extended to work distributively. This iterative method searches for the optimal value by actualizing the weight of the Lagrange multipliers. It can be easily programmed in hardware and does not need to calculate a second derivative [1]. Based on the algorithm proposed by [11], this algorithm identifies the lifted model for tracking and do not need to identify the error.

In this work, we propose a distributed algorithm for voltage and reactive power regulation to track the reference value. The algorithm uses the linearized Koopman representation of the nonlinear voltage model, instead of the error, to design an MPC and a distributed ADMM to solve the optimization problem. The algorithm is proved in an MG within a distributed frame. The rest of this paper is organized as follows: Sect. 2 presents the problem for voltage regulation and the nonlinearities. Section 3 shows the control strategy, first showing the generalities of the Koopman operator and its representation, and presenting the distributed ADMM algorithm. Section 4 shows some simulation scenarios and results. Finally, conclusions are presented in Sect. 5.

2　Problem Statement

In this section, we present the MG model by representing the interconnection of inverters in parallel through a transmission line. Then, some assumptions about the model are made, simplifying the analysis and generating the nonlinear differential equation for the voltage at each inverter.

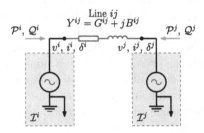

Fig. 1. Equivalent schematic of two parallel microgrids [5].

Based on the connection scheme shown in Fig. 1, where two inverter-based sources are connected in parallel through the transmission line with impedance $Y^{ij} = B^{ij} + G^{ij}$. Each inverter is modeled as a controllable voltage source, for ease of notation, inverters i and j represents the ij^{th} element of the admittance matrix $\mathbb{Y}$. All the generators works at frequency ω^{ref} with phase measurement δ^i, δ^j, and shares active and reactive power $\mathcal{P}$ and $\mathcal{Q}$ according their voltage and phase values. The general expressions for instantaneous active and reactive power are given by [9]

$$\mathcal{P}^i = G^{ii}(v^i)^2 - \sum_{j \in \mathcal{N}_i}(G^{ij}\cos(\delta^{ij}) + B^{ij}\sin(\delta^{ij}))v^i v^j,$$

$$\mathcal{Q}^i = -B^{ii}(v^i)^2 + \sum_{j \in \mathcal{N}_i}(B^{ij}\cos(\delta^{ij}) - G^{ij}\sin(\delta^{ij}))v^i v^j,$$

where $\mathcal{P}^i$ is the active power and $\mathcal{Q}^i$ is the reactive power, and v^i, v^j are the voltage magnitudes. The technical assumption of a predominantly inductive transmission line is made based on the inclusion of a high value inductor at the inverter's output or by the adding a virtual impedance that compensates guarantee this condition by adding a feedback loop at each inverter [6]. Thus, conductance values are zero G^{ij}, and the simplified $\mathcal{Q}^i$ expression is given by

$$\mathcal{Q}^i = -\left\|B^{ii}\right\|(v^i)^2 + \sum_{j \in \mathcal{N}_i} \left\|B^{ij}\right\| \cos(\delta^{ij})v^i v^j,$$

Considering a small change in $\delta^{ij} = \delta^i - \delta^j \approx 0$, the following equation is obtained

$$\mathcal{Q}^i = -\left\|B^{ii}\right\|(v^i)^2 + \sum_{j \in \mathcal{N}_i} \left\|B^{ij}\right\| v^i v^j. \tag{1}$$

Following the hierarchical control frame for MGs, the primary control is based on droop control, a decentralized strategy with a faster response compared with secondary and tertiary control levels. The first control layer subtract (add) from the reference voltage a proportional value to the reactive power demanded (absorbed), deviating the voltage from its reference value. Voltage droop-equations are given by

$$v^i = v^{ref} - n^i \mathcal{Q}^i, \tag{2}$$

where $\mathcal{Q}_i$ is the measured instantaneous reactive power, and n_i is the droop control coefficient. A medium value of the reactive power is calculated using a low-pass filter as

$$\hat{\mathcal{Q}}^i = \frac{1}{1 + \tau s}\mathcal{Q}^i, \tag{3}$$

where τ is the low-pass filter constant. The general expression for voltage regulation that includes reactive power effect is generated by combining (1), (2), and (3) as follows

$$\tau \dot{v}^i = -v^i + v^{ref} - n^i \left(\sum_{j \in \mathcal{N}_i} (v^i)^2 \left\|B^{ij}\right\| + \sum_{j \in \mathcal{N}_i} v^i v^j \left\|B^{ij}\right\| \right).$$

This nonlinear equation depends on the square value of the voltage measured at each inverter and the product with the voltage measured from its neighbors. It can be linearized or, in this case, expressed in a lifted space by using the EDMD algorithm.

3 Control Strategy

In this section, we present the control strategy for the MG. The dynamic model of the inverter is represented in the lifted space by using the Koopman operator and the EDMD algorithm. First, we define the basics of the Koopman operator and the set of basis functions for the EDMD. Then, we present the designing of the MPC for voltage regulation solved using the hands-off algorithm with ADMM.

3.1   Koopman Operator

This work assumes an affine dynamic model of the form

$$\dot{x} = f(x) + g(x)u,$$

where u is the control input.

The Koopman operator is a composition operator that act over a nonlinear system and represents it as a linear one of infinite dimension. The Koopman representation of a system can be determined analytically using the Laplacian average technique. However it is not practical in most cases [2]. Otherwise, this operator can be approximated by using data-driven techniques. This finite-dimensional approximation allows having a matrix representation of the operator, and it is also possible to get a state-space model of the system by determining the input and output matrices.

$$x_{k+1} = g(x_k),$$

where $x \in \mathbb{R}^{n \times n}$, and g is a nonlinear mapping.

It is necessary to gather the vectors of $N - 1$ measurements from the system to approximate the nonlinear map by the Koopman operator, also known as observables

$$X = [x_1 \quad x_2 \quad \cdots \quad x_{N-1}],$$
$$Y = [x_2 \quad x_3 \quad \cdots \quad x_N].$$

Then, it is defined a dictionary of functions $\mathcal{D}$ of the form

$$\mathcal{D} = \{\phi_1 \quad \phi_2 \quad \cdots \quad \phi_M\}$$

These M functions can be nonlinear, polynomials, Fourier, and radial, among others.

All data vectors X, Y is evaluated on the dictionary of functions generating the vector (matrix) of the form

$$\phi = [\phi_1(x) \quad \phi_2(x) \quad \cdots \quad \phi_M(x)].$$

The Koopman operator can be found by solving the following optimization problem

$$\min_{\mathcal{A}} \quad ||\phi(x) - \mathcal{A}\phi(x)||_F$$

For a controlled scenario, the discrete nonlinear controlled system of the form

$$x_{k+1} = f(x_k, u_k),$$

and the Koopman approximation can be found by solving the optimization problem

$$\min_{\mathcal{A}, \mathcal{B}} ||Y_{\text{lift}} - \mathcal{A}X_{\text{lift}} - \mathcal{B}U||_F,$$

where $X_{\text{lift}} = [\phi(x_1), \ldots, \phi(x_{N-1})]$, $Y_{\text{lift}} = [\phi(y_1), \ldots, \phi(y_{N-1})]$. The output matrix can be found of the form $y_k = g(x_k)$ by solving

$$\min_{C} \|X - CX_{\text{lift}}\|_F$$

Finally, the next linear observer is defined by using the founded matrices [8]

$$
\begin{aligned}
z_{k+1} &= \mathcal{A}z_k + \mathcal{B}u_k, \\
y_k &= \mathcal{C}z_k,
\end{aligned}
\tag{3.1}
$$

with $z_0 = \Phi(x_0)$, where z_k is a lifted state vector at time-step k.

For the voltage regulation model, the variable is given by the voltage measured at each inverter and its neighbors $[v^i \quad v^{j \in \mathcal{N}_i}]$. The set of basis functions selected for the EDMD algorithm are given by

$$\Psi = [v^i \quad v^j \quad (v^i)^2 \quad (v^j)^2 \quad v^i v^j]^\top.$$

3.2   ADMM Control

The ADMM algorithm is used to solve the optimization problem set by the MPC. ADMM uses the multipliers method but with the advantage of separating the upgrade of the variable and the multiplier at each iteration. The general form of the optimization problem is given by

$$
\begin{aligned}
\min_{u,\, w} \quad & f(u) + g(w) \\
\text{s.t.} \quad & Au + Bw = c,
\end{aligned}
\tag{4}
$$

whose Lagrangian is given by

$$\mathcal{L}_\rho(u, w, \lambda) = f(x) + g(w) + \lambda^\top(c - Au - Bw) + \frac{\rho}{2}\|c - Ax - Bw\|^2.$$

Last problem can be solved by the ADMM as follows

$$
\begin{aligned}
x_{k+1} &= \arg\min_{x} \mathcal{L}_\rho(x, w_k, \lambda_k), \\
w_{k+1} &= \arg\min_{w} \mathcal{L}_\rho(x_{k+1}, w, \lambda_k), \\
\lambda_{k+1} &= \lambda_k + \rho(c - Ax_{k+1} - Bw_{k+1}),
\end{aligned}
\tag{5}
$$

The optimization problem for node i, using the linear predictor (3.1) is given by

$$
\begin{aligned}
\min_{u^i} \quad & \|v_k^i - v_{ref}\|_Q^2 + \|u_k^i\|_R^2, \\
\text{s.t.} \quad & z_{k+1}^i = \mathcal{A}^i z_k^i + \mathcal{B}^i u_k^i, \\
& v_k^i = \mathcal{C}^i z_k^i,
\end{aligned}
\tag{6}
$$

where

$$J^i\left(u^i\right) = \left\|v_k^i - v_{ref}\right\|_Q^2 + \left\|u_k^i\right\|_R^2, \tag{7}$$

and (6) can be solved by using (5). However, (7) can be rewritten as a Quadratic Programming problem that follows the next form

$$J(u^i) = \frac{1}{2}u^{i\top}H^i u^i + h^{i\top}u^i.$$

and (6) rewritten as

$$\min_{u^i} \quad J^i\left(u^i\right)$$
$$\text{s.t.} \quad A^i u^i \leq c^i,$$

Then, we define a new g_i function and w_i variables given by

$$g^i\left(w^i\right) \;=\; \begin{cases} 0 & w^i \leq c^i, \\ \infty & \text{otherwise,} \end{cases}$$

such that a new optimization problem can be proposed

$$\min_{w} \quad J^i\left(u^i\right) + g^i\left(w^i\right),$$
$$\text{s.t.} \quad A^i u^i - w^i = 0,$$

thus, the previous optimization problem follows (4). Where, H^i and f^i are the matrix and vector related to the control problem, and it can be solved using the following procedure

---

Algorithm 1. ADMM for QP problems based on [4].

Require: $v_0^i, \lambda_0^i \in \mathbb{R}^M, \tau > 0$
   while $\epsilon \geq 0.001$ **do**
$$u_{k+1}^i = \left(H^i + \tau A^{i\top}A^i\right)^{-1}\left(A^{i\top}\left(\lambda_k^i + \rho w_k^i\right) - h^i\right)$$
$$w_{k+1}^i = \min\left(A^i u_{k+1}^i - \frac{\lambda_k^i}{\rho}, \quad c^i\right)$$
$$\lambda_{k+1}^i = \lambda_k^i + \rho\left(w_{k+1}^i - A^i u_{k+1}^i\right)$$

Based on previous definitions, we propose the next general procedure to solve the control problem of agent i

---

Algorithm 2. General Control Procedure.

---

procedure $u^i(V^i, V^j)$ ⊳ Voltage measurements from other inverters
   System Initialization
   Read the value
   Set $\mathcal{A}^i$, $\mathcal{B}^i$, $\mathcal{C}^i$
   Set $\mathbf{V} = [V^i \quad \ldots \quad V^j]$, ⊳ Vector of voltages
   Set V^{ref} ⊳ Voltage of reference
   Set H_p, T ⊳ Prediction Horizon and Sampling Time
   Set Q, R, s ⊳ MPC Gains
   Set $\mathcal{L}$ ⊳ Laplacian Matrix
   while $k \leq H_p$ **do**
      Solve u^i using Algorithm 1 ⊳ Solve by using ADMM
      Select $u_t^i \leftarrow u^i(1)$ ⊳ Select the first optimal value from vector u
      Apply u_t^i ⊳ Apply control action

---

4 Simulations and Results

In this section, we present the simulation results for an MG consisting of five inverters connected in parallel with droop-control. The MG is simulated using Simulink and Matlab code, and represented in Fig. 2: five inverters are connected by transmission lines, each one supplies a local load, the communication graph among inverters is defined by if there is a physical connection among the inverters or not.

For the system's identification using the EDMD algorithm, we generated 1000 different trajectories varying the initial conditions of (2), data are sampled each 0.1 s obtaining a data vector of 10000 values. Also, a control inputs is added using a random signal varying between $-200\,\text{V}$ and $200\,\text{V}$ each 10 s. The parameters for the MPC and MG design are shown in Table 1.

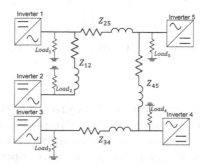

Fig. 2. Microgrid Schematic.

The results for voltage regulation through load changes are shown in Fig. 3. The controller regulates the voltage in a few seconds, when five loads are connected at $t = 0\,\text{s}$. In Fig. 4 is shown the reactive power change at $t = 0\,\text{s}$. The

Table 1. MPC Parameters.

Parameter	Inverter				
	1	2	3	4	5
State difference gain Q	1	1	1	1	1
Input gain R	6	6	6	6	6
Sampling Time (Ts)	0.1	0.1	0.1	0.1	0.1
Voltage restriction	$0.9 \leq v^i \leq 1.1$				
Control Horizon H_p	10	10	10	10	10
Load (kW)	1	1	1	1	1
Line Inductance (mH)	$Z^{12} =1.78$	$Z^{25} =2.15$	$Z^{34} =1.98$	$Z^{45}=2.47$	

algorithm solves the optimization problem by iteration in a few steps and without using any dedicated optimization package (such as Gurobi, Fmincon, quadprog). This aspect makes the algorithm desirable to be implemented in small capacity hardware.

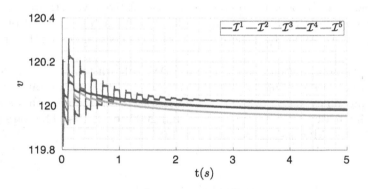

Fig. 3. Voltage Regulation for the MG with load using the control algorithm with ADMM.

The reactive power is supplied by each inverter, and they are also capable of absorbing it. The differences among the reactive power values are given by the impedance's magnitude. Frequency is kept constant during the simulation with a secondary control-loop designed with a consensus approach.

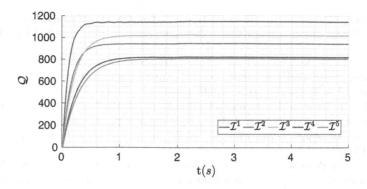

Fig. 4. Reactive Power for the MG with load using the control algorithm with ADMM.

5   Conclusions

This paper presents a data-driven control algorithm for voltage regulation in a MG. Using the V-Q decoupling model for microgrids, the voltage at each inverter is represented by a nonlinear equation which depends on the inverter's impedance and reactive power. The nonlinear model is represented as a linear one in the Koopman space or lifted space using the EDMD algorithm and data collected from simulation experiments. To control the voltage at each inverter was proposed a MPC design based on the Koopman linear representation of the problem. The algorithm also works distributively solved using an ADMM algorithm without any optimization solver. The algorithm was proved in several scenarios for voltage in the MG when there are load changes.

References

1. Anderson, S., Hidalgo-Gonzalez, P., Dobbe, R., Tomlin, C.J.: Distributed model predictive control for autonomous droop-controlled inverter-based microgrids. In: Proceedings of the IEEE Conference on Decision and Control 2019-December(Cdc), pp. 6242–6248 (2019). https://doi.org/10.1109/CDC40024.2019.9028938
2. Budišić, M., Mohr, R., Mezić, I.: Applied Koopmanism. Chaos **22**(4) (2012). https://doi.org/10.1063/1.4772195
3. Farhangi, H.: The path of the smart grid. IEEE Power Energ. Mag. **8**(1), 18–28 (2010). https://doi.org/10.1109/MPE.2009.934876
4. Goldstein, T., O'Donoghue, B., Setzer, S., Baraniuk, R.: Fast alternating direction optimization methods. SIAM J. Imag. Sci. **7**(3), 1588–1623 (2014)
5. Guerrero, J.M., Berbel, N., Matas, J., De Vicuña, L.G., Miret, J.: Decentralized control for parallel operation of distributed generation inverters in microgrids using resistive output impedance. In: IECON Proceedings (Industrial Electronics Conference), vol. 54, no. 2, pp. 5149–5154 (2006). https://doi.org/10.1109/IECON.2006.347859
6. Guerrero, J.M., Vasquez, J.C., Matas, J., De Vicuña, L.G., Castilla, M.: Hierarchical control of droop-controlled AC and DC microgrids - a general approach toward standardization. IEEE Trans. Industr. Electron. **58**(1), 158–172 (2011). https://doi.org/10.1109/TIE.2010.2066534

7. Katiraei, F., Iravani, R., Hatziargyriou, N., Dimeas, A.: Microgrids management. IEEE Power Energ. Mag. **6**(3), 54–65 (2008). https://doi.org/10.1109/MPE.2008. 918702
8. Korda, M., Mezić, I.: Linear predictors for nonlinear dynamical systems: Koopman operator meets model predictive control. Automatica **93**, 149–160 (2018). https:// doi.org/10.1016/j.automatica.2018.03.046
9. Schiffer, J., Zonetti, D., Ortega, R., Stanković, A.M., Sezi, T., Raisch, J.: A survey on modeling of microgrids-From fundamental physics to phasors and voltage sources. Automatica **74**, 135–150 (2016). https://doi.org/10.1016/j.automatica. 2016.07.036
10. Toro, V., Tellez-Castro, D., Mojica-Nava, E., Rakoto-Ravalontsalama, N.: Data-driven distributed voltage control for microgrids: a koopman-based approach. Int. J. Electr. Power Energy Syst. **145**, 108636 (2023)
11. Toro Tovar, B.W.: Data-driven control of interconnected energy systems. Ph.D. thesis, Universidad Nacional de Colombia (2022). https://repositorio.unal.edu.co/ handle/unal/83285

Generalized Nonlinear Rectification Function for Estimating Mel Cepstral Coefficients from Colombian Birdsongs

Jose M. Arias-Arias and Juan P. Ugarte[✉][iD]

GIMSC, Universidad de San Buenaventura, Medellín, Colombia
juan.ugarte@usbmed.edu.co

Abstract. Birds monitoring is important for assessing biodiversity and other ecosystemic aspects. For this purpose, recording and analyzing of birdsongs have become an attractive alternative. There is an ongoing research effort in designing improved signal processing tools for dealing with the problem of recognition of bird species. In this work, we explore the Mel Cepstral coefficients calculation for characterizing bird signals. The Cepstral approach relies on a stage of non-linear rectification which is known to have significant effects on the outcomes of speech processing. Thus, we focus on assessing such stage when processing birdsongs. In this line of thought, we propose two rectification functions that generalize the standard logarithmic and cubic–root functions. These functions are built using homotopic transformation and fractional calculus operators. Numerical experiments reveal that distinct clustering patterns, correlated with birds taxonomic information, can be obtained when adopting different configurations of the proposed rectification functions. Furthermore, the fractional derivative of the logarithmic function yields an improved performance when solving an automatic classification task of Colombian bird species. Therefore, the proposed generalized rectification functions may yield valuable information on distinct bird species. Moreover, the proposed development of the Cepstral analysis can be useful in other fields.

Keywords: Cepstral analysis · multidimensional scaling · fractional calculus · machine learning

1 Introduction

Birds monitoring provides useful information about the state of ecosystems, habitat suitability, and biodiversity [13]. Birds also play an important ecosystemic role such as plant seed dispersal, plant pollination, and insect population control [19]. Through the identification and discrimination of bird species, the extent and distribution of biodiversity can be estimated. Early studies consisted of spotting or hearing birds within their natural habitats. Technological developments yielded the use of camera traps and autonomous sound recorder units,

© The Author(s), under exclusive license to Springer Nature Switzerland AG 2023
J. C. Figueroa-García et al. (Eds.): WEA 2023, CCIS 1928, pp. 251–262, 2023.
https://doi.org/10.1007/978-3-031-46739-4_23

with the advantage of being remotely operated in favor of non-invasive monitoring. These indirect approaches result in a significant amount of digital data from which information about the birds population must be obtained [10]. Thus, there is a current development of computerized tools for processing and extracting quantitative information from this field data.

Acoustic monitoring has become an attractive approach for studying birds population [8,12]. By recording the acoustic landscape, large areas can be covered, far more biodiversity observations can be obtained and the costs are reduced. However, this monitoring procedure is not bird-specific, since the recordings capture the entire acoustical surroundings. Therefore, computerized and automatic solutions for birdsong analysis should consider the content complexity of the underlying data. Fourier transform and spectral analysis are common signal processing tools used when studying birdsongs [13]. The acoustical footprint of distinct bird species can be characterized through the frequency content. This is particularly attractive since machine learning exploits quantitative information that is relevant to the object of interest. Hence, the solution can be developed aiming to automatic classification of bird species. Nevertheless, the optimal set of spectral features, used to fed the learning machine, that solve effectively the bird species classification remains as an open question [10].

Cepstrum analysis is a common tool in acoustic applications [2]. In the case of birdsong processing, Cepstral coefficients have been widely used for characterization and automatic classification tasks [13]. Through the Cepstrum representation the frequency content is characterized, which is especially useful when studying birds since they present a diverse harmonic content. Estimation of Cepstral coefficients implies the implementation of consecutive processes. The configuration of such steps was initially posed for speech processing applications [5] and fine-tuning is required when adopting the Cepstral analysis in other fields. In the case of processing birdsong signals, modifications on the extent of the filterbank and the morphology of the filters have been proposed [3,4,6,7,9]. Less explored, the non-linear rectification has the role of modulating the resulting filterbank energies, so that higher energy frequency bands are emphasized. Cepstral coefficients can be calculated by using logarithmic or cubic–root rectification. In this regard, a study evinced that the type of rectification has a significant effect on the Cepstral analysis outcomes, although those results correspond to speech signals [20]. The role of the Cepstral rectification function for analyzing birdsongs signals has not been scrutinized enough.

Bearing this ideas in mind, in this work, we explore the type of non–linear rectification when calculating the Cepstral coefficients from Birdsong signals. Besides the logarithmic and cubic–root functions, a linear combination of both functions, as a homotopic transformation, is assessed. Furthermore, a generalized logarithmic function is considered by using fractional order derivatives. Fractional calculus adopts real or complex numbers as derivative orders. By exploiting this property, a family of fractional logarithmic functions can be generated which has been effectively applied in other applications [11,18]. In this work, the fractional logarithm is applied as a rectification function during the Cepstrum analysis. The distribution of the Cepstral coefficients representation of birdsong signals is assessed according to the type of rectification by using a dimensional reduction technique for visualization. Then, the effect of the type of rectification is assessed in a task of bird species automatic classification. The evaluated signals correspond to birds from the Colombian ecosystem. The conservation status and threatening due to the illegal trade are considered for selecting the species addressed in this work.

2   Methodology

This section describes the database and the mathematical tools employed in this work. The extraction of the Mel Frequency Cepstral Coefficients (MFCCs) using the standard and the proposed non-linear rectification functions is detailed. The resulting Cepstral coefficients distribution analysis is performed using multidimensional scaling (MDS) as a dimensional reduction technique. Then, a machine learning task is implemented for bird species classification to test the outcomes using the different rectification functions.

2.1   Database

The database was built using acoustic recordings made on field and they are available on the Xeno-canto website www.xeno-canto.org. The species were selected according to the quality of their recordings assigned by the Xeno-canto community. The recordings under Creative Commons license and rated with quality A were used in this work. Quality A indicates loud and clear birdsongs, as established by the repository. The recordings are resampled at 44.1 kHz and manually segmented to extract the vocalization frames. Each frame is divided into non-overlapped windows of $N = 39234$ samples. The segmented signals are normalized to reduce the dependence on variations of sound intensity. The normalization of the i−th window $\hat{x}_i(n), n = 0, \ldots, N-1$ is implemented using the following equation:

$$x_i(n) = \frac{\hat{x}_i(n) - \mu}{\sigma}, \quad i = 0, \ldots, 4680, \tag{1}$$

where, the normalized window $x_i(n)$ is referred as the i−th audio event, and μ, σ are the mean and standard deviation of $\hat{x}_i(n)$, respectively. Table 1 lists the number of recordings (N_r), the number of audio events (N_a), and some metadata related to each specie.

2.2   Mathematical Tools

Mel Cepstral Coefficients. The Mel Cepstral coefficients is a compact representation of the spectral envelope in the Cepstrum domain [1]. Figure 1 shows the flow diagram for calculating the coefficients from an audio event $x_i(n)$.

Each audio event $x_i(n)$ is processed using the Mel filter bank composed of M filters with triangular shape. The filters central frequencies $f_m, m = 1, \ldots, M$

Table 1. Birdsong database description. The conservation status column refers to the conservation status category established by the International Union for Conservation of Nature.

Scientific name	Order	Family	Conservation status	N_r	N_a
Bangsia melanochlamys[a] (Bm)	Passeriformes	Thraupinae	Vulnerable	10	109
Hypopyrrhus pyrohypogaster[a] (Hp)	Passeriformes	Icteridae	Vulnerable	11	106
Icterus chrysater (Ic)	Passeriformes	Icteridae	Least Concern	41	687
Mimus gilvus (Mg)	Passeriformes	Mimidae	Least Concern	66	1671
Penelope perspicax[a] (Pp)	Galliformes	Cracidae	Vulnerable	19	2107
Total				147	4680

[a]Colombian endemic species

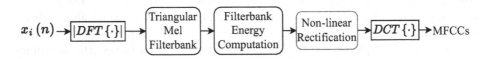

Fig. 1. Flow diagram for calculating Mel Cepstral coefficients.

correspond to equally spaced values on the Mel scale [14]. The Mel frequencies f_m^{mel} are related to the central frequencies f_m as follows:

$$f_m^{\mathrm{mel}} = 2595 \log_{10} \left(1 + \frac{f_m}{700} \right). \tag{2}$$

The spectrum of $x_i(n)$ is obtained through the discrete Fourier transform $X_i(k)$, where k is the bin corresponding to the discrete frequency $f_k = kF_s/N$ and F_s represents the sampling frequency. The $m-$th filter of the Mel filter bank has a frequency response described by the following expression [16]:

$$V(k,m) = \begin{cases} 0, & f_k < f_{m-1}, \\ \frac{f_k - f_{m-1}}{f_m - f_{m-1}}, & f_{m-1} \le f_k < f_m, \\ \frac{f_k - f_{m+1}}{f_m - f_{m+1}}, & f_m \le f_k < f_{m+1}, \\ 0, & f_k \ge f_{m+1}. \end{cases} \tag{3}$$

The $q-$th Mel Cepstral coefficient $\Upsilon_{i,q}$ of the $i-$th audio event is computed using the discrete cosine transform as follows:

$$\Upsilon_{i,q} = \sum_{m=1}^{M} \Phi\{P_{i,m}\} \cos\left[q\left(m + \frac{1}{2} \right) \frac{2\pi}{M} \right], \quad q = 0, \dots, M-1; \tag{4}$$

where, $\Phi\{\cdot\}$ is the non-linear rectification function, and $P_{i,m}$ is the spectral envelope computed using the following expression:

$$P_{i,m} = \frac{1}{\sqrt{A_r}} \sum_{k=0}^{N-1} |V(k,m)\, X_i(k)|^2, \tag{5}$$

where $A_r = \sum_{k=0}^{N-1} |V(k,m)|^2$. The logarithm function or the cubic-root function are commonly used as non-linear rectification function $\Phi\{\cdot\}$. Alternatives for the rectification function can be obtained by linearly combining both functions and through the fractional order derivative of the logarithm function. The following equations describe the resulting functions:

$$\Phi_H\{P_{i,m}\} = a\log(P_{i,m}) + (1-a)\sqrt[3]{P_{i,m}}, \tag{6}$$

$$\Phi_F\{P_{i,m}\} = \frac{\mathrm{d}^\alpha}{dm^\alpha}\left[\log(P_{i,m})\right] = \frac{P_{i,m}^{-\alpha}}{\Gamma(1-\alpha)}\left[\log(P_{i,m}) + \psi(1) - \psi(1-\alpha)\right], \tag{7}$$

where $a \in [0,1]$, $\alpha \in [-1,1]$ is the fractional derivative order, $\Gamma(\cdot)$ and $\psi()$ are the gamma and digamma functions. The non-linear rectification functions Φ_H and Φ_F will be referred to as homotopic and fractional logarithm derivate functions, respectively. It is noteworthy that, in 6, the cases $a = \{0,1\}$ lead to the cubic–root and logarithm rectification functions, respectively. Furthermore, in Eq. 7, the case $\alpha = 0$ yield the logarithm rectification functions. Thus, Φ_H and Φ_F are generalized versions of the standard rectification functions. Figure 2a) shows the standard rectification functions (i.e., $a = \{0,1\}$ in Eq. 6) and the homotopic function for $a = 0.5$. Figure 2b) shows a family of curves generated using different values of α for the fractional logarithm.

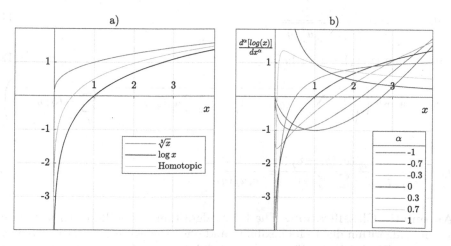

Fig. 2. a) Standard and homotopic rectification functions. b) Family of functions corresponding to the fractional logarithm rectification function.

Dimensional Reduction Analysis. Due to the high dimensional nature of the Mel Cepstral coefficients, the multidimensional scaling (MDS) technique is implemented for data exploration and visualization of the patterns from the estimated values of $\Upsilon_{i,q}$ in low dimensional spaces. The MDS assumes that the initial data is embedded in a normed space. Consider a set of n data points $\mathcal{U} = \{u_1, \ldots, u_n\}$, where each point has κ dimensions. Let $D_{i,j} = d(u_i, u_j)$ be the $n \times n$ matrix containing the distances between pair of elements in $\mathcal{U}$. The MDS algorithm estimates a set of points $\mathcal{V} = \{v_1, \ldots, v_n\}$ with dimension λ $(\lambda < \kappa)$ and $n \times n$ distance matrix $\hat{D}_{i,j} = d_E(v_i, v_j)$, so that $\hat{D} = D$ [15]. The coordinates of the low dimensional set $\mathcal{V}$ result from the optimization process that minimizes a stress function ζ described by the following equation:

$$\zeta = \frac{\sum_{i<j} \left[d(u_i, u_j) - \hat{d}(v_i, v_j)\right]^2}{\sum_{i<j} d(u_i, u_j)^4}. \tag{8}$$

Similar (dissimilar) points in $\mathcal{U}$ are spatially close (far) in $\mathcal{V}$. The values usually adopted for λ are 2 or 3 for yielding data visualization. Several formulations of $d(u_i, u_j)$ can be used to unveil different patterns. In this work, the Euclidean, Dice, signal processing correlation, Chebyshev, Weierstrass, and Jaccard distances are used (denoted as $\{d_E, d_D, d_C, d_{Ch}, d_W, d_J\}$):

$$d_E = \left(\sum_q |u_i(q) - u_j(q)|^2\right)^{1/2}, \tag{9}$$

$$d_D = \frac{\sum_q (u_i(q) - u_j(q))^2}{\sum_q u_i^2(q) + \sum_q u_j^2(q)}, \tag{10}$$

$$d_C = \frac{\sum_q u_i(q) u_j(q)}{\sqrt{\sum_q u_i^2(q) \sum_q u_j^2(q)}}, \tag{11}$$

$$d_{Ch} = \max_q (u_i(q) - u_j(q)), \tag{12}$$

$$d_W = \operatorname{acosh}\left(\sqrt{1 + \sum_q u_i(q) u_i(q)}\sqrt{1 + \sum_q u_j(q) u_j(q)} - \sum_q u_j(q) u_j(q)\right), \tag{13}$$

$$d_J = \frac{\sum_q (u_i(q) - u_j(q))^2}{\sum_q u_i^2(q) + \sum_q u_j^2(q) - \sum_q u_i u_j(q)}. \tag{14}$$

Automatic Classification. The k-NN algorithm is a well-known supervised learning algorithm due to its flexibility and effectiveness in automatic classification tasks. The k-NN classifies an unlabeled data point Υ_j calculating its distance to all the points in the training set Υ_i, and assigning it to that class with the maximum number of nearest neighbors in k neighbors [17]. For the k-NN distance computation, the distances $\{d_E, d_D, d_C, d_{Ch}, d_W, d_J\}$ are tested. Training and test sets are conformed by 70% and 30% of the entire dataset, respectively. Classification classes correspond to the five species presented in Table 1. The classification performance is quantified using sensibility $\mathcal{S}$, precision $\mathcal{P}$, the harmonic mean $F1 = 2\mathcal{SP}/(\mathcal{S} + \mathcal{P})$ and the geometric mean $FM = \sqrt{\mathcal{SP}}$.

3   Results

The results of the dimensional reduction analysis and the automatic classification using the Mel Cepstral coefficients are presented below. The effect of the number of filters M of the Mel filter bank, the non-linear rectification function Φ, and the outcomes of using different distance measures are discussed.

3.1   Mel Cepstral Coefficients

The rectified spectral envelopes $\Phi\{P_{i,m}\}$ of a representative audio event for each bird specie are shown in Fig. 3 using the standard and homotopic rectification, and the fractional logarithm for different values of α. It can be seen the different behavior of the rectification functions mapping in mapping the spectral energy. Visual inspection accounts for significant differences in the amplitude of the curves corresponding to the logarithm rectification concerning the cubic–root and homotopic function. On the contrary, the implementation of the fractional logarithm leads to a finer variation of the resulting spectral envelope.

3.2   Pattern Analysis of Mel Cepstral Coefficients

In this section, the MDS algorithm is used to generate a low dimensional representation of the Mel Cepstral coefficients by using different rectification functions. Figure 4 depicts the MDS maps of the Cepstral Coefficients using the logarithm, homotopic, and cubic–root rectification. Three clusters can be identified in Fig. 4a). A major cluster contains data points of the five species, including sub–clusters related to Pp and Bm species, suggesting acoustic similarities with the Hp, Ic, and Mg species. A second cluster is composed by a significant number of events of the Pp specie and a third cluster at the top of the chart with the remaining points of the Bm specie. Figures 4b) and 4c) present the MDS maps where different colors discriminate the family and taxonomic order, respectively. On the one hand, the Ictaridae, Mimidae, and Thraupidae families belong to the Passeride infraorder and the Passeriforme order as well, the Cracidae family is part of the Galliforme order. Although the Thraupidae family forms a separate sub–cluster, it is still part of the Passeriforme cluster. In addition, the Fig. 4c) depicts the same two groups containing the Pp specie (galliforme order) as in Fig. 4a), but in this case, both clusters are separated from the Passeriforme cluster. It is noteworthy that, through the standard and homotopic rectification, distinct information related to the birds can be discerned from the emerging clusters in the MDS maps.

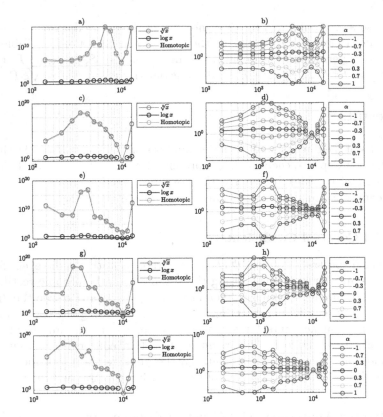

Fig. 3. Rectified spectral envelope $\Phi\{P_{i,m}\}$ using the standard and the homotopic (fractional logarithm) rectifications for a) (b)) Bm, c) (d)) Hp, e) (f)) Ic, g) (h)) Mm, i) (j)) Pp species. Each plot is represented in logarithmic scaled in the horizontal and vertical directions.

Figure 5 portrays the MDS maps corresponding to the fractional logarithm corresponding to distinct configurations of the fractional derivative order α and the number of filters of the Mel filter Bank. In this case, different marker colors discriminate among bird species. The MDS maps suggest that the fractional logarithm rectification in combination with the distinct configuration of the Mel bank filter modulates the dissimilarities of points corresponding to different bird species.

3.3   Automatic Classification

According to the MDS analysis, proper cluster representation of bird species can be achieved by setting the fractional logarithmic rectification and the number of filters in the Mel filter bank. Bearing this outcome in mind, it is reasonable to expect a proper classification using a k-NN algorithm. For this purpose, we

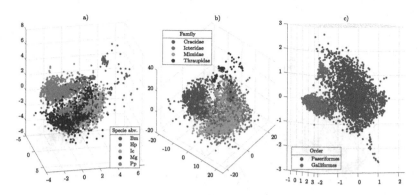

Fig. 4. MDS maps corresponding to $M = 40$ by adopting the a) logarithm rectification and d_E as distance measure, b) Homotopic rectification and d_{Ch} as distance measure, c) cubic-root rectification and d_W as distance measure.

Table 2. Confusion matrix obtained by averaging, over 10 repetitions, the results of the k–NN algorithm by implementing $M = 40$, $\alpha = 0.02$ and d_D as distance measure.

		Predicted Labels				
		Bm	Hp	Ic	Mm	Pp
True Labels	Bm	99.7	0.0	0.0	0.3	0.0
	Hp	0.9	87.8	5.3	1.3	4.7
	Ic	0.0	0.3	93.5	0.2	6.1
	Mm	0.2	0.2	1.8	97.4	0.4
	Pp	0.0	0.0	0.1	0.1	99.9

trained and tested the k-NN algorithm under different configurations by varying the number of neighbors, the type of distance, and the distance weight. In addition, several values of M for configuring the extent of the filters bank were considered. The best classification performance was obtained for $M = 40$ Mel filters for the Cepstral Coefficients computation, a value of $\alpha = 0.02$ for the fractional logarithmic rectification, the distance d_D and $k = 1$ for the k–NN configuration. In order to test reproducibility of such hyperparameterization, 10 repetitions of training and testing are performed, by randomly assigning in each repetition the 70/30% to the training/test sets. In what follows, the performance mean values over 10 iterations are presented. Table 2 presents the confusion matrix in percentage and Table 3 outlines the classification performance for each specie and the macro average values. It can be evinced that, the F_1 and FM metrics for all species are above 91%, whereas the macro averages exceed 95%. Additional experiments revealed that the fractional logarithmic rectification outperforms the classification outcomes using the standard and homotopic rectification configurations.

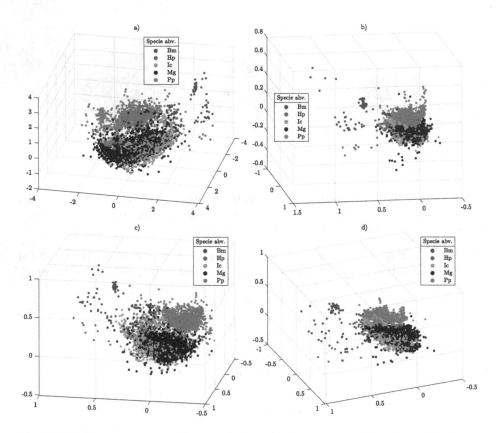

Fig. 5. MDS maps corresponding to the fractional logarithm derivative with a) $\alpha = 0.01$, $M = 13$ and d_E as distance measure, b) $\alpha = 0.01$, $M = 30$ and d_C as distance measure, c) $\alpha = -0.01$, $M = 32$ and d_J as distance measure, d) $\alpha = 0.02$, $M = 40$ and d_D as distance measure.

Table 3. Performance of the k-NN algorithm by implementing $M = 40$, $\alpha = 0.02$ and d_D as distance measure. The last row presents the average of each metric over all species.

Specie.	$\mathcal{S}$	$\mathcal{P}$	F_1	FM
Bm	99.7	96.5	98.1	98.1
Hp	87.8	95.4	91.4	91.5
Ic	93.5	94.4	93.9	93.9
Mm	99.9	99.5	99.7	99.7
Pp	97.4	97.2	97.3	97.3
Macro average	95.6	96.6	96.1	96.1

4   Conclusion

In this work, we assessed the role of the non-linear rectification during the estimation of the Mel Cepstral coefficients for bird species characterization. In addition, a new family of rectification functions is proposed by applying fractional order derivatives. Our numerical experiments revealed that the rectification function leads to different clustering patterns when mapping the Mel Cepstral coefficients into a low dimension space. Furthermore, high performance in classifying five Colombian bird species was achieved by fine tuning the rectification function through the order of the fractional derivative. Future studies must be conducted with a larger dataset for further validation of these results. Moreover, the fractional logarithm enables an additional degree–o–freedom in calculating the Cepstral coefficients that can be exploited in other well known applications of this signal processing tool.

References

1. Instantaneous Features, chap. 3, pp. 31–69. Wiley, Hoboken (2012). https://doi.org/10.1002/9781118393550.ch3
2. Abdul, Z.K., Al-Talabani, A.K.: Mel frequency cepstral coefficient and its applications: a review. IEEE Access **10**(October), 122136–122158 (2022). https://doi.org/10.1109/ACCESS.2022.3223444
3. Arias-Arias, J.M., Ugarte, J.P.: Spectral and cepstral analysis of Colombian birdsongs using multidimensional scaling. In: 2022 12th International Conference on Pattern Recognition Systems (ICPRS), pp. 1–7. IEEE (2022). https://doi.org/10.1109/ICPRS54038.2022.9854072
4. Bang, A.V., Rege, P.P.: Automatic recognition of bird species using human factor cepstral coefficients. Smart Innov. Syst. Technol. **77**, 363–373 (2018)
5. Bogert, B.P., Healy, J.R., Tukey, J.W.: The quefrency alanysis of time series for echoes: cepstrum, pseudo-autocovariance, cross-cepstrum, and saphe cracking. In: Proceedings of the Symposium on Time Series Analysis, pp. 209–243 (1963)
6. Carvalho, S., Gomes, E.F.: Automatic classification of bird sounds: using MFCC and mel spectrogram features with deep learning. Viet. J. Comput. Sci. **10**(01), 39–54 (2023). https://doi.org/10.1142/S2196888822500300
7. Chu, W., Alwan, A.: FBEM: a filter bank EM algorithm for the joint optimization of features and acoustic model parameters in bird call classification. In: 2012 IEEE International Conference on Acoustics, Speech and Signal Processing (ICASSP), pp. 1993–1996. IEEE (2012). https://doi.org/10.1109/ICASSP.2012.6288298
8. Depraetere, M., Pavoine, S., Jiguet, F., Gasc, A., Duvail, S., Sueur, J.: Monitoring animal diversity using acoustic indices: implementation in a temperate woodland. Ecol. Ind. **13**(1), 46–54 (2012). https://doi.org/10.1016/j.ecolind.2011.05.006
9. Graciarena, M., Delplanche, M., Shriberg, E., Stolcke, A., Ferrer, L.: Acoustic front-end optimization for bird species recognition. In: 2010 IEEE International Conference on Acoustics, Speech and Signal Processing, pp. 293–296. IEEE (2010). https://doi.org/10.1109/ICASSP.2010.5495923
10. Kitzes, J., Schricker, L.: The necessity, promise and challenge of automated biodiversity surveys. Environ. Conserv. **46**, 1–4 (2019). https://doi.org/10.1017/S0376892919000146

11. Machado, J.: Fractional order generalized information. Entropy **16**, 2350–2361 (2014). https://doi.org/10.3390/e16042350
12. Mammides, C., Goodale, E., Dayananda, S.K., Kang, L., Chen, J.: Do acoustic indices correlate with bird diversity? Insights from two biodiverse regions in Yunnan Province, south China. Ecol. Ind. **82**(March), 470–477 (2017). https://doi.org/10.1016/j.ecolind.2017.07.017
13. Priyadarshani, N., Marsland, S., Castro, I.: Automated birdsong recognition in complex acoustic environments: a review. J. Avian Biol. **49**(5), 1–27 (2018). https://doi.org/10.1111/jav.01447
14. Rabiner, L., Schafer, R.: Theory and Applications of Digital Speech Processing. Prentice Hall Press (2010)
15. Saeed, N., Nam, H., Haq, M.I.U., Saqib, D.B.M.: A survey on multidimensional scaling. ACM Comput. Surv. **51**, 1–25 (2019). https://doi.org/10.1145/3178155
16. Sigurdsson, S., Petersen, K.B., Lehn-Schiøler, T.: Mel frequency cepstral coefficients: an evaluation of robustness of MP3 encoded music. In: ISMIR, pp. 286–289 (2006)
17. Taunk, K., De, S., Verma, S., Swetapadma, A.: A brief review of nearest neighbor algorithm for learning and classification. In: 2019 International Conference on Intelligent Computing and Control Systems (ICCS), pp. 1255–1260. IEEE (2019)
18. Ugarte, J.P., Tenreiro Machado, J., Tobón, C.: Fractional generalization of entropy improves the characterization of rotors in simulated atrial fibrillation. Appl. Math. Comput. **425**, 127077 (2022)
19. Vallecillo, S., Maes, J., Polce, C., Lavalle, C.: A habitat quality indicator for common birds in Europe based on species distribution models. Ecol. Ind. **69**(2016), 488–499 (2016). https://doi.org/10.1016/j.ecolind.2016.05.008
20. Zhao, X., Wang, D.: Analyzing noise robustness of MFCC and GFCC features in speaker identification. In: ICASSP, IEEE International Conference on Acoustics, Speech and Signal Processing - Proceedings, pp. 7204–7208 (2013). https://doi.org/10.1109/ICASSP.2013.6639061

Optimization

Global Sensitivity Analysis in Optimization – The Case of Positive Definite Quadratic Forms

Milan Hladík[✉][iD]

Faculty of Mathematics and Physics, Department of Applied Mathematics,
Charles University, Malostranské nám. 25,11800Prague, Czech Republic
hladik@kam.mff.cuni.cz
https://kam.mff.cuni.cz/~hladik

Abstract. We consider the problem of minimization of a positive definite quadratic form; this problem has a unique optimal solution. The question here is what are the largest allowable variations of the input data such that the optimal solution will not exceed given bounds? This problem is called global sensitivity analysis since, in contrast to the traditional sensitivity analysis, it deals with variations of possibly all input coefficients. We propose a general framework for approaching the problem with any matrix norm. We also focus on some commonly used norms and investigate for which of them the problem is efficiently solvable. Particularly for the max-norm, the problem is NP-hard, so we turn our attention to computationally cheap bounds.

Keywords: Positive definiteness · Quadratic form · Sensitivity analysis · Tolerance analysis · Matrix norm · NP-hardness

1 Introduction

Sensitivity analysis is a well-known and important discipline in optimization. However, there are still challenging issues, such as involving more complex variations of the data. This paper investigates quite general variations for the unconstrained optimization problem that minimizes a positive definite quadratic form. In order to formulate the problem precisely and to introduce the auxiliary technical tools, we present some preliminaries and notation first.

Sensitivity Analysis. The traditional sensitivity analysis in (linear or nonlinear) mathematical programming [2,5,6,21] studies the effect of variations of one coefficient on the optimal value and the optimal solution. Nowadays, it is a standard and widely used technique and many extensions exist. Among them, the tolerance approach to sensitivity analysis [1,4,10,19,20] was introduced to handle independent and simultaneous variations of certain coefficients. Nevertheless, it is still not clear how to effectively treat possibly all input coefficients and how to perform it by using various measures (in the data space).

Supported by the Czech Science Foundation Grant P403-22-11117S.

J. C. Figueroa-García et al. (Eds.): WEA 2023, CCIS 1928, pp. 265–275, 2023.
https://doi.org/10.1007/978-3-031-46739-4_24

Notation. We use I_n for the identity matrix of size $n \times n$ and $e = (1, \ldots, 1)^T$ for the vector of ones (with convenient dimension). Throughout the paper, the inequalities and the functions min and absolute value are understood entrywise when applied on vectors and matrices.

Vector and Matrix Norms. The vector p-norms are defined for every $p \geq 1$ and $x \in \mathbb{R}^n$ as $\|x\|_p := \left(\sum_{i=1}^{n} |x_i|^p \right)^{\frac{1}{p}}$. Three particular cases are often used: the Manhattan norm ($p = 1$), the Euclidean norm ($p = 2$) and, as the limit case, the maximum norm, which reads $\|x\|_\infty = \max_i |x_i|$.

For two arbitrary vector norms $\|x\|_\alpha$, $\|x\|_\beta$, the subordinate matrix norm [9] is defined as

$$\|A\|_{\alpha,\beta} := \max_{\|x\|_\alpha = 1} \|Ax\|_\beta.$$

If we use it for the vector 1-norm and the maximum norm, we obtain the matrix max-norm

$$\|A\|_{\max} := \|A\|_{1,\infty} = \max_{i,j} |a_{ij}|.$$

In the opposite order, the resulting subordinate matrix norm has the form

$$\|A\|_{\infty,1} := \max_{\|x\|_\infty = 1} \|Ax\|_1 = \max_{y,z \in \{\pm 1\}^n} y^T A z. \tag{1}$$

In contrast to many other basic subordinate norms, this one is NP-hard to compute [3,17].

Provided $\alpha \equiv \beta$, the subordinate matrix norm reduces to the standard induced matrix norm. In particular, the spectral norm $\|A\|_2$ of A is induced by the Euclidean norm. It is known that $\|A\|_2 = \sigma_{\max}(A)$, where $\sigma_{\max}(A)$ stands for the maximum singular value. The induced 1-norm and ∞-norm have simple explicit expressions $\|A\|_1 = \max_j \sum_i |a_{ij}|$ and $\|A\|_\infty = \|A^T\|_1$. The Frobenius norm $\|A\|_F := \sqrt{\sum_{i,j} a_{ij}^2}$ is also a common matrix norm, however, it is not an induced norm.

Interval Analysis. In the matrix max-norm, the unit ball has the form of an interval matrix, so we will also utilize some notation and results from the area of interval analysis [5,14]. An interval matrix is the set of matrices

$$\boldsymbol{A} = [\underline{A}, \overline{A}] = \{A' \in \mathbb{R}^{m \times n}; \ \underline{A} \leq A' \leq \overline{A}\},$$

where $\underline{A}$ and $\overline{A}$ are given lower and upper bound matrices. The midpoint and radius operators are, respectively, defined as

$$\operatorname{mid}(\boldsymbol{A}) = \frac{1}{2}(\underline{A} + \overline{A}), \quad \operatorname{rad}(\boldsymbol{A}) = \frac{1}{2}(\overline{A} - \underline{A}).$$

The set of interval matrices of size $m \times n$ is denoted by $\mathbb{IR}^{m \times n}$, and the set of interval vectors of size n is denoted by $\mathbb{IR}^n$. An interval matrix $\boldsymbol{A} \in \mathbb{IR}^{n \times n}$ is called *regular* if every $A \in \mathbf{A}$ is nonsingular; many conditions on regularity are summarized in Rohn [18]. For a given norm, we define

$$\|\mathbf{A}\| = \max\{\|A\|; \ A \in \mathbf{A}\}.$$

We will particularly utilize the ∞-norm, which has a simple expression

$$\|\mathbf{A}\|_\infty = \||\operatorname{mid}(\mathbf{A})| + \operatorname{rad}(\mathbf{A})\|_\infty.$$

We do not recall the common definition of interval arithmetic; the reader can find it in many papers and books [5,14].

Regularity Radius. Let $A \in \mathbb{R}^{n \times n}$ be a nonsingular matrix and let $\| \cdot \|_*$ be an arbitrary matrix norm. *The regularity radius* is defined as the distance to the nearest singular matrix and we denote it

$$\mathrm{r}(A) := \min\{\|A - B\|_*; \ B \text{ is singular}\}.$$

For the spectral norm or the Frobenius norm (or other orthogonally invariant matrix norms), the regularity radius is equal to the smallest singular value, that is, $\mathrm{r}(A) = \sigma_{\min}(A)$. More generally, by the Gastinel–Kahan theorem [9,12], for any subordinate matrix norm $\| \cdot \|_{\alpha,\beta}$, the corresponding regularity radius can be expressed by the formula $\mathrm{r}(A) = \|A^{-1}\|_{\beta,\alpha}^{-1}$.

Particularly for the max-norm, the regularity radius admits an explicit formula [3,13,15]

$$\mathrm{r}_{\max}(A) = \|A^{-1}\|_{\infty,1}^{-1} = \frac{1}{\max_{y,z \in \{\pm 1\}^n} y^T A^{-1} z}.$$

The formula utilizes exponentially many vectors, but can hardly be avoided because for the max-norm the regularity radius $\mathrm{r}(A)$ is NP-hard. This is the case even on the class of nonnegative symmetric positive definite matrices [15]. Therefore, computationally cheap lower or upper bounds can be useful. A simple lower bound takes the form

$$\mathrm{r}_{\max}(A) \geq \frac{1}{e^T |A^{-1}| e}. \tag{2}$$

Other approximations and special matrices were discussed in [8]. Semidefinite programming relaxation yields bounds with one of the best known approximation ratios [7].

Formulation of the Problem. Consider the unconstrained optimization problem

$$\min \ \frac{1}{2} x^T A x - b^T x, \tag{3}$$

where $A \in \mathbb{R}^{n \times n}$ is positive definite and $b \in \mathbb{R}^n$. Its optimal solution $x^* := A^{-1} b$ is the unique solution of the system $Ax = b$.

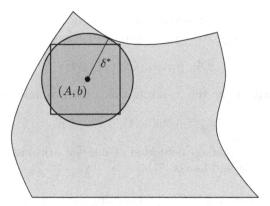

Fig. 1. The space of data (A, b), the set of admissible values in gray and the illustration of the radius of optimality in dark gray. (Color figure online)

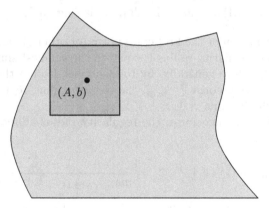

Fig. 2. The space of data (A, b), the set of admissible values in gray and the illustration of the radius of optimality in dark gray for the max-norm. (Color figure online)

We are given the input (A, b), bounds $\ell < x^* < u$ and a matrix norm $\| \cdot \|$. The problem is to find the distance to the nearest data (A', b') for which the optimal solution $x' = A'^{-1}b'$ violates the bounds $\ell \leq x^* \leq u$. This *radius of optimality* is formally defined as

$$\delta^* := \inf\{\|(A', b') - (A, b)\|;\ A' = A'^T \wedge (\det(A') = 0 \vee \neg(\ell \leq A'^{-1}b' \leq u))\}.$$

We need to write "inf" here because it is usually not attained as the minimum. From another perspective, it provides an easy-to-interpret value of the radius of optimality: for every perturbation of the data (A', b') such that $\|(A', b') - (A, b)\| < \delta$ we are sure that the optimal solution x' lies between ℓ and u.

Figure 1 geometrically illustrates the radius of optimality. It depicts the point (A, b) in the space $\mathbb{R}^{n \times n + n}$ and the set of all admissible data (A', b'), that is, that data for which the problem satisfies the bounds $\ell \leq (A')^{-1}b' \leq u$ and nonsingularity of A'. The radius of optimality then graphically represents the radius of the largest ball with center (A, b) and lying inside the admissible set.

Figure 2 then shows the situation when the max-norm is employed. Now, the ball has the form of a box. We also see that the radius of optimality can be attained for a different variation of the data, and also another of the bounds ℓ and u can be active in that case.

Since the computation of δ^* is very hard in general, we will sometimes be content with the calculation of (hopefully tight) lower bounds. Notice the importance of lower bounds – they provide us with safe tolerances of variations of data.

Remark 1. The problem can easily be extended to the problems with equality constraints

$$\min \frac{1}{2}x^T A x - b^T x \ \text{ subject to } \ Cx = d,$$

where $C \in \mathbb{R}^{m \times n}$ has full row rank. Its optimal solution is the unique solution of the system $Cx = d$, $Ax - b = C^T y$, so the problem can be approached in a similar way.

2   General Method

By the definition of the radius of optimality, we can express δ^* as

$$\delta^* := \min_{i=1,\dots,n} \{\delta^0, \delta^\ell(i), \delta^u(i)\}$$

where δ^0 is the radius of positive definiteness, δ_i^ℓ is the radius of non-violence of the lower bound $(A'^{-1}b')_i \geq \ell_i$, and δ_i^u is the radius of non-violence of the upper bound $(A'^{-1}b')_i \leq u_i$. We discuss these quantities in detail below.

Radius of Positive Definiteness. Formally, the radius of positive definiteness is defined as

$$\delta^0 := \inf\{\|A' - A\|; \ A' = A'^T \wedge \det(A') = 0\}.$$

We write δ_*^0 when a particular matrix norm $\| \cdot \|_*$ is used. It is known [11] that

$$\delta^0 = \lambda_{\min}(A),$$

i.e., the smallest eigenvalue of A, provided the matrix norm is consistent (i.e., $\|AB\| \leq \|A\| \|B\|$ for every $A, B \in \mathbb{R}^{n \times n}$) and satisfies the property $\|I_n\| = 1$. For the max-norm (which is not consistent), computation of $\delta^0 = \delta^0_{\max}$ is an NP-hard problem [13, 16]. We have a finite but exponential explicit formula [11]:

$$\delta^0_{\max} = \min_{y \in \{\pm 1\}^n} \frac{1}{y^T A^{-1} y}.$$

As we will see later, it is in general very hard to handle the structured perturbations A'; in our case $A' = A'^T$. However, for the case of the radius of positive definiteness, the symmetry can be relaxed for most of the commonly used norms, including the spectral norm or the max-norm.

Lemma 1. If $\|M\| = \|M^T\|$, then $\|M\| \geq \|\frac{1}{2}(M + M^T)\|$.

Proof. We have $\|\frac{1}{2}(M + M^T)\| \leq \frac{1}{2}\|M\| + \frac{1}{2}\|M^T\| = \frac{1}{2}\|M\| + \frac{1}{2}\|M\| = \|M\|$. □

Let A' be not necessarily symmetric. Then $A + A'$ is positive definite if and only if $A + \frac{1}{2}(A' + A'^T)$ is positive definite. In this case, the corresponding optimal solution is $(A + \frac{1}{2}(A' + A'^T))^{-1}b$. Therefore, for any matrix norm satisfying $\|M\| = \|M^T\|$ we have that δ^0 is the same even when we omit the symmetry condition $A' = A'^T$. For the other norms, relaxing the symmetry of A' results in a lower bound on δ^0.

Proposition 1. If $\|M\| = \|M^T\|$, then $\delta^0 = r(A)$. Otherwise, $\delta^0 \geq r(A)$.

Radius of Optimality for the Upper Bound. Formally, the radius is defined

$$\delta^u(i) := \inf\{\|(A', b') - (A, b)\| < \delta^0; \ A' = A'^T \wedge (A'^{-1}b')_i = u_i\}.$$

We write $\delta^u_*(i)$ when a particular matrix norm $\|\cdot\|_*$ is used.

From the definition, we seek for such a perturbation (A', b'), for which the system

$$A'x = b', \quad x_i = u_i$$

is feasible. Since A' is positive definite, this overdetermined system is feasible if and only if the matrix

$$\begin{pmatrix} A' & b' \\ e_i^T & u_i \end{pmatrix}$$

is singular. We thus reduced the computation to the problem of regularity radius of the matrix

$$A_i^u := \begin{pmatrix} A & b \\ e_i^T & u_i \end{pmatrix}.$$

Here we have two problems. First, the last row is fixed. Second, we should consider the structured perturbations preserving symmetry of A'. Both issues are very difficult problems, however, if we relax them and consider unstructured perturbations, we obtain (hopefully tight) lower approximation

$$r(A_i^u) \leq \delta^u(i).$$

Radius of Optimality for the Lower Bound. This problem is analogous to the previous one, so we do not analyse it in detail. The counterpart of the matrix A_i^u is matrix

$$A_i^\ell := \begin{pmatrix} A & b \\ e_i^T & \ell_i \end{pmatrix}.$$

Summary. In total, the radius of optimality δ^* can be approximated as

$$\delta^* \geq \min\{r(A), r(A_1^u), \dots, r(A_n^u), r(A_1^\ell), \dots, r(A_n^\ell)\}. \tag{4}$$

In this way, the problem is reduced to the computation of the regularity radius of $2n+1$ matrices of size $n \times n$ or $(n+1) \times (n+1)$. For those matrix norms that admit an efficient computation of the regularity radius, the radius of optimality is also efficiently computable. This is not the case for the max-norm, so we discuss it separately.

Example 1. Consider the problem (3) with

$$A = \begin{pmatrix} 5 & 1 & 0 \\ 1 & 3 & 1 \\ 0 & 1 & 4 \end{pmatrix}, \quad b = \begin{pmatrix} 20 \\ 25 \\ 33 \end{pmatrix}, \quad \ell = \begin{pmatrix} 0 \\ 0 \\ 0 \end{pmatrix}$$

and no upper bound u. The corresponding optimal solution is $x^* = A^{-1}b = (3, 5, 7)^T$. Opting for the spectral norm, we compute the particular tolerance radii

$$r(A) = 2.1206, \quad r(A_1^\ell) = 0.31856, \quad r(A_2^\ell) = 0.50574, \quad r(A_3^\ell) = 0.74051.$$

Because of the absence of the upper bounds, we do not need to take care of quantities $r(A_1^u), \dots, r(A_3^u)$. The minimum value of the above radii is $r(A_1^\ell)$, so we have $\delta^* \geq 0.31856$. Therefore, 0.31856 is the guaranteed radius of optimality.

3 Radius of Optimality for the Max-Norm

Recall that the regularity radius is efficiently computable for some matrix norms, but it is NP-hard for the max-norm. That is why we propose an efficiently computable lower bound for $\delta^* = \delta_{max}^*$ in case of the max-norm. First, we recall a useful bound for the solutions of interval systems of linear equations [14].

Lemma 2. *Let $G \in \mathbb{IR}^{n \times n}$, $g \in \mathbb{IR}^n$ and $C \in \mathbb{R}^{n \times n}$. If $\|I_n - CG\|_\infty < 1$, then G is regular and for each $G \in G$ and $g \in g$ we have*

$$\|G^{-1}g\|_\infty \leq \frac{\|Cg\|_\infty}{1 - \|I_n - CG\|_\infty}.$$

Now, we reformulate our problem. Define the interval matrix G and interval vector g as follows:

$$G = [A - \gamma \cdot G_\Delta, A + \gamma \cdot G_\Delta], \quad g = [b - \gamma \cdot g_\Delta, b + \gamma \cdot g_\Delta],$$

where $G_\Delta \geq 0$ and $g_\Delta \geq 0$ are given, and $\gamma \geq 0$ is a parameter. For the max-norm, it corresponds to choosing $G_\Delta = ee^T$ and $g_\Delta = e$, however, our approach works even for general $G_\Delta \geq 0$ and $g_\Delta \geq 0$. Without loss of generality assume that $\min(u - x^*, x^* - \ell) = u - x^*$. We also assume that $u - x^* = \alpha e$ for some $\alpha > 0$, which can be obtained by a suitable scaling. Thus our problem states:

Determine maximal $\gamma \geq 0$ such that G is regular and $\|G^{-1}g - x^*\|_\infty \leq \alpha$ for every $G \in \boldsymbol{G}$ and $g \in \boldsymbol{g}$.

When $G_\Delta = ee^T$ and $g_\Delta = e$, this maximal value is a lower bound on $\delta^*_{\max}$. Since it is NP-hard to compute even this maximal value [3], we focus on the computation of an efficient lower bound.

Proposition 2. *We have*

$$\delta^*_{\max} \geq \frac{\alpha}{\||G_c^{-1}|(g_\Delta + G_\Delta |x^*|)\|_\infty + \alpha \||G_c^{-1}|G_\Delta\|_\infty}.$$

Proof. Consider the substitution $y := x - x^*$. Then the interval system reads as

$$Gy = g - Gx^*.$$

Notice that due to the double occurrences of $\boldsymbol{G}$ the solution set possibly enlarges, but its enclosure serves as an enclosure of the original solution set as well. Applying lemma 2, we get the bound

$$\|G^{-1}g - x^*\|_\infty \leq \frac{\|C(g - Gx^*)\|_\infty}{1 - \|I_n - CG\|_\infty}. \tag{5}$$

Put $C := G_c^{-1}$ and we particularly have

$$\mathrm{mid}(C(g - Gx^*)) = G_c^{-1}(g_c - G_c G_c^{-1} g_c) = 0,$$
$$\mathrm{rad}(C(g - Gx^*)) = \gamma |G_c^{-1}|(g_\Delta + G_\Delta |x^*|),$$

and

$$\mathrm{mid}(I_n - CG) = I_n - G_c^{-1}G_c = 0,$$
$$\mathrm{rad}(I_n - CG) = \gamma |G_c^{-1}|G_\Delta.$$

Thus, in order that $\|G^{-1}g - x^*\|_\infty \leq \alpha$, we get from (5) the sufficient condition

$$\alpha \geq \frac{\|C(g - Gx^*)\|_\infty}{1 - \|I_n - CG\|_\infty} = \frac{\gamma \||G_c^{-1}|(g_\Delta + G_\Delta |x^*|)\|_\infty}{1 - \gamma \||G_c^{-1}|G_\Delta\|_\infty}.$$

From this we express the bound for γ,

$$\gamma \leq \frac{\alpha}{\||G_c^{-1}|(g_\Delta + G_\Delta |x^*|)\|_\infty + \alpha \||G_c^{-1}|G_\Delta\|_\infty}, \tag{6}$$

yielding the bound for $\delta^*_{\max}$.

In order that the derivation is correct, the denominator in (5) must be positive. That is,

$$1 > \|I_n - CG\|_\infty = \gamma \||G_c^{-1}|G_\Delta\|_\infty,$$

whence

$$\gamma < \frac{1}{\||G_c^{-1}|G_\Delta\|_\infty}.$$

From (6) we see that it is satisfied always as a non-strict inequality. However, in view of the definition of δ^* by means of infimum, we can be content with the non-strict inequality. □

It turns out that for the max-norm, the radius of regularity in (4) is implicitly involved in the other optimality radii, so we can omit it.

Proposition 3. *We have*

$$\delta^*_{max} \geq \min\{r_{max}(A_1^u), \ldots, r_{max}(A_n^u), r_{max}(A_1^\ell), \ldots, r_{max}(A_n^\ell)\}. \tag{7}$$

Proof. Denote by r^* the right-hand side value in (7). Our aim is to show that A' is nonsingular whenever $\|A - A'\|_{max} < r^*$. Suppose to the contrary that there is a singular A' such that $\|A - A'\|_{max} < r^*$. Consider a sequence $A_k \to_{k\to\infty} A'$ with $A_1 = A$ and $\|A - A_k\|_{max} < r^*$.

Suppose first that the rank of A' is equal to $n-1$. Denote by i the index of that column of A' that is linearly dependent on the others. Replace the ith column of A' by the vector b and denote the resulting matrix by M. If matrix M is singular, then we perturb the ith column such that it becomes nonsingular (notice that also the vector b can vary such that its variation b' satisfies $\|b - b'\|_{max} < r^*$). By Cramer's rule, the solution x' of $A_k x = b$ satisfies $x_i' = \frac{\det(M_k)}{\det(A_k)}$, where matrix M_k results from A_k by replacing the ith column by vector b. Now, as $k \to \infty$, the entry x_i' diverges. Therefore the condition $\ell_i \leq x_i' \leq u_i$ is violated, which is a contradiction with the definition of r^*.

If the rank of A' is less than $n-1$, then we perturb the corresponding columns such that the rank will be $n-1$. This is easy to achieve since the full column rank matrices form a dense set in matrix space. Then the previous case applies. □

Example 2. Let us reconsider Example 1. Opting now for the max-norm, we calculate

$$r(A) = 0.78462, \quad r(A_1^\ell) = 0.1418, \quad r(A_2^\ell) = 0.19392, \quad r(A_3^\ell) = 0.30591.$$

In accordance with Proposition 3, the calculation of $r(A)$ was redundant. The minimum quantity is attained for $r(A_1^\ell)$, so we have $\delta^*_{max} \geq 0.1418$. This means that the optimal solution of (3) remains nonnegative even if any entry of A and b changes down or up by the amount of at most 0.1418, independently to each other.

In order to apply Proposition 2, we rescale the data such that

$$\tilde{A} = \begin{pmatrix} 5/3 & 1/5 & 0 \\ 1/3 & 3/5 & 1/7 \\ 0 & 1/5 & 4/7 \end{pmatrix}, \quad \tilde{x}^* = \begin{pmatrix} 1 \\ 1 \\ 1 \end{pmatrix},$$

while b and ℓ remain the same. Now, $\tilde{x}^* - \ell = e$, so that we have $\alpha = 1$. The upper bound u is again omitted here. Next, we put

$$G_\Delta = \begin{pmatrix} 1/3 \ 1/5 \ 1/7 \\ 1/3 \ 1/5 \ 1/7 \\ 1/3 \ 1/5 \ 1/7 \end{pmatrix}, \quad g_\Delta = \begin{pmatrix} 1 \\ 1 \\ 1 \end{pmatrix}.$$

Calling Proposition 2, we calculate the lower bound

$$\delta_{\max}^* \geq 0.13143.$$

We see that the result is slightly underestimated, but not too much. In view of intractability of the problem it is expected that an approximate method running in polynomial time will not produce exact bounds.

4   Conclusion

On the one hand, sensitivity analysis is a well-studied discipline in optimization. On the other hand, there are still many challenges. This paper was a contribution to a global approach involving much complex variations in the data. We discussed the unconstrained optimization problem of minimization of a positive definite quadratic form. Even for this (in some sense simple) optimization model it is computationally hard to determine the exact maximal allowable tolerance for the data. That is why we focused on the approximation as well. Anyway, an exact or a tight approximation method is still a challenging problem. Our aim for the future is to address also other important classes of optimization problems.

References

1. Borgonovo, E., Buzzard, G.T., Wendell, R.E.: A global tolerance approach to sensitivity analysis in linear programming. Eur. J. Oper. Res. **267**(1), 321–337 (2018)
2. Fiacco, A.V.: Introduction to Sensitivity and Stability Analysis in Nonlinear Programming. Mathematics in Science and Engineering, vol. 165. Academic Press, New York (1983)
3. Fiedler, M., Nedoma, J., Ramík, J., Rohn, J., Zimmermann, K.: Linear Optimization Problems with Inexact Data. Springer, New York (2006). https://doi.org/10.1007/0-387-32698-7
4. Filippi, C.: A fresh view on the tolerance approach to sensitivity analysis in linear programming. Eur. J. Oper. Res. **167**(1), 1–19 (2005)
5. Floudas, C.A., Pardalos, P.M. (eds.): Encyclopedia of Optimization, 2nd edn. Springer, New York (2009). https://doi.org/10.1007/978-0-387-74759-0
6. Gal, T., Greenberg, H.J. (eds.): Advances in Sensitivity Analysis and Parametric Programming. Kluwer Academic Publishers, Boston (1997)
7. Hartman, D., Hladík, M.: Tight bounds on the radius of nonsingularity. In: Nehmeier, M., Wolff von Gudenberg, J., Tucker, W. (eds.) SCAN 2015. LNCS, vol. 9553, pp. 109–115. Springer, Cham (2016). https://doi.org/10.1007/978-3-319-31769-4_9

8. Hartman, D., Hladík, M.: Regularity radius: properties, approximation and a not a priori exponential algorithm. Electron. J. Linear Algebra **33**, 122–136 (2018)
9. Higham, N.J.: Accuracy and Stability of Numerical Algorithms. SIAM, Philadelphia (1996)
10. Hladík, M.: Tolerance analysis in linear systems and linear programming. Optim. Methods Softw. **26**(3), 381–396 (2011)
11. Hladík, M.: Tolerances, robustness and parametrization of matrix properties related to optimization problems. Optim. **68**(2–3), 667–690 (2019)
12. Kahan, W.M.: Numerical linear algebra. Canad. Math. Bull. **9**, 757–801 (1966)
13. Kreinovich, V., Lakeyev, A., Rohn, J., Kahl, P.: Computational Complexity and Feasibility of Data Processing and Interval Computations. Kluwer, Dordrecht (1998)
14. Moore, R.E., Kearfott, R.B., Cloud, M.J.: Introduction to Interval Analysis. SIAM, Philadelphia (2009)
15. Poljak, S., Rohn, J.: Checking robust nonsingularity is NP-hard. Math. Control Signals Syst. **6**(1), 1–9 (1993)
16. Rohn, J.: Checking positive definiteness or stability of symmetric interval matrices is NP-hard. Commentat. Math. Univ. Carol. **35**(4), 795–797 (1994)
17. Rohn, J.: Computing the norm $\|A\|_{\infty,1}$ is NP-hard. Linear Multilinear Algebra **47**(3), 195–204 (2000)
18. Rohn, J.: Forty necessary and sufficient conditions for regularity of interval matrices: a survey. Electron. J. Linear Algebra **18**, 500–512 (2009)
19. Ward, J.E., Wendell, R.E.: Approaches to sensitivity analysis in linear programming. Ann. Oper. Res. **27**, 3–38 (1990)
20. Wendell, R.E.: Linear programming. III: the tolerance approach. In: Gal et al., T. (ed.) Advances in Sensitivity Analysis and Parametric Programming, chap. 5, pp. 1–21. Kluwer, Dordrecht (1997)
21. Winston, W.L.: Operations Research. Applications and Algorithms, 4th edn. Brooks/Cole, Thomson Learning, Belmont (2004)

MPC-Based Path Tracking of a Differential-Drive Mobile Robot with Optimization for Improved Control Performance

Duván A. Marrugo[ID] and J. L. Villa[(✉)][ID]

Universidad Tecnológica de Bolívar, Cartagena de Indias, Colombia
{marrugod,jvilla}@utb.edu.co

Abstract. This research work presents a novel approach for enhancing the trajectory tracking capabilities of differentially driven mobile robots (DDMR). The proposed methodology combines a model predictive control (MPC) approach with optimization techniques to achieve precise and accurate motion in diverse applications. By incorporating a prediction horizon and a customized cost function, the control algorithm effectively steers the robot along a desired trajectory. The optimization process utilizes an optimization function, to minimize the cost function and refine control inputs. Additionally, parametric trajectory generation is employed to adapt the trajectory based on changing conditions. Simulations conducted in a MATLAB environment using a simulated MBOT-type robot demonstrate the effectiveness and robustness of the proposed approach. The results showcase accurate tracking of desired trajectories, with an average maximum mean squared error (MSE) of 1.68×10^{-4} and an average integral of absolute error (IAE) of 4.25×10^{-3}. Overall, this innovative methodology contributes to the field of DDMR control by offering an advanced solution for trajectory tracking, improving control performance, and enabling various robotic applications.

Keywords: Trajectory tracking · Differentially driven mobile robots · Model predictive control Cost function · Control performance

1 Introduction

In recent years, the field of robotics has witnessed remarkable advancements, particularly in the area of mobile robotics. Mobile robots [11], equipped with the ability to move and navigate autonomously [17], have gained significant attention due to their wide range of applications in various industries [14], including manufacturing [4], logistics [15], and exploration [8]. Among the different types of mobile robots, differential-drive mobile robots have emerged as a popular choice due to their simple mechanical structure and maneuverability [12].

The primary objective of a DDMR is to move from one location to another while accurately tracking a desired trajectory. Achieving precise trajectory tracking is crucial for tasks such as path following, obstacle avoidance, and mapping

J. C. Figueroa-García et al. (Eds.): WEA 2023, CCIS 1928, pp. 276–289, 2023.
https://doi.org/10.1007/978-3-031-46739-4_25

[9]. However, this poses a significant challenge as DDMR are subject to uncertainties, external disturbances, and inherent limitations in their actuation and sensing systems [10]. In [3], autors focus on the control of DDMRs for deforming soft objects, taking into account path tracking. Soft object deformation poses challenges due to its nonlinear, time-dependent, and material-response characteristics. The authors propose a control scheme that involves several steps to address this challenge. First, a position control is designed based on DDMR kinematics to achieve the desired deformation. Then, an alignment control is applied to adjust the orientation of the DDMRs during the deformation process. Two contact points on the object serve as control nodes to achieve the desired shape. Model Predictive Control (MPC) has shown promising results by utilizing dynamic models to predict robot behavior and optimize control actions, surpassing traditional approaches [1]. Reinforcement Learning (RL)-based control, employing algorithms like deep Q-learning and policy gradients, adapts control policies from sensor data and excels in complex and uncertain scenarios [5]. Adaptive and robust control techniques, such as sliding mode control and H-infinity control, have been integrated to compensate for uncertainties and disturbances [16].

In addition to addressing uncertainties and disturbances, research also focuses on the optimization of the MPC-based control strategy for trajectory tracking of DDRMs [7]. This involves considering various factors such as computational efficiency, real-time responsiveness, and stability of the control algorithm. By carefully designing the predictive model and formulating the control optimization problem, the proposed approach aims to strike a balance between accuracy and computational complexity, ensuring that the control algorithm can be implemented efficiently on resource-constrained robotic platforms [13].

The scalability and adaptability of the MPC-based approach for trajectory tracking has been investigated [2]. DDRMs are utilized in various settings, ranging from small-scale indoor environments to large outdoor areas. By assessing the system's behavior in diverse scenarios, Research objective has been to provide information on the applicability and limitations of the MPC-based trajectory tracking approach in practical robotic applications [6].

This research paper focuses on conducting a comprehensive study on the application of model predictive control (MPC) for path tracking in differential-drive mobile robots. The main objective is to develop an MPC-based control strategy that can effectively handle uncertainties while ensuring accurate and robust trajectory following. The proposed approach will be thoroughly evaluated through extensive simulations, considering tracking accuracy, robustness, and computational efficiency as key performance metrics. The paper is structured as follows: Sect. 2 provides a detailed description of the kinematic model of the mobile platform, including its holonomic constraints. In Sect. 3, the design of the MPC control, which incorporates motion constraints for trajectory tracking, is presented. Section 4 focuses on experimental validation conducted in a simulated environment, along with the measurement of controlled performance using appropriate error metrics. Finally, in Sect. 5, the main conclusions drawn from this research are summarized, and potential directions for future work are highlighted.

2   Mobile Robot Modeling

2.1   Mobile Platform

The controller design for this study adopted a similar approach to the Makeblock mBot robot. To model and analyze the robot's kinematics, a prototype design was created using SolidEdge 2022 software. The dimensions of the original robot were replicated, and materials were carefully selected to match its physical properties. This ensured accurate representation and reliable kinematic analysis of the robot.

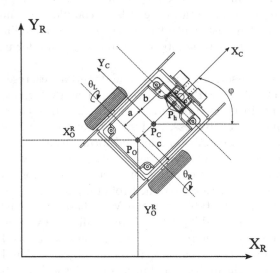

Fig. 1. Geometric Description of mobile robot

The robotic platform under consideration comprises two driving wheels and one passive supporting wheel. Each driving wheel is independently powered by a DC motor equipped with encoders. Figure 1 illustrates the proposed analysis scheme for the robot. The system is described using a global reference frame denoted as $X_R Y_R$. Additionally, a local reference frame $X_C Y_C$ is defined at the center of mass P_C of the robot, which is located at a distance a from the intersection point P_O where the axis of symmetry intersects with the axis of the wheels. The desired reference point for the robot, denoted as P_h, is positioned at a distance b from the center of mass and corresponds to the location of the castor wheel. The distance between the wheels and the axis of symmetry of the robot is denoted as c. The heading angle of the platform, represented by φ, is measured with respect to the X_R axis in the global coordinate system. The angular displacements of the right and left wheels are denoted as θ_R and θ_L respectively.

2.2 Kinematic Model

To develop an effective MPC approach for path tracking, a deep understanding of the differential kinematics of a mobile robot is essential. Differential kinematics deals with the relationship between the velocities of the robot's wheels and its overall motion. By analyzing the robot's geometry and wheel configurations, we can derive kinematic equations that enable us to estimate the robot's position and orientation based on the movements of its wheels. This knowledge forms the foundation for designing a control strategy that can accurately track desired trajectories.

The objective is to establish the relationship between the velocities of the point of interest or control and the velocities of the actuators in the robot system. In the simulation of the robot, the forces acting on the system are not taken into account, and the robot is considered as a point mass. The modeling of this mass is determined by the specific point of interest being analyzed. In our study, we focus on analyzing the trajectory tracking of the castor wheel located at P_h. If the system incorporates additional components such as a robotic arm, camera, or object transport support, the analysis at point P_C can be considered. This allows for a more comprehensive modeling of the system, considering the dynamics of the extended components.

We begin by describing the location of the point of interest with respect to the chosen reference frame $X_R Y_R$. In the Eq. 1 the description of the point P_h is observed.

$$\begin{aligned} h_x &= x_O^R + x_O^h \\ h_y &= y_O^R + y_O^h \end{aligned} \tag{1}$$

Setting the above system as a function of the angle of rotation of the robot φ, we obtain the Eq. 2.

$$\begin{aligned} h_x &= x_O^R + d\cos\varphi \\ h_y &= y_O^R + d\sin\varphi \end{aligned} \tag{2}$$

where $d = a + b$.

Based on the previous equation, we must calculate the velocities of the platform, for this we perform the derivative with respect to the time of the system obtained in the Eq. 2:

$$\begin{aligned} \frac{dh_x}{dt} &= \frac{\partial h_x}{\partial x_O^R}\frac{\partial x_O^R}{\partial t} + \frac{\partial h_x}{\partial \varphi}\frac{\partial \varphi}{\partial t} \\ \frac{dh_y}{dt} &= \frac{\partial h_y}{\partial y_O^R}\frac{\partial y_O^R}{\partial t} + \frac{\partial h_y}{\partial \varphi}\frac{\partial \varphi}{\partial t} \end{aligned}$$

Obtaining as a result the system of equations described in 3.

$$\dot{h}_x = \nu cos\varphi - dw sin\varphi$$
$$\dot{h}_y = \nu sin\varphi + dw cos\varphi \qquad (3)$$
$$\dot{\varphi} = \omega$$

where ν and ω represent the linear and angular velocities of the platform with respect to the reference plane $X_C Y_C$.

The above system of equations can be rewritten for state space. Obtaining the Eq. 4.

$$\underbrace{\begin{bmatrix} \dot{h}_x \\ \dot{h}_y \end{bmatrix}}_{\dot{h}} = \underbrace{\begin{bmatrix} cos\varphi & -dsin\varphi \\ sin\varphi & dcos\varphi \end{bmatrix}}_{J} \underbrace{\begin{bmatrix} \nu \\ \omega \end{bmatrix}}_{\dot{q}} \qquad (4)$$

where J, represents the Jacobian matrix describing the relationship between the velocities between the fixed reference frame and the mobil.

3 MPC Control Design

In the development of an MPC controller for path tracking of mobile robots, two key components play a crucial role: the prediction model and the optimization function.

3.1 Prediction Model

The prediction model forms the basis of the MPC controller, as it captures the dynamics and behavior of the mobile robot. By modeling the robot's motion and incorporating relevant factors such as wheel dynamics, kinematics, and environmental constraints, the prediction model provides a representation of how the robot is expected to behave over a given time horizon. This predictive capability enables the controller to anticipate the robot's future states and plan control actions accordingly, facilitating accurate path tracking. The proposed design is shown in Fig. 2.

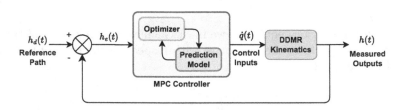

Fig. 2. Block diagram of MPC control.

The prediction model, which is based on model 4, can be expressed as a function of the state errors and the input. This relationship is depicted in Eq. 5.

$$\dot{h}_e = f(h_e, u) \tag{5}$$

where,

$$\begin{cases} h_e = \begin{bmatrix} h_{x_e} & h_{y_e} \end{bmatrix}^T, \\ u = \begin{bmatrix} \nu & \omega \end{bmatrix}^T \end{cases} \tag{6}$$

The primary objective of the path tracking control is to minimize the error. Therefore, the first penalty term of the optimization function is defined in Eq. 7.

$$J_1 = \sum_{i=1}^{N_p} \|h_e(t+i|t)\|^2 \tag{7}$$

To ensure smooth motion of the mobile robot, the second penalty term is incorporated in the optimization function, as illustrated in Eq. 8. This penalty term aims to minimize any abrupt changes or fluctuations in the robot's trajectory.

$$J_2 = \sum_{i=1}^{N_p} \|\Delta u(t+i|t)\|^2 \tag{8}$$

The third penalty term in the optimization function serves to improve the ability of mobile robots to maintain a straight trajectory with minimal disturbances. This penalty term is represented by Eq. 9.

$$J_3 = \sum_{i=1}^{N_p} \|\omega(t+i|t)\|^2 \tag{9}$$

The fourth penalty term in the optimization function serves to ensure that the longitudinal velocity of the mobile robot closely matches the reference longitudinal velocity. This penalty term, as depicted in Eq. 10, helps in achieving the desired speed consistency during trajectory tracking.

$$J_4 = \sum_{i=1}^{N_p} \|\nu(t+i|t) - \nu_{ref}\|^2 \tag{10}$$

where N_p is the prediction horizon.

Finally, the optimization function is obtained as shown in Eq. 11.

$$J = \sum_{i=1}^{4} J_i \tag{11}$$

The control variable output by the path tracking controller can be obtained by solving the optimization problem described in Eq. 12.

$$
\begin{aligned}
& \min_{e,\Delta u,\omega} J \\
& \Delta\nu \in (\Delta\nu_{min}, \Delta\nu_{max}) \\
& \Delta\omega \in (\Delta\omega_{min}, \Delta\omega_{max})
\end{aligned}
\tag{12}
$$

In the optimization problem described in Eq. 12, $\Delta\nu_{min}$ represents the lower limit of the longitudinal velocity increment, $\Delta\nu_{max}$ represents the upper limit of the longitudinal velocity increment, $\Delta\omega_{min}$ represents the lower limit of the heading angle speed increment, and $\Delta\omega_{max}$ represents the upper limit of the heading angle speed increment.

3.2   Optimizer

Algorithm 1: Path Estimation for Differential Mobile Robot

Require: Path h, Initial angular speed ϕ_{init}, Initial linear speed v_{init}
Ensure: Estimated angular speed ϕ_{est}, Estimated linear speed v_{est}
  1: Calculate the error in x-direction: $h_{xe}(k) = h_{xd}(k) - h_x(k)$
  2: Calculate the error in y-direction: $h_{ye}(k) = h_{yd}(k) - h_y(k)$
  3: Define the current position vector: $h = [h_x(k), h_y(k)]$
  4: Define the cost function: $J(q_p) = \text{costFunction}(h_d, h, \phi(k), q_p, a, t_s, k, N)$
  5: Set the optimization options for the `fmincon` function
  6: Optimize the cost function using `fmincon`:
  7:     $q_p = \text{fmincon}(J, q_p, [\omega_{min}, \omega_{max}, \nu_{min}, \nu_{max}], \text{options})$
  8:     where:
  9:     J is the cost function to minimize, which measures the error in following the path
10:     $q_p = $ [angular speed, linear speed] is the initial guess for the angular and linear speeds
11:     $[\omega_{min}, \omega_{max}, \nu_{min}, \nu_{max}]$ indicates no lower and upper bounds for the angular and linear speeds
12:     **options** specify the algorithmic options, such as maximum iterations, convergence tolerance, etc.
13: Separate the control actions:
14:     Reference angular speed: $u_{\text{Ref}}(k) = q_p(1)$
15:     Reference linear speed: $w_{\text{Ref}}(k) = q_p(2)$
16: **return** $\varphi_{\text{est}}, v_{\text{est}}$

In Algorithm 1, fmincon function is utilized to optimize the cost function J, enabling the estimation of the angular and linear speeds of the mobile robot. The cost function is designed based on various factors, including the error in following the desired path, as well as other relevant parameters. The fmincon function is a built-in optimization solver in MATLAB that employs constrained optimization techniques to find the optimal solution within the specified constraints. By iteratively adjusting the control inputs, the algorithm aims to minimize the cost function and achieve accurate trajectory tracking.

4   Results and Discussion

4.1   Simulation Environment

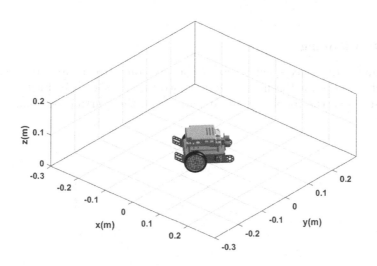

Fig. 3. Virtual environment for simulation developed in MATLAB ©

To simulate robot trajectories accurately, these components were imported in binary STL format, ensuring that their surface dimensions were in meters, matching the working environment specifications. Figure 3 provides a visual representation of the developed environment at a meter-scale. Since the focus is on two-dimensional motion, each component only requires rotation along the Z axis, which is represented by the rotation angle φ. To align each component with the calculated orientation, a rotation matrix $R_z(\varphi)$ is multiplied to achieve the desired orientation.

For the whole simulation, the sampling time $t_S = 0.05$ s was used. In turn, the parameters selected for the evaluation of the MPC and its optimizer are described in the Table 1. The minimum and maximum speed was obtained from the implementation of a PID control in DC Pololu motors with encoders, which allowed to determine the initial dead zone at start-up in order to try to simulate the system with the same conditions as the real one.

Table 1. Parameters of Control System

Parameter	Value	Units
N_p	5	
T	0.05	sec
$\Delta\nu_{min}$	0.1	m/sec
$\Delta\nu_{max}$	1	m/sec
$\Delta\omega_{min}$	3	rad/sec
$\Delta\omega_{max}$	13	rad/sec

4.2   Path Planning

For the simulation, three specific case studies and one special case are proposed. The selected paths for the first three case studies are shown in Figs. 4, 5, and 6. In these cases, the robot initially departs from the starting position of each path.

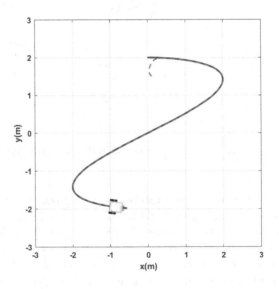

Fig. 4. Simulated Path 1: $y(t) = 2cos(0.3t)$ and $x(t) = 2sin(0.3t)$

In the initial analysis, three types of trajectories are considered. The first is a circular trajectory defined as $y(t) = 2\cos(0.3t)$ and $x(t) = 2\sin(0.3t)$. The second is a sinusoidal trajectory defined as $x(t) = 0.1t$ and $y(t) = 2\cos(0.3t)$. The third is a trajectory with a different frequency, given by $y(t) = 2\cos(0.2t)$ and $x(t) = 2\sin(0.1t)$. These trajectories serve as the basis for evaluating the performance of the proposed control approach in different scenarios.

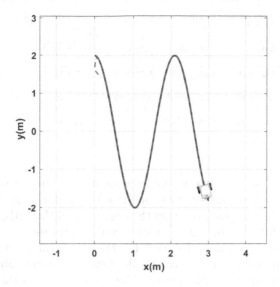

Fig. 5. Simulated Path 2: $x(t) = 0.1t$ and $y(t) = 2cos(0.3t)$

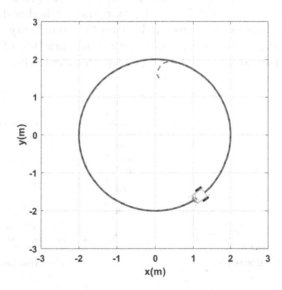

Fig. 6. Simulated Path 3: $y(t) = 2cos(0.2t)$ and $x(t) = 2sin(0.1t)$

4.3 Path Tracking

In the Table 2 we can see the errors obtained for each trajectory according to the location of the P_h. It can be seen that the errors obtained exceed the order of 10^{-4} which indicates that the designed control has a good performance.

Table 2. Performance of a control law based on the error metrics.

Error Metrics	Path 1		Path 2		Path 3	
	X_C	Y_C	X_C	Y_C	X_C	Y_C
Mean Squared Error (MSE)	5.02×10^{-5}	1.68×10^{-4}	4.31×10^{-5}	1.37×10^{-4}	3.96×10^{-4}	1.08×10^{-5}
Root Mean Squared Error (RMSE):	7.08×10^{-3}	1.29×10^{-2}	6.57×10^{-3}	1.17×10^{-2}	1.99×10^{-2}	3.29×10^{-3}
Integral of Absolute Error (IAE)	3.14×10^{-4}	6.57×10^{-4}	8.15×10^{-4}	1.65×10^{-3}	4.52×10^{-3}	7.03×10^{-4}
Integral of Squared Error (ISE)	2.66×10^{-6}	8.923×10^{-6}	6.39×10^{-6}	2.03×10^{-5}	9.18×10^{-5}	2.51×10^{-6}

Furthermore, the errors obtained and the simulation time are documented in Figs. 7, 8, and 9. Each simulation was conducted for a duration of 30 s with 600 samples. Notably, higher peaks occur at the beginning of the path, corresponding to the robot's initial junction with the start of the trajectory.

In Figs. 4, 5, and 6, it can be observed that the robots do not start precisely at the initial position of the trajectory. This deliberate deviation aims to optimize the solution and ensure an efficient start. The peak represents the time required for the robot to reach the starting position of the trajectory.

It is worth mentioning that the path presenting the greatest challenge for the controller is path number 3. Figure 9 demonstrates a higher distortion in the amplitude of the samples over time, indicating the complexity of this circular path. The controller needs to constantly adjust the position of the motors in both coordinate axes to navigate this type of path successfully.

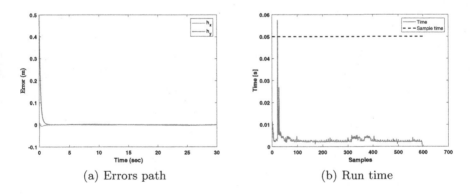

(a) Errors path　　　　　　　　　(b) Run time

Fig. 7. Simulated Results Path 1.

This methodology holds significant value in Differential-Drive Mobile Robot (DDMR) control and finds practical applications in various domains. These exceptionally low errors are particularly useful in autonomous robot navigation in sensitive environments such as hospitals or warehouses, where precision is crucial for obstacle avoidance and safety assurance. They can also be applied

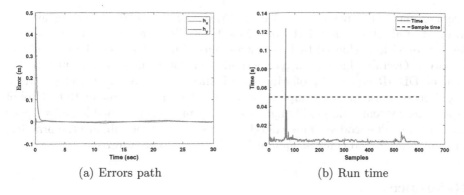

(a) Errors path   (b) Run time

Fig. 8. Simulated Results Path 2.

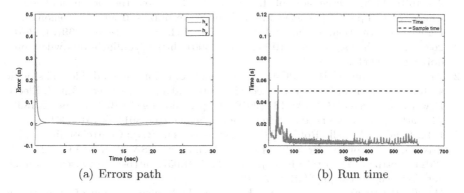

(a) Errors path   (b) Run time

Fig. 9. Simulated Results Path 3.

in critical infrastructure inspection, such as pipelines and power lines, enhancing the robots' ability to follow precise paths and gather accurate data. In summary, these results have valuable potential across a wide range of real-world applications where high precision in mobile robot control is required.

5 Conclusions and Future Works

The research work presented in this study introduces a novel approach for enhancing the trajectory tracking capabilities of differentially driven mobile robots (DDMR). By incorporating a prediction horizon and a customized cost function, the control algorithm effectively steers the robot along a desired trajectory. The optimization process utilizes an optimization function to minimize the cost function and refine control inputs. Furthermore, the research incorporates parametric trajectory generation, which enables the adaptation of the trajectory based on changing conditions. This adaptability enhances the robustness of the control system, allowing the robot to respond effectively to dynamic environments. The results showcase accurate tracking of desired trajectories, with an average maximum mean squared error (MSE) of 1.68×10^{-4} and an average integral of absolute error (IAE) of 4.25×10^{-3}. These results indicate the high level of precision achieved by the control algorithm in tracking the desired trajectories. Overall, this innovative methodology contributes significantly to the field of DDMR control by offering an advanced solution for trajectory tracking. Future work includes implementing the designed control in ROS (Robot Operating System) and modifying the existing prototype to enable motor speed control through encoders. These developments will further enhance the practical implementation and control capabilities of the proposed approach.

References

1. Al-Mufti, O.N.: Discussion of Li et al. (2021) - on the origin and significance of composite particles in mudstones: examples from the Cenomanian Dunvegan formation, sedimentology, 68, 737–754. Sedimentology **69**(6), 2676–2681 (2022). https://doi.org/10.1111/sed.13001, https://onlinelibrary.wiley.com/doi/abs/10.1111/sed.13001
2. Arasteh, F., Riahy, G.H.: MPC-based approach for online demand side and storage system management in market based wind integrated power systems. Int. J. Electr. Power Energy Syst. **106**, 124–137 (2019). https://doi.org/10.1016/j.ijepes.2018.09.041, https://www.sciencedirect.com/science/article/pii/S014206151830615X
3. Felix-Rendon, J., Bello-Robles, J.C., Fuentes-Aguilar, R.Q.: Control of differential-drive mobile robots for soft object deformation. ISA Trans. **117**, 221–233 (2021). https://doi.org/10.1016/j.isatra.2021.01.057, https://www.sciencedirect.com/science/article/pii/S0019057821000677
4. Hercík, R., Byrtus, R., Jaros, R., Koziorek, J.: Implementation of autonomous mobile robot in smartfactory. Appl. Sci. **12**, 8912 (2022). https://doi.org/10.3390/app12178912
5. Huang, J., Junginger, S., Liu, H., Thurow, K.: Indoor positioning systems of mobile robots: a review. Robotics **12**(2), 47 (2023). https://doi.org/10.3390/robotics12020047, https://www.mdpi.com/2218-6581/12/2/47
6. Jeong, Y., Yim, S.: Model predictive control-based integrated path tracking and velocity control for autonomous vehicle with four-wheel independent steering and driving. Electronics **10**(22) (2021). https://doi.org/10.3390/electronics10222812, https://www.mdpi.com/2079-9292/10/22/2812
7. Lee, C., Lin, B., Ng, K., Lv, Y., Tai, W.: Smart robotic mobile fulfillment system with dynamic conflict-free strategies considering cyber-physical integration. Adv. Eng. Inform. **42**, 100998 (2019). https://doi.org/10.1016/j.aei.2019.100998, https://www.sciencedirect.com/science/article/pii/S1474034619305713
8. Liu, S., Li, S., Pang, L., Hu, J., Chen, H., Zhang, X.: Autonomous exploration and map construction of a mobile robot based on the TGHM algorithm. Sensors **20**(2), 490 (2020). https://doi.org/10.3390/s20020490, https://www.mdpi.com/1424-8220/20/2/490
9. Markom, M.A., Adom, A.H., Tan, E.S.M.M., Shukor, S.A.A., Rahim, N.A., Shakaff, A.Y.M.: A mapping mobile robot using rp lidar scanner. In: 2015 IEEE International Symposium on Robotics and Intelligent Sensors (IRIS), pp. 87–92 (2015). https://doi.org/10.1109/IRIS.2015.7451592

10. Ortigoza, R., et al.: Wheeled mobile robots: a review. Latin Am. Trans. IEEE (Rev. IEEE America Latina) **10**, 2209–2217 (2012). https://doi.org/10.1109/TLA.2012. 6418124

11. Ricardo, J.A., Santos, D.A.: Robust collision avoidance for mobile robots in the presence of moving obstacles. IEEE Control Syst. Lett. 1 (2023). https://doi.org/ 10.1109/LCSYS.2023.3275498

12. Rubio, F., Valero, F., Llopis-Albert, C.: A review of mobile robots: concepts, methods, theoretical framework, and applications. Int. J. Adv. Rob. Syst. **16**(2), 1729881419839596 (2019). https://doi.org/10.1177/1729881419839596

13. Salimi Lafmejani, A., Berman, S.: Nonlinear MPC for collision-free and deadlock-free navigation of multiple nonholonomic mobile robots. Robot. Auton. Syst. **141**, 103774 (2021). https://doi.org/10.1016/j.robot.2021.103774, https://www. sciencedirect.com/science/article/pii/S0921889021000592

14. Sarrafan, N., Zarei, J., Saif, M.: Improved finite-time disturbance observer-based control of networked nonholonomic high-order chained-form systems. IEEE Trans. Syst. Man Cybern.: Syst. 1–12 (2023). https://doi.org/10.1109/TSMC.2023. 3268251

15. Wang, C., Du, D.: Research on logistics autonomous mobile robot system, pp. 275–280 (2016). https://doi.org/10.1109/ICMA.2016.7558574

16. Zhang, H.Y., Lin, W.M., Chen, A.X.: Path planning for the mobile robot: a review. Symmetry **10**(10), 450 (2018). https://doi.org/10.3390/sym10100450, https:// www.mdpi.com/2073-8994/10/10/450

17. Zhong, M., You, Y., Zhou, S., Xu, X.: A robust visual-inertial slam in complex indoor environments. IEEE Sens. J. 1 (2023). https://doi.org/10.1109/JSEN.2023. 3274702

A Mixed Integer Linear Programming Model for School Timetable in Cartagena

Manuel Soto-DeLaVega[1]([✉]) [iD], Camilo Molina[2] [iD], Adolfo Tovar Quiroz[1],
Jairo Chegwin Cera[1], and Juan Carlos Luna Marrugo[2]

[1] Universidad Tecnológica de Bolívar, Cartagena, Colombia
msotodelavega@gmail.com
[2] Universidad del Sinú, Cartagena, Colombia

Abstract. This article addresses the school timetable scheduling challenge within an educational institution in Cartagena de Indias, Colombia, which grapples with a lack of technical and technological tools for enhancing educational processes. A thorough literature review underscores the prevalent use of exact models to tackle school timetabling problems. A mathematical model, employing Mixed Integer Linear Programming, was meticulously developed to craft the class timetable. This model accommodated various constraints, including classroom availability, teacher schedules, and subject assignments. The implementation of the model utilized GAMS. Ensuring compliance with teachers' weekly hour restrictions, the generated timetable was subsequently compared to manually created schedules from prior years. Notably, the model generated a higher number of blocks, leading to enhanced efficiency in time utilization. In conclusion, this proposed model streamlines the task of generating school timetables, thereby improving educational quality, and optimizing available resources.

Keywords: Timetable assignment problem · Mixed Integer Programming · Course Scheduling

1 Introduction

The management of educational processes necessitates meticulous attention, given the societal significance of the service rendered. Every decision within the educational sphere must prioritize ongoing enhancement, aimed at delivering high-quality service. To attain this objective, it is imperative that administrative entities within educational institutions allocate all available resources to guarantee service quality.

In Colombia's primary and secondary schools, there is a lack of technical tools, leading to improvised solutions in educational management. Creating class schedules is a major challenge, mainly done manually due to constraints, consuming time, and hindering educational activities [2]. Each institution has unique limitations related to infrastructure, teacher numbers, and courses. To address these challenges effectively and enhance education, computational tools are needed [3, 4]. Various methods like

J. C. Figueroa-García et al. (Eds.): WEA 2023, CCIS 1928, pp. 290–300, 2023.
https://doi.org/10.1007/978-3-031-46739-4_26

heuristics, metaheuristics, and mathematical models can be employed to solve scheduling issues [5, 6], depending on the desired solution level.

The objective of this study is to develop an exact mathematical model for the creation of a class timetable in an educational institution located in the city of Cartagena de Indias, Colombia. First, a literature review was conducted, citing different authors and their approaches to similar problems. The aim is to understand how these issues have been addressed in previous research. Then, we focused on formulating and encoding the mathematical model, considering all the inherent constraints of the problem and the specifications of the case study mentioned in the first chapter. Lastly, an analysis of the mathematical model is performed, and the results obtained through its execution are examined. Finally, general conclusions and recommendations are presented, along with aspects related to potential future work in this field of study.

2 Literature Review

Timetable scheduling is a widely researched field that aims to achieve efficient allocation of temporal resources, such as classes, exams, meetings, and activities. Over the years, various techniques and approaches have been proposed to solve timetabling problems in different contexts [5, 6]. Timetable scheduling problems have been extensively studied due to their practical and theoretical significance. In the educational domain, there are three main scenarios where timetabling is applied: timetable scheduling for schools, timetable scheduling for university courses, and timetable scheduling for university exams. Timetable scheduling for schools, which is the central topic of this study, represents a constant challenge due to the continuous evolution of the educational system. This often gives rise to challenges that require new models and solution methodologies to address them effectively [6].

Timetabling complexities exist in both school and university settings, demanding advanced methods. Heuristic, metaheuristic, and mathematical models prove effective but require customization to institution-specific constraints [7]. Schools involve factors like classroom availability, teacher schedules, and subject assignments. The main distinction lies in the complexity and scope of constraints. Schools focus on limited subjects and teacher schedules, while universities require approaches to additional courses, professors, classrooms, and resources [8].

Mixed Integer Linear Programming (MILP) is widely used for effective scheduling in timetabling. Several studies have employed MILP models for various aspects of timetabling, including course, room, and teacher assignments, and handling specific constraints. For instance, Maldonado-Matute et al. [9] introduced a linear programming model for optimal room and course allocation in a university, considering capacity constraints, resource availability, and teacher preferences. Other works [10, 11] proposed MILP models for school timetables, incorporating room capacity, teacher preferences, and course requirements. MILP models allow simultaneous consideration of multiple constraints, yielding near-optimal solutions that meet all requirements. This approach enhances scheduling efficiency, optimizing resource utilization and overall quality.

In certain scenarios, distinct constraints are addressed. For instance, Marin and Maya [11] employ mixed integer linear programming to maximize consecutive subject blocks.

Alternatively, decomposition techniques efficiently solve timetabling problems, as seen in [12–14], utilizing integer programming models, or adopting column generation, as in [14, 15]. These cases showcase effective mixed integer linear programming applications for generating optimal timetables that meet various constraints and objectives.

3 Case Study

Many educational institutions, including our case study, face complexities when creating class timetables with multiple constraints. This private institution has been providing education from pre-school to high school in the community for 33 years. They prioritize efficient process management to fulfill their academic plan. Timetable scheduling is crucial for teachers, students, and the entire community to follow the annual work plan. Each level of study must comply with a set number of weekly hours, which are regulated and described in the following table (Table 1).

Table 1. Weekly hours per level of study

	Weekly hours	Annual hours
Preschool	20	800
Elementary school	25	1000
Hight school	30	1200

Source: Own elaboration

This number of hours should be allocated either in the morning or in the afternoon, evenly distributed over 5 days of the week (Monday to Friday), within a fixed time frame. Additionally, a daily 25-min break period is scheduled, which must be included within the hours during which the class session takes place. Table 6 shows the distribution of time periods during which the classes are conducted (Table 2).

Table 2. Distribution of class sessions

Session	Level of study	Start time	End time
Morning	**Preschool**	7:00	11:30
	Elementary school	6:30	12:00
	Hight school	6:30	12:45
Afternoon	**Elementary school**	13:00	18:00
	Hight school	13:00	18:55

Source: Own elaboration

Each teacher must allocate 25 weekly class hours, necessitating their presence for a full 6-h session within the institution. Additionally, they are required to dedicate an extra

2 h, either on-site or off-site, for class preparation or related tasks. Each subject's weekly hour allocation is determined by its importance in developing student competencies. Tables 3 and 4 correlate the educational levels (Table 3) with the weekly hour intensity (Table 4) required for different subjects in specific grade levels.

Table 3. Hours of dedication for competencies

	6th	7th	8th	9th
Natural sciences and environmental education	5	5	5	6
Social sciences, history, geography, political constitution, and democracy	4	4	4	5
Artistic and cultural education	1	1	1	0
Ethics and human and religious values	1	1	1	0
Recreation and sports	2	2	2	2
Humanities, Spanish language, and English	9	9	9	8
Math	6	6	6	7
technology and computing	2	2	2	2
Total, weekly hours	**30**	**30**	**30**	**30**

Source: Own elaboration

Teacher rotation per class hour, subject qualifications, and session alignment are essential. Some areas/components subdivide into subjects with weekly hour allocation based on learning relevance.

Table 4. Intensity of weekly hours for sixth to ninth grade

Area	Subjects	Weekly hours	Area	Subjects	Weekly hours
Natural Sciences	Chemistry	2	Humanities and languages	Espanish	4
	Biology	3		English	4
Social Sciences	Social science	3		reading skills	1
	Citizen skills	1	Math	Statistics	1
Artistic education	Art	1		Math	4
Religion and Ethics	religious ethics	1		Geometry	1
Recreation and sports	Physical education	2	Technology	Computing	2

Source: Own elaboration

The institution employs 17 teachers to cover 25 courses across morning and afternoon shifts. Some teachers may instruct in both sessions to meet course demand while adhering to the 48-h weekly limit. Hourly-hired teachers' workload varies yearly. The model must adapt to these changes. Grades 1 and 2 have a single teacher for all subjects, so their scheduling isn't part of the model.

Additional factors to consider include subjects like recreation, sports, and Informatics, often taught in non-standard locations (e.g., computer labs or outdoor areas). These spaces can only accommodate one course at a time. Hence, simultaneous scheduling of the same subject for multiple groups at the same hour should be avoided to ensure exclusive use of these locations. Another specific requirement pertains to the sport subject, which must be scheduled either in the first 4 h of the morning session or the last 4 h of the afternoon session.

4 Model Approach

For this study, we propose to solve the problem using an exact method, specifically Mixed Integer Linear Programming, considering the literature review and the models proposed by Marín and Maya [13] and Kristiansen et al. [16]. Below, we describe the different sets, subsets, parameters, variables, objective function, and constraints of the problem at hand that we aim to solve:

4.1 Set

C : Set of courses c to schedule.
　P : Set of teachers p.
　M : Set of subjects m.
　D : Set of days d.
　T : Set of time periods t in which classes can be assigned (time slots).

4.2 Subsets

$PRIM$: Elementary school courses.
　$SECU:$ High school courses.
　$MES:$ subjects in special classrooms or laboratories.

4.3 Parameters

H_{pmc} : Hours that a teacher $p \in P$ must teach in a subject $m \in M$ in a course $c \in C$.
　A_{pdt} : Availability of each teacher $p \in P$ to be assigned on day $d \in D$ in period $t \in T$.
　N_m : Maximum number of daily hours for a subject $m \in M$.

4.4 Variables

$$X_{td}^{pmc} = \begin{cases} 1; \text{ if professor } p \text{ is assigned to teach subject } m \text{ in course } c \\ \qquad\qquad \text{in period } t \text{ on day } d. \\ \\ 0; \text{ in another case.} \end{cases}$$

$$Y_{td}^{pmc} = \begin{cases} 1; \text{ if a block is started by teacher } p \text{ who dictates a subject } m \text{ in course } c \\ \qquad\qquad \text{in period } t \text{ on day } d. \\ \\ 0; \text{ in another case.} \end{cases}$$

4.5 Objective Function

$$ma'xZ = \sum_{p \in P} \sum_{m \in M} \sum_{c \in C} \sum_{t \in T} \sum_{d \in D} Y_{td}^{pmc} \tag{1}$$

4.6 Restrictions

$$Y_{td}^{pmc} \leq X_{td}^{pmc} \quad \forall p \in P, m \in M, c \in C, t \in T, d \in D \tag{2}$$

$$Y_{td}^{pmc} \leq X_{(t+1)d}^{pmc} \quad \forall p \in P, m \in M, c \in C, t \in T, d \in D \tag{3}$$

$$X_{td}^{pmc} + X_{(t+1)d}^{pmc} - Y_{td}^{pmc} \leq 1 \quad \forall p \in P, m \in M, c \in C, t \in T, d \in D \tag{4}$$

$$\sum_{t \in T} \sum_{d \in D} X_{td}^{pmc} = H_{pmc} \quad \forall p \in P, m \in M, c \in C \tag{5}$$

$$\sum_{t \in T} X_{td}^{pmc} \leq N_m \quad \forall p \in P, m \in M, c \in C, d \in D \tag{6}$$

$$\sum_{p \in P} \sum_{m \in M} X_{td}^{pmc} \leq 1 \quad \forall c \in C, t \in T, d \in D \tag{7}$$

$$\sum_{m \in M} \sum_{c \in C} X_{td}^{PMC} \leq A_{pdt} \quad \forall p \in P, t \in T, d \in D \tag{8}$$

$$\sum_{PRIM \in C} X_{6d}^{pmc} = 0 \quad \forall p \in P, m \in M, t \in T, d \in D \tag{9}$$

$$\sum_{PRIM \in C} Y_{5d}^{pmc} = 0 \quad \forall p \in P, m \in M, t \in T, d \in D \tag{10}$$

$$\sum_{SECU \in C} Y_{6d}^{pmc} = 0 \quad \forall p \in P, m \in M, t \in T, d \in D \tag{11}$$

$$\sum_{MES \in M} X_{td}^{pmc} \leq 1 \quad \forall p \in P, c \in C, t \in T, d \in D \tag{12}$$

$$X_{td}^{pmc} \in \{0, 1\} \quad \forall p \in P, m \in M, c \in C, t \in T, d \in D$$

$$Y_{td}^{pmc} \in \{0, 1\} \quad \forall p \in P, m \in M, c \in C, t \in T, d \in D$$

Equation (1) represents the objective function of the problem, which seeks to maximize the number of blocks, in this case, two consecutive hours of a subject, in the same course, with the same teacher. Equations (2) and (3) restrict the variable Y_{td}^{pmc} so that it can only be activated when a block starts, in addition to allowing a subject to be assigned to any period without necessarily being a block.

Equation (4) requires that, if two periods have the same subject assigned to the same teacher, a block is started. This condition is soft type. Equation (5) means that the hours that a teacher must teach per week in a certain course is equal to that established by the educational institution. This restriction is harsh. Since it is not possible to assign to a course all the hours of the week in the same day, there must be a restriction that limits the number of these time periods, specifically, 2 h maximum per day. Equation (6) oversees this, defining a level for the maximum intensity of hours of the subjects for each day. This constraint is of the hard type. Equation (7) prevents more than one subject or teacher from being programmed on each day and hour.

Equation (8) forces teachers to be scheduled according to the information from the A parameter that contains their time availability. It should be remembered that only the subject Physical Education and, therefore, its teacher also has this condition, which must be assigned in the time periods $t = 1, 2, 3$ and 4.

In Eqs. (5) and (6), the weekly instructional hours for primary and secondary levels are enforced, considering that they are not the same. To limit the number of time slots in which subjects can be assigned to each course, Eq. (9) is utilized, which schedules a break at time slot 6 for all primary level courses.

It is not possible to start a block in the last class period as it would not be completed. Therefore, constraints (10) and (11) are used to prevent scheduling the start of a block at time $t = 6$ for secondary courses and at $t = 5$ for primary courses. It must be ensured that subjects with special classrooms are not taught in two or more courses on the same day and time, regardless of whether they are assigned to different teachers. This is because the institution only has one classroom available to teach each of these subjects.

5   Analysis of Results

The tool used to obtain the schedule was the GAMS program, version 38.1.0. In turn, the Solver used to solve the model was Cplex, which found a solution with a total of 2,857,000 iterations and a relative GAP of 0.035. The computer used to run the model was equipped with an 11th Gen Intel(R) Core(TM) i5-1135. The problem size consisted of 174,295 equations and 116,640 variables.

Verification of program results meeting hard constraints is essential. Figure 1 displays teacher schedules for Monday, detailing subjects, courses, and times. Vertical analysis reveals no overlap; each hour, one teacher teaches one subject. Equation 7 is thus met, prohibiting overlap. To confirm Constraint 5, specifying weekly hours per subject for teachers in specific courses, we examined the teacher's schedule.

	1	2	3	4	5	6
MONDAY						
ALVARO	Soc 3°	Eti 8°	Art 4°	Soc 4°	Soc 4°	
ANDREINA		Bio 3°	Bio 3°		Bio 5°	Bio 7°
KAREN	Ing 10°	Ing 10°	Ing 5°	Ing 5°	Ing 6°	Ing 6°
LICETH	Cas 6°	Cas 6°	Cas 8°	Cas 8°	Cas 10°	Cas 10°
FABIO	Mat 7°	Mat 7°	Est 6°	Geo 6°		
ALEXANDER			Inf 9°	Inf 9°	Inf 8°	Inf 8°
CRISTIAN	Soc 8°		Fil 10°	Fil 10°	Soc 7°	
IUCH			Qui 7°	Qui 7°		
VICTOR	Fis 11°	Fis 11°			Mat 11°	Mat 11°
ANGELICA	Ed. Fis 4°	Ed. Fis 4°				
KATIA	Cas 5°	Cas 5°	Cas 11°	Cas 11°	Cas 9°	Cas 9°
EDITH	Est 9°	Est 9°			Mat 3°	Mat 3°

ALVARO					
	Monday	Tuesday	Wednesday	Thursday	Friday
1	Soc 3°	Soc 5°	Eti 5°	Geo 3°	Eti 6°
2	Eti 8°	Soc 5°	Geo 5°		
3	Art 4°	Geo 4°	Eti 3°	Art 8°	Soc 3°
4	Soc 4°	Soc 4°		Art 6°	Soc 3°
5	Soc 4°	Art 5°	Soc 5°	Art 3°	Eti 4°
6			Eti 7°		Art 7°

Fig. 1. Schedule by teachers generated by the Monday model and Individual schedule for the teacher. Source: Own elaboration

If we sum the time periods in which the teacher is active, it totals 24 h distributed as follows (Table 5):

Table 5. Distribution of hours for the teacher

Subject	Course	Hours	Subject	Course	Hours
Social Sciences	Third grade	3	Geometry	Third grade	1
	Fourth grade	3		Fourth grade	1
	Fifth grade	3		Fifth grade	1
Ethics	Third grade	1	Art	Third grade	1
	Fourth grade	1		Fourth grade	1
	Fifth grade	1		Fifth grade	1
	Sixth grade	1		Sixth grade	1
	Seventh grade	1		Seventh grade	1
	Eighth grade	1		Eighth grade	1

Source: Own elaboration

Figure 3 show the individual schedule for a female teacher, where it can be observed that no classes are scheduled in time periods 5 and 6, as specified in the course constraints. Therefore, Eq. 8 is indeed satisfied.

After generating the schedule using the proposed model, it is compared to previous years' manually created schedules. We notice that the model generates more blocks compared to manual schedules. The number of blocks varies annually due to changes in subject and course distribution among teachers. Each academic period, group and subject assignments change based on institution needs and teacher preferences. This variability requires exploring various combinations to meet all requirements, impacting the number of schedule blocks (Fig. 2).

In addition to the number of blocks, school administrators seek greater efficiency in resource utilization, especially time, and aim to avoid delays in the start of classes caused by the confusion of not having a timely schedule. For this reason, the model proposed in this study emerges as a viable alternative to solve the problem as it streamlines the class assignment process. For comparison purposes, we will analyze the schedules for the ninth grade, with the manually created schedule on the left and the one generated by the model on the right (Fig. 3).

	ANGELICA				
	Monday	Tuesday	Wednesday	Thursday	Friday
1	Ed. Fis 4°	Ed. Fis 9°		Ed. Fis 7°	Ed. Fis 8°
2	Ed. Fis 4°	Ed. Fis 9°		Ed. Fis 7°	Ed. Fis 11°
3		Ed. Fis 5°	Ed. Fis 6°	Ed. Fis 3°	Ed. Fis 10°
4		Ed. Fis 5°	Ed. Fis 6°	Ed. Fis 3°	Ed. Fis 8°
5					
6					

Fig. 2. Individual schedule for the teacher. Source: Own elaboration

	ninth grade				
	Monday	Tuesday	Wednesd	Thursd	Friday
1	Inf	Soc	Cas	Bio	Est
2	Inf	Soc	Cas	Bio	Est
3	E. Fis	Cas	Soc	C. Ciu	Ing
4	E. Fis	Cas	C. Lec	Ing	Ing
5	Mat	Mat	Qui	Qui	Fis
6	Mat	Mat	Geo	Fil	Bio

	ninth grade (mip schedule)				
	Monday	Tuesday	Wednesd	Thursd	Friday
1	Est	E. Fis	Ing	Cas	C. Lec
2	Est	E. Fis	Ing	Cas	Ing
3	Inf	Soc	Soc	Mat	Qui
4	Inf	Bio	Soc	Mat	Qui
5	Cas	Bio	Mat	Fil	Fis
6	Cas	Geo	Mat	Bio	C. Ciu

Fig. 3. Manual vs. Generated Schedules. Source: Own elaboration

In this instance, the manually created schedule has 10 blocks, whereas the generated schedule has 11, the maximum allowable for the ninth grade. The model aims to maximize daily blocks across all courses, a challenging task without computational assistance. Using such tools enhances resource utilization and educational quality.

6   Conclusions

Creating class schedules is undeniably a demanding task, emphasizing the critical importance of a facilitating tool in this process. Through this effort, a model was proposed, building upon the initial concept, which greatly aids the institution in effectively formulating their school schedules. This endeavor involved an extensive and comprehensive study of the institution's unique conditions, thereby laying a solid foundation for the model's formulation.

In formulating the model, an extensive literature search was conducted to find relevant studies related to the topic. A comprehensive review of existing research was undertaken, with the aim of identifying suitable frameworks and approaches that could be adapted to the specific needs identified in the institution through the conducted study.

During this research, a valuable framework was found in one study that showed promise in addressing the institution's unique requirements. The authors' proposed model from that work was implemented with due consideration to the specific conditions of the problem studied.

The GAMS tool was chosen as the primary platform to execute the model, providing a robust and efficient environment for computational analysis. This tool was selected for its capability to handle the complexity of the problem and its flexibility in accommodating specific problem conditions.

With the results obtained from this work, a more effective solution was provided for creating class schedules in the institution. This solution not only enhances the generation of class blocks but also significantly reduces the time required to create the schedules, improving overall efficiency and resource utilization in the educational setting.

In this study, several recommendations are proposed to improve the scheduling process. Firstly, it is essential to consider the needs and preferences of all teachers, particularly their availability for specific class hours. Considering these constraints and preferences can significantly enhance the overall scheduling efficiency. Additionally, for subjects that require a two-hour time slot per week and are taught outside the regular classroom, scheduling them consecutively whenever possible is advisable. This approach helps minimize additional travel time or movement to specialized facilities like laboratories or sports fields, thus optimizing resource utilization and streamlining the scheduling process.

References

1. Sánchez-Otero, M., García-Guiliany, J., Steffens-Sanabria, E., Hernández-Palma, H.: Pedagogical strategies in teaching and learning processes in higher education including information and communication technologies. Informacion Tecnologica 30(3), 277–286 (2019). https://doi.org/10.4067/S0718-07642019000300277
2. Rane, M.V., Apte, V.M., Nerkar, V.N., Edinburgh, M.R., Rajput, K.Y.: Automated timetabling system for university course. In: 2021 International Conference on Emerging Smart Computing and Informatics, ESCI 2021, pp. 328–334. Institute of Electrical and Electronics Engineers Inc. (Mar. 2021). https://doi.org/10.1109/ESCI50559.2021.9396906
3. Reddy, K.P., Krishna, B.T., Sai, T.N., Surekha, Y.T., Kowsalya, G., Reddy, K.D.: An automatic time table generation. Int J Sci Res Sci Technol, 831–835 (Jun. 2021). https://doi.org/10.32628/ijsrst2183183
4. Wiilams, K., Ajinaja, M.: Automatic Timetable Generation Using Genetic Algorithm 8(1) (2019). https://doi.org/10.7176/JIEA
5. Chen, M.C., Sze, S.N., Goh, S.L., Sabar, N.R., Kendall, G.: A survey of university course timetabling problem: perspectives, trends and opportunities. IEEE Access 9, 106515–106529 (2021). https://doi.org/10.1109/ACCESS.2021.3100613
6. Tan, J.S., Goh, S.L., Kendall, G., Sabar, N.R.: A survey of the state-of-the-art of optimisation methodologies in school timetabling problems. Expert Syst. Appl. 165 (Mar. 2021). https://doi.org/10.1016/j.eswa.2020.113943

7. Sørensen, M., Dahms, F.H.W.: A two-stage decomposition of high school timetabling applied to cases in Denmark. Comput. Oper. Res. **43**(1), 36–49 (2014). https://doi.org/10.1016/j.cor. 2013.08.025

8. Oude Vrielink, R.A., Jansen, E.A., Hans, E.W., van Hillegersberg, J.: Practices in timetabling in higher education institutions: a systematic review. Ann. Oper. Res. **275**(1), 145–160 (Apr. 2019). https://doi.org/10.1007/s10479-017-2688-8

9. Maldonado-Matute, J.M., González Calle, M.J., Celi Costa, R.M.: Development of a solution model for timetabling problems through a binary integer linear programming approach. In: Advances in Intelligent Systems and Computing, pp. 510–516. Springer (2020). https://doi. org/10.1007/978-3-030-39512-4_80

10. Rappos, E., Thiémard, E., Robert, S., Hêche, J.F.: A mixed-integer programming approach for solving university course timetabling problems. Journal of Scheduling **25**(4), 391–404 (2022). https://doi.org/10.1007/s10951-021-00715-5. Aug.

11. Algethami, H., Laesanklang, W.: A mathematical model for course timetabling problem with faculty-course assignment constraints. IEEE Access **9**, 111666–111682 (2021). https://doi. org/10.1109/ACCESS.2021.3103495

12. Sørensen, M., Stidsen, T.R.: General rights High School Timetabling: Modeling and solving a large number of cases in Denmark High School Timetabling: Modeling and solving a large number of cases in Denmark. PATAT (2012). [Online]. Available: http://www.lectio.dk

13. Marín-Ángel, J.C., Maya-Duque, P.A.: Modelo lineal para la programación de clases en una institución educativa. Ing Cienc **12**(23), 47–71 (2016). https://doi.org/10.17230/ingciencia. 12.23.3. Feb.

14. Tassopoulos, I.X., Iliopoulou, C.A., Beligiannis, G.N.: Solving the Greek school timetabling problem by a mixed integer programming model. J. Operat. Res. Soci. **71**(1), 117–132 (2020). https://doi.org/10.1080/01605682.2018.1557022. Jan.

15. Dorneles, Á.P., de Araújo, O.C.B., Buriol, L.S.: A column generation approach to high school timetabling modeled as a multicommodity flow problem. Eur J Oper Res **256**(3), 685–695 (2017). https://doi.org/10.1016/j.ejor.2016.07.002. Feb.

16. Kristiansen, S., Sørensen, M., Stidsen, T.R.: Integer programming for the generalized high school timetabling problem. Journal of Scheduling **18**(4), 377–392 (2015). https://doi.org/10. 1007/s10951-014-0405-x. Dec.

Evaluation of a Mixed-Product Production System Performance with Unreliable Machines

Gustavo Alfredo Bula[✉][iD]

Universidad Nacional de Colombia sede Bogotá, Bogotá, Colombia
gabula@unal.edu.co

Abstract. This study analyzes a mixed-product production system with unreliable machines and investigates how certain improvement initiatives impact the enhancement of throughput, reduction of work-in-process inventory, and improvement of overall equipment effectiveness (OEE). The production system studied consists of multiple stages with parallel machines. When a machine fails, it undergoes repairs before being reintegrated into the system. The system must meet the demand for various products, requiring changeover and machine adjustment time during product transitions.

The study aims to measure the impact of improvement efforts on production system deficiencies caused by product variety and periods when a machine is not available or not operational. These improvement initiatives, such as preventive maintenance, regular machine cleaning and lubrication, identification and fixing the root causes of machine breakdowns, use of standardized tools and procedures, and operators training on how to do quick and efficient setups, are intended to enhance the efficiency and stability of a multi-stage production process.

Experimental measurements using discrete event simulation and mathematical modeling provide valuable insights into the impact of improvement initiatives. Increasing the machine uptime reduces WIP. These findings contribute to a better understanding of the relationship between system parameters and performance metrics, supporting informed decision-making for optimizing production system efficiency. This study contributes to the field of production systems engineering, providing insights and strategies for optimizing performance in dynamic manufacturing environments.

Keywords: Production Systems Efficiency · Overall Equipment Effectiveness · Simulation

1 Introduction

Production systems are inherently dynamic, stochastic, and complex in nature [5]. These characteristics pose significant challenges for efficient and effective operations. As dynamic systems they continuously evolve and adapt in response

© The Author(s), under exclusive license to Springer Nature Switzerland AG 2023
J. C. Figueroa-García et al. (Eds.): WEA 2023, CCIS 1928, pp. 301–310, 2023.
https://doi.org/10.1007/978-3-031-46739-4_27

to internal and external factors, requiring to adjust to this constant changes in order to maintain the best possible performance. The stochastic nature of production systems arises from inherent uncertainties such as variations in input parameters, equipment failures, probabilistic processing time among them. Additionally production systems exhibit complexity due to interactions and dependencies among their components, including machine, human, materials and information flows. Understanding and managing this complexity is required for optimizing system performance as it involves balancing trade offs, identifying bottlenecks and ensuring smooth coordination across the entire systems. Recognizing production systems nature highlights the need for advanced modeling, analysis, and control techniques in order to archive enhanced operational efficiencies.

The number of product variety offered by manufacturers has consistently increased. Product variety here is referred as the number of different products that a production system can produce. Product variety can offer the potential to expand markets, increase sales volume and revenues. However, product variety also has some costs. One cost is the cost of setting up the production system to produce different products. Each time a new product is introduced, the production system must be set up to produce that product. Another cost of product variety is the increase in work-in-process inventory [1]. Production systems must be designed to handle such high variety while at the same time achieve mass production performance [6].

In serial multi-stage production systems, where stages are arranged in consecutive order and flow units move sequentially from one stage to the next, throughput is influenced by factors such as the variability of processing times, machine setup times, and unexpected disturbing events such as machine breakdowns. These factors cause production efficiency to fall behind the expected system performance [2]. To have a good approximation of the operational performance of production systems under the influences of such aspects allows us to build predictive and prescriptive models.

This work focuses on the utilization of a mathematical flow models and computer simulation, which has the potential to compute the expected performance of multi-stage production systems with variable throughput due to unreliable machines and setup time. By establishing a more realistic performance baseline, this work serves as a valuable tool for enhancing decision-making processes. Moreover, the integration of optimization functions provides opportunities for cost minimization, thereby improving overall system efficiency while effectively managing and mitigating system losses.

In the subsequent sections of this paper, we will delve into the details of the mathematical model, its underlying principles, and its application within the context of production systems. Through empirical evaluations and case studies, we aim to demonstrate the effectiveness and practical utility of the proposed approach in optimizing system efficiency and enabling informed decision-making for improved manufacturing performance.

2 Production Systems Performance Analysis, Improvement, and Design

System production measurement holds great significance for enterprises as it facilitates monitoring and tracking of business progress while providing crucial real-time information that support decisions. It also serves as the foundation for setting targets that guide system improvement strategies. Precisely defining resource requirements and output expectations is essential in designing and improving production systems. Metrics, monitoring, and alerting are interconnected concepts that form the basis for system improvement. These elements collectively offer visibility into system health, aid in identifying usage and behavioral trends, and enable the assessment of the impact of implemented changes. Robust system production measurement practices provide enterprises with valuable insights and enable effective decision-making for system enhancement and optimization.

Efficiency is one of the most important metrics for measuring manufacturing performance. Many production companies strive to achieve the highest productivity using installed resources under constantly changing circumstances. Common production system performance measures associated to efficiency are: the throughput or the production rate, the number of parts produced in a given time; the total work in process inventory (WIP), the total amount of parts flowing in the system; and the flow time, the time required for flow unit to cross the system [3]. In production systems where machines play a pivotal role in determining production outcomes, metrics such as Overall Equipment Effectiveness (OEE) serve also as valuable indicator for monitoring system efficiency.

Variabilities from sources such as machine failures, shutdowns caused by quality problems, and shutdowns due to required machine changeovers in production systems with product variety exist in almost all production systems, and they have a huge impact on system performance. Even under average operating conditions, the realized performance of production systems often deviates from the theoretically expected performance. Consequently, the availability of tools that enable the quick determination of expected system performance can serve as a decision-support instrument, facilitating a more accurate assessment of system capacity and enabling effective comparisons between actual system performance and the anticipated benchmarks.

2.1 Overall Equipment Effectiveness (OEE)

The OEE concept has been widely used as a quantitative tool essential for measurement of productivity especially in manufacturing operations. The total productive maintenance introduce by Seiichi Nakajima in the 1980s presented a this quantitative metric for measuring productivity of individual equipment in a factory. OEE measures losses over important aspects of production systems based on machines: availability, performance, and quality rate; supporting the equipment effectiveness and thereby its productivity [10]. OEE categorizes reasons for poor performance (losses) and provides the basis for establishing improvement priorities and be the starting point of root cause analysis. Thee perspectives of performance integrated in OEE that are studied in this paper are those related to equipment failure, set up time (changeovers) and machine adjustment (down time losses) and speed losses due to idling and minor stoppage, other speed losses and defect losses are no addressed in this study. OEE can be calculated directly from measured good product output (units), P_g, and theoretical attainable product output (units) in total time, P_a^{th}, without using any other factors; OEE can be calculated in terms of production units as:

$$OEE = \frac{\text{Number of good parts produced}}{\text{Theoretical number of parts produced in total time (TT)}} \quad (1)$$

This expression is the base for measuring the production system productivity [10] by extending the previous expression of OEE (Eq. 2) to the system production level the Overall Throughput Effectiveness (OTE) [8] during the total time of observation.

$$OTE = \frac{\text{Good product output (units) from production system, } P_{g(PS)}}{\text{Theoretical attainable product output (units) from production system, } P_{g(PS)}^{th}} \quad (2)$$

where theoretical number of parts produced in total time is computed by multiplying the theoretical production rate by the total available time. Both model of the productivity, OEE and OTE, metrics can be integrated with computer simulation to facilitate rapid analysis of equipment and manufacturing system productivity, and the investigation of productivity improvement opportunities.

A manufacturing system is usually made up of one or more principal types of manufacturing system architecture, this consists of two or more individual types of equipment and can be classified as *series, parallel, flexible, assembly* and *disassembly*. The OEEs for these principal manufacturing architectures can be calculated using Eq. 2. The average theoretical production rate for actual production system output is a function of the system interconnectivity. Therefore, we consider here simpler systems, namely, serial production lines with M identical exponential machines and infinite buffers. [7].

2.2   Unreliable Machines Performance Metrics

In this work are studied production systems with four (4) stages in series with unreliable M identical machines working in parallel. An unreliable machine has uptime and downtime being random variables with expected values $E[T_{Up}]$ and $E[T_{Down}]$. The machine unplanned downtime is a function of the number of breakdowns within a specified time period and it is related to measures as mean time between failures (MTBF) and mean time to repair(MTTR), both of them are measures of equipment achievement and are related to objectives such as functional performance and process capability, minimizing technical downtime is one of the goal of maintenance [10]. The maintenance function can improve equipments availability by either increasing the MTBF or reducing the MTTR that means reduce planned maintenance time and unplanned downtime in order to have a greater operating time.

The availability rate is determined by three factors, namely reliability, maintainability, and maintenance readiness. The reliability factor is the length of time equipment is able to run without failure and is measured by MTBF. Maintainability is the length of time for which an equipment can be brought back to an operating condition after it has failed, and is measured by MTTR [4]. Since it is the responsibility of maintenance function to ensure the availability of production equipment, the availability rate is related to maintenance effectiveness. The other important time loss is due to changeovers and replacement of routine wear parts. Though the changeover time varies from one operation to another, it takes a considerable amount of time for analysis and reduction. Specialized measurement, analysis, and reduction of each of these losses are important in improving the equipment effectiveness [10].

2.3   Mixed-Product Production Systems

Product variety can be a strategic decision that can have a significant impact on the performance of a production system. However, it is important to weigh the benefits of product variety against the costs before making a decision. Giving a production mix and the demand requirements for each product the total batch size that allows to fulfil the demand can be computed as:

$$Total\ Demand\ Rate = \frac{BS}{Total\ SetUp\ Time + \sum_{i=1}^{n} BS_i \times p_i} \qquad (3)$$

where the total demand rate (K) is the total units the system must provide during a period of time T. The total setup time is the total changeover and adjustment time required to produce all the different product units. BS is the total number of units that compose the bath $(\sum_{i=1}^{n} BS_i)$ and p_i is the expected machine unit processing time. Each time a new product is introduced, the production system must be set up to produce that product. This can be a time-consuming and expensive process. Another impact of product variety is the increase in work-in-process inventory. Work-in-process inventory (WIP)is the inventory of products that are in the process of being produced. When there is a high level of product variety, the work-in-process inventory can also be high. This is because there are more products that need to be produced, and each product takes time to produce. The higher the product variety the higher the WIP. Increased variety in production often implies increased manufacturing complexity. Improvement mus be carried out in order to increase product variety while keeping inventory levels.

The size of each product batch it is computed as:

$$BS_i = \frac{K_i}{K} BS, \; for \; i = 1, \ldots, n \tag{4}$$

In this way it assured that the demand rate for the product i is satisfied.

3   Experiments and Results

A four-stage production system is considered. The throughput of the production system is calculated under the assumption that all machines are of perfect quality (i.e., produce no defective parts), good product output from system during total time period equals the actual product units processed. The first, second and forth stages of the production system are composed of three (3) identical machines, and the third one of two (2) identical machines. At each machine only one product or one flow unit is processed at the same time, and a set up or adjust time exists anytime there is a product change. Product batch arrive at the first stage according to a production-mix, and the batch size for each product is defined in order to meet demand requirements. When a machine fails and the current product or flow unit that have been processed still requires a time to be finished, it is treated as a new entry. The total repair time and the machine set up time include the time to make sure the product can be processed correctly, the adjustment time.

In the system-theoretic approach, a machine is characterized by three independent parameters CT_u, $E[T_{Up}]$, $E[T_{Up}]$. They are used to evaluate machine's efficiency, e, and stand-alone throughput, SAT, according to [9]:

$$e = \frac{E[T_{Up}]}{E[T_{Up}] + E[T_{Down}]} \tag{5}$$

$$SAT = \frac{1}{CT_u} \frac{E[T_{Up}]}{E[T_{Up}] + E[T_{Down}]} \frac{units}{time} \tag{6}$$

However the randomness of the availability time affects the way the system behave and SAT becomes an asymptotic value of real machine throughput. Using $\frac{1}{number \; of \; servers \times SAT}$ as unit cycle time (p) the theoretical batch size (BS) can be calculated from Eq. 3 as:

$$BS = \frac{Total \; Demand \; Rate \times Total \; SetUp \; Time}{(1 - Total \; Demand \; Rate \times p)} \tag{7}$$

The production system must satisfy a daily demand of 165 units of product A and 85 units of products B and C. Machines uptime and downtime time are considered to be random variables Erlang with $\beta = 480$ min and $k = 3$ and Exponential with $\lambda = \frac{1}{48 \, min}$, respectively; this gives as result a machine efficiency $e = 0.97$. The setup time is initially fixed in 15 min independently of product sequence or machine. In the Table 1 the probability distribution function of the

Table 1. Times of the machines in each stage (station) of the process

Station	Parameters (minutes)
1	$N(3.2; 0.15^2)$
2	$N(2.8; 0.15^2)$
3	$N(1.85; 0.10^2)$
4	$N(3.1; 0.15^2)$

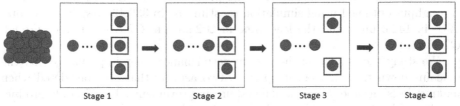

Fig. 1. Production System Configuration

processing unit time for each machine in the four system stages are shown. In Fig. 1) is shown the production system configuration.

Given the capabilities and the number of machines in each stage, the first stage is the one that determines the output flow rate of the production system. Using the machine stand-alone throughput of the first stage, the minimum number of units (assuming a deterministic case) that make up the total process batch is determined. Subsequently, through simulation, the minimum number of units required for the long-term throughput to be equal to or greater than demand requirements is calculated. Under the assumption of deterministic behaviour and machines without breakdowns the production system throughput given by stage one is $450units/day$, $one\ day = 480$ min. If machines breakdowns are taken into account according Eq. 6 the stand-alone throughput for the three machines in parallel corresponds to $435.48units/day$. Given the need of a setup time at each product change, the stage production throughput at long-term is $336.42units/day$ when the total batch size is 154 units, the correspondent batch size for each product is explained ahead.

A discrete event simulation in Python (Jupyter notebook) is used for estimating average performance metrics. In the simulation, the uptime and downtime of the machines are simulated by generating random values from the given probability distribution of the variables $t_{up,i}$ and $t_{down,i}$. The transfer lot is considered as one unit, and the setup time is initialized as soon as the machine finishes processing the last unit of a product batch. The machines do not fail during the setup time. The raw materials required for processing all three products batch size is available at the simulation beginning, each time stage one finishes processing the total batch, a new entry is authorized for the total raw materials needed to process the total batch. The number of simulation iterations was set in such a way that the throughput of each stage was the same or nearly the same. Since stage one determines the input rate of units, the long-term throughput rate of each stage (production system) must be equalized to this value.

To meet the demand rate, the batch size for product A should be at least 76 units, and the batch size for products B and C should be at least 39 units each, a total batch size of 154 units. This values are established through simulation as the minimum integer values for the batch size that meet the daily demand rate. The total batch size must be approximatively 1.12 times the computed batch size using Eq. 7 (137 units) using the single station throughput (SAT) for the first stage, $435.48 unis/day$. For the previous values the expected value of throughput obtained using simulation is estimated in $336.42 unis/day$, the total WIP in 142.6 units and the lead time in 202.93 min. OEE computed through OTE is 74.76%.

We study the impact on the system performance when improving either the machine down time or the set up time, two aspects that are considered when making decisions about production systems improvements. That is, only production losses due to machine break downs and machine changeover and adjustment are considered.

First, we consider increasing the value of e to 98% by augmenting the reliability factor, the length of time machine is able to run without failure. Now the $t_{up,i} \sim Erlang(3, 780)$. In this case the required batch sizes are 72 units for product A, and 37 units for products B and C. That is 1.11 times the computed batch size using Eq. 7. The single station throughput for the first stage is $343.65 units/day$. Now the throughput obtained by simulation is $338.39 unis/day$, the total WIP is 131.02 units, the lead time 185.81 min, and the OEE 75.20%. When increasing the value of e near to 99% by setting the $t_{up,i} \sim Erlang(4, 1200)$, the single station throughput for the first stage is $341.44 units/day$, a batch size for product A of $67 units$, and 35 units for products B and C, 1.08 times the computed batch size using Eq. 7. In this case the throughput obtained by simulation is $337.73 unis/day$, the total WIP is $116.36 units$, the lead time 165.34 min, and the OEE 75.05%.

If the setup time is reduced to 12 min. The required batch sizes are 62 units for product A and 32 units for products B and C. The total batch size must be approximatively 1.16 times the computed batch size using Eq. 7. The single station throughput for the first stage is $345.84 units/day$. In this case the throughput obtained by simulation is $337.55 unis/day$, the total WIP is 123.84 units, the lead time 176.06 min and OEE 75.01%. If the setup time is reduced to 10 min, the single station throughput for the first stage is $349.10 units/day$, the batch size for product A is $54 units$, and 28 units for products B and C; 1.21 times the computed batch size from Eq. 7. In this case the throughput obtained by simulation is $3339.31 unis/day$, the total WIP is $107.72 units$, the lead time 107.72 min, and OEE 75.40%.

As shown in Table 2, the impact of the improvement efforts is a reduction in WIP and lead times, as throughput must be close to the demand rate OEE remains almost the same. The estimated process throughput values obtained using the stand-alone machine throughput (SAT) for the defined process batch

Table 2. Simulations Results

Improvement initiative	Setup Time (minutes)	Batch Size	Machine Efficiency	Throughput Units/day	Total WIP	OEE
None	15	154	0.9677	336.42	142.26	0.7476
Reliability factor	15	146	0.9799	338.39	131.02	0.7520
Reliability factor	15	137	0.9901	337.73	116.36	0.7505
Setup Time	12	126	0.9677	337.55	123.84	0.7501
Setup Time	10	110	0.9677	339.31	107.72	0.7540

sizes to meet the demand rate are always higher than the values yielded by the simulation, as expected. Calculations were performed using the estimated probability of finding stage one in the three possible states-three, two, one, or zero machines operating-and the result was very similar to the estimated process throughput through SAT. However, these last estimated values are slightly smaller in magnitude. In all cases, the values obtained by the simulation are approximately 98% of the estimated value using SAT.

4   Conclusions

This study examined the impact of improving machine downtime and setup time on system performance, throughput, and work-in-process (WIP) inventory in a production system through simulation, several key findings emerged.

First, by increasing the overall system uptime or reducing the setup time, leaded to enhanced throughput and productivity, because it is possible to obtain the required process outputs with a lower work-in-process inventory, thus resulting in a shorter lead time. Secondly, in the experiments conducted to reduce the total batch size by improving machine reliability, the proportion by which work-in-process inventory decreases is greater than the reduction in batch size. In the case of reducing machine setup times, although there is also a reduction in batch size and work-in-process inventory, the reduction in the former is proportionally greater than that in the latter.

Given the simulation results, the calculation of the productive process outputs using the stand-alone throughput is an upper asymptote to the actual process outcome, although the values are very close. This means that they can be used in the initial estimation of the required batch sizes and later fine-tuned through simulation.

Overall, the findings highlight the importance of addressing both machine downtime and setup time in production systems. By minimizing machine downtime, the system can operate at higher efficiency, leading to improved throughput and overall system performance. Simultaneously, optimizing setup time enables smoother product transitions, reducing idle time and enhancing overall productivity.

References

1. Bech, S., Brunoe, T.D., Nielsen, K., Andersen, A.L.: Product and process variety management: case study in the food industry. Procedia CIRP **81**, 1065–1070 (2019). 52nd CIRP Conference on Manufacturing Systems (CMS), Ljubljana, Slovenia, 12–14 June 2019
2. Chen, W., Liu, H., Qi, E.: Discrete event-driven model predictive control for real-time work-in-process optimization in serial production systems. J. Manuf. Syst. **55**, 132–142 (2020)
3. Colledani, M., et al.: Design and management of manufacturing systems for production quality. CIRP Ann. **63**(2), 773–796 (2014)
4. Fleischer, J., Weismann, U., Niggeschmidt, S.: Calculation and optimisation model for costs and effects of availability relevant service elements. In: Proceedings of LCE, pp. 675–680 (2006)
5. Hopp, W.J., Spearman, M.L.: Factory Physics. Waveland Press (2011)
6. Hu, S., Zhu, X., Wang, H., Koren, Y.: Product variety and manufacturing complexity in assembly systems and supply chains. CIRP Ann. **57**(1), 45–48 (2008)
7. Huang, S.H., et al.: Manufacturing productivity improvement using effectiveness metrics and simulation analysis. Int. J. Prod. Res. **41**(3), 513–527 (2003)
8. Huang, S.H., et al.: Manufacturing system modeling for productivity improvement. J. Manuf. Syst. **21**(4), 249–259 (2002)
9. Liu, K.: The (α, β)-precision theory for production system monitoring and improvement. Ph.D. thesis, The University of Michigan (2021)
10. Muchiri, P., Pintelon, L.: Performance measurement using overall equipment effectiveness (OEE): literature review and practical application discussion. Int. J. Prod. Res. **46**(13), 3517–3535 (2008)

Distributionally Robust Optimization for Networked Microgrids: An Overview

Edwin Cervera[1]([✉])[iD], Pablo Morales[1,2], Sebastian Linares-Rugeles[1][iD],
Sergio Rivera[1], and Eduardo Mojica-Nava[1][iD]

[1] Department Electrical and Electronics Engineering, Universidad Nacional
de Colombia, Bogotá, Colombia
{eacerveraf,pabmorales,slinaresr,srriverar,eamojican}@unal.edu.co
[2] Universidad Manuela Beltrán, Bogotá D.C., Colombia

Abstract. Explore the application of Distributed Robust Optimization (DRO) in microgrids and networked microgrids with highly uncertain parameters. Microgrids are small-scale electrical systems with distributed generation, loads, and storage. Optimizing microgrid operation and design involves addressing uncertainties like power demand and renewable generation. DRO offers a solution for robust optimization, ensuring feasible solutions under various scenarios. This paper outlines DRO's key features, benefits, challenges, and its applications in microgrid optimization.

Keywords: Networked Microgrids · DRO · Wasserstein metric

1 Introduction

Conventional fossil fuels like coal, diesel, and gas cannot meet rising electricity demand without harming the environment. The shift to renewable energy is happening, with the use of distributed energy resources (DERs), including both renewables and conventional sources. Microgrids (MGs) are key in Smart Grids. MGs manage distributed energy sources efficiently, including renewables and conventional sources, within a specific area [1]. Interconnecting MGs helps by promoting renewable energy, reducing costs, enhancing system stability, and enabling energy sharing. This interaction is illustrated in Fig. 1.

Networked Microgrids (NMGs) are interconnected to enhance electricity supply resilience, reliability, and efficiency by sharing resources and supporting each other during disruptions. This framework increases reliability through resource redistribution, quick restoration after disruptions, and efficient use of local energy resources. By coordinating operations and resource sharing, NMGs maximize efficiency and minimize costs. However, uncertainties like renewable energy fluctuations and demand changes pose challenges. An energy management system

We want to express our gratitude to the Research Program of Colciencias (code 70169) for their valuable support and funding in the development of this study.

J. C. Figueroa-García et al. (Eds.): WEA 2023, CCIS 1928, pp. 311–323, 2023.
https://doi.org/10.1007/978-3-031-46739-4_28

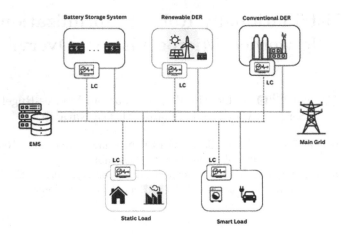

Fig. 1. Physic and communication interaction between MGs and MainGrid

is essential to coordinate generators, loads, and energy trading among NMGs. Operational objectives include cost minimization, renewable integration, loss reduction, and efficient transactions [2]. To model NMGs effectively [3], accounting for uncertainties from renewable generation, demand, and equipment failures is crucial. This enables scenario analysis for informed decision-making. We explore various approaches to tackle optimization challenges in multiple MGs, including line faults, economic dispatch, optimal power flow, investment decisions, and unit commitment using Distributionally Robust Optimization (DRO). Additionally, we propose a method for selecting the appropriate Wasserstein radius for a detailed analysis of DRO problems using a distance-based approach.

2   Dealing with Uncertainty

When assessing uncertainties in networked MGs, we identify two main sources: technical parameters (e.g., energy demand, variable generation, grid events) and economic parameters (e.g., economic growth, energy prices, production costs, economic indicators) [4]. Strategies to address uncertainties fall into three categories. First, stochastic optimization (SO) assumes data follows a specific probability distribution (e.g., Weibull for wind power) to transform problems into deterministic mathematical forms, enabling solutions based on expected performance. These problems can be formulated as.

$$\min_{x \in X} \quad \mathbb{E}_{\mathbb{P}_0}[f(\boldsymbol{x}, \boldsymbol{\xi})] \tag{1}$$

where x is the decision variable, ξ is an uncertain parameter that takes values depending on a known PDF, and $\mathbb{P}$ is a PDF known for ξ parameter. Authors in [5,6] use stochastic methods for energy management under uncertainties. However, solving such problems is challenging due to mathematical complexity, computational demands, and the complexity of analyzing multiple MGs.

Robust optimization (RO) offers an alternative. It aims to find optimal solutions for problems with incomplete or uncertain information. It ensures stability and satisfactory performance in worst-case scenarios by imposing constraints that guarantee a minimum level of performance [7]. This approach minimizes worst-case costs, prioritizing safety and stability in situations with high uncertainty or elevated risks [8].

$$\min_{x \in X} \ \max_{\xi \in \mathcal{U}} f(x, \xi). \tag{2}$$

The uncertainty set $\mathcal{U}$ represents different scenarios for the parameter ξ and allows for a feasible solution. However, this approach, while robust, ignores scenario probabilities and can be computationally challenging for adaptive problems. In contrast, stochastic optimization demands extensive probability distribution information and may lead to biased or suboptimal solutions. Both approaches often involve intractable high-dimensional integration. A to make use of the high quality of the estimator $\hat{\mathbb{P}}_i$, in which the solution is not overfitted to a particular instance of $\mathbf{w}$ is necessary, while acknowledging that $\mathbb{P}$ lies significantly near the estimated distribution, i.e., shares a lot of similarities to it.

Distributionally Robust Optimization (DRO) seeks optimal solutions that perform well under the worst-case scenario, utilizing an ambiguity set of potential distributions. This approach addresses the challenges of estimating distributions in stochastic optimization (SO) and the conservativeness of robust optimization (RO). DRO's worst-case approach regularizes the problem and reduces the error gap seen in SO. DRO problems can be formulated as:

$$\min_{x \in X} \ \max_{\mathbb{P} \in \mathcal{P}} \mathbb{E}_{\mathbb{P}}[f(x, \xi)]. \tag{3}$$

DRO, unlike SO, requires fewer assumptions about the exact probability distribution of variables like distributed generator (DG) output. It uses statistical properties, like moments or bounded deviations, to construct an ambiguity set. This set comprises distributions sharing specific statistical information. As DRO utilizes partial distribution information, its solutions are less conservative than RO but more robust than SO [9].

Figure 2 illustrates the difference. A deterministic approach assumes complete certainty about uncertain parameters. In contrast, SO employs probability density functions, representing uncertainty as a range of parameter configurations (blue polytope). RO models uncertainties by considering parameter value sets (blue polytope) instead of explicit probability distributions, ensuring performance under all scenarios in the uncertainty set.

On the other hand, DRO takes a different approach. DRO represents the ambiguity set as a blue polytope that contains an infinite number of probability distributions. Unlike SO, which directly models the probability density function, DRO focuses on robustness against all possible distributions within the ambiguity set.

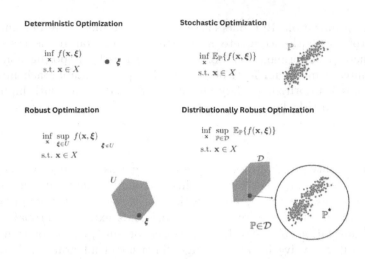

Fig. 2. Different uncertainties modeling approaches

Mean and variance are crucial for characterizing random variables. Moment-determined distributions *M-det* have distributions fully defined by their moments, implying close moment sequences yield similar distributions. Moment-Based DRO uses ambiguity sets representing distributions with common moment-based characteristics, avoiding favoring any particular distribution. Modelers often have access to an empirical distribution from a sample, making ambiguity sets around this empirical distribution common. The goal is for the chosen ambiguity set to statistically encompass the "true" unknown distribution [10].

The Wasserstein distance (EMD) quantifies the difference between probability distributions by measuring the work needed to transform one into another. In DRO, it gauges mismatch between empirical data distribution and candidate distributions representing possible uncertainties. DRO minimizes this distance to find a robust solution amid data distribution uncertainty. The inner maximization problem of (3) can be formulated, using Wasserstein distance as

$$\max_{\mathbb{P} \in \mathscr{P}(\mathbb{U})} \sum_{i=1}^{m} p_i f(\boldsymbol{x}, \boldsymbol{\xi}_i)$$
$$\text{s.t.} \quad W_p(\mathbb{P}, \mathbb{Q}_0) \leq d,$$

where the Wasserstein distance can be defined for general probability measures $\mathbb{P}$ and $\mathbb{Q}$ in $\mathscr{P}(\mathcal{U})$, which are not necessarily discrete distributions over finite support, where $\mathcal{U}$ is a closed subset of $\mathbb{R}^l$. In particular, we define the p-th order Wasserstein distance between $\mathbb{P}$ and $\mathbb{Q}$ as

$$\inf_{\pi \in \mathscr{P}(\mathscr{U} \times \mathscr{U})} \int_{\mathscr{U} \times \mathscr{U}} ||\xi_i - \zeta_j||^p d\pi(\xi, \zeta)$$

$$\text{s.t.} \int_{\{\xi\} \times \mathscr{U}} d\pi(\xi, \zeta) = \mathbb{P}(\xi), \forall \xi \in \mathscr{U}.$$

$$\int_{\mathscr{U} \times \{\zeta\}} d\pi(\xi, \zeta) = \mathbb{Q}(\zeta), \forall \zeta \in \mathscr{U}.$$

In the following sections, different variations will be introduced to develop problems through the implementation of DRO. Then, the main fields of action where this kind of optimization is used to efficiently operate MGs are mentioned.

3   Some Variants of Robust Optimization

Adaptive Robust Optimization. The first variant of the DRO approach is adaptive robust optimization. This optimization seeks to mitigate the consideration of the worst performance by applying an optimization contrary to the uncertainty. For example, suppose we have a cost function to be minimized f, that depends on two vectors of variables to be optimized, y and x; besides of vector of uncertain parameters u. The idea is that before applying the maximization of f with respect to u, to protect ourselves from the worst realization, we perform a minimization of f with respect to y, which in turn can be constrained by x and u (4):

$$\min_{x \in \chi} \max_{u \in U} \min_{y \in Y(x,u)} f(x, y, u). \tag{4}$$

In [11], a transactive energy system (TES) between an MG operator and aggregated MGs minimizes real-time social costs, considering network constraints. Adaptive robust optimization (ARO) addresses uncertainties using alternating direction method of multipliers (ADMM) in each local problem. In [12], researchers use ARO to model renewables' uncertainties for day-ahead scheduling in an MG with various generation sources and batteries, optimizing wait-and-see and here-and-now decisions through a trilevel approach, reducing costs and minimizing cost variability.

Adaptive Robust Stochastic Optimization. When the information on the probabilities of occurrence of the events is available, and a robust optimization methodology is also to be followed, the objective function can be restructured before optimizing with uncertain parameters. Using ARSO, the robustness can be combined with the stochastic nature as follows (5)

$$\min_{x \in \chi} \max_{u \in U} \min_{y \in Y(x,u,\xi)} E_\xi\{f(x, y, u)\}. \tag{5}$$

Stochastic and adaptive robust optimization are integrated in [13,14]. In the first, a model manages an MG, handling continuous uncertainties with adaptive robust optimization and binary uncertainties with stochastic programming. In the second, authors use ARSO for MG operational scheduling, addressing various operational modes and solving optimal power flow problems.

Adaptive Distributionally Robust Optimization. Another variant is ADRO. However, unlike the previous one, the values of the uncertain parameters, although unknown, have known distribution limits, manifesting as restrictions upon the optimization next stage (6) as

$$\min_{x \in \chi} \max_{\mathcal{F} \in \mathcal{D}} \min_{y \in \mathcal{Y}(x, \xi_\mathcal{F})} E_{\xi_\mathcal{F}}\{f(x, y, \xi_\mathcal{F})\}. \tag{6}$$

In [15], authors present a planning model integrating plug-in electric vehicles (PEVs) with the grid. They apply an ADRO-based methodology to address uncertainty, considering network constraints and emphasizing safety and reliability on the Ontario grid. This work highlights the potential enhancement of transactive control theories by incorporating uncertainty treatment in optimization problems.

4 Application of DRO to MG Problems

In this section, we discuss some of the most common applications of DRO in specific MG planning and operation issues.

4.1 Optimal Power Flow

Optimal Power Flow in an MG aims to optimize control variables to achieve various objective functions $f(\boldsymbol{x}, \boldsymbol{\xi})$ like minimizing costs (e.g., fuel, operating), reducing variable variations, transmission losses, emissions, or maximizing utility. Multi-objective approaches often consider operation costs, reliability, and emissions [16].

Numerous distributionally robust (DR) formulations of Optimal Power Flow (OPF) problems have emerged. In [17], scalable DR reformulations for chance-constrained OPF with symmetric forecast errors are introduced and compared. [18] fully reformulates chance-constrained OPF with a moment-based ambiguity set, assessing cost, reliability, and computational time. [19] presents a data-driven DRCC lossless OPF for distribution systems, enhancing reliability with modest cost increase. [20] shows that an unspecified mode significantly affects solution reliability with moment-based ambiguity sets. In [21], a joint-chance-constrained (JCC) second-order-cone approximation optimizes unit commitment and virtual inertia provision from wind. [22] integrates unimodality into moment-based ambiguity sets to reduce conservativeness. [23] explores tractable reformulations of the DR-JCC OPF problem, reducing conservativeness with a moment-based ambiguity set.

DRO with a Wasserstein-metric-based ambiguity set (DROW) was introduced in [24] for a DRCC OPF model, employing a hierarchical power flow model.
In [25], a DRCC linearized OPF model for multi-terminal HVDC (MTDC) systems is developed using a fully data-driven DROW definition. [26] formulates a
multi-stage DRCC linearized OPF problem with model predictive control (MPC)
and Data-driven DROW. [27] proposes a two-stage multi-area dynamic OPF
model using a DR MPC method. [28] presents a two-stage DROW dispatch to
prevent load shedding and renewable spillage, highlighting the preference for
chance constrained energy models [24–28].

4.2   MG Topology Planning and Sizing

Some research has focused on the resilience of MGs and distribution systems
using DRO. In [30], it is applied DRO to maximize expected load restoration in
successive contingencies, improving resilience through proactive MG formation
and reducing cascading impacts, considering line failure probability, generator
allocation, and demand response. In [32], it is used DRO to design and operate
a multiple MG (MMG) system in island mode, optimizing costs from design to
operation, considering the uncertainty of renewable energy.

4.3   Minimizing Operation Costs

Efficiently managing multiple MGs with DRO involves minimizing operational
costs for conventional and uncertain generators like solar and wind [33]. Three
key approaches, long-term unit commitment, economic dispatch, and short-term
Transactive Energy, focus on cost optimization in MGs with uncertainty. They
enable robust decisions that factor in renewable energy variability and enhance
cost efficiency in multi-MG setups [33].

Unit Commitment. The Unit Commitment (UC) is a long-term optimization
problem in power systems that involves deciding which thermal power generation units should be active to meet energy demand and minimize operational
costs [33]. To address uncertainties, data-driven distributionally robust chance-
constrained (DDRC) models are used, as demonstrated by [9]. They employ a
distance-based ambiguity set, constructed through data-driven methods, to capture wind power distribution uncertainty. This approach reformulates the UC
problem into a tractable optimization problem and validates it through case
studies, emphasizing the role of data in controlling conservativeness. By using a
DRO framework for unit commitment, robust decisions can minimize expected
operational costs while considering renewable energy source uncertainties [9].

Economic Dispatch. Economic dispatch optimizes generation outputs in a
MG to minimize costs while considering constraints and demand. In [36], a balance between costs and risk due to uncertain wind power is achieved using confidence intervals and imprecise probability-based ambiguity sets. [37] presents a

security-constrained multiperiod economic dispatch model using moment-based DRO for computational efficiency and security enhancement in renewable energy systems. DRO techniques enable robust solutions that account for uncertainties related to renewable energy sources, reducing operational expenses [36,37].

Transactive Energy Systems. Transactive energy (TE) is a system for balancing power supply and demand using economic control mechanisms. It facilitates decentralized energy management, considering operational costs and enabling distributed energy trading while protecting privacy and security. In [35], a TE framework for scheduling energy between the Distribution System Operator (DSO) and MGs is proposed, utilizing Mathematical Program with Equilibrium Constraints and a distance-based DRO algorithm. Similarly, [38] addresses this problem with an ambiguity set based on moments. DRO improves decision-making, risk management, and system performance in TE, even when the exact distribution is unknown or different from assumptions. The next section introduces a method to calculate and validate the ambiguity set radius, a crucial concept in DRO applications [35,38].

5   Ambiguity Set Radius Selection in DRO: A Cross-Validation Methodology

Choosing the right Wasserstein radius is crucial. A small radius can neglect realistic values of the random variable, as distributions become too close to the expected value. Conversely, a larger radius can yield results distant from actual effects. In this paper, we propose a Cross-Validation algorithm using the empirical distribution $\hat{\mathbb{Q}}_N$ from N data to determine the optimal Wasserstein radius for our optimization problem.

Previous studies, like [35], often treat the Wasserstein radius as an empirical parameter. Our research introduces an algorithm tailored to analyze the radius's effect on the random variable's expected value. Algorithm 1 provides a concise process description as follows: We begin with a set of candidate Wasserstein radii (step 1). The input data is then split into training and testing sets (step 2). Next, we use DROW to calculate upper and lower bounds for the expected value of the random variable ϵ for the first radius in the set (steps 3–5) based on the training data. We compute the expected value of ϵ with the validation set (step 6) and check if it falls within the previously calculated bounds (step 7). Steps 2–7 are repeated with different training and validation sets, and we count how often the expected value falls within the bounds to estimate the reliability parameter (step 8). Finally, we repeat the process (step 9) for all elements in the proposed Wasserstein radii set (step 1). This approach assists in selecting an appropriate Wasserstein radius for empirical data, enhancing decision accuracy for energy managers in MGs (see Fig. 1).

Algorithm 1: Method for estimating the effect of selecting Wasserstein's Radius on the expected value of a random variable.

---

1 A set of Wasserstein radio candidates is presented, $\epsilon = \{\epsilon_1, ..., \epsilon_m\}$
2 Randomly we take two subsets of the same size, T_N and V_N, from sample data $\hat{\xi}$. These subsets will be training and validation sets, respectively.
3 With T_N, we build an ambiguity set $\mathscr{B}_{\epsilon_i}(\hat{\mathbb{Q}}_N)$ with the first element of set ϵ
4 We determine the upper border, $\hat{U}_{\mathscr{B}_\epsilon}$, of the expected value of ξ, through the following optimization problem:

$$\sup_{\mathbb{P} \in \mathscr{B}_{\epsilon_i}(\hat{\mathbb{Q}}_N)} \mathbb{E}_\mathbb{P}[\xi] \tag{7}$$

5 We determine the lower border, $\hat{L}_{\mathscr{B}_\epsilon}$, of the expected value of ξ, through the following optimization problem:

$$\inf_{\mathbb{P} \in \mathscr{B}_{\epsilon_i}(\hat{\mathbb{Q}}_N)} \mathbb{E}_\mathbb{P}[\xi] \tag{8}$$

6 With V_N, the expected value of ξ is determined: $\hat{\mathbb{E}}_{V_N}[\xi]$
7 We repeat K times the steps $2 - 6$, with different T_N and V_N, counting the times (C) that $\hat{U}_{\mathscr{B}_\epsilon} \geq \hat{\mathbb{E}}_{V_N}[\xi] \geq \hat{L}_{\mathscr{B}_\epsilon}$
8 We determine the reliability value: C/K
9 Steps $2 - 8$ are repeated for the next element of set ϵ.

Running Algorithm 1 with 100 data points from wind turbines[1] we obtain the responses depicted in Fig. 3. The reliability curve illustrates how a progressively smaller Wasserstein radius neglects the effects of a portion of the actual domain of the random variable. Conversely, selecting an increasingly larger radius results in optimization distributions extending beyond the upper and lower limits of the average expected value from empirical validation data, which is undesirable. For instance, in this case, if we aim for an acceptable 95% reliability and expect values of the random variable between 90 and 160, the Wasserstein radius should be approximately 35.

Figure 3b demonstrates the significant dependence of the standard deviation of the data on Wasserstein radius reliability. Note that as the standard deviation increases, the required value of the Wasserstein radius to achieve 100% reliability also increases. Additionally, the randomness of reliability values among neighboring radii increases with the increase in standard deviation. These results, obtained from applying Algorithm 1, can be a starting point to determine a selection methodology of Wasserstein's Radius from the statistical parameters of the empirical data set.

---

[1] According to the records available at midnight from August 9 to November 30, 2019, at: https://www.kaggy.com/datasets/jorgesandoval/wind-power-generation.,.

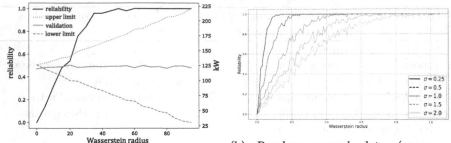

(a) $N = 100$ samples of power generated by wind turbine and k = 50 times.

(b) Random normal data (*mean* = 9) and various standard deviations (200 Wasserstein radius and 200 iterations).

Fig. 3. Application of Algorithm 1.

6 Conclusion

Distributionally Robust Optimization techniques have demonstrated great potential for dealing with uncertainty regarding variable power generation from renewable energy resources, load demand, and other external environmental variables in their use on power systems operations and planning thanks to its distributional approach, which inherently reduces the conservativeness of the robust solutions which can reduce optimal point performance alongside worst-case-cost minimization. Whereas the moment-based ambiguity set definition necessitates at least some accurate empirical distribution information for approximation of the "real" distribution, the Wasserstein-metric-based definition allows fully data-driven approaches, bypassing the need for high accuracy of approximation of the theoretical probability distribution, and even of a high number of sample data [28], whilst also employing the better-performing expectation based cost calculation inherited from stochastic optimization. However, when a "Wasserstein Ball" around an empirical distribution is built too large it includes probability distributions that are too pessimistic, decreasing out-of-sample efficiency as there is no chance-constraint on low-probability distributions. The Wasserstein radius cross-validation selection algorithm provides a much-needed decision-making tool for the definition of the ambiguity set that is fully tunable to the specific use-case data. A complete test study of the algorithm with different parametrizations of the validation dataset generation, such as distribution moments, families, or modalities is still a work in progress.

6.1 Future Work

In future work, we can explore various avenues to enhance distributed transactive control of DERs in distribution systems with uncertainties. This includes investigating advanced forecasting techniques for improved predictions of renewable generation and energy demand, developing more sophisticated control strategies focused on adaptability and real-time optimization, and exploring the integration of robust market frameworks and communication solutions to optimize system operation in uncertain conditions. Additionally, conducting further experimental validation and case studies in larger-scale distribution systems will help assess scalability and real-world effectiveness. Addressing the gap in applying advanced optimization techniques to MGs, distribution, and transmission systems requires designing closed-loop policy frameworks for power system optimization and generating context-specific analyses [26], technique comparisons, and cost-benefit assessments that consider individual agent capabilities and incentives, as well as infrastructure costs.

References

1. Yan, L., Sheikholeslami, M., Gong, W., Shahidehpour, M., Li, Z.: Architecture, control, and implementation of networked microgrids for future distribution systems. J. Mod. Power Syst. Clean Energy **10**(2), 286–299 (2022). https://doi.org/10.35833/MPCE.2021.000669
2. Ma, G., Li, J., Zhang, X.P.: A review on optimal energy management of multi-microgrid system considering uncertainties. IEEE Access **10**, 77081–77098 (2022). https://doi.org/10.1109/ACCESS.2022.3192638
3. Kumar, K.P., Saravanan, B.: Recent techniques to model uncertainties in power generation from renewable energy sources and loads in microgrids - a review. Renew. Sustain. Energy Rev. **71**, 348–358 (2017). https://doi.org/10.1016/j.rser.2016.12.063
4. Zubo, R.H.A., Mokryani, G., Rajamani, H.S., Aghaei, J., Niknam, T., Pillai, P.: Operation and planning of distribution networks with integration of renewable distributed generators considering uncertainties: a review. Renew. Sustain. Energy Rev. **72**, 1177–1198 (2017). https://doi.org/10.1016/j.rser.2016.10.036
5. Xiong, P., Jirutitijaroen, P.: A stochastic optimization formulation of unit commitment with reliability constraints. IEEE Trans. Smart Grid **4**(4), 2200–2208 (2013). https://doi.org/10.1109/TSG.2013.2278398
6. Malekpour, A.R., Pahwa, A.: Stochastic networked microgrid energy management with correlated wind generators. IEEE Trans. Power Syst. **32**(5), 3681–3693 (2017). https://doi.org/10.1109/TPWRS.2017.2650683
7. Zhang, Y., Gatsis, N., Giannakis, G.: Robust energy management for microgrids with high-penetration renewables. IEEE Trans. Sustain. Energy **4**(4) (2013)
8. Lin, F., Fang, X., Gao, Z.: Distributionally robust optimization: a review on theory and applications. Numer. Algorithms Control Optim. **12**(1), 159–212 (2022). https://doi.org/10.3934/naco.2021057
9. Shi, Z.: Data-driven distributionally robust chance-constrained unit commitment with uncertain wind power. IEEE Trans. Power Syst. **34**(2), 1233–1244 (2019). https://doi.org/10.1109/TPWRS.2018.2877045
10. Sun, X.A., Conejo, A.J.: Robust Optimization in Electric Energy Systems. ISORMS, vol. 313. Springer, Cham (2021). https://doi.org/10.1007/978-3-030-85128-6
11. Wang, B., Zhang, C., Li, C., Yang, G., Dong, Z.Y.: Transactive energy sharing in a microgrid via an enhanced distributed adaptive robust optimization approach. IEEE Trans. Smart Grid **13**(3), 2279–2293 (2022). https://doi.org/10.1109/TSG.2022.3152221

12. Ebrahimi, R., Amjady, N.: Adaptive robust optimization framework for day-ahead microgrid scheduling. Int. J. Electr. Power Energy Syst. **107**, 213–223 (2019). https://doi.org/10.1016/j.ijepes.2018.11.029

13. Ebrahimi, R., Amjady, N.: Contingency-constrained operation optimization of microgrid with wind and solar generations: a decision-driven stochastic adaptive-robust approach. IET Renew. Power Gener. **15**(2), 326–341 (2021). https://doi.org/10.1049/rpg2.12026

14. Ebrahimi, M.R., Amjady, N., Hatziargyriou, N.D.: Microgrid operation optimization considering transient stability constraints: a new bidirectional stochastic adaptive robust approach. IEEE Syst. J. **16**(4), 5663–5674 (2022). https://doi.org/10.1109/JSYST.2021.3132908

15. Hajebrahimi, A., Kamwa, I., Delage, E., Abdelaziz, M.M.A.: Adaptive distributionally robust optimization for electricity and electrified transportation planning. IEEE Trans. Smart Grid **11**(5), 4278–4289 (2020). https://doi.org/10.1109/TSG.2020.2987009

16. Prasad, D.: Transient stability constrained optimal power flow using chaotic whale optimization algorithm. In: Handbook of Neural Computation, pp. 311–332 (2017)

17. Roald, L., Oldewurt, F., Parys, B.V., Andersson, G.: Security constrained optimal power flow with distributionally robust chance constraints. arXiv:1508.06061 [math.OC] (2015)

18. Zhang, Y., Shen, S., Mathieu, J.L.: Distributionally robust chance-constrained optimal power flow with uncertain renewables and uncertain reserves provided by loads. IEEE Trans. Power Syst. **32**(2) (2017)

19. Mieth, R., Dvorkin, Y.: Data-driven distributionally robust optimal power flow for distribution systems. IEEE Control Syst. Lett. **2**(3) (2018)

20. Li, B., Jiang, R., Mathieu, J.L.: Distributionally robust chance-constrained optimal power flow assuming unimodal distributions with misspecified modes. IEEE Trans. Control Netw. Syst. **6**(3) (2019)

21. Yang, L., Xu, Y., Zhou, J., Sun, H.: Distributionally robust frequency constrained scheduling for an integrated electricity-gas system. IEEE Trans. Smart Grid **13**(4) (2022)

22. Li, B., Jiang, R., Mathieu, J.L.: Integrating unimodality into distributionally robust optimal power flow. TOP **30**, 594–617 (2022)

23. Yang, L., Xu, Y., Sun, H., Wu, W.: Tractable convex approximations for distributionally robust joint chance-constrained optimal power flow under uncertainty. IEEE Trans. Power Syst. **37**(3) (2022)

24. Duan, C., Fang, W., Jiang, L., Yao, L., Liu, J.: Distributionally robust chance-constrained approximate AC-OPF with Wasserstein metric. IEEE Trans. Power Syst. **33**(5) (2018)

25. Yao, L., Wang, X., Li, Y., Duan, C., Wu, X.: Distributionally robust chance-constrained AC-OPF for integrating wind energy through multi-terminal VSC-HVDC. IEEE Trans. Sustain. Energy **11**(3) (2019)

26. Guo, Y., Baker, K., Dall'Anese, E., Hu, Z., Summers, T.H.: Data-based distributionally robust stochastic optimal power flow-part I: methodologies. IEEE Trans. Power Syst. **34**(2) (2019)

27. Huang, W., Zheng, W., Hill, D.J.: Distributionally robust optimal power flow in multi-microgrids with decomposition and guaranteed convergence. IEEE Trans. Smart Grid **12**(1) (2020)

28. Ordoudis, C., Nguyen, V.A., Kuhn, D., Pinson, P.: Energy and reserve dispatch with distributionally robust joint chance constraints. Oper. Res. Lett. **49**, 291–299 (2021)

29. Babaei, S., Jiang, R., Zhao, C.: Distributionally robust distribution network configuration under random contingency. IEEE Trans. Power Syst. **35**(5), 3332–3341 (2020). https://doi.org/10.1109/TPWRS.2020.2973596
30. Cai, S., Xie, Y., Wu, Q., Zhang, M., Jin, X., Xiang, Z.: Distributionally robust microgrid formation approach for service restoration under random contingency. IEEE Trans. Smart Grid **12**(6), 4926–4937 (2021). https://doi.org/10.1109/TSG.2021.3095485
31. Xie, R., Wei, W., Shahidehpour, M., Wu, Q., Mei, S.: Sizing renewable generation and energy storage in stand-alone microgrids considering distributionally robust shortfall risk. IEEE Trans. Power Syst. **37**(5), 4054–4066 (2022). https://doi.org/10.1109/TPWRS.2022.3142006
32. Shi, Z., Zhang, T., Liu, Y., Feng, Y., Wang, R., Huang, S.: Optimal design and operation of islanded multi-microgrid system with distributionally robust optimization. Electr. Power Syst. Res. **221**, 109437 (2023)
33. Yurdakul, O., Sivrikaya, F., Albayrak, S.: A distributionally robust optimization approach for unit commitment in microgrids (2020). http://arxiv.org/abs/2011.05314
34. Roald, L., et al.: Power systems optimization under uncertainty: a review of methods and applications. IEEE Trans. Power Syst. **33**(6), 6630–6650 (2018). https://doi.org/10.1109/TPWRS.2018.2845278
35. Cao, Y., et al.: Optimal energy management for multi-microgrid under a transactive energy framework with distributionally robust optimization. IEEE Trans. Smart Grid **13**(1), 599–612 (2022). https://doi.org/10.1109/TSG.2021.3113573
36. Li, P., Yang, M., Wu, Q.: Confidence interval based distributionally robust real-time economic dispatch approach considering wind power accommodation risk. IEEE Trans. Sustain. Energy **12**(1), 58–69 (2021). https://doi.org/10.1109/TSTE.2020.2978634
37. Yang, Y., Wu, W.: A distributionally robust optimization model for real-time power dispatch in distribution networks. IEEE Trans. Smart Grid **10**(4), 3743–3752 (2019). https://doi.org/10.1109/TSG.2018.2834564
38. Liu, Z., Wang, L., Ma, L.: A transactive energy framework for coordinated energy management of networked microgrids with distributionally robust optimization. IEEE Trans. Power Syst. **35**(1), 395–404 (2020). https://doi.org/10.1109/TPWRS.2019.2933180

Pickup and Delivery Vehicle Routing Problems in Bike Sharing Systems: A Review

Juan D. Palacio[1]($\boxtimes$) and Juan Carlos Rivera[2]

[1] School of Engineering, Universidad de Medellín, Medellín, Colombia
jdpalacio@udemedellin.edu.co
[2] School of Sciences, Mathematical Modeling Research Group, Universidad EAFIT,
Medellín, Colombia
jrivera6@eafit.edu.co

Abstract. Bike sharing systems (BSSs) have been widely study from their logistic and managerial operations fields. Decisions on transportation and vehicle routing in BSSs are not the exception and there exists an extensive number of publications and research about these type of decisions. Particularly, for the static bicycle repositioning problem (BRP), being one of the most studied problems within a BSS service planning context, is still possible to find research gaps. In this paper, we aim to summarize the main contributions on VRPs for BSS, thus a literature review is presented. Since BRP is essentially a pickup and delivery vehicle routing problem (PDVRP), we firstly review some of the contributions on one–commodity PDVRPs. Next, we describe most relevant research based on the BRP. Finally, we also present some conclusions based on the available literature as well as some interesting research directions.

Keywords: Pickup and delivery · bike sharing systems · vehicle routing optimization

1 Introduction

Bike sharing systems (BSSs) have gained popularity in recent years as an environmentally friendly and cost-effective mode of transportation in urban areas. BSSs have positioned themselves as a convenient and flexible alternative for short-distance travel, promoting a more sustainable mobility and to decrease traffic and pollution caused by combustion-based vehicles transportation. Since 1965, bike sharing systems have continued to evolve and expand worldwide [42]. Many cities around the world have implemented their own bike sharing programs, often customized to meet the specific needs and characteristics of the local environment (e.g., electric bikes, integration with other modes of public transportation).

A BSS is mainly composed by a set of stations with limited capacity (i.e., number of bike slots) distributed along an urban area and a set of bicycles at stations for users. These users can use the system by taking a bike from one of the

J. C. Figueroa-García et al. (Eds.): WEA 2023, CCIS 1928, pp. 324–335, 2023.
https://doi.org/10.1007/978-3-031-46739-4_29

available stations (origin) and then, after a short trip, returning it to the same or a different station (destination). From a logistical perspective, an efficient operation of BSSs requires many challenges, particularly in managing the routing of vehicles to ensure an optimal distribution of bikes across the service area. Precisely, when vehicle routing for the distribution of bikes is required, several bike repositioning problems (BRPs) arise. The BRP can be seen as a generalization of the vehicle routing problem (VRP), which have been extensively studied in the field of operations research. VRPs involve determining the most efficient routes for a fleet of vehicles to deliver and/or collect goods or service. In BSSs context, the VRP focuses on determining the optimal routes for vehicles to rebalance bike stations, distribute bikes based on demand, and perform maintenance operations effectively. It is worth to mention that this paper focuses on station-based routing BSS problems. There exists a different type of service called free-floating BSSs. In the free-floating BSS, bikes are freely parked in defined areas along a urban region. In general, these defined areas are marked with a large rectangle [49]. From now, and since free-floating BSSs are not studied in this paper, we call BSSs to station-based BSSs.

This paper aims to provide a comprehensive review of the vehicle routing problems specifically those arising in BSSs context (i.e., VRPs with pickup and delivery operations). We will explore different variants of VRPs for bike sharing operations emphasizing in the key factors for problem formulations, solution approaches and main results. Furthermore, we will identify current research gaps and challenges, and propose potential directions for future research in this field.

This manuscript is structured as follows: Sect. 2 presents a review on problems, mathematical models and solution strategies for a subset of PDVRPs. Specifically, those in which one commodity and a many to many (M-M) structure is established. Section 3 explores several applications of VRPs in BSSs context. In this case, static and dynamic repositioning problems are reviewed. Finally, Sect. 4 summarize some conclusions and future research paths.

2 Vehicle Routing Problems with Pickup and Delivery Features

This section summarizes three pickup and delivery vehicle routing problems that may fit on BSS contexts. The one-commodity pickup and delivery traveling salesman problem (1–PDTSP), the one-commodity pickup and delivery traveling salesman problem with split demand (SD1PDTSP) and the multi-commodity pickup and delivery traveling salesman problem (M–PDTSP). From a theoretical perspective, these three problems have widely studied and their properties, objectives and constraints can be used to deal with BRPs if commodities are related to bikes.

2.1 One-Commodity Pickup and Delivery Traveling Salesman Problem

Research on 1–PDTSP starts with the work presented in [19]. Authors describe a branch and cut (B&C) algorithm based on an integer linear programming model (ILP). The solution strategy includes Benders cuts, and a heuristic algorithm. Optimal solutions are reported for instances with up to 50 nodes. Then, in [20], authors propose two different heuristics. The first one, based on the *nearest neighbor* algorithm, computes a modified distance matrix in order to penalize movements leading to infeasible solutions (e.g., by avoiding edges connecting nodes with similar demand). The second heuristic consists on modifying the original B&C algorithm described in [19]. Both heuristic strategies are able to find small gaps even when values for the vehicle capacity are tight and the number of nodes is not larger than 60. In [21], authors present new inequalities for the 1–PDTSP adapted from the CVRP (capacitated vehicle routing problem). These inequalities are added to a B&C framework and instances up to 100 customers are optimally solved. Results obtained with this new strategy outperform those reported in [19]. Later, [17] combines a greedy randomized adaptive search procedure (GRASP) with a variable neighborhood descent (VND) procedure to solve the 1–PDTSP. After the constructive phase, the local search is replaced by a VND. After the GRASP scheme is executed, a second VND performs a post-optimization phase. Tested instances include up to 100 nodes while the vehicle capacity goes from 10 to 1000. This GRASP/VND approach is able to find optimal solutions for 96.7% of the instances with up to 50 nodes while new best known solutions are reported for larger instances.

In [51], authors describe a genetic algorithm (GA) with a pheromone-based crossover operator. This operator uses local and global information to generate new offsprings. While the local information includes edge lengths, adjacency relations, and demands on nodes, the global information is based on pheromone trails. Each offspring is locally improved using 2–*opt* moves and then, the mutation procedure is based on a 3–exchange operator. This evolutionary algorithm outperforms the hybrid GRASP/VND presented in [17] for instances up to 500 nodes, and many new best known solutions for large instances are reported. Later, [34] describes a variable neighborhood search procedure with four neighborhoods based on double-bridge and insertion operators. To test this strategy, computational experiments in [34] include 1–PDTSP instances with up to 1000 nodes.

Authors in [44] propose a discrete bacterial memetic evolutionary algorithm (DBMEA) for the 1–PDTSP. The proposed approach is able to solve instances with up to 100 customers and outperforms the GRASP/VND results reported in [17]. Recently, [16] describes a generalization of the 1–PDTSP: the single-vehicle two-echelon one-commodity pickup and delivery problem (2E–1PDP). Authors propose three different mathematical formulations: two mixed-integer linear programming models (MILP) and an ILP. These models are solved within a B&C framework. After solving instances with up to 60 nodes, results show that the B&C based on the ILP outperforms those algorithms based on MILP.

2.2   One-Commodity Pickup and Delivery Traveling Salesman Problem with Split Demand

As mentioned before, in the 1–PDTSP exactly one visit to each location is mandatory. The SD1PDTSP arises when it is possible to split the pickup or delivery quantity if multiple visits are allowed. The SD1PDTSP is introduced in [41] as a generalization of the 1–PDTSP and the *split delivery vehicle routing problem* (SDVRP). Since problems addressed on this manuscript do not include the SDTSP, the reader may find a detailed description of the problem and solution methods in [2,3] and [35].

Research reported in [41] describes an MILP to deal with the SD1PDTSP in which a maximum number of visit to locations is allowed and determined by a parameter. Therefore, the MILP is also able to deal with the 1–PDTSP if that parameter is set to one. As solution strategy, the authors adapt the B&C algorithm in [19] to solve SD1PDTSP instances up to 50 locations. While results are not competitive with other strategies dealing with the 1–PDTSP, this exact approach provides near to optimal results for the split delivery case. Apart from [41], the SD1PDTSP is also study in [25] with a matheuristic algorithm that applies a constructive procedure and then, a refinement phase based on a MILP to improve solution quality. This matheuristic approach is used to solve instances with up 500 locations. Recently, authors in [24] solve SD1PTSP with up to 60 nodes via B&C algorithm. In this algorithm, a relaxed MILP is solved, then feasible and invalid solutions are checked in the subproblem where valid cuts are generated for invalid solutions.

2.3   Multi-commodity Pickup and Delivery Traveling Salesman Problem

Multiple commodities may be also allowed for PDVRPs. Firstly, in [22] the one-to-one M–PDTSP as a generalization of the TSP is presented. In the one-to-one M–PDTSP, each commodity has a single origin and a single destination. In their paper, authors describe two MILPs and decomposition techniques based on path and flow formulations to solve the problem. Instances up to 47 nodes were solved and several scenarios for vehicle capacity and number of commodities were also tested. Next, [40] presents a matheuristic for the one-to-one M–PDTSP. The authors describe a hybrid approach based on a GRASP with a VND for the local search procedure. One of the neighborhoods used within the VND is based on an MILP. This matheuristic is able to deal with instances up to 100 customers. Later, and apart from heuristic techniques, [23] propose an MILP for the one-to-one M–PDTSP. They also present two set of valid inequalities. The first one with the aim of strength the linear relaxation of the mathematical model and the second set aims to remove unfeasible arcs in solutions. This strategy is embedded on a B&C framework and it is tested on instances up to 30 customers and three commodities. Next, authors in [18] deal with the M–PDTSP within a many to many operation. In this case, each commodity can be transported from several sources to several destinations. Authors propose a three-stage heuristic to solve the problem. The proposed algorithm is able to solve instances with up to 400 customers and five products.

3 Vehicle Routing Optimization Models in Bicycle Sharing Systems

This section presents a state of the art on static and dynamic bike repositioning problems. Since free-floating BSSs are not studied in this paper, all the literature presented in this section is devoted to station-based BBS services. Some of the most relevant work in free-floating services may be found in [6, 11, 31, 33, 36, 45].

3.1 Static Bicycle Repositioning Problems

In BSSs, probably the most studied problem is the BRP. The most recent research based on the problem, begin with Raviv et al. [39]. They formulate two MILPs for the BRP which consider the minimization of the weighted sum of operational cost and users dissatisfaction as objective function. To measure the user dissatisfaction with the system, authors propose an index based on the number of shortage events. To solve this problem, two different MILPs models are tested on instances with up to 60 stations based on certain locations of Vélib (BSS in Paris) and then, a complete real instance of 104 stations and one or two vehicles. Relative small gaps are obtained within a maximum time of 18,000 s. A B&C procedure is also coded for the BRP [5]. This algorithm is based on an MILP relaxation for the problem and provides lower bounds when several visits to each vertex are allowed. On the other hand, a tabu search (TS) with four different neighborhoods is also designed to find upper bounds. Instances that vary from 20 to 100 stations are evaluated and it is possible to find small gaps (less than 5% as an average) for instances with up to 60 stations.

In [9], authors present four MILPs for the multi-vehicle BRP in which the total distance of the routes is minimized. They solve these mathematical models via B&C algorithm. The solution strategy was tested in 65 instances adapted from 22 different BSSs around the world and the formulation with best computational performance is able to solve optimally all the instances with up to 50 nodes in less than 15 min. Authors also present a real-world case using data from Reggio Emilia in Italy. Similar to [39], authors in [27] model penalty functions to minimize the cost associated to unsatisfied demand as a single objective function. Nevertheless, they do not consider the operational cost of the route (i.e., total distance). To deal with the single-vehicle case, the authors use a TS procedure and also test an MILP in CPLEX. Computational experiments are based on 156 instances varying from 30 to 400 stations.

A 3-step matheuristic based on: (a) a clustering process supported on savings heuristic, (b) an MILP for vehicles routing though clusters and (c) an MILP (adapted from [39]) for repositioning decisions is also proposed for the BRP [14]. For instances up to 150 stations, the matheuristic outperforms the arc-indexed formulation in [39] obtaining smaller gaps. For some larger instances (up to 200 stations) it was not possible to find optimal solutions but gaps are not larger than 2.52%. In [38], a combined GRASP/PILOT algorithm is proposed to solve the BRP. Authors also develop a VND as a third solution strategy which outperforms GRASP/PILOT in medium size instances. However, GRASP/PILOT finds better solutions than those reported by VND in large instances.

Similar to [5,12] deal with the BRP when several visits to a single node are allowed. Authors describe an exact approach based on a separating algorithm for Bender's cuts. To test the algorithm, instances with up to 60 nodes are solved to optimality within a computational time of two hours. A *branch-and-bound* (B&B) procedure is proposed to solve the BRP when minimizing the total waiting time of stations. To compute upper bounds, authors develop a GA, a greedy search (GS) and a nearest neighbor procedure (NNP). For instances with up to 30 stations the B&B delivers solutions with gap up to 13% from the optimal solution within a maximum computational time of 7,200 s. For larger instances, GS finds better quality solutions than GA and NNP. Nevertheless, GS requires larger computational times.

Later, authors in [10] propose a destroy and repair (D&R) metaheuristic for the BRP with maximum length tour. Initially, the D&R algorithm starts with a constructive phase in which a variant of *savings* heuristic is used. Next, after some nodes are removed from routes, the solution is repaired via insertion procedure or the adapted *savings* algorithm. Finally, local search procedures are embedded in a VND framework. This D&R metaheuristic is tested on instances with up to 500 stations and the previously reported B&C algorithm in [9] is also adapted in order to find lower bounds for problem. For small instances (less than 50 stations) it is possible to find optimal solutions. Larger instances are solved but gaps increase, nevertheless new best known solutions are presented. In 2016, a two-stage methodology to address the rebalancing problem is presented [1]. First, they estimate shortages of bicycles and free slots at each station for each possible number of available bikes at the beginning of a time period. Second, they propose an MILP to find the optimal number of bikes that each station must have in order minimize the total dissatisfaction. Then, the routes for the vehicles are designed minimizing not only the total cost but also the variation over the duration of the set of routes. To do so, these authors solve a minimum cost flow problem to estimate the number of bikes that should be transported along the network. Results for this approach are based on the Palma de Mayorca's BSS case which is a small system with 28 stations. Results show that although a perfect balance on service times is not possible for a time horizon of one week, the routes never differ by more than 15 min. Next, in [13] an MILP to solve the BRP with an heterogeneous fleet is described. In this case, multiple visits to each station are allowed and the objective of the model relies on minimize a non-perfect repositioning operation (i.e., minimize the dissatisfaction of users). The authors tested this MILP on real-world instances with up to 14 stations from a BSS in Oslo, Norway.

Authors in [8] design an iterated local search (ILS) algorithm for the single-vehicle case of the BRP. The proposed ILS includes up to four different perturbation operators and a VND procedure instead of a local search. This ILS outperforms the tabu search presented in [5] for instances with up to 60 stations. Moreover, for larger instances with up to 100 nodes, the ILS finds new best known solutions for instances previously reported in the literature. Finally, in [26] the BRP is also addressed with penalty functions for unsatisfied demand. Authors propose a hybrid large neighborhood search (HLNS) algorithm. This hybrid metaheuristic includes five removal (destroy) operators, five insertion (repair) operators and a TS applied to the most promising solutions. Testing instances with up to 518 stations, the HLNS is able to outperform a proposed MILP coded on CPLEX and the matheuristic described in [14].

In 2018, authors in [46] propose a new variant for the BRP called the green repositioning problem with broken bikes. This study is the first one that includes environmental issues for static and multi-vehicle BRPs. The authors present an MILP for the problem in which the total CO_2 emissions are minimized. The mathematical model is tested using small real-world instances of Citybike in Vienna via commercial solver. The study also analyze multiple-visit to stations and prove that this is a key factor to reduce CO_2 emissions. The multi-vehicle and multiple-visit BRP is solved via ILS in [4]. A B&C algorithm is also described in order to compute lower bounds. These solution strategies jointly finds optimal solutions for most of the real-world instances originally presented in [9] using up to three vehicles. Later, in [48] the green repositioning problem with broken bikes for the single-vehicle version of the problem is tackled. This study includes an enhanced artificial bee colony algorithm to generate the routes and two different methods (one network flow mathematical model and one heuristic) are used to compute the loading and unloading quantities. The authors test the performance of the algorithm solving instances with up to 300 stations.

In 2020, a memetic algorithm (MA) for BRP is described [32]. This algorithm is able to improve best known solutions for 46% of the evaluated instances with up to 564 stations. Computational times also outperform the D&R algorithm described in [10]. In [37], authors develop a TS algorithm and a heuristic algorithm called *capacity range length heuristic*. Results show that TS is able to improve solutions reported with the B&C in [9] and the D&R algorithm in [10] even for large instances with 564 stations. The problem described in [30] is a selective BRP in which not all the pickup stations must be visited. In this study, the authors show that it is possible to improve service level for bikes availability if this repositioning strategy is implemented. The proposed selective pickup and delivery BRP aims to minimize the total travel time and the number of used vehicles for the relocation operation. To solve the problem, a genetic algorithm is coded and real-world instances based on a BSSs from Gangnam-district in Seoul with 95 stations are tested.

Recently, [15] proposed a robust optimization approach to address demand uncertainty by jointly considering strategic and tactical decisions as station location and bike rebalancing, respectively. To deal with this problem, authors present an MILP with non-convex constraints. Therefore, duality theory is applied to reformulate the problem and it is solved via row generation. Tested instances include up to 55 stations. Finally, traffic conditions are included to BRP if a mixed fleet of internal combustion vehicles and electric vehicles is available [28]. The problem is described via MILP and also a hybrid simulated annealing (SA) algorithm. Authors randomly generated nine instances with up to 100 stations and prove that hybrid SA with variable neighborhood structures, outperforms SA and a variable neighborhood search (VNS) as separated algorithms also developed for the problem.

3.2 Dynamic Bicycle Repositioning Problems

Initially, the dynamic BRP motivated by shortages of bikes at some station during peak hours is presented in [7]. The authors present a mathematical formulation able to solve small instances when total unmet demand is minimized. Moreover, they present two decomposition schemes. The first one is based on Dantzig-Wolfe decomposition, while the second strategy follows a Benders decomposition strategy. To test these strategies, authors in [7] solve 120 instances with three different sizes: 25, 50 and 100 stations. Despite decomposition strategies are able to find lower and upper bounds, final gaps increase significantly as the size of the instances also increases.

Later, four different algorithms to deal with the dynamic version of the BRP are proposed: a greedy construction heuristic, a preferred iterative look ahead technique (PILOT) algorithm, a VNS and GRASP [29]. Instances with a number of stations that varies from 30 to 90 were used to test the algorithms. Some scenarios (i.e., demand values) were taken from Vienna BSS. Authors conclude that VNS metaheuristic outperforms the other three proposed algorithms for most of the evaluated instances. Authors in [50] describe a multi-commodity time-space network flow model. Since this formulation is non-linear, authors reformulated it as an MILP. The proposed solution strategy is mainly based on a two-stage approach where firstly a linear relaxation of the MILP is solved and then, routes are assigned to determine upper bounds. Tested instances were taken from real scenarios from Washington and Paris BSSs with up to 200 stations.

A BRP based on the minimization of user dissatisfaction (i.e., unmet demand) and CO_2 emission costs within a bi-objective model is also studied [43]. To compose the dynamic nature of the problem, authors model a multi-period operational horizon in which demands vary at each station and at each period. This problem is split in a set of steps, each step solves a single period of the problem as a static version of the repositioning operation. The solution strategies rely on an enhanced artificial bee colony (ABC) algorithm and a GA. The size of the instances vary from 30 to 180 and for most of the instances, ABC algorithm outperforms the GA. Authors also present an analysis of the impact of several variables (e.g., weight of each objective, length of the service time horizon, time for load and unload bikes) on unmet demand and CO_2 emissions.

Lastly, research in [47] consider a mixed fleet of internal combustion engine vehicles and battery electric vehicles in the dynamic BRP with multiple charging technologies. As objective, this problem aims to minimize the of penalty costs and the charging costs of vehicles within a weighted sum function. The solution strategy is based on a hybrid ABC algorithm and a dynamic programming model. Test instances include a subset of the 100 most active bike stations from Washington BSS.

4   Concluding Remarks and Research Directions

The vehicle routing problem and its associated features in shared mobility contexts as BBSs (e.g., pickup and delivery) have been widely studied. Exact methods made possible to find optimal solutions for small instances of the problem. However, given the complexity of VRPs, many authors consider the use of heuristic, metaheuristic and hybrid strategies to solve instances associated with real case studies of BSSs. On the other hand, solution strategies for BRPs and 1–PDVRPs have been adapted to include other desirable features related to the operation design for BSSs (e.g., split delivery, routes lengths), or related to operation efficiency (e.g., CO_2 emissions, users dissatisfaction).

Future research directions are also based on the study of additional features for static bike repositioning problems and one-commodity vehicle routing problems. The objective behind these research paths is to close gaps between theoretical developments and required facets in real-world BSS scenarios. For example, green-based objective functions for bike repositioning problems would be an interesting study path. CO_2 emissions is still a relevant component for vehicle routing problems and has been emerged as a key metric for decision makers in public and private transportation systems. In line with this motivation on green vehicle routing problems, it could be interesting to explore mixed fleet of internal combustion engine vehicles and battery electric vehicles.

In spite of the extensive research on pickup and delivery vehicle routing optimization within theoretical and practical contexts as in BSSs, there still exist gaps between repositioning problems and solution strategies to solve them. Moreover, so far there is not evidence of publications based on several VRP key features for bike sharing mobility (e.g., collaborative and two-echelon routing). It could be interesting to explore research paths on integrated approaches for static and dynamic repositioning problems. Decisions for static repositioning affects dynamic routing during BBSs operation. Therefore, to design methods that integrates tactical and operational decisions within rebalancing contexts are worth to be explored. Indeed, collaborative operations based on two-echelon structure could mark an initial point to explore how static rebalancing support daily dynamic operation on several zones. Since it is possible to use several vehicles to perform short repositioning routes (with limited length), this strategy remain useful in an intra day operation.

References

1. Alvarez-Valdes, R., et al.: Optimizing the level of service quality of a bike-sharing system. Omega **62**, 163–175 (2016). https://doi.org/10.1016/j.omega.2015.09.007

2. Archetti, C., Bianchessi, N., Speranza, M.G.: Branch-and-cut algorithms for the split delivery vehicle routing problem. Eur. J. Oper. Res. **238**(3), 685–698 (2014)
3. Archetti, C., Speranza, M.G.: Vehicle routing problems with split deliveries. Int. Trans. Oper. Res. **19**(1–2), 3–22 (2012)
4. Bulhões, T., Subramanian, A., Erdoğan, G., Laporte, G.: The static bike relocation problem with multiple vehicles and visits. Eur. J. Oper. Res. **264**(2), 508–523 (2018)
5. Chemla, D., Meunier, F., Wolfler Calvo, R.: Bike sharing systems: solving the static rebalancing problem. Discret. Optim. **10**(2), 120–146 (2013). https://doi.org/10.1016/j.disopt.2012.11.005
6. Cheng, Y., Wang, J., Wang, Y.: A user-based bike rebalancing strategy for free-floating bike sharing systems: a bidding model. Transp. Res. Part E: Logist. Transp. Rev. **154**, 102438 (2021)
7. Contardo, C., Morency, C., Rousseau, L.M.: Balancing a Dynamic Public Bike-Sharing System, vol. 4. Cirrelt Montreal, Canada (2012)
8. Cruz, F., Subramanian, A., Bruck, B.P., Iori, M.: A heuristic algorithm for a single vehicle static bike sharing rebalancing problem. Comput. Oper. Res. **79**, 19–33 (2017)
9. Dell'Amico, M., Hadjicostantinou, E., Iori, M., Novellani, S.: The bike sharing rebalancing problem: mathematical formulations and benchmark instances. Omega **45**, 7–19 (2014)
10. Dell'Amico, M., Iori, M., Novellani, S., Stützle, T.: A destroy and repair algorithm for the bike sharing rebalancing problem. Comput. Oper. Res. **71**, 149–162 (2016)
11. Du, M., Cheng, L., Li, X., Tang, F.: Static rebalancing optimization with considering the collection of malfunctioning bikes in free-floating bike sharing system. Transp. Res. Part E: Logist. Transp. Rev. **141**, 102012 (2020)
12. Erdoğan, G., Battarra, M., Calvo, R.W.: An exact algorithm for the static rebalancing problem arising in bicycle sharing systems. Eur. J. Oper. Res. **245**(3), 667–679 (2015)
13. Espegren, H.M., Kristianslund, J., Andersson, H., Fagerholt, K.: The static bicycle repositioning problem - literature survey and new formulation. In: Paias, A., Ruthmair, M., Voß, S. (eds.) ICCL 2016. LNCS, vol. 9855, pp. 337–351. Springer, Cham (2016). https://doi.org/10.1007/978-3-319-44896-1_22
14. Forma, I.A., Raviv, T., Tzur, M.: A 3-step math heuristic for the static repositioning problem in bike-sharing systems. Transp. Res. Part B: Methodol. **71**, 230–247 (2015). https://doi.org/10.1016/j.trb.2014.10.003
15. Fu, C., Zhu, N., Ma, S., Liu, R.: A two-stage robust approach to integrated station location and rebalancing vehicle service design in bike-sharing systems. Eur. J. Oper. Res. **298**(3), 915–938 (2022)
16. Hernández-Pérez, H., Landete, M., Rodriguez-Martin, I.: The single-vehicle two-echelon one-commodity pickup and delivery problem. Comput. Oper. Res. **127**, 105152 (2021)
17. Hernández-Pérez, H., Rodríguez-Martín, I., Salazar-González, J.J.: A hybrid GRASP/VND heuristic for the one-commodity pickup-and-delivery traveling salesman problem. Comput. Oper. Res. **36**(5), 1639–1645 (2009)
18. Hernández-Pérez, H., Rodríguez-Martín, I., Salazar-González, J.J.: A hybrid heuristic approach for the multi-commodity pickup-and-delivery traveling salesman problem. Eur. J. Oper. Res. **251**(1), 44–52 (2016)
19. Hernández-Pérez, H., Salazar-González, J.J.: A branch-and-cut algorithm for a traveling salesman problem with pickup and delivery. Discret. Appl. Math. **145**(1), 126–139 (2004)

20. Hernández-Pérez, H., Salazar-González, J.J.: Heuristics for the one-commodity pickup-and-delivery traveling salesman problem. Transp. Sci. **38**(2), 245–255 (2004)

21. Hernández-Pérez, H., Salazar-González, J.J.: The one-commodity pickup-and-delivery traveling salesman problem: inequalities and algorithms. Netw. Int. J. **50**(4), 258–272 (2007)

22. Hernández-Pérez, H., Salazar-González, J.J.: The multi-commodity one-to-one pickup-and-delivery traveling salesman problem. Eur. J. Oper. Res. **196**(3), 987–995 (2009)

23. Hernández-Pérez, H., Salazar-González, J.J.: The multi-commodity pickup-and-delivery traveling salesman problem. Networks **63**(1), 46–59 (2014)

24. Hernández-Pérez, H., Salazar-González, J.J.: A branch-and-cut algorithm for the split-demand one-commodity pickup-and-delivery travelling salesman problem. Eur. J. Oper. Res. **297**(2), 467–483 (2022)

25. Hernández-Pérez, H., Salazar-González, J.J., Santos-Hernández, B.: Heuristic algorithm for the split-demand one-commodity pickup-and-delivery travelling salesman problem. Comput. Oper. Res. **97**, 1–17 (2018)

26. Ho, S.C., Szeto, W.Y.: A hybrid large neighborhood search for the static multi-vehicle bike-repositioning problem. Transp. Res. Part B: Methodol. **95**, 340–363 (2017). https://doi.org/10.1016/j.trb.2016.11.003

27. Ho, S.C., Szeto, W.: Solving a static repositioning problem in bike-sharing systems using iterated tabu search. Transp. Res. Part E: Logist. Transp. Rev. **69**, 180–198 (2014)

28. Jia, Y., Zeng, W., Xing, Y., Yang, D., Li, J.: The bike-sharing rebalancing problem considering multi-energy mixed fleets and traffic restrictions. Sustainability **13**(1), 270 (2021)

29. Kloimüllner, C., Papazek, P., Hu, B., Raidl, G.R.: Balancing bicycle sharing systems: an approach for the dynamic case. In: Blum, C., Ochoa, G. (eds.) EvoCOP 2014. LNCS, vol. 8600, pp. 73–84. Springer, Heidelberg (2014). https://doi.org/10.1007/978-3-662-44320-0_7

30. Lee, E., Son, B., Han, Y.: Optimal relocation strategy for public bike system with selective pick-up and delivery. Transp. Res. Rec. **2674**(4), 325–336 (2020)

31. Liu, Y., Szeto, W., Ho, S.C.: A static free-floating bike repositioning problem with multiple heterogeneous vehicles, multiple depots, and multiple visits. Transp. Res. Part C: Emerg. Technol. **92**, 208–242 (2018)

32. Lu, Y., Benlic, U., Wu, Q.: An effective memetic algorithm for the generalized bike-sharing rebalancing problem. Eng. Appl. Artif. Intell. **95**, 103890 (2020)

33. Mahmoodian, V., Zhang, Y., Charkhgard, H.: Hybrid rebalancing with dynamic hubbing for free-floating bike sharing systems. Int. J. Transp. Sci. Technol. **11**(3), 636–652 (2022)

34. Mladenović, N., Urošević, D., Ilić, A., et al.: A general variable neighborhood search for the one-commodity pickup-and-delivery travelling salesman problem. Eur. J. Oper. Res. **220**(1), 270–285 (2012)

35. Ozbaygin, G., Karasan, O., Yaman, H.: New exact solution approaches for the split delivery vehicle routing problem. EURO J. Comput. Optim. **6**(1), 85–115 (2018)

36. Pal, A., Zhang, Y.: Free-floating bike sharing: solving real-life large-scale static rebalancing problems. Transp. Res. Part C: Emerg. Technol. **80**, 92–116 (2017)

37. Pan, L., Liu, X., Xia, Y., Xing, L.N.: Tabu search algorithm for the bike sharing rebalancing problem. IEEE Access **8**, 144543–144556 (2020)

38. Rainer-Harbach, M., Papazek, P., Raidl, G.R., Hu, B., Kloimüllner, C.: PILOT, GRASP, AND VNS approaches for the static balancing of bicycle sharing systems. J. Global Optim. **63**(3), 597–629 (2015)

39. Raviv, T., Tzur, M., Forma, I.: Static repositioning in a bike-sharing system: models and solution approaches. EURO J. Transp. Logist. **2**(3), 187–229 (2013). https://doi.org/10.1007/s13676-012-0017-6

40. Rodríguez-Martín, I., Salazar-González, J.J.: A hybrid heuristic approach for the multi-commodity one-to-one pickup-and-delivery traveling salesman problem. J. Heuristics **18**(6), 849–867 (2012)

41. Salazar-González, J.J., Santos-Hernández, B.: The split-demand one-commodity pickup-and-delivery travelling salesman problem. Transp. Res. Part B: Methodol. **75**, 58–73 (2015)

42. Schuijbroek, J., Hampshire, R.C., Van Hoeve, W.J.: Inventory rebalancing and vehicle routing in bike sharing systems. Eur. J. Oper. Res. **257**(3), 992–1004 (2017)

43. Shui, C., Szeto, W.: Dynamic green bike repositioning problem–a hybrid rolling horizon artificial bee colony algorithm approach. Transp. Res. Part D: Transp. Environ. **60**, 119–136 (2018)

44. Tüű-Szabó, B., Földesi, P., Kóczy, L.T.: The discrete bacterial memetic evolutionary algorithm for solving the one-commodity pickup-and-delivery traveling salesman problem. In: Kóczy, L.T., Medina-Moreno, J., Ramírez-Poussa, E., Šostak, A. (eds.) Computational Intelligence and Mathematics for Tackling Complex Problems. SCI, vol. 819, pp. 15–22. Springer, Cham (2020). https://doi.org/10.1007/978-3-030-16024-1_3

45. Usama, M., Shen, Y., Zahoor, O.: A free-floating bike repositioning problem with faulty bikes. Procedia Comput. Sci. **151**, 155–162 (2019)

46. Wang, Y., Szeto, W.: Static green repositioning in bike sharing systems with broken bikes. Transp. Res. Part D: Transp. Environ. **65**, 438–457 (2018)

47. Wang, Y., Szeto, W.: The dynamic bike repositioning problem with battery electric vehicles and multiple charging technologies. Transp. Res. Part C: Emerg. Technol. **131**, 103327 (2021)

48. Wang, Y., Szeto, W.: An enhanced artificial bee colony algorithm for the green bike repositioning problem with broken bikes. Transp. Res. Part C: Emerg. Technol. **125**, 102895 (2021)

49. Zhang, B., Li, X., Saldanha-da Gama, F.: Free-floating bike-sharing systems: new repositioning rules, optimization models and solution algorithms. Inf. Sci. **600**, 239–262 (2022)

50. Zhang, D., Yu, C., Desai, J., Lau, H., Srivathsan, S.: A time-space network flow approach to dynamic repositioning in bicycle sharing systems. Transp. Res. Part B: Methodol. **103**, 188–207 (2017)

51. Zhao, F., Li, S., Sun, J., Mei, D.: Genetic algorithm for the one-commodity pickup-and-delivery traveling salesman problem. Comput. Ind. Eng. **56**(4), 1642–1648 (2009)

Mathematical Optimization Models for the Design of Industrial Symbiosis Networks: Challenges and Trends

Mestizo-Caro[1]([⊠]) [iD], Orjuela-Castro[2] [iD], and Orejuela-Cabrera[3] [iD]

[1] Universidad Distrital Francisco José de Caldas, Bogotá, Colombia
mymestizoc@udistrital.edu.co
[2] Universidad Distrital Francisco José de Caldas, Bogotá, Colombia
[3] Universidad del Valle, Cali, Colombia

Abstract. This article aims to study the state of the art of the optimization models that have been formulated to address the challenges and problems identified in the application of Industrial Symbiosis models, in terms of their design and implementation, for this, the search for articles is made in the Scopus database, finding a total of 125 articles that are fully detailed, displaying the types of exchanges, the variants in the application of mathematical optimization models, as well as the objective functions, parameters, variables and constraints, with these data, the conclusions and future work to be proposed based on the gaps identified are described. As a conclusion, it is established that greater integration of various types of materials and energy must be done, as well as the integration of various economic sectors and society, seeking a design of Industrial Symbiosis networks based on ecosystems using their metrics and behaviors to closer to the maximum return on the use of materials and energy.

Keywords: Industrial symbiosis · industrial ecology · eco-industrial park · mathematical model · optimization · uncertainty · symbiotic exchanges · energy · water · by-products

Abbreviations

IS	Industrial Symbiosis
EIP	Eco-Industrial Park
AHP	Analytic Hierarchy Process
NGSA III	Non-dominated Sorting Genetic Algorithm 3
MILP	Mixed-Integer Linear Programming
MINLP	Mixed-Integer Nonlinear Programming
FMILP	Fuzzy Mixed-Integer Linear Programming
NLP	Nonlinear Programming
LP	Linear programming
MIP	Mixed Integer Programming
FLP	Fuzzy Linear Programming
FMILQP	Fuzzy Mixed-Integer Linear Quadratic Programming

J. C. Figueroa-García et al. (Eds.): WEA 2023, CCIS 1928, pp. 336–350, 2023.
https://doi.org/10.1007/978-3-031-46739-4_30

1 Introduction

The concept of circular economy has been strengthened in recent years, its principles have been accepted by different actors in society with the aim of coping with the finiteness of resources that exist on our planet by extending the life cycle of products and materials that we consume creating added value, for this objective, work has been done in the search and study of different alternatives translated into policies, practices, methodologies and technologies, a compatible organizational practice is Industrial Symbiosis, a concept that began its application since the early 1970s with the exchange of materials and energy between the plants located in the Kalundborg EIP in Denmark, these plants that traditionally operated separately, work under a collective approach to physically share materials, energy, water and by-products [1], adding value, reducing costs and improving the environment [2]. On the other hand, the EIPs are favorable spaces to apply the concept of IS, since they are designed to generate exchanges and synergies between companies, while facilitating geographic proximity [1]. Although the IS is compatible with the circular economy and with the current needs of the world, it presents several challenges that are immersed within its complex nature promoted by the different exchanges of products that can arise in the network, as well as by interactions between organizations that traditionally work independently and have different objectives. Therefore, this literature review aims to identify the different challenges and trends in terms of mathematical optimization models formulated to face the challenges and complexity in the design and implementation of these networks.

2 Methodology and Results of the Research

The literature review methodology is based on [3], the scope covers the identification and analysis of scientific articles whose focus is the application of mathematical optimization models in the field of IS, the questions to be answered during the review They are: What characteristics are common in the mathematical optimization models applied in the IS?, what are the current trends and gaps related to the mathematical optimization models applied to the IS? The search strategy used is based on the search string TITLE-ABS-KEY (((industrial AND symbiosis) OR (eco and industrial and park)) AND (mathematical OR optimization) AND model), this string is applied in Scopus. From this search, 404 documents are obtained, later the inclusion and exclusion criteria of articles are applied. Conference articles, book chapters, review articles and editorials are excluded, as well as those that do not correspond to the formulation of mathematical optimization models. After applying these criteria, the number of documents chosen for the review is 125.

3 Water and By-Product Exchanges

3.1 Statistical Analysis of the Search Performed

From the use of the search string formulated during the methodology and the use of the Scopus database, it is found that, since 2003, work has been done on the formulation of IS mathematical optimization models, being 2016 and 2020 the years with the highest number of publications with 14 and 15 respectively, there has been a growth in the establishment of networks since 2010 and, since 2015, there have been no fewer than 7 publications per year. On the other hand, Asia and Europe are the continents with the highest number of publications, and China and the USA are the countries with the highest number of publications (see Figs. 1 and 2).

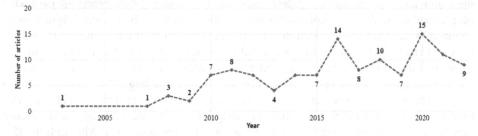

Fig. 1. Number of publications by year and by author applying the search string.

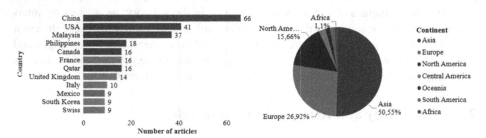

Fig. 2. Number of publications by continent and country.

3.2 Symbiotic Network Configurations Addressed Through Optimization Models

Through the different articles reviewed, three types of exchanges can be characterized, these are: water, energy, and by-products, each of these forms different symbiotic networks that in turn can be integrated to form networks with a greater degree of complexity, generating better recovery results. Figure 3 represents each of the types of exchanges that have been studied over time, and the integrations that may exist between them. Historically, water exchanges have been the most relevant, followed by by-product and energy exchanges, however since from 2018 to the present, models have been proposed to investigate integrations of water and by-products, water and energy and the integration of the three, the use of a new component that has been called in this article as services is also visualized, where does carbon permit trading. Figure 4 shows, in general and specifically, the exchanges studied in the literature, it can be observed that the most studied have been the exchanges of water (43), followed by the energy-by-products integration (32) and finally the integration of the three types of exchanges (19), the exchange of energy occurs through electricity, since for the other types of energy exchange a medium (by-products or water) is required to share it.

1. **Symbiotic water networks.** The integration of water networks between plants led to the origin of the use of mathematical optimization for the structuring of IS networks, the models of water networks have studied different configurations, which can vary according to the number of pollutants [4], the connection configurations of currents loaded with contaminants (sources) in process units (sinks) [5], source-interceptor-sink configurations which have in their structure regenerative units for wastewater treatment acting as centralized hubs within the model [6, 7], as well as units that are owned by the company [8]. Other configurations consider changes in the infrastructure of the networks in the pipelines and technologies used [9] and topological aspects of the location of the different actors and technology [8, 10, 11]. As a new trend in these models, they propose bio-inspired networks that integrate actors with functional roles found in nature, such as artificial wetlands [12].

2. **Exchange of byproducts:** These models have been approached from a general exchange approach, studying the physical exchange of any by-product [13] and from a specific approach taking into account one or more industries or one or more by-products such as exchanges of by-products derived from the chemical industry [14], the exchange of plastic waste for its use through pyrolysis processes [15], the exchange of by-products derived from waste generated by the cement industry [16] and the use, capture, separation and storage of CO2 [17], among others.

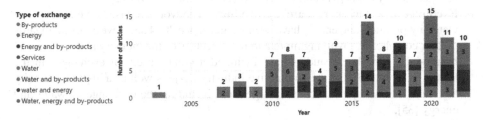

Fig. 3. Number of publications with different exchanges studied per year.

3. **Water and by-product exchange.** The networks of symbiosis of water and by-products have been approached from the perspective of exchange of recovered carbon dioxide and treated wastewater [18], the use of waste generated from treated wastewater, such as sludge and salts [19] and biogas generation through anaerobic digestion of industrial and domestic waste from treated water [20].

4. **Exchange of by-products with energy potential.** Exchanges of organic byproducts that have high energy potential have been studied, these include wood, plastic, coal, hydrogen-based products, palm oil, sugar, among others [21–24]. Other works have focused on the study of energy generation from inorganic byproducts, such as metals and blast furnace gas [25], the use of chemical waste [26].

5. **Exchange of electrical and thermal energy through different means.** The exchanges in this section occur through the use of different equipment by a plant for the generation of steam and electricity as a source of energy for subsequent use by other plants [27], the concept of cogeneration is also widely used in the modeling of these networks, since it takes advantage of the residual heat of conventional

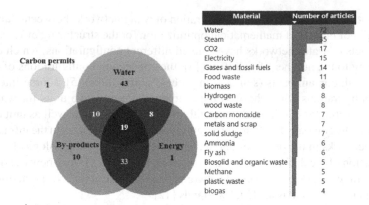

Fig. 4. Frequency of the study of the different types of exchanges and Exchanged materials.

systems to simultaneously obtain electrical energy, as well as thermal energy in the form of steam or hot water for consumption, facilitating compliance. of environmental goals and symbiotic exchanges [28]. There are variants of a technological nature in the modeling application, such as solar energy equipment [29], organic Rankine cycles [30], integration of vapor compression refrigeration systems with absorption refrigeration systems [31] and Hybrid Power Systems (HPS) [32].

6. **Exchange of water, energy, and by-products.** The works focused on exchanges of water, by-products and energy have been studied since 2014 and have evolved towards greater complexity, involving more and more sectors of the industry and a variety of by-products. The latest studies have included a great variety of exchanges in the Forest industry [33] and the automotive industry [34], as well as a high multiplicity of industries and by-products exchanged and including the exchange of water and energy [35].

7. **Symbiotic networks applying the concept of nexus.** Recent work has been formulated under the concept of links, these include water-energy-food links by integrating water networks with the use of biomass from the food sector as an energy source [36] and water-waste-energy nexuses in which wastewater is used as a common source due to its potential to recover energy, water and waste from wastewater [37].

7. **Symbiotic networks based on carbon-hydrogen-oxygen.** The modeling of this special type of network was introduced in 1015, with the argument that carbon, hydrogen and oxygen are main components of many industrial compounds that can be integrated at the atomic level and exchanged and therefore can be modeled in the IS framework ensuring the conversion, separation, treatment, splitting, blending and allocation of streams of compounds made up of these three components [38].

3.3 Preliminary Analysis of the Types of Mathematical Optimization Problems Used in the Literature.

The type of problem most used in the literature studied is the MILP, with 39%, it has maintained a tendency towards being the most used in all the years of evaluation, followed by the MINLP approach with 24%, the FMILP model continues as third most used with a percentage of 9%, giving a tendency that the fuzzy character of the modeling in IS networks has a relative importance. This is ratified since, with a lower participation, there are also FLP and FMILQP models (see Fig. 5).

3.4 Characteristics and Trends of Mathematical Optimization Models Applied in IS Networks.

This section is focused on the study of the objective functions that are used in mathematical optimization applied to IS networks, therefore, a characterization of these and their evolution over time is made. A general description of each type of objective function is made, Fig. 6 describes the types of objective function used, as well as the proportion of use of each objective function in the studied literature. It can be observed that the economic objective functions are the most worked on so far with 56% of the total objective functions found, followed by the environmental objective functions with approximately 33%, other objectives such as those related to infrastructure, uncertainty, demand, social and technical objectives are used in a lesser proportion. Visualizing in the Fig. 6 the behavior of the objective functions used in the literature through the years, it is established that, in 2003, the formulation of mathematical models began with the formulation of economic objectives, in 2007, environmental objectives related to the minimization of resources began to be used and, since then, each year there has been a greater preference towards having objectives of an economic nature. In the years 2020 and 2021 there was a trend towards equilibrium in the use of economic and environmental objectives, however, economic objectives continue to be more used even in these years, in 2020 social objectives were also raised, with the growing concern for investigating networks with an approach oriented towards their integrality being evident.

Analysis of Multi-objective Models. Figure 7 shows that, in recent years, there has been a greater concern to cover a greater number of objectives in an article, making an analysis of the multi-objective functions, there are 37 articles that have this perspective, which it represents approximately 30% of the total articles studied, there are a series of resolution techniques applied for the optimization of IS networks (see Fig. 8), the most used techniques are the Epsilon constraint, fuzzy optimization, and weighted sum. Figure 8 also shows that, when addressing three or more objective functions in multi-objective models, the preference is to do so by means of the epsilon constraint and fuzzy optimization, while the weighted sum is used more for models with two objective functions. The methods that were proposed with a greater number of objective functions were fuzzy optimization and NGSA III as well as the combination of fuzzy optimization and epsilon constraint that addressed 5 objectives in the model, followed by the use of the AHP approach that was used to addressing 4 objectives in the same model, the above demonstrates an affinity between these methods and the models of various objective functions, this aspect is essential for the study of future models with these alternatives.

Fuzzy optimization has been of great importance in the formulation of IS network optimization models, the foregoing because it couples well to the mathematical optimization of IS networks by integrating multiple objectives into one. Objective function and when addressing the conflicts of interest of each participant of the IS since each one has individual objectives, therefore, the models based on fuzzy optimization seek

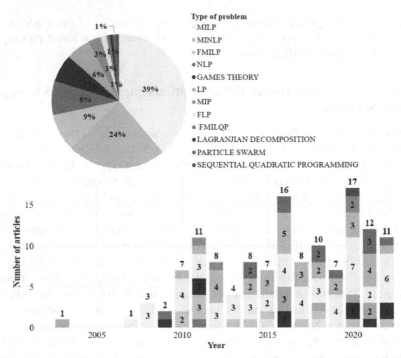

Fig. 5. Proportion and evolution in the use of the types of mathematical optimization problems in IS models.

to maximize the degree of satisfaction of the least satisfied participant, that is, their formulation is based in maximizing a single objective, with different fuzzy goals [39]. There are works that have developed resolution algorithms based on the use of two multi-objective optimization techniques such as lexicographic optimization for the generation of an augmented epsilon constraint method [40] as well as fuzzy optimization in conjunction with the epsilon constraint [41].

Objective Function Approaches. When analyzing the objective functions offered by each proposed IS optimization model, it is observed that the economic component has been widely used, when thinking about working with more than one component in the objective functions, the preference is to address the economic and environmental aspect as a whole, the sustainability approach in two (2) of the articles representing 1.2% of the total, little work being done on the optimization of IS networks. There is only one (1) item that works four of the components; economic, environmental, uncertainty and infrastructure representing 0.8% of the articles (see Fig. 9).

1. Economic objective functions. The objective functions of an economic nature worked on in the optimization of IS networks (see Fig. 10), are largely related to the minimization of the cost of the network, which generally involves the operation and operation costs of the plants, the purchase costs of virgin materials and off-grid energy, capital costs, environmental costs, among others. There are also objective functions focused on the maximization of utilities, profits and profits, on the maximization of

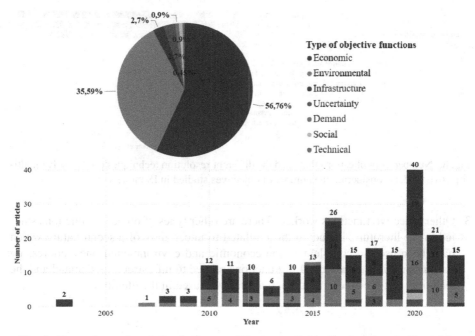

Fig. 6. Proportion and evolution in the use of the types of objective functions in IS models.

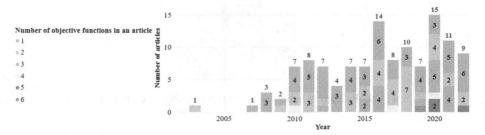

Fig. 7. Number of publications studying one or more objective functions per year.

the net present value (NPV) and the return on investment as an objective function of maximizing the profitability of the investments made, among others.

2. Environmental objective functions. These objective functions have been established in different ways (see Fig. 11), such as the minimization of resource consumption, the minimization of greenhouse gas emissions, the quantification of environmental impacts such as pollution or the depletion of resources. Finally, there are objectives associated with the minimization of emergy, seen as the accumulated energy that is used directly and indirectly to produce a product or service and as a novelty, objectives are formulated aimed at ensuring circularity and maximizing the number of flows between companies in search of ensuring the use of materials and residual energy that can be generated within the network [42].

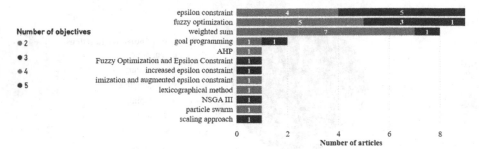

Fig. 8. Number of publications that used the different resolution techniques used to solve multi-objective models considering the number of objectives studied in IS models.

3. Other objective functions worked. There are other types of objective functions studied in the literature, including those related to uncertainty of a social nature which have been used to complement the economic and environmental ones, addressing the sustainability approach [43]. Functions related to infrastructure, demand and the technical part are other formulation alternatives used in the literature.

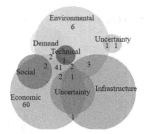

Fig. 9. Proportion in the use of the types of objective functions.

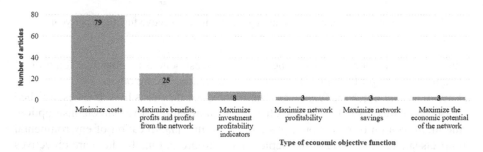

Fig. 10. Frequency of use of different objective functions belonging to the economic type.

Models that Address Uncertainty. Uncertainty is an inherent aspect in Is network optimization models given the complexity and variations that characterize the exchange of materials, information, the interaction of participants in these networks and other aspects of an external nature that are uncertain in decision making. Decisions, thus, of the total articles reviewed, it is found that approximately 23% use the concept of uncertainty from different approaches (see Fig. 12). Among these approaches is multiperiod optimization as the most used (50% of the total) [27, 44], stochastic optimization [45], sensitivity analysis [46], robust optimization [47], parametric robustness analysis [13] and the combination of the stochastic approach and robust optimization in a single model [48].

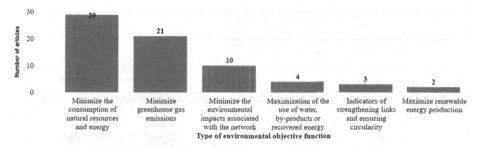

Fig. 11. Frequency of use of different objective functions belonging to the environmental type.

Game Theory-Based Models. Game theory has been applied from early stages in the mathematical models of optimization of IS networks, since it studies the conflict and cooperation that occurs in the interaction between two or more plants participating in said network [27].

Bio-Inspired Models. Recent studies have established bioinspired models, these are based on metrics that are defined in biology to study and measure the behaviors of nature [49].

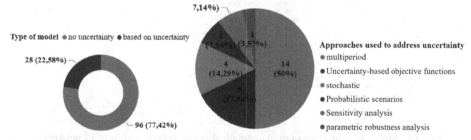

Fig. 12. Proportion of use of models that study uncertainty proportion of use of approaches to address uncertainty in the different models proposed.

Starting from Figs. 13, 14 and 15, It can be seen that both constraints and parameters and variables have been oriented towards establishing models of an economic nature, where flows or flow rates are calculated for the exchanges that are carried out respecting the laws of conservation of matter and energy, as well as the quality of the flows in

terms of contamination and where different characteristics or needs are established by
the plants so that they participate or exchange by-products, water or energy within the
network, making sure that the demands are satisfied and the processing and storage
capacities be respected. Finally, decisions related to the existence of processes and links
or connections between plants also play an important part in the modeling of IS networks.

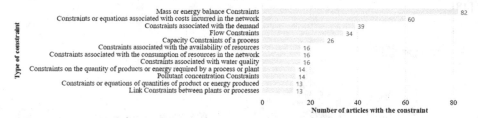

Fig. 13. Most used constraints in mathematical optimization models of IS networks.

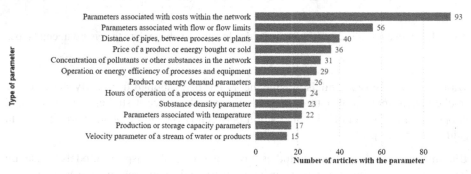

Fig. 14. Most used parameters in mathematical optimization models of IS networks.

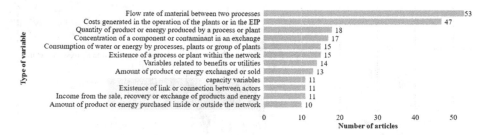

Fig. 15. Most used variables in in mathematical optimization models of IS networks.

4   Conclusions and Future Work

Over the years, the published articles have been oriented mainly to the establishment
of objective functions of an economic and environmental nature; however, under the
rise of the concept of sustainability, the opportunity is presented to cover the social

aspect with greater influence in the formulation. of future models in terms of access to new job opportunities, benefits that the community may have when interacting in IS models, among others, ensuring that there is a greater participation of the needs of the community in inter-company decision-making. To the previous point, the possibility of studying models of 4 or more objectives that integrate, among others, uncertainty components which allow addressing the complexity of the IS, infrastructure components to study the geographical location and other technical aspects and needs is added. of demand, this through alternatives such as metaheuristics, fuzzy optimization, AHP modeling integrated with mathematical modeling or the combination of these at different levels according to the level of complexity to be addressed. The formulation of bioinspired objective functions presents an opportunity in IS modeling and in general in industrial ecology, taking as a reference measures or indicators that have traditionally been studied in nature for their application in this type of models can be transcendental for the companies move closer to the closed loops offered by ecosystems. This can be complemented by the inclusion of behaviors that are studied in ecosystems in the design of IS networks and of resilient, robust and flexible formulations that have been studied in supply chains to deal with the presence of uncertainty.

The integration of the SI with traditional supply chains can be of great relevance in the design of supply chains with a circular or approximate circularity approach, where open cycles and closed cycles of generated waste are promoted [50]. It is also possible to work on having a greater participation by the community as an active participant of the SI and an exchange agent. On the other hand, the models may be increasingly oriented to study the exchanges between multiple companies from different sectors, where the exchanges of waste that include water, multiple by-products and energy, as well as the incorporation and feasibility study of emerging technologies oriented to better use of these residues. According to [51], as in ecosystems, if there is a link between enough separate elements in a complex system, a kind of spontaneous order occurs, so including more and more actors and exchanges in IS models can be beneficial for all participants if the complexity is adequately studied and developed, resulting in interactions and supply chains that in the future change the circular paradigm towards one of an ecosystem nature.

References

1. Chertow, M.R.: Industrials Ymbiosis: Literature. Annu. Rev. Energy Environ. **25**, 313–337 (2000)
2. Jacobsen, N.B.: Industrial symbiosis in Kalundborg, Denmark: A quantitative assessment of economic and environmental aspects. J. Ind. Ecol. **10**(1–2), 239–255 (2006). https://doi.org/10.1162/108819806775545411
3. Mengist, W., Soromessa, T., Legese, G.: Method for conducting systematic literature review and meta-analysis for environmental science research. MethodsX **7**, 100777 (2020). https://doi.org/10.1016/j.mex.2019.100777
4. Ramin, E., et al.: Incremental design of water symbiosis networks with prior knowledge: the case of an industrial park in Kenya. Sci. Total Environ. **751** (Jan. 2021). https://doi.org/10.1016/j.scitotenv.2020.141706

5. Jain, S., Chin, H.H., Bandyopadhyay, S., Klemeš, J.J.: Clustering and optimising regional segregated resource allocation networks. J. Environ. Manage. **322** (Nov. 2022). https://doi.org/10.1016/j.jenvman.2022.116030

6. Salas, D., Van, K.C., Aussel, D., Montastruc, L.: Optimal design of exchange networks with blind inputs and its application to Eco-industrial parks. Comput. Chem. Eng. **143** (Dec. 2020). https://doi.org/10.1016/j.compchemeng.2020.107053

7. Rubio-Castro, E., Ponce-Ortega, J.M., Serna-González, M., El-Halwagi, M.M., Pham, V.: Global optimization in property-based interplant water integration. AIChE J. **59**(3), 813–833 (2013). https://doi.org/10.1002/aic.13874. Mar.

8. Alnouri, S.Y., Linke, P., El-Halwagi, M.: A synthesis approach for industrial city water reuse networks considering central and distributed treatment systems. J. Clean. Prod. **89**, 231–250 (2015). https://doi.org/10.1016/j.jclepro.2014.11.005. Feb.

9. Bishnu, S., Linke, P., Alnouri, S., El-Halwagi, M.: Multi-period water network synthesis for eco industrial parks considering regeneration and reuse. Chem. Prod. Process. Model. (2017). https://doi.org/10.1515/cppm-2016-0049

10. O'Dwyer, E., Chen, K., Wang, H., Wang, A., Shah, N., Guo, M.: Optimisation of wastewater treatment strategies in eco-industrial parks: Technology, location and transport. Chem. Eng. J. **381**(March 2019), 122643 (2020). https://doi.org/10.1016/j.cej.2019.122643

11. Alnouri, S.Y., Linke, P., El-Halwagi, M.M.: Synthesis of industrial park water reuse networks considering treatment systems and merged connectivity options. Comput. Chem. Eng. **91**, 289–306 (2016). https://doi.org/10.1016/j.compchemeng.2016.02.003. Jul.

12. Zhang, K., Malone, S.M., Bras, B., Weissburg, M., Zhao, Y., Cao, H.: Ecologically inspired water network optimization of steel manufacture using constructed wetlands as a wastewater treatment process. Engineering **4**(4), 567–573 (2018). https://doi.org/10.1016/j.eng.2018.07.007

13. Huang, L., Zhen, L., Yin, L.: Waste material recycling and exchanging decisions for industrial symbiosis network optimization. J. Clean. Prod. **276**, 124073 (2020). https://doi.org/10.1016/j.jclepro.2020.124073

14. Pan, M., Sikorski, J., Akroyd, J., Mosbach, S., Lau, R., Kraft, M.: Design technologies for eco-industrial parks: From unit operations to processes, plants and industrial networks. Appl. Energy **175**, 305–323 (2016). https://doi.org/10.1016/j.apenergy.2016.05.019

15. Somoza-Tornos, A., Pozo, C., Graells, M., Espuña, A., Puigjaner, L.: Process screening framework for the synthesis of process networks from a circular economy perspective. Resour. Conserv. Recycl. **164** (Jan. 2021). https://doi.org/10.1016/j.resconrec.2020.105147

16. Lessard, J.M., Habert, G., Tagnit-Hamou, A., Amor, B.: A time-series material-product chain model extended to a multiregional industrial symbiosis: The case of material circularity in the cement sector. Ecol. Econ. **179** (Jan. 2021). https://doi.org/10.1016/j.ecolecon.2020.106872

17. Abraham, E.J., Al-Mohannadi, D.M., Linke, P.: Resource integration of industrial parks over time. Comput. Chem. Eng. **164** (Aug. 2022). https://doi.org/10.1016/j.compchemeng.2022.107886

18. Ahmed, R.O., Al-Mohannadi, D.M., Linke, P.: Multi-objective resource integration for sustainable industrial clusters. J. Clean. Prod. **316** (Sep. 2021). https://doi.org/10.1016/j.jclepro.2021.128237

19. Alnouri, S.Y., Linke, P., El-Halwagi, M.M.: Accounting for central and distributed zero liquid discharge options in interplant water network design. J. Clean. Prod. **171**, 644–661 (2018). https://doi.org/10.1016/j.jclepro.2017.09.236. Jan.

20. Misrol, M.A., Wan Alwi, S.R., Lim, J.S., Manan, Z.A.: An optimal resource recovery of biogas, water regeneration, and reuse network integrating domestic and industrial sources. J. Clean. Prod. **286** (Mar. 2021). https://doi.org/10.1016/j.jclepro.2020.125372

21. Cimren, E., Fiksel, J., Posner, M.E., Sikdar, K.: Material flow optimization in by-product synergy networks. J. Ind. Ecol. **15**(2), 315–332 (2011). https://doi.org/10.1111/j.1530-9290. 2010.00310.x

22. Karayılan, S., Yılmaz, Ö., Uysal, Ç., Naneci, S.: Prospective evaluation of circular economy practices within plastic packaging value chain through optimization of life cycle impacts and circularity. Resour. Conserv. Recycl. **173** (Oct. 2021). https://doi.org/10.1016/j.rescon rec.2021.105691

23. Wang, Q., Tang, H., Qiu, S., Yuan, X., Zuo, J.: Robustness of eco-industrial symbiosis network: a case study of China. Environ. Sci. Pollut. Res. **25**(27), 27203–27213 (2018). https://doi.org/ 10.1007/s11356-018-2764-x

24. Affery, A.P., et al.: Optimal planning of inter-plant hydrogen integration (IPHI) in eco-industrial park with P-graph and game theory analyses. Process. Saf. Environ. Prot. **155**, 197–218 (2021). https://doi.org/10.1016/j.psep.2021.08.016. Nov.

25. Zhang, A., Du, Z., Wang, Z.: Carbon reduction from sustainable consumption of waste resources: An optimal model for collaboration in an industrial symbiotic network. J. Clean. Prod. **196**, 821–828 (2018). https://doi.org/10.1016/j.jclepro.2018.06.135. Sep.

26. Bütün, H., Kantor, I., Maréchal, F.: Incorporating location aspects in process integration methodology. Energies **12**(17) (Aug. 2019). https://doi.org/10.3390/en12173338

27. Galvan-Cara, A.L., Graells, M., Espuña, A.: Application of industrial symbiosis principles to the management of utility networks. Appl. Energy **305** (Jan. 2022). https://doi.org/10.1016/ j.apenergy.2021.117734

28. Afshari, H., Tosarkani, B.M., Jaber, M.Y., Searcy, C.: The effect of environmental and social value objectives on optimal design in industrial energy symbiosis: a multi-objective approach. Resour. Conserv. Recycl. **158**(December 2019), 104825 (2020). https://doi.org/10.1016/j.res conrec.2020.104825

29. Meneghetti, A., Nardin, G.: Enabling industrial symbiosis by a facilities management optimization approach. J. Clean. Prod. **35**, 263–273 (2012). https://doi.org/10.1016/j.jclepro.2012. 06.002

30. Hipólito-Valencia, A.J., Rubio-Castro, E., Ponce-Ortega, J.M., Serna-González, M., Nápoles-Rivera, F., El-Halwagi, M.M.: Optimal design of inter-plant waste energy integration. Appl. Therm. Eng. **62**(2), 633–652 (2014). https://doi.org/10.1016/j.applthermaleng.2013.10.015

31. Chan, W.M., Leong, Y.T., Foo, J.J., Chew, I.M.L.: Synthesis of energy efficient chilled and cooling water network by integrating waste heat recovery refrigeration system. Energy **141**, 1555–1568 (2017). https://doi.org/10.1016/j.energy.2017.11.056. Dec.

32. Mousqué, F., Boix, M., Montastruc, L., Domenech, S., Négny, S.: Optimal design of eco-industrial parks with coupled energy networks addressing complexity bottleneck through an interdependence analysis. Comput. Chem. Eng. **138**, 106859 (2020). https://doi.org/10.1016/ j.compchemeng.2020.106859

33. Yeşilkaya, M., Daş, G.S., Türker, A.K.: A multi-objective multi-period mathematical model for an industrial symbiosis network based on the forest products industry. Comput. Ind. Eng. **150**(October, 2020). https://doi.org/10.1016/j.cie.2020.106883

34. Al-Quradaghi, S., Zheng, Q.P., Betancourt-Torcat, A., Elkamel, A.: Optimization model for sustainable end-of-life vehicle processing and recycling. Sustain **14**(6) (Mar. 2022). https:// doi.org/10.3390/su14063551

35. Cao, X., Wen, Z., Xu, J., De Clercq, D., Wang, Y., Tao, Y.: Many-objective optimization of technology implementation in the industrial symbiosis system based on a modified NSGA-III. J. Clean. Prod. **245**, 118810 (2020). https://doi.org/10.1016/j.jclepro.2019.118810

36. Fouladi, J., AlNouss, A., Al-Ansari, T.: Sustainable energy-water-food nexus integration and optimisation in eco-industrial parks. Comput. Chem. Eng. **146**, 107229 (2021). https://doi. org/10.1016/j.compchemeng.2021.107229

37. Misrol, M.A., Alwi, S.R.W., Lim, J.S., Manan, Z.A.: Multi-objective optimization of an integrated energy-water-waste nexus for eco-industrial park. Chem. Eng. Trans. **89**(June), 349–354 (2021). https://doi.org/10.3303/CET2189059

38. Goh, Q.H., Farouk, A.A., Chew, I.M.L.: Optimizing the bioplastic chemical building block with wastewater sludge as the feedstock using carbon-hydrogen-oxygen framework. Resour. Conserv. Recycl. **176** (Jan. 2022). https://doi.org/10.1016/j.resconrec.2021.105920

39. Tan, Y.D., Lim, J.S., Wan Alwi, S.R.: Multi-objective optimal design for integrated palm oil mill complex with consideration of effluent elimination. Energy **202** (2020). https://doi.org/10.1016/j.energy.2020.117767

40. Kolluri, S.S., Esfahani, I.J., Yoo, C.K.: Robust fuzzy and multi-objective optimization approaches to generate alternate solutions for resource conservation of eco-industrial park involving various future events. Process Saf. Environ. Prot. **103**(Part B), 424–441 (Sep. 2016). https://doi.org/10.1016/j.psep.2016.06.001

41. Tan, Y.D., Lim, J.S., Andiappan, V., Wan Alwi, S.R.: Systematic optimisation framework for a sustainable multi-owner palm oil-based complex. Energy **261** (Dec. 2022). https://doi.org/10.1016/j.energy.2022.125136

42. Dave, T., Layton, A.: Designing ecologically-inspired robustness into a water distribution network. J. Clean. Prod. **254** (May 2020). https://doi.org/10.1016/j.jclepro.2020.120057

43. Afshari, H., Tosarkani, B.M., Jaber, M.Y., Searcy, C.: The effect of environmental and social value objectives on optimal design in industrial energy symbiosis: a multi-objective approach. Resour. Conserv. Recycl. **158** (Jul. 2020). https://doi.org/10.1016/j.resconrec.2020.104825

44. Kachacha, A., Farhat, A., Zoughaib, A., Tran, C.T.: Site wide heat integration in eco-industrial parks considering variable operating conditions. Comput. Chem. Eng. **126**, 304–320 (2019). https://doi.org/10.1016/j.compchemeng.2019.04.013. Jul.

45. Gonela, V., Zhang, J., Osmani, A.: Stochastic optimization of sustainable industrial symbiosis based hybrid generation bioethanol supply chains. Comput. Ind. Eng. **87**, 40–65 (2015). https://doi.org/10.1016/j.cie.2015.04.025

46. Afshari, H., Farel, R., Peng, Q.: Challenges of value creation in Eco-Industrial Parks (EIPs): A stakeholder perspective for optimizing energy exchanges. Resour. Conserv. Recycl. **139**, 315–325 (2018). https://doi.org/10.1016/j.resconrec.2018.09.002. Dec.

47. Aviso, K.B.: Design of robust water exchange networks for eco-industrial symbiosis. Process. Saf. Environ. Prot. **92**(2), 160–170 (2014). https://doi.org/10.1016/j.psep.2012.12.001. Mar.

48. Afshari, H., Farel, R., Peng, Q.: Improving the resilience of energy flow exchanges in eco-industrial parks: Optimization under uncertainty. ASCE-ASME J. Risk Uncertain. Eng. Syst. Part B Mech. Eng. (2017). https://doi.org/10.1115/1.4035729

49. Genc, O., Kurt, A., Yazan, D.M., Erdis, E.: Circular eco-industrial park design inspired by nature: an integrated non-linear optimization, location, and food web analysis. J. Environ. Manage. **270** (Sep. 2020). https://doi.org/10.1016/j.jenvman.2020.110866

50. Farooque, M., Zhang, A., Thürer, M., Qu, T., Huisingh, D.: Circular supply chain management: a definition and structured literature review. J. Clean. Prod. **228**, 882–900 (2019). https://doi.org/10.1016/j.jclepro.2019.04.303

51. Daly, H.E., Farley, J.: Ecological Economics, Second Edition: Principles and Applications (2004)

Simulation

Static and Dynamic Electrical Characterization of Flexible Photovoltaic Panels for Optimization of Their Performance

Fernanda de Carvalho Cirilo and Mariana Amorim Fraga(✉) (iD)

Escola de Engenharia, Universidade Presbiteriana Mackenzie, São Paulo, Brazil
mafraga@ieee.org

Abstract. Flexible photovoltaic panels, also known as thin-film solar panels, have gained attention in recent years due to their unique characteristics and potential applications in emerging fields such as wearable technology. This article reports an experimental study with the aim of analyzing the static and dynamic electrical behavior of three types of flexible photovoltaic panels, namely amorphous silicon (a-Si), copper indium gallium diselenide (CIGS) and organic photovoltaic (OPV). The dynamic measurements were performed using a two-axis solar tracker. The prototype of solar tracker was carefully designed, including the design of the 3D model of the parts of the system and the electronic circuit, created in the Tinkercad software. The tracker logic was implemented using the C + + language, resulting in a simple but functional code to maximize the solar trajectory. The static and dynamic electrical results obtained provide a comprehensive view of the performance of the flexible photovoltaic panels and can help to optimize their use.

Keywords: Solar Energy · Flexible Photovoltaic Panels · Solar Tracker

1 Introduction

Solar energy is a promising renewable source that holds great potential for diversifying the global energy mix. However, the widespread adoption of solar power faces still technical and economic challenges. These challenges encompass the efficiency of solar or photovoltaic panels, their durability, manufacturing costs, and deployment strategies [1, 2]. Currently, photovoltaic panels (PV) can be classified based on four main criteria, as shown in Fig. 1. These classifications help in understanding the different types of photovoltaic panels available in the market and their specific characteristics, which can assist in selecting the most suitable panel for specific applications or requirements.

In terms of material type, the commercial market has classified the photovoltaic panels into panels made from crystalline silicon, such as monocrystalline and polycrystalline silicon panels, and thin-film panels made using thin-film semiconductor materials, such as amorphous silicon (a-Si), cadmium telluride (CdTe), copper indium gallium selenide (CIGS), etc. There is also a new and promising technology in the solar industry, which are the panels made using perovskite [3].

© The Author(s), under exclusive license to Springer Nature Switzerland AG 2023
J. C. Figueroa-García et al. (Eds.): WEA 2023, CCIS 1928, pp. 353–361, 2023.
https://doi.org/10.1007/978-3-031-46739-4_31

In addition to the type of material, photovoltaic panels are also classified according to their efficiency into three categories: (i) high-efficiency panels with higher conversion efficiency above 20%, which includes the monocrystalline silicon panels and some advanced technologies (heterojunction and multi-junction cells), (ii) standard-efficiency panels, between 15% and 20%, which includes most polycrystalline panels and (iii) low-efficiency panels, with lower conversion efficiency below 15%, which generally include thin-film panels [4].

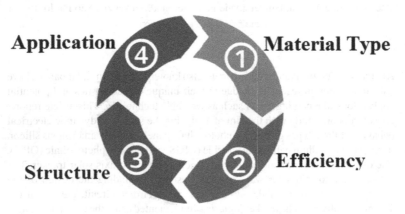

Fig. 1. Main classification criteria of photovoltaic panels (PV)

Another classification of photovoltaic panels is based on their structure and divides them into rigid panels, which are typically installed on rooftops or ground-mounted systems, and flexible panels that are lightweight and can be bent or curved, allowing for applications on irregular surfaces or flexible structures.

There is also a classification based on the application. Photovoltaic panels designed for residential installations, typically smaller in size and power output. Panels suitable for commercial and industrial installations often larger in size and power output. Large-scale panels used in utility-scale solar power plants, capable of generating high amounts of electricity [5].

In this study, our focus is on the flexible photovoltaic panels, also known as thin-film solar panels, due to their outstanding characteristics namely, versatility, lightweight, portability and durability [6]. Among their benefits, it can be highlighted that they can be integrated into a wide range of applications, including building facades, curved structures, vehicles, mobile solar power systems for camping or remote locations, and even clothing. Furthermore, these panels can withstand certain types of impacts and vibrations better than rigid panels. They are less prone to cracking or breaking under stress, which can be beneficial in environments with dynamic conditions, such as on moving vehicles or in areas prone to seismic activity [7]. It been shown that the use de flexible PV opens opportunities for innovative solar energy solutions.

On the other hand, there are still drawbacks associated to flexible photovoltaic such as lower efficiency compared to rigid crystalline silicon, a shorter lifespan compared to rigid panels and relatively higher cost than those of traditional panels.

One way to maximize the solar irradiation is using solar trackers, which are designed to maintain the solar panel's position as close to perpendicular to its plane as possible. This positioning strategy enhances energy capture efficiency throughout the year [8].

In solar energy systems, a single-axis solar tracker is employed to orient and position solar panels in a specific direction, aligning with the apparent movement of the sun throughout the day [9]. It operates along a single axis, often utilizing a horizontal rotating mechanism, enabling the solar panels to rotate and track the sun's path in the sky. This continuous movement maximizes the solar panels' exposure to direct sunlight, resulting in increased energy capture efficiency and enhanced electricity or solar heating production.

Alternatively, a dual-axis solar tracker employs two independent movements to continuously adjust the position of solar panels throughout the day [10]. The azimuth axis facilitates horizontal movement, ensuring alignment with the sun's apparent motion, while the elevation axis allows for vertical adjustment to track the sun's height in the sky. This comprehensive tracking system further optimizes solar panel positioning, enhancing the overall efficiency of energy capture.

This article investigates the electrical characteristics of fixed and mobile flexible photovoltaic panels of a-Si, CIGS and OPV using current-voltage (I-V) measurements. The conversion efficiency and power of the flexible panels are analyzed under different conditions. The goal is determining how to make these panels as efficient as possible with minimal losses. In addition, the impact of the use of a solar tracker on the performance of the flexible panels is also evaluated.

2   Experimental Procedure

In order to perform the static and dynamic electrical analysis of flexible photovoltaic panels, the methodology adopted includes from the research market of these panels to development of a solar tracker prototype.

2.1   Selection of the Materials

After a survey of the types of flexible panels available on the market and the analysis of their datasheets, the following small flexible panels were selected: amorphous silicon (a-Si), copper indium gallium selenide (CIGS), and organic photovoltaic (OPV). Figure 2 shows the used panels.

The a-Si and CIGS were purchased, while the OPV was made available by Institute of Energy and Environment of the University of São Paulo (IEE-USP).

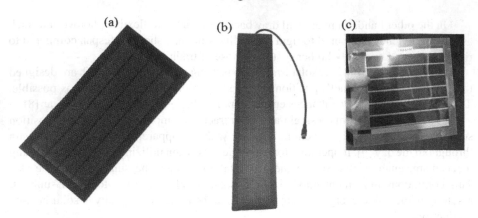

Fig. 2. Flexible photovoltaic panels used: (a) a-Si, (b) CIGS and (c) OPV

2.2 Development of the Solar Tracker

The prototype of a dual-axis solar tracker was designed using Tinkercad software. The goal was to develop a portable, lightweight, and cost-effective system, considering the small dimensions and lightness of the flexible panels that would be tested in this study.

Table 1. Costs for construction of the prototype of solar tracker.

Component	Quantity	Unit cost (USD)	Total cost (USD)
Servo motor	2	4	8
Arduino Uno R3 with Cable	1	15	15
LDR Sensor	4	0.2	0.8
Set of wire Jumpers Male-Male	1	1.5	1.5
Set of wire Jumpers Male-female	1	1.5	1.5
Set of screws and threads	1	0.75	0.75
3M tape	1	1.0	1.5
3D printing costs	-	20	20

After the successful dimensioning of the 3D design, the printing of each solar tracker component was carried out at the Production Engineering Laboratory of Mackenzie Presbyterian University. Subsequently, a simple assembly was carried out by fitting, gluing, and screwing the components together, as needed. Table 1 lists the costs of the components of the solar tracker. Figure 3 shows the printed 3D model and the electronic circuit with Arduino, two servo motors and four Light Dependent Resistor (LDR) sensors.

In the programming logic used in this solar tracker, the LDR sensors will be used at the ends of panel support base, separated in a cross by two buses, in order to collect data and so that the data is executed and applied to the programming logic in C + + applied to Arduino, in order to maximize the direction of the board along the path of the sun during the day.

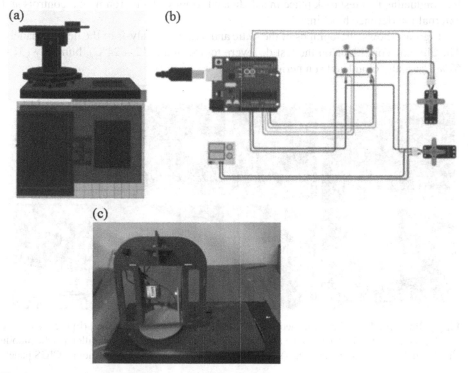

Fig. 3. Design of the solar tracker: (a) 3D model, (b) simulation of the electronic circuit in Tinkercad and (c) photograph of the developed solar tracker

2.3 Electrical Measurements

The I-V characteristic curve is an essential tool for evaluating the efficiency and maximum power of a photovoltaic panel. The key points of the curve are the short-circuit current (I_{SC}), open-circuit voltage (V_{OC}), and the maximum power point (P_{max}), which indicates the highest electrical power that the panel can generate under certain conditions.

Furthermore, characteristic curves are useful for sizing photovoltaic systems and determining the optimal panel arrangement. Temperature and irradiance variations also affect the curves, making their analysis important for understanding the panel's operating condition under different weather conditions.

One of the difficulties encountered with amorphous silicon (a-Si) and OPV flexible panels is the lack of a datasheet with technical specifications for proper practical analysis. Therefore, for these panels, I-V Curve characterization tests were conducted at the Laboratory of Photovoltaic Systems of the IEE-USP.

The I-V curve test performed with the PASAN solar simulator involves applying a variable voltage to a semiconductor device while measuring the corresponding current. These values are then plotted on a graph, forming the I-V curve. From this curve, it is possible to analyze electrical properties of the device such as efficiency. Preparations for conducting this test took place in a dedicated room with environmental controls and external interference blocking.

Figure 4 shows photographs of the static and dynamic analysis of the flexible panels. The climatic conditions on the test day were temperature (12 ~ 24°C), humidity (37 ~ 67%), partially cloud and sun period (6:42 am ~ 5:27 pm).

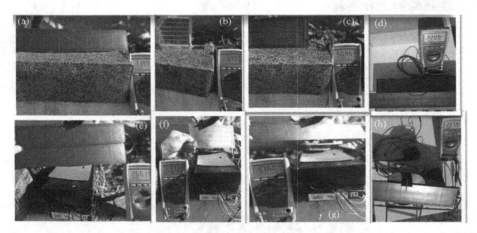

Fig. 4. Photographs of the performed I-V tests for: (a) the fixed CIGS panel, (b) the fixed OPV panel, (c) the fixed a-Si panel, (d) the two fixed CIGS panels connected in parallel, (e) the mobile CIGS panels connected in parallel, (f) the mobile a-Si panel, (g) and (h) the mobile CIGS panel.

3   Results and Discussion

Figure 5 shows the I-V Curve characterization tests for the a-Si and OPV panels obtained using the PASAN solar simulator.

From the I-V curve characterization, it was possible to complete Table 2. This table is an essential tool for the comparison among the main characteristics of the flexible panels and they will be used as a reference for the experimental analysis. The CIGS panel data was maintained as provided in the datasheet of the panel manufacturer Jiang Solar.

In the tests carried out with the fixed static system and the dynamic system using a two-axis solar tracker, the data were collected following the procedure described in Sect. 2.3. As can be observed in Fig. 6, the three types of flexible panels showed the maximum current between the period from 1:00 pm to 2:00 pm, at this time the temperature was close to 24 °C, with full sun.

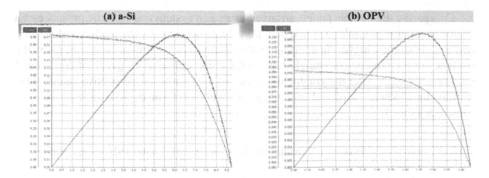

Fig. 5. The I-V characteristics obtained using the PASAN solar simulator.

Table 2. Characteristics of the used flexible photovoltaic panels

Type of panel	a-Si	OPV	CIGS
Size (m x m)	0.19 x 0.10	0.10 x 0.102	0.38 x 0.07
Maximum power (W)	0.862	0.134	2.0
Maximum voltage (V)	6.087	2.287	9.0
Maximum current (A)	0.142	0.058	0.32
Efficiency (%)	17.95	1.25	10

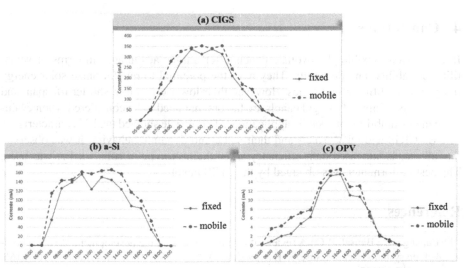

Fig. 6. Graphs of current (mA) behavior of each type of flexible panel as a function of time/radiation

Comparing the flexible panels arranged in a fixed system and with the presence of a solar tracker, it is possible to notice that the voltage obtained by the tracker system with two-axes is slightly higher. In addition, both systems exhibit similar behavior, given the tendency of the presence of straight lines in the construction of the graph of current and radiation per hour. After the graphical analysis of the results, the respective calculations of maximum power (Wp) and efficiency (%) were performed, making it possible to construct Table 3.

Table 3. Results obtained for each one flexible panel analyzed on static and dynamic conditions.

Parameter	a-Si (fixed)	a-Si (mobile)	CIGS (fixed)	CIGS (mobile)	OPV (fixed)	OPV (mobile)
V_{oc} (V)	8.24	8.22	9.14	9.15	2.82	3
I_{sc} (A)	0.144	0.167	0.313	0.353	0.167	0.168
Maximum power (W)	1.187	1.373	2.861	3.23	0.471	0.504
Irradiance (W/m^2)	1000	1000	1000	1000	1000	1000
Efficiency (%)	6.2	7.2	10.8	12.1	4.4	4.7

Analyzing the results obtained, it is possible to observe that the better gain efficiency using the solar tracker was of 1.3% in the CIGS panel and the smaller gain of 0.3% was presented in the OPV panel.

4   Conclusions

In conclusion, flexible photovoltaic panels offer unique advantages in terms of versatility, portability, and durability. They have the potential to revolutionize solar energy integration in different industries. However, their lower efficiency, shorter lifespan, and higher costs compared to rigid panels are factors that need to be considered when evaluating their suitability for specific applications. This article showed the I-V characteristics of a-Si, CIGS and OPV panels and their static and dynamic behavior. It was observed that all panels increased their efficiency when the prototype of solar tracker was used. The best performance was obtained by the CIGS panel.

References

1. Lupangu, C., Bansal, R.C.: A review of technical issues on the development of solar photovoltaic systems. Renew. Sustain. Energy Rev. **73**, 950–965 (2017). https://doi.org/10.1016/j.rser.2017.02.003
2. Mrinalini, M., Islavath, N., Prasanthkumar, S., Giribabu, L.: Stipulating low production cost solar cells all set to retail...! Chem. Rec. **19**(2–3), 661–674 (2018). https://doi.org/10.1002/tcr.201800106
3. Mutalikdesai, A., Ramasesha, S.K.: Emerging solar technologies: perovskite solar cell. Resonance **22**(11), 1061–1083 (2017). https://doi.org/10.1007/s12045-017-0571-1

4. Lee, T.D., Ebong, A.U.: A review of thin film solar cell technologies and challenges. Renew. Sustain. Energy Rev. **70**, 1286–1297 (2017). https://doi.org/10.1016/j.rser.2016.12.028. April
5. Mohammad Bagher, A.: Types of solar cells and application. American J. Opti. Photo. **3**(5), 94 (2015). https://doi.org/10.11648/j.ajop.20150305.17
6. Tsang, M.P., Sonnemann, G.W., Bassani, D.M.: Life-cycle assessment of cradle-to-grave opportunities and environmental impacts of organic photovoltaic solar panels compared to conventional technologies. Sol. Ener. Mater. Sol. Cells **156**, 37–48 (2016). https://doi.org/10.1016/j.solmat.2016.04.024
7. Araki, K., Ji, L., Kelly, G., Yamaguchi, M.: To do list for research and development and international standardization to achieve the goal of running a majority of electric vehicles on solar energy. Coatings **8**(7), 251 (2018). https://doi.org/10.3390/coatings8070251
8. Ramful, R., Sowaruth, N.: Low-cost solar tracker to maximize the capture of solar energy in tropical countries. Energy Rep. **8**, 295–302 (2022). https://doi.org/10.1016/j.egyr.2022.10.145
9. Mehdi, G., Ali, N., Hussain, S., Zaidi, AA., Shah, A.H., Mustafa Azeem, M.: Design and fabrication of automatic single axis solar tracker for solar panel. In: 2019 2nd International Conference on Computing, Mathematics and Engineering Technologies (ICoMET) (January 2019). https://doi.org/10.1109/icomet.2019.8673496
10. Hammoumi, A.E., Motahhir, S., Ghzizal, A.E., Chalh, A., Derouich, A.: A simple and low-cost active dual-axis solar tracker. Energy Science & Engineering **6**(5), 607–20 (2018). https://doi.org/10.1002/ese3.236

Rural Migration in Colombia

Germán Méndez-Giraldo$^{(\boxtimes)}$ (iD), Carolina Suárez-Rendón,
and Michelle González-Velasco

Universidad Distrital F. J. C, Bogotá, Colombia
gmendez@udistrital.edu.co

Abstract. All over the world, various governments have made their own and collective efforts to improve economic, social and environmental conditions, that tend
to a world that, despite the limitations, is more sustainable. However, close to 1
billion people continue to live in conditions of extreme poverty, 80% suffer chronic
hunger, and 281 million people have suffered from difficult migratory processes.
Latin American countries contribute about 12% of these flows; this phenomenon
brings misery and pain to people and their families, increases other social problems
such as insecurity, violence and higher levels of street-begging. According to the
World Migration Report for the year 2022, Colombia has been the main recipient
of the migrants from Venezuela with near to 1.7 million people. But internal displacement in Colombia due to conflict and violence continued to intensify in 2021,
with more than 27,000 people displaced only in the first quarter of the year. There
are some types of migration, with rural migration being one of the most important
to study, because, in addition to creating multiple social phenomena, it is harming
agricultural activities that are essential for food sustainability. The methodology
proposed by the ARCOSES Research Group was implemented; where the variables and indicators were raised in aspects such as insecurity, well-being, economic activities, mainly. This made it possible to identify that Colombia must
seek greater comprehensive development of rural municipalities, to avoid massive
displacements to urban regions that affect the availability of rural labor and collat-
erally the issues of agricultural production and food sustainability. To guarantee
full access and rural develop, prompt and assertive governmental intervention by
the Colombian state is required.

Keywords: Dynamic Simulation · Rural Migration · Rural Well-being · Food
Security

1 Introduction

The problem of migration is of a global order, caused by multiple factors, where poverty,
violence and environmental effects stand out and where the economic effects are the
most important, [1]. An example of the above is presented in the African region, as
referred in [2], in the case of the mass exodus in Zimbabwe, due in part to the economic
crisis and the negative political climate, added to other affectations as stated by [3],
such as climate change and which may be due to rapid-onset events such as floods,

J. C. Figueroa-García et al. (Eds.): WEA 2023, CCIS 1928, pp. 362–375, 2023.
https://doi.org/10.1007/978-3-031-46739-4_32

storms and hurricanes; or slow onset events such as droughts and land degradation. The consequences corm circumstances like these can range from internal to external mobility and from seasonal displacement to definitive resettlement. According to the United Nations in South Africa they project that by 2030, 71.3% of the population will live in urban areas, as many people have abandoned rural areas to find new sources of employment, better educational facilities and relevant medical care. This case is an example of the worrying situation of the future of the rural areas of the region, [4]. But this is not a particular problem of Africa, is a generalized situation in different regions such as in China where rural migrants still have difficulties accessing the civil and social welfare that is only provided to their urban habitants. Many researchers pointed to the lack of institutional protection within the rural work environment as cause of the increase of rural migrants, [5]. Other theories have been built around the phenomenon of rural-urban migration, such as rational individual choice based on cost-benefit relationships, which occurs as a response to the risks derived from agricultural production, or the theory of social network indicating that it is better to live with relates who have been migrants before, [6].

Some causes may be historical, such as the transcontinental migrations that Latin America suffered from colonial times, to the massive migrations after the two world wars. This is a region full of apparent contradictions, since it is the most diverse yet most culturally homogeneous land in the world; it has the highest crime and homicide rates, but the lowest levels of civil wars, holocausts and other forms of mob violence. It has the highest levels of social inequality but also the historically most egalitarian areas, [7]. Of course, not all effects of migration are without negatives for example [8] and [9] express how extremely poor rural households can gain a lot by temporarily relocating to urban areas due to migration subsidies and compensatory action due to higher wages earned by immigrants. This is ratified in [10], where remittances and the development of a country are closely related, as is the case of Indonesia, these become a possible solution and economic development, especially in its rural areas. However, this social phenomenon has brought multiple and varied consequences, it becomes a threat to food security and hinders the achievement of sustainable development goals, [11].

In Colombia, according to the Administrative Department of National Statistics (ADNS), migration is referred to as the geographic movement of people across a specific international border or an internal political-administrative boundary (for example, departments and municipalities) to establish a new habitual residence, [12]. This report indicates that only in three departments of Colombia register a few less than a million of emigrant people. The displacement of people due to violence has affected 90% of the country's municipalities, either by expulsion or by reception of this population, being a force of internally displaced persons who are in a greater degree of vulnerability due to the loss of land, housing and employment opportunities; between 20 and 26% of medium-sized cities have received these internally displaced persons, who in a few years amounted to 20% of their population [13]. In general, the main factors behind IDPs are their exposure to violent events with the objectives of acquiring possession of the land and natural resources to strengthen illegal logging, illegal crops or the increase in livestock; activities that have been associated with ecological changes such as deforestation, [13]. According to the World Migration Report, violence in Colombia, driven in part by territorial control exercised by paramilitary groups, resulted in more than 100,000 new displacements in 2020, [14].

2 Material and Methods

Given the complexity of the system under study, it uses the methodology described in [12]. The structure is showed in Fig. 1, it is composed of three major stages of knowledge acquisition, knowledge representation and decision making. These are described below.

2.1 Knowledge Acquisition Stage

The first item is to state the problem of interest, in this case is to study the phenomenon of rural migration for Colombia. It is review aspects as resources assigned to rural municipalities, availability of employ sources, access to services for rural residents, problems of food availability and decrease in income from agricultural activities. It is intended to develop a simulation model that allows to represent the social problem of rural migration and formulate strategies to guarantee that it is no irreversible problem in the future. A total of 190 bibliographical sources were analyzed, some of them are the most important institution who are worked in this topic as: Latin American and Caribbean Economic Association, World Bank, United Nations Development Program, Food and Agriculture Organization of the United Nations, mainly. In Colombian context were reviewed documents of organizations as: Mission for the design of a strategy for the reduction of poverty and inequality, District Planning Administrative Department, National Planning Department, Colombian Confederation of NGOs, Centro of Research for Development.

The review consisted of 35 experts' documents, between nationals and foreigners, taking into account as a reference their writings on different topics such as: employment, social conflict in rural areas, rural migration, health and education services, government policies, the role of State as a fundamental actor for sustainable development, violence and environmental impact in rural areas. A total of 910 causes were obtained, which were categorized by affinity into 69 selected causes according to the topic relevance, as well as grouping by similar names.

As is the case in [15], where they describe an analysis of the impact of development support for the well-being of small Hungarian regions, another key issue is migration from rural to urban areas as observed in China, the importance of agricultural activity is also highlighted, being one of the most important and most dynamically developing sectors of the economy for reducing migration. Considering the aforementioned, a problem is currently occurring in the Colombian rural is migration of the rural population to the urban areas due to the lack of food, the lack of opportunities, deficient health and education services; and general to disperse from situations of vulnerability induced by poverty. This brings many negative consequences as poor coverage in food security, unsustainable agriculture and rural development, because the deficiency of agricultural labor brings effects on less agricultural production [16].

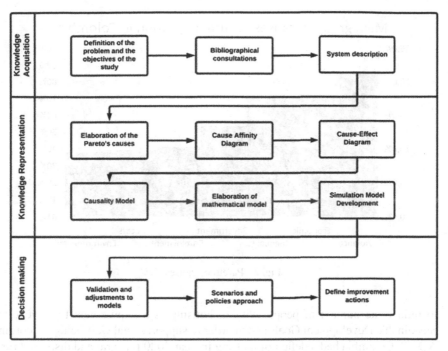

Fig. 1. Methodology used (Taken from the ARCOSES Research Group)

2.2 Knowledge Representation Stage

First activity is the definition of the type of municipality, because is necessary to include as a filter of analysis. Regarding the individual causes, about 880 citations were analyzed, housing variable is cause with most weight in relation to Colombian migration (5.1%), other related variables such as dispossession, loss of their land, quality of housing, services and infrastructure among the main ones. Second cause is food insecurity, since majority of people literally move because they do not have to eat (4.5%), and the violation of rights in all its manifestations appears as the third cause of migration (4.40%). Finally, after affinity process were obtained 59 causes which were grouped into seven sectors: Access, Environmental, Inequality, Economy, Employment, Government and Violence. Variables grouped in sectors are shown in the Pareto Diagram of Fig. 2, explained below.

- Type of Municipality: According ADNS, municipality is understood as the fundamental territorial entity, with political, fiscal and administrative autonomy and whose purpose is the general welfare and improvement of the quality of life of the population in its respective territory. Rural area is characterized by the dispersed disposition of houses and existing agricultural exploitations; it does not have a layout or nomenclature of streets, highways, avenues, and others. Nor does it generally have public services and other types of facilities typical of urban areas, [17]. Colombia has 1,101 municipalities, of which 61% (671) of rural and scattered rural municipalities.
- Access Variables: Access to housing is considered in terms of quantity and quality, and the public services that these dwellings must have in rural areas. It is necessary

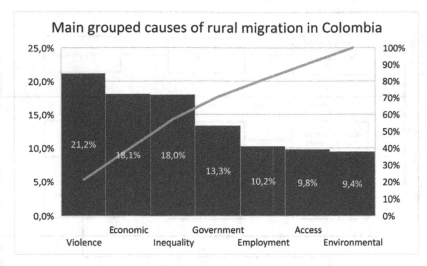

Fig. 2. Pareto of causes

to reduce the number of people without housing as a requirement to achieve the Sustainable Development Goals and in order to support social well-being. According ADNS, Colombia had a deficit of housing in year 2020 for rural and dispersed rural areas near to 2.39 million of households. Of this number, 20.9% and 43.6% were to the corresponded to quantitative and qualitative deficit of housing, respectively.

- Environmental Variables: Colombia is considered one of the countries most affected by climate change due to its location and geographical condition; which affect its population with a high rate of incidence of disasters, which reflects a high vulnerability of its communities, especially rural ones, due to a great climatic variability, determined by influence of Pacific and Atlantic oceans, the Andes Mountain range and the Amazon basin. Internal statistics are out of date, for example, between 2008 to 2012, 6,700,861 people were displaced by floods and 428,738 by droughts according to Colombian authorities as Institute of Hydrology, Meteorology and Environmental Studies.

- Inequality Variables: These refer to the different treatment that has been given to rural regions and that make people from these regions move to others to avoid these gaps. In rural areas, more than poverty, there is indigence; while in the cities the poor are 30% and the indigent 7%; in countryside poor people are 65% and the indigent 33%, as result of decades of neglect. The level of inequality in Colombia, calculated by the Gini coefficient was 0.53, the highest of the OECD countries, and it was also ranked as the second highest in the region only surpassed by Brazil.

- Economic Variables: Level of economic development of a country directly affects quality of life of its inhabitants. In this case, the rural population must move to seek more or better income to survive, generating difficulties to obtain goods and services for family support. The information reported by ADNS in its National Life Survey is interesting, where 38.2% of the heads of household considered themselves poor in 2020.

- Variables of Employment: Rural labor market in Colombia differs significantly from urban one; not only in the composition of employment, but also in its problems: low female labor participation, rural labor informality rate that is significantly higher than urban one, and the child labor. Between 2010 and 2019 was 55.5%, while in the urban sector it was 58.4%; employment rate for rural men was 73% on average, while for urban men it was 67%, and they had a monthly income that is on average 47% of the minimum wage in contrast with the urban areas for the period studied, [18].
- Government variables: A large percentage of the regions of Colombia have been forgotten by the State for years, which is why the living conditions of its inhabitants are deplorable. This is referenced by the null presence of public institutions and services as health and education institutions, in the territory, which entails very serious problems for population that lives there. The reality that Colombia lives in terms of the lack of institutionalist is alarming. For example, Colombia has 1,106 municipalities, and 36% of them have a low or critical institutional capacity and specifically, 137 municipalities of territory have a critical institutional capacity [19].
- Variables of Violence: In the last annual report on Colombia presented to the Human Rights Council in March 2021, the United Nations High Com-missioner for Human Rights indicated an increase in violence carried out by different armed actors in areas rural areas and in some urban centers. In rural areas, some of homicides have caused communities displacement, social leaders murders, by armed actors.

From Pareto diagram, made a cause-effect diagram, see Fig. 3, which allowed creation of causality model that later gave basis to continuous simulation model. This Diagram allows delineating the sectors described above, but it also refines the main variables to be considered in each of these sectors, in order to represent the phenomenon of rural migration. On the other hand, the causal model, see Fig. 4, shows that it is possible to identify factors of the system. In other words, the causes that increase rural migration and that prevent keeping the population available for work in rural areas, but also show the effects of this migration, especially on income and food production, among others.

In this context, the interrelation of demographic variables that affect the population level such as births, deaths, and others variables allow to classify municipal population by gender and age. Variables of the economic sector, refer mainly to the sources and uses of municipalities' economic resources. Variables of access sector refer mainly to access to housing and different public services as health and education, referring not only to quantity but also to quality. Environmental variables show main risks due to the different natural disasters and effects on natural resources, as well as the prevention given to these disasters. Variables of violence of all types and multiple actors already described, including those of common crime. Variables of the inequality sector refer to all the basic needs that are not satisfied and that lead to a condition of poverty and extreme poverty, that are reinforcers of peasant migration. Positive signs indicate that the condition is reinforced, and negative signs where is decreased it. The positive sign explains that a greater increase in a variable will cause increases in the effect variable, and a negative sign when a greater decrease in a variable cause increase in the effect variable. For example, a positive relation is when the greater the population in poverty, the greater the migration of rural inhabitants; the more risk prevention, the lower the vulnerable population will be, in case of a negative relation.

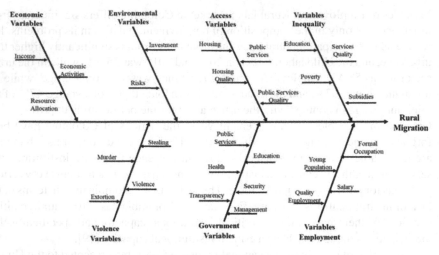

Fig. 3. Cause-Effect Diagram

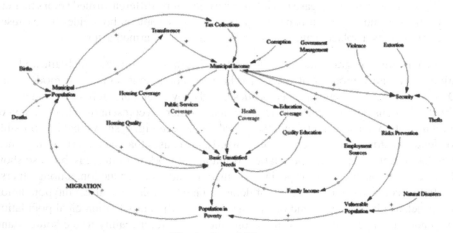

Fig. 4. Causal Diagram

Based on causal diagram, made a simulation model, that is validated and after that the policies are defined and based on the scenario that is evaluated is modifying the independent variables that directly affect the rural migration of the municipalities in Colombia. The causal model is transformed in a Forrester diagram like as in Fig. 5, this model exposes the main variables and the data from for different years through uses of iThink program. Given the complexity and model size measured by the number of necessary variables (municipalities, sectors, time period, scenarios), it was not possible to execute properly in the iThink software; so, it was necessary to build a simulation model in VBA.

A series of conditions that delimit and focus the model dynamic simulation to its objective were taken into account, these are:

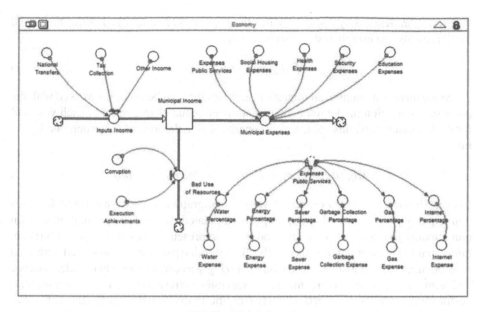

Fig. 5. IThink model

- Colombia has 1101 municipalities, 117 (10.6%) are considered as Cities and Agglomerations; 313 are of the Intermediate type (28.4%) and there are 373 and 298 Rural and Dispersed Rural municipalities, which represent 33.9% and 27.1%, respectively. In other words, municipalities base represents 60.9% of all; however, not all of them are of interest because have immigration process or their percentage of migration are very small.
- After a filtering process only 58 municipalities with the highest levels of rural migration are considered, of which 33 are of the Rural type (56.9%), and the remaining 43.1% are of the dispersed Rural type. These are a representative sample because these are located in 17 of the 32 Departments of the Country.
- The information base is from ADNS, specifically from "TerriData", which is the Territorial Statistics System, and contains information on variables in 16 different dimensions and more than 800 indicators up to the year 2018.
- The main objective of the dynamic simulation model consists on determine the level of migration of the rural municipalities to find its positive and negative impact on the territorial entities in terms of welfare and agricultural production that affects food sustainability and unemployment in rural areas.
- Information will be projected for period between the years 2020 to 2030, and time-based unit is year, because official statistics as migratory movements and agricultural production cycles are found under this unit of measurement.

The initial information for development of simulation model is based on the Colombian population evolution in period study and extracted from ADNS national census of 2005 where the estimates of the Colombian population between 1985 to 2020. Population level is given in Eq. 1. It is estimate for each one of the 58 municipalities and for each year, denoted by $Pop(j, t)$. Once the population function is defined, births and deaths can also be established in a similar way.

$$Pop_{jt} = a_j + b_j t + \varepsilon_t \qquad (1)$$

Since there is no municipal migration statistics that can be used, we worked with the proposed simulation model to obtain an estimated value of migration in each year and for each municipality, this value was compared with a theoretical value denoted by the Eq. 2.

$$Migest_{jt} = Pop_{jt} - Pop_{jt-1} + Death_{jt} - Birth_{jt} \qquad (2)$$

where: $Migest_{jt}$ represents estimated value of migration in each year t and for each municipality j. As indicated, group Pop_{jt} is calculated value of the population of each municipality j in each year t; $Death_{jt}$ and $Birth_{jt}$ represent values of deaths and births in municipality j in each year t, respectively. To determine parameters associated with each type of variable described above, a data analyzing was carried out where independence and homogeneity tests, finding that some variables corresponded to random variables, performing goodness-of-fit tests in most cases fitted a uniform density function of probability (d. f. p.). In other cases, this distribution could also be assumed as a good estimator, so it was decided to use it. Other variables for not passing the independence tests were estimated as time series. Classification is shows below.

- Random variables based on Uniform d. f. p. (RV): Housing Quantity Deficit, Housing Quality Deficit, Aqueduct Coverage, Energy Coverage, Coverage in Secondary Education, Illiteracy Percentage, Social Security Coverage, Personal Theft Rate, Homicide Rate, Violence Rate, Extortion Rate, Access to Education, Integral Risk Index, Investment in Disaster Management, Monetary Poverty Index, Unsatisfied Basic Needs and Population in Misery.
- Variables based on time series (VTS): Percentage of Income from Primary Activities, Coverage in Secondary Education, Quality of Education, Social Security Coverage, Municipal Income, Educational Resources, Health Resources, Water Resources, Municipal Value Added, Occupation People aged 18–28 and Occupation People aged 29–40.

These values are grouped by each of the sectors already described: Access, Environmental, Inequality, Economic, Employment, Government and Violence sectors. For each of these, it is necessary to determine the multipliers $\hat{a}_{ot}$ that positively or negatively affect the simulated rural migration $MigSimul_{jt}$ for period t in municipality j, see Eq. 3.

$$MigSimul_{jt} = \hat{a}_{ot} + \sum_{i1=i}^{k1} \hat{a}_{i1jt} VA_{i1jt} + \sum_{i2=i}^{k2} \hat{a}_{i2jt} VSTA_{i2jt} \qquad (3)$$

All these components of the mathematical model can be transferred to the computational model, this was possible in iThink software for a single representative municipality, but for all 58 municipalities was required to be done in a VBA macro, due to the limitation found in this software.

2.3 Decision Making Stage

To verify its validity, a run sample to estimate the number of replicates necessary obtaining desired level of precision. In this case a number of replicates was 10 for 11 years and 58 municipalities studied. From validation process, was determined that best adjustment is with only 16 variables, these are: Percentage of income from primary activities, housing quantity deficit, housing quality deficit, aqueduct coverage, energy coverage, social security coverage, municipal income, health resources, water resources, homicide rate, violence rate, investment in disaster management, municipal value added, unsatisfied basic needs, population in misery and occupation people aged 18–28. These variables have a high coincidence compared with theoretical background included above, confirming that chosen sectors in causal model represents rural migration, as well as the poor conditions in which the rural population lives. A t-student statistician corresponding to 95% confidence and a relative sampling error of 1% is used. The results of run the number of replicates necessary, are found in Table 1, and these show all variables of interest are statistically valid.

The hypothesis that the simulation model allows obtaining values similar to those based on time series is accepted. It is clear that on annuity average about 380,000 people are forced to migrate from their territories either because of the few opportunities they have, or they search for better well-being, acts of violence, or because of environmental conditions. A fact very interesting is that conditions of violence have a lower incidence in rural migration values. A possible explanation is because official statistics are lower because the peace processes with FARC, the largest group of guerillas in Colombia, this process started in 2012 and ended in 2016. It should be noted that currently violence has intensified for many reasons, but official data correspond from 2012 to 2018. To mitigate the effects of both rural migration and negative impact on food sustainability, three scenarios are proposed: pessimistic, trend and optimistic, modifying parameters selected with −5% for pessimistic scenario, 0% for trend an +5% for optimistic scenario.

Table 1. Values obtained in the Simulation.

Run number	Estimated Average Migration	Simulated Medium Migration
1	380,220	391,295
2	380,209	386,452
3	380,200	390,701
4	380,197	388,733
5	380,218	387,120
6	380,212	381,388
7	380,197	386,367
8	380,203	386,154
9	380,206	389,409
10	380,197	388,829
Average	380,205.9	387,644.8

The proposed policies are:

1. Modify the Housing Quality deficit
2. Modify the Unsatisfied Basic Needs Index
3. Modify the people who are employed between the ages of 18–28
4. Modify Municipal Income

For purposes of improving the level of precision of the simulation, the results will be analyzed from the average of 10 replicates. For the validation is considered 11-years horizon for the 58 municipalities is taken and the values of rural migration and its impacts both on income from primary activities and the amount of food produced, see Table 2.

Table 2. Accumulated Values for the 11 years in the 58 municipalities for each performance measure.

Run	Rural Migration	Tons of Food Lost	Lost Revenue in USD
1	767,284	1,587,990	$ 77,123,238
2	767,142	1,534,894	$ 70,865,010
3	769,462	1,590,298	$ 76,861,360
4	781,238	1,643,119	$ 82,833,823
5	768,346	1,569,496	$ 70,369,891
6	771,144	1,585,913	$ 84,880,849
7	759,628	1,539,579	$ 75,226,277
8	768,730	1,583,069	$ 73,755,724
9	772,714	1,588,606	$ 77,261,953
10	771,882	1,589,189	$ 73,935,171

Table 3 shows results for elected variables for both a pessimistic, trend and optimistic scenario; for this, the accumulated value of the values of all the 11 years and the 58 municipalities is taken. Table 4 shows the same results, but measured in percentage terms.

It is important to indicate that according to ADNS, the production in tons of the different crops, both permanent and transitory, reached the figure of 30,581,176 in 2020, this means that rural migration from these 58 municipalities affects an average of 5% of food production. The main crops affected in order are: Coffee, citrus, passion fruit, rice, mango, plantain, pineapple, banana, tomato, corn, orange, lemon, potato, bulb onion, oil palm and cassava.

3 Discussion

Rural migration at country level has political, economic and social implications that government must face, with the aim of providing well-being to the municipal population and avoiding the appearance of problems derived from the departure of especially young labor and that it can affect food production. Government through its ministries must provide resources for implementation of policies focused on mitigating the unsatisfied needs

Table 3. Results of the Performance Measures with Changing the variables in each Scenario.

Analyzed Scenario	Selected Variable	Average Rural Migration	Average Loss Tons	Average Lost Income in USD
Pessimistic	Housing Quality Change	799,980.4	1,627,717.6	78,292,275.0
	Unsatisfied Basic Needs	792,203.2	1,626,109.2	75,742,662.4
	Employed people aged 18–28	768,208.4	1,571,893.2	75,552,783.0
	Municipal Income	796,530.2	1,627,596.7	78,229,595.0
Trending	None	769,757.0	1,581,215.3	76,311,329.6
Optimistic	Housing Quality Change	747,900.0	1,541,755.8	74,295,482.4
	Unsatisfied Basic Needs	752,355.2	1,545,062.6	75,822,566.2
	Employed people aged 18–28	775,485.2	1,585,852.2	75,613,121.8
	Municipal Income	771,056.9	1,579,567.7	75,770,061.6

Table 4. Percentage Results of the Performance Measures with Changing the variables in each Scenario.

Analyzed Scenario	Selected Variable	Average Rural Migration	Average Loss Tons	Average Lost Income in USD
Pessimistic	Housing Quality Change	103.9%	102.9%	102.6%
	Unsatisfied Basic Needs	102.9%	102.8%	99.3%
	Employed people aged 18–28	99.8%	99.4%	99.0%
	Municipal Income	103.5%	102.9%	102.5%
Trending	None	100.0%	100.0%	100.0%
Optimistic	Housing Quality Change	97.2%	97.5%	97.4%
	Unsatisfied Basic Needs	97.7%	97.7%	99.4%
	Employed people aged 18–28	100.7%	100.3%	99.1%
	Municipal Income	100.2%	99.9%	99.3%

of the rural population, improve municipal in-come where indicators of poverty, health, malnutrition are in more critical situations. In development of the model, the greatest difficulty due to not having updated sources of information is evident. Many factors didn´t include in statistics as COVID-19 pandemic; have affected in rural migration, all of this is fully confirmed with the statements of the UN to the EFE news agency. They report that there were more than 4,300 emergencies due to conflict and disasters in Colombia in 2022 and where 7.7 million people will have humanitarian needs for the year 2023, and 3.1 million with urgent needs; mainly in areas of difficult access and little institutional offer as rural areas. This rural migration model is based on official data sources that, in addition to presenting the phenomenon of having outdated figures, may also show underreporting for political reasons, or because difficulties of the collect process. Results obtained show migration phenomenon especially rural migration, is caused by multiple factors as percentages of change of the selected variables and correspond they to the variation of the three performance measures worked on, such as those of rural migration, losses in food production and the decrease in income in primary activities.

The role played by the quality of housing and the satisfaction of basic needs are highlighted as the best mechanisms to attenuate and mitigate the migration of peasants; this is due to all the inequality in access to services and the search for a decent life of the rural population, this confirms the reinforcing effects between variables, since basic needs include aspects of access and quality of housing. This quality of housing includes some factors such as construction materials, the number of rooms, people who occupied and access to sanitary services, among others. Likewise, the fact of improving the income of the municipalities with a positive effect since part of this income will allow an improvement in the infrastructure of housing and public services, as well as improving access to education and health services and more security in remote municipalities, especially those that are rural and dispersed rural. It is important to stimulate the employment of young people in the field, in addition to accompanying them with a remuneration according to their employability because in some case their work is considered as part of the trades of the peasant family.

The obtained results themselves cannot be ignored, since in these 58 municipalities and 11 years considered, close to 750,000 people will migrate to other places, especially to the cities. This will create an effect already described of a poverty circle, in other words, a greater deficit of basic services in the cities, more unemployment and higher levels of insecurity, mainly. But an important consequence that has not been well measured, is the loss in food production causing a poor food sustainability. This model reflects a decrease of food around of 5%, increasing insecurity in the food supply of the most vulnerable people. State participation is required in order for the well-being of the rural population to develop and strengthen in Colombia, to mitigate these migratory movements guarantying the strengthening of the primary activities that are the main source of rural employment and strengthening production and marketing agricultural products improving the country's food sustainability. As final recommendation is important that model will be run with updated information to include better phenomenon as violence and its impacts in rural migration and food availability.

References

1. Vural, B.M.: Impact of Syrian forced migration on Turkish economy. Sosyoekonomi, pp. 49–64 (2020)
2. Ndlovu, E., Tigere, R.: Economic migration and the socio-economic impacts on the emigrant's family: a case of Ward 8, Gweru Rural district, Zimbabwe. Jàmbá: J. Disaster Risk Stud. **10**(1) (2018). https://doi.org/10.4102/jamba.v10i1.414

3. Cattaneo, C., et al.: Human migration in the era of climate change. Rev. Environ. Econ. Policy **13**(2), 189–206 (2019). https://doi.org/10.1093/reep/rez008
4. Mlambo, V.: An overview of rural-urban migration in South Africa: its causes and implications. Arch. Bus. Res. **6**(4) (2018). https://doi.org/10.14738/abr.64.4407
5. Qi, Z.: An overview of rural to urban migration in China and social challenges. Migration Lett. **16**(2), 273–282 (2019). https://doi.org/10.33182//ml.v16i2.664
6. Huang, X., Liu, Y., Xue, D., Li, Z., Shi, Z.: The effects of social ties on rural-urban migrants' intention to settle in cities in China. Cities **83**, 203–212 (2018). https://doi.org/10.1016/j.cit ies.2018.06.023
7. Xu, D., Yong, Z., Deng, X., Zhuang, L., Qing, C.: Rural-urban migration and its effect on land transfer in Rural China. Land **9**(3), 81 (2020). https://doi.org/10.3390/land9030081
8. Moya, J.: Migration and the historical formation of Latin America in a global perspective. Sociologias **20**(49), 24–68 (2018). https://doi.org/10.1590/15174522-02004902
9. Lagakos, D., Mobarak, A.M., Waugh, M.E.: The welfare effects of encouraging rural–urban migration. Econometrica **91**(3), 803–837 (2023). https://doi.org/10.3982/ecta15962
10. Taylor, J.E., Lopez-Feldman, A.: Does migration make rural households more productive? Evidence from Mexico. J. Develop. Stud. **46**(1), 68–90 (2010). https://doi.org/10.1080/002 20380903198463
11. Hidayati, I.: Migration and rural development: the impact of remittance. In: IOP Conference on Series: Earth Environmental Science, vol. 561, p. 012018 (2020). https://doi.org/10.1088/ 1755-1315/561/1/012018
12. Conceptos Básicos de Estadísticas de Migración. https://www.dane.gov.co/files/investigacio nes/poblacion/migracion/conceptos-basicos-SIEM.pdf
13. Camargo, G., Sampayo, A.M., Peña Galindo, A., Escobedo, F.J., Carriazo, F., Feged-Rivadeneira, A.: Exploring the dynamics of migration, armed conflict, urbanization, and anthropogenic change in Colombia. PLOS One **15**(11), Article no. e0242266 (2020). https:// doi.org/10.1371/journal.pone.0242266
14. McAuliffe, M., Triandafyllidou, A. (eds.): World Migration Report 2022. International Organization for Migration (IOM), Geneva (2021)
15. Bakucs, Z., Fertő, I., Benedek, Z.: Success or waste of taxpayer money? Impact assessment of rural development programs in Hungary. Sustainability **11**(7), 2158 (2019). https://doi.org/ 10.3390/su11072158
16. FAO. FAO Publications series 2021. Rome (2021). https://doi.org/10.4060/cb3916en
17. DANE. MANUAL DE CONCEPTOS. DANE. https://www.dane.gov.co/files/censo2018/inf ormacion-tecnica/cnpv-2018-glosario.pdf
18. Otero-Cortés, A.: El mercado laboral rural en Colombia, 2010–2019. Banco de la República. https://epositorio.banrep.gov.co/bitstream/handle/20.500.12134/9762/DTSERU_281.pdf
19. García Villegas, M., Revelo Rebolledo, J.: LA CONSTRUCCIÓN DEL ESTADO LOCAL EN COLOMBIA. Análisis Político **31**(92), 68–95 (2018). https://doi.org/10.15446/anpol.v31 n92.71098

Investigation of the Conductive Properties of the Electro-Polymerized Thiophene and Pyrrole Derivatives: Correlation Between Experimental and Theoretical Parameters

R. Salgado[1]([✉]) [ID], G. Arteaga[2] [ID], K. Pastor[2] [ID], L. Espitia[2] [ID], C. García[2] [ID], and A. Negrete[2] [ID]

[1] Corporación Universitaria del Caribe, Sincelejo, Sucre, Colombia
rodrigo.salgado@cecar.edu.co
[2] Universidad del Sinú, Montería, Córdoba, Colombia

Abstract. Theoretical and experimental variables determined for the electro-polymerization of thiophene and pyrrole derivatives were correlated. Calculations were performed employing the Density Functional Theory (DFT) method at the B3LYP/6-311G (d, p) level. Theoretical and experimental band gap values were determined to be lower for thiophene derivatives compared to pyrrole derivatives. This low band gap allowed a correlation to be established with the determination of higher conductivity values in thiophene derivatives. Assignment of FTIR vibrational bands and theoretical IR bands for the different polymers of thiophene and pyrrole derivatives are characteristic of this type of polymers.

Keywords: 3,4-ethylenedioxythiophene · 3,4-propylenedioxythiophene · 3,4-ethylenedioxypyrrole · 3,4-propylenedioxypyrrole · theoretical and experimental band gap (Eg)

1 Introduction

Theoretical chemistry provides a solid basis for understanding the fundamental principles governing molecular and atomic interactions. Theoretical models help predict how substances will behave under specific conditions before experiments are carried out [1]. This can save time and resources in focusing experimental research by allowing proper planning of experiments, suggesting key conditions and parameters to be considered, which is of great importance when looking for the synthesis of new compounds or in the design of materials with specific properties [2]. These theoretical models obtained can only be validated through experimentation because when experimental data agree or show similar trends with theoretical predictions, it increases confidence in the theory and demonstrates its usefulness in understanding chemical phenomena. So important has theoretical chemistry become that in 1998, the Nobel Prize in Chemistry was awarded to Walter Kohn, for his development of density functional theory (DFT), and to John Pople, for developing methods that allow us to calculate molecular electronic structure by both the wave function and electron density pathways [3].

© The Author(s), under exclusive license to Springer Nature Switzerland AG 2023
J. C. Figueroa-García et al. (Eds.): WEA 2023, CCIS 1928, pp. 376–387, 2023.
https://doi.org/10.1007/978-3-031-46739-4_33

On the other hand, one of the traditional applications of aromatic heterocyclic compounds such as pyrrole, thiophene and their polymeric derivatives is the control of plant diseases since their ring structure, as well as the presence of N and S heteroatoms increase the biological activity of this type of molecules, which has contributed to an important development of the agrochemical industry [4]. However, since the discovery of conductive polymers (CPs), pyrrole, thiophene and their derivatives, have increased their studies in applications related to the development of sensors, supercapacitors, metal absorption and optoelectronic applications [5–8].

These CPs may be both chemically and electrochemically synthesized [9] using monomers containing different functional groups that allow electrical, optical and magnetic properties to be modulated [10–13]. Thus, pyrrole and thiophene derivatives are an important part of the monomeric units that can be electro-polymerized on different electrode materials such as platinum, gold, glassy carbon, aluminum or AISI 316 steel [14–17]. Arteaga et al. [18] have reported the electro-polymerisation of a series of monomers derived from thiophene and pyrrole with low oxidation potential on steel electrodes, namely 3,4-ethylenedioxythiophene (EDOT), 3,4-propilendioxitiofeno (PRODOT), 3,4-ethylendioxipirrol (EDOP) and 3,4-propylenedioxypyrrole (PRODOP). The deposits were characterized morphologically and electrochemically paying special attention to the respective n-doping/undoping and p-doping/undoping electrochemical responses of the polymeric matrices obtained in each case [18].

On the other hand, the peak potential of the oxidation and reduction of p- and n-doping processes, enabled estimating the ionization potential (IP) and electron affinity (EA) of the studied polymers. Using the Koopman's theorem the frontier orbital energy, HOMO and LUMO, can be respectively evaluated to compare those values [19, 20].

On the other hand, the vibrational properties play an important role in interpreting conformational structures of the various constituents of the polymeric matrix. In this regard, in recent years, theoretical and experimental studies have been carried out concerning the structure and vibrational properties of low band-gap polymers [21–23]. Consequently, in order to obtain information about polymers from pyrrole and thiophene derivatives deposited on the electrode surface, this paper discusses the structural and electronic properties, e.g. band gap energy, conductivity and vibrational properties of the electro-polymeric coatings. Having in mind observations reported in a theoretical-experimental study about the trend of the electro-oxidation potential of thiophene derivatives, the experimental properties are compared with the theoretical parameters obtained from PEDOT, PPRODOT, PEDOP, PPRODOP pentamers.

2 Parte Experimental

2.1 Polymer Synthesis

The experimental part was performed as described elsewhere [11]. All solutions were prepared in acetonitrile (ACN) at room temperature (20 °C). The measurements were conducted in a three-compartment electrochemical cell at room temperature (20 °C) under high purity argon atmosphere, using lithium perchlorate (LiClO4) as supporting electrolyte. The working electrode was an AISI 316 steel disc, ca.0.07 cm^2 geometric area. A Pt wire coil was the counter electrode and, as a reference electrode, an Ag|AgCl in tetramethylammonium chloride, adjusted to match the potential of a saturated calomel electrode at room temperature (20 °C), was utilized [24]. Hence, all potentials quoted herein are related to the SCE at room temperature. EDOT (97%, Aldrich), PRODOT (97%, Aldrich), EDOP (2% w/v in tetrahydrofuran (THF), Aldrich) and PRODOP (2% w/v in THF, Aldrich) monomer units were used as received. Synthesis of their respective conducting polymers was accomplished utlizing cyclic voltammetry (CV) at 50 to 100 mV·s^{-1} within the window potential established as optimal for each starting unit [18].

To calculate the energy of the respective optical band gap and to compare it with the theoretical one, an Analytik Jena, SPECORD 40 UV-vis spectrophotometer was employed. Absorbance measurements were performed within 200 and 1000 nm range for monomers and between 350 to 1000 nm for polymers using 10 mm path length quartz cells. Besides, attenuated total reflectance Fourier transform infrared spectroscopy (ATR FT-IR) measurements were performed on a Bruker IFS 66/S spectrometer. Finally, electrodeposit conductivity was measured on a Jandel RM3-A Four Point probe resistivity meter.

2.2 Computational Methodology

All calculations have been conducted with Gaussian 09 program applying density functional theory (DFT) with B3LYP method The 6-311G (d, p) basis set was used to obtain energy optimized geometries, electronic properties and vibrational wavenumbers of monomer and pentamer polymeric structures.

3 Results and Discussion

Figures 1 and 2 show electrochemical response of thiophene and pyrrole derivatives for *n-doping and p-doping* processes, respectively. En and Ep stand for *p-* and *n-doping* processes peak potentials respectively, i.e. the potential required to partially oxidize or reduce the polymeric matrix, respectively [25, 26].

Given that:

$$\Delta E = E_p - E_n \tag{1}$$

and applying Eqs. 2 and 3, derived by de Leeuw et al. [26]

$$E_{HOMO} = -eV (E_P + 4.4) \tag{2}$$

$$E_{IUMO} = -eV (E_n + 4.4) \tag{3}$$

where the value 4.4 in Eqs. 2 and 3 corresponds to the potential of the SCE reference electrode (saturated calomel electrode), it is possible to calculate the band gap energy, Egap, through Eq. 4.

$$E_{gap} = E_{LUMO} - E_{HOMO} \tag{4}$$

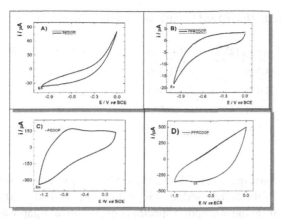

Fig. 1. Electrochemical responses for the *n-doping/undoping* process. SS electrodes modified with electrodeposits of A) PEDOT, B) PPRODOT, C) PEDOP, D) PPRODOP obtained under the previously established optimal conditions.

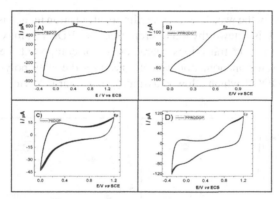

Fig. 2. Electrochemical response for the *p-doping/undoping* process. SS electrodes modified with A) PEDOT, B) PPRODOT, C) PEDOP, D) PPRODOP electrodeposits obtained under the previously established optimum conditions.

Table 1. E_p, E_n, E_{HOMO} and E_{LUMO} values.

Polymer	E_p (V)	E_{HOMO} (eV)	E_n (V)	E_{LUMO} (eV)
PEDOT	0.50	−4.90	−1.00	−3.40
PPRODOT	0.77	−5.17	−1.00	−3.40
PEDOP	1.20	−5.60	−1.30	−3.10
PPRODOP	1.20	−5.60	−0.80	−3.60

Table 1 shows E_p, E_n, E_{HOMO} and E_{LUMO} values obtained from electrochemical experiments.

Table 2. HOMO and LUMO energy values theoretically obtained.

Pentamer	E_{HOMO} (eV)	E_{LUMO} (eV)	dihedrical angle C = C−O−C
PEDOT	−4.419	−1.906	163.6
PPRODOT	−4.421	−1.915	142.0
PEDOP	−3.747	−0.553	164.0
PPRODOP	−3.784	−0.607	144.5

Table 2 shows the respective HOMO and LUMO energy values theoretically obtained for the pentamers of the corresponding thiophene and pyrrole derivatives.

Alternatively, from the absorption spectra (Fig. 3) optical Egap was calculated using Tauc Eq. (5) [27, 28].

$$E_{gap}optical = \frac{1242}{\lambda} \tag{5}$$

where λ stands for the wavelength of maximum absorption in the visible region of the respective spectra. It is noteworthy that, as reported for PEDOT, λ max is observed at ca. 570 nm, assigned to π-π* transitions characteristic of compounds bearing conjugated unsaturation. The same phenomenon was observed for the other polymers, PPRODOT, PEDOP and PPRODOP, which allowed assuming a similar behavior.

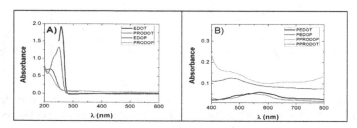

Fig. 3. Absorption spectra of A) monomers and B) polymers, as specified in the inset.

Table 3 shows Egap calculated values using Eq. 4, obtained from electrochemical and theoretical determinations, as well as the optical Egap obtained from Eq. 5.

It is observed that for all determinations that thiophene derivatives always exhibit lower Egap values than pyrrole derivatives and, for better understanding, were summarized in Fig. 4, where Egap values plot obtained utilizing different methods clearly shows that optical values are always higher than those found for electrochemical Egap and also present different trends.

This phenomenon may be explained considering that the optical Egap would be affected only by the type of solvent used during the measurement, while the latter would be affected also by variables such as effects associated with the nature of the supporting electrolyte or type of electrode used. On the other hand, theoretically calculated Egap

Table 3. E_{gap} calculated values using Eq. 4.

Monomer			Polymer				Pentamer
	λ (nm)	E_{gap} optical (eV)	λ (nm)	E_{gap} optical (eV)	E_{gap}^{*} electrochemical (eV)	E_{gap}^{*} theoretical eV
EDOT	285.87	4.34	568.75	2.18	1.50	2.50
PRODOT	277.40	4.48	544.73	2.28	1.77	2.51
EDOP	267.00	4.50	473.84	2.62	2.50	3.19
PRODOP	262.11	4.73	462.80	2.68	2.00	3.17

* *band gap* calculated using Eq. 4.

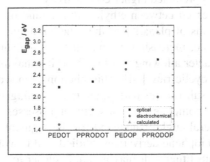

Fig. 4. Optical, electrochemical and theoretical band gap energy of pyrrole and thiophene derivatives.

exhibits the same trend as that observed for optically calculated Eg and, although the theoretical values are always higher, are consistent with the values reported in the literature [29–33].

E_{gap} differences found for thiophene and pyrrole derivatives could be explained by the presence of, respectively, the S and N atoms in the structures [32, 34, 35]. Sulfur, according to valence bond theory, possesses two free nonbonding electron pairs. One of these pairs of electrons is in the unhybridized p orbital and can overlap with p orbitals of carbon atoms of the ring in its structure. This phenomenon brings about the delocalization of this pair of electrons, stabilizing the polymer chain, similarly to what happens with the nonbonding electron pair of N in pyrrole. A second phenomenon would be produced by non-covalent intermolecular attractive interactions between S $\cdot\cdot$ O that would induce a larger stabilization polymer chain planarity increasing thus its aromaticity [36–39]. Aromaticity increase in the oligomer would provide a greater interaction between the chains, creating an efficient π − stacking between aromatic regions. π − stacked structures would favor the electron and charge (hopping) delocalization between different polymer chains, increasing the conductivity of the polymer matrix, as described for other conductive polymers [40–43]. To substantiate this, conductivity measurements were performed on pyrrole and thiophene polymeric derivatives. The obtained results are summarized in Table 4.

Table 4. Conductivity of polymers derived from thiophene and pyrrole electrosynthesized on SS.

Polymer	Conductivity (S cm^{-1})
PEDOT	2.03 ± 0.06
PPRODOT	1.21 ± 0.04
PEDOP	0.5 ± 0.3
PPRODOP	0.3 ± 0.2

It was thus corroborated that conductivity obtained for the various polymeric matrices are consistent with the explanation given above, since the lower band gap values obtained for thiophene derivatives predicted higher conductivity.

The differences observed between ethylenedioxy- and propylenedioxy-derivatives may be explained in terms of planarity of the dihedral angle formed by the segments C = C-O-C (Table 2), i.e. increasing the planarity of the substituent, oxygen would reach a higher sp2 character allowing that its pZ orbital maximizes its interaction with π orbitals of the heterocyclic ring [44]. This phenomenon would enable that oxygen atoms of alkylenedioxy-substituents participate in the conjugated backbone, increasing polymers conductivity (a completely planar segment possesses a dihedral angle of 180°).

Table 2 shows dihedral angles calculated for the segment C = C-O-C of the pentamers of pyrrole and thiophene derivatives studied in this work. The values point out that ethylenedioxy − substituents display an angle closer to planarity than propylenedioxy − substituents, that would explain the smaller band gap of polymers derived from pyrrole and thiophene having the smaller substituent, in addition to predicting a higher conductivity. This phenomenon is also corroborated by the conductivity observed for ethylenedioxy − and propylenedioxy − derivatives from thiophene and pyrrole (Table 4).

To gather information about the vibrational properties of the electro-deposited polymer structures, experimental spectra were recorded utilizing the FTIR-ATR technique and compared with the simulated IR spectra of pentamers from pyrrole and thiophene derivatives, Fig. 5.

As can be seen in the simulated spectra, assigned signals are slightly shifted with respect to the experimental FTIR spectra. One likely explanation for this phenomenon would be that the actual sample corresponds to a complex network of solid phase polymers, while the simulated IR spectra were obtained considering pentamers in gas phase. Table 5 shows FTIR vibrational and IR theoretical bands assignments for the different polymers from thiophene and pyrrole derivatives, verifying that tabulated bands are characteristic for this kind of polymers [45–48].

The agreement between the values of the bands obtained from FTIR and IR-calculated allows postulating oligomers conformational structure in the polymer matrix. Figure 6 shows pentamers structure obtained from DFT/B3LYP/6-311G (d, p) calculations.

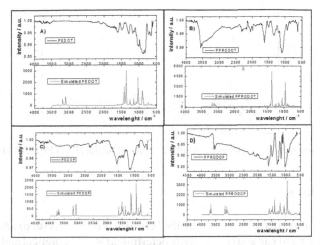

Fig. 5. A) PEDOT, B) PPRODOT, C) PEDOP, D) PPRODOP spectra. Black line (-) experimental FTIR-ATR and red line (-) calculated FTIR.

Table 5. FTIR-ATR and IR-calculated band assignment for thiophene and pyrrole derivatives.

cm^{-1}	PEDOT		PPRODOT		PEDOP		PRODOP	
	FTIR ATR	IR simulated	FTIR ATR	IR simulated	FTIR ATR	IR simulated	FTIR ATR	IR simulated
CH$_2$ wagging	1161	1150	1175	1150	1160	1100	1138	1128
C = C stretching	1619	1611	1586	1625	1527	1545	1648	1634
C-C stretching	1301	1298	1311	1361	1289	1283	1285	1280
C-O-C stretching group	1131	1128	1075	1128	1198	1178	1062	1050
C-S	876	869	823	869	–	–	–	–
C-N	–	–	–	–	1447	1467	1228	1230
CNH	–	–	–	–	3567	3575	3597	3605
C-O bending	929	920	929	920	922	910	918	945

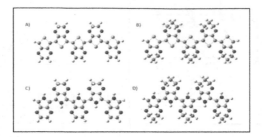

Fig. 6. Conformational structures of A) PEDOT, B) PPRODOT, C) PEDOP, D) PPRODOP.

4 Conclusions

DFT calculations were performed using the base B3LYP/6-311G (d, p) and it was found to correlate with band gap and conductivity determinations. Theoretical and experimental thiophene derivatives band gap is lower than those of pyrrole derivatives, due to non-covalent intramolecular attractive interactions between S·O.

Furthermore, it was found that band gap values difference between derived from the same family are due to backbone geometry of the alkylenedioxy − substitution that modulates the oxygen π-donor character, which directly influences the conductivity increase.

Finally, agreement between the values of the bands obtained from FTIR and IR-calculated was found; this enables postulating the conformational structure of the oligomers in the polymer matrix, verifying that the use of pentamers as comparison model of the polymer may be a valid strategy.

References

1. Suárez, D.: Goals and characteristics of computational chemistry and its application to carbon materials. Dep. Química Física y Analítica 23–28 (2012)
2. Saldívar-González, F., Prieto-Martínez, F.D., Medina-Franco, J.L.: Descubrimiento y desarrollo de fármacos: un enfoque computacional. Educ. Quim. **28**, 51–58 (2017). https://doi.org/10.1016/j.eq.2016.06.002
3. Domínguez, L., Bedolla, C.A.: El Premio Nobel de Química 2013 para Químicos Computacionales. Educ. Química. **25**, 82–85 (2014). https://doi.org/10.1016/s0187-893x(14)70528-2
4. Ashton, M.D., et al.: Controlled bioactive delivery using degradable electroactive polymers. Biomacromol **23**, 3031–3040 (2022). https://doi.org/10.1021/acs.biomac.2c00516
5. Li, X., Liu, Y., Gao, M., Cai, K.: Construction of hierarchical polypyrrole coated copper-catecholate grown on poly (3,4-ethylenedioxythiophene): poly (styrenesulfonate) fibers for high-performance supercapacitors. J. Colloid Interface Sci. **627**, 142–150 (2022). https://doi.org/10.1016/j.jcis.2022.07.050
6. Zhou, Y., Zeng, Z., Guo, Y., Zheng, X.: Selective adsorption of Hg(ii) with diatomite-based mesoporous materials functionalized by pyrrole-thiophene copolymers: condition optimization, application and mechanism. RSC Adv. **12**, 33160–33174 (2022). https://doi.org/10.1039/d2ra05938j

7. Stecko, S., Gryko, D.T.: Multifunctional heteropentalenes: from synthesis to optoelectronic applications. JACS Au **2**, 1290–1305 (2022). https://doi.org/10.1021/jacsau.2c00147

8. Abrama, T., Kacimia, R., Bejjita, L., Bennanib, M.N., M.B.: New organic Materials based on thiophene for photovoltaic devices: theoretical investigation. Turkish Comput. Theor. Chem. **2**, 36–48 (2018)

9. Shirakawa, H., Louis, E.J., MacDiarmid, A.G., Chiang, C.K., Heeger, A.J.: Synthesis of electrically conducting organic polymers: halogen derivatives of polyacetylene, $(CH)_x$. J. Chem. Soc. Chem. Commun. 578–580 (1977). https://doi.org/10.1039/C39770000578

10. Thakur, A.V., Lokhande, B.J.: Effect of the molar concentration of pyrrole monomer on the rate of polymerization, growth and hence the electrochemical behavior of highly pristine PPy flexible electrodes. Heliyon **5**, e02909 (2019). https://doi.org/10.1016/j.heliyon.2019.e02909

11. Xie, A., Lin, X., Zhang, C., Cheng, S., Dong, W., Wu, F.: Oxygen vacancy mediated polymerization of pyrrole on MoO3 to construct dielectric nanocomposites for electromagnetic waves absorption application. J. Alloys Compd. **938**, 168523 (2023). https://doi.org/10.1016/j.jallcom.2022.168523

12. Erdeger, M., Kiskan, B., Gungor, F.S.: Synthesis and characterization of pyrrole-based benzoxazine monomers and polymers. Eur. Polym. J. **179**, 111532 (2022). https://doi.org/10.1016/j.eurpolymj.2022.111532

13. Söyleyici, H.C., Ak, M., Şahin, Y., Demikol, D.O., Timur, S.: New class of 2,5-di(2-thienyl)pyrrole compounds and novel optical properties of its conducting polymer. Mater. Chem. Phys. **142**, 303–310 (2013). https://doi.org/10.1016/j.matchemphys.2013.07.019

14. Aydın, E.B., Aydın, M., Sezgintürk, M.K.: Fabrication of electrochemical immunosensor based on acid-substituted poly(pyrrole) polymer modified disposable ITO electrode for sensitive detection of CCR4 cancer biomarker in human serum. Talanta **222**, 121487 (2021). https://doi.org/10.1016/j.talanta.2020.121487

15. Abdallah, A.B., Ghaith, E.A., Mortada, W.I., Molouk, A.F.S.: Electrochemical sensing of sodium dehydroacetate in preserved strawberries based onin situ pyrrole electropolymerization at modified carbon paste electrodes. Food Chem. **401**, 134058 (2023). https://doi.org/10.1016/j.foodchem.2022.134058

16. Saraç, A.S., Sönmez, G., Cebeci, F.Ç.: Electrochemical synthesis and structural studies of polypyrroles, poly(3,4-ethylene-dioxythiophene)s and copolymers of pyrrole and 3,4-ethylenedioxythiophene on carbon fibre microelectrodes. J. Appl. Electrochem. **33**, 295–301 (2003). https://doi.org/10.1023/A:1024139303585

17. Yaldagard, M.: Green in-situ Fabrication of PtW/Poly Ethylen Dioxy Thiophene/Graphene Nanoplates/Gas Diffusion Layer (PtW/ PEDOT /GNP/GDL) Electrode and its Electrocatalytic Property for Direct Methanol Fuel Cells Application (2019)

18. Arteaga, G.C., et al.: Thiophene and pyrrole derivative polymers electro-synthesized on stainles steel. Doping and morphology characterization. Int. J. Electrochem. Sci. **7**, 7840–7854 (2012)

19. Alemán, C., Casanovas, J.: Theoretical investigation of the 3,4-ethylenedioxythiophene dimer and unsubstituted heterocyclic derivatives. J. Phys. Chem. A **108**, 1440–1447 (2004). https://doi.org/10.1021/jp0369600

20. Nikoofard, H., Sargolzaei, M., Kia, B., Amin, A.H.: DFT study of conjugational electronic structures of aminoalkyl end-capped oligothiophenes up to octamers. Comptes Rendus Chim. **19**, 646–653 (2016). https://doi.org/10.1016/j.crci.2016.01.004

21. Woo, H.Y., Uddin, M.A., Hwang, S.: Density functional theoretical and time-dependent density functional theoretical study on Thiophene–Benzothiadiazole-based polymers. Bull. Korean Chem. Soc. **36**, 427–430 (2015)

22. Scharber, M.C., Sariciftci, N.S.: Low band gap conjugated semiconducting polymers. Adv. Mater. Technol. **6**, 2000857 (2021). https://doi.org/10.1002/admt.202000857

23. Bölke, S., et al.: Influence of the side chain structure on the electronic structure and self-organization properties of low band gap polymers. ACS Appl. Energy Mater. **5**, 15290–15301 (2022). https://doi.org/10.1021/acsaem.2c02919

24. East, G.A., del Valle, M.A.: Easy-to-make Ag/AgCl reference electrode. J. Chem. Educ. **77**, 97 (2000). https://doi.org/10.1021/ed077p97

25. Del-Oso, J.A., Frontana-Uribe, B.A., Maldonado, J.L., Rivera, M., Tapia-Tapia, M., Roa-Morales, G.: Electrochemical deposition of poly[ethylene-dioxythiophene] (PEDOT) films on ITO electrodes for organic photovoltaic cells: control of morphology, thickness, and electronic properties. J. Solid State Electrochem. **22**, 2025–2037 (2018). https://doi.org/10.1007/s10008-018-3909-z

26. de Leeuw, D.M., Simenon, M.M.J., Brown, A.R., Einerhand, R.E.F.: Stability of n-type doped conducting polymers and consequences for polymeric microelectronic devices. Synth. Met. **87**, 53–59 (1997). https://doi.org/10.1016/S0379-6779(97)80097-5

27. Abdel-Aziz, M., Zwawi, M., Al-Hossainy, A., Zoromba, M.: Conducting polymer thin film for optoelectronic devices applications. Polym. Adv. Technol. **32**, 2588–2596 (2021). https://doi.org/10.1002/pat.5290

28. Makuła, P., Pacia, M., Macyk, W.: How to correctly determine the band gap energy of modified semiconductor photocatalysts based on UV–Vis spectra. J. Phys. Chem. Lett. **9**, 6814–6817 (2018). https://doi.org/10.1021/acs.jpclett.8b02892

29. Ding, F., et al.: Benzothiophene and benzosulfone fused pyrazino[2,3-g]quinoxaline: synthesis and semiconducting properties. Chinese Chem. Lett. **34**, 107235 (2023). https://doi.org/10.1016/j.cclet.2022.02.040

30. Mahatme, U.B., Utane, R.D., Rangari, A.H., Tidke, G.D.: Preparation of UV, LASER and white light sensitive conducting polymer poly (3, 4-ethylenedioxythiophene) "PEDOT" nanoparticles. Mater. Today Proc. **49**, 2154–2160 (2022). https://doi.org/10.1016/j.matpr.2021.09.083

31. Bruce, P.G., Scrosati, B., Tarascon, J.-M.: Nanomaterials for rechargeable lithium batteries. Angew. Chemie Int. Ed. **47**, 2930–2946 (2008). https://doi.org/10.1002/anie.200702505

32. Raimundo, J.-M., et al.: Push–pull chromophores based on 2,2′-bi(3,4-ethylenedioxythiophene) (BEDOT) π-conjugating spacer. Tetrahedron Lett. **42**, 1507–1510 (2001). https://doi.org/10.1016/S0040-4039(00)02317-0

33. Stephens, P.J., Devlin, F.J., Chabalowski, C.F., Frisch, M.J.: Ab initio calculation of vibrational absorption and circular dichroism spectra using density functional force fields. J. Phys. Chem. **98**, 11623–11627 (1994). https://doi.org/10.1021/j100096a001

34. Zanuy, D., Alemán, C.: Resolving the subnanometric structure of ultrathin films of poly(3,4-ethylenedioxythiophene) on steel surfaces: a molecular modeling approach. Soft Matter **9**, 11634–11644 (2013). https://doi.org/10.1039/C3SM52477A

35. Zanuy, D., Teixeira-Dias, B., del Valle, L.J., Poater, J., Solà, M., Alemán, C.: Examining the formation of specific interactions between poly(3,4-ethylenedioxythiophene) and nucleotide bases. RSC Adv. **3**, 2639–2649 (2013). https://doi.org/10.1039/C2RA22640E

36. Grossmann, B., Heinze, J., Moll, T., Palivan, C., Ivan, S., Gescheidt, G.: Electron delocalization in one-electron oxidized aniline oligomers, paradigms for polyaniline. A study by paramagnetic resonance in fluid solution. J. Phys. Chem. B **108**, 4669–4672 (2004). https://doi.org/10.1021/jp0379042

37. Roncali, J., Blanchard, P., Frère, P.: 3,4-Ethylenedioxythiophene (EDOT) as a versatile building block for advanced functional π-conjugated systems. J. Mater. Chem. **15**, 1589–1610 (2005). https://doi.org/10.1039/B415481A

38. Demeter, D., Melchiorre, F., Biagini, P., Jungsuttiwong, S., Po, R., Roncali, J.: 3,4-Ethylenedioxythiophene (EDOT) and 3,4-ethylenedithiathiophene (EDTT) as terminal blocks for oligothiophene dyes for DSSCs. Tetrahedron Lett. **57**, 4815–4820 (2016). https://doi.org/10.1016/j.tetlet.2016.09.053

39. Demeter, D., Rousseau, T., Roncali, J.: 3,4-Ethylenedioxythiophene (EDOT) as building block for the design of small molecular donors for organic solar cells. RSC Adv. **3**, 704–707 (2013). https://doi.org/10.1039/C2RA22818A

40. Poater, J., Casanovas, J., Solà, M., Alemán, C.: Examining the planarity of poly(3,4-ethylenedioxythiophene): consideration of self-rigidification, electronic, and geometric effects. J. Phys. Chem. A **114**, 1023–1028 (2010). https://doi.org/10.1021/jp908764s

41. Bendrea, A.-D., Cianga, L., Ailiesei, G.-L., Ursu, E.-L., Göen Colak, D., Cianga, I.: 3,4-Ethylenedioxythiophene (EDOT) End-Group Functionalized Poly-ε-caprolactone (PCL): self-assembly in organic solvents and its coincidentally observed peculiar behavior in thin film and protonated media. Polymers **13**(16), 2720 (2021)

42. Feixas, F., Matito, E., Poater, J., Solà, M.: Quantifying aromaticity with electron delocalisation measures. Chem. Soc. Rev. **44**, 6434–6451 (2015). https://doi.org/10.1039/C5CS00066A

43. Poater, J., Fradera, X., Duran, M., Solà, M.: The delocalization index as an electronic aromaticity criterion: application to a series of planar polycyclic aromatic hydrocarbons. Chem. Eur. J. **9**, 400–406 (2003)

44. Burkhardt, S.E., Rodríguez-Calero, G.G., Lowe, M.A., Kiya, Y., Hennig, R.G., Abruña, H.D.: Theoretical and electrochemical analysis of poly(3,4-alkylenedioxythiophenes): electron-donating effects and onset of p-doped conductivity. J. Phys. Chem. C **114**, 16776–16784 (2010). https://doi.org/10.1021/jp106082f

45. Agalya, G., Lv, C., Wang, X., Koyama, M., Kubo, M., Miyamoto, A.: Theoretical study on the electronic and molecular properties of ground and excited states of ethylenedioxythiophene and styrenesulphonic acid. Appl. Surf. Sci. **244**, 195–198 (2005). https://doi.org/10.1016/j.apsusc.2004.09.139

46. Silva, A.J.C., Ferreira, S.M.F., Santos, D.P., Navarro, M., Tonholo, J., Ribeiro, A.S.: A multielectrochromic copolymer based on pyrrole and thiophene derivatives. Sol. Energy Mater. Sol. Cells **103**, 108–113 (2012). https://doi.org/10.1016/j.solmat.2012.03.024

47. Behera, L., Mohanta, M., Thirugnanam, A.: Intensification of yam-starch based biodegradable bioplastic film with bentonite for food packaging application. Environ. Technol. Innov. **25**, 102180 (2022). https://doi.org/10.1016/j.eti.2021.102180

48. Mohammad, F.: Compensation behaviour of electrically conductive polythiophene and polypyrrole. J. Phys. D Appl. Phys. **31**, 951 (1998). https://doi.org/10.1088/0022-3727/31/8/005

Strategies, Information Technologies and Models for Knowledge Management in Software Development Companies: A Systematic Review of the Literature

Evelin Fragoso[1]([✉]) [iD], Luisa F. Villa[2] [iD], and Lillyana María Giraldo Marín[2] [iD]

[1] Master's Student in Information and Knowledge Management, University of Medellin, Antioquia, Colombia
efragoso378@soyudemedellin.edu.co
[2] Arkadius Research Group, Faculty of Engineering, University of Medellín, Antioquia, Colombia
{lvilla,lmgiraldo}@udemedellin.edu.co

Abstract. Software development companies are currently facing numerous challenges due to rapid technological change, high staff turnover, and brain drain. This means that the key knowledge of the companies is lost and there are difficulties in carrying out the medium and long-term planned projects with the customers, which over time affects the income, productivity, and continuity of these companies. In this scenario, knowledge management, understood as a process that allows the company to identify, collect, store, evaluate, and share valuable information, becomes a critical success factor, as it allows the creation of value through knowledge, thus mitigating the impact of these challenges. This article aims to systematically review the literature to identify what strategies, technologies, and knowledge management models are being used by software development companies to obtain the benefits and capabilities needed to be more solid and competitive in the marketplace. The results of this work show that the most commonly used strategies are collaborative networks, knowledge repositories, training, organizational agility, and peer work. Similarly, it was found that the most commonly used technologies are collaborative tools, information systems, and business intelligence and knowledge management applications. This is embedded in models that promote agility and collaborative working. In addition, according to the articles, increasing productivity, shortening the learning curve for new employees, and developing innovation, absorption, and creativity capabilities were cited as benefits that are fundamental to effective knowledge management. Similarly, challenges for investigation and challenges that should be adopted in future research were found.

Keywords: knowledge management · information technologies · software development methodologies · staff turnover · brain drain · strategies · models · capabilities

© The Author(s), under exclusive license to Springer Nature Switzerland AG 2023
J. C. Figueroa-García et al. (Eds.): WEA 2023, CCIS 1928, pp. 388–398, 2023.
https://doi.org/10.1007/978-3-031-46739-4_34

1   Introduction

With the consolidation of globalized markets, the development of new technologies, and an aggressive competitive culture, knowledge represents the greatest intangible asset of an organization [1]. It is a critical success factor that gives value to companies, as the wealth of an organization is no longer measured based on its financial data, but rather takes into account its intellectual capital, which sets it apart from its competitors and represents a differentiation value [2].

Knowledge plays an important role in organizations and it has been studied by different authors who define it as a set of ideas and experiences at the individual, group, organizational, and social levels about a particular object and situation, tested and contextualized by the subject, that emerge during or as a result of perception, understanding, creative elaboration, conceptualization of their application and transformation [3].

For software development companies, knowledge is the fundamental basis, since implementing software products does not only involve writing lines of code and executing them through different tools; it also requires intellectual and organizational efforts to generate knowledge [4]. Knowledge means understanding the requirements demanded, capturing the ideas of users or customers, and accurately planning the execution of agreed tasks to ultimately deliver a quality product that adds value [5].

The main causes of this phenomenon are that employees have higher salary expectations and seek better working conditions in terms of training, organizational environment, development opportunities, relationships with the work team, better tools, and a balance between life, work, and personal life [6]. This, together with the positioning of foreign companies in developing countries that see the opportunity to hire qualified workers at a lower cost than in their countries of origin, makes it easy for people in the technology sectors to change jobs and take with them all the important knowledge and production capacity of these companies [7]. That makes that the talent deficit in the technology sector, and the gap between the labor market demand for technology and trained personnel [8]; doing that, companies have to face a high costs for training and development of new employees, difficulties in completing projects on time, affecting customers and reducing their intellectual capital [9].

In this way, knowledge management is presented as an alternative, understood as a discipline that promotes an integrated approach to identifying, capturing, assessing, recovering, and sharing all of an organization's knowledge and information assets. These assets may include databases, documents, policies, procedures, and previously captured experiences of individual workers [10], generating new knowledge, which is disseminated in members of the organization, and materialize it into goods, services, and systems [11].

In this sense, knowledge is divided into two types: tacit knowledge, which is rooted in the mind of individuals and is the result of their values, beliefs, life experiences, emotions, procedures, actions and routines [12]. This requires a unique combination of people and information systems that make knowledge available and easily accessible to members. While ensuring an organizational culture that learns the value of "building and thinking together" from work. As a team, mutual respect, communication, empowerment, and the sharing of knowledge to discuss problems to achieve constructive and collective collaboration and consensus, which at this point makes the generation of organizational results more important than individual achievements [14].

This article aims to conduct a systematic review of the literature to identify which strategies, technologies, and knowledge management models are used by software development companies to obtain the benefits and capabilities needed to be more solid and competitive in the market. The article is organized as follows: The introduction, states the general concepts of knowledge management that are presented; in Sect 2, a summary of the systematic literature review (RSL) methodology is presented and how the main steps were performed in the process; in Sect. 3, the results are presented with the findings related to the research question; and finally, in Sect. 4, the conclusions are drawn.

2   Methodology

With this in mind, and considering the importance of knowledge management in software development companies to mitigate the effects of staff turnover and brain drain, this article is presented to identify the state of the art through a systematic literature review, using the methodology proposed by Pérez Rave [16], to answer the following questions:

Q1. What knowledge management strategies are currently used by software development companies?
Q2. What are the technologies that support knowledge management strategies?
Q3. What knowledge management models are these companies using?
Q4. What are the benefits or impacts of using knowledge management strategies and technologies?
Q5. In what application scenarios are knowledge management strategies and technologies used?
Q6. What challenges and issues need to be addressed in future research?

Afterwards, the key terms were defined, and searched in databases such as Scopus Dimensions, Springer and ACM Digital using the following equation: (("knowledge management") AND ("organizational learning") AND ("software development")), including the filter of publications from the last five years (2019–2023) to ensure the validity of the topic, also review articles were excluded, leaving only research studies. As inclusion criteria are defined: Articles with the most citations mentioning knowledge management strategies, knowledge management in software development organizations, knowledge management models in software development, organizational learning strategies, organizational learning models and articles that refer technologies to support knowledge management. As exclusion criteria are defined: Articles that are not digitally accessible, articles without citations, literature that is not indexed in databases, that is not related to the research topic.

The result was 195 articles and then, using the inclusion and exclusion criteria defined, were selected 46 articles were reviewed to determine if they answered the initial questions and a score was assigned for each question as follows: "0" if the question was not answered, "3" if it was partially answered, and "5" if the question was explicitly answered. On this basis, the 25 articles with the highest scores were prioritized and each of them was analyzed, extracting general purpose of the study and its differentiation or relationship with other works, the materials and methods used, the main findings, research challenges and general.

Then the analysis was carried out through the characteristics matrix where the information provided by each article and its relationship with the proposed research questions were crossed. In Chapter 5 references are identified with the notation **N. < ID >** the 25 articles included in the systematic review of the literature.

3 Results

It shows the number of publications identified in the period 2019–2023, in which a very significant increase can be observed in 2022, the year in which 122 investigations were published with an increase of 62.56%, which indicates that this topic has gained relevance as an object of study in recent years. Although in 2023 a decrease in the number of publications is reflected, this is not due to the loss of validity of the topic, but to the cut-off time of the search, that is, 3 months of the current year.

3.1 Answer the Questions Posed

Below are the knowledge management strategies that software development companies are using that are evidenced in the reviewed articles and responses to Q1.

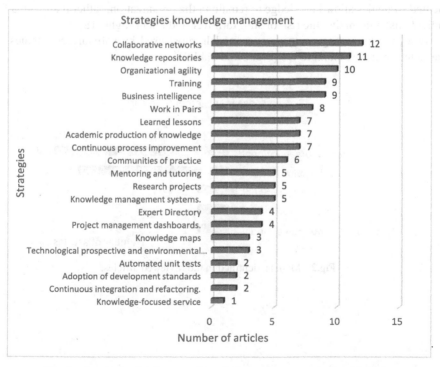

Fig. 1. Strategies that leverage knowledge management in organizations

Figure 1. Shows in general the strategies that software development companies have implemented according to the articles analyzed. In the first place, there are collaborative networks, defined as groups of people and companies that acquire and share information and knowledge [17]. This strategy is mentioned in 12 articles (1,2,3,4,7,8,9,10,15,19,20,22), representing 48% of the articles. These collaboration networks facilitate knowledge sharing, a process that consists in transferring and sharing knowledge between individuals or teams to reduce the time required to solve a business problem [18]. The search for new knowledge requires a personal commitment from each individual, but obstacles can arise in this process, such as the confidentiality of information, since people can share knowledge with unauthorized people [19].

Second place, there are the knowledge repositories of the wiki type, also referred to in 44% of the articles and corresponding to 11 of them (1,2,3,4,5,9,14,15,17, 20,22), which allow the organization, storage, preservation and dissemination of knowledge resources and digital information of an institutional and academic nature in an openform, helping the employees of an organization to identify and access the knowledge resources they need for their daily work [15].

The articles also mention other very relevant strategies such as agility and training, work in pairs, learned lessons, communities of practice, mentoring, tutoring and others, which together enable effective knowledge management and converge in consolidating an agile organizational culture that promotes close collaboration among team members, improving capitalization and sharing of knowledge, emphasizing transparency, continuous improvement, and adaptation to change [21, 23]. These, properly implemented strategies allow knowledge to remain in the organization, rather than with a few individuals, minimizing the risk of staff turnover and talent flight [18].

Next, the knowledge management models most used by software companies are presented, which respond to Q2 (Fig. 2 and Table 1).

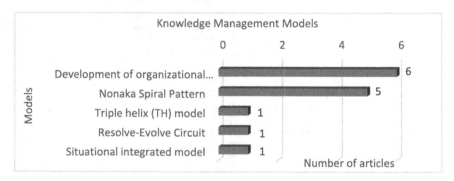

Fig.2. Models identified in the reviewed articles.

Table 1. Models for knowledge management

Model	Author	Description
Capacity development model learning organization	[25]	As seen in Fig. 3, the development of organizational learning capabilities is the most frequently used model by the analyzed companies, mentioned in 24% of the articles (1,4,7,17,21,25). This model is focused on developing organizational learning capacity and is a tool for organizational progress that is consistent with social change and sustainable community development through three dynamic processes: (1) knowledge creation and acquisition, (2) knowledge dissemination and integration," and (3) knowledge storage and application [22]
Spiral pattern of knowledge (Nonaka and Takeuchi)	[26]	The spiral model of knowledge proposed by Nonaka and Takeuchi, referred to in 5 of the articles, representing 20% of the articles (3,5,10,15,17), consists of four phases of the knowledge creation cycle [27]. Socialization: (tacit to tacit) generalization of knowledge through direct interaction, in situations such as observation of activities, tutorials, and sharing experiences in user groups. Exteriorization: (from tacit to explicit) codification of knowledge to pass on to others, in the form of procedure and training manuals, flowcharts, instructions, and self-learning aids. Combination: (from explicit to explicit) it mixes existing information with other knowledge in its explicit form, which can lead to new knowledge, through working meetings, roundtables, seminars, and test groups. Internalization: (from explicit to tacit) internalization of explicit knowledge in individuals through the application, adaptation, and transformation of tacit knowledge; this occurs, for example, in practical exercises, workshops, and pilot tests [28]
Situational Integrated Model (MSI)	[29, 30]	The integrated situation model mentioned in one of the articles (3), which corresponds to 4%, is described as a model with five dimensions: 1) actors, 2) strategic knowledge processes, 3) support processes and culture 4) capital system and 5) system of indicators, these elements enable the generation from the effective management of knowledge as a management tool for professionals to make decisions [31]
Solve and wrap model	[10]	The solve and wrap model mentioned in one of the articles (6), which corresponds to 4%, is described as a model based on knowledge-based service, which using a knowledge base and correct practices can be tightly integrated to solve incident, problems in the software development process, and through metrics that can help identify where knowledge is lacking to direct resources for improvement [32]

(continued)

Table 1. (*continued*)

Model	Author	Description
triple helix (TH),	[19]	In the TH model, the interactions between universities, industry and government are identified as the key to innovation, economic growth and competitiveness. The main benefits for companies that participate in TH networks, especially at the regional level, are based on access to knowledge and a greater capacity to face current challenges [19]

Below are the most used technologies to support knowledge management processes in software development companies that respond to Q3.

Fig. 3. Information technologies that leverage Knowledge Management

Figure 3 shows that the most used technologies in software development companies to support knowledge management are in first place agile collaboration tools, which are referenced in 13 articles (2,3,5,6,9,11,12,1,18,21,22,24,25) which corresponds to 52%. These tools aim to plan, execute, control and analyze the different tasks and processes of a business project, allowing team members to access information from anywhere, make the necessary changes in real time, keep track of the project management and support of agile methodologies [17]. What promotes teamwork, effective communication among its members, continuous process improvement, organizational learning and its evolution through specific functionalities [18].

Secondly related in 12 (2,3,4,6,8,9,11,12,13,16,17,19) articles with 48% are the knowledge databases that are repositories that store the most relevant information for the organization and can include frequently asked questions, manuals, troubleshooting guides, videos and other data that the team may want or need [33].

Thirdly, information systems and business intelligence (BI) systems are identified as one of the relevant technologies. Other technologies such as E-learning learning tools and IOT Internet of Things technologies, industry 4.0, such as intelligent cloud services, knowledge databases. These technologies allow the organization to develop new business and communication schemes with its customers and suppliers, sharing knowledge [12].

Concerned about benefits, the articles show companies obtain when effective knowledge management is carried out through the application of knowledge management strategies and practices, which respond to Q4.

- Increased efficiency and productivity [33].
- Increase in teamwork, innovation and the search for creative solutions [34].
- Reduction in the learning curve through obtaining knowledge in a more systematic way [20, 35].
- Standardization of processes and quick access to information, making decision-making more intelligent [36].
- IT organizations can improve performance metrics and customer service, while enhancing collaboration across fragmented teams and cultivating singular rather than slide vision of the IT ecosystem [22].
- Reduction in training costs and reduction in the losing of vital information for the company [24].

On the other hand, these are the common sceneries where companies apply knowledge management, which respond to Q5.

- **In innovation:** effective knowledge management makes possible the digitization of processes and the development of innovation as part of the transformation since collaborative work allows the acquisition and creation of new knowledge to develop projects that provide solutions to the needs of the organization [37].
- **Development of new products:** the exploitation of knowledge corresponds to the action that ensures the sustainability of the company through: the use of the organization's knowledge in the processes of manufacturing products or providing services; the generation of products and services with high added value and differentiated; the structuring of the processes carried out [38].
- **Development projects:** accumulated knowledge represents a crucial factor in the successful realization of projects, particularly for companies that operate in knowledge-based innovation-intensive sectors [22].
- **Research projects:** the culture exchange represents the organizational principles and theories that development and incorporate new knowledge processes as natural and integrated elements through of the creating the project to look into and resolved common problems [39].
- **Support, Service** Desk, and Incident Ticketing Schemes: Knowledge-Centered Service (KCS, formerly known as Knowledge Centered Support) presents the management and lifecycle of an organization's knowledge base in two rings interdependent: the solve and evolve loops. "resolve" covers day-to-day transaction work with knowledge: customer and service desk, incident tickets, and article creation[40].

Next, the challenges and future work are presented, which respond to Q6.

- It is recommended that future studies target large technology or software development companies and include.
- Increase comparative studies that focus on knowledge management models applied to agile methodologies [18].
- Focus work on better understanding the effects of organizational culture and technological capabilities on organizational learning [13].
- Facing new challenges and opportunities regarding the determination of a technological architecture that supports knowledge management [30].
- Studies on the absorption capacity that allow to deepen the definition of concepts for the formulation of strategies at the organizational level [40].
- Develop studies about knowledge as the ability of people and communities to continually renew themselves [23].

4 Conclusions

The results of the systematic review indicate that the most used knowledge management strategies are collaborative networks, knowledge repositories, training, organizational agility, and business intelligence. Likewise, it was identified that the most used technologies are collaborative tools, information systems, business intelligence applications, and knowledge management systems. With the application of these strategies and the use of these technologies, software development companies can carry out effective knowledge management that facilitates the exchange of ideas and continuous learning among their employees. The effective management of knowledge in software development companies allows to achieve some benefits such as Increased efficiency and productivity, development of more collaborative interaction models and more appropriate processes, Increased teamwork, innovation and of the search for creative solutions, reduction in the learning curve through obtaining knowledge more systematically, standardization of processes and rapid access to information, improvement in decision-making and performance metrics and the customer service.

References

1. Zhang, Z.: Effective requirements development-a comparison of requirements elicitation techniques. Softw. Qual. Manag. XV Softw. Qual. Knowl. Soc. (2007). E. Berki, J. Nummenmaa, I. Sunley, M. Ross G. Staples Br. Comput. Soc.
2. Mizintseva, M.F., Gerbina, T.V.: Knowledge management: a tool for implementing the digital economy. Sci. Tech. Inf. Process. 45(1), 40–48 (2018). https://doi.org/10.3103/S01476882 18010094
3. Rodríguez, D.: Modelos para la creación y gestión del conocimiento: una aproximación teórica. Educar no. 37 (2006)
4. Bermúdez-Arango, A.P., Cuéllar-Torres, C.J., Riascos-Erazo, S.C.: Estrategias de aprendizaje organizacional y tecnologías de la información y las comunicaciones para apoyar la gestión de conocimiento en las pymes del Valle del Cauca, Colombia. Rev. Esc. Adm. Negocios no. 89 (2021). https://doi.org/10.21158/01208160.n89.2020.2818. N.1
5. McGowan Poole, C.D.: "IT outsourcing, knowledge transfer and project transition phases. VINE J. Inf. Knowl. Manag. Syst. 50(2), 219–246 (2020). https://doi.org/10.1108/VJIKMS-04-2019-0053. N.2

6. Sepúlveda Henao, M.: El reto de retener talento en el sector TI Mauricio. Univ. San Buenaventura, Colomb. 18 (2020). **N.3**
7. Martinez, C.: Rotacion laboral en empresas privadas de Colombia. Bogotá (2021)
8. León-Arce, H.G., Mogollón-Pérez, A.-S., Vargas Lorenzo, I., Vázquez Navarrete, M.-L.: Factores que influyen en el uso de mecanismos de coordinación entre niveles asistenciales en Colombia. Gac. Sanit. **35**(2), 177–185 (2021). https://doi.org/10.1016/j.gaceta.2019.06.005
9. Natek, S., Lesjak, D.: Knowledge management systems and tacit knowledge. Int. J. Innov. Learn. **29**(2), 166–180 (2021). https://doi.org/10.1504/IJIL.2021.112994. **N.3**
10. Lineberry, R.: Solve and evolve: practical applications for knowledge-centered service (2019). https://doi.org/10.1145/3347709.3347793. **N.4**
11. Buitrón, S.L., Flores-Rios, B.L., Pino, F.J.: Elicitación de requisitos no funcionales basada en la gestión de conocimiento de los stakeholders. Ingeniare **26**(1), 142–156 (2018). https://doi.org/10.4067/S0718-33052018000100142
12. Lepore, D., Dubbini, S., Micozzi, A., Spigarelli, F.: Knowledge sharing opportunities for industry 4.0 firms. J. Knowl. Econ. **13**(1), 501–520 (2022). https://doi.org/10.1007/s13132-021-00750-9. **N.5**
13. Arrieta Reales, N., Valdés Ortega, J.R.: Diseño y validación de un modelo de gestión del capital intelectual para la calidad de Instituciones de Educación Superior, Colombia. Interdiscip. Rev. Psicol. y Ciencias Afines **37**(1), 1–27 (2020). https://doi.org/10.16888/interd.2020.37.1.10. **N.6**
14. Fteimi, N., Hopf, K.: Knowledge management in the era of artificial intelligence: developing an integrative framework (2021). **N.7**
15. Morfi, D.P., Graupera, E.F., Ortiz, M.: Emprendimiento y Gestión del Conocimiento. Rev. UNIANDES Episteme **3**(3), 422–440 (2016). ISSN-e 1390–9150, vol. 3, no. 3 (Julio - Septiembre) (2016)
16. Pérez Rave, J.I.: Revisión sistemática de literatura en Ingeniería como apoyo a la consultoría basada en investigación. Univ. Cienc. Tecnol. **17**(66) (2013)
17. Natu, S., Aparicio, M.: Analyzing knowledge sharing behaviors in virtual teams: practical evidence from digitalized workplaces. J. Innov. Knowl. **7**(4) (2022). https://doi.org/10.1016/j.jik.2022.100248. **N.8**
18. Khalil, C., Khalil, S.: Exploring knowledge management in agile software development organizations. Int. Entrep. Manag. J. **16**(2) (2020). https://doi.org/10.1007/s11365-019-00582-9. **N.9**
19. Melo, G., Oliveira, T., Alencar, P., Cowan, D.: Knowledge reuse in software projects: retrieving software development Q&A posts based on project task similarity. PLoS One **15**(12) (2020). https://doi.org/10.1371/journal.pone.0243852. **N.10**
20. Ali, I., Musawir, A.U., Ali, M.: Impact of knowledge sharing and absorptive capacity on project performance: the moderating role of social processes. J. Knowl. Manag. **22**(2) (2018). https://doi.org/10.1108/JKM-10-2016-0449
21. Ouriques, R.A.B., Wnuk, K., Gorschek, T., Svensson, R.B.: Knowledge management strategies and processes in agile software development: a systematic literature review. Int. J. Softw. Eng. Knowl. Eng. **29**(3) (2019). https://doi.org/10.1142/S0218194019500153. **N.11**
22. Harb, Y., Abu-Shanab, E.: A descriptive framework for the field of knowledge management. Knowl. Inf. Syst. **62**(12) (2020). https://doi.org/10.1007/s10115-020-01492-x. **N.12**
23. Idrees, H., Hynek, J., Xu, J., Akbar, A., Jabeen, S.: Impact of knowledge management capabilities on new product development performance through mediating role of organizational agility and moderating role of business model innovation. Front. Psychol. **13** (2022). https://doi.org/10.3389/fpsyg.2022.950054. **N.13**
24. Nonaka, I., Takeuchi, H.: La organización creadora de conocimiento. Cómo las compañías japonesas crean la dinámica de la innovación, pp. 61–103 (1995). **N.14**

25. Rubio Arriaga, Z., De la o Burrola, V.G., Ruíz Corrales, M.: Modelo de gestión del conocimiento apoyado en las tecnologías de información y comunicación. Criterio Libr. **16**(28) (2018). https://doi.org/10.18041/1900-0642/criteriolibre.2018v16n28.2132

26. Venkatesh, V., Davis, F.D., Zhu, Y.: A cultural contingency model of knowledge sharing and job performance. J. Bus. Res. **140** (2022). https://doi.org/10.1016/j.jbusres.2021.07.042. **N.15**

27. Modelos teóricos de gestión del conocimiento: descriptores, conceptualizaciones y enfoques. Entreciencias Diálogos en la Soc. del Conoc. **4**(10) (2016). https://doi.org/10.21933/j.edsc.2016.10.181

28. Payró-Campos, P., Fuentes Vasconcelos, F.I.: "Gestión de conocimiento en una empresa de desarrollo de software. Rev. Investig. Académica Sin Front. Div. Ciencias Económ. Soc. (36) (2021). https://doi.org/10.46589/rdiasf.vi36.422. **N.16**

29. Riesco, M.: Gestión del conocimiento en ámbitos empresariales: 'modelo integrado-situacional' desde una perspectiva social y tecnológica (2004)

30. Rabhi, F.A., Bandara, M., Lu, K., Dewan, S.: Design of an innovative IT platform for analytics knowledge management. Futur. Gener. Comput. Syst. **116** (2021). https://doi.org/10.1016/j.future.2020.10.022. **N.17**

31. Jordan-Rivas, J.-A.: Implementación ágil de procesos y gestión del conocimiento (2018). https://doi.org/10.26439/ulima.tesis/8015

32. Koriat, N., Gelbard, R.: Knowledge sharing analytics: the case of IT workers. J. Comput. Inf. Syst. **59**(4) (2019). https://doi.org/10.1080/08874417.2017.1360163. **N.18**

33. Mehmood, M., BB, I.: A review of requirement engineering process models. J. Archit. Eng. Technol., **07**(01) (2018). https://doi.org/10.4172/2168-9717.1000215

34. Mejía, J., Rodríguez-Maldonado, I., Girón-Bobadilla, H., Muñoz, M.: Knowledge management in software process improvement: a systematic literature review. In: Iberian Conference on Information Systems and Technologies, CISTI, vol. 2019 (2019). https://doi.org/10.23919/CISTI.2019.8760614. **N.19**

35. Ouriques, R., Wnuk, K., Gorschek, T., Svensson, R.B.: The role of knowledge-based resources in agile software development contexts. J. Syst. Softw. **197** (2023). https://doi.org/10.1016/j.jss.2022.111572. **N.20**

36. Yao, J., Crupi, A., Di Minin, A., Zhang, X.: Knowledge sharing and technological innovation capabilities of Chinese software SMEs. J. Knowl. Manag. **24**(3) (2020). https://doi.org/10.1108/JKM-08-2019-0445. **N.21**

37. Maciel, C.P.C., de Souza, É.F., de Almeia Falbo, R., Felizardo, K.R., Vijaykumar, N.L.: Knowledge management diagnostics in software development organizations: a systematic literature review (2018). https://doi.org/10.1145/3275245.3275260. **N.22**

38. Chugh, M., Chanderwal, N., Upadhyay, R., Punia, D. K.: Effect of knowledge management on software product experience with mediating effect of perceived software process improvement: an empirical study for Indian software industry. J. Inf. Sci., **46**(2) (2020). https://doi.org/10.1177/0165551519833610. **N.23**

39. Suresh, S., Renukappa, S., Kamunda, A.: Knowledge management: a water industry case study (2019). https://doi.org/10.1145/3325917.3325958. **N.24**

40. Castaneda, D.I., Toulson, P.: Is it possible to share tacit knowledge using information and communication technology tools? Glob. Knowledge, Mem. Commun. **70**(8–9) (2021). https://doi.org/10.1108/GKMC-07-2020-0102. **N.25**

Smart Substation Communication with Virtual Networks

W. A. Vásquez-Barrientos[✉][ID], D. Escobar-Grisales[ID], and J. F. Botero-Vega[ID]

GITA Lab. School of Engineering, University of Antioquia UdeA, Medellín, Colombia
alesander.vasquez@udea.edu.co

Abstract. Power substations are involved in the transmission, control, and transformation of energy. Apart from power equipment, substations have communication networks to control and monitor the whole system; however, this infrastructure requires to have (i) as much backup equipment as the ones working on the substation network, and (ii) expert personnel who is 24/7 watching at the network to immediately react in case of a fault. Virtualized substations emerged as an alternative to overcome these challenges and bring the new challenge of finding alternative communication links/routes in case of a fault. This paper compares two different algorithms, one is a mixture of linear and integer programming and the other one is a metaheuristic algorithm based on ant colonies. Virtualized services (GOOSE, SV, and MMS) were implemented in a substation network and faults in one of the links (one by one, randomly selected) were simulated and two different variables were measured: (i) the computation time that each algorithm took to find alternative routes, and (ii) the path delay for the resulting alternative route. According to our results, the metaheuristic algorithm is faster in finding alternative routes likely because this algorithm is focused on finding a feasible route, not necessarily considering whether it is the optimal one. Regarding the path delay, we did not find statistical differences in the measures of the delays in the paths found by the two algorithms. Further investigation is required to evaluate the suitability of the metaheuristic algorithm to work on more realistic scenarios, where physical and virtualized devices work together.

Keywords: Smart Substations · Virtual Networks · Optimization · Heuristic

1 Introduction

Power substations are perhaps one of the most important components of an electrical network. Their role includes the conditioning, distribution, and transformation of electricity in different levels, namely primary, secondary, and distribution networks [5]. Given the fact that electricity is a critical infrastructure, service providers have to (by law) swiftly respond when any problem or issue happens. Their main objective is to minimize any possibility to suspend the service. Among the existing regulations and standards are IEC61850 [10] and IEEE1588 [7], which highlight and define the maximum number of faults and their corresponding duration such that the service perceived by the final user is not severely affected.

© The Author(s), under exclusive license to Springer Nature Switzerland AG 2023
J. C. Figueroa-García et al. (Eds.): WEA 2023, CCIS 1928, pp. 399–410, 2023.
https://doi.org/10.1007/978-3-031-46739-4_35

Among the main challenges that electricity providers have to face specifically in the power substations are: (i) to minimize the time to solve a given issue or fault such that final users are not (or minimally) affected; and (ii) to reduce costs associated with the administration and maintenance. Traditional power substations require the deployment of the network almost with a mirror implementation that enables the immediate replacement of any equipment in case of a fault. This clearly makes the operation more expensive and also requires the physical presence (all day long, 24/7, and during the whole year), of well-trained experts who need to know how to replace and configure any equipment in the network.

Network virtualization emerged a few years ago as an alternative to tackle the aforementioned challenges. Virtualization of network elements consists in creating virtual versions of physical network components such as routers, switches, firewalls, and others. These virtual versions operate in a virtualized environment and run on underlying physical devices. Communication, protection, and control devices are typical virtualized machines due to the relevant/critical functions they have to perform to assure the continuity of the service [1].

Although the virtualization process is expensive for the electricity company at the beginning, mainly due to the necessity of sophisticated knowledge, clear economical advantages appear in the long term, not only thanks to the removal of physical equipment but also because the response to communication faults becomes faster. Virtualization allows instantiating containers (light virtual machines) with functions of real equipment with the capability of virtualizing and restoring the service in case of a fault. As a key feature of virtual networks, there exist several options to implement algorithms created to automatically react in case of a communication fault. According to the existing regulation regarding virtual networks in power substations, which is mainly based on the IEC61850 standard[1], a restoration algorithm has to react and solve the problem in a given amount of time such that the service is not at risk [12]. One of the most common faults happens in communication links, therefore the restoration algorithm needs to "understand" which kind of messages were being transmitted over the faulty link and make all computations necessary to find an alternative route.

Several alternatives of algorithms and strategies to react in a reasonable amount of time has been proposed in the literature. In [4] the authors propose an approach in which the substation controller is replaced by a virtualized controller. Their experiments allowed the analysis of the delays in the transmission of different services such as GOOSE and MMS. According to their results, when combining GOOSE and MMS messages the delay was 2.17 ms. When the authors sent MMS and GOOSE over different paths, the delay increased to 13.93 ms. Even though the delays obtained by the authors were high, we highlight the fact that this was one of the first works that explored the possibility to virtualize a substation device. Recently, in [11] the authors implemented a communication network for a power substation with routes and functions defined in a network with services based on containers. Apart from the virtualization of services itself, the authors highlight as a contribution, the time that their implementation took to activate a protection relay (max 3 ms). Although the work contributes to the topic of services virtualization, the authors ignored the realistic scenario in which

---

[1] https://libiec61850.com/.

devices are connected to several machines, forming a network and therefore appearing the possibility of different communication failures. In [12] the authors proposed the application of time-sensitive networks to support different functions operating in power substations. This approach allows the evaluation of scenarios with different data flows and network conditions like latency and priority. Their experiments yielded a maximum jitter of 38.7 ms for critical traffic; however, the operation of other network elements is not evaluated.

In this paper, we compared two algorithms created to compute alternative routes in order to keep communication among all network virtualized devices in case of a fault. We introduced a mixed model based on linear programming that calculates the optimal route in case of a fault. The second algorithm is based on the metaheuristic optimization paradigm that involves ant colony. This method is used here for comparison purposes. According to the state-of-the-art, although this approach does not necessarily yields the optimal route [6], it provides an alternative route in times that are below those required by the current standard [10]. Therefore we wanted to verify this and also to compare such an excellent time-to-response with respect to our proposed approach. The two algorithms were implemented upon the Spiderweb topology [8], which was introduced in 2016 by Leal et al. with the aim to overcome several problems previously observed in existing topologies, including star, ring, double ring, and tree. According to our results, the metaheuristic method takes less time to restore the communication.

The rest of the paper is organized as follows: Sect. 2 introduces the concept of substations virtualization. Section 3 introduces the virtualization of services. Section 4 introduces the two optimization methods that are evaluated in this study. Section 5 explains the two experiments performed to evaluate the algorithms, and finally Sect. 6 presents the conclusions derived from the work.

2 Virtualization of Power Substations

Typical substations are composed of power equipment (transform and transmit electricity) and communication devices that are in charge of controlling those power-related equipment. All functions and features related to the transmission and transformation of electricity cannot be virtualized, however, the communication among that equipment is being replaced for several years by virtual machines. This concept of virtualization in the context of power substations requires the definition and implementation of different protocols and rules for the communication network. Virtualization of networks pushed the development of new technologies associated with the process of managing network functions. Software-defined networks (SDN) allow separating control and data planes, which opened the opportunity to develop a number of different features in virtualized networks. The programming protocol-independent packet processors (P4) are another technology that enabled the programming of different virtual devices (routers, switches, filters, etc.) in the data plane. This programming language allows the researchers to manage the traffic in a virtualized network which opens the opportunity to program many different functions and algorithms including those associated with the automatic response in case of a communication fault. The fundamental elements of a virtualized network are listed below:

– Virtual Machines (VM): these are virtual environments that manage their own
  resources (RAM memory, processing, and storage) while executed in a real machine.
  Each VM has its own operating system, applications, and network protocols. Typical VMs can communicate among themselves, and expose services like being a real
  machine but running in a virtual infrastructure.
– Containers: these are light VMs that consume less memory and energy, which enable
  several features including: (i) portability: they can run in any operating system
  excluding unnecessary applications and functions; (ii) lightness: they do not require
  an operating system; (iii) Efficiency: a container only has libraries, files, scripts, and
  necessary configurations to deploy specific functions.
– Virtual switches (VS): they are software components that allow the interconnection
  of VMs and/or containers in a virtual network. They are typically configured to
  manage the traffic among VMs, containers, and the host.
– Network controllers: they are network components in charge of managing and
  controlling the correct operation of a virtualized network. Among their tasks are
  network resources assignment, security policies configuration, and interconnection
  among network devices. Typical controllers SDN are: POX, RYU, OpenDaylight,
  and ONOS.
– Network orchestration: this allows the coordination of virtualized network services
  which implies the automatization of different tasks.

A comprehensive illustration of the functions and tasks executed by these elements
can be found in [2, 11]. Figure 1 illustrates a common virtualized network in the context
of power substations.

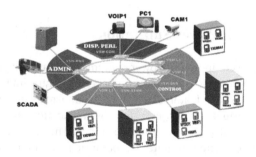

Fig. 1. Virtualized substation.

3   Virtualization of Services in Power Substations

This process consists in implementing services that typically exist in a given physical
machine in the substation and program them in a container. This process allows using
any machine to run different functions and act as different network elements according to the current necessity. Figure 2 shows how a traditional power substation and its
virtualized version looks like. Notice that the virtualized version is implemented and

deployed in the cloud. There is an interface equipment that is physically working in the substation. The main task of this equipment is to interconnect all functions executed by the virtualized devices with the physical machines for which there is no virtual version, e.g., power transformers, actuators, breakers, etc.

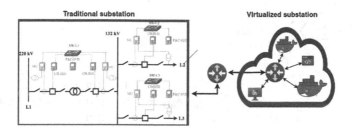

Fig. 2. Virtualized substation.

Virtualized services in power substations are possible via the instantiation of functions typically executed by elements such as Intelligent Electronics Devices (IEDs), meter units (MU), protection and control equipment, and others. The IEC61850 standard provides a set with libraries with the functions that the devices need to execute. These functions enable the communication between physical and virtual equipment (e.g., container) [12].

4   Virtualized Service Optimization

Communication services in virtualized power substations need to be deployed in topologies such that allow real-time services and effective restoration in case of faults, low latency, and high jitter. Scalability and high availability are also among the requirements for an ideal virtualized substation. Different topologies were compared in [8] regarding their reliability. According to the result reported by the authors, the Spiderweb topology is the one that offers more reliability, redundancy, resilience, and feasibility in its administration and inter-operation with different network devices [8]. Based on the results reported in [8], this paper adopted the Spiderweb topology to evaluate the performance of two different optimization algorithms created to find optimal routes that serve as the alternative to communicate two nodes in case of a link fault. The first algorithm is based on the mixed linear programming framework and the second one implements a metaheuristic approach based on an ant colony. Details of these two optimization approaches are presented in the next subsections.

4.1   Optimization Through Mixed Methods

Mixed optimization incorporates concepts of linear and integer programming. Given the fact that in communication networks information is transported from one node to another one, it is necessary to define binary variables to model which links are used, but at the same time, real variables are required to model link's occupation. More realistic models can be defined following mixed optimization strategies and appropriately defining specific restrictions that enable the modeling of robust solutions. For the particular need of finding optimal routes in case of a link fault in the network of a power substation, we defined the following objective function of a mixed optimization model aiming to find the solution in the shortest possible time:

$$\min_{\forall l} K_l = \sum_{s=1}^{S} \sum_{d=1}^{D} \delta_{lds} * h_{ds}$$

subject to

$$\sum_{l=1}^{L} a_{ln} \cdot \delta_{lds} - \sum_{l=1}^{L} b_{ln} \cdot \delta_{lds} = \begin{cases} 1, & \text{if } n = s_d \\ 0, & \text{if } n \neq (s_d y t_d) \quad \forall d, n, s \\ -1, & \text{if } n = t_d. \end{cases}$$

$$\sum_{l=1}^{L} T_l \cdot \delta_{lds} \leq T_{ds} \quad \forall d, s$$

$$\sum_{d=1}^{D} \delta_{lds} \leq 1 \quad \forall l, s$$

$$\sum_{s=1}^{S} \sum_{d=1}^{D} h_{ds} \leq C_l \quad \forall l$$

(1)

where K_l is the variable that accumulates the demands transmitted over the link l. δ_{lds} is a binary variable defined as

$$\delta_{lds} = \begin{cases} 1, & \text{if the link } l \text{ is used to transmit the demand } d \text{ of the service } s \\ 0, & \text{in other cases} \end{cases}$$

h_{ds} is a parameter indicating the quantity of demand d for the service s.

Details of the restrictions defined in the objective function are provided below:

Restriction of flow conservation

$$\sum_{l=1}^{L} a_{ln} \cdot \delta_{lds} - \sum_{l=1}^{L} b_{ln} \cdot \delta_{lds} = \begin{cases} 1, & \text{if } n = s_d \\ 0, & \text{if } n \neq (s_d y t_d) \quad \forall d, n, s \\ -1, & \text{if } n = t_d. \end{cases}$$

(2)

This restriction guarantees flow conservation, i.e., all flow in the input to each node n is equal to the flow at the output of the same node. Indexation about which are the originating and destination nodes per each demand is maintained. a_{ln} is a parameter used to define the origin of a node such that $a_{ln} = 1$ if n is the origin of the link l and $a_{ln} = 0$ otherwise. b_{ln} is a parameter used to define the destination of a node such that $b_{ln} = 1$ if n is the destination of the link l, and $b_{ln} = 0$ otherwise. s_d is the source node for a given demand d, and t_d is the destination node for a given demand d. s_d and t_d values are assigned according to the following rules:

$$s_d = \begin{cases} 1 & \text{if it is the node that originates the demand} \\ 0 & \text{other cases} \end{cases}$$

$$t_d = \begin{cases} -1 & \text{if it is the destination node} \\ 0 & \text{other cases} \end{cases}$$

Restriction of maximum delay

$$\sum_{l=1}^{L} T_l \cdot \delta_{lds} \leq T_{ds} \quad \forall\, d, s \tag{3}$$

This restriction guarantees that the sum of all delays in the links of a given path between s_d and t_d is below the maximum delay T_{ds} defined for the corresponding demand and service.

Restriction of the paths uniqueness for a given service with a given demand

$$\sum_{d=1}^{D} \delta_{lds} \leq 1 \quad \forall\, l, s \tag{4}$$

This restriction guarantees that a given demand does not use the same link twice. This condition also helps in making sure that there will not be an overload on a link because it distributes the demands among different routes.

Restriction of link capacity

$$\sum_{s=1}^{S} \sum_{d=1}^{D} h_{ds} \leq C_l \quad \forall\, l \tag{5}$$

This restriction assures that the sum of all demands in a given link does not exceed its maximum capacity C_l. Table 1 shows the list of services and their corresponding demands within the context of virtualized power substations.

4.2 Metaheuristic Optimization with Ant Colonies

Metaheuristic methods yield acceptable solutions to optimization problems, however, it is not always the case of obtaining the optimal solution. The main reason is that these methods focused on finding a suitable solution but not the optimal one. This is why, in most cases, they find a solution faster than the exact methods [13]. Figure 3 illustrates the particular case of the ant colony optimization algorithm in the context of a graph.

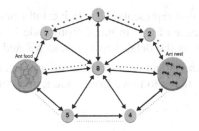

Fig. 3. Ants graph.

Table 1. Description of different service types and their corresponding demands in bytes.

Service	Description	Demand [bytes]	# frames	Protocol
GOOSE	The Generic Object Oriented Substation Event (GOOSE) message reflects the information transmission between intelligent electronic devices (IEDs)	205	4	GOOSE
SV	Sampled Values (SV) are sample values required by control equipment to monitor transformer status	115	∞	IEC61850 SV
MMS	Manufacturing Message Specification (MMS) is the messaging service used to indicate service status and carry low-priority configuration messages	89	4	MMS

A set of artificial ants is created to travel over the whole space of the given problem. While each ant is traveling it can leave pheromones on the visited places to transmit certain information to other ants. A place with a larger number of pheromones indicates to have been visited by more ants. Figure 3 illustrates a general model in which an ant colony searches for the best path from a nest to a food place. Thicker paths illustrate more pheromones on each path, therefore in a given iteration of the algorithm, more ants will take the red-dotted path. It could also be the case that no ant takes a certain path, therefore no pheromones will be placed on it [3].

The process to update the number of pheromones τ_{ij} for the k-th ant on the link between nodes i and j is defined by the following expression:

$$\tau_{ij} \leftarrow (1 - \rho) \cdot \tau_{ij} + \sum_{k=1}^{K} \Delta\tau_{ij}^k$$

where $0 < \rho < 1$ is the pheromones evaporation coefficient, and $\tau_{ij}^k = \frac{1}{L_k}$ if the k-th ant is moving from node i to j. L_k is the length of the path given in terms of the number of links to move from the origin to the destination.

The probability of the k-th ant to choose node j having started from node i is given by

$$P_{ij}^k = \frac{(\tau_{ij})^\alpha \cdot (\eta_{ij})^\beta}{\sum_{l \in N_i^k} (\tau_{ij})^\alpha \cdot (\eta_{ij})^\beta}$$

where α is a parameter that represents the relative influence of a pheromones trace, η_{ij} represents the preference of ants to move from node i to node j and it is defined as $\eta_{ij} = \frac{1}{d_{ij}}$, where d_{ij} is the delay between nodes i and j. $\beta > 0$ is a heuristic parameter that indicates the influence of the heuristic information. N_i^k is the number of available nodes for the k-th ant to move from node i. K is the total number of ants in the algorithm.

5 Experiments and Results

The aforementioned algorithms were evaluated on the Spiderweb topology with the aim to establish their suitability to restore the service in an affordable amount of time, and to find the path with the minimal possible delay, i.e., the optimal path. The Spiderweb topology was defined with a total of 8 nodes and 14 links. All tests were repeated eight times with the aim to verify the robustness of the methods and the stability of the observed results. Two different scenarios were evaluated: (i) the network fully operating with different delays randomly assigned for the links, and (ii) the network operating without one of its links (randomly selected), which is defined as broken with the aim to evaluate the effectiveness of the optimization algorithms to find alternative routes. Details of each experimental scenario are provided in the following subsections.

5.1 Experiment # 1

This experiment intends to show the implementation of different services, e.g., GOOSE, SV, and MMS, in a Spiderweb topology. Different delays were randomly assigned to each link to emulate realistic communication scenarios, then the two algorithms were run to obtain the paths according to the criteria defined on each algorithm. Table 2 shows the delays of the links chosen by each algorithm to connect the evaluated demands (randomly chosen) in the first iteration of the experiment. The main outcome of this experiment is the virtualization of the services, which is already a positive result according to other studies in the state-of-the-art. [9]

Table 2. Delays in paths chosen by mixed vs. metaheuristic algorithms. d_{ij}: demand from node i to node j. l: link. T: delay in [ms]. $\sum T$: sum of delays of all links within a given path. Avg.: average.

Mixed algorithm				Metaheuristic algorithm				
d_{ij}	$l\colon T$	$l\colon T$	$l\colon T$	$\sum T$	$l\colon T$	$l\colon T$	$l\colon T$	$l\colon T$	$\sum T$
4–1	11: 0.01	8: 0.01	–	0.02	3: 0.1	2: 0.05	9: 2.5	8: 0.01	2.66
8–4	11: 0.01	–	–	0.01	8: 0.01	1: 1.5	2: 0.05	3: 0.1	1.66
1–5	7: 0.01	6: 2	5: 0.3	2.31	8: 0.01	12: 0.01	–	–	0.02
2–8	1: 1.5	8: 0.01	–	1.51	9: 2.5	–	–	–	2.5
2–3	2: 0.05	–	–	0.05	2: 0.05	–	–	–	0.05
Avg.				0.72	Avg.				1.38

Notice that, in this case, where there is no fault in any of the links, the mixed algorithm selects paths that are on average faster than those selected by the metaheuristic algorithm. This result confirms the fact that even though heuristic algorithms can solve the problem of finding alternative paths in less time than other algorithms, their result is not necessarily the optimal one (the fastest one). The next experiment will compare these two algorithms when there is a fault in one link, therefore it is expected the metaheuristic algorithm to find the solution faster than the mixed one.

5.2   Experiment # 2

In this experiment, we randomly selected and broke links (one by one) and run the two optimization algorithms introduced in Sect. 4 to evaluate what is their capability to (i) restore the service in the minimal possible time, and (ii) find the optimal path such that its total delay is the minimum possible among all options in the network. Figure 4 illustrates the topology of the network and highlights link 8 which is considered as one of the fault scenarios.

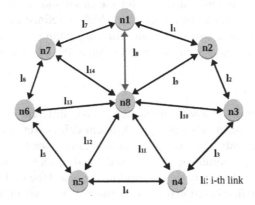

Fig. 4. Network topology.

Table 3 indicates the routes selected by each algorithm when there is no fault in any link vs. when there is a fault in link $l = 8$. All demands are considered in this evaluation; however, notice that not all paths use the link 8, although the algorithms compute a new route in every case because the alarm of a broken link implies that a new path needs to be computed regardless of the involved links in a given path. This is necessary because the distribution of the services may change in every iteration.

Routes where link 8 is involved and a fault is produced, are marked as $\cancel{8}$. The next row indicates the alternative route computed by the corresponding optimization algorithm. Delay times are shown for comparison purposes and also the difference between the time without fault and with fault is included. The last rows of Table 3 show the computation times obtained with each algorithm in the two scenarios (with and without fault). Notice that computation times are clearly lower for the case of the metaheuristic algorithm. The reason is that this algorithm takes the first alternative path that appears as a feasible option, without considering whether it is optimal in terms of the path delay. Conversely, when estimating the average delay over the whole demand, it can be observed that, for the iteration that we are showing, the mixed algorithm finds faster paths than the metaheuristic one. With the aim to validate this observation, we decided to analyze the statistical behavior of the path delays over all iterations for all demands when link 8 is broken. Figure 5 shows the distribution of those delays obtained with the two algorithms. A Mann-Whitney U test was performed and the result showed that there are no significant differences between these two distributions ($p = 0.34$). Therefore, in case of a fault, both algorithms select similar routes regarding the path delay.

Table 3. Results obtained with the two optimization algorithms when link $l = 8$ is broken. P_T: Path delay. $\Delta(P_T)$: Difference between the path delay with and without fault.

	Mixed			Metaheuristic		
Demand	Links	P_T	$\Delta(P_T)$	Links	P_T	$\Delta(P_T)$
4-1	8̸–11	0.02		3–2–9–8̸	2.66	
Alt. route	3–2–1	1.65	+1.63	3–2–1	1.65	-1.01
8-4	11	0.01		8̸–1–2–3	1.66	
Alt. route	11	0.01	0	11	0.01	-1.65
1-5	7–6–5	2.31		8̸–12	0.02	
Alt. route	7–14–12	2.11	-0.2	7–14–13–5	4.81	+4.78
2-8	1–8̸	1.51		9	2.50	
Alt. route	9	2.50	0.99	2–3–11	0.16	-2.34
2-3	2	0.05		2	0.05	
Alt. route	2	0.05	0	2	0.05	0
Average	–	1.02	–	–	1.36	–

Comp. time without fault: 36.3ms   Comp. time without fault: 7.9ms

Comp. time with fault: 49.8ms   Comp. time with fault: 12.3ms

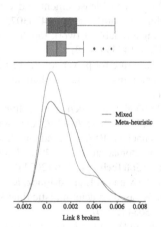

Fig. 5. Path delay distributions.

6 Conclusions and Discussion

The virtualization of services in the context of power substations is introduced in this paper. A state-of-the-art topology is implemented with the aim to compare two optimization algorithms (mixed and metaheuristic) when one of the links in the network is broken. According to our results, the metaheuristic algorithm is faster in finding alternative routes. The main reason is because this strategy is not focused on finding optimal routes but feasible alternatives such that restore the communication between origin and destination nodes. Finally, we did not find statistical differences between the path delays measured in the alternative routes found by the two algorithms. As a future work, we envision the implementation of a more realistic scenario in which physical and virtualized machines are working.

References

1. Bouffard-Vercelli, Y.E., André, B.: Future architectures of electrical substations. In: 2021 Petroleum and Chemical Industry Conference Europe (PCIC Europe), pp. 1–6. IEEE (2021)
2. Chica, J.C., Imbachi, J.C., Botero, J.F.: Security in SDN: a comprehensive survey. J. Netw. Comput. Appl. **159**, 102595 (2020)
3. Dorigo, M., Gambardella, L.M.: Ant colony system: a cooperative learning approach to the traveling salesman problem. IEEE Trans. Evol. Comput. **1**(1), 53–66 (1997)
4. Dorsch, N., Jablkowski, B., Georg, H., Spinczyk, O., Wietfeld, C.: Analysis of communication networks for smart substations using a virtualized execution platform. In: 2014 IEEE International Conference on Communications (ICC), pp. 4239–4245. IEEE (2014)
5. Huang, Q., Jing, S., Li, J., Cai, D., Wu, J., Zhen, W.: Smart substation: state of the art and future development. IEEE Trans. Power Delivery **32**(2), 1098–1105 (2016)
6. Hussain, K., Mohd Salleh, M.N., Cheng, S., Shi, Y.: Metaheuristic research: a comprehensive survey. Artif. Intell. Rev. **52**, 2191–2233 (2019)
7. Institute of Electrical and Electronics Engineers: IEEE Standard for a Precision Clock Synchronization Protocol for Networked Measurement and Control Systems. Standard 1588. IEEE (2008). https://ieeexplore.ieee.org/document/4753073
8. Leal, A., Botero, J.F.: Defining a reliable network topology in software-defined power substations. IEEE Access **7**, 14323–14339 (2019)
9. Leal, A., Botero, J.F.: An architecture for power substations communication networks based on SDN and virtualization paradigms. Revista Facultad de Ingeniería Universidad de Antioquia **100**(100), 48–66 (2021)
10. libIEC61850: libIEC61850/lib60870-5—open source libraries for IEC 61850 and IEC 60870-5-104. https://libiec61850.com/libiec61850/. Accessed 14 July 2023
11. Rösch, D., Nicolai, S., Bretschneider, P.: Combined simulation and virtualization approach for interconnected substation automation. In: 2021 6th International Conference on Smart and Sustainable Technologies (SpliTech), pp. 1–6 (2021)
12. Sanchez-Garrido, J., Jurado, A., Medina, L., Rodriguez, R., Ros, E., Diaz, J.: Digital electrical substation communications based on deterministic time-sensitive networking over ethernet. IEEE Access **8**, 93621–93634 (2020)
13. Talbi, E.G.: Metaheuristics: From Design to Implementation. Wiley, Hoboken (2009)

Development of a Farm Animal Tracking Device Using LoRaWAN

Rejane Sá[✉][iD], Lucas Noé[iD], Narcelio Silva[iD], Rogério Diogenes[iD],
Wendell Rodrigues[iD], and Elianderson Silva[iD]

Instituto Federal do Ceará, Fortaleza, Brazil
{rejane_sa,rogerio.diogenes,wendell,elianderson.lima}@ifce.edu.br,
{lucas.noe.santos08,narcelio.lima.silva05}@aluno.ifce.edu.br
https://ifce.edu.br/

Abstract. This project aims to develop an ox tracking system using LoRaWAN (Low Power Wide Area Network) technology to monitor the locomotion of animals on farms. The system's goal is to provide accurate information about the location and behavior of the oxen, assisting breeders in efficiently managing the herd. The device is designed to track and locate the ox through an earring that will be installed in the animal's ear. Initially targeting beef cattle, the product aims to monitor the animal's location for two primary reasons: identifying issues (such as theft or diseases) and preventing intrusion into environmentally protected areas. Laboratory and field tests were conducted to validate communication and data accuracy.

Keywords: IoT · LoRaWAN · Monitoring GPS

1 Introduction

The tracking of animals, mandated by international trade regulations within the meat supply chain, necessitates the intensification of management practices on rural properties. This involves stringent control measures for animals, including the prompt and accurate individual identification of each animal.

Besides trade regulations, in [6], Aleluia et al. highlight a critical issue in the context of global agriculture and urbanization trends. They start by drawing attention to the significant shift of the global population towards urban areas, with an estimated increase to over 2.5 billion urban dwellers by 2050, according to the Food and Agriculture Organization (FAO). This shift has consequences for agriculture, as most agricultural activities traditionally occur in rural areas. The paper suggests that rural abandonment could adversely affect agricultural production, potentially leading to challenges in meeting the rising demand for agricultural products, such as dairy, which has seen a notable increase in consumption over the years.

Supported by IFCE and NEPEN.

Moreover, the text emphasizes the need for sustainable strategies to address the growing demand for agricultural products while considering the decreasing labor force available for farming. It hints at the concept of optimizing production to minimize waste and meet consumption growth. The mention of traditional animal monitoring methods being cumbersome and costly on medium and large farms underscores the practical challenges facing modern agriculture. Overall, they emphasize the urgency of adopting innovative and efficient solutions, such as advanced monitoring technologies, to ensure the sustainability of agricultural production in the face of urbanization and changing consumption patterns.

LoRaWAN (Low Power Wide Area Network) allows several features and applications to solve problems with low power communication [1–3]. Currently, in addition to commercial issues, the international market has been demanding that producers ensure that the cattle do not devastate/treade in areas of environmental preservation. This is only possible through tracking techniques and software with position log, which records the map of steps throughout the animal's useful life. Large consumers, especially in the European market, demand control of the animal's traceability, even failing to buy if there is any suspicion about the process, especially if it is not reliable or auditable. The main point is the guarantee that the animal was not created in places of environmental preservation. Any kind of suspicion about this suspends beef exports.

In addition to the commercial factor, which would already justify the application of the product to be generated by this project, tracking cattle provides the customer with an alarm tool against animal theft and the possibility of identifying possible diseases. This is because, with the locations and accelerometer, it is possible to know the precise location of the animal. In addition, if the animal is not moving for several hours straight, it is possible to indicate the occurrence of some problem, illness or even attack by snakes and other animals. Works with animal monitoring are seen in [4] and [5], for example.

The report [7] states the global livestock monitoring market has experienced remarkable growth, with an estimated value of USD 5.6 billion in 2022. Projections (Fig. 1) indicate that this market is poised to witness substantial expansion, reaching approximately USD 23.35 billion by 2032. This growth trajectory is attributed to the adoption of smart IoT sensors, signaling a significant revolution in the field of animal agriculture. With a compound annual growth rate (CAGR) of 15.4% anticipated over the forecast period from 2023 to 2032, the livestock monitoring sector is set to play a pivotal role in the modernization and enhancement of animal farming practices worldwide.

Thus, this project aims to develop an ox tracking system using LoRaWAN technology to monitor the locomotion of animals on farms. The system aims to provide accurate information about the location and behavior of the oxen, helping breeders in the efficient management of the herd. The use of tracking devices with LoRaWAN technology offers significant advantages compared to other solutions due to its low power consumption rate and long data transmission distance. These features allow the devices to be implanted in steers without causing discomfort or interfering with their natural behavior.

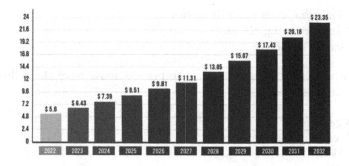

Fig. 1. Livestock Monitoring Market Size, 2022 to 2032 (USD Billion). Source: [7]

The project is organized as follows: Sect. 1 the introduction, Sect. 2 the description of the developed device. In Sects. 3 and 4 the results and conclusion of the project, respectively.

2 Device

The tracking system consists of earring-shaped devices equipped with GPS location sensors and a battery powered by a small solar panel. This device collects data on the animal's geographic position and movement patterns. Information is transmitted over the LoRaWAN network to a centralized base station on the farm.

The base station receives data from tracking devices and forwards it to a server for processing and storage. On this server, data is analyzed and transformed into useful information for livestock farmers. Data processing algorithms can identify patterns of behavior such as preferred grazing sites, migration routes or abnormal activities such as the animal being immobile for an extended period.

Livestock farmers can access the information through an app or web platform, allowing them to remotely monitor the herd. This facilitates decision-making related to the health, nutrition, reproduction and management of the animals. Furthermore, in cases of theft or loss of animals, the tracking system can help locate them quickly, minimizing financial losses.

All data will be uploaded and made available to be consumed in a data cloud. A dashboard will be developed for data visualization, including the following functionalities:

- Cattle herd registration and management;
- Visualization of cattle tracking;
- Register of virtual fences;
- Generate alarms and basic reports:
- Cattle theft alarms;

– Alarms for anomalous cattle behavior;
– Virtual fence crossing alarms;
– Bovine status report;

For hardware and encapsulation, the project must have the following components/functionalities:

– Battery powered;
– NB-IoT communication;
– Geolocation;
– Acceleration measurement;
– Low power consumption;
– Maximum weight of 40 g;
– IP68 enclosure.

2.1 Hardware e Firmware

The earring's 3D design was developed with the lowest possible weight for the ox in mind. The entire 3D device design is seen in Fig. 2 and the solar panel seen in Fig. 3.

For TAG processing, the STM32WB15CC was used and the Cinterion TX62 for LPWAN communication. In the schematic called peripherals, along with the connections, there are the power supply circuits for the microcontroller and the peripherals and the accelerometer circuit. For the accelerometer function, we use the LIS2DE12, which is a high-performance, ultra-low power, three-axis linear accelerometer belonging to the "femto" family, with standard I2C/SPI digital serial interface output. The self-test capability allows the user to verify sensor functionality in the final application. In this schematic, there is also the electrical diagram of the LED circuit, which serves as our HMI, the reed switch circuit, which is for commissioning using magnet, the AC modem and the DC-DC converters.

A small panel was used to power an internal battery. For the converters, the SN74LV1T34DCKR was used, which is a low voltage CMOS logic gate that operates in a wider voltage range for industrial, automotive, telecommunications and portable applications. For battery charging we use the SiP32510. It is a slew rate controlled load switch designed for 1.2 V to 5.5 V operation. It features a smooth controlled slew rate of 1.6 ms typical, which limits inrush current for charging designs. heavy capacitive and minimizes the resulting voltage drop on the power rails.

In the firmware, the functionalities, state machine and optimization of memory consumption, processing and physical space were studied. Also built all communication drives with GPS, Accelerometer and NB-IoT communication, implemented low consumption.

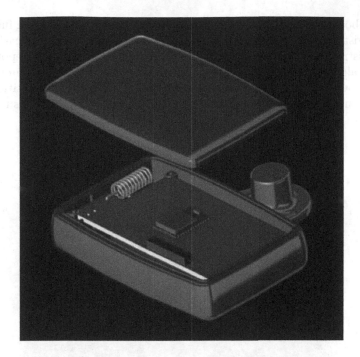

Fig. 2. 3D design of the structure.

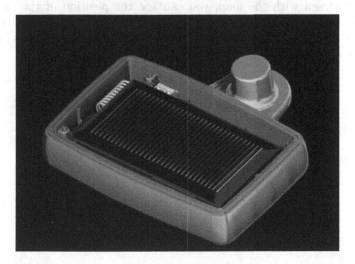

Fig. 3. 3D drawing of the structure seen from the photocell.

2.2   Monitoring System

In this stage, data integration and visualization systems were developed. Generated windows of the project's integration and monitoring system are presented.

The dashboard developed for data visualization includes the following functionalities: Registration and management of cattle herd; Visualization of cattle tracking; Registration of virtual fences; Generating alarms and basic reports: Cattle theft alarms; Bovine anomalous behavior alarms; Virtual fence overtaking alarms; Bovine status report; seen on the screen in Fig. 4. The position of the ox is seen in Fig. 5. SPACEVIS is the software developed for web visualization.

Fig. 4. Animal visualization screen in SPACEVIS.

On the screen with the map, you can see the position of the ox with the location reference, and it is also possible to see the entire trajectory traveled by the animal. The images in Figs. 6 and 7 show the farm image with the LoRaWAN network mapping and the position of the ox, respectively.

Fig. 5. Animal registration screen in SPACEVIS.

Fig. 6. View from the farm.

Fig. 7. Image with the location of the animal.

3   Results

In the integration and testing stage, tests were carried out in the laboratory and in the field with the device installed in the animal. Commissioning test, battery analysis, communication test and mechanical structure in the field. In Fig. 8 you can see an image of the LoRa gateway installed on the farm.

The device commissioning process is the process of installing and registering the equipment in the software and it will have three flows, commissioning in the application, commissioning in the backend and commissioning in the device.

In the application, the operator must open the TagVis application at the installation site, scan the device's QR CODE, select the COMMISSIONING option and enter the animal's information. In the device commissioning process there are more steps. The device leaves the factory in SHUTDOWN mode.

Fig. 8. Gateway installed on the farm. No need of complex infrastructures.

The device will exit this mode after feeling the magnet approach 3 times. For each approximation, the LED must flash and wait 1 s and it will wait up to 5 s for the next approximation of the magnet. If the process is completed successfully, the device should keep the LED on for 5 s and then it will start the commissioning process. If the process is interrupted during one of the three attempts, the device should flash 5 times very quickly and return to shelf mode.

In tests with the first version of the device there were some problems with communication and location of components. In the second version the problem with the PCI was solved. Figures 9 and 10 show the first version of the device. In Figs. 11 and 12 the final version.

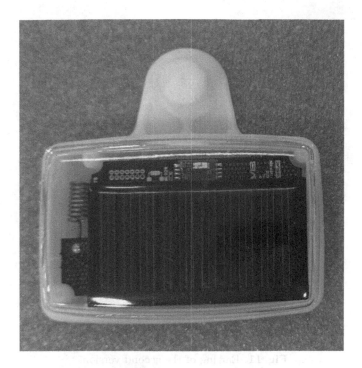

Fig. 9. Earring of the first version.

Fig. 10. Earring on the animal in the first version of the device.

Fig. 11. Earring of the second version.

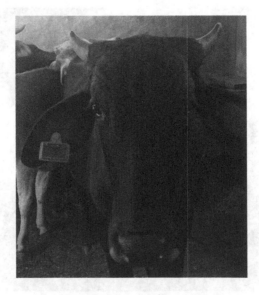

Fig. 12. Earring on the animal in the second version of the device.

4 Conclusion

In this project, we developed an innovative cattle tracking system using LoRaWAN technology and solar energy, aiming to verify the locomotion of animals on farms in an efficient and sustainable way.

Through the implementation of the tracking system with LoRaWAN, we were able to monitor the geographical position and behavior of the oxen accurately and in real time. This information is essential for cattle breeders, allowing for more efficient management of the herd and decision-making based on concrete data.

Additionally, the integration of solar panels into the system provides a clean, renewable source of energy to power the tracking devices. This eliminates the need for frequent battery replacement and significantly reduces operating costs, making the system more sustainable and economically viable in the long term.

The use of LoRaWAN technology provided wide communication coverage, allowing tracking devices to send data even in remote rural areas. This is important on large farms where comprehensive monitoring is required to ensure animal welfare and optimize production.

Throughout the project, we faced technical challenges such as developing low-power tracking devices and configuring an efficient LoRaWAN network. However, with dedication and teamwork, we overcame obstacles and achieved satisfactory results.

The successful implementation of this LoRaWAN and solar panel steer tracking system has potential in the livestock industry. Livestock farmers can now monitor their herds more accurately, improving animal health and management, reducing financial losses and contributing to sustainable practices.

Acknowledgment. We would like to express our acknowledgment to the IFCE research department and the Master Program PROFNIT. Also, we highlight the dedicated team at the LIT laboratory, and the support provided by NEPEN throughout this research endeavor. Their contributions and assistance have been instrumental in the successful completion of this project.

References

1. Niles, K., Ray, J., Niles, K., Maxwell, A., Netchaev, A.: Monitoring for analytes through LoRa and LoRaWAN technology. Procedia Comput. Sci. **185**, 152–159 (2021). Big Data, IoT, and AI for a Smarter Future
2. Zakaria, M., Jabbar, W., Sulaiman, N.: Development of a smart sensing unit for LoRaWAN-based IoT flood monitoring and warning system in catchment areas. Internet Things Cyber-Phys. Syst. **3**, 249–261 (2023)
3. Guevara, N., Bolaños, Y., Diago, J., Segura, J.: Development of a low-cost IoT system based on LoRaWAN for monitoring variables related to electrical energy consumption in low voltage networks. HardwareX **12**, e00330 (2022)
4. Alipio, M., Villena, M.: Intelligent wearable devices and biosensors for monitoring cattle health conditions: a review and classification. Smart Health **27**, 100369 (2023)

5. Valchev, E., Malinov, P., Glushkova, T., Stoyanov, S.: Approach for modeling and implementation of an intelligent system for livestock cattle on pastures. IFAC-PapersOnLine **55**, 211–216 (2022). 7th IFAC Conference on Sensing, Control and Automation Technologies for Agriculture AGRICONTROL 2022
6. Aleluia, V., Soares, V., Caldeira, J., Rodrigues, A.: Livestock monitoring: approaches, challenges and opportunities. Int. J. Eng. Adv. Technol. **11**, 67–76 (2022)
7. Livestock Monitoring Market Size, Growth, Trends, Report By 2032 (2023). https://www.precedenceresearch.com/livestock-monitoring-market

In-Silico Study of the Effect of Particulate Matter from Medellín on Virtual Ventricular Tissue

Angela M. Gómez[1], Juan P. Ugarte[2] (iD), Robison Buitrago-Sierra[3] (iD),
Isabel C. Ortiz-Trujillo[4], Natalia Acevedo[4], and Catalina Tobón[5]([✉]) (iD)

[1] Universidad de Antioquia, Medellín, Colombia
[2] GIMSC, Universidad de San Buenaventura, Medellín, Colombia
[3] MATyER, Institución Universitaria ITM, Medellín, Colombia
[4] Universidad Pontificia Bolivariana, Medellín, Colombia
[5] MATBIOM, Universidad de Medellín, Medellín, Colombia
ctobon@udemedellin.edu.co

Abstract. In this work, the effect of air particulate matter (PM) from Medellín City on ventricular electrophysiological properties was studied. Computational simulations were implemented using single-cell and two-dimensional models of human ventricular tissue, in combination with previous experimental findings about the effect of PM collected in Medellín City on cardiac cultures. The results showed a concentration-dependent proarrhythmic effect of PM. As the concentration of PM increases, a greater block effect of the calcium current is observed, generating reductions in action potential duration (APD) and conduction velocity, flattening the electrical restitution curve, and favoring the onset of arrhythmic episodes by increasing tissue vulnerability to reentries. In-silico studies may contribute to a better understanding of the mechanisms by which air pollutants have unhealthy effects on cardiac tissue.

Keywords: In-silico study · particulate matter · ventricular models

1 Introduction

Air pollution is defined as a mixture of dust, gases, and suspended particles, typically associated with negative effects on human health [3]. Particulate matter (PM) is the set of liquid and solid particles emitted into the air and it is considered one of the six polluting substances with the greatest risk to public health. The increase in the concentration of PM is related to increased premature mortality. A study developed by the Global Burden of Disease estimated that environmental pollution was responsible for 9 million deaths in the world in 2019 [16]. Accordingly in most countries, acceptable levels of pollutants are established based on their impact on health, however, in several major cities, these established limits are frequently exceeded.

Air pollution in Colombia, specifically in the city of Medellín is considered one of the most significant environmental challenges. In order to address this situation,

J. C. Figueroa-García et al. (Eds.): WEA 2023, CCIS 1928, pp. 423–433, 2023.
https://doi.org/10.1007/978-3-031-46739-4_37

Medellín has Air Quality Monitoring Systems, which are responsible for monitoring reference pollutants. Among these, concern for PM stands out, whose concentration has exceeded in recent years the maximum limits allowed both nationally and internationally at different times of the year, even presenting orange or red air quality indices, which are considered critical [13].

PM exposure has been recognized as an important risk factor for the development and worsening of cardiovascular diseases [6]. A few studies in vitro and in animal models have provided evidence that PM exposure can negatively affect cardiac system [4, 21, 24]. These findings suggest the existence of mechanisms through which PM could influence the excitability and electrical function of the cardiac ventricle [12]. Therefore, it is necessary to expand the knowledge about the effects of PM on human cardiac tissue and its possible proarrhythmic effects. However, experimental studies in vitro, in vivo, and clinical studies in humans have important ethical limitations, limitations in terms of costs, infrastructure, and time. In this sense, in silico experimentation through computational simulations using mathematical and virtual models is presented as an efficient and effective tool to tackle those limitations. Therefore, biophysically detailed in-silico cardiac models could provide a deeper understanding of the negative effects of PM on cardiac tissue.

This work aims to study the effect of air PM from Medellín city on ventricular electrophysiological properties, implementing computational simulations, using single-cell and two-dimensional models of human ventricular tissue, in combination with previous experimental findings about the effect of PM collected in Medellín City on cardiac cell cultures. This study helps to understand the underlying mechanisms through which PM affects cardiac electrical activity. Furthermore, it is intended to contribute, as scientific support, for decision-making on air pollution mitigation strategies by government entities, in order to reduce the health risks associated with exposure to PM.

2   Methods

2.1   Model of PM Effect Based on In-Vitro Previous Results

Based on a study in ventricular myocytes, which indicates that PM affects the cardiac electrical activity by blocking the L-type calcium channels (I_{CaL}) [4], we developed a basic model of the PM effect on I_{CaL} using the steady-state fraction of block (b_{PM}). The Hill equation was adopted to fit the concentration-response relationships for PM block. In this model, the channel kinetics will be considered unchanged in the presence of the PM.

$$b_{PM} = \frac{1}{1 + \left(\frac{IC_{50}}{D_{PM}}\right)^h},$$

where IC_{50} is the half maximal inhibitory concentration for the I_{CaL} current block by PM, and D_{PM} is the PM concentration with values of 0 nM, 1.5 nM, 3 nM, 4.5 nM, and 6 nM. A Hill coefficient (h) of 1 indicates completely independent binding.

The value of IC_{50} was obtained from a previous study where PM filters from different monitoring stations located in the city of Medellín were provided by the Early Warning

System (SIATA), the agency in charge of monitoring air quality and weather forecasts in the city. The PM was extracted from a total of 42 filters from the central zone of the city between January and June 2022. The PM was extracted from filters using the Soxhlet method, which is commonly employed for the extraction of PM [5, 14]. Afterward, the extract was concentrated using a rotary evaporator and dried at 80 °C in an oven overnight. From the PM extract, 15 serial dilutions (1:1) were made, starting from a concentration of 25 mg/ml of complete PM and diluted in dimethyl sulfoxide (DMSO) until obtaining a concentration of 0.002 mg/ml. A positive control (pure DMSO), a negative control (cells without treatment), a solvent control (DMSO 0.19%), and a medium control (without cells) were adopted.

The assays to evaluate the cytotoxic effect of PM on cardiac cells were performed with the exposed cultures. The MTT assay was implemented following the protocol reported by Muelas et al. [15], to assess cell viability. In a 96-well plate, 10000 cells per well were seeded. Treatments were applied 24 h after seeding and consisted of adding 10 μl of each of the 15 dilutions of the PM samples for 24 h. Then, the culture medium was discarded and 50 μl of MTT solution (1 mg/ml) was added, this dish was incubated for 2 h at 37 °C isolated from light. Subsequently, the medium was discarded with MTT and 100 μl of isopropanol was added to each well to dissolve the formazan crystals that formed, stirring constantly for 30 min. Finally, the optical density was read with a Multiskan-go spectrophotometer with a wavelength of 570 nm.

This assay is performed with the purpose of finding the lethal dose 50 (LC50) after exposure to PM, that is the concentration at which viability decreases by 50%. From the results of mean viability versus concentration of PM, where viability decreased as the PM concentration increased, it was possible to obtain through regression analysis an LC50 of 1.44 mg/ml, this value was considered in this study as the IC_{50} value for the model.

2.2 Single-Cell Ventricular Model

The O'Hara-Rudy model of the human ventricular action potential [19] was chosen for this study because of the large number of human ventricular experimental data obtained from more than 140 healthy hearts used in its construction and evaluation, and its application within the CiPA initiative [23]. The model has 41 state variables and its equations are all smoothly varying functions, free of singularities and "if" conditionals. The model describes in detail the passage of the different ions through channels, exchangers, and electrogenic pumps located in the cellular sarcolemma. It considers the changes in the ionic concentrations of potassium (K^+), sodium (Na^+), and calcium (Ca^{2+}) in the cytoplasm as in the sarcoplasmic reticulum and the variation of the intracellular and extracellular concentrations of the different ions, as well as the dynamics Ca^{2+} release associated with contraction. Thus, the O'Hara-Rudy model can reproduce the ventricular action potential.

The equation that allows to obtain the action potential (V) is deduced from the application of Kirchoff first law to the equivalent electrical circuit of the cell membrane:

$$C_m \frac{dV}{dt} + I_{ion} + I_{st} = 0,$$

where C_m is the membrane capacitance, I_{st} is the external stimulation current, and I_{ion} is the total ionic current given by the sum of all the currents that participate in the generation of the action potential:

$$I_{ion} = I_{Na} + I_{to} + I_{CaL} + I_{CaNa} + I_{CaK} + I_{Kr} + I_{Ks} + I_{K1} + I_{NaCa}$$
$$+ I_{NaK} + I_{Nab} + I_{Cab} + I_{Kb} + I_{pCa}.$$

This model represents electrical activity at the cellular level, under normal physiological conditions. The Hill equation was included within the mathematical equation for I_{CaL} current in the human ventricular cell model of O'Hara-Rudy, where the fractional blockage was included as a factor $(1 - b)$ as follows:

$$I_{CaL} = (1 - b_{PM}) \frac{\frac{g_{CaL} \cdot d \cdot f \cdot fCa \cdot 4 \cdot V \cdot F^2}{R \cdot T} (Ca_i \cdot e^{\frac{2 \cdot V \cdot F}{R \cdot T}} - 0,341 \cdot Ca_o)}{e^{\frac{2 \cdot V \cdot F}{R \cdot T}} - 1},$$

where g_{CaL} is the maximum conductance of I_{CaL}, d is the activation gate, f is the voltage-dependent inactivation gate, f_{Ca} is the calcium-dependent inactivation gate, R is the gas constant, T is the temperature, V is the transmembrane potential, F is the Faraday constant, Ca_i is the intracellular calcium concentration, and Ca_o is the extracellular calcium concentration.

2.3 2D Ventricular Tissue Model

The simulations were performed using a 2D model to simulate the electrical behavior of ventricular tissue. The model consists of a 6×6 cm square mesh, composed by 192×192 elements, with a spatial discretization of 312.5 μm. An isotropic tissue was considered, where the conduction velocity is the same in the longitudinal and transverse directions. The previously modified cell model was coupled to this model. The propagation of the action potential in a 2D model can be modeled by the reaction-diffusion equation, as follows:

$$K \left(\frac{\partial^2}{\partial x^2} + \frac{\partial^2}{\partial y^2} \right) V = C_m \frac{\partial V}{\partial t} + I_{ion} + I_{st},$$

where K is the conductivity value of the tissue. To solve the equation numerically, a previously reported semi-spectral scheme [26] was applied and implemented in the MATLAB® software. The integration time step was 0.01 ms. The K value was adjusted to obtain a realistic conduction velocity of 43.5 cm/s under normal conditions (without PM).

Figure 1 shows a representation of the 2D tissue model and the O'Hara-Rudy model of the human ventricular cell, indicating the effect of PM on I_{CaL} current.

2.4 Stimulation Protocol

For the single-cell simulations, the modified cell model was implemented in the free software OpenCOR® from CellML, where the equation for the action potential was solved through the forward Euler method with a time step of 0.001 ms. An S1-S1 stimulation protocol was applied, which consists of a train of 10 rectangular pulses with duration of 2 ms and amplitude of −2000 pA, at a basic cycle length (BCL) of 1000 ms. Measurements of action potential duration at 90% repolarization (APD_{90}), and ionic currents were performed at the tenth potential for each PM concentration. Subsequently, the BCL was reduced to generate electrical restitution curves and thus evaluate the effect of PM at different concentrations on the restitution property of the ventricular action potential.

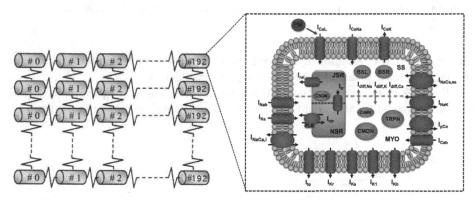

Fig. 1. Representation of tissue and cell ventricular models. The effect of PM on I_{CaL} is shown.

To assess tissue vulnerability to reentry in the 2D model, a cross-field S1-S2 stimulation protocol was implemented [9], where S1 is a flat stimulus applied to the left end of the tissue, and S2 is a flat premature stimulus applied to the top of the tissue when the repolarization wavefront generated by S1, exceeds half the domain. The time elapsed between the application of S1 and S2 is called the coupling interval. This protocol generates an excitation-refractoriness gradient in order to form reentrant waves. The vulnerable window to reentry is considered as the period of time within which it is possible to generate a reentry.

This study was performed using MATLAB R2018b on a MacBook Pro 2,3 GHz Intel Core i7 Quad Core, 16 GB 1600 MHz DDR3.

3   Results

The quantitative effects of PM on ionic currents and action potential when simulating progressive increases in PM concentration in the human ventricular cell model can be observed in Table 1.

Under control conditions (without PM), the I_{CaL} peak had a value of −1.708 pA/pF, and the APD_{90} had a value of 264 ms. However, as the PM concentration increases, downregulation of I_{CaL} was observed. When the highest PM concentration was applied (6 nM), the I_{CaL} peak reached a value of −0.366 pA/pF, indicating a decrease of 78.6%, which caused an APD shortening, reached a value of APD_{90} of 215 ms, indicating a

Table 1. PM effects under simulated action potential and I_{CaL} and I_{K1} currents at different PM concentrations.

[PM]	APD_{90}	Reduction	I_{CaL} peak	Reduction	I_{K1} left shift
0 nM	264 ms	–	−1.708 pA/pF	–	–
1.5 nM	235 ms	11.0%	−0.894 pA/pF	47.7%	32 ms
3.0 nM	223 ms	15.5%	−0.605 pA/pF	64.6%	44 ms
4.5 nM	217 ms	17.8%	−0.456 pA/pF	73.3%	50 ms
6.0 nM	215 ms	18.6%	−0.366 pA/pF	78.6%	52 ms

decrease of 18.6%. Additionally, the peak of I_{K1} current had a left shift of 52 ms. The resting membrane potential did not show significant changes.

Figure 2 shows the simulated action potential and I_{CaL} and I_{K1} currents at PM concentrations of 0 nM, 1.5 nM, 3 nM, 4.5 nM, and 6 nM, measured in the tenth S1 stimulus.

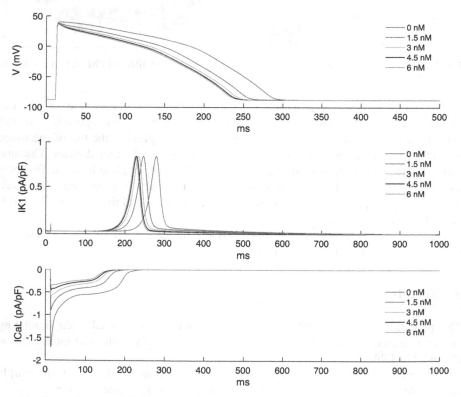

Fig. 2. Action potential duration and I_{CaL}, I_{K1} currents at different PM concentrations.

The effect of PM on the dynamics of electrical restitution of the ventricular action potential can be observed in Fig. 3, where the values of APD_{90} obtained for each concentration of PM at BCL of 1000 ms, 800 ms, 500 ms, 400 ms, and 350 ms are plotted.

For all PM concentrations, as the BCL decreases, or equivalently, as the pacing rate increases, the restitution curve becomes increasingly steeper, indicating that the APD shortens. However, this effect is reduced as the PM concentration increases, where the curves are flatter, observing a reduction in APD between the BCL values of 1000 ms and 350 ms of 11.1% for control conditions (without PM), and only of 4.8% for the 6 nM PM concentration.

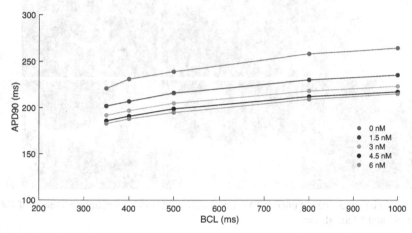

Fig. 3. Electrical restitution curves of the action potential at different BCL values for each concentration of PM.

By applying the S1-S2 cross-field protocol to the 2D model of ventricular tissue, it was not possible to generate a reentry in the control condition (i.e., without PM). Under such conditions, the wavefront generated by S2 turns on itself, but it collides with its own refractory tail (unexcitable tissue) and it extinguishes because the refractory period is larger than the turning trajectory.

On the other hand, when we applied PM at high concentrations (4 nM and 6 nM), the conduction velocity decreased slightly (42.6 cm/s), and it was possible to generate reentries within a vulnerable window of 44 ms. The wavefront that has a shorter refractory period, due to the APD shortening and slightly reduced conduction velocity, encounters excitable tissue and continues to turn, generating reentry. Figure 4 depicts the reentry sequence obtained by applying the 6 nM of PM concentration at a coupling interval (time between S1 and S2) of 400 ms.

4 Discussion

Epidemiological studies have reported effects such as heart failure, generation of cardiac arrhythmias, and decreased heart rate variability [1, 22]. Experimental studies also have shown that exposure to atmospheric pollutants increases the probability of occurrence of cardiac arrhythmias [4, 6, 12, 21, 24], however, the mechanisms underlying these effects are poorly understood. In-silico studies facilitate the study of these mechanisms since they allow the development of experiments that would not be possible to do in reality, accessing physiological variables that are difficult to manipulate under experimental conditions. The mathematical models developed in this work of the effects of PM on ionic currents and action potential, provide an appropriate digital platform to evaluate the arrhythmogenicity of this pollutant.

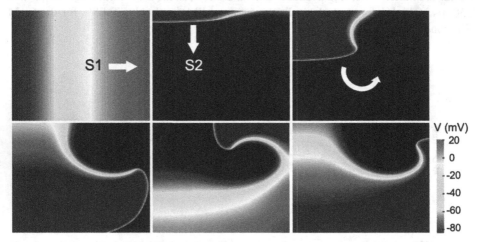

Fig. 4. Reentry sequence obtained at PM concentration of 6 nM at a coupling interval of 400 ms. Stimuli S1 and S2 are shown.

In this work, we evaluated the effects that PM at different concentrations causes on ion channels, action potential, and vulnerability to reentry, using computational simulations. Our computational experiments implemented the results of a previous in vitro study in cardiac cell cultures exposed to different concentrations of PM extracted from Medellín air filters. Such experimental data was used for developing a mathematical formulation of the PM effect at the cellular level, and cell and tissue ventricular models.

The results evinced a concentration-dependent proarrhythmic effect of PM. As PM concentration increases a greater block of the I_{CaL} current was observed, generating APD and conduction velocity reductions, flattening the electrical restitution curve, and favoring the initiation of arrhythmic episodes by increasing tissue vulnerability to reentries. Our results at the single-cell level are in agreement with experimental in-vitro studies [4, 8], where the blocking of the I_{CaL} current in a larger fraction as the concentration of PM components increases, leads to a shortening of APD [4]. Another study with ventricular myocardium of rats suggests that PM administration reduces myocardial contractility by reducing sarcolemmal calcium influx and the myosin ATPase activity [27]. In neurons has been observed that PM components may alter the bioelectrical properties by blocking high voltage-activated calcium currents, particularly L-type [20]. To the knowledge of the authors, there are no in-silico studies of PM effect on the human ventricular tissue.

The flattening of the APD restitution curve with increasing values of PM concentration indicates that the APD undergoes slight changes as the BCL decreases. This suggests a loss of sensitivity of the action potential to changes in the stimulation frequency, suggesting that a high concentration of PM favors stimulation by premature stimuli. APD restitution and conduction velocity have been shown to be dominant factors regulating the dynamic instability and therefore play an important role in predisposing to tachycardias [29].

Reduction of APD can also reduce significantly the theoretical limit of the path length required for the development or maintenance of reentry, which initiates and sustains cardiac arrhythmias [2, 17]. The APD and refractory period decrease in human cardiac tissue is the most likely cause for the small number of reentries underlying cardiac arrhythmias [25]. Vulnerability to cardiac arrhythmias caused by PM has been addressed by different studies, which agree with the findings of the simulations of this work, where a high concentration of PM increases the vulnerability to reentries. In an experimental study in rats exposed to PM [10], an increase in sensitivity to cardiac arrhythmias was recorded through electrocardiogram monitoring. Watkinson et al. [28] demonstrated that PM exposure leads to premature ventricular and atrial arrhythmias. Kim et al. [11] showed a close relationship between cardiovascular disease in 12 rats due to PM exposure, observing premature ventricular contractions and tachycardia. In an epidemiological study between 2015 and 2016, coal combustion was identified as the primary source of PM associated with arrhythmias, with PM generated from combustion being significantly linked to the generation of cardiac arrhythmias [7]. In the long term, PM is responsible for the loss of contractile capacity through myocardial infarction [18].

5 Conclusions

The results of this in-silico study show that the blocking effect on calcium current yielded by atmospheric pollutant PM, causes reductions in action potential duration and conduction velocity, a concentration-dependent effect. Consequently, the higher the concentration of the contaminant, the more vulnerable the ventricular tissue to reentries, which favors the initiation of reentrant mechanisms in a piece of ventricular tissue, showing a concentration-dependent proarrhythmic effect.

This study contributes to a better understanding of the effects of PM present in the air of Medellín on ventricular cardiac tissue, highlighting the importance of considering PM as a significant risk factor in the development of cardiac diseases in the city. These conclusions provide a foundation for future research in this field.

Acknowledgments. This work was supported by the *Ministerio de Ciencia Tecnología e Innovación* (MINCIENCIAS) from Colombia, through grant No. 120677757994.

References

1. Ansari, M.A., et al.: The role of aryl hydrocarbon receptor signaling pathway in cardiotoxicity of acute lead intoxication in vivo and in vitro rat model. Toxicology **306**, 40–49 (2013)
2. Antzelevitch, C., Burashnikov, A.: Overview of basic mechanisms of cardiac arrhythmia. Card. Electrophysiol. Clin. **3**(1), 23–45 (2011). https://doi.org/10.1016/j.ccep.2010.10.012

3. Bai, L., et al.: Air pollution forecasts: an overview. Int. J. Environ. Res. Public Health. **15**(4), 780 (2018). https://doi.org/10.3390/ijerph15040780
4. Bernal, J., et al.: Full reversal of Pb++ block of L-type Ca++ channels requires treatment with heavy metal antidotes. J. Pharmacol Exp. Ther. **282**(1), 172–180 (1997)
5. Cavanagh, J.-A.E., et al.: Exploratory investigation of the chemical characteristics and relative toxicity of ambient air particulates from two New Zealand cities. Sci. Total. Environ. **407**(18), 5007–5018 (2009). https://doi.org/10.1016/j.scitotenv.2009.05.020
6. England, P.H.: The Effects of Long-Term Exposure to Ambient Air Pollution on Cardiovascular Morbidity: Mechanistic Evidence. London (2018)
7. Feng, B., et al.: High level of source-specific particulate matter air pollution associated with cardiac arrhythmias. Sci. Total. Environ. **657**, 1285–1293 (2019). https://doi.org/10.1016/j.scitotenv.2018.12.178
8. de Mattos, G.F., et al.: Lead poisoning: acute exposure of the heart to lead ions promotes changes in cardiac function and Cav1.2 ion channels. Biophys. Rev. **9**(5), 807–825 (2017). https://doi.org/10.1007/s12551-017-0303-5
9. Greisas, A., Zlochiver, S.: Modulation of spiral-wave dynamics and spontaneous activity in a fibroblast/myocyte heterocellular tissue—a computational study. IEEE Trans. Biomed. Eng. **59**(5), 1398–1407 (2012). https://doi.org/10.1109/TBME.2012.2188291
10. Hazari, M.S., et al.: TRPA1 and sympathetic activation contribute to increased risk of triggered cardiac arrhythmias in hypertensive rats exposed to diesel exhaust. Environ. Health Perspect. **119**(7), 951–957 (2011). https://doi.org/10.1289/ehp.1003200
11. Kim, J.B., et al.: Particulate air pollution induces arrhythmia via oxidative stress and calcium calmodulin kinase II activation. Toxicol. Appl. Pharmacol. **259**(1), 66–73 (2012). https://doi.org/10.1016/j.taap.2011.12.007
12. Link, M.S., et al.: Acute exposure to air pollution triggers atrial fibrillation. J. Am. Coll. Cardiol. **62**(9), 816–825 (2013). https://doi.org/10.1016/j.jacc.2013.05.043
13. López, R.A., et al.: Informe de calidad de vida de Medellín. Medellín (2016)
14. Masih, A., et al.: Concentrations, sources, and exposure profiles of polycyclic aromatic hydrocarbons (PAHs) in particulate matter (PM10) in the north central part of India. Environ. Monit. Assess. **163**(1–4), 421–431 (2010). https://doi.org/10.1007/s10661-009-0846-4
15. Muelas, S., et al.: In vitro and in vivo assays of 3,5-disubstituted-tetrahydro-2H-1,3,5-thiadiazin-2-thione derivatives against Trypanosoma cruzi. Mem. Inst. Oswaldo Cruz **97**(2), 269–272 (2002). https://doi.org/10.1590/S0074-02762002000200023
16. Murray, C.J.L., et al.: Global burden of 87 risk factors in 204 countries and territories, 1990–2019: a systematic analysis for the global burden of disease study 2019. Lancet **396**(10258), 1223–1249 (2020). https://doi.org/10.1016/S0140-6736(20)30752-2
17. Nattel, S.: New ideas about atrial fibrillation 50 years on. Nature **415**(6868), 219–226 (2002). https://doi.org/10.1038/415219a
18. Newby, D.E., et al.: Expert position paper on air pollution and cardiovascular disease. Eur. Heart J. **36**(2), 83–93b (2015). https://doi.org/10.1093/eurheartj/ehu458
19. O'Hara, T., et al.: Simulation of the undiseased human cardiac ventricular action potential: model formulation and experimental validation. PLoS Comput. Biol. **7**(5), e1002061 (2011). https://doi.org/10.1371/journal.pcbi.1002061
20. Parvin, Z., et al.: The effect of lead (Pb2+) on electrophysiological properties of calcium currents in F77 neuron in Helix aspersa. Physiol. Pharmacol. **4**(2), 145–160 (2000)
21. Peters, A., et al.: Increased particulate air pollution and the triggering of myocardial infarction. Circulation **103**(23), 2810–2815 (2001). https://doi.org/10.1161/01.CIR.103.23.2810
22. Qin, X., et al.: Gender-specific differences of interaction between obesity and air pollution on stroke and cardiovascular diseases in Chinese adults from a high pollution range area: a large population based cross sectional study. Sci. Total. Environ. **529**, 243–248 (2015). https://doi.org/10.1016/j.scitotenv.2015.05.041

23. Sager, P.T., et al.: Rechanneling the cardiac proarrhythmia safety paradigm: a meeting report from the cardiac safety research consortium. Am. Heart J. **167**(3), 292–300 (2014). https://doi.org/10.1016/j.ahj.2013.11.004
24. Thurston, G.D., et al.: Ambient particulate matter air pollution exposure and mortality in the NIH-AARP diet and health cohort. Environ. Health Perspect. **124**(4), 484–490 (2016). https://doi.org/10.1289/ehp.1509676
25. Ten Tusscher, K.H.W.J., et al.: Organization of ventricular fibrillation in the human heart: experiments and models. Exp. Physiol. **94**(5), 553–562 (2009). https://doi.org/10.1113/expphysiol.2008.044065
26. Ugarte, J.P., et al.: Atrial rotor dynamics under complex fractional order diffusion. Front. Physiol. **9** (2018). https://doi.org/10.3389/fphys.2018.00975
27. Vassallo, D.V., et al.: Lead reduces tension development and the myosin ATPase activity of the rat right ventricular myocardium. Braz. J. Med. Biol. Res. **41**(9), 789–795 (2008). https://doi.org/10.1590/S0100-879X2008000900008
28. Watkinson, W.: Cardiac arrhythmia induction after exposure to residual oil fly ash particles in a rodent model of pulmonary hypertension. Toxicol. Sci. **41**(2), 209–216 (1998). https://doi.org/10.1006/toxs.1997.2406
29. Xie, F., et al.: Electrical refractory period restitution and spiral wave reentry in simulated cardiac tissue. Am. J. Physiol. Circ. Physiol. **283**(1), H448–H460 (2002)

Author Index

© The Editor(s) (if applicable) and The Author(s), under exclusive license
to Springer Nature Switzerland AG 2023
J. C. Figueroa-García et al. (Eds.): WEA 2023, CCIS 1928, pp. 435–436, 2023.
https://doi.org/10.1007/978-3-031-46739-4

Printed in the United States
by Baker & Taylor Publisher Services